C000271769

PRACTICAL GUIDE TO EVIDENCE

Second Edition

Cavendish
Publishing
Limited

London • Sydney

PRACTICAL GUIDE TO EVIDENCE

Second Edition

Christopher Allen, LLM, PhD, Barrister
Senior Lecturer, Inns of Court School of Law, City University

Cavendish
Publishing
Limited

London • Sydney

First published in Great Britain 2001 by Cavendish Publishing Limited, The Glass House, Wharton Street, London WC1X 9PX, United Kingdom
Telephone: +44 (0)20 7278 8000   Facsimile: +44 (0)20 7278 8080
Email: info@cavendishpublishing.com
Website: www.cavendishpublishing.com

© Allen, C   2001
First edition   1998
Second edition   2001

All rights reserved. No part of this publication may be reproduced, stored in a retrieval system, or transmitted, in any form or by any means, electronic, mechanical, photocopying, recording, scanning or otherwise, except under the terms of the Copyright Designs and Patents Act 1988 or under the terms of a licence issued by the Copyright Licensing Agency, 90 Tottenham Court Road, London W1P 9HE, UK, without the permission in writing of the publisher.

British Library Cataloguing in Publication Data

Allen, Christopher, 1944–
Practical guide to evidence – 2nd ed
1 Evidence (Law) – England 2 Evidence (Law) – Wales
I Title
347.4'2'06

ISBN 1 85941 604 7

Printed and bound in Great Britain

To Felix

Rules capable of rendering right decisions secure are what the nature of things denies. To the establishment of rules by which misdecision is rendered more probable than it would otherwise be, the nature of man is prone. To put the legislator and the judge upon their guard against such rashness is all that the industry of the free inquirer can do in favour of the ends of justice.

Jeremy Bentham

It may safely be laid down as an universal position, that the less the process of inquiry is fettered by rules and restraints, founded on extraneous and collateral considerations of policy and convenience, the more certain and efficacious will be its operation.

Thomas Starkie

PREFACE TO THE SECOND EDITION

The three years since the publication of the first edition of this book have seen substantial changes in the law of evidence. The European Convention on Human Rights has been incorporated into English law by the Human Rights Act 1998, and the courts have already considered it in relation to a number of topics, including reversal of the burden of proof in criminal cases, evidence obtained by entrapment, improperly obtained evidence and the protection from disclosure of journalists' sources. The Youth Justice and Criminal Evidence Act 1999 has simplified the law relating to competence and compellability in criminal cases. It has introduced new provisions to protect vulnerable and intimidated witnesses, and it has further restricted the evidence that may be given of a complainant's previous sexual behaviour in trials where the defendant is charged with a 'rape offence'. This statute is being brought into effect in stages. To avoid an unnecessarily complex presentation, this edition follows the London University syllabus for LLB external students and the Inns of Court School of Law Bar Vocational Course syllabus by stating the law as if the statute were fully in force.

There have been significant developments in case law also, especially in relation to the rule against hearsay. In *R v Ward* (2001), the Court of Appeal avoided the rule on the basis of the quality of the evidence that was affected by it, thus creating the possibility of future relaxation that depends not on law, but on what are perceived to be the merits of the case. In *R v Callender* (1998), the court attempted unconvincingly to unify the *res gestae* exceptions. In *R v Derodra* (2000), the court found a way round the inconvenient decision of the Divisional Court in *Brown v Secretary of State for Social Security* (1994). Evidence of identification has continued to be a developing area; the conflicts within the Court of Appeal over the interpretation of para 2.3 of Code D have only just been resolved by the House of Lords, which held in *R v Forbes* (2001) that this provision means what it says. The scope of s 78(1) of the Police and Criminal Evidence Act 1984 still remains far from clear, not least because of the much-criticised decision of the Court of Appeal in *R v Chalkley and Jeffries* (1998). The decision in *R v Z* (2000) expands still further the scope of similar fact evidence, and 'background evidence' has now emerged as an independent category of admissibility. In a number of important decisions, the Court of Appeal has limited the operation of s 34 of the Criminal Justice and Public Order Act 1994.

These are only some of the developments that this second edition takes into account. My object remains as before: to explain evidence law in a way that will make for sound understanding and the creative use of argument, whether in court or in an examination.

CJW Allen
Gray's Inn
August 2001

PREFACE TO THE FIRST EDITION

With evidence it is easy to miss the wood for the trees. One of the main reasons for this is that the subject is as much about reasoning with facts, the use of language, and the application of principles as it is about rules of law. I have tried to write a book that will make this clear. My experience of teaching and examining has shown that many students find it hard to understand Evidence outside the context of factual situations, and even harder to apply what has been learned to different sets of facts in problem questions. I have tried to cope with these difficulties by providing detailed illustrations from the cases. Where a point has seemed particularly important I have provided several examples of the law at work, in the hope that if one example fails to make things clear another may succeed. I have tried to keep particularly in mind the needs of students who are studying part time or for an external degree. In a full time class any obscurities or ambiguities in a text can be resolved quickly before they develop into difficulties with the subject. But for the part time or external student it is vital to get things as clear as possible from the start. I cannot claim to have achieved this completely, but I have tried to do so. The book may be used with my *Sourcebook on Evidence* and I have indicated where a case or extract from an article appears there. I have also provided pointers to a wider range of literature for those who need to research a particular topic or to prepare for essay questions in an examination. I owe a special debt of gratitude to Stephen Guest, who has read much of my manuscript. It has benefited greatly from his comments. Of course, he must not be taken to endorse all the opinions here, and any errors that remain are mine alone. Many of the chapters have their origins in lectures and seminars given at the Inns of Court School of Law, at University College London and on London University's External Programme. I am grateful to my students for helping me to clarify my ideas about how to present this subject. Finally, I should like to thank Cavendish Publishing Limited for all their help in the production of this book.

CJW Allen
Gray's Inn
April 1998

CONTENTS

Contents

TABLE OF CASES

TABLE OF STATUTES

STATUTORY INSTRUMENTS

EUROPEAN LEGISLATION

CHAPTER 1

INTRODUCTION

Law cannot be properly understood without some knowledge of the context in which it operates. Just as the student of commercial law needs to understand something of what is involved in ordinary commercial transactions, so the student of evidence needs some understanding of what is involved in ordinary processes of proof.

Those processes will therefore be my first concern in this chapter. I shall then turn to a more traditional topic: the definition of 'evidence'. This will be followed by a section which covers the concepts of relevance, admissibility and weight. These are fundamental to the consideration of all aspects of our subject. The fourth section contains a short glossary of some of the technical terms commonly encountered in studying evidence. The fifth discusses two characteristics of evidence law which it is helpful to appreciate at the outset: its limited application and the way in which it is constructed. The last section is concerned with a particular contextual topic: the functions of judge and jury in a Crown Court trial.

EVIDENCE AND PROOF

A useful way of approaching this topic is by looking at a case which was notorious at the beginning of the 20th century and for some decades afterwards. The defendant was Dr Crippen, who was charged in 1910 with the murder of his wife.[1] According to the prosecution, Crippen had fallen in love with his young secretary, Ethel Le Neve, and had decided to kill his wife to leave himself free to marry Ethel. One night, therefore, he put poison in a glass of stout – his wife's regular nightcap. The poison might have been sufficient to kill her, or it might merely have made her unconscious. At any rate, by the time Crippen had finished with her she must have been dead, because he drained the blood from the body, dissected it, and separated the flesh from the bones. He buried the pieces of flesh in the cellar of the house where they lived. The bones and the head were never found; it was assumed that they had been burned. To explain his wife's absence, Crippen at first told her friends that she was staying with her sister in America; later he said that she had died there. When the police began to make inquiries, he told them that his wife had left him and that he had been too embarrassed to tell the

---

1   See Cullen, T, *Crippen: The Mild Murderer*, 1988.

truth to friends and neighbours. Crippen had not yet been arrested, and shortly after his interview with the police he hurriedly left the country with Ethel Le Neve. Meanwhile, the police dug up the cellar floor and discovered the human remains buried there. Crippen was followed and brought back to England to stand trial.

Imagine yourself now in the position of a lawyer for the prosecution in that case. You know, of course, what constitutes murder in English law. But, given these facts and that law, what had to be established before a jury could find Crippen guilty of murder? The first thing that had to be proved was that Mrs Crippen was dead. Crippen maintained when questioned by the police and later at trial that his wife had left him and that he knew nothing of the remains in the cellar. So it was necessary for the prosecution to establish that the remains were those of Mrs Crippen. They also had to show that it was her husband who had killed her and that he had done so intentionally. This meant they had to prove that Mrs Crippen had died from poison administered by the accused with the intention of causing her death.[2]

The task faced by the prosecution is illustrated by Figure 1.1. Item 1 represents 'the thing that has ultimately to be proved'. This expression can be shortened by adopting a term used by JH Wigmore:[3] the *ultimate probandum*. In this case, it is expressed by the proposition 'Crippen murdered his wife.' Items 2 to 5 inclusive represent what Wigmore called *penultimate probanda*.[4] These are the propositions which, taken together, go to prove the ultimate probandum. Unless there was some evidence to support each one of the penultimate probanda, a defence submission that there was no case to answer would have been likely to succeed.

---

2   To keep this analysis as simple as possible, I have ignored the possibility that she did not die until Crippen dismembered her body.

3   Wigmore (1863–1943) was a Professor of Law at Northwestern University in Chicago from 1893 until his death nearly 50 years later. He was the author of many works, including a famous *Treatise on Evidence* (1st edn, 1909–15; 3rd edn, 1940) and *The Principles of Judicial Proof* (1913, 1931; later *The Science of Judicial Proof*, 1937). His system for analysis of evidence, described in the latter work, is best studied today in Anderson, T and Twining, W, *Analysis of Evidence*, 1991. See also Twining, W, *Theories of Evidence: Bentham and Wigmore*, 1985.

4   Note the plural form. The singular is penultimate *probandum*.

Figure 1.1

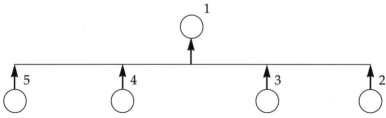

Key list

1 Dr Crippen murdered his wife (*ultimate probandum*).
2 Mrs Crippen was dead.
3 Poison had caused her death.
4 Dr Crippen had administered the poison.
5 He had done so with the intention of causing death.

It is not necessary, for the purpose of understanding the process of proof, to show how all the penultimate probanda were proved in the Crippen case. It is enough to concentrate on the first of these, which appears as item 2 in Figure 1.1. The proof of this item is illustrated by Figure 1.2.

Figure 1.2

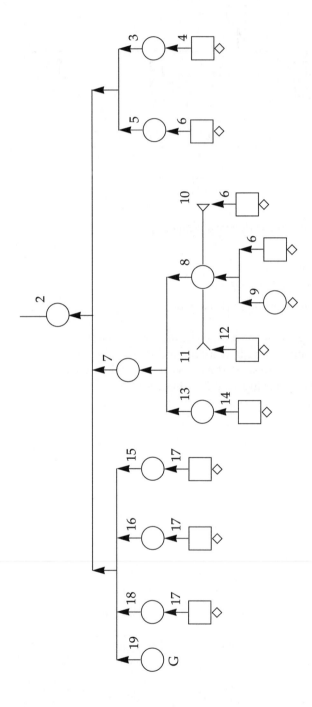

Key list

2   Mrs Crippen was dead.

3   Some remains were found in the cellar.

4   Police testimony to this effect.

5   The remains came from a human body.

6   Prosecution expert's testimony to this effect.

7   The body was that of Mrs Crippen.

8   A piece of the abdomen bore the mark of an operation scar.

9   Item of real evidence.

10 The shape of the mark was more consistent with a scar than with a fold.

11 The mark may have been caused by folding.

12 Defence expert's testimony to this effect.

13 Mrs Crippen had an operation scar on her abdomen.

14 Her sister's testimony to this effect.

15 No one had seen Mrs Crippen since 31 January 1910.

16 Mrs Crippen had friends and relations.

17 Prosecution testimony to this effect.

18 Mrs Crippen had a friendly, outgoing personality.

19 Someone with such a personality who has not communicated with any friends or relations for some months may be dead.

The following points should be observed:

(a) Proof is made by establishing several sets of inferences which ultimately converge on item 2.

(b) Each set of inferences rests on a foundation, which is marked in Figure 1.2 either by a diamond shape or by the letter G.

(c) There are three types of foundation on which sets of inferences can be based:

- the testimony of a witness at trial, represented by a square with a diamond beneath it. Examples are the testimony of the forensic scientists on each side (items 6 and 12);

- an item of 'real evidence', ie, something which the jurors can examine for themselves. An example is a piece of flesh collected with the other pieces from the cellar and said by the prosecution to bear an identifying scar. This type of foundation is represented by a circle with a diamond beneath it (item 9);

- a generalisation about the way things are in the world, for example, item 19, represented by a circle with the letter G beneath it.

(d) All three types of foundation have in common the fact that the members of the jury rely on their own perception for experience of them. The jurors can see and hear the witnesses giving oral evidence in the witness box. They are able to see the items of real evidence. They rely on their own previous perceptions, that is, their experience, when deciding whether or not to accept the truth of a proposed generalisation. If they recognise it as something that is either already part of the way in which they understand the world, or as something that at least fits with their understanding, they are likely to accept it. Otherwise, it is likely to be rejected. In these ways, members of a jury are in direct touch with all foundational items. But they are in direct touch with nothing else. Every item not foundational has to be inferred, and every process of inference is open to error and so apt to produce a false conclusion. The majority of items in Figure 1.2 are, like the majority of items of evidence in any case, non-foundational and therefore to be regarded with particular care before their truth is accepted. Direct perceptions are open to error too, of course, but inferences about events in the past provide additional scope for error.

(e) Just as a set of inferences is based on a foundation, so each inference in the set is based on those immediately below it. This basing relationship is hard to define, but for these purposes it will be enough to say that a basing item, often taken in conjunction with other items of evidence, makes another item in the chain of proof to some degree likely. For example, you probably feel instinctively that once it is established that a piece of the abdomen bore the mark of an operation scar (item 8) and that Mrs Crippen had an operation scar on her abdomen (item 13), it is likely that the remains came from the body of Mrs Crippen (item 7). How likely you feel any particular inference to be will depend on how cautious you are in forming beliefs and what weight you think ought to be attached to the data on which you base the inference in question. Someone who wishes to prove something will ideally be able to rely on an accumulation of different items of evidence from different witnesses. So here, if items 15 to 19 (relating to Mrs Crippen's disappearance) stood alone, we might be willing to accept Mrs Crippen's death as no more than a remote possibility. But the likelihood that she is dead becomes much stronger when evidence of the discovery in the cellar is added. 'Likelihood' in this context is often referred to as 'probability', meaning probability of any degree, however slight. This sense of 'probability' is different from the more colloquial one where it stands for something with a greater than 50% chance of being the case – a probability rather than a possibility.[5]

(f) The significance of an item of evidence lies in the fact that it makes a particular inference either more or less likely to be true. Look at the inference represented by item 8 in Figure 1.2. The prosecution needed to show that the remains found in the cellar were those of Mrs Crippen. They

---

5   See generally Eggleston, R, *Evidence, Proof and Probability*, 2nd edn, 1983, Chapter 2.

hoped to establish this by proving that Mrs Crippen had an operation scar on her abdomen and that an identical scar was to be found on one of the pieces of flesh found by the police. The defence countered this argument by calling expert evidence to the effect that the mark on the flesh was not a scar, but a fold that had developed after burial. Items 10 and 11 represent the experts' evidence on this question. Whether the jury accepted the truth of the inference represented by item 8 was going to depend on which expert they found the more persuasive.

Wigmore's chart system is one way of thinking methodically about the facts of any case in which you may be instructed. As an advocate and a lawyer, you must be able to ensure, so far as possible, that your client has available all the evidence needed to establish or rebut a claim. You have to be aware of the weaknesses in your own case and in that of your opponent. Does too much depend on the evidence of one witness? What grounds might there be for questioning that person's reliability? It will very rarely be the case that one particular inference must inevitably be made from certain facts; what other possible inferences might be made which would do your client less damage or your opponent more harm? To what extent are you or your opponent relying on the truth of hidden and hitherto unconsidered generalisations about the way things are in the world as the basis for making inferences? We shall return to these questions, but at this stage, having already used the word 'evidence' in several contexts, it is desirable to break off in order to say something about attempts to define this word.

DEFINING EVIDENCE

Wigmore thought it 'of little practical consequence to construct a formula defining what is to be understood as "evidence"', and he may well have been right. He nevertheless attempted a definition[6] and writers of textbooks on evidence have traditionally taken this to be one of their first tasks. The most satisfactory attempt was probably made in the 19th century by WM Best, who, influenced by Jeremy Bentham, defined evidence as 'any matter of fact, the effect, tendency, or design of which is to produce in the mind a persuasion, affirmative or disaffirmative, of the existence of some other matter of fact'.[7]

6　'What we are concerned with is the process of presenting evidence for the purpose of demonstrating an asserted fact. In this process, then, the term Evidence represents: any knowable fact or group of facts, not a legal or a logical principle, considered with a view to its being offered before a legal tribunal for the purpose of producing a persuasion, positive or negative, on the part of the tribunal, as to the truth of a proposition, not of law or of logic, on which the determination of the tribunal is to be asked.' (Wigmore, JH, *A Treatise on the System of Evidence in Trials at Common Law*, Tillers, P (ed), 1983, Vol I, section 1.)

7　Best, WM, *A Treatise on the Principles of the Law of Evidence*, 4th edn, 1866, p 10. Cf Bentham, J, 'Rationale of Judicial Evidence', in Bowring, J (ed), *The Works of Jeremy Bentham*, 1838–43, Vol 6, p 208.

More recent attempts at defining 'evidence' have included: 'that which makes evident a fact to a judicial tribunal';[8] 'information by which facts tend to be proved';[9] 'any material which tends to persuade the court of the truth or probability of some fact asserted before it';[10] 'something which may satisfy an inquirer of [a] fact's existence'.[11] This sort of thing is helpful up to a point, but the word 'evidence' can be used in different ways, depending on the context. Take, for example, the following:

(a) 'In August of last year, Bywaters, according to the evidence, made a statement to his mother about the unhappy life of Mrs Thompson.'

(b) 'The damp mud on his boots was evidence that he had left the house earlier that evening.'

(c) '"You must not tell us what the soldier, or any other man, said, sir," interposed the judge, "it's not evidence".'

In the first of these examples, 'evidence' was used to refer to what had been said in court by one or more witnesses. In the second, 'evidence' referred to a relationship of relevance between the fact of there being damp mud on boots and the fact that he had left the house earlier that evening. In the third example, 'evidence' was used in a restricted sense to cover only those legally admissible things that a witness could say in court.

As lawyers, you will be concerned with evidence in all these senses. You may have to advise on what information should be obtained from potential witnesses to substantiate or rebut a claim at trial. You may have to challenge the evidence of an opponent's witness on the basis that it is irrelevant, or construct an argument to demonstrate the relevance of what your own witnesses have to say. You may have to consider whether the law permits an admittedly relevant item of information to be given in evidence, or whether the item is caught by some rule or principle of exclusion.

RELEVANCE, WEIGHT AND ADMISSIBILITY

The concepts distinguished

It will help you to analyse problems and to develop arguments if I begin with a brief outline that distinguishes between these three concepts, even though we shall see later that judges have sometimes appeared to erode their boundaries so that one concept merges with another.

---

8   Nokes, GD, *An Introduction to Evidence*, 4th edn, 1967, p 1.
9   Keane, A, *The Modern Law of Evidence*, 5th edn, 2000, p 1.
10   Murphy, P, *Murphy on Evidence*, 1995, p 1. Cf the different approach in later editions.
11   Tapper, C, *Cross and Tapper on Evidence*, 9th edn, 1999, p 1.

Let us suppose that Charlie is being prosecuted for burglary of a shop in London. The likelihood that he committed the crime can be expressed by means of a scale running from 1 to -1 thus:

Figure 1.3

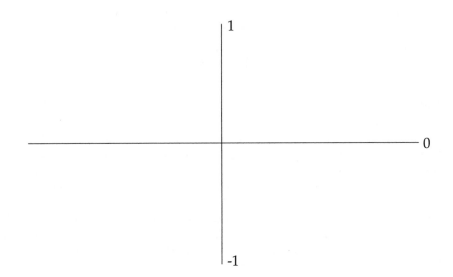

At the top of the scale, the point marked '1' represents the mental condition of being certain that it was Charlie who did the burglary. At the bottom of the scale, the point marked '-1' represents the mental condition of being certain that Charlie did not commit the burglary. Any item of evidence that makes it either more or less likely that Charlie did what the prosecution allege will have a place on the scale at some point between 0 and 1 or between 0 and -1, and will, in principle, be relevant at Charlie's trial. So, for example, if a prosecution witness says that he saw Charlie near the shop shortly before the burglary, that will be relevant and will have a place somewhere between 0 and 1. If Charlie produces a witness who says that she was with him several hundred miles away at the time the offence was committed, that piece of information will be relevant and will have a place somewhere on the scale between 0 and -1. It is important to note that neither item of evidence is *conclusive* of the matter in issue. For an item of evidence to be *relevant* it is *never* necessary that it should be conclusive. In other words, it is no argument against the relevance of an item of evidence that it can be explained in a way that does not support the proposition that it is being put forward to prove. An alternative explanation can always be found for what appears to be the most compelling piece of evidence. Notorious miscarriages of justice based on evidence of confessions by the accused are obvious illustrations of this.

An item of evidence that makes neither the Crown's case nor Charlie's case more likely to be true will be *irrelevant* and will have no place on the scale.

The *extent* to which a piece of evidence makes the case of one of the parties more likely to be true is not a matter of relevance but of *weight*. It is relevance that gets the item onto the scale in the first place, but it is weight that dictates the position it takes there. The weightier the evidence, the nearer it will be to one or other extremity. Generally, while questions of relevance are for the judge to decide, questions of weight are left to the jury.

Although an item of evidence may be relevant, sometimes its legal *admissibility* may be in doubt. Problems of this kind are decided by the judge.

Relevance[12]

According to Lord Simon in *DPP v Kilbourne*,[13] 'Evidence is relevant if it is logically probative or disprobative of some matter which requires proof'. But since courts can deal only in probabilities, not certainties, this must mean that relevant evidence is that which makes the matter requiring proof more or less probable.[14] It may be important to be able to establish by argument the relevance of a contested item of evidence. The reason for this is that, although relevance does not always, because of the way the law works, make an item of evidence admissible, any item of evidence that *is* admitted *must* be relevant.[15] So one way of excluding an item of an opponent's evidence is to argue that it is irrelevant; hence the need to be able to make convincing submissions on this subject. But how are we to know what is, in Lord Simon's words, logically probative or disprobative? The question can almost never be answered by reference to a rule of law. In the vast majority of cases the law furnishes no test of relevance but refers, tacitly, to logic and general experience.[16]

The key to relevance is an understanding of the importance of *generalisations about the way things are in the world*: the sort of things exemplified by item 19 in Figure 1.2. That item was needed to make sense of items 15, 16 and 18. You will remember that the immediate object was to

---

12 See Choo, AL-T, 'The notion of relevance and defence evidence' [1993] Crim LR 114.

13 [1973] AC 729, p 756.

14 Cf Stephen, JF: The word 'relevant' means that 'any two facts to which it is applied are so related to each other that according to the common course of events one either taken by itself or in connection with other facts proves or renders probable the past, present, or future existence or non-existence of the other', Stephen, JF, *A Digest of the Law of Evidence*, 3rd edn, 1877, p 4.

15 *R v Turner* [1975] QB 834, p 841; *Sourcebook*, p 401. See also *R v Sandhu* [1997] Crim LR 288.

16 Thayer, JB, *A Preliminary Treatise on Evidence at the Common Law*, 1898, p 265.

prove that Mrs Crippen was dead. To this end, the prosecution wished to adduce evidence to show that she had not been seen by anyone since 31 January 1910, that she had friends and relations, and that she possessed a friendly, outgoing personality. But those facts are meaningless if you do not accept that item 19 says something true about the way things are in the world. If you do not accept that someone with a friendly, outgoing personality who has failed for some time to communicate with any friends or relations may be dead, it follows that it is irrelevant to prove those facts about Mrs Crippen.

An advocate needs to be familiar with the structure of arguments about relevance. It follows that, as part of your preparation of a case, you will have to think through matters that you might hitherto have accepted instinctively so that, if necessary, you can justify or challenge a claim that something is relevant. If your object is to exclude a particular item of evidence, a denial of relevance may be an effective weapon. If you can show that your opponent must rely on a generalisation that is absurd, or at least questionable, in order to establish relevance, that evidence is likely to be excluded.

An example of this approach can be seen in *R v Bracewell*.[17] Two men, Bracewell and a man named Lockwood, were charged with burglary and murder. The case for the prosecution was that they had agreed to burgle a house occupied by a man named Blakey, that in the course of the burglary Blakey had been killed, and that both men were responsible for his death. Both defendants admitted burglary, but each said the other was solely responsible for Blakey's death. The deceased had suffered death from a violent attack. One of the witnesses for the prosecution was Lockwood's mistress, a Mrs Firth. Her statement to the police referred to the fact that Lockwood was a very violent man. She described occasions when he had been violent to her and added: 'Once he started these assaults he did not appear to be able to stop himself.' This part of her statement was inadmissible as evidence for the prosecution, because normally evidence of an accused's general criminal disposition is inadmissible to show that he has committed the crime for which he is being tried. But although the prosecution could not use this evidence, the question arose whether Bracewell could. His counsel, in order to support Bracewell's defence that Lockwood had been the sole cause of the death, applied to cross-examine Mrs Firth with a view to making these matters known to the jury. The trial judge refused to allow this, and in due course Bracewell was convicted of murder. He appealed, arguing that the judge's decision had been wrong.

Counsel for Bracewell argued before the Court of Appeal that Mrs Firth's evidence on these matters was relevant to his client's case, and so admissible. In order to establish relevance he relied on the generalisation that: 'A man who, when he uses violence to his mistress, does not know when to stop, is

---

17   (1978) 68 Cr App R 44; *Sourcebook*, p 336.

more likely to have been guilty of a violent assault on a man in the course of a burglary than a man who has not used violence to his wife or mistress.' Of this generalisation, Ormrod LJ said that opinions on its validity might differ widely. Without the benefit of statistical evidence, it could only be a matter of opinion. The onus of satisfying the judge as to the relevance of evidence was on the party tendering it. The Court of Appeal clearly thought that this burden had not been satisfied and that the decision of the trial judge to exclude the evidence had been correct.

The decision shows several things. First, counsel and judges recognise the significance of generalisations in establishing relevance. Secondly, the burden is on the party who tenders evidence to show that it is relevant; it is not for the party challenging relevance to show that the evidence is irrelevant. Thirdly, a judge may be unwilling to accept the truth of an appropriate generalisation without the support of expert evidence.[18]

Is there a concept of legal relevance?

Everything that I have written so far suggests that any arguments about relevance are going to be about facts, not law. This is a view that has been challenged in the past and on which two great American evidence scholars, JB Thayer and JH Wigmore, were divided. Thayer defined the law of evidence as 'a set of rules and principles affecting judicial investigations into questions of fact',[19] but he thought that these rules and principles did not regulate the process of reasoning, save to the extent of helping to select the factual material on which the processes of reasoning were to operate. The principle forbidding the reception of irrelevant evidence was not so much a rule of evidence as a presupposition involved in the very conception of a rational system of evidence.[20] According to Thayer, the law furnished no test of relevance. Instead, the law tacitly referred to logic and general experience, the principles of which were presumed to be known.[21]

Wigmore accepted that relevance had originally been a matter of logic and common sense. But he argued that there were so many instances in which the bearing of particular facts on particular issues had been ruled upon by courts that the united logic of a great many judges and lawyers furnished evidence of the sense common to a great many individuals, and so acquired the authority of law. It was therefore proper, he argued, to talk of legal relevance.[22]

---

18 On generalisations, see further Tapper, *op cit*, fn 11, pp 55–56; Twining, *Theories of Evidence*, pp 142–46, extracts in *Sourcebook*, pp 11–13.

19 Thayer, *op cit*, fn 16, p 263.

20 Thayer, *op cit*, fn 16, pp 264–65. Cf the *dicta* of Lawton LJ in *R v Turner* [1975] QB 834, p 841; *Sourcebook*, p 401.

21 Thayer, *op cit*, fn 16, p 265.

22 Wigmore, *op cit*, fn 6, section 12.

It is certainly the case that, in some instances, judges have laid down rules about what is relevant or irrelevant. For example, in *DPP v Camplin*,[23] it was decided that age and sex were always relevant when considering the defence of provocation. Further, in ss 41–43 of the Youth Justice and Criminal Evidence Act 1999, Parliament has provided a statutory framework for determining the relevance of a complainant's previous sexual history where the defendant is on trial for a 'rape offence'.[24] But in addition to specific rules like this, it is also necessary to take into account the courts' practice of rejecting evidence of minimal weight on the ground that it is 'irrelevant'. Judges have pragmatic reasons for not admitting every item of logically relevant evidence, however slight its weight. The best reason is that if the field of judicial inquiry is too wide, confusion leading to misdecision may result. Another reason is that concessions have to be made to the shortness of life, as well as to the financial resources of the litigants or the legal aid fund.

An old case illustrating an approach of this kind is *Hollingham v Head*.[25] The plaintiff sold a quantity of guano to the defendant. When he sued the defendant for the price, the defendant alleged that he was entitled, by the terms of the contract, to refuse payment. He alleged that the guano, which had been sold under the name of 'Rival guano', was of a new kind and that in order to persuade him to place an order, the plaintiff had sold it at £7 per ton on the condition that if it was not equal to Peruvian guano, the price of which was £14 per ton, the defendant was not to pay for it. The plaintiff denied that this had been a condition of the contract. The question arose whether, in order to prove the existence of the condition, the defendant could cross-examine the plaintiff about sales of Rival guano to other customers on the same condition, and whether evidence could be called as part of the defendant's case to this effect. The Court of Common Pleas held that such evidence and cross-examination were inadmissible as not being relevant to the issue between the parties. But the judgments of Willes and Williams JJ showed that the court was mainly concerned with the need to save time and ensure that the jury was not distracted from the point in issue.

Willes J appeared to base his judgment on the ground of relevance by saying: 'I do not see how the fact that a man has once or more in his life acted in a particular way makes it probable that he so acted on a given occasion.' But this is unconvincing. There may be circumstances where the fact that someone has done X in the past *does* make it more likely that, where X has been committed, he, rather than someone who has not done X before,

---

23 [1978] AC 705. But a more usual approach is that of the Court of Appeal in *R v Guney* [1998] 2 Cr App R 242, p 265, where it was emphasised that questions of relevance do not depend on 'abstract legal theory but on the individual circumstances of each particular case'.

24 *Hansard*, HL Deb, 23 March 1999, col 1216. See Chapter 4 below.

25 (1858) 27 LJCP 241; *Sourcebook*, p 20.

committed X on this occasion. That was not the type of problem found in *Hollingham v Head* but, even so, the conclusion seems odd. It seems likely – the report has insufficient detail for the reader to be sure – that the defendant wanted to show that the contract he had made with the plaintiff was part of something like a promotion campaign for Rival guano. It would surely have been relevant to the existence of the alleged condition to prove that the contract with the defendant had been part of such a campaign, during which contracts had been made on identical terms with other purchasers. The real reason for exclusion seems to have been the fear of inconvenience if the inquiry had to be extended in this way.

Another move which appeared to limit the concept of relevance in law was made by the House of Lords in *R v Blastland*.[26] The body of a boy who had been buggered and strangled was found and in due course the defendant was charged with buggery and murder. He denied murder, but admitted some sexual activity with the boy not far from where the body was later found. According to the defendant, after having oral sex with the boy he noticed another man nearby, whereupon he panicked and ran home. He gave a description of the other man which corresponded closely to that of a man referred to throughout the proceedings as 'Mark'. The case for the defence was that it was Mark, and not the accused, who had committed buggery and murder. In order to support this, the defence wished to call evidence of persons to whom Mark had spoken after the murder had taken place. It was hoped that this evidence would show that Mark knew things about the murder that only the murderer could have known.

The House of Lords held that this evidence was inadmissible because, amongst other reasons, it was irrelevant. What the defence witnesses could say would amount to evidence of Mark's knowledge, and so of his state of mind. But, said Lord Bridge, for that state of mind to be relevant, it had to be itself directly in issue in the trial, which it clearly was not, or it had to be 'of direct and immediate relevance' to an issue arising in the trial. The issue at the trial was whether it was proved that the defendant had buggered and murdered the deceased. But Mark's knowledge was not, *per se*, of any relevance to this issue. What was relevant was not the fact of Mark's knowledge but how he had come by that knowledge. He might have done so in a number of ways, but the two most obvious possibilities were either that he had witnessed the commission of the murder by the appellant or that he had committed it himself. The statements which it was sought to prove that Mark made, indicating his knowledge of the murder, provided no rational basis whatever on which the jury could be invited to draw an inference as to the source of that knowledge. To admit the evidence would have been a mere

---

26 [1986] AC 41; *Sourcebook*, p 22; Carter, PB, 'Hearsay, relevance and admissibility' (1987) 103 LQR 106, pp 108–13.

invitation to speculate.[27] Accordingly, the evidence was irrelevant and therefore inadmissible.

A problem arising at once is what we are to understand by the qualifying words 'direct and immediate' in relation to relevance. What the prosecution had to prove in this case was, as Lord Bridge said, that Blastland had buggered and murdered the deceased. It was devastatingly clear that anything tending to prove or disprove that proposition was relevant to the issue with which the trial court was concerned. What did the requirement that the relevance be 'direct and immediate' add? Nothing. Some things, of course, point more clearly to a particular conclusion than others. But this is a matter of weight, not relevance. Ought we to take Lord Bridge as stipulating that for evidence to be relevant, it must have some minimum weight? But while 'weight' in relation to evidence can usually be understood, the metaphor cannot be pressed too far. A requirement of a minimum weight presupposes an ability to measure exactly. At this point the metaphor breaks down. While physical objects may be capable of exact measurement, items of evidence are not.

Another way of reading what Lord Bridge said is to stress the inconclusiveness of the information tendered. Mark's knowledge was relevant because it opened up a possibility that he had come by it in a way that was inconsistent with the defendant's guilt. But because the jury had no means of telling whether that possibility was likely to be right or not, it was 'irrelevant'. Lord Bridge appears to have assumed that an ambiguity which is incapable of resolution can never, to any significant degree, tend to the disproof of a fact in issue. But it is absurd to suggest that an ambiguity which cannot be resolved is incapable of providing a reasonable doubt, and if there was a reasonable doubt the accused was entitled to a verdict of not guilty.

There have been other suggestions that relevance may be a matter of law. In *Vernon v Bosley*,[28] Hoffmann LJ appeared to acknowledge a concept of legal relevance that in some cases would involve qualifying a party's right to choose how to present his case by reference to other public or private interests. For example, in any litigation, the general public and the party's opponent would have an interest in keeping down the length and cost of the proceedings. To defend this interest a judge might have to rule inadmissible the exploration of side issues which, though probably having potential relevance, did not appear sufficiently relevant to justify the time and expense

---

27 [1986] AC 41, p 54; *Sourcebook*, p 24. The idea that inconclusive evidence may be irrelevant is a potential weapon in the defence armoury. It could be used to exclude prosecution evidence on the basis that a jury could only speculate about its significance. For another case recognising the impropriety of jury speculation see *R v Woodward* (1994) *The Times*, 7 December.

28 (1994) *The Times*, 8 April. A full transcript of the judgment has been relied on for the passage in the text.

needed to investigate them. Relevance might also have to be balanced against other interests where a question involved a witness in breaking a confidence imposed by his religion, profession or conscience. Hoffmann LJ insisted that as a matter of legal analysis this was not an exercise of a discretion but the application of the law: the concept of relevance employed by the law would sometimes involve the need to carry out such balancing exercises.[29]

Is it desirable to recognise a concept of 'legal relevance' that is stricter than logical relevance? Two principal difficulties stand in the way of such a development. The first is that a concept of this kind would be impossible to define. The second is that since each case would depend so much on its own facts, there would be considerable difficulty in developing a body of case law about what was legally relevant.[30] Cases where a court has made a general rule about the relevance in certain circumstances of a particular kind of evidence, such as *DPP v Camplin,* are better seen as defining substantive law than as saying something about a concept called 'legal relevance'. Cases where relevance has been used as a cloak for pragmatic decisions should simply be marginalised in favour of greater openness.

There are other potential disadvantages in acknowledging a concept of legal relevance. There is a danger that such a concept would exclude logically relevant evidence unless legal precedent authorised its admission. Further, if, despite difficulties, a body of case law were to develop, it would give rise to a large number of cumbersome rules and exceptions. But perhaps the greatest disadvantage arises from the fact that, since the decisions of judges about relevance tend to reflect the prevailing value judgments of the society in which they live, relevance can become a useful instrument for discarding arguments and evidence that challenge important, but perhaps unexpressed, values. To fix relevance in a straitjacket of case law would make it even more difficult than it already is to adapt the law to changing circumstances.[31]

---

29 A problem with this view is that the decision of a trial judge on a question of relevance amounts to a decision on a question of law. Hoffmann LJ could not face the implications of this for the work of the Court of Appeal and swiftly added that the judge's decision would be entitled to 'the same respect as the exercise of a discretion'. In other words, a judge's decision on relevance would not generally be reviewable by the Court of Appeal. The other members of the Court of Appeal (Farquharson and Ralph Gibson LJJ) showed no inclination to adopt Hoffmann LJ's views on this subject. The practical problem has been solved in civil proceedings by the new Civil Procedure Rules, which give the court a broad discretion to exclude otherwise admissible evidence: see CPR, r 32.1 and *Grobbelaar v Sun Newspapers Ltd* (1999) *The Times,* 12 August.

30 In *R v Batt* [1994] Crim LR 592, for example, the Court of Appeal held that evidence of finding £50 in the defendant's house had no relevance to intent to supply in the future the drugs that had been discovered. On the other hand, the Court of Appeal held in *R v Wright* [1994] Crim LR 55 that evidence of finding £6,000 could have given rise to an inference of dealing, and tended to show that the drugs in the defendant's possession were intended to be supplied to others. For further discussion, see Redmayne, M, 'Drugs, money and relevance' (1999) 3 E&P 128.

31 See James, GF, 'Relevancy, probability and the law' (1941) 29 Cal L Rev 689; Trautman, HL, 'Logical or legal relevancy – a conflict in theory' (1952) 5 V and L Rev 385; Weyrauch, WO, 'Law as mask – legal ritual and relevance' (1978) 66 Cal L Rev 699.

Sometimes courts avoid a full challenge to the relevance of an item of evidence, but attempt to distinguish between evidence with a 'direct' relevance to the principal question in dispute and evidence relevant to 'collateral facts', which will, if established, tend to elucidate that question. It is then said that, while it is the right of the party tendering evidence of the former kind to have it admitted, there is not the same absolute right when a party tenders evidence of facts collateral to the main issue. In order to entitle him to give such evidence, he must first satisfy the court that the collateral fact which he proposes to prove will, when established, be capable of affording a reasonable inference as to the matter in dispute. He is also bound to satisfy the court that the evidence will be reasonably conclusive, and will not raise a difficult and doubtful controversy of precisely the same kind as that which has to be determined on the main issue.[32] The reasons for this approach are the practical ones that have already been shown to affect decisions about relevance itself: collateral inquiries can confuse a jury and lengthen trials. The investigations undertaken in any trial have to be kept within reasonable limits, so as to secure 'promptitude, precision and satisfaction in the administration of justice'.[33]

The application in practice of this distinction may not be easy, as was shown by *Managers of the Metropolitan Asylum District v Hill and Others*.[34] In that case the plaintiffs, who were landowners in Hampstead, brought an action for nuisance, allegedly caused by the construction and maintenance in the vicinity of a hospital for smallpox patients. The trial judge had rejected their application to call evidence as to the effect of other similar hospitals on their surrounding neighbourhoods. Although this was not the main issue in the appeal, various observations about this ruling were made by members of the House of Lords. The Lord Chancellor, Lord Selborne, said: 'If evidence could be given of any similar or other facts, from which the effect (or absence of effect) of other hospitals ... on the surrounding neighbourhoods, could either positively or approximately be ascertained, it would ... be admissible and material.'[35]

Lord O'Hagan was not prepared to say that the trial judge had been wrong in rejecting the evidence. Even supposing there to have been proof as to the state and management of the other hospitals, so as to establish a similarity between them and the hospital at Hampstead, he thought that such evidence would not have been pertinent. It would, he said, 'have involved the jury in a multitude of collateral inquiries, calculated to confuse and embarrass

---

32 *Managers of the Metropolitan Asylum District v Hill* (1882) 47 LT 29, p 35, *per* Lord Watson.
33 *Ibid*, p 31, *per* Lord O'Hagan.
34 *Ibid*.
35 *Ibid*, p 30.

them; and it might have been endlessly prolonged by an indefinite multiplication of objects of comparison'.[36]

Lord Blackburn thought that the plaintiffs could derive no benefit from evidence that other hospitals had led to the spread of the disease in the surrounding neighbourhood unless they could show that the disease had spread despite the taking of those precautions that had been taken at the Hampstead hospital. The defendant, on the other hand, should be able to give evidence that, in the case of other hospitals, the disease had not been communicated to the neighbourhood, so as to show that a hospital did not inevitably lead to the spread of disease. He added, however, that he was aware that such inquiries might make the trial of such an issue by a jury impracticable, and so declined to say whether the evidence was properly rejected or not. Lord Watson also declined to decide the point.

The problem whether facts were collateral or directly relevant to facts in issue arose more recently in *R v Funderburk*.[37] The defendant was charged with having unlawful sexual intercourse with a girl aged 13, the daughter of a woman who was lodging with him and his partner, a Miss Potts. The girl's evidence made it clear to the jury that she had been a virgin before her first act of intercourse with the defendant. The defence case was that she was lying in order to support her mother, who had a grudge against the defendant. A difficulty the defence had to meet was the detailed account that the girl gave of the alleged acts of intercourse. One answer suggested by the defence was that, despite her age, she was sexually experienced, and had transposed experiences that she had had with other men onto the defendant. In order to substantiate this theory, the defence wished to call Miss Potts to give evidence that, before the first alleged act of intercourse with the defendant, the girl had had a conversation with Miss Potts. During this conversation, she had told Miss Potts that she had had sexual intercourse with two named men, and consequently wanted a pregnancy test. The trial judge refused to permit either evidence or questions in cross-examination on the subject of this conversation. He ruled that whether or not the girl was a virgin at the time of the first incident was irrelevant to the charge of unlawful sexual intercourse.

The Court of Appeal accepted that in order to keep criminal trials within bounds, and to assist the jury to concentrate on what mattered without being distracted by doubts about marginal events, it was necessary wherever possible to avoid a multiplicity of issues. But was the evidence that Miss Potts would have given directly relevant to a fact in issue, or was it evidence of collateral facts that were relevant, if at all, only to the girl's credibility? The court said that the answer to a question of this kind must be 'an instinctive one based on the prosecutor's and the court's sense of fair play, rather than

---

36 *Managers of the Metropolitan Asylum District v Hill* (1882) 47 LT 29, p 31.
37 [1990] 1 WLR 587; *Sourcebook*, p 378. Cf *R v Neale* [1998] Crim LR 737.

any philosophic or analytic process'.[38] On the facts of this case, the challenge to the girl's loss of virginity was sufficiently closely related to the subject matter of the indictment for justice to require evidence to be called to substantiate the challenge. The defence should therefore have been allowed to cross-examine the girl about her conversation with Miss Potts, and to call Miss Potts to rebut any denial.[39]

Weight

Although relevance and weight are distinct concepts, the weight of an item of evidence may still be connected to relevance. Even if it is accepted that there is no separate concept of legal relevance and that a clear distinction exists between relevance and weight, there remains at least some connection between relevance and weight, because the weight of an item of evidence may be affected by the form of any generalisation that is relied on to make it relevant. The bolder the generalisation, the weightier the evidence is likely to be. But the trouble with bold generalisations is that they are less likely than cautious ones to be true. When arguments about weight are addressed to juries, an overly analytical approach by an advocate is likely to be inappropriate. But further analysis can be required for purely practical reasons: arguments about weight are addressed to judges in civil trials, and in criminal trials weight may be of importance when a judge has to consider admissibility. The reason for this is that judges in criminal cases have a discretion to exclude evidence presented by the prosecution against the defendant if they think its probative worth will be outweighed by any improperly prejudicial effect it is likely to have on the jury.[40]

An example will illustrate the connection between relevance-supporting generalisations and the weight of evidence. Suppose Ronnie is charged with theft. The prosecution can show, among other items of evidence, that at a time immediately before the theft Ronnie was badly in debt. What line are you going to take about this if you are defending him? My own view is that it would be better if the jury heard nothing of this. There is always a danger of speculation – of some unjustified assumption being made. It will therefore be tempting to challenge the admissibility of this evidence on the basis that it is irrelevant. The prosecution will then have to defend its relevance. They may do so by saying, 'Of course it's relevant. It provides a motive for committing theft'. Pressed further, this may be elaborated by a generalisation on these lines: 'Persons who are in debt are highly likely to commit theft to relieve

---

38 [1990] 1 WLR 587, p 598.

39 Whether a matter is collateral or directly relevant to an issue in the case also affects rules about cross-examination and calling evidence in rebuttal: see below, Chapter 4.

40 *R v Sang* [1980] AC 402.

themselves of their burdens.' This, if true, would certainly make the evidence of debt relevant and weighty. But is this generalisation true? Surely not. Another, more acceptable, generalisation is needed. This time the prosecution come up with: 'Persons who are in debt are fairly likely to commit theft to relieve themselves of their burdens.' Most people would probably agree that this was still too sweeping a generalisation to be accepted as true. So the prosecution try again: 'Persons who are in debt are more likely than those who are not to commit theft.' This might be accepted as true. By now, however, the generalisation has become so weak that the value of the evidence of debt is highly questionable. In particular, the generalisation says nothing about *how much more likely* are persons in debt to commit theft than those who are not in debt.

At this stage, a different line will be taken by the defence in their attempt to get the evidence of debt excluded. 'Your Honour, I do not concede that this item of evidence is relevant. But even if it is, the weight of the evidence must be very slight because of the weak, inconclusive nature of the generalisation needed to make it so. That in itself is a reason for exclusion, because the probative worth of the evidence is very small when set against its possible prejudicial effect.' More will be said about the judge's discretion to exclude evidence later.[41] The important thing at this stage is to see that the defence have available an argument for exclusion based on weight, which itself is founded on the form of the argument relied on to establish relevance.

Admissibility

I have been discussing admissibility so far mainly in connection with relevance. But it is possible to have an item of evidence which is clearly relevant but which is nevertheless inadmissible because of some rule of law. You might think that this situation, at least, could be dealt with merely by knowing the law, but you would be mistaken. The reason for this, as we shall see in more detail in later chapters, is that the application of some of the most important rules of exclusion is governed by the probative job that the questioned item of evidence has to do.[42] It is wise, therefore, when considering the possibility of exclusion on legal grounds, to clarify first the way in which the questioned item of evidence is relevant; that is, in effect, to discover its probative job. Failure to do this is likely to lead to misapplication of the law. In particular, any argument based on a previous judicial decision is foolhardy unless you are satisfied that the analogy between your own case and the earlier one is proper. And it is unlikely to be proper if the probative jobs done by the evidence in the two cases are different.

---

41 See below, Chapter 9.
42 See, in particular, the law relating to hearsay and similar fact evidence.

An example will show what I mean. Suppose in your present case you want to call Charlie. If permitted, he will say, 'Danny told me that he saw Edward breaking into the bank'. Now suppose that you had doubts about the admissibility of this. You have done some research and you have found a Court of Appeal decision which has not been overruled and which held on its facts that Gerald could say in evidence, 'Harry told me that he saw Jim breaking into the post office'. If you were interested in the *form* of the words rather than in their *function in the case as a whole* you might well conclude that there was no significant difference between these two statements and that by virtue of the earlier decision Charlie should be able to give evidence of what Danny told him.

But suppose you check the *probative job* of the evidence in each case. In the present case you are prosecuting Edward for burglary. But the Court of Appeal case concerned a civil action for defamation brought by Jim against Harry. The probative job is different in each case. In the civil action, Jim wanted to prove that Harry had made a defamatory allegation of robbery against him. The last thing he wanted to prove, if he were to recover damages for defamation, was that what Harry said was true. The function of the evidence was solely to prove that the particular allegation had been made. In the present criminal case, however, the function of the evidence is to prove that Edward is guilty of burglary. The words are being relied on for the truth of what they allege, not just for the fact that they were uttered. The result of the difference in function is that the earlier piece of evidence was admissible but the later is not. The evidence in the criminal case is inadmissible because it offends the rule against hearsay. Put simply, this is a rule which forbids calling evidence of what was asserted by someone outside court in order to establish *the truth of the matters asserted*, as opposed to *the fact of assertion*.

It is clear from this example that the form of words alone will not reveal the probative job of the item of evidence in question. This will be revealed only when you look at what the parties are trying to prove in the case and see what is the relevance of the particular item of evidence to one or more of those objectives. In other words, until you know what is the relevance of the proposed evidence, you do not know the probative job and you cannot apply the law.

SOME TERMINOLOGY

It may be helpful at this stage to provide simple explanations of some of the technical terms most commonly encountered in this subject. They are arranged alphabetically. Usage varies to some extent and what I have provided should be regarded as a guide, not as a set of closed definitions.

Best evidence rule[43]

This was an old rule of evidence requiring that the best evidence that the nature of the case allowed should always be presented to the jury. It did not require the greatest quantity of evidence that could possibly be given of any fact; the object of the rule was to prevent the introduction of any evidence which, from the nature of the case, suggested that better evidence was in the possession of the party producing it. So, for example, oral evidence of the physical condition of certain objects was rejected when the objects could have been produced in court.[44] The best evidence rule was also one of the traditional justifications for rejecting hearsay evidence.[45] The rule has long since fallen into abeyance.[46]

Circumstantial evidence

This expression refers to evidence of a fact that is not itself a fact in issue[47] but is a fact from which the existence or non-existence of a fact in issue can be inferred. For example, in the Crippen case, one of the facts in issue was the fact that Mrs Crippen was dead. But the prosecution could not produce a witness who had seen her die, or who had seen and identified her dead body. It was therefore necessary to rely on circumstantial evidence of the fact of death. This was provided by the discovery of the remains in the cellar, including the piece of scarred flesh, and the fact that no one had seen or heard from Mrs Crippen for some time.

Collateral facts[48]

These are facts relating to some subsidiary matter which itself affects the question of whether a fact in issue will be established or not. Examples are facts affecting a witness's competence,[49] or the weight to be attached to a witness's evidence. For example, evidence about a witness's bias would generally be held to fall within this category.

---

43 Twining, W, *Rethinking Evidence: Exploratory Essays*, 1994, pp 35–36; Nance, DA, 'The best evidence principle' (1988) 73 Iowa L Rev 227; Imwinkelreid, EJ, 'The worst evidence principle: the best hypothesis as to the logical structure of evidence law' (1992) U Miami L Rev 1069.

44 *Chenie v Watson* (1797) Peake Add Cas 123.

45 See below, Chapter 6.

46 *Garton v Hunter* [1969] 2 QB 37, p 44. But see Nance, *op cit*, fn 43.

47 See below, p 23.

48 See above, pp 17–19.

49 Some writers call these 'preliminary facts'.

Documentary evidence[50]

This expression refers to evidence of the contents of documents. Obvious examples of documentary evidence are written contracts, correspondence and memoranda. 'Documentary evidence' refers to anything in which information of any description is recorded, and may therefore include such items as films, tapes and video recordings.[51] The contents of documents may be proved by either 'primary' or 'secondary' evidence. 'Primary evidence' refers to the original document itself, produced for the inspection of the court. 'Secondary evidence' refers to evidence of the contents of the original document which comes by report, or in some other second hand or derivative way. Examples would be a copy of the original document, or oral evidence from a person who has seen the original and can recall its contents.

Facts in issue

In a civil action, this expression refers to those facts alleged in the statements of case by the parties, including facts necessary to establish pleaded defences, that are either denied or not admitted by the other party. In criminal cases the effect of a plea of not guilty is to declare everything that the substantive law makes material to the offence a fact in issue.[52] In practice today, this statement of the effect of a plea of not guilty does not represent the whole picture. There are informal procedures for clarifying issues in any complex criminal case at a pre-trial hearing. There are also statutory procedures for the same purpose where a criminal case involves serious or complex fraud, or where the indictment reveals a case of such complexity or length that a preparatory hearing would be of substantial benefit.[53] There is also a duty of defence disclosure under s 5 of the Criminal Procedure and Investigations Act 1996.

Original evidence

A distinction has traditionally been drawn between evidence which is 'original' and evidence which comes before the tribunal at second hand or in

---

50 See below, Chapter 17.

51 Criminal Justice Act 1988, Sched 2, para 5(1), as amended, and Civil Evidence Act 1995, s 13. In fact the common law included within the class of documentary evidence 'all material substances on which the thoughts of men are represented by writing, or any other species of conventional mark or symbol'. So, eg, the wooden tally sticks used as receipts in the Exchequer counted as documentary evidence: Best, *Treatise*, pp 297–98.

52 *R v Sims* [1946] KB 531, p 539, *per* Lord Goddard CJ.

53 *Practice Direction (Crown Court: Plea and Directions Hearings)* [1995] 1 WLR 1318; Criminal Justice Act 1987, ss 7–11; Criminal Procedure and Investigations Act 1996, ss 29–31.

some other derivative way. An example of this distinction is the division of documentary evidence into primary and secondary categories. The expression 'original evidence' is also used to refer to evidence of words uttered by someone other than the testifying witness, where the object of adducing such evidence is not to prove the truth of anything asserted by the person who first uttered the words, but merely to prove the fact that the assertion was made. For example, ss 4 and 18 of the Public Order Act 1986 make it an offence in certain circumstances for a person to use threatening, abusive or insulting words. In a prosecution under the Act, evidence could be given by a bystander who was able to remember and repeat the words which he had heard the defendant use.

Real evidence[54]

This term is used to refer to items of evidence that are presented to the senses of the tribunal and that may be examined by it. A good example was the piece of scarred flesh in the Crippen case. Original documents such as letters, contracts or memoranda may also become items of real evidence if they are adduced to show their condition rather than the truth of their contents. In the latter case, it would be more appropriate to refer to them as documentary evidence. The use of real evidence as a means of persuasion can be most effective. A famous American trial lawyer once observed that 'jurors learn through all their senses, and if you can tell them and show them, too, let them see and feel and even taste or smell the evidence; then you will reach the jury'.[55]

Testimony

'Testimonial evidence', or 'testimony', was traditionally defined as the sworn statements of witnesses in court.[56] There are several difficulties with this definition today. First, not all statements in court are sworn. The evidence of children under 14, for example, cannot be given on oath in criminal trials.[57] Secondly, evidence today can be given in certain circumstances by video-link. Thirdly, the old definition tended to obscure the fact that in some civil proceedings, especially at pre-trial applications, the sworn statement of the witness was in writing. Such statements were called 'affidavits' (from the medieval Latin *affidare*, meaning 'to declare on oath'). Under the new Civil Procedure Rules, at pre-trial applications, written, unsworn, witness

---

54 See below, Chapter 17.
55 See the obituary of Melvin Belli (1996) *The Times*, 11 July, p 19.
56 See, eg, Stone, S and Wells, WAN, *Evidence: Its History and Policies*, 1991, p 84.
57 See below, Chapter 3.

statements are generally used instead, and these now constitute the evidence on which the court will base its decision at that stage. Perhaps 'testimony' is ceasing to be a useful term.

Voir dire

The *voir dire* is a trial within a trial, in which the court determines disputed facts that have to be established before certain items of evidence can be admitted. Examples are disputed questions of fact in relation to the competence of a witness, or in relation to the admissibility of a confession or a tape recording. The name of the procedure comes from the old form of a special oath taken by witnesses on such occasions. In trials on indictment, the *voir dire* is held in the absence of the jury, as the decision on the question is one for the judge alone.

TWO IMPORTANT CHARACTERISTICS OF EVIDENCE LAW

Evidence law has only a limited application and evidence law is a mixture of principles, rules and discretions.

Evidence law has only a limited application

It applies in its fullest form only in contested Crown Court cases. In such cases, questions about evidence law arise in two principal contexts: in arguments about admissibility and in arguments about what directions the judge should give to the jury in summing up. Whatever the historical origins of rules of exclusion, the fact remains that for over a century at least they have been justified as a way of controlling the supposedly erratic reasoning of juries. In civil cases, which are only very exceptionally tried by a jury, there is virtually no need for this protective approach. Gradually, this has had its effect on the law of evidence, and now many of the restrictions on admissibility which still operate in criminal cases have been abolished in civil cases. For example, the Civil Evidence Act 1995 has abolished the operation, in civil proceedings, of one of the most entrenched of the exclusionary rules – the rule against hearsay.[58] In magistrates' courts, the strict rules of evidence apply in the hearing of criminal cases, but arguments about evidence law are less frequent than in Crown Court trials because the magistrates are judges of both law and fact. There can be no question of keeping them in ignorance, as a jury

---

58 See below, Chapter 6.

can be kept in ignorance, of an item of evidence whose admissibility is contested. Further, because there is no summing up in a trial before magistrates, arguments about directions on evidence cannot arise. In practice, a law of criminal evidence that has been developed by appellate courts in the context of Crown Court trials may not always be easy, or even possible, to apply in magistrates' courts.[59]

In addition, much dispute resolution goes on outside courts. Arbitrators and tribunals of various kinds have, from the beginning, adopted a much more flexible approach to the admissibility of evidence. Even within the criminal process, important pre-trial decisions are made which affect citizens, but which are governed only very loosely, if at all, by evidence law. For example, evidence law has little or nothing to say that will affect decisions to arrest or charge a suspect.

Evidence law is a mixture of principles, rules and discretions

Students sometimes hope that evidence law is merely a system of rules that can be packed neatly into a handbook and memorised. Whatever the position may have been in the past, the truth of the matter these days is very different. As Lord Griffiths said in *R v H*:

> In the past when jurors were often uneducated and illiterate and the penal laws were of harsh severity, when children could be transported, and men were hanged for stealing a shilling and could not be heard in their own defence, the judges began to fashion rules of evidence to protect the accused from a conviction that they feared might be based on emotion or prejudice rather than a fair evaluation of the facts of the case against him. The judges did not trust the jury to evaluate all the relevant material and evolved many restrictive rules which they deemed necessary to ensure that the accused had a fair trial in the climate of those times. Today with better educated and more literate juries the value of those old restrictive rules of evidence is being re-evaluated and many are being discarded or modified.[60]

It should be said that, as a historical account, this is highly misleading.[61] What is important, however, is the current judicial attitude towards exclusionary rules that it illustrates. Our starting point must be the distinction between rules and principles, which is a common feature of any developed legal system and which has been made familiar since the 1960s by Ronald Dworkin[62] The

---

59   See Darbyshire, P, 'Previous misconduct and magistrates' courts – some tales from the real world' [1997] Crim LR 105; Darbyshire, P, 'An essay on the importance and neglect of the magistracy' [1997] Crim LR 627.

60   [1995] 2 AC 596, p 613.

61   See Allen, C, *The Law of Evidence in Victorian England*, 1997, Chapter 2.

62   See, eg, Dworkin, RM, 'Is law a system of rules?', in *The Philosophy of Law*, Oxford Readings in Philosophy, 1977, pp 38–65.

distinction is this. Rules are applicable in an all-or-nothing fashion. If the facts are those stipulated in the rule, then the rule applies. A rule can have exceptions, but an accurate statement of the rule will take these into account. For example, it is a rule that, in criminal proceedings, the evidence of a child aged under 14 shall be given unsworn.[63] So if little Johnnie, aged 13, has to give evidence in a criminal trial, he must do so unsworn, however intelligent or religious he may be. There are no two ways about it.

Principles, on the other hand, do not necessitate a particular decision in the way that rules do. They do not apply in an all-or-nothing way. All we mean when we say that something is a principle of our law is that it is something which officials, including judges, must take into account if it is relevant in a particular situation. For example, it is a principle of evidence law that the prosecution may not call evidence to show that the accused has been guilty of earlier criminal acts for the purpose of leading to the conclusion that the accused is a person likely, from his criminal conduct or character, to have committed the offence which is the subject of the current indictment.[64] This, like every other legal principle, has a dimension that rules lack. That dimension is one of weight, or importance. We cannot say that, within a system of rules, one rule is more important than another, so that when two rules conflict one supersedes the other because of its greater weight. If two rules conflict, one of them must be an invalid rule. The position is entirely different with principles. Because a principle is simply something that must be taken into account if relevant, it does not point conclusively to a particular result in the way that a rule does. Nor can it, strictly speaking, conflict with other principles. The existence of another, different, principle does not entail that the first one should be ignored because it is irrelevant. Both principles are to be taken into account, but, on the facts of a particular case, the judge will give greater weight to one principle rather than the other. For example, it is also a principle of evidence law that the mere fact that an item of prosecution evidence shows the commission by the accused of crimes other than those in the indictment should not render that evidence inadmissible if it is relevant to an issue before the jury.[65]

To illustrate the application of principles, let us suppose that Charlie is charged with the murder of a young girl by strangulation. There was no sign of a struggle, nor of any attempt at sexual interference. There was no other apparent motive for the crime. No attempt had been made to conceal the body, although this could easily have been done. Charlie was seen near the place where the body was found, but there were other people around who

---

63   Youth Justice and Criminal Evidence Act 1999, s 55(2)(a).

64   *Makin v AG for New South Wales* [1894] AC 57, p 65, *per* Lord Herschell LC; *Sourcebook*, p 228. In this interpretation I am following Williams, CR, 'The problem of similar fact evidence' (1979) Dalhousie LJ 281, extracts from which are reprinted in *Sourcebook*, pp 229–34.

65   *Makin v AG for New South Wales* [1894] AC 57, p 65.

might have committed the crime. However, we know something more about Charlie. Last year, he was charged with the murder by strangulation of two other young girls, whose bodies were found in similar circumstances – no sign of a struggle, no attempt at sexual interference, and no attempt to conceal the bodies. He was tried, found guilty of manslaughter by reason of diminished responsibility and sent to a mental hospital under a restriction order without limit of time.[66] Just before the current murder, Charlie had escaped from the mental hospital, which was only a few miles away. Both principles are relevant in the prosecution of Charlie for this most recent murder, but the judge will have to give one greater weight than the other if the prosecution argues that evidence of Charlie's convictions for the earlier killings is relevant and admissible in the current case.[67]

The difference between rules and principles is of the utmost importance when considering whether, or to what extent, a previous case should be used in arguing a point of evidence law. If the earlier case is at appellate level and *defines or modifies a rule*, the ratio of the case becomes part of the rule and therefore binding in relevantly similar circumstances. But if the earlier case involves *the application of a principle* to a particular situation, that decision will reinforce the principle, but is not likely to be of much help in deciding a later case. There are two main reasons for this. The first is that the application of the principle in the first case does not make irrelevant other competing principles in the later case. The second reason is that, when principles have to be chosen and applied, courts are more sensitive to the facts of the particular case under consideration and less likely to be influenced by the preferences made in earlier cases where the facts inevitably were different. At best, an earlier decision will be only persuasive; at worst, it will be irrelevant.

It is clear that if a principle-based approach is adopted rather than one that is rule-based, the court is less constrained. Where a principle has to be chosen and applied, argument will be about the facts of the particular case rather than about other cases. This is a radically different style of argument from that adopted in some other legal contexts, but it is the kind of argument that has become increasingly important in evidence law. Not only have the courts moved away from a rule-based approach to one based on principle, but the legislature has encouraged this process. At common law, for example, the law relating to similar fact evidence[68] has undergone radical change since the 1970s. The willingness of Parliament to adopt an approach based on principles rather than on rules can be seen in s 78 of the Police and Criminal Evidence Act 1984, which allowed judges to exclude prosecution evidence on the ground of unfairness in relation to the proceedings, and in s 32 of the Criminal Justice and Public Order Act 1994, which permitted the development of a

---

66 For restriction orders, see Mental Health Act 1983, s 41.

67 Cf *R v Straffen* [1952] 2 QB 911.

68 See below, Chapter 10.

system of informal warnings in place of the old law of corroboration.[69] A principle-based approach to the law inevitably gives the trial judge greater discretion than does a rule-based approach to admit or exclude evidence. The Court of Appeal recognises this, and has on several occasions said that it will not interfere with decisions about admissibility made in exercise of a discretion except on the familiar public law grounds.[70] The effect of this is that the advocate will often have to argue about admissibility at trial *on the facts* and without the assistance of binding precedents. This will generally be the only opportunity for his submission to succeed; in the absence of public law grounds he is unlikely to have a second chance in the Court of Appeal.

Of course, it may not always be clear whether a particular part of evidence law is governed by principles, by rules, or by a mixture of the two. The situation may be in flux. Even if this does not appear to be so, students should be on their guard against assuming over-readily that the topic under investigation is rule-based. Judges who have become familiar over the years with a rule-based system of evidence may talk without meaning to do so as if that system still applies in all its original force. Care needs to be taken also in reading expositions of law in standard textbooks. Writers of such works have traditionally favoured a rule-based approach to their subject, not least because this makes for simplicity of organisation.[71] In fact, simplicity was often only superficially attained. There is a strong argument in favour of a principle-based approach to evidence law, since an overly rule-based approach is likely to lead to frustration from attempts to reconcile the irreconcilable. If, for example, you adopted a rule-based approach towards the cases on the admissibility of evidence about finding cash when a defendant is charged with possession of drugs with intent to supply, not only would you have to memorise the particular facts of all the cases where such evidence was allowed or disallowed, but you would have to try to construct from the cases a system of rules without any contradictions. It is much simpler, and it makes far more sense, to regard these cases as attempts, more or less successful, to apply basic principles of relevance, without in themselves establishing any binding rules about admissibility.[72]

---

69 See below, Chapters 8 and 9.

70 See, eg, *R v Rankin* (1995) *The Times*, 5 September; *R v Khan and Others* [1997] Crim LR 508. Those grounds are that the person with a power of decision took into account something that should have been ignored, failed to take into account something that should have been considered, or reached a decision that no reasonable person could have reached.

71 Simpson, AWB, 'The rise and fall of the legal treatise: legal principles and the forms of legal literature' (1981) U Chicago L Rev 632; Sugarman, D, 'Legal theory, the common law mind and the making of the textbook tradition', in Twining, W (ed), *Legal Theory and Common Law*, 1986, pp 26–61.

72 See, eg, the cases cited above, fn 30. These are only the tip of the iceberg. The effect of this shift in favour of principles and judicial discretion has been to increase the importance for advocates of being able to develop arguments about the relevance and weight of evidence as well as the more traditional arguments based on case law and statute. Cf above, pp 8–20.

THE FUNCTIONS OF JUDGE AND JURY

In jury trials the judicial function is divided between the judge, whose decision on matters of law is (subject to the right of appeal) final, and the jury, who are in principle the sole judges of fact. Every summing up should contain a direction to the jury about these separate functions. The suggested direction, prepared by the Criminal Committee of the Judicial Studies Board and revised in June 1991, encouraged the judge to explain the position as follows:

> It is my job to tell you what the law is and how to apply it to the issues of fact that you have to decide and to remind you of the important evidence on these issues. As to the law, you must accept what I tell you. As to the facts, you alone are the judges. It is for you to decide what evidence you accept and what evidence you reject or of which you are unsure. If I appear to have a view of the evidence or of the facts with which you do not agree, reject my view. If I mention or emphasise evidence that you regard as unimportant, disregard that evidence. If I do not mention what you regard as important, follow your own view and take that evidence into account.[73]

It is particularly important that this division of functions be made clear to juries, because the law permits the trial judge to comment on the evidence in his summing up. Subject to an overriding obligation to be fair, a judge is entitled to give his opinion to the jury on a question of fact and to express it strongly, so long as he makes it clear that this is advice, rather than a direction that must be followed.[74] In *R v Sparrow*, Lawton LJ recommended a robust approach by trial judges:

> [I]n our experience a jury is not helped by a colourless reading out of the evidence as recorded by the judge in his notebook. The judge is more than a mere referee who takes no part in the trial save to intervene when a rule of procedure or evidence is broken. He and the jury try the case together and it is his duty to give them the benefit of his knowledge of the law and *to advise them in the light of his experience as to the significance of the evidence* ...[75]

There are, however, at least two important situations where, despite the general principle, the judge in a criminal trial makes rulings that involve decisions about facts. In the first place, it is sometimes necessary to establish the existence of certain facts before a particular witness's evidence, or a

---

73 Quoted in *R v Jackson* [1992] Crim LR 214. This is only a suggested direction; it does not have to be followed verbatim. But failure to give a direction conveying the gist of what is expressed by these words is likely to give rise to a successful appeal. In fact, the message is not new. See the charge to the jury of Buller J in *De La Motte's Trial* (1781) 21 St Tr 687, col 809.

74 *Chandler v DPP* [1964] AC 763, p 804, *per* Lord Devlin. Cf the summing up of Devlin J, as he then was, in the trial of Dr Bodkin Adams in 1957: Devlin, P, *Easing the Passing: the Trial of Dr John Bodkin Adams*, 1986, p 177. But the Court of Appeal has said that a judge should not give his own views about whether witnesses have told the truth or not: *R v Iroegbu* (1988) *The Times*, 2 August. See also *Mitchell v R* [1998] 2 Cr App R 35, p 42.

75 [1973] 1 WLR 488, p 495. Emphasis supplied.

particular item of evidence, can be admitted. Here it is for the judge to decide whether the condition is satisfied. For example, it is for the judge to decide whether a witness is competent to give evidence.[76] It is also for the judge, not the jury, to decide whether the prosecution has proved those matters which have to be established before evidence can be given of a confession by an accused person.[77]

Secondly, it is the judge's task to decide, on a defence submission that there is no case to answer, whether there is sufficient evidence to allow the case to proceed or whether the jury should be instructed to return a verdict of not guilty without waiting to hear the case for the defence. The approach of a trial judge to such a submission was set out in *R v Galbraith* and approved in *R v Fulcher*.[78] If there is no evidence that the alleged crime has been committed by the defendant, the judge should stop the case by directing the jury at that stage to return a verdict of not guilty. Where there is some evidence of a tenuous character, for example because of an inherent weakness or vagueness, or because it is inconsistent with other prosecution evidence, he should stop the case if he decides that it is not such as would allow a properly directed jury to convict. But where the strength or weakness of the prosecution case depends on the view to be taken of a witness's reliability, and where on one possible view of the facts there is evidence on which a jury could properly conclude that the defendant was guilty, the case should be allowed to proceed.[79]

Finally, it should be noticed that although the judge's directions on the law are his responsibility, it has become increasingly common for the judge to invite prosecution and defence advocates to address him on the content of those directions where there is room for more than one view about what that should be. In *R v N*,[80] the Court of Appeal observed that it had frequently said that difficulties would be avoided, and cases conducted with clarity, if discussion took place between judge and counsel at the end of the evidence about points of law and, more particularly, about the points of evidence that had arisen. (Such discussion should, of course, be in open court, but in the absence of the jury.) The effect of this development has been to increase the amount of preparation required for a criminal jury trial. Not only must

---

76 Youth Justice and Criminal Evidence Act 1999, s 54.

77 Police and Criminal Evidence Act 1984, s 76(2) and (3).

78 [1981] 1 WLR 1039; [1995] 2 Cr App R 251.

79 These are not the only, or even the only important, instances when a judge makes a decision about facts in a criminal trial. Other instances include the balancing between probative value and likely prejudicial effect when a judge is asked to exercise his common law discretion to exclude evidence: see below, Chapter 9; see also the discussion of relevance in this chapter, above, pp 10–19. If there is no special concept of legal relevance, it looks very much as if a judge's decision on this subject is a decision about facts rather than law.

80 [1998] Crim LR 886. See also *R v Islam* [1999] 1 Cr App R 22, p 23.

advocates prepare arguments for or against the admissibility of problematic items of evidence; arguments will also have to be prepared about the directions which the judge should give to the jury on admissible items of evidence that may call for special guidance.

THE EUROPEAN CONVENTION ON HUMAN RIGHTS

The Convention was incorporated into English law by the Human Rights Act 1998. Section 6(1) of the Act provides that it is unlawful for a public authority to act in a way which is incompatible with a Convention right. By s 6(3), 'public authority' includes a court or tribunal. Courts must therefore have regard to the Convention in all their decisions. This will include taking into account relevant decisions of the European Court of Human Rights in which provisions in the Convention have been interpreted and applied. If English case law is inconsistent with Convention rights, the Convention prevails. The position of legislation is different. By s 3(1), so far as it is possible to do so, primary and subordinate legislation must be read and given effect in a way that is compatible with Convention rights. If this is not possible, the legislation must be applied, but the court can make a declaration of its incompatibility with the Convention. It is expected that this will trigger an amendment to remove the incompatibility.

The impact of the Convention on evidence law is potentially considerable. Of particular significance are Art 6, which provides a right to a fair trial, and Art 8, which provides a right to respect for private and family life. Article 6 has been held to provide, by implication, a privilege against self-incrimination.[81] Article 8 is of importance when considering the admissibility of evidence obtained by intrusive surveillance devices. At various stages throughout this book, the impact of the Convention is considered in relation to specific problems. However, it will be helpful at the outset to have some understanding of the general approach of the European Court of Human Rights to its interpretation. A fundamental point to grasp is that the Court adopts a flexible approach, despite the apparently absolute character of some of the articles. Convention rights tend to be regarded as principles to be applied in the particular circumstances of individual nation states.[82]

In *Brown v Stott*, Lord Steyn observed that the preambles to the Convention reveal two basic aims. The first is to maintain and realise human rights and fundamental freedoms. The second is to foster effective political democracy. The makers of the Convention, he said, realised that from time to time, the fundamental right of one individual may conflict with the rights of

---

81 *Brown v Stott (Procurator Fiscal, Dunfermline)* [2001] 2 All ER 97, pp 115, 119 (PC).
82 *Ibid*, p 115.

others. For example, the principles of free speech and privacy may be in conflict in a particular set of circumstances. A single-minded concentration on the pursuit of individuals' fundamental rights, to the exclusion of the interests of the wider public, might be subversive of the ideal of a tolerant liberal democracy. So, the Convention requires that where difficult questions arise, a balance must be struck.[83]

Some applications of Art 6 can be used to illustrate this. The right to be presumed innocent of a criminal offence until proved guilty under Art 6(2) appears to be an absolute requirement. But it has been held that it does not prohibit rules that transfer the burden to the accused to establish a defence, provided the overall burden of proof remains on the prosecution.[84] The admissibility of evidence has been recognised as generally a matter for national systems to regulate. Unlawfully obtained evidence may be admissible without affecting the fairness of the trial as a whole.[85] The right of silence is not absolute.[86] Lord Hope has summarised a three-step approach, based on decisions of the European Court, to be followed when issues are raised about an alleged incompatibility with a right under Art 6:

- is the right in question an absolute right, or is it a right which is open to modification or restriction?;

- if it is not absolute, does the modification or restriction contended for have a legitimate aim in the public interest?;

- if so, is there a reasonable relationship of proportionality between the means employed and the aim sought to be realised?[87]

Provisions of the Convention ought not to be used by themselves in an attempt to make an argument seem stronger. In *Barclays Bank plc v Ellis*,[88] the Court of Appeal said that mere reference to the Convention does not help the court. Counsel has a duty to formulate arguments *based on European decisions*; only in that way can an argument be persuasive.[89]

---

83   *Brown v Stott (Procurator Fiscal, Dunfermline)* [2001] 2 All ER 97, p 118. See also Lord Bingham at p 115. But see also *Heaney and McGuinness v Ireland* [2001] Crim LR 481, where the ECHR held that in some circumstances the very essence of a Convention right may be destroyed, and so give rise to a violation.

84   *Ibid*, p 105.

85   *Ibid*, pp 107–08.

86   *Ibid*, p 119.

87   *Ibid*, p 130.

88   (2000) *The Times*, 24 October.

89   The same applies to examination candidates.

CHAPTER 2

DEVELOPMENT AND CURRENT OBJECTIVES

The purpose of this chapter is to provide an outline of the way in which evidence law has developed, and to say something about its possible objectives today. Some knowledge of the development of a legal subject is useful because it can make the present law easier to understand. It can also be helpful in practice if you have to argue a point of law. An opponent will sometimes try to rely on an earlier decision that appears to be against you. It may not be possible to show that it has been overruled, and it may be difficult to distinguish it from your case on the facts. What you may be able to do, though, is show that the legal context in which it was decided was different from that of today; the law moves on, and your opponent's 'authority' is no more than a relic of an outdated approach.[1] Thinking about the possible *objectives* of evidence law can have a use beyond that of answering examination questions. In a subject that is increasingly governed by discretion and based on principles as well as rules, a wide perspective can be useful in argument, as the statute and case law on improperly obtained evidence shows.[2]

DEVELOPMENT

In 1983, Dennis Butler was tried for raping and indecently assaulting two women, each on a separate occasion. Various sexual activities were alleged against him. In an interview with the police Mr Butler denied everything. He refused to take part in an identification parade, so confrontations were arranged between him and the complainants. One failed to recognise him. The other was rather doubtful about his appearance but recognised him more definitely by his voice. No doubt because it was clear that identification would be an issue at trial, the prosecution wished to rely on evidence of 'similar facts' to strengthen the case against the accused. Leave was requested to call a woman who had previously had a sexual relationship with Mr Butler. She, it was hoped, would describe a variety of sexual practices in which they had freely indulged, but which closely resembled those that the complainants said their attacker had forced them to perform. The defence objected to the admissibility of this evidence. Later, in the Court of Appeal, Sir Ralph Kilner Brown described the way in which this question had been determined:

---

1   See, eg, *R v Butler* (1987) 84 Cr App R 12.
2   See below, Chapter 9.

At the trial, and to some extent before us, there was an unnecessary citation of lengthy extracts from numerous authorities, one or two of which go back nearly a hundred years. Encouraged by the very full and detailed treatment of the subject in *Archbold* (42nd edn), Chapter 13 and Chapter 14, para 12, application to call the evidence took a long time and went into a second day. The argument before the judge occupied no less than 15 pages of transcript, and the ruling by the judge another 13 pages of the transcript.[3]

Even a decade earlier, such an extensive citation of cases would probably have attracted no comment because evidence of 'similar facts' had, for much of the 20th century, been regarded as governed by a detailed system of *rules*, established by binding decisions of appellate courts. But Sir Ralph Kilner Brown observed that the leading case of *DPP v Boardman*[4] and other authorities had established *principles* that were well known, and that within those principles, every case was to be decided *on its own particular circumstances*.

A year after Dennis Butler's trial, Parliament emphasised the place of principle and discretion in evidence law. In s 78 of the Police and Criminal Evidence Act 1984, it was enacted that a judge might exclude evidence on which the prosecution proposed to rely if it appeared that its admission would have such an adverse effect on the fairness of the proceedings that it ought to be excluded.[5] Despite some setbacks (in particular, the decision of the House of Lords on hearsay evidence in *R v Kearley* and some recent statutory provisions),[6] evidence law today is less rule-based than at any time since the formation of the Court of Criminal Appeal in 1907. This more flexible approach is not a complete novelty. Courts for much of the 18th century adopted a far less restricted approach than they did later towards the evidence of competent witnesses. For example, although the leading treatise stated that 'a mere hearsay' was 'no evidence', such evidence was nevertheless widely admitted.[7] From quite early in the 19th century, however, this approach gave way in civil cases to an increasingly rule-based system. A study of the development of modern evidence may therefore conveniently begin in the 18th century and try to follow the ways in which a more rigid system became established, from which we have only fairly recently begun to be released.

---

3   *R v Butler* (1987) 84 Cr App R 12, p 16.

4   [1975] AC 421.

5   See also Criminal Justice Act 1988, ss 25 and 26.

6   [1992] 2 AC 228.

7   Gilbert, Sir J, *The Law of Evidence*, 3rd edn, 1769, p 152. For the admissibility in practice of hearsay, see Langbein, JH, 'The criminal trial before the lawyers' (1978) 45 U Chi L Rev 236; Langbein, JH, 'Shaping the eighteenth-century criminal trial: a view from the Ryder sources' (1983) 50 U Chi L Rev 1; Langbein, JH, 'Historical foundations of the law of evidence: a view from the Ryder sources' (1996) 96 Columbia Law Rev 1168.

Counsel in the 18th century regularly appeared in civil cases in the superior courts of common law and at *nisi prius*,[8] and in doing so followed a well established practice. This is reflected in the work on evidence by Gilbert, which was published posthumously in 1754 and was the leading work on the subject for about 50 years.[9] Gilbert's *Law of Evidence* was not primarily a work of theory. It was a practical work, in which the longest section was taken up with a consideration of the evidence admissible to prove or disprove issues arising in different forms of action. Gilbert shows us what evidential matters were important to lawyers acting for parties in 18th century civil proceedings.

Apart from the large section dealing with substantive law, two features indicate a way of looking at evidential problems that was strikingly different from our own. The first is a substantial body of rules excluding not classes of *evidence*, but classes of *witnesses*. Two major groups were affected. Those who would not give evidence on oath were generally excluded, whether their refusal was due to religious scruples or to lack of any religious belief. In addition, anyone with a financial or proprietary interest in the outcome of a case was incompetent to testify as a witness in it, however small the interest might be. One of the effects of this rule was, of course, to bar the parties to the litigation from testifying. In addition, some potential witnesses might be excluded because of past criminal convictions. Some idea of the reasons for these exclusions can be gathered from arguments that were raised against subsequent proposals for reform. Evidence had to be given on oath because it was thought that people with the wrong sort of religious belief – or, worse, no religious belief at all – could not be trusted as responsible members of society. The oath was a fundamental safeguard of truth; to make it optional would be to encourage infidelity and irreligion.[10] Treatise writers tended to justify the exclusion of interested persons from testifying on the basis of their supposed lack of integrity or impartiality.[11] However, when reform was mooted a different argument was put forward: people ought not to be put in a position where they might be tempted to commit perjury.[12] This argument may in fact have been closer to the original purpose of the rule than that suggested by the

---

8   Juries in civil cases were traditionally summoned to appear on a fixed day at Westminster, but it became the practice to add to the summons, 'unless before then [*nisi prius*] the King's justices should have come' into the county as commissioners of assize and gaol delivery. Baker, JH, *An Introduction to English Legal History*, 3rd edn, 1990, pp 24–25; Milsom, SFC, *Historical Foundations of the Common Law*, 2nd edn, 1981, p 49.

9   See above, fn 7 and see also Twining, W, 'The rationalist tradition of evidence scholarship', in *Rethinking Evidence: Exploratory Essays*, 1994, pp 32, 35–38; Landsman, S, 'From Gilbert to Bentham: the reconceptualization of evidence theory' (1990) 36 Wayne L Rev 1149.

10 See the comment by Taylor, JP, *Treatise on the Law of Evidence*, 6th edn, 1872, Vol II, para 1248, in which he regretted the reforms that had by then been made.

11 See, eg, Phillipps, SM, *A Treatise on the Law of Evidence*, 7th edn, 1829, Vol I, p 45; Starkie, T, *A Practical Treatise of the Law of Evidence*, 3rd edn, 1842, Vol I, p 17.

12 See, eg, Lowndes, J, *A Few Brief Remarks on Lord Denman's Bill for Improving the Law of Evidence*, 1843.

treatise writers. Steven Shapin has shown the importance of truthfulness as a characteristic of gentility in the 17th century;[13] it may be that the exclusion of interested witnesses in the superior courts of common law was not to protect the courts from being misled, but to protect the gentry from the embarrassment of being found to be liars. In inferior courts, where small claims were heard, the ban did not apply.[14]

The second feature of Gilbert's treatise that marks it out from later writings on evidence is the emphasis placed on written testimony. Gilbert's basic principle was that proof should be by the best available evidence. In his hierarchy of sources, written evidence was preferred because he thought it less likely to be fallible than mere oral testimony. This preference is reflected in the amount of space devoted to the two subjects: written evidence was given about three times as much space as oral evidence. He first considered sealed public records, then other public documents such as affidavits and depositions, and then private documents such as deeds. Only afterwards did he turn to the subject of oral evidence.[15]

In criminal courts, the position was very different. Research by John Langbein has thrown light on the conduct of criminal trials in the 18th century.[16] In the early decades of the century, it appears that anything like modern adversary procedure was entirely absent. Adversary procedure has been described as containing three fundamental elements. In the first place, the decision maker remains neutral and passive during the trial. Secondly, the litigants themselves are responsible for the production and quality of the proof upon which the case will be decided. The third element is the existence of an elaborate set of rules to govern the trial and the actions of the advocates.[17] Langbein concluded that in relation to criminal trials:

> ... adversary procedure cannot be defended as part of our historic common law bequest. The criminal lawyer and the complex procedures that have grown up to serve him are historical upstarts.[18]

This was so of necessity. In situations where it was rare for the prosecution to be represented by a lawyer, let alone the defence, the evidence had to be obtained from a mixture of judicial questioning and confrontation between the accused and his accusers. It is clear that, although the prisoner could not be sworn, he was expected to answer questions and make out the facts relied

---

13 Shapin, S, *A Social History of Truth: Civility and Science in Seventeenth-Century England*, 1994; see especially pp 3–125.

14 Winder, WHD, 'The courts of requests' (1936) 52 LQR 369.

15 Cf Landsman, *op cit*, fn 9, p 1153.

16 See above, fn 7.

17 Landsman, S, 'The rise of the contentious spirit: adversary procedure in eighteenth-century England' (1990) 75 Cornell L Rev 497, pp 500–01. See also Damaska, MJ, *The Faces of Justice and State Authority: A Comparative Approach to the Legal Process*, 1986, Chapter 4.

18 Langbein, JH, 'Criminal trial before the lawyers' (*op cit*, fn 7), p 316.

on in his defence.[19] Further, in the absence of counsel, there was a much greater opportunity for informal judicial control of the jury. Not only could the judge provide advice and comment throughout the trial, but it was rare for a jury to retire from court in order to discuss its verdict. Most verdicts were discussed by jurors while remaining in the jury box, and this also allowed a judge to give guidance where he thought it necessary. Nothing like our modern system of evidence could have grown in those circumstances. Then, as Langbein has shown, from about the mid-1730s counsel began to appear on behalf of some accused persons. At first they were allowed only to examine and cross-examine witnesses. It was not until 1836 that counsel for persons accused of felony were given statutory authority to address the jury on their clients' behalf. The extent of their participation until then depended on the discretion of the trial judge and the practices of the various circuits. There was clearly a great variety of modes of trial in the early 19th century. Here, for example, is an attorney's account, published in 1833, of trials at the Old Bailey:

> For several sessions I made a calculation of the average time which each trial occupied; I never found it exceed eight and a half minutes, notwithstanding many cases engage the court a whole day ... The rapidity with which the trials are dispatched throws the prisoners into the utmost confusion. Fifty or sixty of them are kept in readiness in the dock under the court, to be brought up as they may be called for. These men, seeing their fellow prisoners return tried and found guilty in a minute or two after being taken up, become so alarmed and nervous, in consequence of losing all prospect of having a patient trial, that in their efforts at the moment to rearrange their ideas and plan of defence, and put the strongest features of their cases before the court as speedily as possible, they lose all command over themselves, and are then, to use their own language, taken up to be knocked down like bullocks, unheard ... The evident anxiety of all the city judges to proceed with indecent and unjudicial haste with the business of this court makes them frequently petulant at any interruption or impediment to their usual dispatch, which manifests itself in much acrimony between themselves and counsel ...[20]

As a contrast, we have a description of what a French observer, Charles Cottu, saw when he was a guest of the Bench and Bar on the Northern Circuit in the early 1820s. The judge remained 'almost a stranger' to what was going on. He took notes of examination-in-chief and cross-examination. Sometimes he would ask questions of a witness, but his object was 'more to obtain an explanation of the witness's depositions than to establish any additional circumstance against the prisoner'. At the end of each deposition the prisoner was told to ask the witness whatever questions he pleased, but, since an accused person was generally represented by counsel, Cottu concluded that the prisoner did so little in his own defence that 'his hat stuck on a pole might

---

19 See, eg, the fictional account of a criminal trial in Fielding, H, *The History of Tom Jones*, 1749, Book VIII, Chapter 11.

20 Anon, *Old Bailey Experiences* (1833), quoted in (1833) X Law Magazine, pp 276–77.

without inconvenience be his substitute at the trial'. According to Cottu, prisoners in London were only very rarely represented by counsel, and this, rather than any cynical attempt to impress a foreign visitor, probably accounts for the vivid differences between these two descriptions from the early 19th century.[21]

The intervention of counsel in criminal trials may have been accepted initially because judges were aware of imperfections in criminal procedure, especially the use of accomplices who volunteered to give evidence for the prosecution in the hope of obtaining a pardon for themselves. But adversary procedure probably came to be established in criminal trials chiefly as the result of a population explosion at the Bar during roughly the first half of the 19th century.[22] In these circumstances, young barristers would have been eager to break into work wherever they could, and it is likely that criminal work, especially on circuit, appeared as an attractive new market.[23]

The growth of adversary procedure in criminal trials was a large step towards the development of our modern law of evidence. But one important element remained lacking: until 1907, there was no effective system of criminal appeals. Without such an appellate system, a rule-based system of law could scarcely develop to match the one that was growing rapidly in the civil courts.

Before the 19th century the common law was generally regarded as being in continuous process of growth, flexible enough to operate as an instrument of reform and better suited to that task than Parliament. These views depended on the belief that common law was essentially a *system of reasoning*, which might be partially expressed by way of maxims, and of which the decisions of the judges were only evidence.[24] There was little scope for binding authority because the three common law courts developed separately, and law reporting was inadequate.[25] However, a line of authority might be strong enough to be considered binding, and in this situation there was room for the idea to develop that decisions of the courts formed the *substance* of the

---

21 Cottu, C, *On the Administration of Criminal Justice in England; and the Spirit of the English Government*, translated from the French, 1822, pp 88–90.

22 Duman, D, 'Pathway to professionalism: the English Bar in the eighteenth and nineteenth centuries' (1980) Journal of Social History 615.

23 In addition to the works cited on the growth of adversary procedure in criminal trials, see Baker, JH, 'Criminal courts and procedure at common law 1550–1800', in Cockburn, JS (ed), *Crime in England 1550–1800*; Post, JB, 'The admissibility of defence counsel in English criminal procedure' (1984) 5 J Leg Hist 23; Beattie, J, 'Scales of justice: defence counsel and the English criminal trial in the eighteenth and nineteenth centuries' (1991) 9 Law and History Review 221; Cairns, DJA, *Advocacy and the Making of the Adversarial Criminal Trial 1800–1865*, 1998.

24 Baker, JH, *Introduction to Legal History*, pp 226–29; Lieberman, D, *The Province of Legislation Determined: Legal Theory in Eighteenth-Century Britain*, 1989, pp 43–46, 84–86, 102; Lobban, M, *The Common Law and English Jurisprudence 1760–1850*, 1991, pp 2–15, 47–49; Postema, GJ, *Bentham and the Common Law Tradition*, 1986, Chapter 1.

25 On law reporting, see Megarry, Sir R, *A Second Miscellany-at-Law: A Further Diversion for Lawyers and Others*, 1973, pp 117–33.

law, and were not merely *evidence* of it. The 19th century saw a change in attitude to case law,[26] and this affected the way in which evidence law developed. In this development treatise writers, law reporters and judges all played a part.

Treatise writers attempted to present their subject as a rule-based system derived from case law.[27] Passages in the works of WM Best and of other writers show that the authors regarded their subject as having been recently developed by the judges, although based on older principles.[28] The treatise writers' increasingly rule-based approach left less room for judicial discretion in the admission of testimony. The writers themselves appear to have realised that this was a novel development. Several of them argued in favour of exclusionary rules, relying on the supposed lack of weight possessed by certain types of testimony, the difficulties experienced by jurors in assessing evidence, and the need for clear, general rules in the interests of certainty. There was a perception that uncertainty was a great defect in English law.[29] For various reasons, this could not be remedied by codification. Not least of these reasons was the fact that, in criminal evidence, the case law was underdeveloped through lack of an effective appellate system. In addition, Members of Parliament were unwilling to allow significant changes in the law to be made without thorough examination, for which there was insufficient parliamentary time. Among the judges, codification was supported only by a minority.

Any increase in the certainty of the common law had therefore to be made by the judges. In the law of civil evidence, they tried to achieve this by developing an increasingly rule-based system of exclusions. In this they were assisted by institutional changes that made for a more uniform approach to civil appeals.[30] However, because the criminal courts lacked an effective appellate structure until 1907, the judges were unable to develop rules of criminal evidence to anything like the same extent. There were informal common practices, but no more. On the formation of the Court of Criminal Appeal in that year, criminal evidence law began to develop in the same way. Only in recent decades have the benefits of a more discretionary approach to admissibility been appreciated. The result is that modern criminal evidence law is a mixture of statute law, of common law rules (mainly developed after 1907), and more recent discretionary powers. As for civil evidence, the rule-

---

26 Evans, J, 'Change in the doctrine of precedent in the nineteenth century', in Goldstein, L (ed), *Precedent in Law*, 1987, pp 35–72.

27 Simpson, AWB, 'The rise and fall of the legal treatise: legal principles and the forms of legal literature' (1981) 45 U Chi L Rev 632; Sugarman, D, 'Legal theory, the common law mind and the making of the textbook tradition', in Twining, W (ed), *Legal Theory and Common Law*, 1986, pp 26–61.

28 Best, WM, *A Treatise on the Principles of Evidence*, 1849, pp 117–18, 125–29. For other treatise writers, see Twining, W, *Rethinking Evidence*, pp 33–70.

29 Daniel, WTS, *The History and Origin of the Law Reports* (undated), p 32.

30 Evans, *op cit*, fn 26, p 64; Allen, CK, *Law in the Making*, 7th edn, 1964, pp 219–21.

based, exclusionary system that had developed during the 19th century could no longer be justified after the virtual abolition during the 20th century of trial by jury in civil actions. Gradually it was demolished by statute, and today comparatively little of importance remains.

The other great change in evidence law during the 19th century was the gradual abolition of the old restrictions on competence. This was a long and piecemeal process. The religious bars were removed in two stages. Attention was focused during the first on the relief of those who, like Quakers, had religious scruples against taking an oath. After some partial reforms, complete success was achieved for civil proceedings when the Common Law Procedure Act 1854 made an affirmation an acceptable replacement for a religious oath. This reform was extended to criminal trials in 1861. Attention then turned to the relief of those who refused to take an oath because they subscribed to no religious belief. These attempts succeeded with the passing of the Evidence Further Amendment Act 1869.

The 19th century also saw the removal of witness disqualifications based on criminal convictions and financial interest in the outcome of the litigation. Three main stages can be seen. The first was reached in 1843; in that year, Lord Denman's Act abolished the rule whereby persons with certain criminal convictions had been disqualified from giving evidence. The Act also made a substantial inroad on the rule that an interested witness could not testify. The second stage was reached in 1851, when the Evidence Amendment Act (also known as Lord Brougham's Act) made competent the parties to most civil proceedings in the superior courts of common law. The third stage was reached only in 1898, when the Criminal Evidence Act permitted the accused to give evidence in all criminal cases.

The traditional view, represented for example by Holdsworth,[31] was that these statutory reforms were largely inspired by the critique of Jeremy Bentham, many of whose writings on evidence were published during the 1820s. There is no doubt that, for the student of jurisprudence or intellectual history, Bentham is a formidable figure.[32] It is likely, however, that the traditional view exaggerates Bentham's role in the story of evidence law reform. Debates in Parliament, as well as in pamphlets, journals and newspapers, show that those supporting the various proposals for reform had widely different concerns from those expressed by Bentham. He had wanted competence to be extended as part of a grand campaign for reform, which was aimed at the destruction of what he called the 'sinister interests' of Church and State. The statutory reforms were achieved for pragmatic reasons that had nothing to do with such a radical programme. Success depended on

---

31 Holdsworth, Sir WS, *A History of English Law*, 1903–72, Vol XIII, p 42; Vol XV, pp 138, 307. See also Hart, HLA, *Essays on Bentham*, 1982, p 31.

32 For his work on evidence, see Twining, W, *Theories of Evidence: Bentham and Wigmore*, 1985.

convincing enough lawyers and politicians that increased social stability made change both safe and desirable, and, so far as the 1898 reforms were concerned, that what was proposed involved no threat to the relatively new balance of power in criminal trials between judge, counsel and the accused.[33]

CURRENT OBJECTIVES

Evidence law is part of what is known as 'adjective' law, at least one of the purposes of which is to enforce the 'substantive' law of rights and duties. One of the aims of evidence law, therefore, will be to help courts to make accurate findings of fact, to which the relevant substantive law will then be applied. This objective is often referred to as 'rectitude of decision', but it cannot be the sole aim of evidence law. There are bound to be other aims, which will be determined by what are conceived to be the fundamental objectives of civil and criminal procedures. These will obviously include respect for individuals' legal rights, but it is arguable that they will also include respect for individuals *in themselves* because the best interpretation of our legal institutions involves the fundamental principle that individuals exist as ends in themselves, and not merely as means to be arbitrarily used by the will of some other persons or institutions.[34]

The main function of civil process in the English legal system today is conflict resolution. According to this theory, civil proceedings are primarily a method of achieving peaceful settlement of private disputes. The aim of adjective law must therefore be to encourage parties to litigation to accept the adjudication (subject to a right of appeal), and to encourage others to resort to litigation rather than self-help as a means of dispute resolution.[35] These aims require that adjective law should be efficient and should provide procedures that are accepted as fair by actual and potential litigants. Such procedures will include a right to be heard, a right to legal representation (at public expense, if need be), an impartial hearing, a reasoned judgment, and a right of appeal. Efficiency requires procedures that, so far as possible, achieve accuracy of outcome but also avoid waste of time and delay. Justice that is delayed harms the litigants in the case in question, who must pay increased costs, and other litigants, who have to wait longer for a hearing. In addition, delayed justice

---

33   Allen, C, *The Law of Evidence in Victorian England*, 1997.

34   Cf Kant, I, *Foundations of the Metaphysics of Morals*, trans Beck, LW, 2nd edn, 1990, pp 45–46.

35   There may, of course, be acceptable alternatives to litigation in the courts, such as arbitration.

harms those parties whom it continues to keep out of their rights while they await adjudication.[36]

This is not the place for a full discussion of the objectives of criminal law.[37] But for the purpose of understanding evidence law it is useful to see the criminal process as having at least two major objectives. These have been described in terms of the conceptual models of Due Process and Crime Control.[38] Both take into account the risk of erroneous outcomes. The Due Process model is concerned to protect defendants by minimising the risk of erroneous convictions; the Crime Control model is concerned with protecting the community by minimising the risk of erroneous acquittals. The problem for any judicial system is not, of course, which model to choose and which to reject, but how to find the right balance between the two. Someone who claims that the sole aim of evidence law is rectitude of decision fails to say everything that needs to be said. While it is obvious that a criminal case cannot be properly decided in accordance with the law unless the relevant facts are correctly determined, this is an incomplete statement of aims because it leaves unexplained how it is proposed to minimise the overall risk of error – in other words, what mixture of the two models of criminal process should be adopted. An attempt to state the aims of evidence law fully must take into account the seriousness of the risk of erroneous convictions on the one hand, and of erroneous acquittals on the other. In doing so it must consider what value judgments *in addition to rectitude of decision* are to be taken into account when determining the parts played by the two models in decisions about aims.

It is likely that there is quite a high risk of erroneous conviction in criminal cases that varies, probably, with the tribunal and the nature of the offence charged.[39] A major reason for this is almost certainly that there is regularly a substantial imbalance of resources between the prosecution and the defendant. Imbalance may occur in civil proceedings also, as where a major corporation and a private individual are in dispute, but such imbalance is a

---

36 Another way of regarding the civil process is to see it as a means of altering behaviour by imposing costs on people. On this view, the court is not so much concerned with the resolution of the immediate dispute as with its effect on others' future conduct. The imposition of legal liability is then a way of making individuals take into account the costs of their actions. In this way the State encourages appropriate attitudes of care towards others as well as compliance with obligations. See Scott, KE, 'Two models of the civil process' (1974–75) 27 Stanford L Rev 937. Something of this approach can occasionally be found in English procedure (eg, in cases where a plaintiff is entitled to exemplary damages), but it is too rare to have much, if any, effect on procedural objectives.

37 A good starting point for wider investigation is Ashworth, A, *The Criminal Process: An Evaluative Study*, 2nd edn, 1998, Chapter 2.

38 Packer, HL, 'Two models of the criminal process' (1964) 113 U of Pa L Rev 1.

39 In the nature of things this has to be guesswork, but see, eg, Woffinden, B, *Miscarriages of Justice*, 1989, p 485; Baldwin, J and McConville, M, *Jury Trials*, 1979.

matter of chance. It is not, as it is in criminal prosecutions, a built-in feature.[40] Because of this imbalance, there is a permanent danger that a defendant will be wrongly convicted because he is unable through lack of resources to gather the evidence he needs to combat the case put forward by the State. This is not to say that the State always uses its power efficiently. The point is that, when it comes to the crunch, the State can pull out all the stops; most defendants cannot. The imbalance is particularly dangerous because of the temptation for police to pursue only those lines of investigation that support their preconceived theories of the case. Nor is this a temptation confined to members of the police. The State's scientific experts may also be partisan, ignoring lines of inquiry that might assist the defendant and even suppressing evidence that weakens the prosecution case. The prosecution has a duty to disclose evidence that may assist the defence, but this is now governed by the Criminal Procedure and Investigations Act 1996, and some scepticism has been expressed about the effectiveness of this legislation to protect defendants.

Another reason why there is a risk of wrongful conviction is the special difficulty of evaluating evidence in criminal trials. Problems may arise both from the nature of the evidence itself and from the way in which it is presented. 'Similar fact' evidence provides a classic example of the difficulties involved in evaluation.[41] This type of evidence tends to show that the defendant committed the offence alleged, but can also show that the defendant is guilty of other offences, not the subject of the current charge, or of some other conduct of which the jury is likely to disapprove. Suppose Bertie is charged with committing a robbery in London. His defence is that he was on holiday with his girlfriend in Plymouth at the time. Bertie has been convicted of a number of robberies in the recent past. On each occasion, he gave evidence of a similar alibi defence. Or suppose Freddie, a married man, is charged with indecently assaulting the family's babysitter. Part of the prosecution case is that just before the alleged assault, Freddie tried to get the babysitter to look at pornographic photographs with him. Freddie vigorously denies this, but the prosecution have statements from two other women who did babysitting for his family and who say that, although Freddie never assaulted them, he did try to get them to look at pornographic photographs. If the jury hear the supporting evidence in the cases of Bertie and Freddie, there is a danger that they may give it too much weight, and so convict the defendants. Alternatively, they may decide that the defendants are such anti-social characters that even if they did not commit the offence charged, they are likely to have committed others for which they were not caught. They therefore convict.

---

40 Most criminal prosecutions are against individuals. It is possible that where a corporation is prosecuted, the imbalance may be less pronounced.

41 See below, Chapter 10.

Problems of evaluation may arise if evidence is not given by an eye witness, but by someone who heard an earlier account from an eye witness. The testifying witness can obviously be questioned about whether he heard the eye witness accurately, but there will generally be little point in asking questions designed to discover how reliable the eye witness was. The evidence of what the testifying witness heard may be relevant because it makes a fact in issue to *some* degree more or less likely to be true. But how is that degree to be assessed?

A more general problem arises from the way evidence is presented in an adversary system. Under such a system, evidence may have a built-in risk of misleading, because the parties, not the court, are responsible for producing evidence, and neither party is likely to be willing for the whole truth to emerge. An advocate who examines his own witness in court will be doing so on the basis of a statement of facts which have already been selected during the pre-trial stage. He knows that he will move outside that framework at his peril, because if he asks the witness a question on a topic not covered in the statement he will risk getting an answer that damages his client's case. Cross-examining counsel is likely to rely substantially on questions to which a plain 'yes' or 'no' answer is appropriate, and he will generally try to deny the witness any chance of providing wider explanations for fear that the witness may say something that damages the party on whose behalf he is conducting the cross-examination.[42] Where evidence is presented in so partial and restricted a way, there is a risk that truth will suffer. One result of that may be a wrongful conviction.

A defendant found guilty in criminal proceedings is subjected to some degree of moral condemnation, which may damage his reputation, and to punishment, which may involve loss of property or liberty. However, the harm resulting from a wrongful conviction is not suffered by the defendant alone. Although, in a criminal trial, there is a conflict that has to be resolved between prosecution and defence, it is an important objective of the proceedings to affect the future conduct of the defendant and others and not merely to resolve the dispute. To satisfy this additional objective the public must have justifiable confidence in the criminal process, and in the behaviour of the police and others supporting the power of the State. Wrongful convictions destroy trust in the criminal process and in those representatives of State authority who have most to do with the preservation of security. Wrongful acquittals may also diminish the public's sense of security, but are far less likely to do so. Wrongful acquittals are not revealed in the same dramatic way as wrongful convictions, and so impinge on public consciousness far less vividly. What tends to happen is that the public, or

---

42 See Stone, M, *Cross-Examination in Criminal Trials*, 1988, pp 106–07; Boon, A, *Advocacy*, 1993, p 88; Law Commission Consultation Paper No 138, 1995, paras 6.42–6.49.

some part of it, gets the idea (often from the abuse of statistics by some politician or policeman with a career to advance, or by some journalist with a column to complete) that 'criminals are getting away with it'.

Should measures be adopted to guard against the danger of wrongful convictions, even if this means increasing the probability of wrongful acquittals? This might be justifiable on the purely consequentialist basis already referred to: the object of the criminal law is to maintain security, and widely publicised wrongful convictions defeat that object more than vague impressions from time to time that 'criminals are getting away with it'. But there are at least two problems with this argument. The first is the difficulty, some might say impossibility, of measuring levels of insecurity. Secondly, even if insecurity could be quantified, it would be open to manipulation. A reduction in the protection of suspects could be justified, for example, even though insecurity at the prospect of widespread crime had been generated in a hysterical political campaign. Another consequence might be that the protection afforded to suspects could fluctuate significantly over a relatively short period of time, depending on the state of 'public opinion' – however that might be gauged.

Security alone will be a very weak basis for the protection of suspects and defendants. Is it possible to rely on *rights* as a more solid foundation? To support a rights-based claim effectively we need to be clear about the argument being used. In particular, it is necessary to avoid being misled by language. To take an obvious example, I do not 'have' a right in the same way that I 'have' a computer or a car. To say that I 'have a right' is a way of referring to a state of affairs that is entirely different from possession of a physical object. Things are further complicated because to 'have a right' is capable of referring not just to one particular state of affairs, but to several quite different ones, and agreement about what these are may be difficult to find.

The easiest state of affairs to understand exists where someone has a *legal* right. To say 'X has a legal right to R' is to say that some person has a legal duty to provide X with R, and that the law will enforce this. Thus if I sell my car to Alice for £7000, she has a legal right to the car and I have a legal right to the price. If I let her have the car before she pays me the price and she subsequently fails to pay, I can enforce my right by suing her for breach of contract. Some writers have argued that, in the absence of a legal right of this kind, I have *no* rights. Jeremy Bentham, for example, claimed that '*Natural rights* is simple nonsense: natural and imprescriptible rights, rhetorical nonsense – nonsense upon stilts'.[43] But there seems absolutely no reason at all to confine the concept of rights to legal contexts. As well as describing types of

---

43 Bentham, J, 'Anarchical fallacies', Article II, in Waldron, J (ed), *Nonsense Upon Stilts: Bentham, Burke and Marx on the Rights of Man*, 1987, p 53.

legal arrangement, this concept can be used to assert moral claims. For example, the expression can be used to argue for the *moral desirability* of creating a new *legal* right. Thus even before the relevant legislation had been passed, it would have been possible to argue coherently that workers had a right to a minimum amount of paid leave. The more obvious way of putting this is to say that talk about rights can be used to express a *principle of morality that advances or protects some individual interest.*

Assertions about morality will almost inevitably give rise to much argument, but this does not mean that talk of moral rights is nonsense. The person who says that only legal rights can exist is talking as if rights were *things* with essential identifying characteristics, such as corresponding legal duties. But rights are not *things* at all. The expression 'right' can be used in a number of different contexts to convey different ideas. To ignore this leads to an impoverishment of language and of political morality.[44] In some contexts, 'right' refers simply to a special interest that has greater weight than ordinary interests, and so counts for more in utilitarian calculations. As such, it can be outweighed, either by a similar interest opposed to it or by a large enough quantity of ordinary interests. In other contexts, 'right' refers to a special type of protected interest that has priority over other interests, in that the protected interest has to be promoted to the greatest possible extent before other interests are even taken into consideration. Where this is the case, rights have absolute priority over considerations of the general good, while leaving open the possibility of adjustment if they appear to conflict among themselves. A slightly different approach is to say that, while considerations of the general interest normally determine the way in which political decisions are taken, rights operate like trump cards. Persons have rights when the general good is not a sufficient justification for denying them what they wish to have or do, or for imposing some loss or injury on them. This does not mean that rights can always withstand overwhelming considerations of general welfare, but they can never be overridden merely because, on balance, the proposed action is likely to benefit the community.[45] In other contexts, rights can be regarded as the basis of strict constraints on action. They exclude even from consideration certain types of behaviour towards others. The result is that certain options are always ruled out, come what may.

It is against this background that rights-based claims in respect of legal process have to be assessed. Most people would want to argue that legal process should take rectitude of decision into account not just because truth is valuable in itself, but because it is instrumental in securing fundamental

---

44 See further, Benn, SI, 'Rights' in Edwards, P (ed), *The Encyclopedia of Philosophy*, 1967, Vol 7, pp 195–99; Waldron J, 'The philosophy of rights', in Parkinson, GRH (ed), *An Encyclopaedia of Philosophy*, 1988, pp 713–37; Waldron, J (ed), *Theories of Rights*, Oxford Readings in Philosophy, 1984, pp 1–20.

45 Dworkin, R, *Taking Rights Seriously*, 1977, pp xi, 191–92.

rights. Process values such as fairness and human dignity should also be taken into account, because the law ought to treat citizens as rational autonomous agents – to be persuaded, if possible, not merely coerced. Just as the criminal *law* needs to be justified to those on whom it is binding, so a criminal *verdict* needs to be justified to the defendant and to others. It must carry moral authority, and it cannot do this if the criminal process concentrates solely on factual accuracy, to the exclusion of all other considerations. Truth finding is, then, a major means by which the legitimacy of the verdict is secured, but it is not an end in itself. If this is the case, there may, for example, be circumstances where evidence should be excluded because, although reliable, it was obtained by iniquitous means. Suppose that vital evidence used in the trial of a dangerous robber had been obtained by torturing his wife and children. Could the verdict against him be morally justifiable?[46]

---

46 See Dennis, IH, 'Reconstructing the law of criminal evidence' (1989) CLP 35, and Duff, RA, *Trials and Punishments*, 1986, especially Chapter 4.

CHAPTER 3

COMPETENCE AND COMPELLABILITY

What persons are permitted by law to give evidence? This question is considered in the topic known as *competence*. This is a technical term and should not be used to refer to the question whether a witness who does give evidence is *reliable* or not. What persons may be compelled by law to give evidence, or risk punishment for contempt of court if they refuse? This question is considered in the topic known as *compellability*.

All evidence must generally be given on oath or affirmation unless a witness in a criminal trial is aged under 14.[1] The Oaths Act 1978 requires that the oath be administered in the manner provided in s 1, unless the witness objects or is physically incapable of taking the oath in the prescribed way. Persons who wish to affirm, or to swear in the manner prescribed by a religion other than Judaism or Christianity, may do so.[2] An oath administered otherwise than in accordance with s 1 will be administered in a lawful manner, provided it appears to the court to be binding on the witness's conscience, and provided the witness himself considers it to be binding on his conscience.[3] However, the effect of s 4(1) is to make binding any oath that has been administered in a form that the witness has declared to be binding. By s 4(2), the validity of an oath is not affected if the person swearing has no religious belief. By s 5(4), an affirmation has the same force and effect as an oath. It follows that it would be improper for a judge to make any distinction in summing up between witnesses who gave evidence on oath and witnesses who affirmed. Evidence given on affirmation is subject to the law against perjury in the same way as evidence on oath.

Inability to testify has always been regarded as the exception rather than the rule. When the modern law of evidence was beginning to develop in the 18th century, the exception was a wide one whose rationale was probably twofold: a desire to keep people away from a situation where they might be tempted to commit perjury, and the view that certain types of people were so unreliable that any testimony from them would be worthless. Those excluded from testifying were the parties to civil actions and their spouses, and any other persons with a financial interest in the outcome of the proceedings; the accused and their spouses in criminal cases; certain persons with criminal convictions; and many people who would not, or could not, take a Christian oath before giving evidence. This last category included those, such as

---

1 See Youth Justice and Criminal Evidence Act 1999, s 55.
2 Oaths Act 1978, ss 1(3) and 5(1).
3 *R v Kemble* [1990] 1 WLR 1111.

children, who were unable to satisfy the court that they understood the nature and significance of an oath.

Subject to some exceptions, a witness who was competent was also compellable. The primary rule of universal competence and compellability was stated by Willes J in *Ex p Fernandez*:[4]

> Every person in the kingdom except the sovereign may be called upon and is bound to give evidence to the best of his knowledge upon any question of fact material and relevant to an issue tried in any of the Queen's courts, unless he can shew some exception in his favour ...

In civil actions, this primary rule applies to the parties themselves and their spouses. The Evidence Act 1851 allowed the parties to a civil action in the superior courts of common law to give evidence, but left their spouses incompetent as witnesses. This state of affairs was clearly unsatisfactory. A contemporary critic noted:

> Among the middle classes matters of business are often conducted by [the wife] for her husband. Yet in such cases we have the practical absurdity that the husband, who knows *nothing* about it, *may* be called, while the wife, who knows *all* about it, *may not*.[5]

The Evidence Amendment Act 1853 was passed to meet this sort of criticism. Section 1 provided that on the trial of any matter, husbands and wives of the parties were to be both competent and compellable as witnesses. This section remains in force. The result is that, if thought appropriate, one party can compel the other, or the other's spouse, to testify. Of course, although the witness can be compelled to testify, he or she cannot be compelled to co-operate by giving a witness statement in advance. A party would need to have a strong reason for calling somebody without knowing for sure what that person might say in the witness box; nevertheless, it can be done.

For the last two centuries the tendency has been to increase the scope of competence while maintaining a few cases where a competent witness is not compellable. Four classes of witness require special consideration:

(a) defendants in criminal cases;

(b) spouses of defendants in criminal cases;

(c) children;

(d) persons of defective intellect.

---

4 (1861) 10 CBNS 3, p 39. See also *Hoskyn v Commissioner of Police for the Metropolis* [1979] AC 474, pp 484, 500–01.

5 (1851–52) *Law Times* 18, p 122.

DEFENDANTS IN CRIMINAL CASES

Accused persons as a general class were not allowed to give evidence at their trials until the Criminal Evidence Act 1898. It is a mistake, however, to state that they were always unable to testify in their own defence prior to this Act. During and after the 1860s, statutes from time to time created new offences and specifically allowed defendants charged under the statute in question to testify in their own defence. This gave rise to some curious anomalies which in the end helped to ease the path of the 1898 Act.[6]

By s 1 of the Criminal Evidence Act 1898, all defendants were made competent, but not compellable, witnesses in their own defence. An accused person is also a competent, but not compellable, witness for any co-accused.[7] This assumes that two or more persons who have pleaded not guilty are being tried together on the same indictment. Once one of the defendants has been separated from the others (for example, by changing his plea to guilty, or by being discharged at the end of the prosecution case on a submission of no case to answer, or by severance of the indictment), he will become compellable, as well as competent, for any of the remaining defendants.[8]

Accused persons are incompetent as witnesses for the prosecution.[9] In a case where several persons are charged, and the prosecution wish to use the evidence of one of them against the other, it is necessary to separate the potential witness from his companions, so that he is not, or is no longer, liable to be convicted of any offence in the proceedings.[10] This may be done in several ways. The prosecution may discontinue proceedings against their potential witness. A more usual way of obtaining an accomplice's evidence is to persuade the accomplice to plead guilty when his co-defendant pleads not guilty. Because of his plea, the accomplice will no longer be *liable to be convicted* of any offence in the proceedings, and will thus be available as a witness for the prosecution. The question has arisen whether, in such circumstances, the accomplice should be sentenced before giving evidence at his former companion's trial. Judicial practice has varied, but it is clear that whether sentence has been passed or not has no effect on the competence of an accomplice. It may, of course, affect the weight that a jury attaches to his evidence.

---

6   The Criminal Law (Amendment) Act 1885 produced particularly blatant anomalies. This Act created a number of new sexual offences. A person charged with any of these was allowed by the statute to give evidence in his own defence, but a person charged with the common law offence of rape was incompetent to testify.

7   *R v Macdonnell* (1909) 2 Cr App R 322; Criminal Evidence Act 1898, s 1(1).

8   *R v Boal* [1965] 1 QB 402; *R v Richardson* (1967) 51 Cr App R 381; *R v Conti* (1973) 58 Cr App R 387.

9   Youth Justice and Criminal Evidence Act 1999, s 53(4).

10 *Ibid*, s 53(5).

The effect of a defendant's giving evidence

Where a defendant gives evidence, he must do so on oath or affirmation and he will be liable to cross-examination.[11] His testimony will be evidence at the trial *for all purposes*. Thus, he may incriminate himself in the witness box and anything he says there may be used as evidence against any co-defendant.[12] Counsel for the prosecution is entitled to cross-examine with a view to incriminating not only the defendant giving evidence but a co-defendant also.[13] The defendant who gives evidence may also be cross-examined on behalf of any co-defendant.

The effect of a defendant's failure to give evidence

Under the 1898 Act, the judge and counsel for any co-accused were always permitted to comment on a defendant's failure to testify. The judge, however, had a duty to warn the jury that they were not entitled to infer guilt from silence at trial.[14] In certain cases, provided this basic point had been made, some criticism was regarded as acceptable. For example, in *R v Brigden*,[15] the accused's case, put to the appropriate witnesses in cross-examination, was that the police had planted incriminating evidence on him. The accused himself did not testify. The Court of Appeal approved the trial judge's comment to the effect that the jury had not heard from the accused, and that this might help them in deciding whether there was any truth in the allegation against the police.

Similar criticism was permitted where the accused did not testify, but relied on facts that must have been within his knowledge. Thus, in *R v Martinez-Tobon*,[16] the accused was charged with the illegal importation of cocaine in a packet. The defence was that he had thought the packet contained emeralds, but the accused chose not to testify. The trial judge commented in his summing up that if the defendant had thought the drugs were emeralds, one might have thought that he would be very anxious to say so. On appeal against conviction it was argued that the judge's comment had gone beyond what was permissible, but the Court of Appeal disagreed. Provided the judge made the basic point that guilt should not be inferred from silence, it might be appropriate to make a stronger comment where the defence case involved alleged facts which: (a) were at variance with the Crown's evidence or were

---

11 Criminal Justice Act 1982, s 72.
12 *R v Rudd* (1948) 32 Cr App R 138, *Sourcebook*, p 78.
13 *R v Paul* [1920] 2 KB 183, *Sourcebook*, p 77.
14 *R v Wickham* (1971) 55 Cr App R 199, *Sourcebook*, p 76; *R v Bathurst* [1968] 2 QB 99.
15 [1973] Crim LR 579.
16 (1993) 98 Cr App R 375.

additional to it and exculpatory; and (b) must, if true, be within the defendant's knowledge.

The law was changed by s 35 of the Criminal Justice and Public Order Act 1994. The court or jury, in determining whether the accused is guilty of the offence charged, may now draw such inferences as appear proper from the accused's failure to give evidence at trial, or his refusal without good cause to answer any question when giving evidence.[17]

Certain conditions have to be satisfied for this provision to apply. The defendant must:

(a) have pleaded not guilty;[18]

(c) be physically and mentally fit to testify;[19] and

(d) be aware of the risks attached to silence.[20]

Where an accused gives evidence but fails to answer a certain question, no inferences can be drawn if he is entitled to refuse to answer the question by virtue of any enactment, or on the grounds of privilege, or where the court in the exercise of its general discretion excuses him from answering it.[21] For example, the defendant might be entitled to refuse to answer a question about his previous convictions under s 1(3) of the Criminal Evidence Act 1898, or he might be able to claim legal professional privilege,[22] or the judge might excuse him from answering a question because it was oppressive or likely to produce information whose probative worth would be outweighed by its likely prejudicial effect on the jury.[23]

In *R v Cowan*,[24] Lord Taylor CJ, in delivering the judgment of the Court of Appeal, accepted that it would be open to a court to decline to draw any adverse inference from silence at trial and for a judge either to direct or merely to advise a jury against drawing such an inference if the circumstances of the case justified it. But for either course to be taken, at least one of two conditions would have to be satisfied. There would have to be some evidential basis for taking that course. It would not be proper for a defence advocate to give to the jury reasons unsupported by evidence for his client's silence at trial. Alternatively, there would have to be some exceptional factors in the case, making it fair not to draw any adverse inferences.

---

17 Criminal Justice and Public Order Act 1994, s 35(3).

18 *Ibid*, s 35(1)(a).

19 *Ibid*, s 35(1)(b).

20 *Ibid*, s 35(2). For the procedure to ensure that the defendant is aware of these risks, see *Practice Direction* [1995] 1 WLR 657.

21 Criminal Justice and Public Order Act 1994, s 35(5).

22 See Chapter 13.

23 See below, p 239.

24 [1996] QB 373.

As the Court of Appeal emphasised in *R v Napper*,[25] the general rule is that it should be open to a jury to draw adverse inferences when a defendant fails to testify. Attempts to minimise or marginalise the operation of the section are contrary to the spirit of its provisions. The judge, in any direction under the section, must tell the jury that:

(a) the defendant is entitled to remain silent;

(b) an inference from silence cannot prove guilt on its own;[26] and

(c) they must be satisfied there is a case to answer before drawing any inferences from silence. (Of course, the judge must have thought there was, or the case would already have been stopped. But the jury may not believe the witnesses whose evidence the judge considered sufficient to raise a *prima facie* case.)

The importance of this last requirement has been emphasised on at least two occasions by the Court of Appeal. In *R v Birchall*,[27] a conviction was quashed because the trial judge had omitted to tell the jury that they had to be satisfied there was a *prima facie* case to answer before they could draw any inferences from the defendant's failure to testify. The Court of Appeal said that this failure gave rise to a clear risk of injustice. An appeal was allowed for the same reason in *El-Hannachi and Others*[28]. In delivering the judgment of the court, May LJ said that some omissions from a summing-up were more important than others. The drawing of inferences from silence was a particularly sensitive area, not least in the light of Arts 6(1) and 6(2) of the European Convention on Human Rights. Inescapable logic demanded that a jury should not start to consider whether to draw inferences from a defendant's silence at trial until they had concluded that the Crown's case against him was sufficiently compelling to call for an answer.[29]

The judge must also tell the jury that if they conclude that the silence 'can only be sensibly attributed to the defendant's having no answer, or none that would stand up to cross-examination', they *may*, but not must, draw an adverse inference. The effect of this appears to be that the jury must be told that no inference is to be drawn unless they are sure that there is no other reasonable explanation, consistent with innocence, to account for it.[30]

The requirement under s 35(1)(b) that the defendant be physically and mentally fit to testify presupposes, of course, that he is fit to plead. If the

---

25 [1996] Crim LR 591.

26 Criminal Justice and Public Order Act 1994, s 38(3).

27 [1999] Crim LR 311.

28 [1998] 2 Cr App R 226.

29 *Ibid*, pp 240–41. Article 6(1) provides for a fair and public hearing. Article 6(2) provides that everyone charged with a criminal offence shall be presumed innocent until proved guilty.

30 *R v Cowan* [1996] QB 373, p 381.

defence wish to argue that s 35 does not apply because of the defendant's physical or mental condition, they must be able to point to some admissible evidence in support of this contention.[31] It will be for the judge to decide on the *voir dire* whether the defendant's condition makes it undesirable that he give evidence, so as to make s 35 inapplicable. Undesirability does not follow automatically from the defendant's low mental age. But it might be undesirable for a defendant to testify if there were medical evidence that giving testimony would involve the risk of an epileptic attack, or, where a defendant suffers from latent schizophrenia, if the experience of testifying might cause his mental illness to develop further.[32] It has been suggested that it might also be undesirable if the defendant's mental condition were such that he might create a highly unfavourable impression in the witness box, for example, because of inability to control outbursts of aggression.[33]

SPOUSES OF DEFENDANTS IN CRIMINAL CASES

The current law is to be found in s 80 of the Police and Criminal Evidence Act 1984 (PACE), as amended by the Youth Justice and Criminal Evidence Act 1999, and in s 53(1) of the 1999 Act.

Section 53(1) provides that at every stage in criminal proceedings, *all* persons are (whatever their age) *competent* to give evidence. It follows that an accused's husband or wife ('spouse') is always competent for the prosecution. The only possible exceptions to this would occur where the spouse failed to satisfy the requirements for competence contained in s 55(3), or where he or she was a defendant in the same proceedings. In that case, the spouse would be incompetent for the prosecution by virtue of s 53(4). It follows from the very wide terms of s 53(1) of the 1999 Act that an accused's spouse will also be competent for the accused and for any co-accused.

By s 80(2) of PACE, the accused's spouse is always compellable as a witness for the accused. But this provision is subject to s 80(4), which provides that no person who is charged in any proceedings shall be compellable under s 80 to give evidence in those proceedings. So, if a husband and wife are both charged in the same proceedings, the husband cannot compel the wife under s 80(2) to give evidence for him, and she cannot compel him to give evidence for her.

The accused's spouse will, again subject to sub-s (4), be compellable for the prosecution and for her spouse's co-accused, but only in relation to offences

---

31 *R v A* [1997] Crim LR 883.

32 *R v Friend* [1997] 2 All ER 1011, p 1020.

33 See the commentary on *R v Friend* [1997] Crim LR 817, p 819.

that are 'specified'.[34] In other words, the accused's spouse is compellable for a co-accused only in those circumstances where he or she would be compellable for the prosecution. The reason for this is that since the prosecution cannot compel the spouse to give evidence in trials for offences that are not 'specified', it would be wrong for someone jointly charged with the accused to be able to do so, because the result would be to give the prosecution an indirect advantage through the opportunity for cross-examination.[35] For example, if the husband and a co-accused are charged with handling, the wife would not be a compellable witness for the prosecution because handling is not a 'specified' offence. But if the co-defendant could compel the wife to give evidence in his defence, she could be cross-examined by the prosecution, and during the course of that cross-examination she might have to provide answers that would support the case against her husband.

The 'specified' offences are set out in s 80(3) of PACE. They are offences where:

(a) the offence charged involves an assault on, or injury or a threat of injury to, the spouse of the accused or a person who was at the material time under the age of 16;

(b) the offence charged is a sexual offence alleged to have been committed in respect of a person who was at the material time under the age of 16;

(c) the offence charged consists of attempting or conspiring to commit either of the above, or being a secondary party to or inciting either of the above.

There is at least one problem with the interpretation of these provisions. It concerns what is referred to in sub-s (3)(a) as an offence which '*involves* an assault on, or injury or a threat of injury to' the spouse of the accused or a person who was at the material time under the age of 16. The sub-section clearly covers an offence such as robbery, where violence or the threat of it is an essential element of the offence. But it is unclear whether 'involves' covers an offence where this is not the case, and the violence is only an incidental element.[36] In *R v McAndrew-Bingham*,[37] the same wording in s 32(2)(a) of the Criminal Justice Act 1988 was given the broader interpretation, but this was in the context of a provision for the use of video and live-link TV wherever a child witness was likely to be traumatised by confrontation with the accused. The court adopted a purposive construction, but it is by no means clear that a purposive construction of s 80(3) of PACE would have the same result.

In any proceedings, a person who has been, but is no longer, married to the accused shall be competent and compellable to give evidence as if that

---

34   See PACE 1984, s 80(2A).

35   May, R, *Criminal Evidence*, 4th edn, 1999, p 455.

36   Andrews, JA and Hirst, M, *Criminal Evidence*, 3rd edn, 1997, p 233; Creighton, P, 'Spouse competence and compellability' [1990] Crim LR 34, pp 38–39.

37   (1998) *The Times*, 28 December.

person and the accused had never been married.[38] Marriage persists until grant of decree absolute.

By s 80A of PACE, the failure of an accused's spouse to give evidence shall not be made the subject of any comment by the *prosecution*. The judge, and counsel for any co-accused, can comment. In *R v Naudeer*,[39] the Court of Appeal said that, save in exceptional circumstances, a judge should exercise a great deal of circumspection if he chooses to make any comment. (The reason for this is that, as with any other potential witness, there may have been some good reason why that person was not called.) But counsel for a co-accused may, presumably, comment as strongly as he thinks fit.

CHILDREN[40]

A distinction is drawn between civil and criminal cases.

Civil cases

The first question that will arise is whether the child is competent to give sworn evidence. The test is the one which used to govern both civil and criminal cases and which was laid down in *R v Hayes*:[41] does the child understand *the solemnity of the occasion* and *the special duty to tell the truth*, over and above the ordinary social duty to do so? Belief in a divine sanction is unnecessary. If the child does not satisfy these conditions, the court must then rely on the Children Act 1989. Section 96 applies to a child (defined in s 105 as a person under the age of 18) who is called as a witness in any civil proceedings and who does not, in the court's opinion, understand the nature of an oath. Such a child's evidence may be heard if, in the court's opinion, the child understands that it is his duty to speak the truth and he has sufficient understanding to justify his evidence being heard.

Criminal cases

The current law is contained in ss 53–57 of the Youth Justice and Criminal Evidence Act 1999. The fundamental provision is contained in s 53(1): at every stage in criminal proceedings, all persons are, *whatever their age*, competent to give evidence.

---

38 PACE 1984, s 80(5).

39 (1984) 80 Cr App R 9, p 13.

40 Spencer, J and Flin, R, *The Evidence of Children: the Law and the Psychology*, 2nd edn, 1993; Birch, D, 'Children's evidence' [1992] Crim LR 262; Brennan, 'The battle for credibility' [1993] NLJ 623.

41 [1977] 1 WLR 234.

By sub-s (3), a person is *not* competent to give evidence if it appears to the court that he is not a person who is able to:

(a) understand questions put to him as a witness, and

(b) give answers to them which can be understood.

Any question whether a witness in criminal proceedings is competent may be raised either by a party to the proceedings, or by the court of its own motion (that is, by the judge, even if none of the parties raises the issue). If such a question arises, the procedure set out in s 54 will be followed. It is for the party calling the witness to satisfy the court that, *on a balance of probabilities*, the witness is competent.[42] It should be noted that this civil standard applies to both defence and prosecution. The issue must be determined in the absence of the jury, if there is one.[43] Expert evidence may be received on the question.[44] Any questioning of the witness, where the court considers that necessary, shall be conducted by the court in the presence of the parties.[45] In other words, the potential witness will not be submitted to examination and cross-examination by counsel, but may be questioned by the judge.

Assuming a child is competent to give evidence, will that child's evidence be sworn or unsworn? By s 55(2), no witness may be sworn unless:

(a) he has attained the age of 14, and

(b) he has a sufficient appreciation of the solemnity of the occasion and of the particular responsibility to tell the truth which is involved in taking an oath.

This is, in essence, the test applied in *R v Hayes*,[46] so belief in a divine sanction is unnecessary. However, witnesses aged 14 and over are likely to take the oath without further question, because sub-s (3) provides that if the witness is able to give intelligible testimony, he shall be presumed to have satisfied condition (b) if no evidence tending to show the contrary is adduced by any party. The effect of this is that children aged 14 and over will be treated as adults, and no inquiry will be made into their capacity to take the oath unless an objection, supported by evidence, is made. If any question as to the satisfaction of either of the conditions in sub-s (2) arises, it is for the party wishing to have the witness sworn to satisfy the court that, on a balance of probabilities, those conditions are satisfied.[47] Again, the standard is the same for both defence and prosecution, and the proceedings to determine the

---

42 Youth Justice and Criminal Evidence Act 1999, s 54(2).

43 *Ibid*, s 54(4).

44 *Ibid*, s 54(5).

45 *Ibid*, s 54(6).

46 [1977] 1 WLR 234.

47 Youth Justice and Criminal Evidence Act 1999, s 55(4).

question will be conducted under the same rules as proceedings to determine competence.[48]

If a person is competent to give evidence, but fails to satisfy the tests for giving sworn evidence, his evidence may be given unsworn.[49]

PERSONS OF DEFECTIVE INTELLECT

Here, also, a distinction is drawn between civil and criminal cases.

Civil cases

The old common law, formerly applicable to both criminal and civil cases, still applies. A person who is mentally disordered or defective will not inevitably be incompetent to testify. Competence depends on the nature and severity of the disability, which may be investigated in open court before testimony is received. If there is a doubt about the ability of a witness to give reliable evidence because of his mental condition, expert evidence should be called on the *voir dire* to deal with the matter. It should not normally be necessary at that stage to call the witness whose mental condition has given rise to the problem.[50]

The crucial test is whether the potential witness understands the nature of the oath in the light of the test stated in *R v Hayes*. Thus, in an old case, the prosecution wished to call an inmate of a lunatic asylum. One of the attendants was called first and gave evidence that the man in question had the delusion that spirits continually conversed with him. But, he added, he believed that the inmate was capable of giving an account of anything that had happened before his eyes. The man was allowed to testify because the court found that he had a clear understanding of the obligation of an oath and was rational on all subjects except his particular delusion.[51]

More recently, in *R v Bellamy*,[52] a rape complainant aged 33 had a mental age of 10. The Court of Appeal held that she should have been allowed to give sworn evidence because it had been clear from her answers to initial questions from the trial judge that she had satisfied the *Hayes* test. The Court of Appeal was particularly impressed by the fact that she had realised that if she told a lie when she gave evidence she could, as she had said, be 'put away'.

---

48 Youth Justice and Criminal Evidence Act 1999, s 55(5)-(7).

49 *Ibid*, s 56.

50 *R v Barratt and Sheehan* [1996] Crim LR 495.

51 *R v Hill* (1851) 2 Den 254.

52 (1985) 82 Cr App R 222.

Criminal cases

Sections 53–57 of the Youth Justice and Criminal Evidence Act 1999 constitute a code governing the competence and capacity to be sworn of all persons tendered as witnesses in criminal cases. Where a potential witness has a defective intellect, therefore, the tests to be applied and the procedure for determining them are the same as have already been described in relation to children. It follows that a person with defective intellect may be able to give evidence in criminal, but not in civil, proceedings. In criminal proceedings, provided he satisfies the basic test for competence, he will be able to give evidence – if not sworn, then unsworn. In civil proceedings, an adult witness with defective intellect must be able to satisfy the *Hayes* test and be sworn; if he cannot do so, there is no provision enabling him to give unsworn evidence.

CHAPTER 4

THE COURSE OF TESTIMONY

There are three golden rules which, if followed faithfully, will ensure that you understand this part of evidence law:

(a) leave your books and go into a court;

(b) once there, watch and listen carefully; and

(c) repeat this process frequently.

If you do these things, the rather dry topics covered in this chapter will make more sense, and so will be more easily remembered. Watching films of trials, whether fictional or not, is no substitute. Nearly all are American, or influenced by American procedure. American and English procedures and terminology differ, and it is indiscreet to confuse the two.

Behind the rules governing the way in which evidence is given, there exist certain assumptions, listed below. An understanding of these can be useful, because they go some way towards giving shape to an otherwise amorphous topic. These are ideas that have shaped the way the law developed; whether they are good ideas or not is, for present purposes, immaterial:

(a) It is the responsibility of the parties, not the court, to produce the evidence. It follows from this that the examination of witnesses is the job of the advocate, not the judge.

(b) Testimony is best evaluated when it is fresh, and this is taken to mean when it emerges orally from the witness at trial. There was originally, therefore, reluctance to rely on pre-trial accounts from witnesses of the events in question. In civil cases this reluctance has substantially diminished, and even in criminal cases the courts today adopt a more relaxed attitude than in the past.

(c) The credibility of a witness is one of the relevant facts in any trial. One of the most important guides to a person's credibility is his moral character. A conviction for any criminal offence is relevant to moral character, and so to credibility.

(d) Trials, and criminal trials in particular, should be over quickly. If they are not, the wheels of justice will grind to a halt. There must therefore be a limit to the number of issues that can be pursued in a trial.

I have divided this chapter into eight sections. The first three deal with the various stages of witness examination: examination-in-chief, cross-examination and re-examination. I then turn to four particular problems: the rules governing the way in which a witness may refresh his memory before and during testimony; the admissibility of a witness's previous statements to support his testimony in court ('previous consistent statements'); 'hostile' witnesses; and questions on 'collateral' matters. Finally, I deal in outline with procedural measures that have been adopted for the protection of vulnerable or intimidated witnesses.

EXAMINATION-IN-CHIEF

This is the first stage in the examination of a witness at trial, and is conducted on behalf of the party who has called him. In civil actions a witness's pre-trial written statement may stand as the evidence-in-chief.[1] Where this happens, the witness will usually be called and sworn, asked for his name and address and whether the contents of his statement are true, and then tendered for cross-examination. However, before tendering the witness for cross-examination it may be necessary to ask some questions about matters that have become relevant since the statement was served, or to apply for leave to ask questions about matters that should have been included in the statement but were omitted. In all cases the trial judge has an unfettered discretion to require a witness to give oral evidence-in-chief, and in *Cole v Kivells*,[2] the Court of Appeal said that this discretion might usefully be exercised in relation to evidence about matters where there are conflicts on the facts. It is also not unknown for a judge hearing a complicated case to ask that the evidence-in-chief be given orally so as to gain more time to absorb its details.

A witness will very frequently be favourable to the cause of the party who has called him. Because of this, two rules that are peculiar to examination-in-chief have developed. These are the rules against leading questions and against discrediting one's own witness.

The rule against leading questions

The best account of leading questions that I know was given in 1813 by Lord Ellenborough CJ in a speech in the House of Lords:

> I have always understood, after some little experience, that the meaning of a leading question was this, and this only, that the Judge restrains an advocate who produces a witness on one particular side of a question, and who may be supposed to have a leaning to that side of the question, from putting such interrogatories as may operate as an instruction to that witness how he is to reply to favour the party for whom he is adduced. The counsel on the other side, however, may put what questions he pleases, and frame them as best suits his purpose, because then the rule is changed, for there is no danger that the witness will be too complying.[3]

---

1   CPR, r 32.5(2).
2   (1997) *The Times*, 2 May.
3   Lord Campbell, *The Lives of the Chief Justices of England*, 1849–57, Vol III, pp 209–10.

A leading question, then, is one that suggests to the witness the answer that is wanted, and an advocate must not ask leading questions of his own witness.[4] Obviously, if an advocate does obtain evidence from his own witness by a leading question, that evidence is likely to have less weight than evidence adduced without such assistance.

It is, of course, necessary to a certain extent to 'lead' the mind of the witness to the subject of the inquiry, but this is permissible provided the answer is left open to the witness. It is not always easy in practice to decide how far to go. Suppose you want the witness to say, 'I was in Trafalgar Square on 1 December 2000'. A clearly leading question would be: 'You were in Trafalgar Square on 1 December 2000, weren't you?' but what about, 'Where were you on 1 December 2000?' or, 'Have you been in Trafalgar Square recently?' or, 'Were you in Trafalgar Square on 1 December 2000?'. It could be argued that the last of these questions suggests neither a negative nor affirmative reply, and is therefore not a leading question. On the other hand, it clearly directs the witness's attention to a particular time and place, both of which may be contested, and it could be argued that, for that reason, it falls under the ban on leading questions. Whether the other questions are permissible will depend on the extent to which the assertion is contested. If, for example, the witness is an alibi witness, the date will be all-important. The prosecution may be ready to accept that at some time the witness was in Trafalgar Square, but will vigorously contest that it was on 1 December 2000. In those circumstances, the examination should be conducted on these lines:

Q Do you remember a time when you were in Trafalgar Square?

A Yes.

Q When was that?

Suppose instead that the witness is appearing for the prosecution, and the case against the defendant is that he attempted to drown his girlfriend in one of the fountains in Trafalgar Square on 1 December 2000. The defence is self-defence. The date of the contested events will not be in issue, but their nature most certainly will. If the prosecution witness has been called to give an account of what he saw on that date, the accuracy of his perception is very likely to be contested. In that case, the place from which he observed what was happening will be important. The examination should then go like this:

Q Do you remember 1 December 2000?

A Yes.

Q Where were you on that day?

In both cases, a leading question has been avoided *on a matter in contention*.

---

4   The rule was established by at least the late 17th century: see *R v Rosewall* (1684) 10 St Tr cols 147, 190.

This suggests an exception to the rule against leading questions during examination-in-chief. Questions on non-controversial matters, which will frequently include matters of an introductory nature, may be the subject of leading questions. Leading questions are also permissible where a witness proves to be 'hostile' to the party calling him.[5]

A less usual, but always illegitimate, form of leading question is one that assumes that something has already been established by evidence when that is not the case. Thus, if it is in issue that a particular custom existed, and the witness has not yet given evidence of that fact, it is improper to ask whether certain conduct was in accordance with the custom, because that question assumes the custom to exist.[6]

The rule against discrediting one's own witness

A witness called by a party will have been chosen as a witness by that party and put forward by him as a truthful witness. If a party has reason to think a particular person is not to be believed on his oath, that party ought not to try to support his case by the testimony of such a witness. So if a witness's evidence unexpectedly turns out to be against the interest of the party who has called him, the latter cannot repair the damage by trying to show that the witness is of bad character. As Lord Denman CJ said in *Wright v Beckett*,[7] 'You shall not prove that man to be infamous whom you endeavoured to pass off to the jury as respectable'. However, the party who called the witness may call other witnesses to contradict the damaging testimony and, in certain circumstances, he may to some extent discredit the witness by cross-examining him about a former statement of the witness that is inconsistent with his testimony in court.[8]

CROSS-EXAMINATION

The objects of cross-examination are to complete and correct the story told by the witness during evidence-in-chief. The business of the cross-examiner is therefore to test the accuracy and honesty of that evidence and to give an opportunity to the witness to bring out matters that are favourable to the case of the party on whose behalf the cross-examination is being conducted. If, for example, you are defending someone charged with burglary and your defence is an alibi, you must give the prosecution witnesses who identified

---

5   See below, p 93.
6   *Curtis v Peek* (1864) 29 JP 70.
7   (1834) 1 M&Rob 414, p 425.
8   See below, pp 93–94.

your client at the scene of the crime an opportunity to concede that they may have been mistaken. In addition, of course, you will try to bring out those facts, such as poor lighting and short periods of observation, that you hope will lead the jury to have a reasonable doubt about the accuracy of the witnesses' identifications. Because the objects of cross-examination are to complete and correct a witness's story, the right to cross-examine can be exercised by anyone whose interests have been affected by the testimony in question. If co-plaintiffs or co-defendants have conflicting interests, the evidence of one may affect others, and it is only fair that those affected should have the right to cross-examine.[9] Another rule that follows from the objects of cross-examination is that its scope is not confined to those matters that have been covered by evidence-in-chief, but extends to all relevant matters.[10]

Unlike examination-in-chief, cross-examination operates on the assumption that the witness does not favour the cause of the party on whose behalf it is conducted. There is no danger that such a witness will simply follow the questioner's lead and accept without thinking the suggestions put to him, and the reason for excluding leading questions from examination-in-chief is therefore absent in cross-examination. Further, since the cross-examining party has not been responsible for bringing the witness before the court, he cannot be understood to vouch for that witness's character, and so is free to discredit him by all proper means at his disposal. There may be another reason why leading questions are permitted in cross-examination. Counsel appearing for accused persons in trials for felony were allowed to cross-examine prosecution witnesses, but were not allowed to address the jury until 1836. Sir James Stephen's theory was that while counsel were confined to cross-examination alone, 'the cross-examination tended to become a speech thrown into the form of questions', and that it retained that character afterwards to a greater or less extent.[11]

But there are limits to what can be done in cross-examination. Its purpose to complete and correct evidence-in-chief is to be achieved by eliciting evidence, not by indulging in argument. The advocate who is cross-examining should therefore avoid questions that invite argument. In *R v Baldwin* Lord Hewart CJ said:

> One so often hears questions put to witnesses by counsel which are really of the nature of an invitation to an argument. You have, for instance, such questions as this: 'I suggest to you that ...' or 'Is your evidence to be taken as suggesting that ...?' If the witness were a prudent person he would say, with the highest degree of politeness: 'What you suggest is no business of mine. I am not here to make any suggestions at all. I am here only to answer relevant

---

9   *Lord v Colvin* (1855) 3 Drew 222; *R v Hadwen* [1902] 1 KB 882.

10   *Berwick-upon-Tweed Corporation v Murray* (1850) LJ Ch 281, p 286.

11   Sir JF Stephen, *A History of the Criminal Law of England*, 1883, Vol I, p 431. See also Cairns, DJA, *Advocacy and the Making of the Adversarial Criminal Trial 1800–1865*, 1998, p 48.

questions. What the conclusions to be drawn from my answers are is not for me, and as for suggestions, I venture to leave those to others.' An answer of that kind, no doubt, requires a good deal of sense and self-restraint and experience ... It is right to remember in all such cases that the witness in the box is an amateur and the counsel who is asking questions is, as a rule, a professional conductor of argument, and it is not right that the wits of the one should be pitted against the wits of the other in the field of suggestion and controversy. What is wanted from the witness is answers to questions of fact.[12]

Cross-examination should consist of questions only, and never statements of fact. The time for statements such as 'The defendant will say that ...' is during an opening speech, not during cross-examination.[13] The way to avoid such expressions is to put your allegations in the form of a question. So, if it is your case that the police planted the gelignite on your client, you ask: 'You planted the gelignite on my client, didn't you?'[14]

Another restriction that must be borne in mind is that, although the methods of obtaining evidence are wider in cross-examination than in examination-in-chief, the evidence that is obtained must still be admissible under the ordinary rules of evidence. Hearsay, for example, does not suddenly become admissible just because it is obtained during cross-examination. This presents a special problem in criminal trials where there are several defendants, because evidence may be admissible in relation to some of the defendants but not to others. The judge must tell the jury in his summing up to ignore such evidence when considering those defendants against whom it is inadmissible. It follows from this that a defendant must not be cross-examined about evidence that is inadmissible in relation to the case against him, even though it has been held admissible in relation to some other defendant.

In *R v Windass*,[15] for example, the appellant was one of several persons charged with conspiracy to steal. He had been stopped in a motor car carrying a quantity of stolen clothes. His girlfriend, a Miss Findlay, was a co-defendant. More stolen clothing was found at her flat. A diary was also found in her possession. This contained material that showed her complicity in the conspiracy, but the trial judge held it to be admissible only against her, because it was no more than a private record and was not a document created

---

12 (1925) 18 Cr App R 175, pp 178–79.

13 *Archbold: Criminal Pleading, Evidence and Practice*, 2001, p 1097.

14 In my view this is preferable to 'Did you plant the gelignite on my client?'. The leading question (permissible, remember, in cross-examination) gives an impression of quiet confidence, suggesting that you know the truth of the matter, and if only the police were honest, they would come clean and agree with you. I once heard an elegant variation on this from a very distinguished QC, thus: '[In world weary tones] I suppose, officer, if I suggested that you'd planted the gelignite on my client, you'd disagree with me, wouldn't you?' But this style is probably not suitable for beginners.

15 (1989) 89 Cr App R 258.

to further the conspiracy.[16] Despite the fact that the diary was admissible only in relation to the girlfriend, the prosecution were allowed to use it in their examination of the appellant. His attention was drawn to an entry for 27 May, which read: 'Finished with Knocky for good now, he's found other new shoplifters, so let him get on with it.' It was admitted that the appellant's nickname was 'Knocky'. He was asked whether he had any idea of what the entry meant, and he attempted an explanation. Prosecuting counsel was even allowed to give copies of the diary entry to the jury so that they could follow the cross-examination better.

The Court of Appeal held that this line of cross-examination had been improper for two reasons:

(a) It was wrong to ask a witness what a third party meant in a document written, without any contribution from that witness, by the third party.

(b) It was even more wrong for counsel to take a statement that was inadmissible in relation to the witness he was cross-examining, and then to ask the witness to explain the inadmissible, but highly damaging, statements that the maker of the document had written.

R v Windass was applied in *R v Gray and Evans*,[17] where the Court of Appeal held that one defendant should not have been cross-examined by the prosecution about statements relating to him that a co-defendant had made in a police interview.

Sometimes it may initially be unclear whether an item of evidence is admissible or inadmissible against a particular defendant. It is necessary then to establish the conditions that will make it admissible before proceeding to ask any questions about it. This applies to cross-examination as well as examination-in-chief. For example, in *R v Cooper*[18] the defendant was charged with an offence involving the importation of cannabis concealed in a television set. As part of its case, the prosecution relied on two letters, which had not been posted and which had been found in a room occupied by the defendant with his wife. They were written by the wife, but in the joint names of herself and the defendant. The prosecution argued that the jury could infer from what had been written that the defendant was expecting the arrival of a consignment of drugs. For example, one letter said: 'We have been hashless for a couple of weeks (all the houses) and the strain was showing. There was a sharp increase in the consumption of alcohol and general erratic behaviour. But, Ali's contact came thru [sic] for us last Friday and had us all smiling.'

The trial judge held that the letters were admissible. In evidence, the defendant said that he did not know that his wife had written the letters; he was not aware of their contents and was not responsible for them. The judge in

---

16 See also below, Chapter 7, p 171.
17 [1998] Crim LR 570
18 (1985) 82 Cr App R 74.

summing up told the jury that unless they were satisfied that the defendant knew of the contents of the letters, they should ignore them. It was argued on appeal that the letters should never have been admitted. They were inadmissible as hearsay, and were an attempt to get round the general rule under which one spouse was not a compellable witness against the other. The Court of Appeal made it clear that before a defendant can be cross-examined on a third party's account of events, he must have accepted that account as true. The prosecution should have proved as part of their case the finding of the letters in the place where they were found, so as to give notice to the defendant of the use that might eventually be made of them. But initially there should have been no indication to the jury of their contents. Then, at an appropriate stage in the cross-examination of the defendant, the letters should have been placed before him, and he should have been asked if he was aware of their contents. Only if he had said that he was aware of their contents could he have been asked about the passages suggesting drug shortages in the past.[19]

The scope of cross-examination can be limited by common law or statute. An example of a common law limitation is the restrictive approach adopted towards attempts to cross-examine police witnesses about their conduct in other cases. Important statutory restrictions are contained in the Youth Justice and Criminal Evidence Act 1999.

Cross-examining the police on other cases

In *R v Edwards*,[20] the defence at trial had been that alleged admissions had been concocted by the police, who were members of the West Midlands Serious Crimes Squad. By the time of the appeal, police officers involved in the case were the subject of a large number of allegations, which were being investigated by the Police Complaints Authority. One of the officers had been charged with perjury, and it was known that other trials involving members of this squad had resulted in acquittals or the quashing of convictions on appeal. The Court of Appeal said that if that information had been available to the defence at trial, the court would have had to consider what questions could properly have been asked of the police witnesses in cross-examination.

The court said that it would be unwise to lay down hard and fast rules as to how a trial judge should exercise his discretion to secure a balanced picture of a witness's reliability. But the court went on to say that it would not have been proper to ask the appropriate officers about either an untried charge of perjury or complaints not yet ruled on by the Police Complaints Authority. Nor should police witnesses have been asked about allegedly discreditable conduct by other officers, whether serving in the same squad or not. There

---

19   See also *R v Cross* (1990) 91 Cr App R 115.
20   [1991] 1 WLR 207; *Sourcebook*, p 368.

was no legal basis on which the defence could adduce evidence of an habitual course of conduct, designed by police to defeat the provisions of the Police and Criminal Evidence Act 1984.[21]

In relation to other cases where the same police officer had given evidence 'unsuccessfully', the court laid down the following propositions:

(a) The acquittal of a defendant in case A, where the prosecution case depended largely or entirely on the evidence of a police officer, does not normally render that officer liable to cross-examination as to credit in case B.

(b) However, where a police officer, who has allegedly fabricated an admission in case B, has also given evidence of an admission in case A, where there was an acquittal, *by virtue of which his evidence is demonstrated to have been disbelieved*, it is proper that the jury in case B should be made aware of the fact.

(c) However, where the acquittal in case A does not 'necessarily' indicate that the jury disbelieved the officer, such cross-examination should not be allowed. A verdict of not guilty may mean no more than that the jury had some doubt about the prosecution case, not that they believed any witness was lying.[22]

What appears to be required is a verdict that *entails* perjury by a police officer, rather than a verdict that is merely *consistent with* perjury. But in the absence of any reasons for a jury's verdict this is an impossible test to satisfy. The Court of Appeal suggested as much in *R v Meads*.[23] In this case, counsel for the appellant and counsel for the prosecution both accepted that, where the circumstances of an earlier acquittal *pointed to* fabrication of evidence by a police officer, cross-examination should be permitted.

It was accepted by both sides that cross-examination about unproved allegations against a police officer should not be permitted, nor should cross-examination about the misconduct of other officers. The Court of Appeal observed that it might be necessary on another occasion to consider whether an acquittal could ever demonstrate that the evidence of a prosecution witness should be disbelieved.

The problem was indirectly considered in *R v Guney*,[24] where one of the issues raised on appeal related to the disclosure of relevant material by the prosecution. The Court of Appeal said that the defence were entitled to be informed of convictions of any officers in the case or of disciplinary findings against any of them. However, the court said that it would be wholly

---

21 See also *R v Clancy* [1997] Crim LR 290.
22 [1991] 1 WLR 207, p 217.
23 [1996] Crim LR 519.
24 [1998] 2 Cr App R 242.

unrealistic for the prosecution to attempt to maintain records of every occasion when any police officer gave evidence that was 'successful or unsuccessful (whatever that may mean)'. In the court's opinion, 'the records available to the Crown Prosecution Service should include transcripts of any decisions of the Court of Appeal Criminal Division in which convictions have been quashed on the express basis of misconduct or lack of veracity of identified police officers as well as with cases which have been stopped by the trial judge or been discontinued on the same basis'.[25] The court took *R v Edwards*[26] as the starting point for the contemporary approach to the problem of discreditable behaviour by a police witness. The court went on to consider the problem that arose where the witness had given evidence 'unsuccessfully' in earlier cases. In relation to successful appeals, the court endorsed an earlier statement by Lord Lane CJ. He had said that the fact that the Court of Appeal 'was not satisfied' about aspects of the police evidence could not be the subject of cross-examination. From this, it followed that the quashing of a conviction 'should be less likely to found a proper basis for cross-examination than an acquittal by the jury, not least because the witness whose conduct is impugned has not normally had any opportunity to give evidence'.[27]

Thus, the Court of Appeal envisaged circumstances when an earlier acquittal in a different case *might* be the subject of cross-examination, but said nothing about the nature of those circumstances. On the other hand, because the court clearly considered itself bound by *R v Edwards*,[28] it could be argued that the test in that decision has been endorsed, with all its difficulties. But the point did not arise directly, and *R v Meads*[29] appears not to have been cited. The law remains unsettled.

The law is also unsettled on the subject of cross-examination of particular officers about unresolved allegations of impropriety against them. In *R v Edwards (Maxine)*,[30] the Court of Appeal had to consider the safety of a conviction after a trial in which evidence had been given by members of the Stoke Newington Drugs Squad. The defence had been that officers in the case had fabricated incriminating evidence. After the trial, an investigation into this squad had begun, and the officers in the defendant's case were among those investigated. At the end of the investigation, no charges were made, or disciplinary proceedings taken, against them. But at one stage, the degree of suspicion as to the trustworthiness of one of these officers was such that the

---

25   [1998] 2 Cr App R 242, p 258.

26   [1991] 1 WLR 207.

27   *Ibid*, p 262.

28   [1991] 1 WLR 207.

29   [1996] Crim LR 519. See also *R v Twitchell* [2000] 1 Cr App R 373; *R v Malik* [2000] 2 Cr App R 8.

30   [1996] 2 Cr App R 345.

Crown Prosecution Service had offered no evidence in two cases in which he had been involved and had not resisted an appeal in another. The Court of Appeal held the defendant's conviction to be unsafe. Beldam LJ said that it was impossible to be confident that there would have been a conviction had the jury known the facts and circumstances of the other cases in which this officer had been involved. Thus, the court assumed that information about the unresolved investigations in other cases would have been admissible at the defendant's trial if it had been available.[31] On the other hand, in *R v Guney*, Judge LJ stated that: 'Cross-examination of police officers on the basis of unresolved criminal charges or complaints to the Police Complaints Authority is not permitted.'[32]

Cross-examination of complainants in trials for sexual offences

The credibility of a witness is a relevant fact in any case because it is something that makes that witness's testimony about other relevant matters more or less likely to be true. At common law, cross-examination of a witness may be relevant either solely to credibility, or solely to an issue in the case, or to a mixture of both. For some centuries moral character was regarded as relevant to credibility, and witnesses in any type of case could therefore be cross-examined about sexual promiscuity (amongst other things) with a view to showing that their evidence was not worthy of belief. Thus in *R v Castro* (1874)[33] the question was whether the defendant committed perjury in swearing that he was Sir Roger Tichborne. A witness, Lord Bellew, stated that he had made tattoo marks on the arm of Roger Tichborne when they were at school together. No such marks were on the defendant's arm. It was held that Bellew could be asked and compelled to answer the question whether, many years after the alleged tattooing and many years before the occasion on which he gave evidence, he had committed adultery with the wife of one of his friends.[34] The position was no different in cases where a complainant alleged rape or a similar offence. So a complainant could be cross-examined about being a prostitute, or about indiscriminate promiscuity, simply in order to show that she was not to be trusted. Such evidence might, on the facts of a particular case, be thought relevant not merely to her credit, but to the issue of guilt itself. This was particularly likely to be so where the act of intercourse was admitted by the defendant, but was alleged to have been with the

---

31 A similar decision was reached in *R v Whelan* [1997] Crim LR 353, in which *R v Edwards (Maxine)* was approved.

32 [1998] 2 Cr App R 242, p 260.

33 *Charge of the Lord Chief Justice of England in the Case of The Queen against Thomas Castro ... printed from the shorthand writer's notes*, 1874, Vol II, p 4764.

34 But Cockburn CJ disapproved of counsel's behaviour in exercising that right. See below, Chapter 11, p 303.

complainant's consent. Whatever might be the position today, it is probably true that for much of the 20th century jurors would quite readily accept that a woman who was in the habit of committing fornication or adultery with different men was more likely than one who did not have that habit to have consented to sexual intercourse with a man to whom she was not married. On that basis, her sexual habits would have been relevant not only to her credit but to the issue of the defendant's guilt as well. Even today, where consent is in issue, a woman's previous sexual relations with *the defendant* are likely to be thought relevant, on the basis that a habit of consensual intercourse with a particular man makes another act of intercourse with that man more likely to have been consensual than if there had been no previous history of sexual relations between them. It will, of course, be remembered that an item of evidence does not have to be conclusive, or even very weighty, to be relevant.[35]

The common law was first changed by the Sexual Offences (Amendment) Act 1976, which applied where the defendant was charged with a 'rape offence'. Broadly speaking, this included rape, attempted rape, and aiding and abetting rape. It did not include other sexual offences, such as indecent assault. Section 2 of the Act provided that the defendant could not call any evidence, or ask any questions in cross-examination, about any 'sexual experience' of the complainant with a person *other than* the defendant unless the judge gave leave. On an application for leave, the judge was bound to grant it if he was satisfied that it would be unfair to the defendant to refuse.

In *R v Viola*,[36] the Court of Appeal said that leave should be given if the evidence or questions might reasonably lead the jury to take a different view of the complainant's evidence. It said that the Act was aimed primarily at protecting the complainant from questions that were relevant only to credibility. So if the proposed line of questioning was relevant to an issue in the trial in the light of the way the case was being run, it was likely to be admitted. The court acknowledged that there was a grey area in such cases between relevance to credit and relevance to an issue in the case. Evidence of promiscuity might be so strong, or so closely contemporaneous to the event in issue, as to reach the border between credit and issue. Conversely, relevant evidence might have such slight weight that it would not be unfair to exclude it. Later cases showed that the complainant's sexual history might become relevant because her evidence of circumstances surrounding the alleged offence had a 'ring of truth' that gave credibility to her story as a whole. For example, if, during her evidence, she claimed or gave evidence suggesting that the encounter had led to the loss of her virginity, a jury might think in relation to a particular defendant, 'It's not likely she'd have chosen him for a first experience; it must have been rape'.[37]

---

35 See above, Chapter 1, pp 8–10.
36 [1982] 1 WLR 1138.
37 See *R v SMS* [1992] Crim LR 310.

The relevant provisions of the 1976 Act have now been repealed by ss 41–43 of the Youth Justice and Criminal Evidence Act 1999.[38] Section 41(1) puts a significant restriction on the way the defence can conduct its case where the defendant is charged with what the Act calls a 'sexual offence'. This is defined in s 62 of the 1999 Act and includes, among other offences, rape, indecent assault, unlawful sexual intercourse and any attempt to commit these offences. The new Act applies to a wider range of offences than the Act of 1976.

The restriction imposed by s 41(1) is that, except with the leave of the court, no evidence may be adduced by the defence, nor any questions asked in cross-examination, 'about any sexual behaviour of the complainant'. 'Sexual behaviour' is defined in s 42(1)(c) as:

> ... any sexual behaviour or other sexual experience, whether or not involving any accused or other person, but excluding (except in s 41(3)(c)(i) and (5)(a)) anything alleged to have taken place as part of the event which is the subject matter of the charge ...

The expression 'sexual behaviour' appears to be wider than 'sexual experience', which was used in the 1976 Act. For example, it seems capable of including flirtatious behaviour and perhaps even suggestive conversation. The scope of exclusion in s 41(1) is significantly wider than that provided in the 1976 Act. In particular, the 1976 Act expressly allowed questions about a complainant's previous sexual experience with the defendant. This is now subject to the general ban. The effect of this is very likely to be that where rape is alleged as an incident within a long standing consensual sexual relationship, the jury would be kept in ignorance of this background.[39]

By s 41(2), the court may give leave to adduce evidence of the complainant's sexual behaviour, or to allow cross-examination about it if, and only if, it is satisfied of two matters: first, that either sub-s (3) or sub-s (5) applies; *and*, secondly, that a refusal of leave might have the result of rendering unsafe a conclusion of the trier of fact on any relevant issue in the case. These are not *alternative* conditions; for leave to be given, *both* must apply. It has been argued, notably by Lord Ackner,[40] that the Act creates, potentially, a situation where refusal of leave might render a conclusion of fact unsafe, but where leave must still be refused because the conditions laid down for admissibility in sub-s (3) or (5) are not satisfied. The government answer to that criticism, given by Lord Williams of Mostyn in the House of Lords, was

---

38 See Geddes, A, 'The exclusion of evidence relating to a complainant's sexual behaviour in sexual offence trials' (1999) 149 NLJ 1084; Kibble, N, 'The sexual history provisions ...' [2000] Crim LR 274.

39 See the speech of Lord Ackner in the debate on the Bill, *Hansard*, 23 March 1999, col 1210. But see also fn 52, below.

40 *Ibid*, col 1209.

that the provisions allowed enough scope for all *relevant* evidence about a complainant's sexual behaviour to be introduced. However, he immediately qualified this by claiming that the provisions now contained in s 41 provided a statutory framework for determining relevance.[41] He repeated this later in his speech, adding that the government believed that in the past, the law had not been sufficiently balanced between respective interests.[42] It looks very much as if the government is accepting that some facts may be *logically* relevant, but, to preserve a 'balance' between the interests of the complainant and the defendant, they are not allowed to be *legally* relevant. On the other hand, if either of sub-s (3) or (5) applies, it is difficult to imagine circumstances in which a refusal of leave would not render a conclusion on an issue in the case unsafe.

The expression 'any relevant issue in the case' is defined by s 42(1)(a) as 'any issue falling to be proved by the prosecution or defence in the trial of the accused'. In a rape trial, of course, the defence has no burden of proof, but this is not the case with all the sexual offences covered by the Act. See, for example, the offence created by s 128 of the Mental Health Act 1959, which makes it unlawful for a member of hospital staff to have sexual intercourse with a woman receiving treatment for mental disorder at that hospital.

The scope of sub-s (3)

The sub-section distinguishes between cases where the evidence or question in cross-examination relates to a relevant issue, but that issue is *not* one of consent, and those cases where the relevant issue *is* one of consent. The expression 'issue of consent' is defined in s 42(1)(b) as 'any issue whether the complainant in fact consented to the conduct constituting the offence with which the accused is charged (and accordingly does not include any issue as to the belief of the accused that the complainant so consented)'. So, if the defence is not that the complainant consented, but that the defendant *believed that she was consenting*, the sole test is whether the evidence or question relates to a relevant issue in the case, and the restrictions imposed by s 41(3)(b) and (c) will not apply.

However, the test of relevance where such a defence is put forward has been strictly applied. In *R v Barton*,[43] the defence to a rape charge was mistaken belief that the complainant had consented. The defendant wanted to call evidence of the complainant's sexual experiences with other men to establish the foundation for that belief, but the trial judge refused leave. The Court of Appeal upheld this decision and drew a distinction between belief that a woman *would consent if asked*, and belief that a woman *is consenting* to a

---

41 *Hansard*, 23 March 1999, col 1216.
42 *Ibid*, col 1220.
43 (1987) 85 Cr App R 5.

particular act of intercourse. If a defendant wishes to establish that he was getting the wrong message from a complainant's responses, the evidence will have to be relevant to that issue. It will be no good establishing that the woman is promiscuous; that would be relevant only to a belief that she *would consent if asked*, not to a belief that she *was consenting on a particular occasion*. To establish the latter, evidence would be needed of the defendant's knowledge of her idiosyncratic behaviour on other occasions that might have led him to believe, for example, that when she said 'no', she meant 'yes'.

Sub-section 41(3) applies if the evidence or question in cross-examination relates to a relevant issue in the case *and either*:

(a) that issue is not an issue of consent; *or*

(b) it is an issue of consent, and the sexual behaviour of the complainant to which the evidence or question relates is alleged to have taken place at or about the same time as the event which is the subject matter of the charge; *or*

(c) it is an issue of consent and the sexual behaviour of the complainant is alleged to have been, in any respect so similar:

    (i) to any sexual behaviour of the complainant which the defendant alleges took place *as part of the event* which is the subject matter of the charge, *or*

    (ii) to any other sexual behaviour of the complainant which the defendant alleges took place *at or about the same time as* that event,

that the similarity cannot reasonably be explained as a coincidence.

Sub-section (3)(b) allows the court to look, but only to a limited extent, at the context in which the event which is the subject matter of the charge is alleged to have taken place. The bill originally provided for a 24 hour framework on either side of the alleged offence. If the complainant's sexual behaviour did not fall within that period, it was automatically excluded. Section 41(3) is more flexible, but only slightly so. Lord Williams, speaking for the government, said that anything that happened more than 24 hours before or after the alleged offence should only rarely be considered to have taken place 'at or about the same time' as the event giving rise to the charge. He referred to the possible inclusion of events happening 'a few minutes – or at the very most, a few hours – outside the 24 hour limit'. (Conversely, if something had occurred just within 24 hours of the alleged offence, the court might not consider it to have taken place 'at or about the same time'.) In particular, Lord Williams said, the sub-section was not intended to include evidence of behaviour three, four or five days before the alleged offence. So if a complainant had had sexual intercourse with four different men a few days before the alleged offence, that evidence would not be admissible to support a defence of consent.[44]

Sub-section (3)(c) allows the court to look at sexual behaviour of the complainant on other occasions where that behaviour is so similar to the behaviour of the complainant on the occasion under investigation that the similarity cannot be explained as a coincidence. The behaviour may match either some element alleged by the defendant to have been part of the event that has led to the charge, or some feature of its surrounding circumstances within the limitations just described. It appears to cover behaviour either before or after the alleged offence. The test here is effectively one of 'striking similarity' – a concept originating in some of the cases on similar fact evidence.[45] Such evidence must be of an unusual and specific nature. According to Lord Williams, it could not include 'evidence of a general approach towards consensual sex', such as a taste for one night stands or for having sex on a first date. It certainly could not include the fact that the complainant had previously consented to sex with people of the same race as the defendant. Nor could it include, where the allegation was of rape in a car, the fact that the complainant had previously had consensual sex in a car. He said that to be admitted under this provision, behaviour had to be 'the sort of behaviour that is so unusual that it would be wholly unreasonable to explain it as coincidental'. As an example, he took a complaint alleging gang rape where one of the defendants alleged consent. If the defence had 'specific factual evidence' that the complainant had previously engaged in consensual group sex under similar circumstances, this might be relevant for the jury to consider.[46] One disadvantage of the 'striking similarity' test that Lord Williams did not consider is the burden that it will place on judges, who will have to decide what sort of sexual behaviour, homosexual as well as heterosexual, is now so unusual that it ought to be admitted.[47]

By s 41(4), no evidence or question shall be regarded as relating to a relevant issue in the case if it appears to the court to be reasonable to assume that the sole or main purpose of the defence is to impugn the credibility of the complainant as a witness. Of course, in one sense, evidence and questions about a complainant's sexual behaviour are bound to be designed to impugn the credibility of the complainant: the whole purpose of such questioning and evidence will be to create a reasonable doubt about whether the complainant is telling the truth when he or she says that sexual intercourse took place without consent. This can hardly be what the sub-section refers to. It presumably refers to the old common law rule, originally abolished for

---

44 *Hansard*, 23 March 1999, col 1217.

45 See below, Chapter 10.

46 *Hansard*, 23 March 1999, col 1218.

47 By s 142 of the Criminal Justice and Public Order Act 1994, it is an offence for a man to rape a woman *or another man*. See the refusal of Lord Cross in *DPP v Boardman* [1975] AC 421 to determine what were usual practices for middle-aged homosexual men.

complainants in rape offences under the 1976 Act, that permitted evidence of immorality to be adduced to discredit generally what a witness said on oath.

Sub-section (5)

This exception to the general prohibition applies if the evidence or question relates to any evidence adduced *by the prosecution* about any sexual behaviour of the complainant. So if during examination-in-chief the complainant states that she was a virgin before she was raped, the defence may cross-examine with the object of rebutting that assertion, and call evidence to do so if need be. But what is the position where the complainant makes a statement about her sexual behaviour during cross-examination? Suppose that when counsel for the defendant puts it to her that she consented, she replies, 'That's a lie! I'd never have sex with anyone but my husband!'. The defence know that the complainant has in fact had sexual relations with at least three other men in the last six months. But can this be put to her? It does not appear to be evidence *adduced by the prosecution*, unless you regard everything said by a prosecution witness as such. If it was adduced by anyone, it was by defence counsel. More probably, it is wrong to think of it as adduced by anybody; rather, it has been volunteered by the witness. But in neither case could the statement, on a literal construction of sub-s (5), be rebutted. Yet the statement with nothing to contradict it could powerfully influence the jury.

Sub-section (6)

This provides that, for the purposes of sub-ss (3) and (5), the evidence that is permitted to be called must relate to *specific* instances of alleged sexual behaviour by the defendant. The question is, how specific? Would it be sufficiently specific to refer to an adulterous relationship with Charlie during summer last year? Or must there be greater particularity, stating, for example, the date and place of every act of adultery relied upon?

Procedure

By s 43, an application for leave under s 41 shall be heard in private and in the absence of the complainant. Nothing is said of the defendant's presence; *presumably* Parliament did not intend to exclude him, and the application will be made to the court after members of the press and public have been excluded. Where such an application has been determined, the judge must state in open court, but in the absence of the jury if there is one, his reasons for giving or refusing leave, and, if leave is granted, the extent to which evidence may be adduced or questions asked. Presumably, this also will take place in the presence of the defendant, but in the absence of the complainant, who would otherwise be alerted to questions she or he would face in cross-examination.

I have already suggested that ss 41 and 42 of the 1999 Act make it possible that probative evidence will be excluded, to the disadvantage of the defence. For example, a long standing sexual relationship between the complainant and the defendant could be concealed from the jury. Another example of potential injustice was given in the House of Lords by Lord Thomas of Gresford. Suppose, he said, a man and a woman live happily together for a period of time, but that the woman subsequently goes to live with another man. In due course that man leaves her and she returns to her first partner. A little later she has a row with that partner about having left him for another man. After the row she goes to the police and complains that her first partner has raped her. At the trial for rape, counsel for the defendant wants to put to the complainant that she made the complaint because of the row she had over her going away with the other man. Naturally, the defendant wants to give evidence explaining what the row was about. However, the effect of s 41 is to exclude both cross-examination and defence evidence on that matter.[48]

It is hardly surprising that, as Baroness Mallalieu said, there is 'profound dismay' at the Criminal Bar, and among many judges, about these provisions.[49] At some stage, the question whether they are compatible with the European Convention on Human Rights is bound to be litigated. Article 6 provides that everyone charged with a criminal offence has certain minimum rights. These include the right to examine or have examined witnesses against him, and to obtain the attendance and examination of witnesses on his behalf under the same conditions as witnesses against him. A law that privileges the prosecution by excluding cross-examination or evidence that is relevant to the defence case, and may be of such probative weight as to raise a reasonable doubt about the defendant's guilt, sits uneasily with this provision. But the outcome of a challenge cannot be easily predicted. It is well settled that the public interest may be taken into account in deciding what the right to a fair trial requires in a particular context. In *Doorson v Netherlands*,[50] it was said that 'principles of fair trial also require that in appropriate cases the interests of the defence are balanced against those of witnesses or victims called upon to testify'. What might tip the balance in favour of defendants is the fact that where the defence is the defendant's *belief* in the complainant's consent, the defendant is not precluded from adducing evidence that he and the complainant had recently taken part in consensual sexual activity with each other. To admit such evidence where the defence is belief in consent, but to exclude it where the defence is simply that the complainant consented, seems illogical. Where both defences are raised, a jury would have to be directed that the evidence of the previous relationship was relevant to one defence but not

---

48 *Hansard*, 23 March 1999, col 1214.
49 *Ibid*. See also the speech of Lord Thomas at col 1215.
50 (1996) 22 EHRR 330, p 358.

the other. As Rose LJ said in *R v Y*,[51] a summing-up in such terms would have more of a flavour of Lewis Carroll than a rehearsal of matters of jurisprudence.

Cross-examination on previous inconsistent statements

Any witness may be cross-examined about an earlier statement of his that is inconsistent with his testimony in court. If the witness then admits that his earlier account is the true one, no problem arises. But what if he does not? In civil proceedings the previous inconsistent statement will be evidence of the truth of its contents,[52] so the trial judge can choose between the earlier and the later account. But this is not so in criminal cases. How, then, should a jury be directed about a previous inconsistent statement that the witness does not accept as true? In *R v Golder*,[53] the Court of Appeal said that when a witness is shown to have made previous inconsistent statements, the jury should be directed that the previous statements do not constitute evidence on which they can act. But the court assumed that, in such a case, the jury would be directed that the witness's evidence at trial should be regarded as unreliable. However, in *R v Governor of Pentonville Prison ex p Alves*,[54] Lord Goff, in a speech with which the other Law Lords agreed, said that this was not an invariable requirement. He approved the decision of the Court of Appeal in *R v Pestano*,[55] in which it was held that the credibility of such testimony was a matter for the jury to consider, subject to a proper warning as to weight by the judge.

The manner in which a witness should be cross-examined about previous inconsistent statements is governed by provisions in the Criminal Procedure Act 1865.[56] Section 4 applies to both oral and written statements[57] and provides as follows:

> If a witness, upon cross-examination as to a former statement made by him relative to the subject matter of the indictment or proceeding, and inconsistent with his present testimony, does not distinctly admit that he has made such statement, proof may be given that he did in fact make it; but before such proof

---

51 [2001] Crim LR 389. *R v Y* reached the House of Lords after this section was written and has been reported as *R v A* [2001] 3 All ER 1. The House held, applying the interpretative obligation under s 3 of the Human Rights Act 1998, that where the evidence and questioning is so relevant to the issue of consent that to exclude it would endanger the fairness of the trial under Art 6 of the Convention, it should not be excluded under s 41(3)(c) of the 1999 Act.

52 See below, Chapter 7.

53 [1960] 1 WLR 1169; *Sourcebook*, p 366.

54 [1993] AC 284; *Sourcebook*, p 367.

55 [1981] Crim LR 397.

56 This Act, which applies to civil as well as to criminal proceedings, re-enacted the Common Law Procedure Act 1854, ss 23 and 24, which applied only to civil cases.

57 *R v Derby Magistrates' Court ex p B* [1996] AC 487.

can be given the circumstances of the supposed statement, sufficient to designate the particular occasion, must be mentioned to the witness, and he must be asked whether or not he has made such statement.

Section 5 applies to written statements only and provides as follows:

> A witness may be cross-examined as to previous statements made by him in writing or reduced into writing relative to the subject matter of the indictment or proceeding, without such writing being shown to him; but if it is intended to contradict such witness by the writing, his attention must, before such contradictory proof can be given, be called to those parts of the writing which are to be used for the purpose of so contradicting him: provided always, that it shall be competent for the judge, at any time during the trial, to require the production of the writing for his inspection, and he may thereupon make such use of it for the purposes of the trial as he may think fit.

These provisions are intended to protect a witness against being unfairly surprised during cross-examination. Under s 4, the 'circumstances' which are to be mentioned to the witness include such details as the time of the earlier statement, the place where it was made, and particulars of other persons present when it was made.[58] The section applies if the witness does not 'distinctly admit' the earlier statement, and can therefore be used if the witness says merely that he does not remember, or if he refuses to answer. Under s 5, the witness can be shown the earlier statement, asked to read it silently, and then asked if he stills stands by what he has just said in the witness box. That may be enough for the witness to change his testimony. If he does not, the advocate must decide whether he wants to use the writing to establish the inconsistency. If he does, the document must be put in evidence. The disadvantage of this is that it will then be available to the court in its entirety, and its overall effect may be to show far more consistency than inconsistency between what the witness said first and what he has later said in the witness box.

The Law Commission has recommended that previous inconsistent statements should be evidence of the truth of their contents in criminal as well as civil proceedings.[59] One reason for this recommendation was the difficulty for fact finders in observing the distinction between a statement going to credit and a statement going to the issue. But the Commission also argued that if jurors or magistrates are trusted to decide that a witness has lied throughout, and to disregard that witness's testimony, they should be free to decide, on the basis of other evidence or the witness's response under cross-examination, that an earlier statement was true.[60]

---

58 *Angus v Smith* (1829) Moo&M 473; *Carpenter v Wall* (1840) 11 A&E 803. Section 4 was declaratory of the common law (*Cross & Tapper on Evidence*, 1999, p 295).

59 Law Commission, *Evidence in Criminal Proceedings: Hearsay and Related Topics*, Law Com No 245, 1997, Cm 3670.

60 Law Com No 245, 1997, para 10.89.

RE-EXAMINATION

The object of re-examination is to clarify and complete matters which were referred to in cross-examination, but which were left in an ambiguous or incomplete state. Re-examination should not be used merely as an opportunity to repeat evidence-in-chief. An advocate is not allowed, in re-examination, to ask questions that do not arise from the matters covered in cross-examination. If a subject was raised during examination-in-chief but not covered in cross-examination, it cannot be referred to in re-examination. Still less can a wholly new subject be raised in re-examination. For example, in *R v Fletcher and Others*,[61] the defendant's cross-examination of a prosecution witness was limited to the witness's credit only. The prosecution were not allowed, in re-examination, to ask their witness further questions so as to incriminate the defendant.

REFRESHING MEMORY

A witness may want to refresh his memory in the witness box about the events to which he is testifying. Typically, such a witness is a police officer, but the same rules apply if any other person wants to use a memory-refreshing note. To establish that a note may be used, the advocate must prove that it is a 'contemporaneous' one. This does not mean that the note must have been made literally contemporaneously, but it should have been made as soon as possible after the events recorded, at a time when the matters were still fresh in the witness's memory.[62] The advocate whose witness wants to use a memory-refreshing note will therefore usually ask the witness three questions:

(a) Do you wish to use a note?

(b) When was that note made?

(c) When you made the note, were the matters then still fresh in your memory?

The last question should not, of course, be asked when the note was a contemporaneous note in the strict sense; in other words, a note made while a conversation or events were proceeding. Sometimes a police witness will want to use a note compiled by another officer. This is permissible, provided the testifying witness verified its accuracy at a time when the matters were still fresh in that witness's memory.

'Refreshing memory' for these purposes can refer to two different situations. The first is where the witness's memory is actually jogged by the

---

61 (1829) 1 Lewin 111.

62 *R v Richardson* [1971] 2 QB 484.

words on the page. The second situation is where the events recorded were too long ago for the memory to be jogged, but the witness says he is sure that the matters he recorded are true. For example, in *Maugham v Hubbard*,[63] the question arose in a civil action whether the witness had received £20 from the plaintiff six years earlier. A cash book kept by the plaintiff had an entry that gave the date and recorded the transaction. The witness had acknowledged the transaction by writing his initials at the side of the entry, but he said that he had no recollection of receiving the money. He continued, 'I know nothing but by the book; but seeing my initials, I have no doubt that I received the money'. The paper on which this entry had been made was not stamped as a receipt, and so could not be produced to prove by itself the receipt of the money. But the trial judge held that the witness might use it to refresh his memory, and his decision was upheld by the Court of King's Bench.

Refreshing memory *outside* court was discussed in *R v Richardson*.[64] The defendant was being tried for offences committed about 18 months earlier. The civilian witnesses called for the prosecution were told outside court before giving evidence that they might refresh their memories, if they wished, by reading the statements they had made to the police a few weeks after the offences were committed. Each of the witnesses did so. On appeal, the question arose whether this had been proper. The court accepted that the statements were not sufficiently 'contemporaneous' to have been used as memory-refreshing documents while giving evidence. The Court of Appeal approved of what had happened and made several points:

(a) The court recognised the difference in approach towards documents used in the witness box and those used outside it. But there was no compulsion to aim for consistency in what was only a matter of practice, if that would produce results that would hinder the course of justice.

(b) To refuse to offer a chance of reading their statements to witnesses would tend to hinder justice: it would make testimony a test of memory rather than truthfulness. It would create difficulties for honest witnesses but do little to hamper dishonest ones.

(c) It would be wrong if several witnesses were handed statements in circumstances enabling one to compare with another what each had said.

In *R v Westwell*,[65] the Court of Appeal said that there was no rule that witnesses *must* be allowed to see their statements before giving evidence. There might be cases where there was reason to suppose that the witness had an improper purpose in wishing to see it; in those circumstances he should be

---

63 (1828) 8 B&C 14; *Sourcebook*, p 346.
64 [1969] 1 QB 299; *Sourcebook*, p 347.
65 [1976] 2 All ER 812; *Sourcebook*, p 349.

denied the opportunity. The court also said that it was desirable, though not essential, for the prosecution to tell the defence if witnesses had been shown their statements. In *R v Thomas*,[66] the Court of Appeal approved a trial judge's decision that a child aged eight should not be shown her statement before giving evidence. Presumably this was on the basis that so young a child might not appreciate that her testimony had to be about what she remembered of the day in question, and not about what she had read.

Suppose the original note that the witness would have used in the witness box has been destroyed or lost. Can a substitute be used? This question arose in *R v Cheng*.[67] The defendant was charged with selling heroin in Soho. Over a considerable period of time, police officers had kept observation, making detailed notes of what they saw. The defendant did not stand trial until some three years after the alleged offences. During this time, one of the officers in the case transferred from the Metropolitan Police to another police force. At the time of his transfer, he handed in the relevant notebook, with all his others, to the Metropolitan Police. The notebook was then lost, but there existed a statement made by the officer with the assistance of his notes. It was not a full transcript of the notes, because the statement omitted references to other persons who had also been under observation. The prosecution did not claim that this statement was a 'contemporaneous' document within the requirements of the memory-refreshing rules, but the trial judge nevertheless allowed the officer to refresh his memory from it while giving evidence. The Court of Appeal held that he had been right to do so. Provided there is evidence that the statement or transcription contains substantially what was in the notes, the witness should be allowed to refresh his memory from it. But if it bears little relation to the original notes, the judge should refuse leave to use such an imperfect source.

Suppose a witness who has *not* seen his statement before going into the witness box dries up or goes adrift while testifying. Can anything be done? In *R v Da Silva*,[68] the Court of Appeal held that in such circumstances, a witness can be permitted to break off his testimony and refresh his memory. However, certain conditions have to be satisfied:

(a) The witness must state that he cannot now recall the details of events because of the lapse of time since they took place.

(b) The witness must have made a statement much nearer the time of those events. It need not be a 'contemporaneous' one, but it must represent his recollection at the time he made it.

(c) The witness must wish to have an opportunity to read the statement before continuing with his evidence.

---

66 [1994] Crim LR 745.
67 (1976) 63 Cr App R 20; *Sourcebook*, p 350.
68 [1990] 1 All ER 29; *Sourcebook*, p 351.

Even if these conditions are satisfied, once the witness has read his statement it should be taken away. He cannot use it continuously to refresh his memory as if it were a contemporaneous note.

It was also said that the witness could refresh his memory in this way only if he had *not* read his statement before going into the witness box. But in *R v South Ribble Magistrates ex p Cochrane*,[69] the Divisional Court took the view that, while the satisfaction of all the conditions referred to in *R v Da Silva* was *sufficient* for a trial judge to exercise his discretion to allow a witness to refresh his memory from his statement, it did not follow that it was *necessary* for all those conditions to be satisfied before a judge could allow a witness to refresh his memory in that way. No rigid rule of law precludes a court in a criminal trial from exercising a broad discretion to permit a witness who has begun to give evidence to refresh his memory from his witness statement, even though it is not a 'contemporaneous' statement, and even though he *has* read it before going into the witness box. There should be no difference between someone who has read his statement and not taken it in properly and someone who has not read it at all.

Where a note is relied on to refresh a witness's memory, the advocate who cross-examines may wish to look at it. May he do so? What use may he make of the document? And in what circumstances can the document itself become an item of evidence in the trial? In order to understand how the rules about these matters work, three things must be appreciated. The first is that if the memory-refreshing document becomes a physical item of evidence (often called 'an exhibit') in the case, it becomes something that the jury can take with them to examine when they have retired to consider their verdict. The judge should direct the jury when summing up that such a document has only a limited use: it is not evidence of the truth of the matters stated in it, but only evidence of the consistency (and so of the credibility) of the witness who used it.[70] But this will not alter the fact that a prosecution witness's memory-refreshing document that has become an exhibit can harm the defence considerably. Most of the time the defence will want the jury to forget the details of the prosecution case, and a permanent reminder to them of what a prosecution witness has said will often be most undesirable.

Secondly, a document used to refresh a witness's memory may cover a variety of matters, not all of which will be obviously relevant to the trial of any particular defendant. The original police officer's notes in *R v Cheng*,[71] for example, contained records of observations involving other suspects who were not being tried with Cheng.

Thirdly, for a document to become an exhibit in the case, application must be made to the judge by the party who wants this. In the sort of situation

---

69 [1996] 2 Cr App R 544.

70 *R v Virgo* (1978) 67 Cr App R 323; *Sourcebook*, p 355.

71 (1976) 63 Cr App R 20; *Sourcebook*, p 350.

under discussion, that party will often be the one whose witness has been cross-examined. Talk about a document 'becoming an exhibit' is a shorthand device that I use to refer to a procedure of this sort where the judge allows the application. It does not mean that the document becomes an exhibit *automatically*.

The rules about the use of memory-refreshing documents were summarised as follows by Sir Jocelyn Simon P in *Senat v Senat*:[72]

(a) Where a document is used to refresh a witness's memory, cross-examining counsel may inspect the document in order to check it. This will not make the document an exhibit. (Where a witness has given evidence without referring to notes, but has used notes to refresh his memory before going into the witness-box, counsel may call for and inspect those notes and cross-examine on them.)[73]

(b) Counsel may cross-examine on the contents of such a document without making it an exhibit, provided the cross-examination does not go beyond the parts that are being used to refresh the witness's memory. For example, if counsel finds among the memory-refreshing parts something favourable to his client that has not yet been mentioned in evidence by the witness, he can cross-examine about it, and the document will not become an exhibit.

(c) However, where cross-examination is on parts of the document that have not been used to refresh the witness's memory, there is a risk that the document *will* be made an exhibit.

The effect of all this is that you may sometimes have to balance the possible advantage to be gained from cross-examination on the non-memory-refreshing parts of a document against the disadvantage of having the document put in as an exhibit, and becoming a permanent reminder to the jury of a witness's testimony.

The operation of these rules can be seen in *R v Britton*.[74] The defendant had been charged with assault during a political demonstration. After he was released from the police station, he typed out his recollection of events. At trial he was allowed to use this note, because it was regarded as sufficiently contemporaneous, to refresh his memory while giving evidence of what happened prior to his arrest. On cross-examination, counsel for the prosecution inspected the note and asked questions about matters in it that had not been relied on to refresh the defendant's memory while giving evidence-in-chief. The defence applied to have the typed note made an exhibit, but the trial judge refused. The Court of Appeal held that this was wrong. Cross-examining counsel had gone beyond the parts used to refresh

---

72 [1965] P 172; *Sourcebook*, p 353.

73 *Owen v Edwards* (1983) 77 Cr App R 191; *Sourcebook*, p 354.

74 [1987] 2 All ER 412.

the witness's memory, and the defence were therefore entitled to have the whole document put in as an exhibit.

The Law Commission considered the problems associated with 'memory refreshing' in its report on hearsay and related topics.[75] The Commission adopted a realistic approach to this part of the law, observing:

> It may be a fiction that it is the oral evidence that counts; the best evidence may well be the earlier statement. If the witness cannot remember the matters stated even with the help of the statement, the statement is effectively hearsay.[76]

The Commission recommended that if a witness does not, and cannot reasonably be expected to, remember a matter well enough to be able to give oral evidence of it; *and* the witness previously made a statement about that matter when it was fresh in the witness's memory; *and* the witness indicates while giving evidence that, to the best of his belief, he made the statement and it is true, then the statement should itself be admissible as evidence of that matter.[77] Under this recommendation, the rules about refreshing memory would become less important. In many cases today, it is a fiction that the memory is jogged by the note, for in truth there is no independent recollection of the matters referred to. Many notes would be treated as evidence of the matters contained in them. But a genuine memory-refreshing element might remain in some instances, and the Commission did not recommend that the existing rules on the use of memory-refreshing documents should be abolished. However, where a memory-refreshing document becomes evidence in the case (because cross-examination went beyond the memory-refreshing parts), the Commission thought that the document should be evidence not just of consistency, but of the truth of the matters contained in it. If this were not so, the evidential status of a document would differ, depending on whether the old rules or the new rules applied to it.[78] One of the side effects of this recommendation would be to create an imbalance between prosecution and defence. Where a document is admitted as evidence of the truth of its contents, it would be an exhibit in the trial. Since the documents to which this recommendation is most likely to apply will be the notes or statements of police officers, the jury would often have a permanent reminder of part of the prosecution evidence, but usually none of that provided by the defence. To avoid this, the Commission recommended that where a statement previously made by a witness in a document is admitted, the document should not accompany the jury when they retire to consider their verdict, unless the court considers it appropriate or all the parties agree that it should do so.[79]

---

75 Law Com No 245, 1997.

76 Law Com No 245, 1997, para 10.66. The statement will effectively be hearsay if it evokes no recollection at all because what is really happening is that the court is relying on the *statement*, which was made outside court, for the truth of its contents.

77 *Ibid*, para 10.80.

78 *Ibid*, para 10.82.

79 *Ibid*, para 10.62.

PREVIOUS CONSISTENT STATEMENTS

There is a rule that evidence may not be given of the fact that a witness, on some occasion before the trial, made a statement that was consistent with his later testimony at trial. Such statements are usually referred to as 'previous consistent statements' and the rule is sometimes referred to as 'the rule against narrative'. The purpose of the rule is to avoid a situation in which a potential witness might be tempted to manufacture evidence, and artificially increase the weight of what he says in court, by telling the same story to any number of people before the trial takes place. The application of this rule is illustrated by the decision of the Court of Criminal Appeal in *R v Roberts*.[80] The defendant was tried for the murder of his former girlfriend by shooting her with a rifle. His defence was that the death had been an accident. At trial, the defence wished to call evidence from the defendant's father to the effect that his son, shortly after being arrested, had told him that there had been an accident. The trial judge held this evidence inadmissible and was upheld by the Court of Criminal Appeal. Humphreys J said that the law was well settled: a party is not permitted to make evidence for himself.

Despite the decision in *R v Roberts*, it has been the practice to admit in evidence all unwritten and most written statements made by an accused person to the police, whether they contained admissions of guilt or denials. But in *R v Pearce*,[81] the trial judge excluded two voluntary statements and part of an interview on the ground that they were self-serving statements, and so inadmissible under the general rule.[82] The Court of Appeal held that this was wrong, and summarised the law as follows:

(a) A statement containing an admission is evidence of the facts admitted.

(b) A statement that is not an admission is admissible to show the attitude of the accused at the time when he made it. This should not be limited to statements made on first encounter with the police, though the longer the time that has elapsed since the first encounter, the less weighty the denial is likely to be. It is the duty of the prosecution to present the case fairly to the jury, and it would be unfair to give evidence of admissions but exclude answers favourable to the defendant.

(c) Although, in practice, most statements to the police are given in evidence even when they are largely self-serving, there may be a rare occasion when a defendant produces a carefully prepared written statement to the police with a view to making it part of the evidence in the case. The trial judge

---

80 [1942] 1 All ER 187; *Sourcebook*, p 356.

81 (1979) 69 Cr App R 365; *Sourcebook*, p 357.

82 Confessions would have been admissible as an exception to the rule against hearsay: see below, Chapter 9.

would plainly exclude such a statement as inadmissible.[83] (This was said before the passing of ss 34, 36 and 37 of the Criminal Justice and Public Order Act 1994. Since the change in the law effected by these sections, it is unlikely that even a statement of the sort described would be ruled *inadmissible*, though the weight to be attached to it would probably not be great.)

Suppose the defendant makes a statement containing a mixture of inculpatory and exculpatory matters. For example, he admits that he drove his co-defendants to the scene of the crime and drove them away afterwards, but says that he did so only because they threatened to kill him if he refused. What should the jury be told about the evidential status of that? On the basis of the law just described, it seems that the inculpatory part is evidence of the truth of its contents but the exculpatory part is not – it is evidence only of the defendant's reaction when questioned by police. But in *R v Sharp*,[84] the House of Lords accepted that it was unrealistic to expect a jury to understand the distinction, and said that the jury should be told to consider the whole statement in deciding where the truth lies. However, the judge should usually point out that the excuses are unlikely to have the same weight as the incriminating parts.

There are other exceptions to the rule against admitting previous consistent statements. If, in cross-examination, a witness's account is challenged as being a recent invention, he may support his credibility by reference to earlier statements to the same effect as his evidence. A case in point is *R v Oyesiku*.[85] The defendant had been arrested and taken into custody for assaulting a police officer. About two days later, before he was given bail, his wife went to his solicitors and made a written statement. The effect of it was that the policeman, who had been in plain clothes, was the aggressor, and that her husband did not realise that he was dealing with a police officer. At that stage the wife had not seen her husband. At trial she gave evidence on these lines in his defence. She was cross-examined on the basis that she had invented her evidence to help her husband. To rebut this suggestion, the defence asked for leave to put her statement to the solicitors before the jury. The trial judge refused, but the Court of Appeal held that he had been wrong. Following an Australian case,[86] the court said that if the credit of a witness is attacked on the ground that his testimony is a recent invention or has been recently devised or reconstructed, even though not with conscious dishonesty, evidence of an earlier statement will be admissible to rebut the suggestion made in cross-examination. If, however, the prosecution alleges that the defendant's story was fabricated from the outset, rather than

---

83 (1979) 69 Cr App R 365, pp 369–70.
84 (1988) 86 Cr App R 274; *Sourcebook*, p 358. The decision was followed by the House of Lords in *R v Aziz* [1996] AC 41.
85 (1971) 56 Cr App R 240; *Sourcebook*, p 360. See also *R v Tyndale* [1999] Crim LR 320.
86 *Nominal Defendant v Clements* (1961) 104 CLR 476.

at a later date, the usual rule applies: a previous consistent statement will be inadmissible.[87]

Another exception occurs where a complainant of either sex alleges the commission of a sexual offence. Evidence of an earlier complaint by that person may be given if certain conditions are satisfied. This type of evidence has only a limited value. It has what Buxton LJ called in *R v Islam*[88] an 'odd and difficult status'.[89] It may be adduced, not as evidence of the fact complained of, but for the purpose of showing consistency in the complainant's conduct and consistency with the evidence she has given.[90] In the earlier case of *R v Osborne*,[91] the Court for Crown Cases Reserved held that such evidence was also admissible to negative consent. Though not expressly overruled, a direction to this effect is unlikely to be given today.[92] The Judicial Studies Board standard direction encourages judges to direct juries that such evidence 'may possibly help you to decide whether she has told you the truth. It cannot be independent confirmation of X's evidence since it does not come from a source independent of her'.[93] In *R v Islam*, the Court of Appeal emphasised that such a direction is essential; the matter is one of law, not discretion. The court also noted that 'on occasion judges may also think it appropriate to remind the jury that a person fabricating an allegation may support it by an equally false complaint'.[94]

Since the sole value of the complaint is to show consistency, no evidence that it was made can be given if the complainant does not give evidence.[95] In *White v R*,[96] the Privy Council held that a complainant may not give evidence of making a complaint unless the person to whom it was made is called to prove its terms.

To be admissible, the complaint has to be made as soon after the event complained of as could be reasonably expected. The mere fact that the statement was made in answer to a question does not make what was said inadmissible, provided the question was not of a suggestive or leading nature. For example, 'What is the matter?' or 'Why are you crying?' would be unobjectionable. But 'Did Charlie assault you?' would lead to the rejection of the complaint – at least if Charlie, and not another person, was being

---

87 See, eg, *R v Williams* [1998] Crim LR 494.
88 [1999] 1 Cr App R 22.
89 *Ibid*, p 28.
90 *R v Wallwork* (1956) 42 Cr App R 153, p 161; *R v Islam* [1999] 1 Cr App R 22, p 26.
91 [1905] 1 KB 551.
92 But the rule in *R v Osborne* was re-stated in *White v R* [1999] AC 210.
93 Cited in *R v Islam* [1999] 1 Cr App R 22, p 27.
94 *Ibid*, p 27.
95 *R v Wallwork* (1956) 42 Cr App R 153.
96 [1999] 1 Cr App R 153.

prosecuted.[97] The trend since the beginning of the 20th century has been to make it easier to admit complaints under this exception. It became clear quite soon that a complaint can be 'recent', and so admissible, even though not made at the first opportunity that presents itself. It is enough if it is made at the first *reasonable* opportunity. What that is in a particular case will depend on the circumstances, including the character of the complainant, the relationship between the complainant and the person to whom the complaint was made, and the relationship between the complainant and persons to whom he or she had an opportunity to complain, but did not, before making the complaint of which evidence is tendered.

A complaint will not be inadmissible merely because, at an earlier stage, the victim told someone *part* of the story, but without being specific, provided the complaint that *was* specific was made as soon as could reasonably be expected. In *R v Valentine*,[98] the complainant, who had been raped after being threatened with a knife, told no one when she arrived at 2.30 am at the house where she lived with her parents and elder brother. The following morning she told her brother that she had been attacked by a man with a knife, but said that she did not want their parents to know. She made no reference at that stage to rape. She went to work in the afternoon, and in the evening met two male friends. At first she told one of them what she had told her brother and no more. Only later that evening, when she was alone with this friend, did she tell him that she had been raped.

It was argued on appeal that this complaint had not been made at the first reasonable opportunity, but the Court of Appeal agreed with the trial judge that, on those particular facts, it had. Roch LJ explained the decision as follows:

> We now have greater understanding that those who are the victims of sexual offences, be they male or female, often need time before they can bring themselves to tell what has been done to them; that some victims will find it impossible to complain to anyone other than a parent or member of their family, whereas others may feel it quite impossible to tell their parents or members of their family.[99]

In such cases, evidence of a complainant's distress shortly after or at the time of the complaint may also be given. This is similarly treated. It is admissible to show consistency with the description of the incident given in evidence by the complainant, but it cannot be regarded as confirming that evidence from an independent source.[100]

---

97   *R v Lillyman* [1896] 2 QB 167, *Sourcebook*, p 166; *R v Osborne* [1905] 1 KB 551; *Sourcebook*, p 167.

98   [1996] 2 Cr App R 213.

99   *Ibid*, p 224.

100 *R v Keast* [1998] Crim LR 748; *R v Islam* [1999] 1 Cr App R 22, p 27.

Other previous consistent statements may be admitted as part of the *res gestae*,[101] or as evidence of a previous identification by the witness.[102]

HOSTILE WITNESSES

An advocate who calls a witness in support of his client's case will not, save in exceptional circumstances, conduct his examination-in-chief in ignorance of what the witness is expected to say. He will have with his papers a written statement of that witness's evidence about the matters in issue. But sometimes a witness fails to say what is expected of him; he may even say the contrary of what is expected. Reasons for this may be that he is honest but muddled, or that his recollection of events has genuinely changed. Such a witness is described as 'unfavourable', but the advocate can do nothing to discredit him, and his only remedy will be to call other witnesses to give a different account of events.[103]

Sometimes, however, a witness will fail to say what is expected of him, or say the contrary, because he is *not desirous of telling the truth to the court at the instance of the party calling him*. Such a witness is described as 'hostile' and may be discredited to a limited extent. This definition of a hostile witness by Sir James Fitzjames Stephen[104] is the most useful one to remember, because it makes no assumption about the motive for the witness's lack of co-operation. Some writers have stated that a witness is hostile 'when he shows animus against the party calling him',[105] but this is misleading. If Freddie is due to appear as a witness for the prosecution against Charlie, but is warned by Charlie's sisters, cousins and aunts of the unspeakable things they will do to him if he testifies, he may very well lack the desire to tell the truth when prosecuting counsel examines him. But this will be because he wants to save his skin, not because he has an 'animus' against the prosecution. He will be 'hostile', nevertheless. The key to avoiding confusion on this topic is to remember that 'unfavourable' and 'hostile' are technical terms and are not to be given their ordinary meanings.

A witness ruled hostile by the judge may be cross-examined by the party calling him with a view to showing that he said something different on an earlier occasion. But he may not be cross-examined with a view to discrediting

---

101 See below, Chapter 7. The court may allow the defence to cross-examine on a witness's previous consistent statement where it would be fair to do so (*R v Evans and Caffrey* [2001] 6 Archbold News 2, CA).

102 See below, Chapter 8. For the recommendations of the Law Commission in relation to all three categories, see Law Com No 245 (1997), paras 10.41–10.60.

103 *Ewer v Ambrose* (1825) 3 B&C 746; *Greenough v Eccles* (1859) 5 CBNS 786.

104 Stephen, Sir JF, *A Digest of the Law of Evidence*, 12th edn, 1936, Art 147. It was adopted by the Court of Appeal in *R v Prefas* (1988) 86 Cr App R 111.

105 Nokes, GD, *An Introduction to the Law of Evidence*, 4th edn, 1967, p 143.

him generally, for example, by asking him questions about any previous convictions he may have.[106] The power to cross-examine hostile witnesses can be found in both statute and common law. The statutory provision is contained in s 3 of the Criminal Procedure Act 1865. Like ss 4 and 5, this applies in civil proceedings also. The advocate calling such a witness may, by leave of the judge, 'prove that he has made at other times a statement inconsistent with his present testimony'.

Sometimes a problem may arise because the hostile witness fails to provide enough 'present testimony' to be inconsistent with the previous statement. Such a person may be treated as hostile and cross-examined by virtue of common law. For example, in *R v Thompson*,[107] the daughter of the defendant, who was charged with incest, took the oath and gave her name and address, but then refused to testify against her father. The Court of Appeal decided that the judge had power at common law, as well as under the 1865 Act, to allow her to be cross-examined by the prosecution, who had called her.

The object of cross-examination will very often be to put to a hostile witness his earlier statement, in hope that the witness will revert to his original story. According to s 3 of the 1865 Act, the witness must first be reminded of the occasion when he made the statement, and asked whether he did in fact make such a statement on that occasion. It is useful to remember that if a witness is hostile through fear, it is possible to put in his statement to the police as evidence under provisions in the Criminal Justice Act 1988.[108] If an unimportant witness is hostile it may be better tactics to stop questioning the witness, rather than make it obvious to the jury that he is giving evidence unwillingly.

A judge may conclude that a witness is hostile without a *voir dire*; it is in his discretion to hold one or not.[109]

---

106 See above, p 66, for references to the rule against discrediting one's own witness.
107 (1976) 64 Cr App R 96; *Sourcebook*, p 362.
108 See s 23(3) of the Act and below, Chapter 7.
109 *R v Honeyghon and Sales* [1999] Crim LR 221.

COLLATERAL QUESTIONS AND EVIDENCE IN REBUTTAL[110]

A multiplicity of issues in a case will lengthen the proceedings and is likely to confuse a jury. For this reason there is a rule that a witness's answers to questions on collateral matters (for example, matters that are relevant only to credit and not to an issue in the case) are 'final'. In other words, evidence may not subsequently be adduced by the party who asked the question to rebut the answer given by the witness. Unfortunately, it is not always easy to determine what is relevant to an issue in the case, and what is relevant only to a collateral matter.[111] There are some exceptions to the rule that answers to questions on collateral matters are 'final':

(a) Section 6 of the Criminal Procedure Act 1865 allows previous convictions (usually relevant only to credit) to be proved where the witness denies them or refuses to answer.

(b) If a witness denies that he is *biased*, either for or against a party, evidence may be called to disprove him. Thus, in *R v Phillips*,[112] where the defendant was charged with incest, his daughters denied in cross-examination that they had been 'schooled' in their evidence by their mother. The Court of Criminal Appeal held that the defendant should have been allowed to call witnesses to say that the daughters had told them that their mother had done this.[113]

(c) Evidence may be given of a witness's general reputation for untruthfulness. If Q is the witness whose reputation for truth is challenged, another witness, R, may be asked whether he has knowledge of Q's general reputation for truthfulness and whether, from such knowledge, he would believe Q's sworn testimony. R may also express his own opinion, based on personal knowledge, as to whether Q is to be believed upon his oath. In either case, however, R may not, during examination-in-chief, refer to facts forming the basis of his opinion, although he may be cross-examined about them.[114]

---

110 See Seabrooke, S, 'The vanishing trick – blurring the line between credit and issue' [1999] Crim LR 387.

111 For further discussion, see the references to *Managers of the Metropolitan Asylum District v Hill and Others* (1882) 47 LT 29 and to *R v Funderburk* [1990] 1 WLR 587, above, Chapter 1. See also *R v Nagrecha* [1997] 2 Cr App R 401; *R v Neale* [1998] Crim LR 737; *R v Somers* [1999] Crim LR 744.

112 (1936) 26 Cr App R 17.

113 See also *Thomas v David* (1836) 7 C&P 350; *R v Yewin* (1811) 2 Camp 638n; *R v Shaw* (1888) 16 Cox CC 503.

114 *R v Richardson* (1968) 52 Cr App R 317; *Sourcebook*, p 384.

(d) Evidence may be given of a physical or mental disability affecting a witness's reliability.[115] So, for example, if an identifying witness denies in cross-examination that he is short sighted or suffers from delusions, evidence may be called to prove that he does suffer from those disabilities.

PROTECTING VULNERABLE OR INTIMIDATED WITNESSES[116]

Sections 16–33 of the Youth Justice and Criminal Evidence Act 1999 provide special measures to protect vulnerable or intimidated witnesses. Witnesses may be eligible for assistance either on the grounds of age or incapacity, under s 16, or on grounds of fear or distress about testifying, under s 17. A witness is eligible under s 16 if he is under the age of 17 at the time of the hearing, or if the court considers that the quality of evidence given by the witness is likely to be diminished because the witness suffers from mental disorder or otherwise has a significant impairment of intelligence and social functioning, or if the witness has a physical disability or is suffering from a physical disorder. Under s 17, a witness other than the accused is eligible for assistance if the court is satisfied that the quality of evidence given by the witness is likely to be diminished by reason of fear or distress on the part of the witness in connection with testifying in the proceedings. A complainant in respect of a sexual offence is also eligible for assistance in relation to proceedings in respect of that offence.

The court may make 'special measures directions' in respect of eligible witnesses under s 19. It also has powers under s 21 to make special provisions for child witnesses, that is, witnesses under the age of 17 at the time of the hearing, if the trial is for one of the offences specified in s 35, which includes, *inter alia*, sexual offences and kidnapping. The primary rule in such a case is that evidence-in-chief must be video recorded, and any evidence not given in that way must be given by means of a live link.

As well as video recorded evidence and evidence by live link, the special measures available to the court include screening the witness from the accused, excluding the public from court (but only where the proceedings relate to a sexual offence or it appears to the court that there are reasonable grounds to fear intimidation of the witness), removal of wigs and gowns and examination through an interpreter or some other intermediary. As a final

---

115 *Toohey v Metropolitan Police Commissioner* [1965] AC 595; *Sourcebook*, p 385.

116 See McEwan, J, 'In defence of vulnerable witnesses: the Youth Justice and Criminal Evidence Act 1999' (2000) 4 E&P 1; Birch, D, 'A better deal for vulnerable witnesses' [2000] Crim LR 223; Hoyano, L, 'Variations on a theme by Pigot: special measures directions for child witnesses' [2000] Crim LR 250; Birch, D, and Leng, R, *Blackstone's Guide to the Youth Justice and Criminal Evidence Act 1999*, 2000, pp 25–89.

sweeping-up provision, s 30 provides that a special measures direction may provide for 'such device as the court considers appropriate with a view to enabling questions or answers to be communicated to or by the witness despite any disability or disorder or other impairment which the witness has or suffers from'.

By s 32, where on a trial on indictment evidence has been given in accordance with a special measures direction, the judge must give the jury such warning (if any) as he considers necessary to ensure that the accused is not prejudiced by that fact.

Sections 34–39 of the Act protect certain witnesses, such as complainants in trials for sexual offences and some child witnesses, from cross-examination by the accused in person.

CHAPTER 5

BURDEN AND STANDARD OF PROOF AND PRESUMPTIONS

Every contested case, civil or criminal, must give rise to at least one contested issue of fact, but many cases of both kinds give rise to several issues of fact to be decided between the parties. This is particularly frequent in civil cases, because a defendant against whom a claim is made will often not only defend that claim but raise one of his own against the claimant, formerly the 'plaintiff', – called a 'counterclaim' – to be decided in the same action. This chapter deals with two questions which arise in relation to every issue of fact:

(a) Who has the burden of adducing evidence to prove the fact in question?

(b) What test will be applied to determine whether sufficiently weighty evidence has been called to discharge that burden?

THE BURDEN OF PROOF

The 'burden of proof' is the obligation which rests on a party in relation to a particular issue of fact in a civil or criminal case, and which must be 'discharged', or 'satisfied', if that party is to win on the issue in question. This burden is often referred to as 'the legal burden'. It is to be distinguished from what is called 'the evidential burden' which, as we shall see, is something completely different. Unfortunately for students of this subject, there are several synonyms for 'legal burden'. This concept can also be referred to by any of the following expressions: 'persuasive burden', 'probative burden', 'ultimate burden', 'burden of proof on the pleadings', and 'risk of non-persuasion'. Remember, though, that 'evidential burden' does *not* refer to the same concept.

Remember also that talk about the burden of proof in any given case makes no sense *unless you relate that burden to a particular issue of fact*. It is dangerous to talk of the burden of proof in relation to a case as a whole, because in many civil cases, and in some criminal cases also, one party will bear the burden of proof on some issues and another party will bear it on others. For example, in a simple case of negligence arising from a road traffic accident there are quite likely to be at least two fundamental issues. The claimant will say that there was a collision between the defendant's car and his own, that this was caused by the negligence of the defendant, and that as a result the claimant suffered injury, loss and damage. In response to this, the defendant may admit that there was a collision, but deny that he was guilty of any negligence, saying that the only person guilty of negligence was the claimant. And he may go on to say that as a result of the claimant's negligence, he, the defendant, suffered injury, loss and damage. He will have, in other words, a counterclaim against the claimant.

How many issues are there here? To establish his claim the claimant will have to prove that:

(a) there was a collision between the two cars;

(b) the collision was caused by the defendant's negligence; and

(c) as a result of the collision, he suffered loss.

The defendant admits the collision. But to establish his counterclaim he must then go on to prove that:

(d) the collision was caused by the claimant's own negligence; and

(e) as a result, he (the defendant) suffered injury, loss and damage.

So there are five issues, four of which are disputed. (The collision is admitted.) Who has the burden of proof in this case? An answer to this question can be given only by reference to the issues. In fact, the claimant has the burden of proof on issues (b) and (c), and the defendant has the burden of proof on issues (d) and (e).

It is very important to remember that, in relation to any particular issue, the burden of proof can rest on only *one* party. Thus, in relation to a single issue, you cannot have a burden on one party to prove the existence of a state of affairs and a burden on the other party to prove its non-existence. In particular, you should note that a counterclaim raises issues that are entirely separate. If the claimant fails to satisfy the judge that the accident was caused by the negligence of the defendant, the claimant will not recover damages from the defendant. But this does not mean that the defendant will recover from the claimant. To do so, the defendant must satisfy the judge that the accident was the claimant's fault, and he may fail to achieve this. It might be a perfectly rational result for both claim and counterclaim to fail, because on neither side was the evidence strong enough to persuade the judge that one party was at fault rather than the other.[1]

Deciding burdens of proof in civil cases

In some cases the point may already be covered by case law or statute. Many commercial transactions are undertaken according to a standard form of contract. For example, standard forms of contract are in use for building and

---

1   *Morris v London Iron and Steel Co Ltd* [1987] 2 All ER 496; *Sourcebook* p 31. But see also *Sewell v Electrolux Ltd* (1997) *The Times*, 7 November, where the Court of Appeal said that a judge cannot avoid his duty to resolve conflicts of evidence by resorting to the burden of proof as a means of deciding a case.

construction works and for the carriage of particular commodities. Where your client entered into a standard form of contract, the contract may already have been the subject of appellate decisions which will bind a subsequent court on points of interpretation. However, such decisions will be binding *only* if you are dealing with a contract which is of the standard form in question. Just because a particular form of words was used in *one* type of contract, it does not follow that a decision about the interpretation of *that* contract will be persuasive, let alone binding, where the court has to interpret a *different* contract. Interpretation takes place *in a context*; words and phrases do not have immutable meanings wherever they may appear.

Statutes sometimes impose burdens of proof in civil proceedings. Suppose, for example, an insolvent debtor has preferred one creditor over others (as by paying that creditor in full while others went completely unpaid). The Insolvency Act 1986 provides that if the debtor is subsequently made bankrupt, the trustee in bankruptcy may apply to the court for an order restoring the position to what it would have been if that preference had not been made.[2] The court cannot make such an order unless the debtor who gave the preference was influenced in deciding to give it by a desire to put the creditor into a better position than he would otherwise have had in the event of the debtor's bankruptcy. Ordinarily, therefore, the burden will be on the trustee in bankruptcy to prove that desire. However, where the preferred creditor was an 'associate'[3] of the debtor, the Act provides that the appropriate desire shall be presumed 'unless the contrary is shown'. The effect of this is to put onto the preferred creditor the burden of proving that at the time the preference was made, the debtor did *not* have the appropriate desire.

In the absence of precedent or statutory provision, resort must be had, in doubtful cases, to general guidelines. At least two can be perceived, but unfortunately they are only of the most tenuous kind. The first is that the burden should lie on the party who affirms a proposition rather than on the party who denies it.[4] The second is that 'the burden of proof in any particular case depends on the circumstances under which the claim arises'.[5]

Quite properly, the courts have avoided a mechanical approach to the 'affirmation or denial' test. In particular, the court's decision will not be determined by the form of words used in the statements of case, formerly known as 'pleadings'. In *Soward v Leggatt*,[6] a landlord claimed against his tenant under a repairing covenant in a lease. In his pleading he alleged that

---

2   Insolvency Act 1986, s 340.
3   Defined in the Insolvency Act 1986, s 435.
4   *Constantine (Joseph) SS Line Ltd v Imperial Smelting Corpn Ltd* [1942] AC 154, p 174, *per* Viscount Maugham.
5   *Ibid.*
6   (1836) 7 C&P 613; *Sourcebook*, p 31.

the defendant 'did not repair' and 'did not paint' the premises. To this the defendant pleaded that he 'did ... well and sufficiently repair' and that he 'did paint' the premises. Thus, on paper, it looked as if the plaintiff was making denials and the defendant the positive assertions.

At trial, the defendant's counsel claimed that he had the burden of proof and so the right to open the case. Lord Abinger CB said:

> Looking at these things according to common sense, we should consider what is the substantive fact to be made out, and on whom it lies to make it out. It is not so much the form of the issue which ought to be considered, as the substance and effect of it. In many cases, a party, by a little difference in the drawing of his pleadings, might make [his allegation] either affirmative or negative, as he pleased. The plaintiff here says 'You did not repair'; he might have said 'You let the house become dilapidated.' I shall endeavour by my own view to arrive at the substance of the issue, and I think in the present case that the plaintiff's counsel should begin.[7]

In other words, despite the form of the pleadings, the burden of proof was on the plaintiff to prove breach by the defendant of the covenants in the lease.

It may be particularly difficult to predict how a judge will allocate the burdens of proof in a case where contractual provisions exclude or limit liability. The cases often referred to on this topic in the books show no more than the application in differing circumstances of the second guideline referred to above: that where the burden of proof lies will depend on the circumstances of the particular claim.

A case often cited is *The Glendarroch*.[8] The plaintiffs had bought a consignment of cement, which was to be carried to them by the defendant shippers. But the ship carrying the cement became stranded and the cement was so damaged as to be worthless. No bill of lading had in fact been signed, but the trial judge found that the contract was governed by the terms of an ordinary bill of lading. Under a contract of this type, shippers were exempt from liability for damage caused by perils of the sea unless the damage was due to the shippers' own negligence.

The shippers denied liability on the ground that the ship had become stranded and the cement damaged by reason of perils of the sea. But the trial judge ruled that in order to excuse themselves they had to show not just a peril of the sea, but that the peril had not been occasioned by their negligent navigation. The shippers thereupon called no evidence and the plaintiffs were awarded judgment. Had the trial judge been right?

In the Court of Appeal, Lord Esher MR dealt first with the contractual structure. He agreed with the trial judge that the case had to be treated as if the contract had been on the ordinary terms of a bill of lading. Such a bill of

---

7   (1836) 7 C&P 613, p 615.

8   [1894] P 226; *Sourcebook*, p 32.

lading expressly excluded the shippers from liability caused by perils of the sea. The next question was whether a term was to be implied in an ordinary bill of lading that the perils of the sea should not have been occasioned by the shippers' negligence. Lord Esher thought that such a term did exist by necessary inference. Further, it was to be read into the contract as an exception to an exception. The contract had to be read as if it stated that the shippers would be liable *unless* the loss was caused by perils of the sea, *unless that loss was the result of the negligence of the shippers*.

In those circumstances, it was for the plaintiff to prove the contract and non-delivery. The defendants had the burden of showing that the loss had been caused by perils of the sea, so as to exclude them from liability. It was then for the plaintiffs to make out the exception to that exception by proving that the shippers had been negligent.

What swayed Lord Esher was the way in which actions of that kind had for many years been pleaded. The plaintiff would allege the existence of a bill of lading and the fact of non-delivery under it. The defendant would then plead that the loss had been by perils of the sea. No plea that could be found in the books had ever gone on to say that the loss by perils of the sea was not caused by negligence. Yet if the contention were true that the burden of proof to that extent lay on the defendant, every one of those pleas without that allegation had been no answer to the plaintiff's pleading and had thus been open to demurrer.[9] But in no such case had a demurrer been pleaded. From this it could be inferred that there was no burden on shippers in such circumstances to prove that the perils of the sea had not been caused by their own negligence. Instead, a long succession of similar cases showed the plaintiff setting out a replication[10] saying in effect, 'True there was a loss by perils of the sea within the *prima facie* exception, but that was brought about by the negligence of the shippers'. This practice of pleading reflected where, as a matter of law, the burdens lay. The judge had been wrong. The onus had been on the plaintiffs to prove negligence. It had not been for the shippers to prove absence of negligence on their part.

In this case, the Court of Appeal reached its decision by treating the contract as one in a standard form and by looking to see where the burdens had been placed in other contracts of the same nature. In adopting this approach the judges were no doubt influenced by the need felt by commercial men for legal predictability in their dealings with each other.

9 A demurrer was a written plea to the effect that the facts pleaded failed as a matter of law to establish a cause of action or a defence, as the case might be.

10 Another technical term from the old forms of pleading. The first pleading, in which the plaintiff stated his case, was the 'declaration'. The defendant would reply with either a demurrer or a 'plea'. Various pleas could be used to avoid liability. The type used by a defendant in this sort of case was a 'confession and avoidance', ie, the defendant *confessed* that the goods had been lost, but hoped to *avoid* liability by relying on the fact that the loss had been caused by perils of the sea: Holdsworth, Sir WS, *A History of English Law*, 1903–72, Vol III, pp 629–30.

But later cases showed that *The Glendarroch* was not to be used blindly as a precedent in different contractual circumstances. In *Hurst v Evans*,[11] the defendants had insured the plaintiff, a jeweller, against loss of or damage to his jewellery and other property, 'arising from any cause whatsoever ... except breakage ... and except loss by theft or dishonesty committed by any servant ... in the exclusive employment' of the plaintiff. Those were the only two exceptions.

A robbery was committed at the plaintiff's premises and jewellery was stolen. The plaintiff had two employees, Brown and Mason. There was no suggestion that Brown had had any part in the crime, but the insurers called evidence to show that about the date of the offence, Mason had been associating with notorious and highly skilled safe breakers.

Counsel for the jeweller argued that the burden was on the insurers, if they wished to avoid liability, to show that Mason had been either the actual perpetrator of the crime or an accomplice. The insurers argued that this was wrong, and that the burden was on the plaintiff to show that his servant Mason had not been dishonest.

Lush J relied on a long established rule for pleading claims on policies of marine insurance which required that the plaintiff should state the contract accurately, with all exceptions to the defendant's liability, and should allege that the defendants did not come within any of those exceptions. *The Glendarroch* had been cited, but Lush J said that there was nothing in that case to show that the rule on which he relied should not apply. However, what was Lush J thinking of to rely on standard form contracts of *marine* insurance in a claim on insurers for loss of a jeweller's goods? The answer lies later in the report and shows that the legal justification was simply a support for a decision that turned on the facts.

'Looking at the policy,' the judge said, 'it is impossible to hold that the onus is on the defendant. To do so would produce absurd results'. It was not a case of insurance against loss by some specified peril such as fire or theft. The insurance was against *any* loss due to *any* cause, except the two specified – breakage and servants' dishonesty. If the plaintiff was right, he would only have to prove a loss of jewellery and it would be for the defendants to prove that amongst the multitude of possible causes the actual cause was either breakage or servants' dishonesty. To avoid such a situation the burden was on the plaintiff to prove that the loss was one against which the insurers had agreed to indemnify him. In other words, he had the burden of proving that the loss had not been occasioned by the dishonesty of his servant Mason. Although Lush J did not explicitly say so, his decision was clearly influenced

---

11 [1917] 1 KB 352; *Sourcebook*, p 34. Cf *Munro Brice & Co v War Risks Association Ltd* [1918] KB 78.

by the consideration that it would be easier for the plaintiff to prove that his servant had not been involved than for the insurers to prove that he had.

Another case in which reliance was placed on *The Glendarroch* was *Joseph Constantine SS Line Ltd v Imperial Smelting Corpn Ltd.*[12] The appellants were owners of a steamship which had been chartered to the respondents to carry a cargo from Australia to Europe. The ship duly sailed to pick up the cargo, but before it could do so there was an explosion on board which utterly disabled it from carrying out the charterparty. The respondent charterers claimed damages from the owners for failure to load the cargo. The owners relied on the doctrine of frustration to excuse them from performance. The charterers argued that this would not work unless the owners could show that the explosion had occurred without any fault on their part. But the owners argued that once the frustrating event was proved, the burden was on the charterers to prove negligence by the owners so as to bar them from relying on frustration as a defence.

The arbitrator was unable to make a finding as to the cause of the explosion. At that point the allocation of burdens of proof became decisive.

The speeches in the House of Lords showed that the desire to achieve a just result was uppermost in the Law Lords' minds. Viscount Simon LC observed that if the party relying on frustration had to show that the event happened without his default, he would often fail in his action because of the difficulty of proving a negative:

> Suppose that a vessel, while on the high seas, disappears completely during a storm. Can it be that the defence of frustration of the adventure depends on the owner's ability to prove that all his servants on board were navigating the ship with adequate skill and that there was no 'default' which brought about the catastrophe? Suppose that a vessel in convoy is torpedoed by the enemy and sinks immediately with all hands. Does the application of the doctrine require that the owners should affirmatively prove that those on board were keeping a good lookout, were obscuring lights, were steering as directed, and so forth?[13]

Viscount Simon added that frustration depended on whether, from the express terms of the particular contract, a further term should be implied which, its conditions fulfilled, would end the contract. Such an implied term in this case might well be: 'This contract is to cease to be binding if the vessel is disabled by an overpowering disaster, provided that disaster is not brought about by the default of either party.' Having drafted the notional clause in this way, Viscount Simon was then able to draw an analogy with 'perils of the sea' clauses like the one in *The Glendarroch* and say that the implied clause should affect the burden of proof in a similar way. The effect of this analogy was to place a burden on the charterers to prove negligence by the owners in order to

---

12 [1942] AC 154; *Sourcebook*, p 37.
13 [1942] AC 154, pp 161–62.

defeat the owners' reliance on frustration as an excuse for their failure to load the goods.

But the implied clause might equally well have said: 'This contract is to cease to be binding if the vessel is disabled by an overpowering disaster *for which neither party is responsible.*' If a form of words was to dictate where the burden lay, this would have produced a different result. But the result was not based on a form of words; the case was not, despite superficial appearances, decided by a piece of notional drafting and a precedent. Instead, notional drafting and the precedent were brought in to support a decision that was justifiable on pragmatic grounds. As Lord Wright said in the same case: 'The court is exercising its powers, when it decides that a contract is frustrated, in order to achieve a result which is just and reasonable.' Once again, the crucial consideration appears to have been ease of proof. To make the party relying on frustration in such circumstances prove absence of fault would have been unreasonable.

Ease of proof was the determining consideration in *Levison v Patent Steam Carpet Cleaning Co.*[14] In this case the plaintiffs had sent an expensive Chinese carpet to the defendants for cleaning. The defendants failed to return it and ultimately concluded that it had been stolen. They relied on a clause in their contract with the plaintiffs limiting their liability for loss, the effect of which was to make them liable for only £44 rather than £900 – the value of the carpet. A clause like this could be relied on only if the party relying on it had carried out the substance of the contract and had not been guilty of a fundamental breach of it. But was it for the plaintiffs to prove fundamental breach or for the defendants to negative it?

Lord Denning MR thought that it should be for the cleaners to prove that they had not been guilty of fundamental breach. The plaintiffs did not know what had happened to the carpet. The cleaners were the ones who knew, or should have known, what had happened. The burden should therefore be on them to show that they had used proper care in their handling of the carpet; it was not for the plaintiffs to prove that the defendants had been guilty of negligence. The legal hook on which Lord Denning hung this result was a point about bailment. This transaction had been a bailment for reward, and the cases showed clearly that, in such circumstances, the bailee was absolutely liable for loss of or damage to the goods which were the subject of the bailment. He could avoid his liability only by proving that he had used all due care when handling the goods.[15]

Orr LJ agreed. The bailee in such circumstances was more likely to know the facts and be in a better position to ascertain them than the bailor. And Sir David Cairns added that however difficult it might sometimes be for a bailee

---

14 [1978] 1 QB 69; *Sourcebook,* p 40.
15 [1978] 1 QB 69, pp 81–82.

to prove a negative, he was at least in a better position than the bailor to know what happened to the goods while they were in his possession.

These cases show that the courts' approach to problems about the burden of proof in civil actions is likely to be determined on the basis referred to by Viscount Maugham in the *Joseph Constantine* case. It depends on 'the circumstances under which the claim arises'.[16] The only hard and fast conclusion that can be made is that 'where the burden of proof should rest is merely a question of policy and fairness based on experience in the different situations'.[17] In looking at those situations it is likely that a court will be chiefly concerned with the question of which of the parties will find it easier to discharge a burden of proof, even if sometimes that may involve proving a negative.

That 'he who asserts must prove' may involve having, in effect, to prove a negative can be seen from the decision of the House of Lords in *Pickford v Imperial Chemical Industries plc*.[18] In this case, the plaintiff had been employed by the defendants as a secretary. She developed a disease in both hands, which was recognised by the DHSS for the purposes of industrial injury benefit and which was known as 'PDA4'. It consisted of cramp caused by repetitive movements. She sued the defendants for negligence, claiming that the disease was organic in origin and so had been reasonably foreseeable by them. The defendants said that it was psychogenic in origin, and so could not have been reasonably foreseen. (A disease that is organic has its origin in the physical body; one that is psychogenic has its origin in the mind.) Both sides produced medical experts. The plaintiff's expert said that her disease was organic in origin. The defendants' expert said that it was psychogenic, and gave a particular reason for this conclusion. The trial judge said that he was not satisfied that the defendants' explanation was correct, but he said also that he was not satisfied that the disease was organic in origin. He therefore found for the defendants.

The Court of Appeal allowed the plaintiff's appeal by a majority. Stuart-Smith LJ said that all the judge had to do was decide on the evidence which of the two explanations actually advanced was the more probable. He had therefore approached the burden of proof wrongly. Waite LJ agreed. He asked this question: why should a plaintiff who has established PDA4, and who has satisfied the court that the only psychogenic explanation relied on against her did not apply, be under any duty to prove a negative and show by positive evidence that her complaint had no psychogenic origin?

---

16 *Constantine (Joseph) SS Line Ltd v Imperial Smelting Corpn Ltd* [1942] AC 154, p 174.

17 *Rustad v Great Northern Ry Co* 122 Minn 453; 142 NW 727 (1913), opinion by Dibell J, quoted in Morgan, EM, *Some Problems of Proof under the Anglo-American System of Litigation*, 1956, p 76.

18 [1998] 3 All ER 462.

However, a majority of the House of Lords held that the trial judge's approach had been right. The basis of the plaintiff's claim was that her disease was organic in origin, and so foreseeable. The Court of Appeal had effectively reversed the burden of proof. It had, of course, been open to the defendants to adduce evidence to rebut the plaintiff's claim about the cause of her disease, but they did not have to prove any particular psychogenic explanation. Failure to prove the explanation that they did put forward still left open the question whether the plaintiff had proved that her disease was organic in origin. The burden of proving this remained with her and, since she had failed to discharge it, the trial judge's decision in favour of the defendants had been correct.

The burden of proof in criminal cases[19]

The basic *rule* was laid down by Viscount Sankey LC in *Woolmington v DPP*:[20] 'Throughout the web of the English criminal law one golden thread is always to be seen, that it is the duty of the prosecution to prove the prisoner's guilt.' That is the rule. But is it supported by any *principle*?

It would be possible to justify the rule as part of a policy to avoid embarrassing criticisms of the administration of justice by minimising wrongful convictions. These are more likely to be avoided if the burden is fixed in this way than if an accused person has to prove his innocence. It is also possible to justify the rule by appeal to principle. For example, it would be a necessary feature of the law if it were accepted that, in Dworkin's words, 'people have a profound right not to be convicted of crimes of which they are innocent'.[21] Do our politicians, or even our judges, recognise a basis of principle rather than policy for this rule? The story of the exceptions to it does not provide an encouraging answer.

Viscount Sankey said that the rule was subject to exceptions in the case of the defence of insanity and subject also to any statutory exception. But there have been challenges to the idea that it is ever just to place a legal burden of proof on defendants.

The best starting point is that put forward by Paul Roberts: placing the burden of proof on the prosecution restricts 'the power of the State to intervene in the lives of individuals and their families in the far-reaching and

---

19 In addition to the books and articles cited below, reference may also be made to the following: Criminal Law Revision Committee, 11th Report, *Evidence (General)*, Cmnd 4991, 1972, paras 137–42; Williams, CR, 'Offences and defences' (1982) 2 LS 233; Campbell, K, 'Offence and defence' in Dennis, I (ed), *Criminal Law and Criminal Justice*, 1987, p 73; Stein, A, 'After *Hunt*: the burden of proof, risk of non-persuasion and judicial pragmatism' (1991) 54 MLR 570; Williams, G, 'Evidential burdens on the defence' 127 NLJ 182.

20 [1935] AC 462, p 481; *Sourcebook*, p 43. For the importance of a correct direction to the jury on the burden of proof, see *R v Bentley (deceased)* [2001] 1 Cr App R 307, p 326.

21 Dworkin, R, 'Principle, policy, procedure', in *A Matter of Principle*, 1986, p 72.

sometimes catastrophic ways sanctioned by the machinery of criminal justice'.[22] But where a burden of proof rests on a defendant in relation to any issue, he must be convicted even though the magistrates or jury are left undecided about facts that are relevant to that issue. The Criminal Law Revision Committee, in their 11th Report, were strongly of the opinion that burdens on the defence should be evidential only. They pointed out that in the typical case under the existing law, where the essence of the offence is that the offender has acted with blameworthy intent and the defence that the defendant must prove is that he acted innocently, it was 'repugnant to principle' that a court, left in doubt as to the defendant's intent, should be bound to convict.

Statute has already adopted this principle to a limited extent. Under the pre-Theft Act law, a person charged with the statutory offence of possession of housebreaking implements had the legal burden of proving lawful excuse.[23] But s 25(3) of the Theft Act 1968 provides that proof that the accused had with him any article made or adapted for use in committing a relevant offence shall be merely evidence that he had it with him for such use. In other words, the legal burden of proving the offence remains with the prosecution. Consistency suggests that existing statutory provisions placing a legal burden on defendants should be amended so as to place on them an evidential burden only. Such a change would also be in general accordance with the common law, which, with the sole exception of insanity, has not found it necessary to impose any legal burden on the defence.

The Criminal Law Revision Committee thought that the real purpose of casting burdens on the defence in criminal cases was to prevent the defendant from submitting that he had no case to answer in a situation where, as a matter of common sense, his conduct called for explanation, but where the prosecution had not adduced evidence to negative the possibility of an innocent explanation. This applied especially to cases where the defence related to a matter peculiarly within the knowledge of the defendant. The Committee thought it entirely justifiable to impose a burden on the defence for this purpose, but said that the purpose was sufficiently served by making the burden an evidential one. Further, a change would remove the existing need for the judge to give a complicated direction to the jury on the different standards of proof.[24]

Another reason for placing only an evidential burden on the defence is that it is easier for the prosecution to discharge the legal burden of proof. The prosecution dictates the nature of the proceedings, and it has far greater resources than the defendant to further them and bring them to a successful

---

22 Roberts, P, 'Taking the burden of proof seriously' [1995] Crim LR 783, p 785.

23 Larceny Act 1916, s 28(2).

24 CLRC, 11th Report, para 140. See also Williams, G, 'The logic of "exceptions"' [1988] 47 CLJ 261, pp 263–67; *Sourcebook*, pp 44–46. For the standard of proof where the defendant has a legal burden, see p 119, below.

conclusion. The prosecution employs professional investigators to detect crime and gather evidence; it has scientific resources unavailable to most defendants and the manpower to conduct detailed and lengthy inquiries. It has legal advisers to shape the charges to fit the evidence. Innocent people are not generally concerned to prove their innocence until called upon to do so, and by then it may be too late to collect the necessary evidence. The defendant's access to physical evidence may be restricted, as where the prosecution has destroyed all available samples during testing or has failed to collect samples at all. To *know* that your state of mind was an innocent one is not the same as being able to *prove* that that was the case.

Legal burdens on defendants may have to be considered in the light of the European Convention on Human Rights, which is now incorporated into English law under the Human Rights Act 1998. By Art 6(2), 'Everyone charged with a criminal offence shall be presumed innocent until proved guilty according to law'. The effect of this provision was considered by Lord Hope in *R v DPP ex p Kebilene and Others*.[25] After noting that Art 6(2) is wholly consistent with the common law as stated by Viscount Sankey in *Woolmington*, he added that, as Viscount Sankey had recognised, it has always been open to Parliament, by way of a statutory exception, to transfer the burden of proof on a particular issue from the prosecution to the defendant. Until now, the only check on Parliament's freedom to do so has been political. However, the Human Rights Act changes this, and it will apply to *all* legislation, whether before or after the Act.

To see if a statutory provision is incompatible with Art 6(2), it is necessary to see what it says. Some provisions encroach more on the presumption of innocence than others. Broadly speaking, three kinds are possible:

- A mandatory presumption of guilt as to an essential element of the offence. This is a presumption that *must* be applied if the basis of fact on which it rests is established. This will be inconsistent with the presumption of innocence.

- A discretionary presumption of guilt as to an essential element of the offence. Here the court may or may not rely on the presumption, depending on its view as to the weight of the evidence.

- Presumptions that relate to an exemption or proviso which the defendant must establish if he wishes to avoid conviction, but which is not an essential element of the offence. Examples are the provisions that the courts had to consider in *R v Edwards* and *R v Hunt*.[26]

---

25 [2000] 1 Cr App R 275, pp 321–33.
26 [1975] QB 27; [1987] AC 352: see below.

But Lord Hope emphasised that even if the court decides that a particular provision breaches the presumption of innocence, this will not lead inevitably to incompatibility with Art 6(2). The decisions of the European Court of Human Rights show that other factors have to be considered. By what is known as the 'margin of appreciation', the European Court has acknowledged that national authorities are better placed to evaluate local needs and conditions than an international court. For this reason, the Convention does not have to be applied uniformly by all States. Instead, its application may vary according to local needs and conditions. National courts should see the Convention as an expression of fundamental principles rather than as a set of mere rules. Application of these principles will involve balancing competing interests: those of the individual and those of society. In some circumstances, the courts should recognise that there is an area of judgment within which they should defer, on democratic grounds, to the considered opinion of the elected body or person whose act or decision is said to be incompatible with the Convention, and this will be the case *even where the Convention states a right in unqualified terms*. The cases decided by the European Court show that although Art 6(2) is expressed in absolute terms, it is not regarded as imposing an absolute prohibition on reverse burden provisions. In order to consider whether a provision is reasonable in balancing the interests of the individual and those of society, it may be useful to consider these questions:

- What does the prosecution have to prove in order to transfer the burden to the defendant?
- What is the nature of the burden on the defendant? Does it relate to something that is likely for him to be difficult to prove? Or does it relate to something that is likely to be within his knowledge, or to which he readily has access?
- What is the nature of the threat faced by society that the provision is designed to combat?

In *R v Lambert, R v Ali* and *R v Jordan*,[27] the Court of Appeal had to consider the application of Art 6(2) to s 2(2) of the Homicide Act 1957 and ss 5(4) and 28 of the Misuse of Drugs Act 1971, which provided defendants who could prove certain specified facts with a defence to a charge of murder or possession of drugs. Lord Woolf CJ relied on the speech of Lord Hope in *Kebilene*, and said that in taking into account the jurisprudence of the European Court of Human Rights, it was necessary to take a broad and purposive approach to the language of the Convention. In this way, the Convention would be a valuable protection of the fundamental rights of individual members of the public and of society as a whole. He added that the courts were entitled under the Convention to pay a degree of deference to Parliament's view about what was

27 [2001] 1 All ER 1014.

in the interest of the public generally, and should do so as a matter of constitutional principle.[28]

Subject to the Convention, there is at least no problem in seeing where the burdens lie if a statute provides, for example, that an accused person shall be guilty of an offence 'unless the contrary is proved'.[29] But the question whether Parliament in any given case has *impliedly* overridden the *Woolmington* principle is more difficult to resolve.

A convenient starting point for discussion of this topic is s 101 of the Magistrates' Courts Act 1980 (formerly s 81 of the Magistrates' Courts Act 1952). It provides that where the defendant relies for his defence on any 'exception, exemption, proviso, excuse or qualification', whether or not it is part of the description of the offence, the burden of proving such a defence shall be on him. In *R v Edwards*,[30] the Court of Appeal held that this principle was not confined to cases heard in magistrates' courts; the provision was a statutory statement of a common law rule applicable in *all* criminal courts.

Lawton LJ spoke of the need, when applying this principle, to 'construe the enactment under which the charge is laid' in determining where the burden of proof lay.[31] This task of interpretation was subsequently emphasised by the House of Lords in *R v Hunt*.[32] In *R v Hunt*, the prosecution proved that the defendant was in possession of powder containing morphine. But their evidence did not prove whether or not this powder was of a type covered by a provision in the relevant legislation that exempted preparations containing not more than 0.2% of morphine. There was a submission of no case to answer, which the trial judge rejected. The defendant then changed his plea to guilty and appealed against his conviction on the basis that the trial judge had erred in law in rejecting the submission. The Court of Appeal dismissed the appeal on the basis that the effect of the Act was to place the burden of proving that the powder fell within the exception on the defendant, and he had failed to discharge it. The House of Lords allowed the appeal on the ground that the rule about exceptions contained in s 101 of the Magistrates' Courts Act 1980 did not apply. The 0.2% provision was part of the definition of the essential ingredients of the offence, which the prosecution had to prove to make out a case against the defendant.

In reaching this conclusion, the House of Lords said that the classification of defences for s 101 purposes is not constrained by the form of words used or their location in the statute creating the offence. A more subtle approach to

---

28 The Court held that Art 6(2) had not been infringed in any of the cases.

29 See, eg, Prevention of Corruption Act 1916, s 2. For further examples with slightly different wording, see Prevention of Crime Act 1953, s 1; Sexual Offences Act 1956, s 30; Homicide Act 1957, s 2; Misuse of Drugs Act 1971, s 28; Criminal Justice Act 1988, s 139.

30 [1975] QB 27; *Sourcebook*, p 47.

31 [1975] QB 27, p 40.

32 [1987] AC 352; *Sourcebook*, p 47.

interpretation was required, one which would pay regard to the wording of the Act, but would also take into account the mischief at which it was aimed, as well as practical matters affecting the burden of proof. Some guidelines were suggested by Lord Griffiths:

(a) Courts should be 'very slow' to classify a defence as falling within s 101, because Parliament can never lightly be taken to have intended to impose an onerous duty on a defendant to prove his innocence in a criminal case.

(b) Ease and difficulty to be encountered by the parties in discharging the legal burden are of great importance.

(c) The gravity of the offence must be considered. Offences involving the misuse of hard drugs were 'among the most serious in the criminal calendar' and, subject to certain special defences where the burden of proof was specifically placed on the defendant, they were absolute offences. In those circumstances any ambiguity should be resolved in favour of the defendant.[33]

The task of interpretation is a difficult one. There are at least four reasons for this. First, the question whether a given statutory provision falls within the class of 'any exception, exemption, proviso, excuse or qualification' is inherently problematic, as *Nimmo v Alexander Cowan and Sons Ltd*[34] shows.

This case was concerned with the interpretation of s 29(1) of the Factories Act 1961, which provided: 'There shall, so far as is reasonably practicable, be provided and maintained safe means of access to every place at which any person has at any time to work and every such place shall, so far as is reasonably practicable, be made and kept safe for any person working there.' The House of Lords had to decide whether, under this provision, the defendant employers had a burden of proving that it was *not* reasonably practicable for them to make the workplace safe, or whether the plaintiff employee had to prove that it *was* reasonably practicable for his employers to make the workplace safe. As the section also created a summary offence, the same question could have arisen in a prosecution.

The House divided, three to two, on the construction of the section. The minority held that it required the plaintiff or prosecution to prove that it was reasonably practicable to make the workplace safe. The majority held that, once the plaintiff or prosecution had proved that the workplace was not safe, it was for defendants to excuse themselves by proving that it was not reasonably practicable to make it safe. All agreed that if the words of a statute did not clearly state on whom the burden should lie, the court should look to other considerations to determine the intention of Parliament, such as the mischief at which the Act was aimed, and at practical considerations affecting

---

33 [1987] AC 352, pp 374, 378.
34 [1967] 3 All ER 187; *Sourcebook*, p 53.

the burden of proof: in particular, the ease or difficulty the respective parties would have in discharging the burden.

A second difficulty of interpretation arises from the fact that s 101 has been only haphazardly applied. In cases involving offences on highways, for example, two very similar statutory provisions have been differently construed. *Gatland v Metropolitan Police Commr*[35] was concerned with s 140 of the Highways Act 1959, which made it an offence 'if a person, without lawful authority or excuse, deposits any thing whatever on a highway'. The Divisional Court held that the effect of s 101 of the Magistrates' Courts Act was that it was for the accused to prove that he had lawful authority or excuse. *Nagy v Weston*[36] was concerned with s 121(1) of the Highways Act 1959. This made it an offence 'if a person without lawful authority or excuse, in any way wilfully obstructs' a highway. In this case, the Divisional Court held, without reference to the Magistrates' Courts Act, that it was for the prosecution to prove the absence of lawful authority or reasonable excuse.[37]

Cases involving criminal damage constitute another anomaly. Definitions of various offences under the Criminal Damage Act 1971 begin with the words 'A person who, without lawful excuse ...'. Neither the Law Commission nor, in one case, the Divisional Court, thought that these provisions were covered by the principle in s 101 of the Magistrates' Courts Act.[38] Other legislation has imposed a burden of proof on defendants, even though this would have been unnecessary if s 101 had been regularly enforced.[39]

A third reason for difficulty in interpretation is that the project of distinguishing between rules and exceptions for s 101 purposes may be logically flawed. Glanville Williams has argued that the courts have allowed themselves to become ensnared by words. There is no intrinsic difference between the elements of an offence and an exception, or defence, to that offence. All the exceptions or defences can be stated in negative form as part of the definition of an offence instead of as something outside the offence. A rule that is subject to an exception is only partly true if stated without the

---

35 [1968] 2 QB 279.

36 [1965] 1 All ER 78.

37 The decision was subsequently approved by the Court of Appeal and the Divisional Court. See *Hirst & Agu v Chief Constable of West Yorkshire* (1987) 85 Cr App R 143; *Carey v Chief Constable of Avon and Somerset* [1995] RTR 405.

38 *Criminal Law: Report on Offences of Damage to Property*, Law Com No 29 (1970) para 48; *Jaggard v Dickinson* [1981] QB 527, 530.

39 Prevention of Crime Act 1953; Sexual Offences Act 1956. See, generally, Smith, JC, 'The Presumption of Innocence' (1987) 38 NILQ 223; *Sourcebook*, pp 56–59.

exception.[40] The exception is, rationally regarded, part of the rule. There are no characteristic features of exceptions – they are just linguistic constructs.

An example will illustrate the point. Suppose some future government in the UK wishes to gratify citizens who pay tax at the higher rate. It decides to do so by conferring on them a privilege of a trivial nature and accordingly enacts a statute, s 1 of which provides: 'Only citizens who pay tax at the higher rate shall be permitted to wear gold watches.' The statute also provides in s 2 that it shall be an offence for any person to wear a gold watch in breach of s 1. The parliamentary draftsman might equally well have provided: 'No citizen shall wear a gold watch unless he pays tax at the higher rate.' Now suppose that Tim has been discovered wearing a gold watch and is prosecuted under the Act. If the distinction between rules and exceptions can be maintained, the allocation of the burden of proof will depend entirely on the whim of the draftsman. If the first formula is used, the burden will be on the prosecution to prove that Tim did not pay tax at the higher rate. But if the second formula is used, the burden will be on Tim to show that he does pay tax at the higher rate and so comes within the exception.

On a true analysis of the situation, you have in either case an offence package which consists of the offence elements and the negative of any defences or exceptions. It is an indivisible whole and should be treated as such. Section 101 rests on a false premise.

Finally, the reliance on policy that was authorised by the Law Lords in *Nimmo v Alexander Cowan and Sons Ltd* and *R v Hunt* makes for uncertainty in interpretation. There are pointers: for example, the ease or difficulty that the respective parties would encounter in discharging the burden may be significant. But this is a question of fact on which there may be different opinions in different cases. In *R v Hunt* itself the Court of Appeal, unlike the House of Lords, thought that the burden should be on the defendant to prove that a preparation of morphine in his possession was in a form permitted by the statute. Their reason was that sometimes it would be easier for a defendant to discharge that burden than for the prosecution to prove that the preparation was in a form not permitted by the statute, for example, where there was evidence that the defendant had possessed the substance but where he had refused to surrender it for examination.[41]

Although a just result appears to have been reached on the facts in *R v Hunt*, the decision has been criticised for the effect that it may have had on the

---

40　Williams, *op cit*, fn 24; *Sourcebook*, pp 59–64. Cf Dworkin: 'Of course a rule may have exceptions (the batter who has taken three strikes is not out if the catcher drops the third strike). However, an accurate statement of the rule would take this exception into account, and any that did not would be incomplete. If the list of exceptions is very large, it would be too clumsy to repeat them each time the rule is cited; there is, however, no reason in theory why they could not all be added on, and the more that are, the more accurate is the statement of the rule.' Dworkin, RM, 'Is law a system of rules?', in *The Philosophy of Law*, 1977, pp 45–46.

41　[1986] 1 All ER 184, p 191.

Woolmington principle. One problem is its assumption that an implied allocation of an issue to the defendant involves a legal, rather than an evidential, burden. But the main thrust of the criticism is that it failed to establish a clearly defined rule of limited application to allow for implied statutory exceptions to *Woolmington*. Instead, it established a broad rule that allows an uncertain range of policy criteria to be adopted by the courts in their interpretation of legislation. The effect has been to authorise judicial policy making under the guise of statutory interpretation. This significantly undermines *Woolmington*, because it makes it possible for judges to adopt utilitarian policies that ignore, or at any rate give less weight to, the principles that justify placing the burden of proof on the prosecution.[42]

The strength of this criticism has been weakened by the way in which the European Convention has been interpreted. Both the European Court of Human Rights and the House of Lords and Court of Appeal have accepted that where a reverse burden question arises, judges may have to take into account such considerations as the threat faced by society that the legislation was designed to correct, and the right balance to be struck between the interests of the individual and those of society.[43] The suggestion that judges ought not to concern themselves with public policy sounds increasingly like an argument from another world. But there is at least one argument that can be used to enforce the principle contained in Art 6(2). The effect of s 35 of the Criminal Justice and Public Order Act 1994 has been to put defendants under greater pressure to offer an explanation where *prima facie* evidence of an offence has been adduced. The former disadvantage of the prosecution where the defendant had special knowledge may now have been substantially reduced, if not removed altogether. If a reverse burden is thereby made unnecessary, it is difficult to see how it could be supported if a breach of Art 6(2) is alleged.[44]

THE EVIDENTIAL BURDEN

The evidential burden is not strictly a burden of *proof* at all. It is best seen as a *rule of common sense* which says that there must be *some* evidence for a particular issue to become a live one so as to be fit for consideration by a jury or other tribunal of fact. It is sometimes said that an evidential burden is on a party 'to adduce' some evidence to support a particular issue. This can be

---

42 See particularly Healy, P, 'Proof and policy: no golden threads' [1987] Crim LR 355. A more optimistic view was taken in Birch, D, 'Hunting the snark: the elusive statutory exception' [1988] Crim LR 221.

43 See the references to *Ex p Kebilene* and *Lambert*, above.

44 For a discussion of this in relation to s 2 of the Prevention of Corruption Act 1916, see *Legislating the Criminal Code: Corruption*, Law Com No 145 (1997), Part XI. See also s 34, referred to in Chapter 9, below.

misleading; it is not essential that the evidence be adduced by the party who has the evidential burden. The evidence could come from witnesses on the other side, either in cross-examination or even when giving evidence-in-chief. All that a party with an evidential burden needs to be able to do is to *point to* some evidence making the issue in question a live one.

Whether an evidential burden has been satisfied is a matter for the judge alone. It follows that there should never be any reference to it in a summing up. The evidential burden governs what the judge *does*, in leaving the question to the jury or withdrawing it from them. The legal burden governs what he *says* when directing the jury about how they are to reach their verdict.[45]

The effect of having an evidential burden can be seen in an illustration. Suppose, first, that Mr Whitewig is defending Charlie on a charge of assault. Charlie has decided not to give evidence and there is no suggestion from the prosecution witnesses or anyone else that he might have been acting in self-defence when he struck his victim. In an impassioned closing speech to the jury, Charlie's counsel says: 'Members of the jury, you cannot convict my client because there is always the possibility that he might have been acting in self-defence. And so long as that possibility remains, how can you be satisfied so that you are sure of his guilt?' At that stage the judge would be likely to interrupt and say, 'Mr Whitewig, there is not a scrap of evidence to support the suggestion that the accused might have been acting in self-defence and I shall have to tell the jury in due course that that issue is not open for their consideration'.

In practice, the question of whether an evidential burden has been satisfied is more likely to arise on a defence submission, at the end of the prosecution case, that there is no case to answer. As well as having the legal burden of proof, the prosecution also have an evidential burden to adduce some evidence fit to go to a jury of every element necessary to establish their case against the accused. If, at the end of their case, there is no evidence of an essential element of the offence, the judge will allow the submission and direct the jury to return a verdict of not guilty without hearing the case for the defence.[46]

Questions are sometimes asked about the weight of evidence required to satisfy an evidential burden. Judges have occasionally referred to this, but what they have said has not been very helpful and it can be misleading if it encourages students to think of the evidential burden as a burden of *proof*. It would, for example, be wholly wrong to suggest that the evidential burden has to be discharged 'on the balance of probabilities' or 'beyond reasonable doubt'. The simplest line to take is that, because the evidential burden is not a

---

45 Williams, G, 'The evidential burden: some common misapprehensions' (1977) 127 NLJ 156.

46 See *R v Galbraith* [1981] 1 WLR 1039, approved in *R v Fulcher* [1995] 2 Cr App R 251; above, Chapter 1, p 31.

burden of proof, it does not make sense to talk of a standard of proof in relation to it. The only qualification to this is that where non-insane automatism is relied on as a defence, a judge is unlikely to leave that defence to the jury in the absence of medical or scientific evidence in support.[47]

When does an evidential burden rest on the defence? The answer is that the defence will have such a burden *in relation to any issue that the prosecution are not required to raise*. One obvious case is where the defence have a *legal* burden to satisfy in relation to a particular issue. But even where the defence has no legal burdens, it may still, in relation to some issues, have an evidential burden. General defences (such as self-defence, duress, and non-insane automatism), which are applicable to more than one offence, will place an evidential burden on the defendant.[48] The same is true of the defence of provocation as a defence to a murder charge.[49] These 'defences' operate by way of what, in a civil action, would be called 'confession and avoidance': they admit certain facts, but raise a new issue to avoid the likely consequence of what has been admitted. The placing of an evidential burden on a defendant is compatible with Art 6(2) because it does not breach the presumption of innocence.[50] An example of a defence that does *not* work in this way is the defence, where rape is alleged, that the complainant consented to the act of sexual intercourse. The absence of consent in rape is an essential element of the offence, in respect of which the prosecution has both a legal and evidential burden.[51] It should be remembered that an evidential burden, like a legal burden, can rest on only one party in respect of one issue. There is therefore no evidential burden on the defendant in a rape trial to show consent, though obviously a defendant is likely to be convicted if that is the defence and there is not at least *some* evidence of consent.

Where an alibi defence is raised, there is no legal burden of proof on the defendant. The judge must tell the jury in summing-up that it is for the prosecution to disprove the alibi beyond reasonable doubt before there can be a conviction.[52]

---

47 *Hill v Baxter* [1958] 1 All ER 193, p 197; *Bratty v AG for Northern Ireland* [1963] AC 386, pp 413–14.
48 *R v Lobell* [1957] 1 QB 547; *R v Gill* [1963] 1 WLR 841; *Bratty v AG for Northern Ireland* [1963] AC 386.
49 *Mancini v DPP* [1942] AC 1.
50 *R v DPP ex p Kebilene and Others* [2000] 1 Cr App R 275, p 324.
51 *DPP v Morgan* [1976] AC 182.
52 *R v Popat* (No 2) [2000] 1 Cr App R 387.

THE STANDARD OF PROOF

Standard of proof in criminal cases

Two formulas are traditional. Jurors may be told, 'You must be satisfied so that you are sure', or 'You must be satisfied beyond reasonable doubt' of the accused's guilt. *But it is the effect of the summing up as a whole that matters.* A direction that does not follow one of these formulas exactly may still be a good one.[53] The overall effect of the summing up may be particularly important where the judge refers to the standard of proof several times. A single reference which, taken alone, would be insufficient, may be cured by the presence in other parts of the summing up of accurate statements of the law.

Some directions will be obviously wrong and, if they stand alone, may cause a conviction to be quashed on appeal. For example, it is not enough for the judge to tell the jury merely that they must be 'satisfied' that the prosecution has proved its case, because this would allow the jury to convict if satisfied to the civil standard on a mere balance of probabilities.[54] Where there is a legal burden on a defendant in a criminal case in respect of any issue, that burden will be discharged by proof on the balance of probabilities – the civil standard.[55]

Why should there be two different standards of proof? Having two standards reflects a fundamental assumption that our society makes about the comparative costs of erroneous factual decisions. In any judicial proceeding in which there is a dispute about the facts of some earlier event, the fact finder can never acquire unassailably accurate knowledge of what happened. All he can acquire is a belief about what *probably* happened. The strength of this belief can vary. A standard of proof represents an attempt to instruct the fact finder about the degree of confidence our society thinks he should have in the correctness of factual conclusions for a particular type of adjudication. The expressions 'proof on the balance of probabilities' and 'proof beyond reasonable doubt' are quantitatively imprecise. Nevertheless, they do communicate to the fact finder different ideas concerning the degree of confidence he is expected to have in the correctness of his conclusions. Any trier of fact will sometimes, despite his best efforts, produce a decision about facts that is wrong. In a law suit between two parties, a factual error can make a difference in one of two ways. First, it can result in a judgment in favour of the plaintiff when the true facts warrant a judgment for the defendant. The corresponding result in a criminal case would be the conviction of an innocent

---

53 *Walters v The Queen* [1969] 2 AC 26; *Sourcebook*, p 64.

54 *R v Hepworth and Fearnley* [1955] 2 QB 600; *R v Gourley* [1981] Crim LR 334.

55 *R v Carr-Briant* [1943] KB 607; *Sourcebook*, p 65.

man. On the other hand, a factual determination that is wrong can result in a judgment for the defendant when the true facts justify a judgment in the plaintiff's favour. The result corresponding to this in a criminal trial would be the acquittal of a guilty man.

The standard of proof influences the relative frequency of these two types of erroneous outcomes. If the standard of proof in a criminal trial was proof on a balance of probabilities rather than proof beyond reasonable doubt, there would be a smaller risk of factual errors resulting in the release of guilty persons, but greater risk of factual errors resulting in conviction of the innocent. The standard of proof in a particular type of litigation therefore reflects society's assessment of the harm attaching to each kind of error. It is this that explains the difference between criminal and civil standards of proof. In a civil suit we generally regard it as no more serious for there to be an erroneous verdict in the defendant's favour than for there to be such a verdict in the plaintiff's favour. Proof on the balance of probabilities therefore seems the appropriate standard. But in a criminal case we do not view the harm that results from the conviction of an innocent man as equivalent to the harm that results from acquitting someone who is guilty. The defendant in a criminal trial generally has more at stake than a defendant in a civil trial, and so the margin of error must be reduced in his favour by placing on the prosecution the burden of proving guilt beyond reasonable doubt.[56]

Standard of proof in civil cases

The criminal courts have produced many decisions which have attempted to clarify the criminal standard of proof, because judges have to instruct the jury correctly about both burden and standard in summing up.[57] Idiosyncratic approaches, or ones that were plainly wrong, headed straight for the Court of Appeal in the event of a conviction. But because very few civil cases are heard with a jury, the opportunity to define the civil standard has not often arisen. An attempt sometimes referred to is that of Denning J in *Miller v Minister of Pensions*.[58] There he said that, in a civil case, the evidence 'must carry a reasonable degree of probability, but not so high as is required in a criminal case. If the evidence is such that the tribunal can say: "We think it more probable than not," the burden is discharged, but, if the probabilities are equal, it is not.'[59]

The application of this standard has sometimes given rise to difficulty where an allegation has been made in civil proceedings of exceptionally bad

---

56   *In Re Samuel Winship* 397 US 358 (1970), pp 369–72, opinion of Harlan J.
57   See, eg, *R v Hay* (1983) 77 Cr App R 70.
58   [1947] 2 All ER 372; *Sourcebook*, p 65.
59   [1947] 2 All ER 372, p 374.

conduct. Examples in the past have included allegations of adultery, of fraud, or of conduct which would have amounted to a criminal offence. More recently the problem has arisen in connection with allegations of child abuse in care proceedings or in matrimonial disputes. The problem can be put in this way: where a particularly serious allegation has been made, is it still the case that the burden of proof can be satisfied on a mere balance of probabilities? The courts have tended to answer this question in two ways. One approach is to say that, although the standard in all civil cases is proof on the balance of probabilities, there may be different degrees of probability within that standard. The other approach is not to emphasise degrees of probability, but the weight of evidence required to satisfy a court that a particular allegation has been proved.

A useful starting point is *Hornal v Neuberger Products Ltd*.[60] In this case, the question arose of whether one party to a contract had made a representation about the contract goods to the other. The representation, if it had been made, was false. The trial judge was prepared to hold that, on the balance of probabilities, the representation had been made. But if it had been made, it followed that the person who had made it was guilty of fraud and could in theory have been prosecuted for the offence of obtaining money by false pretences. The judge said that if he had to be satisfied to the criminal standard that the representation had been made, the evidence was insufficient and the plaintiff had not proved his case. But he then went on to hold that, as it was a civil case, the civil standard applied, and according to *that* standard he *was* satisfied that the representation had been made. He therefore gave judgment for the plaintiff.

On appeal it was argued that the criminal standard should have been applied, since the allegation was of conduct amounting to a criminal offence. The Court of Appeal rejected this argument. Denning LJ said that the more serious the allegation, the higher the degree of probability required, but it need not, in a civil case, reach the very high standard required by the criminal law. Hodson LJ said simply that in a civil case, the balance of probability standard was correct. Morris LJ said that the gravity of the allegation was part of the whole range of circumstances which have to be weighed in the scale when deciding on the balance of probabilities.

Current opinion favours the approach of Morris LJ rather than that of Denning LJ. In *Re H and Others*,[61] a majority of the House of Lords supported the opinion that, 'the more serious the allegation, the less likely it is that the event occurred and, hence, the stronger should be the evidence before the court concludes that the allegation is established on the balance of probability'.[62] As Lord Nicholls put it: 'Fraud is usually less likely than

---

60   [1957] 1 QB 247; *Sourcebook*, p 67.
61   [1996] AC 563, pp 586–87.
62   *Ibid*, p 586.

negligence. Deliberate physical injury is usually less likely than accidental physical injury.'[63] He added that, although the result was much the same, this did not mean that where a serious allegation was in issue the standard of proof required was higher. It meant only that the inherent probability or improbability of an event was itself a matter to be taken into account when weighing the probabilities and deciding whether, on balance, the event had occurred. If a third standard were substituted in some civil cases, it would be necessary to identify what that standard was and when it applied. The formulation of such a standard would risk causing confusion and uncertainty; it was better to stick to 'the existing, established law on this subject'. Contrary observations were not an accurate statement of the law.[64] Strictly, the Law Lords' opinion on this point was *obiter*. But this had been the view of the Court of Appeal[65] and it had been assumed without argument by counsel for all parties in the House of Lords.[66]

PRESUMPTIONS

It is possible for both legal and evidential burdens to be affected by *presumptions*. Nevertheless, presumptions fit awkwardly into an evidence course. When lawyers in the 18th century first started to write books on evidence, they used to include large amounts of substantive law on such subjects as trespass, nuisance, bailment, actions on the case and so forth. Their object was to include not only what we should recognise as rules or principles of evidence, but rules about what had to be proved in order to establish particular claims or defences. There was no unifying principle other than the convenience of the arrangement for practitioners. Evidence textbooks today have sections entitled 'presumptions', and this at first glance looks like a suitable topic to cover. In fact, apart from the impact of presumptions on evidential and legal burdens, it is not. These bits and pieces are simply a survival from the older style of writing. No successful attempts have been made to find an all-embracing theory that would make 'presumptions' a true part of evidence law. What you see are several quite distinct chunks of

---

63 [1996] AC 563, p 586.

64 *Ibid*, p 587. Lord Goff and Lord Mustill agreed with Lord Nicholls. Lord Browne-Wilkinson dissented on a different point.

65 [1995] 1 FLR 643.

66 Lord Lloyd said that, in the absence of argument and in the light of earlier decisions, including some in the House of Lords, he was not prepared to say that, contempt of court apart, it was never necessary to prove facts in a civil case beyond a balance of probabilities. (A person who disobeys a court order in civil proceedings will be guilty of contempt of court and may be sent to prison as punishment. Since *Re Bramblevale Ltd* [1970] Ch 128, it has been clear that an alleged contempt must therefore be proved beyond reasonable doubt, and this was accepted by the House of Lords in *Re H and Others* [1996] AC 563.)

substantive law, selected for no other reason than habit, which have little or no connection with each other and which are apt to mislead, because they can obscure the fact that there are many other similar devices in statutory sources of law that never get mentioned in evidence textbooks.

Because this is an area where attempts to find unifying features have been made so unsuccessfully, you may find classification confusing. When a writer refers to a presumption, you need to be sure how the word is being used. The sort of presumption that you will be trying to learn about because it appears in an examination syllabus – for example, of marriage, legitimacy and death – is usually what is often called a *rebuttable presumption of law*. Talk of any other type of presumption is unnecessary and leads to confusion. A 'presumption of fact' is merely *an inference* from facts, which is part of an ordinary reasoning process. For example, it would be possible, though unhelpful, to say that where the fingerprints of the accused are found at the scene of a crime, there is a presumption of fact that the accused was at some time present there.

Another 'presumption' of this kind is an inference that may be drawn from the possession of property that has recently been stolen. Judges and writers have quite often referred to this as 'the doctrine of recent possession', thereby inflating even more its apparent importance. As will be seen, there are good reasons for thinking that this part of the law has become obsolete since ss 34 and 35 of the Criminal Justice and Public Order Act 1994 came into force. The rule affected cases of handling and theft and worked as follows:

(a) there had to be proof, or an admission, of the fact that the defendant was found in possession of stolen property; and

(b) the defendant's possession was so soon after the property had been stolen that it could fairly be described as 'recent'. (This was a question of fact, depending on the circumstances of each case.)

If those conditions were satisfied, the jury were to be directed that:

(a) such possession called for explanation; and

(b) if the defendant gave no explanation, or gave an explanation that the jury were sure was untrue, they were entitled to infer that the defendant was guilty of either handling or theft.

The burden of proof remained on the prosecution, so that if the defendant's explanation left the jury in doubt as to his dishonesty, they were bound to acquit.[67]

In *R v Raviraj*,[68] the Court of Appeal said that this rule was only a particular aspect of a general proposition that where suspicious circumstances appear to demand an explanation, the lack of a credible explanation may

---

67 *R v Schama* (1914) 84 LJKB 396; *R v Garth* [1949] 1 All ER 773; *R v Aves* [1950] 2 All ER 330.

68 (1986) 85 Cr App R 93, p 103.

warrant an inference of the defendant's guilty knowledge. This proposition was itself only part of a wider proposition that guilt may be inferred from the unreasonable behaviour of a defendant when confronted with facts that seem to accuse him. That is one line on which the common law was developing some years before the Criminal Justice and Public Order Act, and it was a controversial one. It differed significantly from the later legislation, in that no inference could be drawn from a suspect's silence after he had been cautioned.[69] The effect of s 34 of the 1994 Act changed that position because, while retaining the right to silence, it removed much of its usefulness by allowing inferences to be drawn from its exercise.[70] Thus if a defendant provides no explanation to the police for his possession of property that has recently been stolen, and produces one for the first time only at trial, inferences may be drawn under s 34. And if no explanation is provided even at trial, inferences can be drawn under s 35.[71] For this reason, it is likely that the common law 'doctrine of recent possession' will fall into disuse.

Another 'presumption of fact' is that people intend the natural consequences of their acts. This was formerly a common law 'presumption' and was put on a statutory basis by s 8 of the Criminal Justice Act 1967, which provides as follows:

A court or jury, in determining whether a person has committed an offence–

(a) shall not be bound in law to infer that he intended or foresaw a result of his actions by reason only of its being a natural and probable consequence of those actions; but

(b) shall decide whether he did intend or foresee that result by reference to all the evidence, drawing such inferences from the evidence as appear proper in the circumstances.[72]

If someone refers to an 'irrebuttable presumption of law', that is just the same as referring to some principle or rule of substantive law. So, for example, the 'presumption of innocence' refers to the principle that the burden of proof generally rests on the prosecution in a criminal case.

When dealing with true presumptions – rebuttable presumptions of law – we shall not understand them unless we realise that they serve different purposes. One purpose is to save judicial time and effort. For example, according to the presumption of legitimacy it is presumed that a child born in lawful wedlock is legitimate in the absence of evidence to the contrary. Given the fact of birth in those circumstances, it would be unreasonable and time wasting not to presume the legitimacy of the child. But another, quite

---

69 *R v Raviraj* (1986) 85 Cr App R 93.

70 See below, Chapter 9, p 240.

71 See above, Chapter 3, p 54.

72 The section was inserted in the Act to overrule the decision of the House of Lords in *DPP v Smith* [1961] AC 290, which had the effect of making the presumption irrebuttable in some circumstances.

different, function is to resolve a dilemma which arises from the complete lack of evidence about a fact in issue. For example, according to the presumption of death a person will be presumed to have died if it is proved that:

(a) there is no acceptable evidence that he has been alive at some time during a continuous period of at least seven years;

(b) there are persons likely to have heard of him, had he been alive, who have not heard of him during that period; and

(c) all due inquiries have been made with a view to finding the person in question, but without success.[73]

The presumption in this case operates by artificially increasing the probative value of the basic facts – absence for seven years, etc – in the absence of any contrary evidence. So far as probative worth goes, there is nothing special about seven rather than six years' absence. But seven years gives rise to a rebuttable presumption of law, while six years gives rise only to a possible inference of fact. The reason is that it would be inconvenient to suspend indefinitely the rights of someone who has disappeared. What the law has done is to provide, by a rule affecting the burden of proof, a limitation period. Another example of a presumption that has been created to resolve a dilemma in the absence of evidence is s 184(1) of the Law of Property Act 1925. This provides that where two or more persons have died in circumstances where the order in time of the deaths is uncertain, then for all purposes affecting title to property the deaths shall be presumed to have occurred in order of seniority, with younger persons surviving older ones.[74]

A dilemma-resolving presumption is only needed if a dilemma truly exists. The existence of this sort of presumption should not blind you to the fact that a court may make the inference you want from the facts that are available. So if you can prove that X took a flight on an aeroplane that exploded in mid air, you are not going to have to wait for seven years to pass before a court can find as a fact that X is dead.

Because presumptions are creatures of substantive law, the best place to find out about them is in books about the relevant substantive law and not in books of evidence. The fact that presumptions are creatures of substantive law can be seen from the fact that by far the most important of them are statutory and behave according to the provisions of the legislation in which they are to be found. The lack of any unifying feature, even among the common law presumptions, is emphasised by the fact that the same common law presumption can operate differently in civil and criminal contexts. For example, in *Dillon v The Queen*,[75] the Privy Council held that the common law

---

73 *Chard v Chard* [1956] P 259, p 272.

74 See further, Tapper, C, *Cross and Tapper on Evidence*, 9th edn, 1999, p 123; Zuckerman, AAS, *The Principles of Criminal Evidence*, 1989, pp 110–21.

75 [1982] AC 484.

presumption of regularity[76] could not be relied on by the prosecution to establish a central element of the offence alleged in that case against the accused. And it is unlikely that the prosecution would be able to rely on the presumption of legitimacy in a case of incest.[77]

Some examples of statutory presumptions have already been mentioned. It may be convenient at this stage to describe briefly some common law examples.

Presumption of marriage

Where a man and a woman have gone through a ceremony of marriage followed by cohabitation, there is a presumption that the ceremony was valid. It has been said that to rebut the presumption evidence is required that is 'strong, distinct, satisfactory and conclusive', or at least 'clear, distinct and satisfactory'. The presumption is not to be shaken by 'a mere balance of probability'.[78] But this test was applied at a time when concern for status was greater than it is today. In *Piers v Piers*, for example, Lord Campbell referred to the 'tremendous responsibility' borne by a court having to decide the validity of a marriage and the peril of holding that a woman was a concubine and the children bastards.[79] Further, in *Re H and Others*[80] the House of Lords favoured a single standard of proof in civil cases and, in the unlikely event of a litigant's having to rely on the presumption today, rebuttal on the balance of probabilities would almost certainly suffice.

Even where there is no evidence that a ceremony of marriage has been performed, a presumption that a man and woman were lawfully married will arise from evidence of cohabitation, coupled with their reputation as man and wife.[81]

Presumption of legitimacy

There is a presumption that a child born or conceived during wedlock is the child of the woman's husband. The presumption applies not only where the husband and wife are living together, but also where they are living apart, whether by virtue of a formal or informal agreement. The presumption does not apply where the parties are separated under a court order. But it will

---

76 See below, p 129.
77 Tapper, *op cit*, p 124.
78 *Piers v Piers* (1849) 2 HLC 331, pp 362, 370, 379–80.
79 *Ibid*, p 381.
80 [1996] AC 563.
81 *In Re Taylor, decd* [1961] 1 WLR 9.

apply after the presentation of a petition for divorce or nullity and even after the granting of a decree nisi, as opposed to a decree absolute, of divorce or nullity. The reasoning behind this is that 'the law contemplates spouses as fulfilling their marital duties to each other unless there has been an actual order of the court dispensing with the performance of such duties'. So long as the law presumes the parties to a marriage to be performing their duties to each other, so long also will the law presume that if the woman bears a child she will be bearing it as the result of intercourse with her husband.[82]

The presumption of legitimacy may be rebutted by evidence which shows that it is more probable than not that the person in question is legitimate or illegitimate, as the case may be.[83] This presumption, therefore, affects the legal burden of proof.

Presumption of death

Some statutory provisions require a court to presume the death of a person in certain circumstances.[84] In matters where no statute lays down an applicable rule, the question of whether a person is to be presumed dead or not is generally simply a question of fact. However, from a long line of judicial statements, it appears to be accepted that there is a common law presumption of death in certain cases where a person has been absent for seven years.

The presumption operates as follows. Where as regards a certain person there is no acceptable evidence that he was alive at some time during a continuous period of seven years or more, then he will be presumed to have died at *some* time during that period if it can be proved that:

(a) there are persons who would be likely to have heard of him during that period;

(b) those persons have not heard of him; and

(c) all due inquiries have been made appropriate to the circumstances.[85]

The presumption is merely that death occurred *at the latest* by the end of seven years. It says nothing as to when during that period death occurred.[86]

A presumption casts a burden on the party against whom it operates. That burden may be 'evidential' or 'persuasive'. If evidential, the presumption may be rebutted by evidence sufficient to show that the question which the

---

82 *Knowles v Knowles* [1962] P 161, pp 166–67.

83 Family Law Reform Act 1969, s 26.

84 See, eg, Matrimonial Causes Act 1973, s 19(3), in relation to proceedings on a petition for presumption of death and dissolution of marriage; Offences Against the Person Act 1861, s 51, in relation to prosecutions for bigamy.

85 *Chard v Chard* [1956] P 259, p 272.

86 *In Re Phene's Trusts* (1870) 5 Ch App 139, pp 144, 152.

presumption was meant to resolve is still a live issue. It has been suggested that the common law presumption of death is merely evidential.[87] If that is correct, once *some* evidence has been adduced sufficient to raise an issue whether or not the person in question is alive, the presumption is rebutted and the party who wishes to rely on the fact of death must prove that fact on the balance of probabilities. If, however, a presumption is 'persuasive', it affects the legal burden of proof so that the fact presumed must be found to exist, once the foundational facts have been proved, unless the court is satisfied by the evidence on the balance of probabilities that it does not. There is no satisfactory authority on the effect of the presumption of death. But this is hardly surprising, because any evidence showing a person to be alive is likely to prevent the presumption from arising at all since one or more of the conditions referred to in *Chard v Chard* will remain unsatisfied. In practice, problems posed by a person's unexplained disappearance allow room for a good deal of judicial manoeuvre. Where there is no direct evidence of either life or death, a judge sitting alone will be able to reach a conclusion which he thinks desirable on the facts of the case. The result is that the common law presumption of death has now little practical effect in litigation, and this is shown by the undeveloped state of the law on this subject.[88]

Res ipsa loquitur

This maxim, meaning 'the thing speaks for itself', was traditionally regarded as giving rise to some kind of presumption in actions for negligence. Where something which had caused an accident was shown to have been under the management of the defendant or his servants, and the accident was such as in the ordinary course of things did not happen if those who had management used proper care, the accident itself led to an inference of negligence.[89]

More recently, in *Lloyde v West Midlands Gas Board*,[90] approved by the Privy Council in *Ng Chun Pui v Lee Chuen Tat*,[91] the maxim was described as 'no more than an exotic, although convenient, phrase' to describe a common sense approach, not limited by technical rules, to the assessment of evidence. It means that a claimant *prima facie* establishes negligence where:

(a) it is not possible for him to prove precisely what was the relevant act or omission that set in train the events leading to the accident; but

---

87 Stone, D, 'The presumption of death: a redundant concept?' (1981) 44 MLR 516, p 519, citing *Cross on Evidence*, 1974, p 126.

88 *Ibid*.

89 *Scott v London and St Katherine's Docks Co* (1865) 3 H&C 596; *Moore v R Fox & Sons* [1956] 1 QB 596. See further *Witting* [2001] 117 LQR 392.

90 [1971] 1 WLR 749, p 755.

91 [1988] RTR 298, p 301.

(b) on the evidence as it stands at the close of the claimant's case it is more likely than not that the cause of the accident was some act or omission of the defendant, or of someone for whom the defendant is responsible, involving failure to take proper care for the claimant's safety.

The effect of the maxim was formerly uncertain. Some judges thought that it affected the legal burden of proof so that, once the accident had been proved, the defendant could avoid liability only by showing that he had not been negligent, or at least by providing a reasonable explanation of the accident which was consistent with the absence of any negligence on his part.[92] Others took the view that the legal burden of proof was not affected and that only an evidential burden was created.[93]

The latter view received the approval of the Privy Council in *Ng Chun Pui v Lee Chuen Tat*. In an advice delivered by Lord Griffiths, the Privy Council said that it was misleading to talk of the burden of proof shifting to the defendant in a case where *res ipsa loquitur* applied. In any action for negligence the burden of proof rests throughout on the claimant. In an appropriate case the claimant will establish a *prima facie* case by relying on the fact of the accident. If the defendant adduces no evidence, there will be nothing to rebut the inference of negligence and the claimant's case will have been proved. But if the defendant *does* adduce evidence, that evidence must be evaluated to see if it is still reasonable to draw the inference of negligence from the mere fact of the accident.[94]

Presumption of regularity

This is a loose expression which appears at present to refer to two different presumptions. One is the presumption that official appointments have been properly and formally made, and that official acts have been properly and formally performed.[95] According to one writer, the reasons for making these presumptions are that it is improbable that any person would carry out public functions unless he had been duly appointed, and it is improbable that somebody who had been properly appointed would be guilty of a dereliction of duty by carrying out one of his tasks improperly.[96] A more realistic view is that it is simply a rule of convenience.

---

92 See, eg, *Woods v Duncan* [1946] AC 401, p 419; *Barkway v South Wales Transport Co* [1948] 2 All ER 460, p 471; *Colvilles Ltd v Devine* [1969] 2 All ER 53, pp 56–57.

93 See, eg, *Colvilles Ltd v Devine* [1969] 2 All ER 53, p 58; *Henderson v Henry E Jenkins* [1970] AC 282, p 301.

94 [1988] RTR 298, pp 300–01.

95 It is sometimes referred to by the Latin maxim '*Omnia praesumuntur rite esse acta*'.

96 Nokes, GD, *An Introduction to Evidence*, 4th edn, 1967, p 70.

So, for example, in *R v Verelst*,[97] where the defendant was charged with committing perjury while giving evidence in an ecclesiastical court, Lord Ellenborough CJ held that the prosecution did not have to prove that the court official who administered the oath had been properly appointed. The fact of his having acted in that capacity for some years was 'sufficient *prima facie* evidence that he was duly appointed and had competent authority to administer the oath', because it was 'a general presumption of law that a person acting in a public capacity is duly authorised so to do'.[98]

The status of the presumption is less clear. After Lord Ellenborough's initial ruling in *R v Verelst*, the defendant adduced evidence that, in fact, the official in question had not been properly appointed (and so had had no authority to administer an oath). In the face of this evidence, Lord Ellenborough said that the presumption stood only 'till the contrary is proved'. On the evidence, he found that the official's lack of authority had been proved. The question that arises is whether the presumption is a persuasive presumption, or merely an evidential one: must the defendant rebut it by proving on the balance of probabilities that the contrary is the case, or merely by adducing *some* evidence that that is so, with the result that the party relying on the presumption must prove the proper appointment to the appropriate civil or criminal standard?

R v Verelst suggests that the presumption is persuasive. Support can be found in the decision of the Court of Appeal in *Harris v Knight*,[99] in which it was held that, just as the presumption is not needed where due observance of the formalities has been proved, so it has no place 'where such observance is proved'.[100] However, in the same case, Lopes LJ said that the presumption 'applies with more or less force according to the circumstances of each case', which suggests that in some cases its effect might be to place an evidential burden only on the party against whom it is used. A further complication arises from the decision of the Privy Council in *Dillon v The Queen*.[101] In this case the defendant was a police officer charged with negligently permitting the escape of prisoners in his lawful custody. No formal proof was provided at trial of the lawfulness of the prisoners' custody. The Privy Council held that this was fatal to the prosecution case and allowed the defendant's appeal against conviction. Both the trial magistrate and the Jamaican appeal court had relied on the presumption of regularity to support the conviction, but the Privy Council said that a central element of an offence could not be established in this way.[102] It is likely that this decision would now be

---

97 (1813) 3 Camp 432.
98 *Ibid*, p 433.
99 (1890) 15 PD 170.
100 *Ibid*, p 180.
101 [1982] AC 484.
102 See also *Swift v Barrett* (1940) 163 LT 154; *Scott v Baker* [1969] 1 QB 659.

preferred to that in *R v Verelst* in a criminal trial, but the effect of the presumption in a civil action is unclear.

The second presumption under this head is that a mechanical instrument, provided it is of a kind that is usually in working order, was in working order at a particular time that is relevant in the litigation. Its effect is to place an evidential burden on the party against whom the presumption is used. The justification is its convenience. In *Nicholas v Penny*,[103] for example, the Divisional Court said that the courts will presume, in the absence of contrary evidence, that a watch or speedometer was in working order at the material time. And in *Tingle Jacobs & Co v Kennedy*,[104] in a *dictum* with which the other members of the Court of Appeal agreed, Lord Denning MR said, in relation to a set of traffic lights, 'when you have a device of this kind set up for public use in active operation, I should have thought that the presumption should be that it is in proper working order unless there is evidence to the contrary'. Evidence from computers, formerly regarded as suspect, is no longer subject to special provisions to ensure reliability, either in civil or criminal proceedings.[105] It seems to follow that the presumption of 'working order' now applies to computers, as well as to such instruments as watches, speedometers and traffic lights.

---

103 [1950] 2 KB 466.
104 [1964] 1 All ER 888, p 889.
105 Civil Evidence Act 1995, Sched 2; Youth Justice and Criminal Evidence Act 1999, s 60.

CHAPTER 6

HEARSAY: THE SCOPE OF THE RULE[1]

STATEMENT OF THE RULE

As good a statement of the hearsay rule as any was given originally in *Cross on Evidence* and adopted by Lord Havers in *R v Sharp*:[2] 'An assertion other than one made by a person while giving oral evidence in the proceedings is inadmissible as evidence of any fact asserted.'[3]

Although a strict system of exclusionary rules and exceptions did not develop before the 19th century, by the end of the 17th century, there appears to have been a recognition that the admission of hearsay evidence was generally undesirable, and this was sometimes expressed by statements to the effect that hearsay was not evidence.[4] The principal reasons for its undesirability were that the original assertion was not on oath, and the person making it was not available for cross-examination.[5]

It is important to notice that the rule against hearsay excludes an item of evidence *only if the purpose of adducing that evidence is to establish the truth of the facts asserted.* It follows that in relation to any item of evidence that you suspect may be caught by the rule, you need first to ask: 'What is *the job of proof* that this item of evidence is being put forward to do?' Only when you know what this is can you see whether the evidence is caught by the hearsay rule, which is brought into operation not by any particular form of words, but by the use that is going to be made of them. Thus, the hearsay rule is essentially a *rule about the use of language.*

---

1 See Law Commission, *Evidence in Criminal Proceedings: Hearsay and Related Topics*, Law Com No 245 (1997). A useful monograph is Choo, AL-T, *Hearsay and Confrontation in Criminal Trials*, 1996. See also Weinberg (1973) 9 Melbourne ULR 268, Tribe (1974) 87 Harv LR 957, Park (1981) 65 Minn LR 423, Guest (1985) 101 LQR 385, Ashworth and Pattenden (1986) 102 LQR 292, Williams (1987) 11 Adel LR 113, Guest (1988) 41 CLP 33, Hirst (1993) 13 LS 521, Pattenden (1993) 56 MLR 138, Rein (1994) 110 LQR 431, Jackson (1998) 2 E&P 166, Peysner (1998) 2 E&P 232.

2 (1988) 86 Cr App R 274, p 278; *Sourcebook*, p 190.

3 Section 1(2) of the Civil Evidence Act 1995 defines hearsay, for the purposes of that Act, as 'a statement made otherwise than by a person while giving oral evidence in the proceedings which is tendered as evidence of the matters stated'. The use of 'statement' rather than 'assertion' does not seem to be significant.

4 See, eg, *R v Charnock* (1696) 12 St Tr, cols 1377, 1454.

5 Morgan, EM, *Some Problems of Proof under the Anglo-American System of Litigation*, 1956, pp 109–14. Justifications for the exclusion of hearsay evidence are more fully considered below, p 153.

A clear example of the operation of the rule is *Sparks v R*.[6] The defendant was charged with indecently assaulting a girl just under four years old. Before the examining magistrate, the mother gave evidence that her daughter told her that she had been taken out of the car by the person who had assaulted her. The mother went on: 'I then asked her what did the person look like, and she said that it was a coloured boy.' At trial, the girl herself did not give evidence because of her age, and the mother's evidence of what her daughter had said was ruled inadmissible because it infringed the hearsay rule. The defendant, who was white, was convicted and appealed. He argued that it was unjust for the jury to be left throughout the whole trial with the idea that the child could not give any clue as to the identity of her assailant. But obviously the great relevance of the girl's statement was to make it very much less likely that the defendant had done what was alleged. He was relying on the girl's statement for the truth of what had been asserted and the hearsay rule therefore applied. The Privy Council upheld the trial judge's ruling.[7]

Another case where the defence wanted to rely on the truth of something that had been asserted by someone not giving evidence at trial was *R v Turner*.[8] In this case, one of the defendants, Donald Barrett, appealed against his conviction for robbery. He argued that the trial judge had wrongly excluded evidence that a man called Saunders had told the police that he, and not Barrett, had been involved in the robbery. The Court of Appeal held that evidence of what Saunders had said to the police was caught by the rule. Obviously, the reason for adducing it was to establish that Saunders, not Barrett, had been involved. In other words, the defence were relying on what Saunders had said to establish the truth of his assertions. The Court of Appeal emphasised that the hearsay rule applied to both prosecution and defence equally.

Sparks v R and *R v Turner* show that the application of the rule can make it impossible for a defendant to put before the court evidence, which may be very cogent, pointing to his innocence. This could deprive a defendant of a fair trial and is a serious objection to the existing law.[9]

A case to be distinguished is *Subramaniam v Public Prosecutor*.[10] The defendant was prosecuted for possession of ammunition contrary to emergency regulations. His defence was that he had been captured by terrorists, that he had been acting under duress, and that at the time of his capture by the security forces he had been attempting to surrender. He gave evidence describing his capture and how he had been forced to accompany

---

6   [1964] AC 964; *Sourcebook*, p 93.
7   The appeal was allowed on other grounds.
8   (1975) 60 Cr App R 80; *Sourcebook*, p 95.
9   Cf *Evidence in Criminal Proceedings: Hearsay and Related Topics,* Law Com No 138 (1995), paras 7.34–7.73; Law Com No 245 (1997), paras 4.4–4.13.
10   [1956] 1 WLR 965; *Sourcebook*, p 96.

the terrorists. The trial judge ruled inadmissible as hearsay any evidence of his conversation with the terrorists. He was convicted and appealed. But the Privy Council held that the trial judge had been wrong and allowed the appeal. They emphasised that:

> Evidence of a statement made to a witness by a person who is not himself called as a witness may or may not be hearsay. It is hearsay and inadmissible when the object of the evidence is to establish the truth of what is contained in the statement. *It is not hearsay and is admissible when it is proposed to establish by the evidence, not the truth of the statement, but the fact that it was made.* The fact that the statement was made, quite apart from its truth, is frequently relevant in considering the mental state and conduct thereafter of the witness or of some other person in whose presence the statement was made.[11]

In this case statements could have been made to the defendant by the terrorists which, whether true or not, might have affected his mind by *causing him to believe* that he would suffer instant death should he disobey their orders. Such evidence would have supported his defence of duress. The judge had been wrong, therefore, to rule out all evidence of conversations with the terrorists.

Another case where the rule was inapplicable was *Mawaz Khan v The Queen*,[12] in which two defendants were prosecuted for murder. Circumstantial evidence connected them both with the scene of the crime, but the prosecution relied strongly on the fact that each defendant had made a statement to the police setting up the same false alibi for both of them. The Crown relied on these statements as evidence from which the jury could infer a joint attempt to set up a false alibi, and so joint guilt. Evidence of the statements was given by the police as part of the prosecution case, and the trial judge ruled that each statement was admissible in relation to both defendants. The Privy Council upheld this ruling. The hearsay rule catches only those assertions that are adduced to prove the *truth* of the facts asserted. These statements were adduced by the prosecution, not to show that their contents were *true*, but to show that they were *false*. Accordingly they did not come within the hearsay rule.

The cases referred to so far were relatively straightforward. But hearsay law has been described as 'exceptionally complex and difficult to interpret'.[13] What we need is some method of approach to the subject which will enable us to understand why some cases were decided as they were and why others are open to criticism. Above all, we need a technique for thinking about hearsay, either in relation to problems that may be encountered in an examination or subsequently in practice. Hearsay law is, as we have already seen, essentially

---

11 [1956] 1 WLR 965, p 970. Emphasis supplied.
12 [1967] 1 AC 454; *Sourcebook*, p 97.
13 Report of the Royal Commission on Criminal Justice, Cm 2263, 1993, London: HMSO, ch 8, para 26.

law about the use of language and it is in language that the key to its understanding can best be found. As will be explained below, the decision of the House of Lords in *R v Kearley*[14] extended the rule against hearsay to 'implied assertions'. This decision has been widely criticised, and the Law Commission has recommended its reversal. In trying to explain how the rule against hearsay works, I have initially left this complication to one side. The beginner is advised to take *R v Kearley* on board only after the groundwork has been done. If the Law Commission's recommendations are carried into effect, the basic explanation of the hearsay rule will remain undisturbed. Even if they are not, the explanation will remain useful as a foundation for analysis and for critical appraisals of the law.

HEARSAY AND LANGUAGE

Cross's statement of the rule, adopted in *R v Sharp*,[15] refers to an 'assertion', and the definition in the Civil Evidence Act 1995 refers to a 'statement'.[16] In the first place, therefore, we should get clear what these words mean. The proper understanding of an assertion or statement is that it is generally an *utterance* (ie, a production of spoken or written words) which is made in such a way as *deliberately to convey the impression* that it is made *with the object of saying something that is true*.[17]

Two points need to be emphasised here. The first is that assertions are either true or false.[18] The second point to emphasise is that not all utterances are assertions. When in doubt in relation to a particular utterance, ask whether it makes sense to say of it either that it is true or that it is false. If it makes no sense to say either of these, you have a non-assertive utterance.

Take the following examples:

(a) When is the next train for Birmingham?

(b) Good morning, Felix.

(c) Ouch!

---

14 [1992] 2 AC 228.

15 (1988) 86 Cr App R 274, p 278.

16 Civil Evidence Act 1995, s 1(2).

17 Cf Dummett, M, *Frege: Philosophy of Language*, 2nd edn, 1981, p 300. Assertions or statements may be oral or written, but the use of words is not essential: they can be made by signs, such as sign language, semaphore or morse code. For a simple example, see *Chandrasekera v R* [1937] AC 220, where at a murder trial evidence was admitted under an exception to the hearsay rule that the victim, unable to speak because of her injuries, had made signs indicating that it was the defendant who had cut her throat.

18 Another way of stating this is to say that an assertion has a 'truth value'. From now on, the word 'assertion' should be taken to include 'statement'.

(d) Rest eternal grant to them, O Lord.

(e) The house is up there, round the corner.

Only in relation to (e) does it make sense to say that the utterance is true or false. Try putting the words 'It is true that ...' or 'It is false that ...' before any of the others and you will see readily that you have, literally, made a nonsense. Only (e) is an assertion.[19] Another test for an assertion is whether what is said operates as a piece of narrative or description, however short.

If a truth value cannot be assigned to a particular utterance, it follows that the utterance *cannot* be repeated for the purpose of asserting the truth of its contents, because no such truth exists. The utterance cannot, therefore, be caught directly by the rule against hearsay.[20] At this stage confusion sometimes arises, because it is not appreciated that in relation to *any* utterance it is always possible to ask: 'Is it true *that it was said*?' But that is irrelevant when considering whether the rule against hearsay applies. The relevant question in such cases is, instead: 'Given that it is true that the speaker said X, *is X itself true*?' Of course, in relation to questions, greetings and so forth you can ask the question: 'Was that said?' But if you get an affirmative answer you cannot, except in relation to utterances like the one above at (e), sensibly go on to say: 'Is what the speaker said true?'

There is a special form of utterance which has particular significance for the hearsay rule: this is the 'performative' utterance.[21] What is involved here is a combination of words and context that often has the *appearance* of a mere description or narrative but is more than that, because *those* words in *that* context amount to the performance of an *action*. Examples can be found in social, religious and legal contexts:

(a) 'I will,' when uttered in the course of a marriage ceremony.

(b) 'I name this ship *The Queen Elizabeth*,' uttered by someone launching a ship while smashing a bottle of champagne against it.

(c) 'There will be judgment for the claimant,' when uttered by a judge at the end of a trial.

(d) 'I'm prepared to sell you my car for £750,' when uttered by the owner of a car while negotiating its sale to another.

In all these cases, the words used operate as an action which has the effect of making things in the world different from the way they were before. Thus in the above examples, the person who says, 'I will,' gives consent to be married;

---

19   The others from (a) to (d) are respectively a question, a greeting, an exclamation and a prayer. This, of course, makes certain assumptions about context, for example, that these expressions do not operate as part of a code.

20   It may in the current state of the law be caught indirectly, as an implied assertion: see below, p 142.

21   Some writers use the expression 'operative words' or 'verbal act' instead of 'performative utterance'.

a new ship is named; the defendant becomes legally bound to pay damages; and the owner of the car creates a situation where a contract can be brought into existence by the other party's acceptance.

As said, performative utterances can have the appearance of describing or narrating, and so of asserting things. But this is not always so. 'Let's set fire to the Houses of Parliament!' may be a performative utterance, because in an appropriate context it can constitute the act of incitement to arson; it changes the way things are in the world because the words make the speaker criminally liable. Even where performative words do appear to be assertive, they differ from assertions in the sense already described – that of narrative or descriptive utterances – because generally the overriding intention of the speaker is not to describe what he or she is doing or to state that he or she is doing it: the intention is to do it.[22] When I say 'I will,' before the vicar, I am not reporting on a marriage; I am indulging in it.[23] It is for this reason that performative utterances, like other more obviously non-assertive utterances such as questions or exclamations, do not have a truth value.[24]

If a performative utterance has no truth value, it is not possible to rely upon it as evidence of the truth of the matters that it asserts, because it *asserts* nothing, and for this reason it cannot be caught by the rule against hearsay. This is the best explanation for the decision in *Woodhouse v Hall*.[25] The charge against the defendant was that she had acted in the management of a brothel, contrary to the Sexual Offences Act 1956. The premises in question were a sauna in Wanstead and the defendant was the manageress. Two other women were also employed there with her. Over a period of time, four police officers kept observation and also entered the premises, pretending to be genuine customers. There they were massaged by the defendant and by the two other women. They were prepared to give evidence that while being massaged they had been offered masturbation, referred to as 'hand relief', by the defendant and by the two other women. They had, apparently, been quoted prices of £6 for 'hand relief' and £10 for what was called 'topless hand relief'. It was said,

---

22 I say 'generally', because there may be circumstances where the law makes a party's intention irrelevant. For example, according to contract law, if X behaves in a way that would lead a reasonable man to believe he was agreeing to terms proposed by Y, and Y has that belief, X will be bound, even though he had no 'real intention' to enter into that agreement: see *Smith v Hughes* (1871) LR 6 QB 597, p 607.

23 Cf Austin, JL, *How to Do Things with Words*, 2nd edn, 1975, p 6. The best introduction to the concept of performative utterances is in Austin, JL, *Philosophical Papers*, 3rd edn, 1979, pp 233–52.

24 It may be objected that an utterance can be assertive as well as performative. For example, 'I'm willing to sell you my car for £750' can be seen on one level as an assertion about a state of mind, which may or may not be true, and also as a performative utterance (an offer), which has no truth value. But the key question is, 'What probative job is this evidence being put forward to do?'. If for some reason the utterance is not relied on for its performative qualities, but merely as an assertion, it will be caught by the hearsay rule.

25 (1980) 72 Cr App R 39; *Sourcebook*, p 39. See also *R v Chapman* [1969] 2 QB 436.

however, that none of the officers had accepted and that each had made some excuse.

The question arose whether the evidence of the officers, as to the offers made by the two other women, was admissible. Those other women were not called by the prosecution. The magistrates held that this evidence was caught by the hearsay rule and so was inadmissible. The prosecution accepted that, in the absence of police evidence about offers from the other women, they could not establish that the sauna satisfied the common law definition of a brothel: an establishment at which two or more persons were offering sexual services. The Divisional Court had to consider whether the magistrates had been right.

It was held that the magistrates had been wrong, because the hearsay rule did not apply. The relevant issue, because of the common law definition of a brothel, was whether the women had made these offers. The police officers had been entitled to give evidence of them.

The key to understanding this decision lies in the concept of performative language. The women who told the men that they could have 'hand relief' for £6 and 'topless hand relief' for £10 were not concerned simply to describe the way things were in the world at Wanstead. Their overriding interest was not to *describe* offers of sexual services, but to *make* them. Having made the offers, they changed the way things were in the world, because what they said had the legal effect of turning the sauna into a brothel.

HEARSAY AS A RULE OF USE

A question of hearsay arises only when the words spoken are adduced in evidence in order to establish some fact *narrated* or *described* by them. This was emphasised by the Privy Council in *Ratten v The Queen*.[26] The defendant was charged with the murder of his wife by shooting. It was clear that her death had been caused by a wound from a shotgun held by him. But his defence was that the gun had gone off accidentally while he was cleaning it. His evidence was that he had immediately telephoned for an ambulance and that shortly afterwards the police had telephoned him, whereupon he had asked them to come at once. *He denied that any telephone call had been made by his wife.* To rebut his account the prosecution were allowed to call evidence from a telephonist on the local exchange concerning a call made from the house at about 1.15 pm. Other evidence showed that the shooting took place no later than about 1.20 pm.

The telephonist's evidence was to the effect that she had heard a hysterical woman's voice say, 'Get me the police please'. On appeal it was argued that

---

26   [1972] AC 378; *Sourcebook*, p 101.

this evidence was hearsay; in the opinion of the Privy Council it was not. It was evidence that a telephone call *had* been made by the deceased. The telephonist's evidence also showed that the deceased had been at that time in a state of emotion or fear. This fact explained the making of the call. It was argued that this evidence amounted to an assertion by the deceased that she was being attacked by the accused, but the Privy Council rejected that, saying that there was no hearsay element in the evidence. From the fact that the woman's voice had been sobbing and hysterical and the fact that she had said 'Get me the police please', the jury were entitled to infer, if they thought fit, that the caller had been in a state of emotion or fear as the result of some existing or impending emergency. In the absence of any explanation from the defendant, it was for the jury to decide what light, if any, that threw on the situation at the time.

On the *R v Sharp*[27] definition of the hearsay rule this appears to have been correct. What had been uttered by the woman had involved not an assertion but a request, or perhaps something more appropriately described as a cry. A cry cannot be called a *description* because it is more primitive than any description, and words, such as 'I am afraid' or 'Get me the police please' may approximate more or less to a cry.[28]

The question whether written words were relied on as assertions, so as to be caught by the hearsay rule, or relied on in some other way, so as to be admissible, arose in *R v Rice*.[29] Rice and another man called Moore were convicted on two counts of conspiracy to steal motor cars and to obtain log books by false pretences. The case for the Crown was supported by a mass of evidence. Amongst other things, it was alleged that in furtherance of the conspiracy, Rice had made a journey to Manchester by air. At the trial, evidential problems arose in connection with an airline ticket that was produced to prove this. The trial judge's treatment of the ticket was later the basis of Rice's unsuccessful appeal against conviction. The ticket was for two seats on a flight from London to Manchester in the names of 'Rice' and 'Moore' for 10 May 1961. The ticket was produced by an airline representative whose job it was to deal with flight tickets returned after use. It was produced from the file where tickets used by passengers would in the 'ordinary course' be found. Rice said he had never flown to Manchester and knew nothing of the ticket or how it had come to be booked.

The Court of Criminal Appeal held that the ticket (besides being obviously relevant) was admissible, because an airline ticket which has been used on a flight and which has a name on it has more likely than not been used by a man of that name, or by one of two men whose names are on it. On the other

---

27 (1988) 86 Cr App R 274.

28 Cf Wittgenstein, L, *Philosophical Investigations*, trans Anscombe, GEM, 3rd edn, 1967, Part II, p 189.

29 [1963] 1 QB 857; *Sourcebook*, p 99.

hand, the court said that the document could not be treated as 'speaking its contents', for what it might say could only be hearsay. The ticket could not be treated as saying 'I was issued to Rice and Moore'.

This appears to be a fine distinction, but the result can be defended in another way. The ticket involved a written utterance, but its main point was not to provide a narrative about the persons to whom the ticket had been issued. The main purpose of creating the ticket was to provide a *licence* to its holders to be where otherwise they would have been trespassers, namely, on the aeroplane. As a licence it amounted to a legal act. In other words, it was a *performative utterance* from which it was legitimate, as the law then stood, to infer another fact – the use of the ticket by a person whose name appeared on it.

The use of the ticket in this way depended, of course, on one of its identifying features – the names written on it – and it is useful to compare *R v Rice* with other cases where identifying features have been held to infringe the rule against hearsay in order to highlight the difference between performative utterances and mere assertions.

In *Patel v Comptroller of Customs*,[30] the defendant was convicted of making a false declaration in a customs import document. The case against him was that, in respect of five bags of coriander seed, he had declared their country of origin to be India when in fact they had come from Morocco. The evidence that the coriander had come from Morocco consisted of labels on interior bags which stated 'produce of Morocco'. The Privy Council held that this was hearsay evidence and inadmissible to prove the country of origin.[31] In *R v Brown*,[32] the Court of Appeal held that the rule against hearsay was similarly infringed where the prosecution had relied on the names of hospital patients on shoes to establish the identity of the owners of the shoes.

In both cases the only purpose of putting the words on the articles had been to assert the truth of what was stated – in *Patel v Comptroller of Customs* the purpose had been to assert the country of origin of the coriander seed, and in *R v Brown* the purpose had been to assert ownership of the shoes. In these cases the rule against hearsay had clearly been infringed. The difference between these cases and *R v Rice* is that in the latter case the reason the ticket came into existence was not to provide a narrative or description, but to change the way things were in the world by granting a licence.

A performative utterance is only one example of an utterance that is outside the (direct) scope of the hearsay rule. Another example occurs where the *interest* shown by a party in an utterance is probative, regardless of the

---

30 [1965] AC 356.

31 See also *Comptroller of Customs v Western Lectric Co Ltd* [1966] AC 367.

32 [1991] Crim LR 835.

truth (if any) of what was uttered. This appears from *R v Lydon*.[33] In 1985, a robbery, carried out by two men, took place at a post office in Oxfordshire. The question was whether Lydon had been one of the robbers. There was substantial identification evidence, but the Crown also relied on the discovery, about a mile from the scene of the robbery, of a gun on a grass verge by the edge of the road used by the getaway car. The gun was in four pieces. Immediately in the vicinity two pieces of rolled up paper were found which had written on them, 'Sean rules' and 'Sean rules 85'. The defendant's first name was Sean. On an inside surface of the broken gun barrel, there was a heavy smear of blue ink, which expert witnesses said was similar to that on the pieces of paper, so that the ink could have originated from the same pen.

It was argued for the defendant that the references to 'Sean' were hearsay, but the trial judge admitted the evidence. The Court of Appeal held that he had been right to do so. The writing was relevant *not as an assertion of the state of facts expressed by the words but as itself a fact providing circumstantial evidence* upon the basis of which the jury might reach relevant conclusions. Here the conclusions they were invited to reach were that the paper had been in the possession of someone wishing to write 'Sean rules', and that that person was someone either named Sean himself or associated with a person of that name.

This appears to be right. If 'Sean rules' was an assertion at all, it was not one that had any relevance, even indirect, to the issues raised by those proceedings.

Similar reasoning can be found in *R v McIntosh*[34] In that case, the defendant was charged with being concerned in the importation of cocaine. At a house where he had been living before his arrest, police found hidden in the chimney a piece of paper on which were written calculations of the price and weight of a quantity of drugs. The handwriting was *not* that of the defendant. The Court of Appeal held that this was admissible evidence for the prosecution. The document was not admitted for the truth of its contents, but it nevertheless had probative value because its possession by the defendant showed that he had an interest in the information contained in it. This fact was relevant because it tended to strengthen the prosecution case that he had been involved in dealings involving drug importation.[35]

IMPLIED ASSERTIONS AS HEARSAY

In *Ratten v The Queen, R v Rice, R v Lydon* and *R v McIntosh* we can see a pattern of cases emerging where an utterance was not a direct assertion of

---

33   (1987) 85 Cr App R 221; *Sourcebook*, p 104.
34   [1992] Crim LR 651. Cf *R v Balogun* [1997] Crim LR 500.
35   See also *Roberts v DPP* [1994] Crim LR 926.

anything at issue in the criminal proceedings, but was seen as *circumstantial evidence from which inferences could be drawn that were relevant to matters in issue.* However, the question has arisen whether what can be inferred from reported, non-assertive utterances should also be caught by the rule against hearsay. The argument that it should be caught is that whether the reported utterance is assertive or not, it will still have generally been made by someone who is not available to the court. The device for bringing such utterances within the scope of the hearsay rule is the concept of 'implied assertion'. Here is a simple example: if from my office I hear someone shout, 'Shut that window!' I am likely to infer that the speaker *believes* that there is an open window nearby, and thus that there *is* an open window nearby. On the analysis under discussion, the command 'Shut that window!' is an implied assertion that there is a window open nearby.

When the House of Lords decided *R v Kearley*,[36] they took the same line as the Court of Appeal in the earlier case of *R v Harry*.[37] But as their main authority the Lords relied on a much earlier decision of the Court of Exchequer Chamber in *Wright v Doe d Tatham*[38] and, in particular, on the judgment of Parke B in that case. To understand this recent development, we need to look at all three cases.

In *R v Harry*,[39] the accused was charged with the possession and supply of drugs. The case for the prosecution was that he and his co-defendant, a man called Parmar, had been in joint possession of a quantity of cocaine from which either could draw at will. Parmar had rented a flat in Chelsea and one afternoon had been present there with the accused, a third man and a woman. Early in the evening a disturbance of some kind arose, and a neighbour telephoned the police to complain. In due course some police arrived. Their visit might have been uneventful, but for the fact that while they were there the third man jumped out of the window.

Since the flat was on the fourth floor, the police wanted to find out what might have led to this behaviour. It then emerged that Parmar and his guests had been taking cocaine. The flat was searched. Various items were found, including 53 g of cocaine hidden in a lavatory brush holder in the bathroom. This was said by the prosecution to be part of a pool of drugs possessed by both Parmar and Harry, from which Harry had supplied at least one other person. Harry's case was that he had not had anything to do with such a large quantity of drugs. He admitted taking cocaine and providing small amounts for his friends, but he insisted that it was Parmar who was the big dealer.

---

36 [1992] 2 AC 228; *Sourcebook*, p 113.
37 (1988) 86 Cr App R 105; *Sourcebook*, p 107.
38 (1837) 7 A&E 313; *Sourcebook*, p 109.
39 (1988) 86 Cr App R 105; *Sourcebook*, p 107.

After Parmar and Harry had been arrested, some police officers stayed in the flat that night and the next evening to carry out further investigations. While they were there, they received about 20 telephone calls from would-be purchasers of drugs, none of whom asked for Harry and many of whom asked for Parmar. The prosecution did not rely on this evidence at trial. But counsel for Harry was anxious to elicit it from the officers in cross-examination in order to support his client's claim that it was Parmar who was the big dealer. The trial judge allowed counsel for Harry to ask the police if they had received any telephone calls while in the flat, and whether any of those calls had been for Harry. But beyond that he was not permitted to go, and this ruling formed the basis for Harry's appeal after he was convicted of the offences involving the large amount of cocaine.

The Court of Appeal dismissed the appeal. They thought it was a borderline case, but decided against the appellant for the following reasons. It was common ground that the flat was being used for dealing. Both prosecution and defence accepted that. The live issue for Harry was *who* was doing the dealing. The only benefit he could get from evidence of the calls was by reference to their contents, most of which referred to Parmar. He was therefore relying on the contents of the telephone calls to establish that it was his co-accused and not himself who was doing the drug dealing on the premises. In other words, he was proposing to rely on the words 'testimonially', to use Lord Wilberforce's expression in *Ratten v The Queen*.[40] The evidence that Harry's counsel had wanted to adduce was thus inadmissible hearsay.

In fact the judgment does not get to grips with the implied assertion point. The crucial question in *R v Harry* was whether what was said by the telephone callers could properly be described as assertions. The report does not go into detail, but it is clear that some at least of the utterances overheard were non-assertive. In Lawton LJ's words, 'the inquirers were asking questions, the effect of which was that they wanted to know whether any cocaine or other drugs were available for sale'. The court seems to have *assumed* that questions could operate as narratives. Perhaps the point was not argued, but it was certainly there to be taken.

In *Wright v Doe d Tatham*,[41] the court was concerned with the testamentary capacity of a man named Marsden. In order to help establish testamentary capacity, counsel for those trying to support the validity of Marsden's will wanted to produce in evidence some letters that had been written to Marsden during his life. These letters were written in terms suggesting that the writers

---

40 [1972] AC 378, p 387. 'Words spoken are facts just as much as any other action by a human being. If the speaking of the words is a relevant fact, a witness may give evidence that they were spoken. A question of hearsay only arises when the words spoken are relied on "testimonially", ie, as establishing some fact narrated by the words.'

41 (1837) 7 A&E 313; *Sourcebook*, p 109.

believed Marsden to be sane and capable of managing his own affairs. For example, one of the correspondents had written asking Marsden to carry out certain business transactions for him.

The Court of Exchequer Chamber held that these letters had been rightly excluded. The point is clearly made in the judgment of Parke B, which was later relied on in *R v Kearley*. His view was that the contents of the letters were not admissible to prove the facts in issue in the litigation in question. He acknowledged that, *by implication*, they stated that Marsden possessed qualities relevant to testamentary capacity, but they were to be treated on the same footing as if they had contained *direct and positive statements* to that effect. For the purpose of establishing Marsden's testamentary capacity, they were mere hearsay because they were statements of the writers, not on oath, of the truth of the matter in question.

Because of the form the argument for admissibility had taken, Parke B went on to consider whether evidence of *actions* might be admissible as a way of avoiding the rule against hearsay. He was firmly of the opinion that evidence of actions could be caught as much as evidence of statements. Evidence that a doctor had allowed a will to be executed by a sick testator would be inadmissible to establish the testator's testamentary capacity; evidence from the doctor at trial would be needed. And, in a famous illustration, Parke B invented a situation where the fact in issue was the seaworthiness of a ship. Suppose the deceased captain had first examined every part of the vessel and only then had embarked in it with his family? Such evidence would be caught also. He concluded that 'proof of a particular fact, which is not of itself a matter in issue, but which is relevant only as implying a statement or opinion of a third person on the matter in issue, is inadmissible in all cases where such a statement or opinion not on oath would be of itself inadmissible ...'.[42]

In *R v Kearley*, drugs had been discovered on the accused's premises. He was charged, amongst other things, with possessing them with intent to supply. In the hours following his arrest, police officers remaining at his house while he was at the police station answered 15 telephone calls. Ten of those calls were for the accused and were made by persons who asked for drugs. According to the police, there were also nine persons who called at the premises asking for the accused, seven of whom indicated that they wished to buy drugs. At trial, the police officers were allowed to give evidence of all the calls, including evidence of what had been said by the callers. With one irrelevant exception, the callers did not give evidence. The question for the House of Lords was whether that police evidence should have been given.[43] It

---

42 (1837) 7 A&E 313, pp 388–89.
43 The words had not been spoken in the presence of the defendant; if they had, both the words and the defendant's reactions might have been admissible: see below, Chapter 9.

was accepted that the purpose of adducing the evidence had not been to establish the truth of any fact narrated by the words. Instead, the purpose had been to invite the jury to infer from the fact that the words were uttered that the accused had been supplying drugs.

A majority of the House of Lords held that the evidence should not have been admitted because it was caught by the hearsay rule. 'Implied' assertions can be caught just as much as express assertions. Another reason given was that the evidence had been irrelevant. What the callers said had shown their intention to buy, but not the accused's intention to sell. The conclusive answer to this latter argument can be found in the dissenting speech of Lord Griffiths:

> It is of course true that it is almost certain that the customers did believe that they could obtain drugs from the appellant, otherwise they would not have telephoned or visited his premises. But why did all these people believe they could obtain drugs from the appellant? The obvious inference is that the appellant had established a market as a drug dealer ...[44]

The Law Commission has noted that the principal difficulties with implied assertions are practical: it is hard to recognise them, and the application of the rule leads to the exclusion of cogent evidence.[45] Further, the Commission thought that the concept of 'implied assertion' was misleading in at least two ways:

(a) It assumes that the words or conduct in question do, somehow, constitute an assertion of the fact that they are adduced to prove. But it is arguable that they do not amount to an assertion at all, and are instead directly probative, in which case they should not be caught by the hearsay rule.

(b) 'Implied' is used in an unusual sense. Normally it refers to an assertion that is not made expressly, but is *intended by the speaker or agent* to be understood from what is said or done. But in the context of hearsay it is used quite differently in relation to utterances or actions where there may be no such intention, but where what is referred to is an *inference drawn by the hearer or observer*.

In the view of the Law Commission, the crucial question is not whether any particular kind of assertion should be excluded from the ambit of the hearsay rule, but whether words or conduct not *intended* to assert a fact should be treated, for the purposes of the rule, as amounting to an assertion of that fact at all.[46]

An important object of the hearsay rule is to exclude evidence where there is a substantial risk of fabrication. It follows that the rule should extend to any conduct by a person (an 'agent') that is *intended* to give the impression that a particular fact is true. But if the agent did not intend that anyone should infer

---

44 [1992] 2 AC 228, p 238.
45 Law Com No 245 (1997), paras 4.19–4.25.
46 *Ibid*, para 7.17.

that fact, then he cannot have been trying to mislead anyone about it. If he cannot have been trying to mislead anyone, a court ought not to be prevented from inferring the existence of a fact merely because the agent may have been mistaken in believing it.[47]

So an agent's words or conduct should not be regarded as asserting a fact, and therefore should not be caught by the hearsay rule if adduced as evidence of that fact, unless the agent intended to assert that fact. An intention to assert a fact should be understood as an intention to convey the impression that the fact now sought to be inferred from the words or conduct was true.[48] Only if the agent did not intend to convey that impression can it be safely assumed that he was not deliberately trying to mislead. The form of words used is not important. What matters is the impression the words or conduct were intended to convey. Did the agent intend to cause someone else to believe that the fact in question was true?[49]

There may be cases where a statement is fabricated without the intention of making someone believe that it is true, but where there is merely an intention that someone should act on the basis that it is true. For example, a clerk handling claims for expenses may be concerned only to see that the right procedure has been followed and may have no belief, one way or another, about the contents of any statements provided as part of the claim. The hearsay rule should therefore also apply where a statement is made with the intention that some action should be taken on the basis of the truth of the fact stated, including cases where a machine is caused to operate by 'feeding' it with information.[50]

Finally, the Law Commission argued that a distinction should be drawn between 'purpose' and 'intention'. 'Purpose' refers to the objective that an agent hopes to achieve by acting as he does. 'Intention' can refer to this, but it can refer also to consequences that an agent may not wish to bring about, but which he knows to be an inevitable side effect of what he desires. If we were to include within the hearsay rule the case where an agent knows that a particular inference *will* be drawn, even though that may not be what he wishes to bring about, it is hard to see why the rule should not extend to cover cases where an agent knows that a particular inference *may* be drawn. For the purposes of the rule against hearsay, the most defensible place to draw the line is between those consequences that it is the agent's *purpose* to bring about, and those that it is not.[51]

---

47 Law Com No 245 (1997), para 7.20.
48 Cf Dummett, *op cit*, fn 17.
49 Law Com No 245 (1997), paras 7.25–7.32.
50 *Ibid*, paras 7.33–7.35.
51 *Ibid*, paras 7.36–7.38.

In the light of these conclusions, the Law Commission has recommended:

(1) that (subject to exceptions) in criminal proceedings a statement not made in oral evidence in the proceedings should not be admissible as evidence of any matter stated; and

(2) a matter should be regarded as stated in a statement if (and only if) the purpose, or one of the purposes, of the person making the statement appears to the court to have been:

    (a) to cause another person to believe the matter; or

    (b) to cause another person to act, or a machine to operate, on the basis that the matter is as stated.[52]

The House of Lords provided no definition of 'implied hearsay', but the judgment of Parke B in *Wright v Doe d Tatham* is an obvious starting point. However, that case was concerned only with non-assertive verbal utterances, and the same was the case in *R v Kearley*. There is no need to defy common sense more than we are bound to and it ought not to be assumed that what Parke B said, *obiter*, about hearsay by *conduct*, that is, non-verbal behaviour like that of the imaginary sea captain, is good law. It can therefore tentatively be suggested that an argument based on implied hearsay operates in the following way (where 'p' stands for any proposition):

(a) A speaker (S) made a non-assertive out-of-court utterance (NA).

(b) S would not have made NA if he had not believed that p.

(c) S believed that p.

(d) Therefore it is likely that p.

Example:

(a) Richard asked Miranda if she had any Russian Blue kittens for sale.

(b) Richard would not have asked Miranda this if he had not believed that she was a breeder of Russian Blue cats (and so likely to have kittens for sale).

(c) Therefore Richard believed that Miranda was a breeder of Russian Blue cats.

(d) Therefore it is likely that Miranda *was* a breeder of Russian Blue cats.

This can be contrasted with the pattern of argument involved in 'straightforward' hearsay:

(a) A speaker (S) made an out-of-court *assertive* utterance that p.

(b) S believed that p.

(c) Therefore it is likely that p.

---

52 Law Com No 245 (1997), para 7.40.

Example:

(a) Richard said that Miranda was a breeder of Russian Blue cats.

(b) Therefore Richard believed that Miranda was a breeder of Russian Blue cats.

(c) Therefore it is likely that Miranda *was* a breeder of Russian Blue cats.

With this suggested analysis of the pattern of argument involved in implied hearsay, we can review some of the cases dealt with under the last section to see how they might fare today.

In *Ratten v The Queen*,[53] the relevant non-assertive utterance was: 'Get me the police please.' It was said to be possible from that utterance to infer that the speaker was at that time in a state of emotion or fear as the result of some existing or impending emergency. It is very likely that belief in the existence of just such a situation led to the utterance. The implied hearsay pattern of argument was exactly reproduced and, subject to any relevant hearsay exceptions, evidence of what the speaker said would not now be admissible, although the fact that the telephone operator had been contacted from that number would remain admissible.

In *R v Rice*,[54] for the reasons given above, the ticket amounted to a performative utterance. It was thus the equivalent of an *act*. On that analysis, the first step in the implied hearsay pattern of argument is missing and the ticket would be admissible today for the same purpose as was allowed by the Court of Criminal Appeal.

This assumes that Parke B's *obiter dicta* would not be followed. If, following Parke B, there *can* be hearsay by conduct, the question arises whether the airline company would have issued the ticket had it not believed that a man named Rice or Moore would be on the flight in question. It seems most likely that it *would* have issued the ticket without any such belief. What almost certainly led the airline to issue the ticket was the belief that somebody (his name did not matter) had paid the correct price. On this analysis, the implied hearsay argument falls at the second stage and the ticket would still be admissible today.

In *R v Lydon*,[55] the writing was an assertive utterance that was not adduced to prove the truth of its contents. It would be admissible on the general principle that requires the assertion to be adduced in order to establish the truth of its contents before the hearsay rule can apply.[56]

---

53 [1972] AC 378; *Sourcebook*, p 101.

54 [1963] 1 QB 857; *Sourcebook*, p 99.

55 (1987) 85 Cr App R 221; *Sourcebook*, p 104.

56 It could also be argued that people are more likely to have in their possession a piece of paper or other article that has their name on, rather than the name of some other person. This was essentially the argument of the Court of Appeal in *R v Rice*.

It is unclear whether the utterances on the paper in *R v McIntosh*[57] were of an assertive or non-assertive kind. If they were assertions, the problem is readily solved: they were not being adduced to prove the truth of their contents but to prove something about the state of mind of the person in whose possession the paper was found. The question of hearsay would not arise. If the utterances were non-assertive, the question would then be whether they would have been made if the writer had not believed that the defendant would be interested in them. If we look at the utterances alone, apart from the circumstances in which the paper was found, there appears to have been nothing to suggest this. The document was quite unlike those with which the court was concerned in *Wright v Doe d Tatham*,[58] for those were letters *addressed to Marsden*. On this analysis, the implied hearsay argument would break down at the second stage. The hearsay rule would not apply and the evidence would still be admissible.

EVIDENCE PRODUCED BY MACHINES[59]

The hearsay rule does not exclude tapes, films or still photographs that have *directly* recorded an incident under investigation as it actually took place. So, for example, in *R v Dodson*,[60] film from a security camera that had been operating during a robbery was admitted in evidence. In *Taylor v Chief Constable of Cheshire*,[61] witnesses who had watched a video recording of an offence during its commission were allowed to give evidence of what they had seen where the tape itself had been accidentally erased; the court took the view that they had been in exactly the same position as someone watching the commission of a crime through a pair of binoculars.

The hearsay rule does not apply to documents produced by machines that automatically record some process or event, such as a print-out from a computer recording telephone calls made from a given number,[62] or from an Intoximeter recording the level of alcohol in breath.[63] Nor are readings from a machine that simply carries out arithmetical procedures caught by the hearsay rule.[64] In none of these cases was the court being asked to accept the truth of

---

57 [1992] Crim LR 651.
58 (1837) 7 A&E 313; *Sourcebook*, p 109.
59 Law Com No 245 (1997), paras 7.42–7.50. See also below, Chapter 17.
60 (1984) 79 Cr App R 220.
61 [1987] 1 WLR 80.
62 *R v Spiby* (1990) 91 Cr App R 186.
63 *Castle v Cross* [1984] 1 WLR 1372. In *Owens v Chesters* (1985) 149 JP 235, the machine reading was held to be outside the hearsay rule, and so was the oral evidence of the officer as to what the reading had been.
64 *R v Wood* (1982) 76 Cr App R 23.

an assertion made by a *person*, so the hearsay rule was inapplicable. It makes no sense to insist on rules devised to cater for human beings where humans have been replaced by machines.[65]

The position is different, however, where there has been some human intervention in the process: for example, where an employee has previously compiled records and someone else has transferred them to a computer. Thus, in *R v Coventry JJ ex p Bullard*,[66] a computer print-out stating that a person was in arrears with his poll tax was held to be inadmissible hearsay because it must have been based on information fed into the computer by a person, which had not been properly proved. The Law Commission has recommended that this distinction should continue to be observed, and that where a representation of any fact is made otherwise than by a person, but depends for its accuracy on information supplied by a person, it should not be admissible as evidence of the fact unless it is proved that the information was accurate.[67]

NEGATIVE HEARSAY[68]

Sometimes a party, usually the prosecution in a criminal case, will wish to prove that an event did *not* occur. The only way practically to do this may be to examine records to see if there is an appropriate entry to show that the event occurred and, in the absence of such an entry, to infer that it did not. There is somewhat unsatisfactory authority that in certain circumstances such an inference may be made without being 'negative hearsay' – an infringement of the hearsay rule to establish a negative rather than a positive fact.

In *R v Patel*,[69] the prosecution had to prove that a man named Ashraf was an illegal immigrant. It called an immigration officer to say that Ashraf's name did not appear in Home Office records and that it could be inferred from this that he was an illegal immigrant. The Court of Appeal held this evidence to be hearsay. But Bristow J said that if an officer with personal knowledge of the compilation and custody of the records had been called, he could have given non-hearsay evidence of the absence of the name and its significance.

---

65 Cf *The Statue of Liberty* [1968] 2 All ER 195, p 196, *per* Sir Jocelyn Simon P: 'The law is bound these days to take cognisance of the fact that mechanical means replace human effort.'

66 (1992) 95 Cr App R 175.

67 Law Com No 245 (1997), para 7.50.

68 *Ibid*, paras 7.10–7.12.

69 [1981] 3 All ER 94.

This approach was followed in *R v Shone*.[70] In that case, a stock clerk and sales manager were called to give evidence that entries would have been made on record cards if certain vehicle parts had been properly disposed of rather than stolen, that there were no such entries, and that the parts had therefore been stolen. The Court of Appeal held this evidence to be not hearsay but 'direct evidence' of those matters.

Thus, although an inference as to facts in issue may not be drawn from a document because that would be hearsay,[71] an inference may be drawn from the non-existence of a document or entry, because that is 'direct evidence'. Some people might think this bizarre. They would be right.

THE RULE IGNORED

In *Myers v DPP*,[72] the House of Lords held that it was not permissible for judges to create new common law exceptions to the hearsay rule even where the reliability of the evidence seemed secure: that power lay with Parliament alone. The courts, for reasons of convenience, have nevertheless sometimes ignored the problem.[73] This is apparent, for example, from the rules that have developed about allowing witnesses to 'refresh their memories' when giving evidence;[74] from the evidential status of 'mixed' statements made by accused persons to the police;[75] from the rules relating to expert opinion evidence;[76] and from various decisions about identification evidence.[77]

A case in which the rule against hearsay was evaded rather than ignored was *R v Ward*,[78] in which it was held that evidence tending to confirm the defendant's presence near the scene of the crime, but which was *prima facie* hearsay, might nevertheless be admissible on the basis, apparently, of the weight of the evidence. The defendant had been charged with conspiracy to steal. On three occasions, and in relation to two cars, a passenger in a car gave his name as 'Michael Kevin Ward', the defendant's full name, when the car was stopped and passengers were asked to identify themselves. The passenger also gave a date of birth and an address which were those of Ward. Objection was taken to the admissibility of these answers on the basis that

---

70 (1983) 76 Cr App R 72.
71 *Wright v Doe d Tatham* (1837) 7 A&E 313; *Sourcebook*, p 109.
72 [1965] AC 1001.
73 See generally Ashworth, J and Pattenden, R, 'Reliability, hearsay evidence and the English criminal trial' (1986) 102 LQR 292.
74 See above, Chapter 4, p 83.
75 See above, Chapter 4, p 89.
76 See below, Chapter 12.
77 See below, Chapter 8.
78 [2001] Crim LR 316.

they were hearsay. The Court of Appeal said that that difficulty could not be overcome by arguing that the purpose of admitting the statements was to prove that they had been made. The evidence was clearly relied on to prove that Ward was in the cars at the relevant times. The court then considered the possibility of admitting the evidence as admissions.[79] A problem with this, as the court recognised, was that the argument for admissibility assumed the very thing that had to be proved. To establish that Ward had made an admission, it was necessary to rely on the very evidence that was in dispute because of the hearsay rule. What was said was inadmissible unless it could be shown by some independent evidence that the speaker was Ward, and there was no independent evidence. But the Court of Appeal found an answer in the quality of the evidence. If a man gave his full name, a date of birth which was that of the person with the full name, and an address which was also that of the person with that name, the evidence was strong enough to establish an admission.

JUSTIFICATIONS FOR THE RULE

Several justifications have traditionally been given.[80]

Hearsay is not the best evidence[81]

According to this objection, hearsay is inferior to direct evidence and should therefore be inadmissible in criminal proceedings. In many cases this is a persuasive argument, but in some cases hearsay will be the best evidence *available*, and in some cases hearsay may actually be more reliable than direct evidence. An example of the latter situation occurred in *Myers v DPP*,[82] where a contemporaneous record made by workers in a motor car factory of cylinder block and chassis numbers was held to be inadmissible hearsay. Even if it had been possible to trace the workers who had stamped the parts with numbers and then recorded them, their recollection several years later of parts and numbers must have been non-existent.

---

79 An admission in a criminal case is generally referred to as a confession and is admissible as an exception to the rule against hearsay under s 76(1) of the Police and Criminal Evidence Act 1984. See Chapter 9, below.

80 See, eg, *Teper v R* [1952] AC 480, p 486, *per* Lord Normand.

81 Law Com No 245 (1997), paras 3.2–3.4.

82 [1965] AC 1001.

Hearsay evidence would be easy to invent[83]

In *R v Kearley*,[84] one of Lord Ackner's reasons for excluding evidence of the telephone calls was that evidence of that kind could be easily invented by the police. It would, of course, be equally open to a defendant to manufacture hearsay statements with a view to creating a reasonable doubt about the prosecution case. The risk of manufacture does increase if the original source of information is unavailable for cross-examination. However, the Law Commission has suggested that this risk could be reduced by limiting new exceptions to the rule to first hand hearsay, by imposing requirements for admissibility such as giving advance notice of any hearsay evidence, and by the exclusion of the hearsay evidence of unidentified witnesses. 'First hand' hearsay evidence is hearsay at one remove from the original speaker. For example, A makes an assertion to B, who then wishes to repeat it in court to establish the truth of what A asserted. 'Multiple' hearsay occurs when the evidence is at more than one remove from the original speaker. For example, A makes an assertion to B, who reports it to C. C then wishes to repeat it in court to establish the truth of what A originally asserted. (Multiple hearsay is sometimes referred to by the number of removes from the original speaker: second hand hearsay, third hand hearsay, and so on.)

The risk of errors in transmission[85]

Someone who reports the words of another person may have misheard or misinterpreted them. But the existing hearsay rule can exclude statements, such as those in letters or tape-recordings, where there may be no doubt about what was said. The Law Commission's view is that this is an objection to multiple hearsay only.

The demeanour of the original source is lost[86]

The appearance and unconscious behaviour of a witness while giving evidence have traditionally been thought to help in assessing the weight of his testimony. Today, when 'body language' has assumed the kind of significance formerly attached to phrenology or numerology, this opinion may still be widely held. But some persons, including some judges, have disagreed, and psychological research suggests that they are right. It seems that demeanour is an unreliable guide to sincerity and is even more unreliable in relation to accuracy.

---

83   Law Com No 245 (1997), paras 3.5–3.8.
84   [1992] 2 AC 228; *Sourcebook*, p 113.
85   Law Com No 245 (1997), paras 3.5–3.8.
86   *Ibid*, paras 3.9–3.12.

Hearsay statements are not on oath[87]

Historically, this was the main reason for rejecting hearsay evidence, but it seems improbable that nowadays an oath is any guarantee that the witness will tell the truth. It is more to the point that people are likely to be less careful about the accuracy of what they say in private conversations than in court, where they can be cross-examined publicly.

The absence of cross-examination[88]

The fact that the maker of the original statement cannot be cross-examined is the chief objection today to the admission of hearsay evidence. It depends on an assumption that the weaknesses in such evidence will not be apparent to juries or magistrates in the absence of cross-examination. Since almost no research has been done into the ways in which juries or magistrates assess evidence, the assumption is difficult to accept or reject.

There are four potential defects in direct (non-hearsay) testimony which cross-examination may be able to expose:

(a) insincerity – the witness may be lying;

(b) ambiguity – the testimony may be unclear and so misunderstood;

(c) faulty perception – the witness may be honest but mistaken; and

(d) faulty memory – the witness may no longer accurately recall what he perceived.

If a witness (W) purports to repeat in court what he has been told about an event by an out-of-court speaker (S), the possible sources of error are doubled. Either W or S could be lying. S's original statement may have been misunderstood by W and/or W may himself give unclear testimony. S may have been mistaken in what he thought he saw. W may be mistaken in what he thought S said. The memories of both W and S may be at fault.[89]

But in cases where the witness's truthfulness and accuracy of observation are not in issue, and where there is no ambiguity, little can be gained from

---

87 Law Com No 245 (1997), paras 3.13–3.14.

88 *Ibid*, paras 3.15–3.18.

89 Where W purports to narrate in court a non-hearsay statement made by S to W – ie, a statement whose relevance depends not on the fact that it is true, but only on the fact that it was made – the possible sources of error are not doubled. Since the court is not concerned with the truth of what S said to W, questions about S's sincerity, perception and memory do not arise. Only ambiguity remains as a possible source of error. See, generally, Tribe, LH, 'Triangulating hearsay' (1974) 87 Harv LR 957; Choo, *op cit*, fn 1, Chapter 2.

cross-examination.[90] The Law Commission's view is that absence of cross-examination does not justify the *whole* of the present rule.

The defendant's right of confrontation[91]

Although not part of the common law, there is a view that it is fundamental to justice that an accused person should be able to confront the witnesses who accuse him, and that to bring the witness and the accused together makes the accused and the public feel that justice is being done.[92] The Law Commission's view is that, although it is desirable that witnesses should give their evidence in the presence of the accused if possible, other factors, such as the impossibility of obtaining evidence directly from a witness in court, may outweigh this consideration.

---

90 And although cross-examination may be effective in exposing faulty perception or memory, or ambiguity in narration, it is less likely to be effective at exposing insincerity (Choo, *op cit*, fn 1, pp 32–33).

91 Law Com No 245 (1997), paras 3.34–3.35; Friedman, RD, 'Thoughts from across the water on hearsay and confrontation' [1998] Crim LR 697.

92 See also Choo, *op cit*, fn 1, pp 37–42.

CHAPTER 7

HEARSAY EXCEPTIONS

COMMON LAW EXCEPTIONS

The common law developed a number of exceptions to the hearsay rule, several of which are now virtually obsolete. Since the Civil Evidence Act 1995 abolished the hearsay rule in civil proceedings, the common law exceptions are now of significance only in criminal cases. The main relevant exceptions are certain statements by deceased persons, statements admitted as 'part of the *res gestae*', and statements made in furtherance of a common purpose (for a complete list, see Law Com No 245 (1997), para 2.8).

STATEMENTS BY DECEASED PERSONS

There is no *general* exception at common law for the admissibility of statements by persons who have died since making them. To be admissible, the statement must fall into one of several categories developed by the courts during the 19th century or earlier. Of these, only two are likely to be of any significance: declarations against pecuniary or proprietary interest, and dying declarations in cases of murder or manslaughter.

Declarations against pecuniary or proprietary interest[1]

A declaration against pecuniary or proprietary interest by a person since deceased is admissible as evidence of the truth of its contents, subject to four conditions:[2]

(a) The deceased must have had a 'peculiar' (ie, particular or special) means of knowing the facts stated.

(b) The interest against which the declaration was made must be either pecuniary or proprietary. According to the old cases,[3] a declaration that was merely against what was called penal interest – a declaration that would expose the declarant to criminal penalties – was not enough. It is not clear what the position would be if admission of a criminal act would

---

1   See Stone, J and Wells, WAN, *Evidence: Its History and Policies*, 1991, pp 391–99.
2   *R v Rogers* [1995] 1 Cr App R 374, pp 378–80.
3   Eg, the *Sussex Peerage* case (1844) 11 Cl&Fin 85.

expose the declarant to civil as well as criminal proceedings, or what the effect of pecuniary penalties, awards of compensation, or forfeiture of property under the criminal law might be. The pecuniary or proprietary interest does not have to be a legal or even moral one. Even if the declaration was an admission of an obligation enforceable only by 'the strong arm tactics of the criminal fraternity', it would be enough.

(c) The declaration must be against the interest of the deceased at the time when it was made; that is, it must refer to a present obligation and not one arising in the future.

(d) The declarant must know that the declaration is against his interest.

A declaration against pecuniary or proprietary interest may be adduced to prove not only the truth of its contents, but the truth of other facts connected to it. But this will be the case only where the connected facts are necessary to explain the nature of the declaration. Two cases may be compared.

Higham v Ridgway[4] involved litigation concerning real property, in the course of which it became necessary to prove the date of birth of a man named William Fowden Junior who had died some years before the trial of the action. The question arose whether proof could be made by adducing as evidence entries in the records kept by a male midwife who had attended at the birth of the deceased. The entries showed the date when he had delivered the child. They also showed his fee, against which appeared the word 'paid'. The Court of King's Bench held that these entries constituted a declaration against the midwife's pecuniary interest, because by making them he had provided evidence that could have been used to defend any further claim for fees he might have made in respect of that occasion. In order to understand the word 'paid', it was necessary to look at all the entries to see what was the demand to which they referred. When that was done, the date of birth was incidentally revealed and the entries could be used to prove that as well as the fact of payment.

In *R v Rogers*,[5] the defendant was charged with possessing heroin with intent to supply. He had been arrested after visiting premises that were shortly afterwards found to have drugs hidden underneath the floorboards. The defence was that Rogers knew nothing of them. He said that they had been in the exclusive possession of a man called Law, who had since died. In support of his defence, Rogers called Law's widow and asked the judge to admit, under this exception to the hearsay rule, evidence of a statement made to her by Law about two weeks before he died. The gist of that statement was that some men were after him for the money for the heroin that the police had found, and that the defendant knew nothing about this source of supply.

---

4   (1808) 10 East 109; *Sourcebook*, p 137.
5   [1995] 1 Cr App R 374.

The Court of Appeal agreed with the trial judge that the deceased's words did not amount to a declaration against pecuniary interest because to say that someone is being pursued for money does not mean that he owes it. The court went on to say, however, that even if this did amount to a statement against pecuniary interest, the rest of the statement, to the effect that Rogers knew nothing of the drugs, would be inadmissible. Counsel for Rogers had argued that if the declaration itself was admissible it made admissible 'collateral' (that is, connected) evidence. In support, he had relied on *Higham v Ridgway*.[6] But the Court of Appeal distinguished that case on the basis that there the collateral matter (the date of birth of the child) had been necessary to explain the nature of the transaction indicated by the word 'paid'. The court said that collateral matters were admissible *only if necessary to explain the transaction in question*. In this case, it was plain that the heroin Law had been talking about was that seized by the police; there was no need of any further identification. Accordingly, even if Law's declaration that he was being pursued for money had amounted to a declaration against interest, the rest of what he said would have been inadmissible.

Dying declarations in cases of murder or manslaughter[7]

A declaration as to the circumstances of his death made by a declarant under a settled, hopeless expectation of death is admissible to prove the cause of death.[8] The reason for this exception was the belief that a settled, hopeless expectation of death would encourage truthfulness.

Such evidence will be admitted only 'where the death of the deceased is the subject of the charge'.[9] It is unclear whether a dying declaration would be admissible in a prosecution for causing death by dangerous driving as well as in cases of murder or manslaughter. Since, in such a case, death would be the subject of the charge, there seems to be in principle no reason why it should not, except unwillingness to extend an anachronism.

Any hope of recovery at the time when the declaration is made will make it inadmissible. In *R v Jenkins*,[10] a magistrates' clerk was present at the deathbed of a victim in order to take her statement. He prefaced it by writing words saying that it was made 'with no hope of my recovery'. The victim, trying no doubt to take a slightly more optimistic view of things, insisted that this be amended to read 'with no hope at present of my recovery'. The

---

6   (1808) 10 East 109; *Sourcebook*, p 137.
7   See Stone and Wells, *op cit*, fn 1, pp 421–25; Choo, AL-T, *Hearsay and Confrontation*, pp 106–12; Law Com No 138, paras 3.9–3.32.
8   *R v Woodcock* (1789) 1 Leach 500, p 502; *Mills v R* [1995] 3 All ER 865, p 875.
9   *R v Mead* (1824) 2 B&C 605, p 608, *per* Abbott CJ.
10   (1869) 20 LT 372.

statement was held inadmissible on the ground that the additional words suggested that the declarant did have some faint hope of recovery.

Problems of interpretation are likely to arise here, as elsewhere in evidence law. An example is *R v Perry*[11] where the deceased had said to a companion: 'Oh, Gert, I shall go, but keep this a secret. Let the worst come to the worst.' She then said what the defendant had done to her. The Court of Criminal Appeal, looking at the opening words as a whole, held that the victim's state of mind satisfied the conditions for a dying declaration. A recent example is *R v Lawson*.[12] The defendant was charged with the murder of his wife. The case for the prosecution was that he had started a fire in his flat, where his wife was confined to a wheelchair. After being rescued by the fire brigade, both she and her husband (who was suffering from smoke inhalation) were placed in an ambulance. Ambulance staff heard her say, 'You have really got me now,' and at the hospital she said, 'Murder, murder'. She was then sedated and she died several hours later. The trial judge held that the wife's words in the ambulance and at the hospital were admissible, among other reasons, as dying declarations. The Court of Appeal upheld this ruling.[13]

So long as the state of mind was the correct one at the time when the declaration was made, it does not matter if the victim developed hopes of recovery at some later stage.[14] Nor does it matter that the victim was expected to recover or was even told that he would recover – provided, of course, he did not believe what he was told.[15] The fact that death did not occur for some time is also irrelevant: in *R v Bernadotti*,[16] for example, the declarant lived for nearly three weeks after making the declaration, which was nevertheless held to be admissible.

The declarant must have been someone who would have been competent as a witness.[17] This requirement is now unlikely to present a difficulty. The dying declaration of a very young child will be problematic, not because of the rule about competence, but because it would be difficult to satisfy the court that such a declarant had a settled, hopeless expectation of death.

Occasionally, dying declarations may assist the defence: they are admissible even if partly adverse to the declarant. For example, in *R v Scaife*,[18] the deceased had said that the defendant 'would not have struck me but that I provoked him to it'. This was admitted.

---

11 [1909] 2 KB 697.

12 [1998] Crim LR 883.

13 But the courts appear reluctant to infer a settled, hopeless expectation of imminent death merely from the extent of the victim's injuries: see, eg, *R v Morgan* (1875) 14 Cox CC 337.

14 *R v Austin* (1912) 8 Cr App R 27.

15 *R v Mosley & Morrill* (1825) 1 Mood 97; *R v Peel* (1860) 2 F&F 21.

16 (1869) 11 Cox CC 316.

17 *R v Pike* (1829) 3 C&P 598.

18 (1836) 2 Lewin 150.

RES GESTAE STATEMENTS[19]

The Latin expression *'res gestae'* may be loosely translated as 'events occurring' or 'things happening'. If a statement is said to be part of the *res gestae*, what is meant is that it is an out-of-court statement so closely associated with the circumstances in which it was made that it is likely to be more reliable than other evidence of out-of-court statements, and so may safely be admitted. The psychology lying behind this notion may be suspect, but that, historically, is the rationale for this cluster of exceptions.[20] Having said that, it might be better to forget the rationale altogether and regard the four exceptions which are described under this head as standing independently. The reason for this is that it is often assumed that the 'excited utterance' conditions (see below) have somehow got to apply to the other three situations as well. This is not so.

Excited utterances

These are the spontaneous exclamations of the victim of an offence or of an observer. Most of the cases are about victims' utterances, but this exception is not confined to them. Earlier civil cases are still relevant for the interpretation of this exception and there are, for example, collision cases where the words came not from one of the parties to the litigation, but from a passenger or bystander.[21]

The leading case is *R v Andrews*,[22] in which the test for admissibility under this head was laid down by Lord Ackner. It is as follows:

(a) The primary question that the judge must ask is whether the possibility of concoction or distortion can be disregarded.

(b) To answer that question, the judge must first consider the circumstances in which the particular statement was made, in order to satisfy himself that the event was *so unusual, startling or dramatic* as to dominate the thoughts of the speaker to the extent that *his utterance was an instinctive reaction to that event*, giving no time for reasoned reflection. In such a situation, the judge would be entitled to conclude that the involvement or pressure of the event excluded the possibility of concoction or distortion, provided the statement was made in conditions of approximate contemporaneity.

---

19 See Stone [1939] 55 LQR 66, Nokes [1954] 70 LQR 370, Gooderson [1956] CLJ 199, [1957] CLJ 55, Ormerod [1998] Crim LR 301.

20 I have referred to *res gestae* statements as an exception to the hearsay rule because it is convenient to do so. There has been some dispute – unimportant for practical purposes – as to whether such statements amount to an exception or fall outside the rule altogether. The Law Commission has taken it as settled that the latter view is correct: Law Com No 138 (1995), para 3.38, n 78.

21 Stone and Wells, *op cit*, fn 1, p 381.

22 [1987] AC 281; *Sourcebook*, p 128.

(c) For the statement to be sufficiently spontaneous, it must be *so closely associated with the event that excited it* that the mind of the speaker was still dominated by that event. The fact that a statement was made in answer to a question is only a factor to be taken into consideration under this head.

(d) Quite apart from the time factor, there may be *special features* in the case that relate to the *possibility of concoction or distortion*: for example, the speaker may have had a motive for fabrication, such as malice. The judge must be satisfied that, having regard to any such special feature, there was no possibility of any concoction or distortion to the advantage of the speaker or the disadvantage of the defendant.

(e) The ordinary fallibility of human recollection goes to the *weight* to be attached to the statement by the jury, not to its *admissibility*. But there may be *special features* that give rise to the *possibility of error*: for example, where the original speaker has drunk to excess or where he made an identification in particularly difficult circumstances. If there are special features such as these, the judge must consider whether he can still exclude the possibility of error before admitting the evidence.

(f) Where the trial judge has properly directed himself as to the correct approach to the evidence, and there is material that entitles him to reach his conclusions, his decision will not be interfered with on appeal.

Obviously, an 'excited utterance' argument cannot succeed where the utterance precedes the dramatic event by any significant period of time. In *R v Newport*,[23] the appellant's wife left their house after an argument. The case for the prosecution was that the appellant pursued her with a bread knife. At some stage during the flight, the wife suffered a stab wound, which caused her death. The prosecution said that she had been murdered; the defence said that there had been an accident. The prosecution applied for evidence to be admitted that the wife had made a telephone call to a friend that evening. The friend said that she had sounded agitated and frightened, and had asked if she could come to the friend's house if she had to leave her own in a hurry. This evidence was admitted on the basis that what the wife said to her friend had been part of the *res gestae*, but the submission and the judge's ruling proceeded under a misconception that the call had been made immediately before the wife left the house, whereas in fact it had taken place 20 minutes earlier. In the light of this new evidence, the Court of Appeal held that the wife's utterance was plainly not part of the immediate incident and should have been excluded. It was in no sense a spontaneous and unconsidered reaction to an immediately impending emergency.

The nature of the event itself, and the lapse of time between the event and the utterance, are likely to feature in arguments about admissibility. The less dramatic the event and the greater the lapse of time, the less likely it is that the

---

23   [1998] Crim LR 581.

speaker's mind was still dominated by the event so as to rule out any opportunity for concoction or distortion. For example, in *Tobi v Nicholas*,[24] the *res gestae* exception was held not to apply where a statement was made 20 minutes after a relatively undramatic traffic accident.

Tobi v Nicholas may be contrasted with *R v Carnall*,[25] where the defendant was charged with the murder by beating and stabbing of a man who had known him well. Part of the evidence against the defendant was of what the victim had said between the attack and his subsequent death. Two witnesses had seen him in the street outside their house. He was bleeding and asking for help. He said that he had been attacked with knives and baseball bats and that it had taken him about an hour to crawl to the house. The witnesses asked him who his attacker had been, and he named the defendant. A policeman went with the victim to hospital. In reply to the officer's questions, the victim again named the accused and gave details of the background to the attack. The judge ruled that both items of evidence formed part of the *res gestae*. On appeal it was argued that this had been wrong. Reliance was placed mainly on the length of time that had elapsed between the attack and the statements by the victim.

The Court of Appeal held that the trial judge had applied the *R v Andrews* principles and that there had been material entitling him to reach his decision. In those circumstances, the court would not interfere. The crucial question was whether there was any real possibility of concoction or distortion, or whether the judge felt confident that this could be ruled out because the speaker's thoughts were so dominated by what had happened. In answering this question, the judge had taken into account the nature of the attack, the injuries inflicted, the pain suffered by the victim and his obsession with trying to get help and stay alive. The time factor was not conclusive.

Statements relating to the maker's contemporaneous state of mind or emotion

It has been said that, 'Wherever it is material to prove the state of a person's mind, or what was passing in it, and what were his intentions, there you may prove what he said, because that is the only means by which you can find out what his intentions were'.[26] So, for example, where it is alleged that a bankrupt has made a fraudulent preference, his knowledge at the time of the transaction that he was insolvent may be proved by his statements to that effect.[27]

---

24   (1987) 86 Cr App R 323.
25   [1995] Crim LR 944.
26   *Sugden v Lord St Leonards* (1876) LR 1 PD 154, p 251, *per* Mellish LJ.
27   *Thomas v Connell* (1838) 4 M&W 267.

In criminal cases, however, the application of this principle has been erratic. Several old decisions at first instance can be cited in support, but the argument in them was virtually non-existent. For example, in *R v Dixon*,[28] a soldier had killed a corporal. The jury were directed that his statement immediately afterwards, 'I know what I have done and am not sorry for it', was admissible to prove an intent to kill. It was presumably thought that those words showed his state of mind very shortly after the event, and from his state of mind at *that* stage could be inferred his state of mind at the *earlier* stage, just before the killing.

In *R v Vincent, Frost and Edwards*,[29] the defendants were charged in relation to a number of political meetings where they had spoken. One of the counts in the indictment alleged that they had conspired to procure large numbers of persons to assemble for the purpose of inciting terror and alarm in the minds of the Queen's subjects. Evidence having been given of several meetings at which the defendants had been present, it was proposed to ask a superintendent of police whether persons had complained to him of being alarmed by these meetings. It was argued for the defence that the prosecution should have called the persons who had been alarmed, but Gurney B held the superintendent's evidence admissible.

Again, it seems necessary to spell out the reasoning. It had to be shown that the defendants had encouraged persons to assemble for the purpose of inciting terror and alarm among other persons, who were present but not participating – let us call them 'law-abiding citizens'. In order to establish this, it was helpful, though not *necessary*, to show that the assembly had actually caused terror and alarm to some law-abiding citizens. To establish *that* fact, the police superintendent was allowed to give evidence of the complaints he had received, because these reflected the states of mind of a number of law-abiding citizens at the time when they made the complaints.

In *R v Edwards*,[30] the defendant was charged with the murder of his wife. A neighbour was allowed to testify that a week before the death the wife had come to the neighbour's house with a carving knife and a large axe, which she had asked the neighbour to keep. She explained her actions by saying, 'My husband always threatens me with these and when they're out of the way I feel safe'.[31]

---

28   (1869) 11 Cox CC 341.

29   (1840) 9 C&P 275.

30   (1872) 12 Cox CC 230.

31   If declarations of contemporaneous mental feelings are to be treated in the same way as declarations about bodily feelings, it was surely wrong to admit her explanation for the way she felt. Cf *R v Gloster* (1888) 16 Cox CC 471, and see below, p 170. The case could also be regarded as involving a statement accompanying and explaining a relevant act (see below, p 171) but a difficulty with this is that the act must first be shown to have at least some possible relevance to the matters in issue without any reference to the accompanying statement: see *Wright v Doe d Tatham* (1837) 7 A&E 313, p 361, *per* Coltman J.

A more obvious case would occur where the defendant, charged with the murder of a victim, could be shown to have expressed feelings of antipathy towards the deceased shortly before the death. During the course of argument in *R v Ball*, Lord Atkinson said:

> Surely in an ordinary prosecution for murder you can prove previous acts or words of the accused to shew he entertained feelings of enmity towards the deceased, and that is evidence not merely of the malicious mind with which he killed the deceased, but of the fact that he killed him. You can give in evidence the enmity of the accused towards the deceased to prove that the accused took the deceased's life.[32]

An expression of intention to do something has sometimes been relied on to prove that the speaker carried out the act in question. An expression of intention is, of course, an expression of the speaker's state of mind at the time he announces his intention. That state of mind is one of having decided to act in some way at some time in the future. Precisely what inference, if any, can be drawn from an expression of intention depends on the facts of the particular case. This is another example of a problem that will not be resolved by an appeal to precedent. Some examples, though, may be given by way of illustration.

In *R v Buckley*,[33] the defendant was charged with the murder of a police constable. A year earlier the constable had been the principal witness against the defendant in a prosecution that led to the defendant's imprisonment. Evidence was adduced, apparently without objection by the defence, that after the defendant was released from prison he had been heard to mutter threats of vengeance against the constable. The prosecution also wanted to prove that on the night when he had met his death the constable had gone to keep watch on the defendant. The only evidence of this was a statement of that intention made by the constable to his superior officer earlier in the day. Lush J, after consulting with Mellor J, held the superior officer's evidence to this effect admissible, but gave no reasons for his decision.

In *R v Wainwright*,[34] two brothers were tried for the murder of a woman named Harriet Lane. Evidence was available from a person who had seen Lane on the afternoon of 11 September 1874 as she was leaving her lodgings. After that date Lane was not seen alive again, and that was the date alleged by the prosecution to be the date of the murder. The witness was ready to say that Lane had told her that she was going to a certain address. Other evidence showed that that was the address of premises occupied by one of the defendants. The prosecution appears to have argued that Lane's statement about where she was going was admissible as part of the act of leaving her own lodgings; they appear, therefore, to have relied on a different hearsay

---

32   [1911] AC 47, p 68.
33   (1873) 13 Cox CC 293; *Sourcebook*, p 130.
34   (1875) 13 Cox CC 171; *Sourcebook*, p 132.

exception – that which covers statements relating to the maker's performance of an act (see below, p 171). But it could be argued that the words of the trial judge were relevant to this exception also. In excluding as hearsay the evidence of Lane's expression of intention, he said that it 'was only a statement of intention which might or might not have been carried out'.

In *R v Thomson*,[35] the defendant was charged with using an instrument on a woman for the purpose of procuring a miscarriage. The woman died before trial, but not as a result of the miscarriage. The defence was that the defendant had done nothing and that the woman had performed the operation on herself. At trial, counsel for the defence wished to cross-examine a prosecution witness in order to establish that the deceased had stated earlier that she intended to perform an operation on herself to procure a miscarriage. The trial judge ruled this evidence inadmissible. The defendant was convicted and appealed. Before the Court of Criminal Appeal it was argued that an accused person is entitled to adduce any evidence that will prove his defence, whether it is admissible according to the strict rules of evidence or not. This got short shrift from the court, which dismissed the appeal. But no attempt was made to argue on the narrower ground that the deceased's words were admissible as an expression of her intention, and *R v Buckley*[36] was not cited. The prosecution did cite *R v Wainwright*[37] but, as already stated, it is not clear that in that case the court had this particular exception clearly in mind.

More recently, however, the Court of Appeal upheld the proposition that a statement of intention may be admissible under this exception. In *R v Moghal*,[38] the defendant and his mistress, Sadiga, were jointly charged with the murder of a man named Rashid. Separate trials were ordered and Sadiga was tried first. Her defence was that Moghal had been solely responsible. She was acquitted. Then Moghal was tried. His defence was that Sadiga had been solely responsible. On appeal from his conviction, the Court of Appeal considered *obiter* whether the evidence could have been given, in support of his defence, of Sadiga's state of mind and feeling at times before and after the killing.

The killing took place on 30 October 1975. Evidence was available that at a family conference in March 1975, Sadiga had declared her intention to kill Rashid and had prophesied his death within months. There was also available evidence of a confession made by Sadiga to police who had investigated the crime. The trial judge excluded evidence of the confession on the basis that what Sadiga told the police about her previous murderous state of mind was hearsay. This decision was upheld by the Court of Appeal. Scarman LJ

35   [1912] 3 KB 19; *Sourcebook*, p 132.
36   (1873) 13 Cox CC 293; *Sourcebook*, p 130.
37   (1875) 13 Cox CC 171; *Sourcebook*, p 132.
38   (1977) 65 Cr App R 56; *Sourcebook*, p 131.

accepted the statement in *Cross on Evidence* (4th edn) that, to be admitted, such statements must relate to the maker's *contemporaneous* state of mind or emotion. He added that, although contemporaneity was a matter of degree, what Sadiga had said to the police was far too long after the event to be admitted as evidence of her state of mind before and at the time of the killing. But the court disapproved of the judge's view that what Sadiga had said at the family conference was also inadmissible. The words uttered by Sadiga on that occasion had reflected her state of mind and feelings *at that time*. Her words and mental state had therefore been contemporaneous and her statements on that occasion were admissible.

It should be noted that the evidence of what was said at the family conference was not held admissible because it was thought to be contemporaneous with the *murder*. It is the state of mind and the utterance that expresses it that have to be contemporaneous, not the state of mind and the event under investigation. This situation should not be confused with 'excited utterances' in the kind of circumstances illustrated by *R v Andrews*.[39]

It does not, of course, follow from this decision that a statement of intention made seven months before the crime will now invariably be regarded as relevant evidence. As we have seen above, in Chapter 1, previous decisions do not generally determine relevance. It may be significant that in this case it was the *defence* that wanted to use the statement of intention. It remains to be seen whether such a statement would be so readily admitted at the request of the prosecution.

A difficult case where evidence relating to a person's state of mind was discussed was *R v Gilfoyle*.[40] The defendant, Norman Gilfoyle, was charged with the murder of his wife, Paula. He had produced to the police a suicide note in her handwriting after she had been found hanging from a beam in their garage. Nevertheless, in due course he was convicted of murder. On appeal, the Court of Appeal made observations about witness statements that had been available to the prosecution but had not been used at trial because it had been thought that they infringed the hearsay rule.

A friend of the deceased woman had stated that some time before her death, Paula had told her that Norman was doing a project on suicide as part of his work as an auxiliary nurse and had asked for her help in writing examples of suicide notes. In the view of the Court of Appeal this was relevant to the state of mind of the deceased when she wrote the suicide note produced by her husband. Accordingly, it should have been admitted under this exception to the hearsay rule.

While this might have been an attractive result, it seems to have extended the scope of the exception significantly. The rationale of the exception lies in

---

39   (1987) AC 281; *Sourcebook,* p 130.
40   [1996] 1 Cr App R 302.

the idea that an expression of *contemporaneous* state of mind or emotion is likely to be spontaneous, and therefore true. But the evidence thereby adduced is no more than evidence of the speaker's mind *at that particular time*, and *R v Moghal*[41] supports the proposition that one of the conditions of admissibility is that the declaration must relate to the condition of the speaker's mind at the time of making the declaration. What the court in *R v Gilfoyle* did was to use the evidence of the earlier conversation because it was thought to be relevant to the state of mind of the deceased, not at the time of the conversation, but at the stage when she wrote the suicide note. There was therefore a break in the connection between the utterance and the state of mind under investigation. More than that, the utterance in question, though clearly relevant to the speaker's state of mind at the time when she wrote the suicide note, was not in itself a direct expression of the speaker's state of mind at all; it was an assertion about something that the defendant had done.[42]

Another difficult decision is *R v Callender*.[43] Callender and another man were tried for conspiracy to commit arson. Callender was convicted; his co-defendant was acquitted. The prosecution case was that Callender, an animal rights activist, had conspired with others to make incendiary devices. These were to be placed in a number of locations, but principally at premises where factory farming was carried on. In May 1994, Callender and his co-defendant had leased a house, which, according to the prosecution, was used to plan an arson campaign. Police kept watch on the house until mid-October, when both men were arrested. On the premises was equipment designed, according to the prosecution, for the making of incendiary devices. There were kitchen timers, theatrical maroons, containers, flammable liquid, cotton wool, nails and fire lighters. An explosives expert gave evidence that, although each of these items could have had an innocent use, the combination of them indicated an intention to construct incendiary devices. Callender's defence at trial was that it had not been his intention to commit arson, but to make dummy devices. These were to have been left at a number of premises in order to attract publicity in a campaign to oppose factory farming. Callender's co-defendant gave evidence. He said that Callender, whatever he in fact intended, had told *him* that the intended devices were specifically designed not to ignite.

Although Callender did not himself give evidence, he called several witnesses. One of them, a Mrs Hammond, was also concerned with animal rights. She said that she and Callender had met on 2 October 1994. During this meeting, Callender told her that he was planning a campaign against a particular company, against which Mrs Hammond was herself planning a lawful protest. He told her that he intended to remove files from the

---

41 (1977) 65 Cr App R 56; *Sourcebook*, p 131.

42 It is clear that these observations were made *obiter* and it may well be that they will not be followed in subsequent decisions. *R v Moghal* was not referred to.

43 [1998] Crim LR 337, LEXIS 6 Nov 1997.

company's premises and place dummy incendiary devices in lorries at the back of the premises in order to gain publicity for his cause. He explained to her that the devices were not dangerous. Another witness gave evidence of a similar conversation.

The trial judge held that Callender's purpose in adducing evidence of what he had said to Mrs Hammond and the other witness was to support the assertion that he intended to assemble dummies, not incendiary devices. He then ruled that this evidence was *prima facie* hearsay in relation to Callender, and that although it occurred during the period when the conspiracy was alleged to have been taking place, it did not form part of the *res gestae* because it lacked any element of spontaneity. The evidence was admissible only in relation to the co-defendant, because the fact that Callender had made statements about dummy devices to others tended to support the co-defendant's case that that was what Callender had said to him.

It was argued on appeal that the evidence of conversations about dummy devices was admissible for Callender's defence because admissibility was not governed by the principles set out in *R v Andrews*. It was submitted that there were at least two other categories of *res gestae*. One contained 'statements concerning the maker's frame of mind or the maker's emotions. Where the knowledge or emotions of a person were in issue in a trial, then evidence of statements made by such a person would be admissible to prove that person's state of mind'. In relation to this submission, counsel apparently said nothing about statements of *intention*. Indeed, he appears not to have relied on it at all for the admissibility of Callender's conversations. Instead, he relied on another category of *res gestae*: statements accompanying and explaining relevant acts. He argued that the relevant acts were Callender's visits to the witnesses, and that these were explained by what Callender had said on those occasions. The trial judge had been wrong to apply the *Andrews* test to this category.

For the prosecution, it was submitted that *res gestae* was 'a single doctrine' and the *Andrews* test applied in all categories. In reply, Callender's counsel made a significant concession. If, he said, there are grounds for a judge to think that a statement in any of the categories of *res gestae* had been concocted, that statement should not be admitted. This concession, said Roch LJ when delivering the judgment of the Court of Appeal, concluded Callender's appeal. However, he went on to say that the *res gestae* principle was a single principle, and that for evidence to come within that exception, the trial judge must be satisfied that there had been no opportunity for concoction or distortion by the speaker.

This decision is unsatisfactory, not least because the appeal was argued on the wrong basis. For a statement accompanying and explaining an act to be admissible, the act must be relevant apart from the words accompanying it. In *Wright v Doe d Tatham*,[44] Coltman J said:

---

44   (1837) 7 A&E 313, p 361.

Where an act done is evidence *per se*, a declaration accompanying that act may well be evidence if it reflects light upon or qualifies the act. But I am not aware of any case, where the act done is, in its own nature, irrelevant to the issue, and where the declaration per se is inadmissible, in which it has been held that the union of the two has rendered them admissible.

In *R v Bliss*,[45] evidence was tendered, to prove the nature of a certain road, that someone had planted a tree at a particular point, saying simultaneously that it marked the boundary between his land and the highway. It was held that the mere planting of the tree was irrelevant apart from the declaration. Accordingly, neither evidence of the planting, nor of the declaration accompanying it, could be given. So here, Callender's encounters with the witnesses were irrelevant to any fact in issue apart from what he stated on those occasions.

A better argument would have been that Callender's statements were expressions of his contemporaneous state of mind – in particular, of his *intentions*. His state of mind was relevant, of course, because that was what was being investigated by the court hearing the conspiracy charge. Admittedly, such expressions might have been concocted, but so might any expression of intention. The authorities before *R v Callender* do not support either the concession made by Callender's counsel or the view of the Court of Appeal that the *Andrews* test applies to all categories of *res gestae*.[46]

The decision is particularly unfortunate because it further confuses the law relating to *res gestae* at a time when that law is by no means clear, but when the Law Commission has proposed its retention in any reform of the rule against hearsay.

Statements relating to the maker's contemporaneous physical sensations

The usefulness of this exception is limited because, while such statements are admissible as evidence of the sensations, they are inadmissible to prove their *cause*. In *R v Gloster*,[47] for example, statements made by a woman who was dying from the effects of an illegal abortion, and who named the person responsible, were held inadmissible. Charles J held that to be admissible, such statements had to be confined to contemporaneous symptoms and should not include any sort of narrative about how the symptoms had been brought about. It is possible that 'contemporaneous' may be flexibly interpreted; during argument in *R v Black*,[48] Salter J said that it should not be confined to

---

45 (1837) 7 A&E 550.
46 See the commentary on this decision in [1998] Crim LR 338–39.
47 (1888) 16 Cox CC 471; *Sourcebook*, p 134.
48 (1922) 16 Cr App R 118; *Sourcebook*, p 134.

feelings experienced at the actual moment when the statement was made and should include an expression such as, 'Yesterday I had a pain after meals'.

Statements relating to the maker's performance of an act[49]

A statement that is made at the time of performing a relevant act is admissible to explain the act, provided it is made contemporaneously by the person who performs the act.[50] As already stated,[51] the act has to be relevant to the facts in issue apart from the declaration accompanying it. In an old case, evidence was admitted of words accompanying the transfer of a sum of money in order to explain the nature of the transaction.[52] A recent example[53] is *R v McCay*.[54] The accused had been identified on an identification parade by a witness who had observed the parade through a glass screen. People on the parade could not see through the screen or hear what was being said on the other side of it. The accused, who occupied the position numbered 8 on the parade, was identified when the witness said to the inspector conducting the parade, 'It is number 8'. At trial, the witness could remember identifying someone but could not remember the number of that person on the parade. The trial judge allowed the inspector to fill the gap by telling the court what the witness had said. On appeal it was argued that this infringed the hearsay rule. The Court of Appeal held that the evidence had been properly admitted. The statement had accompanied a relevant act – that of identification – and was necessary to explain it. The court regarded identification as involving both a physical and an intellectual activity – seeing and recognising – which were explained by the accompanying words.

STATEMENTS IN FURTHERANCE
OF A COMMON PURPOSE

Where defendants are charged with conspiracy, or charged jointly with an offence where the prosecution allege a common enterprise, evidence of acts done or statements made by one defendant in furtherance of the common enterprise will be admissible against other defendants, even though those other defendants were not present at the time when the act was done or the

---

49 Choo, *op cit*, fn 7, pp 118–19.

50 *Rawson v Haigh* (1824) 2 Bing 99; *Walters v Lewis* (1836) TC&P 344; *R v Bliss* (1837) 7 A&E 550; *Howe v Malkin* (1878) 40 LT 196.

51 See above, pp 169–70.

52 *Walters v Lewis* (1836) 7 C&P 344.

53 Which, however, appears to be inconsistent with earlier decisions: see Choo, *op cit*, fn 7, pp 118-19.

54 [1990] 1 WLR 645; *Sourcebook*, p 135.

statement made. The reason for this is that a combination of persons for the purpose of committing a crime is regarded as implying an authority in each to act or speak in furtherance of the common purpose on behalf of the others.[55]

There must always be some evidence other than the hearsay evidence of a party to the alleged common enterprise to prove that a particular defendant *is* a party to that enterprise,[56] but evidence of the *acts*, including verbal acts, of the defendants can establish this.[57]

It has been suggested[58] that where what was said by one defendant is no more than a narrative of some event that has already taken place, this principle is unlikely to apply, because such a statement would only rarely be *in furtherance* of the enterprise. This would certainly be true of a confession, made by one of the defendants to the police, that referred to the actions of other defendants. But it has been said that an account of events narrated by one of the parties to another, while the common enterprise was continuing, in order to bring him up to date, might be regarded as in furtherance of the enterprise, and so admissible against all the parties referred to in it.[59]

An example of the operation of this exception to the hearsay rule can be seen in *R v Devonport and Pirano*.[60] The appellants were two of five defendants convicted of conspiracy to defraud a bank. One of the items of evidence in the case was a document found in the possession of a girlfriend of one of the defendants. The prosecution's case was that it had been dictated to her by her boyfriend and that it showed the proposed division of the proceeds of the conspiracy. It referred to all five defendants. There was no suggestion that either of these two appellants had prepared the document himself or been a party to its preparation, and no link between either of them and the document was ever established. The only conspirator with any knowledge of, or connection with, the document was the one who had dictated it. Was the document evidence against all the conspirators?

The Court of Appeal held that it was, provided: (a) it constituted an act or declaration by the conspirator who brought it into existence in furtherance of the conspiracy; and (b) there was some further evidence beyond the document itself that the persons to whom it referred were parties to the conspiracy alleged against them. In fact, such evidence was available. Since the document appeared to be *not a record of distribution after the conspiracy* but an indication of the *intended distribution* of the proceeds of the conspiracy *when it had been fulfilled*, it was *prima facie* prepared in furtherance of the conspiracy and so admissible.

---

55 *R v Gray and Others* [1995] 2 Cr App R 100.

56 *R v Murray and Others* [1997] 2 Cr App R 136.

57 See, generally, Smith, JC, 'Proving conspiracy' [1996] Crim LR 386; Smith, JC, 'More on proving conspiracy' [1997] Crim LR 333.

58 *Tripodi v R* (1961) 104 CLR 1, approved in *R v Gray and Others* [1995] 2 Cr App R 100.

59 *R v Jones and Others* [1997] 2 Cr App R 119, pp 128–29.

60 [1996] 1 Cr App R 221.

STATUTORY EXCEPTIONS

The application of the hearsay rule has been considerably affected by legislation. What follows is not an exhaustive list of exceptions; it concentrates on those provisions most likely to be important in examinations and in practice.

DOCUMENTARY HEARSAY UNDER THE CRIMINAL JUSTICE ACT 1988

Sections 23 and 24 of the Criminal Justice Act 1988 allow for the admissibility of written, *but not oral*, hearsay in certain cases. Both sections have to be read in the light of either s 25 or s 26. A two-stage analysis is involved:

(a) Does this item of documentary hearsay come within either s 23 or s 24?; If yes,

(b) Which of ss 25 or 26 applies, and what will be its effect? (They operate in different ways.)

Sections 23 and 24 are both confined to 'a statement' in a 'document'. 'Statement' means any representation of fact, however made, and 'document' means anything in which information of any description is recorded.[61] Where documentary hearsay is admitted under either s 23 or s 24, the judge in summing-up must draw attention to the fact that the maker of the statement was not in court to be cross-examined on its contents. The jury should be warned to take particular care, for that reason, when considering that item of evidence. It is not sufficient merely to remind the jury that the evidence was given by way of a witness statement.[62]

Section 23

The section provides that, subject to certain conditions, a statement made by a person in a document shall be admissible in criminal proceedings as evidence of any fact of which direct oral evidence *by him* would be admissible. A fundamental question will therefore be whether the maker of the *written* statement could have given *oral* evidence of the matters to which it relates, had he appeared in person at the trial. One effect of this provision is to confine the exception to *first hand* documentary hearsay. If the document itself

---

61 Criminal Justice Act 1988, Sched 2, para 5(1), as amended by Civil Evidence Act 1995, Sched 1, para 12.

62 *R v Curry* (1998) *The Times*, 23 March.

contains hearsay[63] *that* will not be something of which oral evidence could usually be given. But if the hearsay falls within one of the exceptions to the rule – if, for example, it came within the *res gestae* exception – oral evidence *could* be given of it, and it might therefore be admissible as part of a statement in a document under s 23.[64]

Whether the statement has been 'made' by the relevant person may be a matter for argument. In *R v McGillivray*,[65] the victim of a crime had suffered burns. He gave a police officer an account of what had happened; the officer wrote down what the victim said and then read it back to him. The victim agreed that the officer's record was accurate, but could not sign it because of his injuries. He died shortly afterwards. It was held that the statement had been made by the victim in a document for the purposes of admissibility under s 23. The key to understanding this decision is to see the police officer as the victim's agent in making the statement. However, an unverified note of a conversation, or a conversation that is secretly recorded, is unlikely to have been 'made by a person in a document' within s 23.[66]

Section 23 applies only where the person who made the statement (M) is unavailable for a reason set out in sub-s (2) or (3). There may be a dispute about the existence of an appropriate condition. If so, this will have to be resolved at a *voir dire* (a trial within a trial) in the absence of the jury.[67] Although it is necessary for the prosecution to prove the existence of an appropriate condition to the criminal standard if they wish to use s 23, if the defence wish to rely on the section *they* have to prove the existence of an appropriate condition only on the balance of probabilities.[68]

The conditions in sub-s (2) are that:

(a) M is dead or unfit to attend as a witness by reason of his bodily or mental condition;

(b) M is outside the UK and it is not reasonably practicable to secure his attendance;

(c) all reasonable steps have been taken to find M but he cannot be found.

---

63 Eg, 'X told me that he had seen the defendant breaking into the house'.

64 Cf *The Ymnos* [1981] 1 Ll Rep 550. This interpretation was adopted in *R v Lockley* [1995] 2 Cr App R 554 and *R v James* [1996] 2 Cr App R 39. But see Law Com No 245 (1997), paras 8.25–8.26.

65 (1993) 97 Cr App R 232.

66 See *Re D (a Minor)* [1986] 2 FLR 189 and *Ventouris v Mountain (No 2)* [1992] 1 WLR 887, which interpreted a similar provision in Part I of the Civil Evidence Act 1968 (now repealed).

67 *R v Minors* [1989] Crim LR 360.

68 *R v Mattey and Queeley* [1995] 2 Cr App R 409.

The condition in sub-s (3) is that:

(a) the statement was made to a police officer or some other person charged with the duty of investigating offences or charging offenders; *and*

(b) the person who made the statement does not give oral evidence through fear or because he is kept out of the way.

Not reasonably practicable to secure attendance (s 23(2)(b))

The mere fact that it is *possible* for a witness to attend does not mean that his attendance is reasonably practicable. To determine this question the judge has to consider several factors. These include:

(a) the importance of the evidence and the extent to which the witness's non-attendance is prejudicial to the defence;

(b) the expense and inconvenience of securing the witness's attendance, though it may be that this should not be a major concern where the witness is part of the 'prosecution team';[69] and

(c) the reasons why it is not convenient or reasonably practicable for the witness to attend.[70]

Does not give evidence through fear (s 23(3)(b))

The main problems under s 23 have arisen in connection with the requirement of 'fear' in sub-s (3)(b). In *R v Acton JJ ex p McMullen*,[71] it was argued that those relying on the sub-section had to satisfy the court that the maker of the statement was in fear owing to attempts made *since* the making of the statement to put him in fear. It was also argued that the fear had to be based on reasonable grounds. The Divisional Court rejected both arguments, saying that it was wholly inappropriate to introduce a concept of reasonable grounds and that it was sufficient for the court to be sure that the witness was in fear as a consequence of the commission of the material offence, or of something said or done subsequently in relation to that offence.

The decision of the Court of Appeal in *R v Martin*[72] shows that although it will be *sufficient* that the witness's fear was a consequence of the commission of the offence, or of something said or done subsequently in relation to that offence, it is not *necessary* that the fear should arise in either of these ways. Provided fear is established, there is no need for the court to inquire into the

---

69 Presumably someone such as a police officer or prosecution expert witness.

70 *R v Castillo and Others* [1996] 1 Cr App R 438.

71 (1990) 92 Cr App R 98.

72 [1996] Crim LR 589.

basis of it. So if a witness's fear arises, for example, from a mistaken belief by the witness that he is being followed in the streets, the sub-section will still apply. It is enough that a witness is afraid and fails to testify as a result.[73]

The sub-section can be relied on even though the witness has already begun to give evidence. In *R v Waters*,[74] the Court of Appeal said that the sub-section is available so long as there remains any relevant evidence that the witness is still expected to give.

Sometimes proof of fear can present problems. In *Neill v North Antrim Magistrates' Court*,[75] two witnesses to a robbery had given written statements to the police identifying the appellant and the other accused persons as participants. They were tendered to the magistrates at the preliminary inquiry, but the appellant's solicitor requested that the witnesses should attend and give oral evidence. The magistrates, having heard evidence from a police officer, admitted the statements pursuant to the relevant Northern Ireland legislation on the ground that the witnesses had refused to give evidence through fear. The police officer had testified that on the previous day the mothers of the witnesses had told him that their sons were afraid to come to court because of threats made against them. The officer added that the mothers had come to court and had confirmed that their sons were still afraid to attend. The witness statements were admitted, and the appellant and the other accused committed for trial.

The House of Lords held that if the police officer's evidence had been that the two young men *had spoken to him directly* of their fear, the officer would have been able to prove their fear by admissible evidence, namely, evidence of their declarations as to their contemporaneous states of mind. But no such evidence had been given – only an account of what the mothers had been told by their sons. That was hearsay and so inadmissible.

The position was different in *R v Fairfax*[76] where two witnesses had made statements to the police against the defendant. Neither witness appeared at trial and the prosecution applied to have their statements admitted under s 23. Two further statements by the witnesses were read, in which they said they were too frightened to give evidence. This was confirmed by police officers who gave evidence in relation to the question of admissibility. These further statements, made both in writing and orally to the police, were sufficient to prove fear. They were hearsay, but within the exception covering declarations about contemporaneous states of mind.

---

73 It is thus possible for the fear to arise in a way that is almost wholly unconnected with the offence. Apparently the condition would be satisfied if a witness gave a statement to the police but subsequently had a dream, as a result of which he feared some disaster if he should give evidence against the defendant and so refused to do so.

74 [1997] Crim LR 823.

75 [1992] 4 All ER 846.

76 [1995] Crim LR 949.

In *R v Belmarsh Magistrates' Court ex p Gilligan*,[77] the Divisional Court held that in order to satisfy the requirements of s 23, it is necessary for the court to hear oral evidence as to fear, for example, from a police officer who has spoken to the witness. A second written statement from the witness asserting his state of fear was held to be insufficient to justify the admission of an earlier statement, in which the witness had provided evidence against the accused. It is difficult to account for this decision. The second written statement, just as much as any oral statement to a police officer, fell within the common law hearsay exception that admits evidence of a person's contemporaneous state of mind. In *R v Rutherford*,[78] although the point was not directly raised, the Court of Appeal held that there was sufficient evidence of fear where a potential witness had made a second written statement expressing his fear. In *R v Greer*,[79] the Court of Appeal said that there was no reason why a judge should not hear 'unsworn evidence' from the witness who is in fear, even though a statement made in this way would not be evidence in the case (because unsworn).

R v Greer is an eccentric decision. The view usually taken is that the s 23 conditions must be proved by evidence, and, further, *by evidence that is admissible without relying on the statute.* That answer was given in relation to another of the s 23 conditions in *R v Case*.[80] The defendant was charged with theft of a purse from a Portuguese tourist. The prosecution tendered the witness statements of the victim and another Portuguese tourist, who had been with her at the time of the theft. The statements showed that the two witnesses lived outside the UK. The judge admitted the statements under s 23(2)(b), having inferred that it was not reasonably practicable to secure the witnesses' attendance.

The Court of Appeal held that there was no admissible evidence that the witnesses were outside the UK. It was not permissible to look to the statements whose admissibility was in question for evidence that would satisfy a precondition of admissibility.[81]

---

77 [1998] 1 Cr App R 14.
78 [1998] Crim LR 490.
79 [1998] Crim LR 572.
80 [1991] Crim LR 192.
81 Before the statements could be used as evidence for any purpose it was necessary to establish the conditions in s 23(2)(b) by admissible evidence. This could not be done by using the statements, because they were inadmissible until the conditions had already been proved. The defence are, of course, entitled to cross-examine witnesses who have been called to establish the conditions for applying s 23: *R v Wood and Fitzsimmons* [1998] Crim LR 213 (CA).

Kept out of the way

This expression is wider than the earlier provision in s 13(3) of the Criminal Justice Act 1925, which allowed a deposition to be read at trial where the witness had been 'kept out of the way by means of the procurement of the accused or on his behalf'. It now seems to be sufficient if the witness is 'kept out of the way' by anyone, but it is unclear whether this condition would be satisfied if the police had decided to keep a witness out of the way for his own protection.

Section 24

Section 24 makes admissible in certain circumstances documents *created* or *received* by a person in the course of a trade, business, profession or other occupation, or as the holder of a paid or unpaid office. Section 24 statements may include information that has passed through more than one person before being recorded in the document, provided: (a) each person supplying the information had, or may be reasonably supposed to have had, personal knowledge of the matters dealt with;[82] and (b) each person supplying the information received it in the course of a trade, business, profession or other occupation, or as the holder of a paid or unpaid office.[83]

The inclusion of documents 'received' by a person in the course of a trade, etc, will cover the situation where there has been correspondence between someone who is in a trade, etc, and someone who is not. If it were not for this provision, only one side of the correspondence would be admissible. But the effect of the provision may well be wider than that. If read literally, for example, all letters to the editor of *The Times* are admissible, provided their authors have personal knowledge of their contents.[84]

By s 24(4), a document prepared for the purposes of pending or contemplated criminal proceedings or a criminal investigation shall be inadmissible under s 24(1) unless one of the requirements set out in s 23(2) is satisfied, or the requirements of s 23(3) are satisfied, or the person who made

---

82 Section 24 statements, therefore, unlike s 23 statements, may include multiple as well as first hand hearsay.

83 Section 24(1)(ii); s 24(2).

84 Birch, D, 'The Criminal Justice Act 1988: (2) documentary evidence' [1989] Crim LR 15, p 25, quoting Professor JC Smith.

the statement cannot reasonably be expected to have any recollection of the matters dealt with in the statement.[85]

There is a distinction, drawn in s 24(1)(ii), between the maker of a statement and a supplier of information. In *Brown v Secretary of State for Social Security*,[86] the Divisional Court held that the maker of the statement – the one who must be unavailable or unable to remember – is the person who brings into existence the document that a party wishes to produce in evidence; it is *not* the person who supplied the information contained in the document (where that person is not the same as the person who brought the document into existence). But the Court of Appeal disapproved of *Brown* in *R v Derodra*.[87] In that case, the defendant was charged on an indictment that alleged, essentially, fraud on an insurance company by making a claim in respect of a burglary that had taken place before the policy was taken out. In order to establish the date of the burglary, the prosecution wished to rely on the contents of a computerised record of crimes, known as a 'CRIS' report. The relevant entry in the computer record had been made by a PC Gable from information provided by the defendant's lodger, a Mr Baloyi. The prosecution argued that this report was admissible under s 24 of the Criminal Justice Act 1988, on the basis that the relevant condition under s 23(2)(c) was satisfied: namely, that all reasonable steps had been taken to find the maker of the statement, but that he could not be found. The trial judge found that this applied to Mr Baloyi. But the defence argued that, on the proper construction of s 24, the maker of the statement was not Mr Baloyi, but PC Gable. He *was* available, but the only condition that would have permitted the CRIS report to be admitted if he was the maker of the statement was contained in s 24(4)(iii), and that did not apply. It was therefore crucial to determine whether the maker of the statement for s 24 purposes was Mr Baloyi or PC Gable.

The Court of Appeal held that it was Mr Baloyi. It said that when the Divisional Court in *Brown v Secretary of State* drew attention to the distinction in s 24 between the supplier of information and the maker of the statement, that court had been wrong to assume that the 'maker of the statement' meant the maker of the document, however mechanical a role he played. The correct view of the 'maker of the statement' is that it is the person who makes, or vouches for, the representation of fact that the statement consists of. Who that is will depend on the circumstances of each particular case. In the present

---

85 The Law Commission has noted (Law Com No 138 (1995), para 4.32) that it is uncertain whether or not witness statements created or received by police officers fall within s 24. The words of the section suggest that they do; indeed, if they were not covered, the Act would be inapplicable in situations where it was clearly intended to apply. See Smith, JC, 'Sections 23 and 24 of the Criminal Justice Act 1988: (1) some problems' [1994] Crim LR 426; McEvoy, D, 'Sections 23 and 24 of the Criminal Justice Act 1988: (2) a reply' [1994] Crim LR 430.

86 (1994) *The Times*, 7 December. See also *R v Bedi* (1992) 95 Cr App R 21; *R v Field* [1992] Crim LR 299.

87 [2000] 1 Cr App R 41.

case, Mr Baloyi was in that sense the maker of the statement. It was therefore in relation to him, not to PC Gable, that the condition in s 23(2)(c) had to be satisfied. It was satisfied, and thus the CRIS report was admissible under s 24.

While under s 23 the existence of the appropriate conditions of admissibility must be proved by admissible evidence,[88] the existence of the conditions set out in s 24(1) can be inferred from the document under consideration. In *R v Foxley*,[89] it was argued for the appellant that, for documents to be admissible under s 24, it must be separately proved that they were created in the course of a trade, etc, that the information contained in them was supplied by persons with personal knowledge, and that the documents were authentic. The Court of Appeal drew a distinction between the two sections. It may be, Roch LJ said, that direct evidence of the requirements of s 23(2) and (3) is necessary. But the purpose of s 24 is to enable a document to speak for itself. The court was assisted in coming to this conclusion by the wording of condition (ii) of s 24(1)[90] which, Roch LJ said, demonstrates that Parliament anticipated that courts would draw inferences as to the personal knowledge of the person supplying the information.

A good example of a document that was allowed to speak for itself occurred in *R v Ilyas and Knight*.[91] A diary had been found on a counter at business premises containing, the Court of Appeal said, the sort of entries one would expect to find in a document created by a person in the course of a business, and in circumstances where the information would have been supplied by a person who might reasonably be supposed to have had personal knowledge of the matters dealt with. It was held admissible without further explanation as a document created in the course of a business, although the court did say that there might be circumstances in which a document would have to be explained in evidence before it could be admitted under s 24.

Sections 25 and 26

As said earlier, if you have to consider either s 23 or s 24 you must always go on to consider the application of either s 25 or s 26. The difference between the two was emphasised by the Court of Appeal in *R v Cole*.[92] By s 25, if, having regard to all the circumstances, the court is of the opinion that a statement admissible under s 23 or s 24 'in the interests of justice ought not to be

---

88 See *R v Case* [1991] Crim LR 192, but cf *R v Greer* [1998] Crim LR 572.

89 [1995] 2 Cr App R 523.

90 The condition refers to a person 'who may reasonably be supposed to have had personal knowledge of the matters dealt with'.

91 [1996] Crim LR 810.

92 [1990] 2 All ER 108; *Sourcebook*, p 146. See also *R v Radak and Others* [1999] 1 Cr App R 187, p 195.

admitted', it may direct that it be not admitted. The court, in considering that question, must have regard to the matters set out in s 25(2). These include the nature, source and likely authenticity of the document containing the statement; the extent to which the statement appears to supply evidence that would otherwise not be readily available; the relevance of the evidence; and any risk of unfairness to a defendant from its admission or exclusion, having regard in particular to whether it is likely to be possible to controvert the statement if the person making it does not attend to give oral evidence. Thus, if s 25 applies, there is a presumption in favour of *admitting* the evidence; to be excluded, 'the court must be made to hold the opinion that the statement ought not to be admitted'.

By contrast, under s 26, which deals with documents prepared for the purpose of criminal proceedings or investigations, a statement that is admissible in principle under s 23 or s 24 shall not be given in evidence unless the court is of the opinion that the statement 'ought to be admitted in the interests of justice'.[93] The matters to which the court must have regard are the contents of the statement; any risk of unfairness to a defendant from its admission or exclusion, having regard in particular to whether it is likely to be possible to controvert the statement if the person making it does not attend to give oral evidence; and any other relevant circumstances. Thus, if s 26 applies, the presumption is in favour of *exclusion*; the court is not to admit the statement unless made to hold the opinion that in the interests of justice it *ought to be admitted*.[94]

The existence of a discretion means that cases are decided very much on their own facts,[95] but it has been said that the crucial factor for determining the exercise of the discretion is the quality of the evidence.[96] An example of this appears in *R v Lockley and Corah*.[97] At a trial for murder, evidence of a confession by one of the defendants was given by a witness who had shared a cell with that defendant. A re-trial became necessary, and by that time the witness had absconded. The trial judge admitted a transcript of the evidence she had given at the first trial. The Court of Appeal accepted that this evidence was potentially admissible under both s 23, as first hand hearsay, and s 24, as a business document. The exercise of discretion had to be considered for the first time because the trial judge had failed to consider it. The Court of Appeal

---

93 There may be borderline cases where it is unclear whether the statement was one made for the purpose of criminal proceedings: eg, a statement prepared as part of an internal investigation when it was not known whether or not a suspected offender would be reported to the police. See Law Com No 138 (1995), para 4.48.

94 *R v Cole* [1990] 2 All ER 108, pp 115–16.

95 The Law Commission has commented that the considerations to be taken into account tend to cancel each other out, so that a judge is left without clear guidance: Law Com No 138 (1995), para 4.50.

96 *Scott v R* [1989] AC 1242, p 1259, applied in *R v Cole* [1990] 2 All ER 108.

97 [1996] Crim LR 113.

held that s 26 applied because a 'statement made in contemplation of criminal proceedings' included a statement made in the course of such proceedings. The court said that although the character of a witness was not an overriding consideration, there was significant evidence of this witness's dishonesty and it was important that the jury should have been able to see the witness and observe her demeanour while she gave oral evidence. As this was not possible, the transcript should have been excluded.

But decisions are unpredictable. In *R v Kennedy and Burrell*,[98] the trial judge had admitted the statement of a deceased witness who had consumed a considerable amount of alcohol at the time of the incident that he related, and whose account was inconsistent in important respects with accounts of other witnesses. The Court of Appeal said that, on balance, it would not have disturbed the decision to admit this evidence, and allowed the appeal only because the judge had failed to warn the jury in summing up of its specific weaknesses.

If the quality of the evidence is good enough, a documentary statement *may* be admitted even where it forms the main evidence against the defendant.[99]

When considering under s 25 or 26 whether it will be possible for a defendant to controvert the evidence of the statement maker, the court takes into account the fact that there are various opportunities for controversion. They include, in addition to the defendant's own testimony, cross-examination of prosecution witnesses, calling other defence witnesses, and putting the credibility of the statement maker in issue under para 1 of Sched 2 of the Act.[100] The failure of the prosecution authorities to give the defence an opportunity to controvert evidence by cross-examination led the Court of Appeal in *R v Radak and Others*[101] to hold that a witness statement should have been excluded under s 26. In that case, a prosecution witness living in the USA refused to attend to give evidence. The trial judge found that it was not reasonably practicable to secure his attendance and allowed his statement to be admitted in the exercise of his discretion under s 26. But the prosecution had known from the outset that the witness might not attend. It was argued successfully on an interlocutory appeal that steps should have been taken to obtain his evidence on commission in the USA,[102] because that would have provided the defence with an opportunity for cross-examination. The Court of Appeal held that this consideration should have led to the exclusion of the witness statement in a proper exercise of the trial judge's discretion under s 26.

---

98   [1994] Crim LR 50.

99   *R v Dragic* [1996] 2 Cr App R 232.

100   *R v Cole* [1990] 2 All ER 108; *R v Gokal* [1997] 2 Cr App R 266.

101   [1999] 1 Cr App R 187.

102   Under the Criminal Justice (International Co-operation) Act 1990, s 3.

Discrediting a witness whose statement is admitted

Where documentary hearsay is admitted under s 23 or 24, Sched 2 of the Act makes admissible 'any evidence which, if *the person making the statement* had been called as a witness, would have been admissible as relevant to his credibility'.[103] In addition, if the court gives leave, evidence may be given of any matters relevant to credibility about which that person could have been cross-examined, even though they would have been collateral matters on which his answer would have been final.[104] Evidence may also be given of any oral or written contradictory statements made by that person either before or after he made the statement admitted as documentary hearsay.[105]

THE CIVIL EVIDENCE ACT 1995

This Act implements the recommendations of the Law Commission's report on the hearsay rule in civil proceedings.[106] Section 1(1) of the Act provides that in civil proceedings[107] evidence shall not be excluded on the ground that it is hearsay. Multiple as well as first hand hearsay is now admissible.[108] Before the Act there existed particular statutory provisions that rendered hearsay admissible in certain circumstances. Many provisions, such as the Births and Deaths Registration Acts 1836–1953, had the effect of making certain documents evidence of their contents in particular contexts. The most significant modern provision of this kind was s 96(3)–(7) of the Children Act 1989 and the orders made under it. These allowed hearsay evidence to be given in civil proceedings in connection with the upbringing, maintenance or welfare of a child. The Law Commission was unwilling to disturb these convenient provisions and therefore ensured, by s 1(3), that existing statutory provisions making hearsay admissible should not be affected.[109]

Sections 2–4 make provision for safeguards in relation to hearsay evidence. The object of s 2 is to enable parties to make any necessary pre-trial inquiries arising from the fact that some evidence will be hearsay. A general duty is imposed on parties by s 2(1) to give warning, where reasonable and practicable, that they intend to adduce hearsay evidence. Section 2(2) allows

---

103 Eg, evidence of previous convictions.

104 See above, Chapter 4, p 86.

105 Criminal Justice Act 1988, Sched 2, para 1.

106 Cm 2321, 1993.

107 By s 11, 'civil proceedings' means civil proceedings, before any tribunal, in relation to which the strict rules of evidence apply, whether as a matter of law or by agreement of the parties.

108 Civil Evidence Act 1995, s 1(2).

109 But Part I of the Civil Evidence Act 1968, making limited general provisions for the admissibility of hearsay evidence, was repealed: see Sched 2.

for rules of court to be made to govern this duty. By s 2(3), the duty may be excluded by agreement.[110] Section 2(4) provides that a failure to comply with this duty shall not affect the admissibility of the evidence, but may be penalised in costs or in other ways at the court's disposal.[111] Section 3 provides a power to call for cross-examination a person whose statement has been tendered as hearsay evidence. Section 4 provides courts with statutory guidelines to assist in weighing hearsay evidence.

Sections 5–7 contain supplementary provisions. By s 5(1), the maker of a statement adduced as hearsay evidence must have been competent to give direct oral evidence at the time when the statement was made. Section 5(2) provides for the admissibility of evidence to attack or support the credibility of the maker of a hearsay statement, as well as evidence tending to show that such a person made previous or later inconsistent statements.

By s 6(1), previous consistent and inconsistent statements of persons called as witnesses are admissible as evidence of the matters stated; but by s 6(2), a party who calls a person as a witness may not adduce evidence of a previous statement made by that person without leave of the court, unless the purpose is to rebut a suggestion that his evidence has been fabricated. However, this shall not prevent a written statement of oral evidence which a party to the proceedings intends to adduce from being adopted by a witness in giving evidence or being treated as his evidence.[112]

The operation of the provisions of ss 3, 4 and 5 of the Criminal Procedure Act 1865 is preserved by s 6(3). These provisions of the 1865 Act apply to civil as well as to criminal proceedings and deal with the extent to which a witness may be discredited by the party producing him, the proof of contradictory statements made by a witness and cross-examination about previous statements in writing.[113]

Section 7 deals with evidence formerly admissible at common law by way of exception to the hearsay rule. The most important of these provisions is that the common law rule relating to the admissibility of admissions adverse to a party is superseded by the provisions of the Act. Such admissions are now admissible as hearsay statements under s 1 and are subject to the provisions of the Act in relation to notice and weight.

Sections 8–10 deal with other matters. The effect of s 8 is that, where a statement contained in a document is admissible as evidence in civil proceedings, it can be proved by the production of the original document or a

---

110 Eg, in an arbitration agreement.

111 Eg, by granting an adjournment to enable the party who has suffered from the surprise to gather fresh evidence to deal with it.

112 The object of this provision is to facilitate the current practice in civil proceedings of avoiding a formal and full examination-in-chief.

113 For details see above, Chapter 4.

copy authenticated in such manner as the court shall approve. It is immaterial how many removes there are between a copy and the original.

Section 9 concerns the proof of records of a business or public authority. Its effect is that documents, including those stored by a computer, forming part of the records of a business[114] or public authority, are admissible as hearsay evidence under s 1, and the ordinary notice and weighing provisions apply. Unless the court otherwise directs, a document shall be taken to form part of the records of a business or public authority if there is produced to the court a certificate to that effect signed by an officer of the business or public authority. The *absence* of an entry in the records of a business or public authority may be proved in civil proceedings by affidavit of an officer of the business or public authority to which the records belong.

By s 14(1), nothing in the Act affects the exclusion of evidence on grounds other than that it is hearsay. In other words, evidence that would be inadmissible for some other reason does not become admissible just because it is in the form of hearsay.

PROPOSALS FOR REFORM[115]

The major issue of principle that the Law Commission had to consider when reviewing exceptions to a rule against hearsay was whether the law should be discretionary or rule-based. The chief advantage of a discretionary approach is that it enables a court to tailor decisions to the individual case. The major disadvantage is that, where discretions are available, they will be exercised differently by different judges and magistrates, so making for inconsistency and unpredictability. Judicial discretion was a significant feature of the documentary hearsay provisions of the Criminal Justice Act 1988, but the Commission discovered that there was great variety in the way these powers were exercised.[116] The Commission decided to turn away from a discretionary-based approach, and recommended that there should be an exclusionary hearsay rule, with specified exceptions and a limited inclusionary discretion. There are four types of exception:

(a) categories of automatic admissibility where the declarant's oral evidence is, for one of certain specified reasons, unavailable ('the unavailability exception');

---

114 'Records' means records in whatever form; 'business' includes any activity regularly carried on over a period of time, whether for profit or not, by any body (whether corporate or not) or by an individual: see s 9(4). So the regular cleaning of my cat's litter tray is now a business.

115 CLRC, 11th Report, paras 224-65; Law Com No 245 (1997); Carter (1993) 109 LQR 573; Osborne [1993] Crim LR 255; Spencer [1994] Crim LR 628; Zuckerman [1996] Crim LR 4; Ormerod [1996] Crim LR 16; Spencer [1996] Crim LR 29; Murphy (1997) 1 E&P 107.

116 Law Com No 245 (1997), paras 4.28–4.31.

(b) an exception under which statements made by witnesses who are in fear may be admitted with the leave of the court;

(c) a business documents exception;

(d) certain preserved exceptions, such as confessions, statements that are part of the *res gestae*, and statements made by parties to a common enterprise.[117]

The unavailability exception

The Law Commission thought it a major limitation of the present law that only documentary evidence can be admitted under the Criminal Justice Act 1988, and they recommended that the unavailability exception should be extended to oral as well as documentary hearsay. Before this exception could be relied on, however, the declarant would have to be identified, thus enabling the opposing party to challenge credibility and reliability. The Commission also recommended that the exception should not apply to a statement of any fact of which the declarant could not have given oral evidence at the time when the statement was made. Thus, the unavailability exception will not allow multiple hearsay. Further, the exception should not be available where, in order to prevent the declarant from testifying, the party who wishes to adduce the evidence himself caused the declarant to be unavailable. Causes of unavailability should be death, physical or mental illness, and absence abroad in circumstances where it is not reasonably practicable to secure attendance. The Commission also recommended that the unavailability exception should apply where the declarant cannot be found, and where reasonably practicable steps have been taken to find him.[118]

Fear

The Commission's inquiries showed that a major problem in the administration of criminal justice was that many witnesses were too frightened to give evidence. But proving that intimidation has taken place can be extremely difficult, as the consequence of successful intimidation is often that the witness disappears without any clear reason. The Commission concluded that there should be a hearsay exception to cover the situation where a witness failed through fear to give oral evidence. However, it would be undesirable to have an *automatic* exception, because that would enable witnesses to give statements to the police and later avoid having to go to court and be cross-examined by falsely claiming to be frightened. The leave of the court should therefore be required before hearsay evidence could be given for

---

117 Law Com No 245 (1997), para 8.1.
118 *Ibid*, paras 8.3–8.43.

this reason. 'Fear' is to be widely construed; in particular, fear of the death or injury of another, or of financial loss, will suffice. Under the present law, contained in s 23(3)(a) of the Criminal Justice Act 1988, the statement of a frightened witness can be adduced only if it was made to a police officer or some other person charged with the duty of investigating offences or charging offenders. This condition can have the effect of putting the defence at a disadvantage, because defence witnesses are sometimes fearful of antagonising the police or others with an interest in the prosecution. The Commission accordingly recommended the abolition of this restriction.[119]

Business documents[120]

The Law Commission concluded that there should continue to be an exception for statements contained in business documents, but that there should be less room for the exercise of discretion. Their recommendation was that statements falling within the business documents exception should be automatically admissible, but that the court should have power to direct that a statement is not admissible as a business document if satisfied that the reliability of the statement is doubtful. The Commission also recommended reversing the effect of the present interpretation of 'maker of the statement' in s 24(1)(ii) of the 1988 Act.[121]

Preserved exceptions

The Commission recommended that the current law be preserved in respect of admissions, confessions, mixed statements, and evidence of reaction. The admissibility of a confession by one co-accused at the instance of another should be governed by provisions similar to s 76 of the Police and Criminal Evidence Act 1984, but taking into account the standard of proof applicable to a defendant. Under the Commission's proposals, a relevant confession made by a third party could be admitted if the person making it has died, is too ill to attend court, cannot be found or is outside the UK. Such statements would be automatically admissible to the extent that oral evidence by that person would be admissible. Where the person confessing is too frightened to testify, the confession could be admitted with leave of the court. But in other cases (for example, where the person confessing refuses to obey a witness order, or testifies but refuses to answer questions which may incriminate him) the

---

119 Law Com No 245 (1997), paras 8.48–8.70.

120 *Ibid*, paras 8.71–8.83.

121 See *R v Bedi* (1992) 95 Cr App R 21; *R v Field* [1992] Crim LR 299; *Brown v Secretary of State for Social Security* (1994) *The Times*, 7 December. According to these decisions, the maker is the person who does the physical act of recording, not the supplier of the information that is recorded.

confession could be admitted only by the 'safety valve' mechanism. The Commission recommended the retention of the existing *res gestae* exceptions, the common enterprise exception, and a number of other common law exceptions, including reputation as evidence of a person's good or bad character.[122]

The safety valve[123]

The Commission recommended a limited inclusionary discretion to admit hearsay which falls within no other exception. Its purpose would be to prevent potential injustice that could arise through the exclusion of hearsay evidence. It should extend to oral as well as documentary hearsay, and to multiple as well as first hand hearsay. It should be available to both prosecution and defence if the court is satisfied that, despite the difficulties there may be in challenging the statement, its probative value is such that the interests of justice require it to be admissible. The Commission gave three examples of cases where an application might be made under such a provision:

(a) D is prosecuted for indecent assault on a child. The child is too young to testify, but she initially described her assailant as 'a coloured boy'. The defendant is white.

(b) D is prosecuted for the murder of his girlfriend. He denies that it was he who killed her. Fixing the time of the murder is an essential part of proving that D must have done it. A child aged eight tells the police that she saw the victim leaving her home at a time after the prosecution says she was dead. By the time the case comes to trial, the child can remember nothing about when she saw the victim.

(c) D is charged with assault. X, who is not charged, admits to a friend that he, X, committed the assault. D and X are similar in appearance. X's confession is inadmissible hearsay without the safety valve.

---

122 Law Com No 245 (1997), paras 8.84–8.99, 8.114–8.132.
123 *Ibid*, paras 8.133–8.149.

CHAPTER 8

HAZARDOUS EVIDENCE

All evidence, without exception, is hazardous because it is inherently liable to mislead. There are several reasons for this. The first is that all evidence emerges as a result of some kind of selection. One kind may be loosely described as 'natural selection'. Not all the evidence that is relevant to a particular inquiry will have survived. Witnesses may have died; documents may have been destroyed; the physical features of a building may have been altered. Another kind of selection is human selection. In any investigation someone has to gather the evidence that *has* survived; but to gather effectively, you have to be intelligent enough to recognise what may be significant, and honest enough to do the job without preconceived ideas of what the outcome of the investigation should be. Natural selection and human frailty between them ensure that no court ever sees more than a part of the whole picture, and that part may be a very small, misleading one.[1]

Another reason for the hazardous nature of evidence is that too much has to be taken on trust. It is not always appreciated that the only direct experience on which a tribunal of fact can rely in a legal inquiry is its perception of witnesses testifying in the witness box, and sometimes the perceptions resulting from its own examination of items of real evidence. In relation to a testifying witness two difficulties arise. The first comes from uncertainty about whether the witness can trust the evidence of his own senses. He may believe that he saw the defendant stab the victim, but what guarantee has he that things were not otherwise? The second difficulty comes from the fact that the court has to rely on the witness for an insight into what happened on the occasion under investigation. But all the triers of fact can perceive is the witness giving evidence. What is their justification for inferring from the witness's testimony that the defendant did in fact stab the victim?

A third reason for the hazardous nature of evidence is that, save for some items of real evidence, it is presented through the medium of language. But language is notoriously ambiguous. Words, it has been said:

> ... may be easily misunderstood by a dull man. They may be easily misconstrued by a knave. What was spoken metaphorically may be apprehended literally. What was spoken ludicrously may be apprehended seriously. A particle, a tense, a mood, an emphasis, may make the whole difference between guilt and innocence.[2]

---

1   Cf Carr, EH, *What is History?*, 2nd edn, 1987, pp 7–30.
2   Lord Macaulay, *The History of England from the Accession of James II*, 1849–55, repr 1880, Vol 2, Chap 5, p 161.

But more than this, the adversary system adopted in our courts tends to perpetuate ambiguity. One of the earliest lessons learned by the student of advocacy is how to avoid giving the witness whom he is cross-examining a chance to explain his testimony. Closed, leading questions requiring a 'yes' or 'no' answer are recommended. These may be good trial tactics, but they are ill-designed for the discovery of truth.[3]

Politicians and lawyers have usually turned a blind eye to these defects. Attempts to make verdicts a little more reliable have been made only erratically and on a piecemeal basis. But there have been attempts to remove the hazards involved in the selection by police and prosecuting authorities of evidence to be used against defendants in criminal trials. There have also been attempts to control the way in which juries think about kinds of evidence that at various times have been considered particularly unreliable.

From the first of these attempts, there developed a duty on the prosecution to disclose to the defence matters coming to light during their investigations that might assist the defence case.[4] The second kind of attempts gave rise to law compelling judges to warn juries in a particular way when they had to consider certain types of evidence, or evidence from certain types of witness.

In the 18th century, when the beginnings of our modern law of evidence can be seen, both prosecution and defence in criminal proceedings were often unrepresented by counsel, and the judge played a much larger part than in the 19th century and later. In particular, judges had greater control over juries' deliberations. Summings up could contain much more of the judge's opinion than would now be thought proper. Where it appeared that a deliberation was likely to be short, the jury would often not leave the jury box. Either then or in the course of testimony itself there was opportunity for informal dialogue with the judge about the evidence.[5]

This informal procedure, with its strong inquisitorial element, in time gave way to a system more like the one we are used to today, although there was one major difference: until 1898, there was no general right for a defendant to testify in his own defence. Prosecution and defence were increasingly represented by counsel, probably in part because of an increase in the size of the Bar, and the judge lost some of his control over the jury's deliberations. But because jurors were free to weigh the evidence without judicial intervention, it became more necessary to warn them during summing up

---

3   See, eg, Stone, M, *Cross-Examination in Criminal Trials*, 1988, p 107; Boon, A, *Advocacy*, 1993, pp 113–14. Cf McEwan, J, *Evidence and the Adversarial Process: The Modern Law*, 1992, pp 16–19; Law Com No 138 (1995), paras 6.42–6.49.

4   For further information about the prosecution's duty of disclosure, see the standard works on criminal procedure. The safeguards developed by the judges have recently been cut down by politicians: see the Criminal Procedure and Investigations Act 1996.

5   See above, Chapter 2.

about the weight to be attached to certain types of witnesses and testimony and of the danger of convicting on the basis of such evidence without some independent support. Warnings were thought to be necessary in three main cases: those involving the evidence of children, those involving the evidence of accomplices, and those involving complaints of a sexual crime. In these cases, juries were generally invited to look for evidence that supported, or, to use the technical expression, 'corroborated' the evidence regarded as hazardous, and were warned of the danger of convicting solely on uncorroborated evidence.

For a long time the content of the warning, and even whether a warning was given at all, was a matter solely for the trial judge's discretion. The mechanism for converting judicial discretion into rules of law did not exist: Parliament was an unsuitable institution to deal with the minutiae of criminal law reform, and there was no effective system of criminal appeals until the Court of Criminal Appeal was established in 1907. Only then did discretionary practices begin to harden into rules of law. It was not until 1916 that the law of 'corroboration' began to be clearly formed. From that time, however, it was settled that what was needed was some independent evidence implicating the accused in a material particular.[6]

Before long a highly complex body of law developed, the effect of which was that in the absence of an accurate warning, a conviction was very likely to be quashed. Reform came about only when fashionable opinion began to take a more trusting view of children's evidence and to regard as unconvincing the suggestion that some women might, for malicious reasons or for no reasons at all, concoct allegations against men of sexual offences. Corroboration law has now been very largely abolished by s 34(2) of the Criminal Justice Act 1988[7] and s 32 of the Criminal Justice and Public Order Act 1994.[8]

Alongside the strict law of corroboration there had grown up a less formal body of law about warnings that should be given to a jury where a witness might be unreliable, even though he did not fall within the limited classes to which corroboration law applied. For example, it was held that an informal warning should be given where witnesses had a purpose of their own to serve

---

6   *R v Baskerville* [1916] KB 658. For the development of corroboration law generally, see Allen, C, *The Law of Evidence in Victorian England*, 1997, Chapter 2.

7   In relation to the evidence of children.

8   In relation to evidence of complainants of sexual offences and evidence of accomplices. There was no pressure of opinion to change the law concerning accomplices' evidence, but it was presumably felt that the fewer opportunities judges had to get things wrong, the better it would be for criminal trials. There remain three cases where a conviction cannot be secured without corroboration: high treason, perjury and speeding. See Treason Act 1785, s 1; Perjury Act 1911, s 13; and Road Traffic Regulation Act 1984, s 89(2). See, generally, CLRC, 11th Report, para 183; Law Commission, *Corroboration of Evidence in Criminal Trials*, 1991, Cm 1620; Dennis, I, 'The Criminal Justice and Public Order Act 1994: the evidence provisions' [1995] Crim LR 4; Mirfield, P, '"Corroboration" after the 1994 Act' [1995] Crim LR 448.

in giving evidence, or where they suffered from mental disorder.[9] This body of law remained unaffected by the statutory provisions that abolished most of the old corroboration law. But it is unlikely now to have any independent existence. In *R v Makanjuola*,[10] the Court of Appeal emphasised that trial judges have a wide discretion to adapt warnings about the testimony of any particular witness to the circumstances of the case. It may be that the old, less formal body of law will be suggestive when considering whether a judge should now give a warning to the jury. But it cannot be put higher than that. What is clear is that if the judge decides in his discretion to give or not to give a warning, the exercise of that discretion will only exceptionally be reviewed by the Court of Appeal. Quite amazingly, it was initially suggested by some writers that all the old law about corroboration might still apply once a judge had decided to give a discretionary warning under the new system. The Court of Appeal abruptly rejected this notion in *R v Makanjuola*.

There remains one type of evidence where a warning is required which is still governed by a rule-based rather than a discretionary system. Identification evidence, falling within the principles set out in *R v Turnbull*[11] and subsequent cases, must be the subject of a particular type of judicial warning in the summing up. The reason for this is that the dangers of misidentification became a fashionable worry earlier than fears that insufficient credence was being attached to the evidence of children or of complainants in cases involving allegations of sexual misconduct. In the 1970s, the law of evidence was more rule-based than it later became, and so a rule-based remedy was applied to achieve reform.

Code D of the current Codes of Practice made under the Police and Criminal Evidence Act 1984 (PACE) is likely to be relevant to any problem involving identification. The whole of the Code is important, but special attention should be paid to Annex A (identification parades) and Annex D (showing photographs). The importance of the Code lies in the fact that evidence obtained in breach of its provisions is likely to be unreliable, and so likely to be excluded under s 78(1) of PACE.[12]

DISCRETIONARY WARNINGS TO THE JURY

Since *R v Makanjuola*,[13] it is clear that the effect of s 32(1) of the Criminal Justice and Public Order Act 1994 is that it is now a matter for the judge's

---

9   *R v Beck* [1982] 1 WLR 461; *R v Spencer* [1987] AC 128. See also Law Commission, *Corroboration of Evidence in Criminal Trials*, 1991, Cm 1620, Appendix C.

10   [1995] 3 All ER 730; *Sourcebook*, p 172.

11   [1977] QB 224; *Sourcebook*, p 174.

12   See further under the discussion of 'ill-gotten' evidence, below, Chapter 9.

13   [1995] 3 All ER 730; *Sourcebook*, p 172.

discretion what, if any, warning should be given in relation to *any* witness in whatever type of case. Such witnesses include co-defendants who give evidence.[14] But for a warning to be given, there must be some evidential basis for suggesting that the witness's testimony may be unreliable. It will not be enough merely to rely on the fact that the witness complains of a sexual offence, nor will the fact that a witness is an accomplice inevitably require a warning. Where the judge decides that some warning is required, its strength and terms are also a matter for his discretion. In particular, the warning does not have to follow the old corroboration rules. However, where a judge advises a jury to look for independent evidence that supports a particular witness's evidence, he should identify any evidence which, if believed by the jury, would be capable of giving such support.[15] Finally, the Court of Appeal said it would be slow to interfere with a judge's exercise of discretion in this respect except on the basis of *Wednesbury* unreasonableness.[16]

For these reasons, a detailed study of pre-*Makanjuola* case law is as unnecessary as it would be tedious. However, one type of evidence potentially supportive of the prosecution case has recently been considered by the courts on several occasions: a body of case law has developed concerning warnings that may be needed where lies have been told by a defendant.

Evidence of a defendant's lies

Evidence of lies told by a defendant either inside or outside court can have probative value, but it will often require a warning from the judge to ensure that the jury approaches such evidence carefully and does not give it more weight than is appropriate. The direction given by a judge on this subject is often called a '*Lucas* direction' after the name of a case[17] where the problem was discussed in the context of the old corroboration law. A more recent case, *R v Burge and Pegg*,[18] has restated the law in the following way.

The gist of the direction contains two points:

(a) the lie must be admitted by the defendant, or the jury must find it proved beyond reasonable doubt, before it can be taken into account; and

(b) the jury must be warned that the mere fact that the defendant has lied is not in itself evidence of guilt, because defendants may lie for innocent reasons. Only if the jury is sure that the defendant did *not* lie for an innocent reason can a lie support the prosecution case.

---

14 *R v Warwick Muncaster* [1999] Crim LR 409.
15 *R v B(MT)* [2000] Crim LR 181.
16 It confirmed this in *R v R* [1996] Crim LR 815.
17 *R v Lucas* [1981] QB 720; *Sourcebook*, p 169.
18 [1996] 1 Cr App R 163.

This cannot mean that the jury must find that the defendant lied *because he was guilty of the offence charged* before they can take the lie into account, for then they would already have come to the conclusion that the prosecution had proved its case and it would be unnecessary to refer to the lie at all. What it must mean is that the prosecution have to negative any innocent explanation for the lie given by the defendant or on his behalf before the jury can take the lie into account.

According to *R v Burge and Pegg*, a direction on these lines is usually required in four circumstances:

(a) Where the defendant relies on an alibi.

(b) Where the judge, in exercise of the wide discretion that he now has as a result of s 32 of the Criminal Justice and Public Order Act, suggests that the jury look for something to support a hazardous item of prosecution evidence and points to an alleged lie by the defendant as potential support.

(c) Where the prosecution try to show that the defendant has told a lie, either in or out of court, about a matter separate and distinct from the offence charged, but which points to the guilt of the defendant on that charge. For example, suppose George is charged with the murder, by shooting, of a bank clerk. He tells the police that he has never handled a gun in his life; in fact he has won several prizes in shooting competitions. The prosecution would argue that George lied to try to get out of trouble because he knew he was guilty.

(d) Where, although the prosecution have not used an argument like the one in (c), the judge thinks that the jury might adopt such an argument independently.

A direction is not required in every case where a defendant gives evidence merely because the jury might conclude that some of his evidence contained lies. Except, apparently, where the defence at trial is an alibi (the first of the four circumstances referred to in *R v Burge and Pegg*), a direction is not required if rejection by the jury of the defendant's evidence leaves them no choice but to convict. This will be the case where the prosecution witnesses' evidence is in direct and irreconcilable conflict with the evidence of the defendant and his witnesses. In such a case, a direction about lies would be unnecessary and confusing. If the jury comes to the conclusion that the prosecution witnesses are telling the truth, the outcome of the case is settled. For a direction to be appropriate, the lie generally has to be about a *subsidiary* matter so as to provide *additional* evidence of the defendant's guilt. Where there is no distinction between the issue of guilt and the issue of lies, a direction on the lines indicated in *R v Burge* will usually only confuse.[19]

---

19   *R v Harron* [1996] 2 Cr App R 457.

For example, suppose Bertie is charged with assaulting Freddie, whom he knows, in a bar. Bertie's case throughout has been that, although he was in the bar, he did not assault Freddie. He has said consistently that Freddie is trying to frame him because of a grudge arising from a quarrel about a business deal. On these facts the issue of lies and the issue of guilt exactly overlap. If the jury believe Freddie they are bound to convict Bertie, and it will follow that they must have believed that Bertie was lying in the witness box. But these lies did not relate to a subsidiary matter; they related to the central question of whether Bertie assaulted Freddie. Here the judge should *not* give a *Lucas* direction.

Now suppose that the charge is as before, but Bertie at first tells the police that he was never in the bar at all; he was at a cinema with his girlfriend Edith. When Edith is interviewed by the police, she fails to support his alibi. Bertie then admits that he gave a false alibi and produces in its place the defence described above. That false alibi is a subsidiary matter, capable of pointing to guilt on the charge of assault, but not entailing it. (In the first example, if the jury concluded that Bertie was lying, he was *inevitably* guilty as charged; not so in this example.) Here the judge *should* give a *Lucas* direction.[20]

IDENTIFICATION AND *TURNBULL* GUIDELINES

It has been recognised for many years that evidence of identification presents particular difficulties for any tribunal of fact. In its Eleventh Report, the Criminal Law Revision Committee stated: 'We regard mistaken identification as by far the greatest cause of actual or possible wrong convictions.'[21] A similar view was taken in the Devlin Report.[22] The reason is that evidence of identification is exceptionally difficult to assess. As the Devlin Report put it, there are two ways of testing a witness. The first is by the nature of his story – is it probable and coherent? The second is by the demeanour of the witness – does he appear to be honest and reliable? Eye-witnesses of an event can differ widely about the details of it. Normally, when a court has to reach a conclusion about an incident or event, it does not have to make a finding on each detail. It is enough if out of the evidence as a whole, there can be

---

20 For further examples, see *R v Robinson* [1996] Crim LR 417; *R v Hill* [1996] Crim LR 419; *R v Lesley* [1996] 1 Cr App R 39. In *R v Middleton* [2001] Crim LR 251, the Court of Appeal said that when deciding whether or not to give a *Lucas* direction, it would be more useful to consider the question in the context of the individual case, rather than by 'laboriously trawling through hosts of reported and unreported cases'. Where a *Lucas* direction would confuse the issue for the jury, it should not be given.

21 Criminal Law Revision Committee, Eleventh Report, *Evidence (General)*, 1972, Cmnd 4991, para 196.

22 *Report to the Secretary of State for the Home Department of the Departmental Committee on Evidence of Identification in Criminal Cases*, 1976, para 8.1.

extracted as much of the story as is necessary to know in order to determine the point in issue. But with identification evidence there is no story. The issue rests on a single piece of observation:

> The state of the light, the point of observation and the distance from the object are useful if they can show that the witness must be using his imagination; but otherwise where there is a credible and confident assertion, they are of little use in evaluating it. Demeanour in general is quite useless. The capacity to memorise a face differs enormously from one man to another ... If a man thinks he is a good memoriser and in fact is not, that fact will not show itself in his demeanour.[23]

English law now tries to protect defendants from wrongful convictions that are based on mistaken identification evidence in two ways: by a system of judicial warnings to juries, and by a Code of Practice governing identification procedures.

In *R v Turnbull*,[24] the Court of Appeal acknowledged that evidence of visual identification presented special difficulties in criminal cases and had led to miscarriages of justice. To deal with this problem, the court laid down guidelines for judges summing up in cases where the prosecution rely on contested identification evidence. Failure to follow the guidelines is likely to lead to the quashing of a conviction as unsafe. Two questions arise: (a) When do the guidelines apply? (b) What do they require the judge to do?

When do the guidelines apply?

They apply whenever the prosecution case depends 'wholly or substantially' on the correctness of one or more identifications of the defendant, and the defence allege that the identifying witnesses are mistaken. The words 'wholly or substantially' were used by Lord Widgery CJ in *R v Turnbull*. On the face of it, they suggest that a *Turnbull* direction would *not* be required where identification evidence was only a small item in a mass of other evidence against the defendant. But it is unlikely that a judge would invite an appeal by omitting the direction in a case where the prosecution placed *any* reliance on disputed identification evidence.

A *Turnbull* direction must be given in cases where identification is based on *recognition*, as well as in other situations where it might be thought that the risk of error was greater: for example, where there has been a mere fleeting glimpse by the identifying witness.[25]

---

23 Devlin Report, para 4.25.

24 [1977] QB 224; *Sourcebook*, p 174. The dangers inherent in identification evidence may also have to be considered in a civil context: *R v Cardinal Newman's School Birmingham ex p S* (1997) *The Times*, 26 December (DC).

25 *Shand v The Queen* [1996] 1 WLR 67, p 72.

The full direction does not have to be given where the jury itself is asked to make the identification. In *R v Blenkinsop*,[26] the jury was asked to identify the defendant, whom they had seen in court, as the person shown in a video film and various 'still' photographs taken at the scene of a demonstration. The Court of Appeal held that a full *Turnbull* warning was not required because the jury did not need to be told things such as whether the photograph was of good or poor quality, or whether the person alleged to be the defendant was shown in close up or not: they could see for themselves. But a jury should still be warned of the risk of mistaken identification and the need to exercise particular care in any identification which they make for themselves.

The need for a *Turnbull* direction arises generally where the issue is whether the defendant was present at a particular place or not. Where his presence at the scene is not disputed, but his participation in the offence is, the direction does not have to be given automatically. It *will* be necessary where there is the possibility that a witness has mistaken one person for another: for example, because of similarities of clothing, colour or build,[27] or because of confused action, such as a fight during a wedding reception.[28]

The *Turnbull* direction came into existence to deal with the problem posed by the honest but mistaken witness. Suppose, however, the defence is that the prosecution witnesses who purport to have identified the accused as being present are lying. In *Shand v The Queen*,[29] the Privy Council stated the position in this way. There may be exceptional cases where a *Turnbull* direction is unnecessary, or where it is sufficient to give it more briefly than where honest mistake is alleged, but the cases in which the warning can be wholly dispensed with must be exceptional. Even where the defence say that there has been perjury rather than an honest mistake, the judge should normally tell the jury to consider whether they are satisfied that the witness was not mistaken.

But there are cases where the Court of Appeal has recognised that, on the facts and because of the nature of the defence, the *Turnbull* warning *could* be omitted altogether. A recent case was *R v Cape and Others*[30] where the defendants were charged with violent disorder in a public house. The prosecution case depended solely on the evidence of the licensee, who knew the defendants. Each defendant said that, although he had been in the public house at the relevant time, he had not been involved in violence. Two said that the licensee was lying as the result of a grudge. The Court of Appeal said that, in relation to those two defendants, no issue of identification arose,

---

26 [1995] 1 Cr App R 7.
27 *R v Slater* [1995] 1 Cr App R 584.
28 *R v Thornton* [1995] 1 Cr App R 578.
29 [1996] 1 WLR 67.
30 [1996] 1 Cr App R 191.

because the allegation was that the licensee was framing them. Accordingly, no *Turnbull* direction had been required.[31]

It seems that a *Turnbull* warning is not required where a witness does not identify the suspect, but merely gives evidence of aspects of someone seen which point to the suspect as the person guilty of an offence. In *R v Byron*,[32] the defendant was charged with assaulting four children of the woman with whom he was living. Evidence was given by a witness who had seen a man with a large tattoo on his upper left arm striking two of the children. The defendant was one of only two adult males living in the house. He had such a tattoo, whereas the other did not. The Court of Appeal said that the evidence was 'descriptive' and was evidence of 'elimination' rather than of 'identification'.

The distinction was more fully considered in *R v Gayle*,[33] where the defendant was charged with burglary. The case for the prosecution was that he had entered a school classroom and there had stolen a handbag. The bag, without the money that it had contained, was found in the rubbish bin of a nearby public house in the following circumstances. Between 3.00 pm and 3.10 pm on the same day, a cook in the public house was preparing food for a customer whom she had not, at that stage, seen. While doing so, she saw a man by the rubbish bins in the yard. She described him as a black man, who was wearing a black nylon jacket with a brightly coloured capital 'K' on the back. She saw him put something in one of the bins. When she took the food that she had been preparing to the customer, she recognised him as the man she had seen in the yard. After serving him, she went to look in the rubbish bin. There she found the stolen handbag. The defendant, when interviewed by the police, admitted that he had been the man in the yard, but he said that he had gone to urinate there and had found the bag on the ground. He said that he had never seen it before and had put it in the bin.

There were certain internal difficulties with this account, but it was clearly desirable to establish some link between the defendant and the school. A possible link was the evidence of the school caretaker. He said that he had seen a man at about the relevant time on the school premises, going towards the exit that led to the public house, but that the man had been too far away for him to see his actual features. He was able to say, however, that it had been a black man in his late 20s to early 30s, six feet tall, stocky in build, wearing a black bomber jacket with the 'Kangol' logo on the back. Thus, it was possible for the jury to infer from this evidence that the man he had seen was the defendant. He had accurately described the jacket, he had seen the man walking towards the public house, and he had given a good general description that fitted the defendant.

---

31 See also *R v Courtnell* [1990] Crim LR 115.

32 (1999) *The Times*, 10 March. See also *D v DPP* (1998) *The Times*, 7 August; *R v Doldur* [2000] Crim LR 178.

33 [1999] 2 Cr App R 130.

No identification parade was held, and at trial the question arose whether there should have been a parade. The defence relied on Code D, para 2.3, of the Codes of Practice issued under the Police and Criminal Evidence Act 1984. This states that whenever a suspect disputes *an identification*, an identity parade shall be held, save in certain exceptional cases.[34] The trial judge held that a parade would have been inappropriate because the caretaker had not *identified* the defendant as the burglar. It was argued on appeal that the trial judge had been wrong, but the Court of Appeal disagreed. The caretaker had not identified as the defendant the person whom he had seen and described. Henry LJ said that there was a qualitative difference between identification evidence and 'evidence of description'.

He added:

> The special need for caution before conviction on identification evidence is because, as experience has often shown, it is possible for an honest witness to make a mistaken identification. But the danger of an honest witness being mistaken as to distinctive clothing, or the general description of the person he saw … [is] minimal. So the jury can concentrate on the honesty of the witness, in the ordinary way.[35]

If, where there is evidence that is merely evidence of description, the jury can 'concentrate on the honesty of the witness, in the ordinary way', it follows not only that an identification parade is inappropriate, but that a *Turnbull* warning is inappropriate also. This is consistent with the decision of the Court of Appeal in *R v Browning*,[36] where it was said that *Turnbull* warnings are inappropriate in cases involving the identification of motor cars.

Where identification is by voice, there is no obligation to hold a 'voice identification parade',[37] but evidence obtained in this way is not inadmissible.[38] Where evidence of identification by voice is relied on, the judge should direct the jury on suitably adapted *Turnbull* lines.[39]

What does a *Turnbull* direction require?

When a judge has to give a *Turnbull* direction he must do three things:

(a) He must warn the jury of the special need for caution before convicting the accused in reliance on the evidence of identification.

---

34 For a full discussion of this provision, see Chapter 9, below.

35 *R v Gayle* [1999] 2 Cr App R 130, p 135.

36 (1992) 94 Cr App R 109, pp121–23.

37 *R v Deenik* [1992] Crim LR 578; *R v Gummerson and Steadman* [1999] Crim LR 680.

38 *R v Hersey* [1998] Crim LR 281.

39 *Ibid; R v Gummerson and Steadman* [1999] Crim LR 680. See also *R v Roberts* [2000] Crim LR 183, where the Court of Appeal appeared to acknowledge that there are even greater difficulties with voice identification than with visual identification.

(b) He must tell the jury the reason for needing such a warning. Some reference should be made to the possibility that a mistaken witness can be a convincing one, and that a number of such witnesses can all be mistaken. In *R v Pattinson and Exley*,[40] the Court of Appeal allowed appeals and criticised a direction on identification for failing to make adequate reference to the risk of miscarriages of justice resulting from mistaken identification evidence.[41]

(c) He must direct the jury to examine closely the circumstances in which each identification came to be made.

The court in *R v Turnbull* suggested the following as possible subjects of judicial comment, and they can be used as a checklist, provided it is remembered that it is not an *exclusive* list.

(a) *Previous sightings.* Had the accused been seen by the witness before? Recognition may be more reliable than a fleeting glance, but the jury should still be reminded that mistakes in recognising relations and close friends are sometimes made.

(b) *Impediments.* Was observation impeded, for example, by passing traffic or people?

(c) *Distance.* How far away from the person identified was the identifying witness?

(d) *Discrepancies.* Is there a match between the witness's first description of the suspect to the police and the defendant's actual appearance?

(e) *Light.*

(f) *Extents of time.* How long did the observation last? How much time passed between the original observation and the witness's subsequent identification of the defendant to the police at an identification parade or by some other means?

(g) *Specific weaknesses.* Is the identification evidence weakened by any special circumstances: for example, because the identifying witness had been drinking or had weak sight?

However, it is not necessary in *every* case for the judge to summarise for the jury all the weaknesses in the identification evidence. If he does choose to summarise the identification evidence, he should point to strengths as well as weaknesses.[42] Having warned the jury in accordance with the guidelines, the

---

40 [1996] 1 Cr App R 51.

41 But *R v Turnbull* does not require the incantation of a formula. The judge has a broad discretion to express himself in his own way when directing a jury on identification. All that is required is that he should comply with the sense and spirit of the guidance in *R v Turnbull*. (*Mills v R* [1995] 3 All ER 865.)

42 *R v Pattinson and Exley* [1996] 1 Cr App R 51; *R v Qadir* [1998] Crim LR 828. But in some cases, a failure to point out weaknesses can be the basis of a successful appeal: see, eg, *R v Popat (No 2)* [2000] 1 Cr App R 387. So a judge who does not want to be successfully appealed should, to be safe, refer to weaknesses in all cases.

judge should go on to direct them to consider if the identification evidence is supported by any other evidence. At this stage he should identify for them the evidence that is capable and incapable of providing such support. Supporting evidence might include a rejected defence alibi,[43] or, today, the defendant's silence, either under police questioning or at trial.[44]

It was said in *R v Turnbull* that where the quality of the identification evidence is good, the jury can safely be left to assess it even without any supporting evidence, subject to an adequate warning. But where the quality is poor, the judge should withdraw the case from the jury at the end of the prosecution case unless there is other evidence to support the correctness of the identification.

IDENTIFICATIONS INSIDE AND OUTSIDE COURT

The law concerning identifications made inside and outside court is inevitably a compromise. On the one hand, it tries to ensure by the Code of Practice that such evidence is reliable. On the other hand, there is reluctance to exclude evidence of identification on technical grounds where there is little danger of unreliability. This can be seen, for example, in cases where the hearsay rule has either been ignored or treated in a cavalier fashion.

Dock identification

The rule here is often misunderstood. Identification of an accused person *for the first time* when he is in the dock at trial is to be avoided.[45] But once there has been an out-of-court identification, there can be no objection to asking a witness to identify the accused in court as part of the background to his account of events. The same would be true where identification was not an issue: for example, in a shoplifting case where the defendant does not deny being in the shop or taking the goods but says that he forgot to pay.[46]

---

43 But in that case the jury should be warned that a false alibi is sometimes invented to bolster a true defence: see *R v Lesley* [1996] 1 Cr App R 39.

44 Criminal Justice and Public Order Act 1994, ss 34 and 35.

45 *R v Cartwright* (1914) 10 Cr App R 219. But see *Barnes v Chief Constable of Durham* [1997] 2 Cr App R 505 (dock identifications customary in magistrates' courts).

46 Typically, the questioning would go somewhat as follows where the store detective is being examined: Where were you on such and such a date? Did you see anybody on that occasion? Do you see that person here in court today?

Evidence of previous identifications

It has long been settled that evidence of a previous out-of-court identification of the defendant can be given by the person who made the identification. The reason is that it shows that the witness was able to identify the accused at a time nearer to the events under investigation, so reducing the chance of mistake.[47]

Lax application of the hearsay rule

In various respects the law about identification has been only loosely controlled by the hearsay rule. Two examples can be given:

(a) The rule against hearsay has been relaxed, or ignored, to allow evidence to be given by a bystander of someone else's out-of-court identification. In *R v Christie*,[48] the defendant was charged with indecently assaulting a boy, who shortly after the incident had identified the defendant to his mother and a police officer as his assailant. In court, he identified the defendant again as his assailant, but for some reason was not asked about his earlier identification. It was held that evidence of this incident could be given by the police officer and the mother to confirm the identification made by the boy in court.

This approach was extended in *R v Osbourne and Virtue*[49] where it was held that if an identifying witness can remember picking someone out on an identification parade but cannot remember whom, evidence of someone who observed the parade may be given to fill the gap in the identifying witness's evidence. That case also held that even if a witness who identified the defendant on a parade cannot remember taking part in a parade at all and cannot identify the defendant in court, evidence may be given by another witness that the first witness did take part and picked out the defendant.

Even if the first part of the decision in *R v Osbourne and Virtue* can be justified on pragmatic grounds,[50] there are no grounds on which the second part can be supported. It goes beyond the decision of the House of Lords in *R v Christie* and leads to the admission of hearsay evidence where the defence have no opportunity of cross-examining the person who made the identification. Nevertheless, it is by now an established part of evidence law and likely to be followed in the future.

---

47 See the speech of Viscount Haldane in *R v Christie* [1914] AC 545; *Sourcebook*, p 176.

48 [1914] AC 545; *Sourcebook*, p 176.

49 [1973] 1 QB 678; *Sourcebook*, p 178.

50 Delays between identification parades and trial may cause a witness to forget the person he identified at the parade.

(b) Neither the hearsay rule nor the rule against previous consistent statements applies to sketches, whether made by the witness himself or by a police artist on the basis of instructions from the witness, or to photofit pictures of a suspect. In *R v Cook*,[51] the Court of Appeal held that sketches and photofits were in a class of their own and outside the scope of the rules. This is odd. A *verbal* description given by a witness to a police officer would be caught by the hearsay rule, and neither the police artist's picture nor the photofit specialist's image have the independence from a particular observer that is associated with a still photograph or video film (which are admissible as original evidence: see below, Chapter 17).

Neither a photofit nor a sketch amounts, by itself, to an identification of the defendant, and a *Turnbull* warning is therefore inappropriate. It has been suggested that a jury should be directed that the significance of a sketch or photofit is that it shows the witness's impression of the offender soon after the offence.[52]

Code D

Section 66 of the Police and Criminal Evidence Act 1984 provides that the Secretary of State shall issue codes of practice in connection with various matters, including the identification of persons. By s 67(11), any code shall be admissible in evidence, and if any provision of such a code appears to the court to be relevant to any question, it shall be taken into account in determining that question. There are currently five Codes of Practice. Code D is concerned with identification procedures. Usually, the defence will want to rely on a breach of Code D to argue that identification evidence is so unreliable that it ought to be excluded under s 78(1) of the Police and Criminal Evidence Act 1984. This provides:

> In any proceedings the court may refuse to allow evidence on which the prosecution proposes to rely to be given if it appears to the court that, having regard to all the circumstances, including the circumstances in which the evidence was obtained, the admission of the evidence would have such an adverse effect on the fairness of the proceedings that the court ought not to admit it.[53]

After a number of general provisions, Code D deals with identification by witnesses. By para 2.0, a record has to be made of the description of the suspect as first given by a potential witness. This must be done before the witness takes part in any formal identification process.

---

51 [1987] QB 417; *Sourcebook*, p 181.
52 May, R, *Criminal Evidence*, 4th edn, 1999, p 389.
53 This provision is more fully discussed in Chapter 9, below.

In a case that involves disputed identification evidence, and where the identity of the suspect is known to the police and he is available, there are four methods of formal identification by witnesses available. The first, and most favoured, is an identification parade. If a suspect refuses or fails to attend an identification parade, or the holding of a parade is impracticable, arrangements must if practicable be made to allow the witnesses the opportunity to see him in a 'group identification', a video film, or a 'confrontation'.[54]

Paragraph 2.3 provides as follows:

> Whenever a suspect disputes an identification, an identification parade shall be held if the suspect consents unless paragraphs 2.4 or 2.7 or 2.10 apply. A parade may also be held if the officer in charge of the investigation considers that it would be useful, and the suspect consents.

Under para 2.4, a parade need not be held if the 'identification officer', as defined in para 2.2, considers that it would not be practicable to assemble sufficient people who resemble the suspect to make the parade fair. So if the suspect is six feet seven inches tall and has red hair, the police are likely to be excused from holding a parade. Paragraphs 2.7 and 2.10 deal with the circumstances in which a 'group identification' and a video film identification respectively can be made.

Paragraph 2.3 is mandatory, unless one of the exceptions contained in that paragraph applies. There was formerly a division of opinion in the Court of Appeal over its interpretation. In *R v Popat*,[55] the court held that para 2.3 did not require an identification parade to be held where a suspect had previously been 'properly and adequately' identified by the relevant witness, or where there had been an 'actual and complete' identification by a witness. This view was rejected by a differently constituted court in *R v Forbes*,[56] where it was held that an identification parade was mandatory where the suspect asked for one, regardless of any previous identifications, unless one of the exceptions contained in the Code applied. The conflict was resolved by the House of Lords in *R v Forbes*,[57] which supported the decision of the Court of Appeal in that case and rejected *R v Popat*. However, it was said that para 2.3 did not cover all situations. It might be futile to have an identification parade if a witness to a crime had made it clear that he would not be able to recognise the culprit if he saw him again, or if the case was one of pure recognition of someone well known to the witness.

The Code does not prevent an initial street identification shortly after the commission of the offence. For example, in *R v Kelly*,[58] the defendant was

---

54   Paragraphs 2.1, 2.6.
55   [1998] 2 Cr App R 208.
56   [1999] 2 Cr App R 501.
57   [2001] 1 All ER 686.
58   [1992] Crim LR 181.

charged with attempted rape. The offence took place in a street and the attacker was disturbed before he could complete the full offence. The victim called for the police, who arrived shortly afterwards. As she was talking to the police, she saw the accused in the street and said, 'I think it's him'. One of the officers questioned, but did not arrest, the defendant. Meanwhile the victim was brought nearer to him, where the light was better, in a police car. She was asked to look hard and confirm that the man she saw was her attacker. She said she was sure and the accused was arrested.

On appeal, it was argued that the defendant should have been arrested as soon as the victim had pointed him out on the first occasion. The defendant would then have had the benefit of a properly conducted identification parade. The second stage of her identification had amounted to a confrontation, which according to the Code should not have taken place unless other forms of identification were impracticable. The Court of Appeal dismissed the appeal. It said that when a complainant made a tentative identification within minutes of her ordeal, but in a situation where distance and lack of light made the task difficult, the natural and sensible reaction was to take her closer for a better look. Where a suspect was found within minutes of the crime, and close to the scene, it might well be that the provisions of the Code did not apply.

In *R v Hickin and Others*,[59] the Court of Appeal took a similar view, saying that Code D catered largely for formal identification procedures and should not be interpreted so as to require the police to behave in a way that was an affront to common sense. In that case, the defendants were charged with violent disorder. The offence had been committed at night. Two men had been seriously injured in the disorder, and shortly after police learned of this they arrested a large group of suspects. Two members of the public saw the assaults and reported them to other police officers who, within minutes of the assaults, took the witnesses to the large group of suspects to see if they could identify participants. There were no identification parades.

The Court of Appeal approved of the course taken. It was clearly impracticable to set up that night the large number of identification parades that would have been required under Code D. It would have been undesirable to postpone the attempts at identification because recollections might become weaker, and later identifications would deprive the witnesses of the opportunity to see the suspects' clothing, which could be a valuable aid. The court observed, however, that in situations of this kind the police should record the information first received from the witnesses, as well as the precise steps taken afterwards. It also suggested that where there was more than one witness it might be advisable to reserve one or more for an identification parade – thus in effect providing a filter for suspects picked out by the informal procedure.

---

59 [1996] Crim LR 584. See also *R v Malashev* [1997] Crim LR 587; *R v Anastasiou* [1998] Crim LR 67.

The conduct of identification parades is governed by Annex A to Code D. It should be noted, in particular, that the parade must consist of at least eight persons, in addition to the suspect, 'who so far as possible resemble the suspect in age, height, general appearance and position in life'.[60]

A group identification takes place where the suspect is viewed by a witness amongst an informal group of people. For example, a witness in London might be asked to stand at the head of an escalator on the underground railway and observe the people travelling up it to see if he could identify anyone. The procedure may take place with the consent of a suspect, or covertly if the suspect has failed or refused to go on an identification parade. A group identification may also be arranged if the officer in charge of the investigation considers that it will be more satisfactory than a parade, whether because of fear on the part of the witness or for some other reason.[61]

The identification officer may show a witness a video film of the suspect if he considers that this would be the most satisfactory course of action – for example, if the suspect had refused to take part in an identification parade or a group identification. The suspect should be asked for his consent, but if this is refused, the identification officer has a discretion to proceed without it, if it is practicable to do so.[62] If a video identification is to be made, the film must include the suspect and at least eight other people who, so far as possible, resemble the suspect 'in age, height, general appearance and position in life'. The suspect and other persons shall as far as possible be filmed in the same positions or carrying out the same activity and under identical conditions.[63]

If neither a parade, a group identification nor a video identification is arranged, the suspect may be confronted by the witness. Such a confrontation does not require the suspect's consent, but it may not take place unless none of the other procedures is practicable.[64] But the police may not use force to make a suspect submit to a confrontation by a witness.[65] The suspect should be confronted independently by each witness, who should be asked, 'Is this the person?'. A confrontation should normally take place in a police station, either in a normal room or in one equipped with a screen permitting a witness to see the suspect without being seen.[66]

Where the identity of the suspect is not known, a police officer may take a witness to a particular neighbourhood or place to see whether he can identify the person he saw on the relevant occasion. Before doing so, a record should be made, where practicable, of any description given by the witness of the

---

60 Paragraph 8.
61 Paragraph 2.7.
62 Paragraphs 2.10, 2.11.
63 Annex B, paras 3, 4.
64 Paragraph 2.13.
65 *R v Jones and Nelson* (1999) *The Times*, 21 April.
66 Annex C, paras 3, 4.

suspect. Care must be taken not to direct the witness's attention to any individual.[67]

A witness must not be shown photographs or photofit, identikit or similar pictures if the identity of the suspect is known to the police and he is available to stand on an identification parade. If the identity of the suspect is not known, the showing of such pictures to a witness must be done in accordance with Annex D.[68] In particular, it should be noted that only one witness should be shown the photographs at any one time. He should be allowed as much privacy as is practicable, and should not be allowed to communicate with other witnesses.[69] He should be shown not less than 12 photographs at a time, which should, so far as possible, all be of a similar type.[70] If a witness makes a positive identification from photographs, then, unless the person identified is eliminated from inquiries, other witnesses must not be shown photographs. But both the identifying witness and the other witnesses should be asked to attend an identification parade (or group or video identification).[71]

Where the Code applies, failure to comply with its provisions will not be a breach where to comply would be futile. Thus, in *R v Montgomery*,[72] the Court of Appeal held that a suspect would not be entitled to a parade where there was no reasonable possibility that a witness would be able to make an identification.[73]

The fact that photographs have been used at some stage in the identification process will not usually be brought out at trial by the prosecution. The reason, of course, is that to disclose their use shows that the defendant has a criminal record. Where photographs have been used, the defence should be informed and left to decide for themselves whether any reference to this fact should be made.[74]

---

67 Paragraph 2.17.
68 Paragraph 2.18.
69 Annex D, para 2.
70 *Ibid*, para 3.
71 *Ibid*, para 5.
72 [1996] Crim LR 507.
73 The witness had made a statement, but said that she did not think she would be able to recognise the man again. See also *R v Nicholson* [2000] 1 Cr App R 182; *R v Forbes* [2001] 1 All ER 686.
74 *R v Lamb* (1980) 71 Cr App R 198; *Sourcebook*, p 183. But there is no absolute ban on reference by the prosecution to photographs: see *R v Allen* [1996] Crim LR 426. The best justification for this is that such evidence, though it may be probative, will normally be outweighed by the prejudicial effect on the jury when they hear something that shows the defendant to have a criminal record. But, as with all evidence, prejudicial effect is capable of being outweighed in a particular case by probative value: see the commentary on this case at p 427.

CHAPTER 9

CONFESSIONS AND ILL-GOTTEN EVIDENCE[1]

Although confessions are out-of-court statements adduced to prove the truth of their contents, they are admissible as an exception to the hearsay rule.[2] However, it is recognised that considerations of fairness or reliability may make it undesirable to admit evidence of a particular confession, or other items of evidence on which the prosecution proposes to rely. The law on these matters reflects a tension between the need to ensure the conviction of the guilty and the need to ensure that people are not convicted on evidence that is unreliable, or as a result of proceedings that are unfair.

To try to ensure reliability and fairness, Codes of Practice have been brought into existence under ss 60(1)(a) and 66 of the Police and Criminal Evidence Act 1984 (PACE).[3] They are aimed at controlling the way in which certain kinds of evidence are obtained. It is important to be familiar with their provisions, especially in relation to police questioning and identification, because breaches *may* lead to the exclusion of evidence under either s 76 or s 78 of PACE. It is also important to be aware of the right to legal advice, granted by PACE, that is reflected in some of the provisions of the Codes. But it is not enough merely to be able to point to a breach, either of a provision in PACE or of the Code: the breach must be used as part of a more complex argument. It is arguments of this kind that are the subject of this chapter.

Sections 76 and 78 of PACE deal respectively with confessions and with a discretion to exclude, for reasons of fairness, evidence on which the prosecution proposes to rely. These sections are very often relied on in the alternative. It was decided in *R v Mason*[4] that s 78 applies to confessions just as much as to any other evidence. The cases, therefore, cannot be read on the basis that one group is relevant to s 76 and another to s 78, and some overlap is inevitable in what follows.

---

1   The leading treatises are *Wolchover and Heaton-Armstrong on Confession Evidence*, 1996, and Mirfield, P, *Silence, Confessions and Improperly Obtained Evidence*, 1997. See also: CLRC, 11th Report, pp 34–47, 212–14; Royal Commission on Criminal Procedure, Cmnd 8092, 1981, Chapter 4; Royal Commission on Criminal Justice Report, Cm 2263, 1993, pp 57–68; Allen [1990] 49 CLJ 80; Pattenden [1991] 107 LQR 317; Choo [1991] Crim LR 867; Dennis [1993] PL 291; Birch (1994) 47 CLP, Part 2, 73; Hunter [1994] Crim LR 558; Sharpe [1994] Crim LR 793; Robertson [1994] Crim LR 805; Dennis [1995] 54 CLJ 342; Sharpe (1997) 1 E&P 149; Carter [1997] 113 LQR 468; Grevling [1997] 113 LQR 667; Easton (1998) 2 E & P 109; Birch [1999] Crim LR 769; Choo [1999] Crim LR 929; Jennings [2000] Crim LR 879.

2   Police and Criminal Evidence Act 1984 (PACE), s 76(1).

3   *Ibid*, ss 60(1)(a) and 66: Codes of Practice, revised edition, 1995.

4   [1988] 1 WLR 139.

A preliminary warning is necessary. In reading cases where evidence has been excluded under either section, but particularly under s 78, you are not reading precedents that will have to be followed in later cases. You cannot step twice into the same river. No situation is ever exactly repeated, no defendant is exactly like another, and the effect of acts or omissions by the police is likely to vary greatly from case to case. Knowledge of some previous decisions is helpful because they give some idea of the ways in which courts have behaved. But such knowledge is no substitute for careful thought about the facts of your own particular case, including the nature of your particular defendant. You cannot avoid the struggle to work out a satisfactory argument which will bring *your particular facts* within the scope of either s 76 or s 78. It is clear that the effect of s 76(2)(b) is to require the court to take into account the particular circumstances of the defendant who relies on the sub-section (see below). And, in relation to s 78, it has been said that the decision of a judge whether or not to exclude evidence is made as a result of the exercise by him of a discretion based upon the particular circumstances of the case and upon his assessment of the adverse effect, if any, it would have on the fairness of the proceedings. Judges may well take different views in the proper exercise of their discretion, even where the circumstances of two cases are similar. This is not an apt field for hard case law and well founded distinctions between cases.[5]

It is in relation to a confession that an argument for exclusion will very often have to be made. By s 76(2):

... if in any proceedings where the prosecution proposes to give in evidence a confession made by an accused person it is represented to the court that the confession was or may have been obtained–

(a) by oppression of the person who made it; or

(b) in consequence of anything said or done which was likely, in the circumstances existing at the time, to render unreliable any confession which might be made by him in consequence thereof,

the court shall not allow the confession to be given in evidence against him except in so far as the prosecution proves to the court beyond reasonable doubt that the confession (notwithstanding that it may be true) was not obtained as aforesaid.

This puts the burden of showing that a confession was *not* obtained in the vitiating circumstances referred to in (a) and (b) on the prosecution. By sub-s (3), the court may 'of its own motion' (that is, without the point being taken on the defendant's behalf) require the prosecution to satisfy it that a confession was not made in the vitiating circumstances.

By sub-s (4), the fact that a confession is wholly or partly excluded under sub-s (2) shall not affect the admissibility in evidence of any facts discovered

---

5   *R v Jelen and Katz* (1989) 90 Cr App R 456, pp 464–65; approved in *R v Roberts* [1997] 1 Cr App R 217, p 231 (CA).

as a result of the confession. Suppose Charlie confesses to stealing some jewellery and tells the police that he hid it under the floor in his bedroom. The police search his bedroom and recover the jewellery. The fact that the stolen jewellery was found in that place is admissible as evidence against Charlie, even if his confession is excluded under sub-s (2). What the police cannot say, if Charlie's confession is excluded, is that they found the jewellery in his bedroom *as the result of what he told them.*

By the same sub-section, where a confession has a relevance that goes beyond the truth of its contents because it shows that the defendant speaks, writes or expresses himself in a particular way, so much of the confession as is necessary to show that he does so will be admissible. Suppose Bertha has been raped. She tells the police that her attacker spoke English poorly, with a strong German accent. Hans is interviewed by the police and makes several damaging admissions. The interview is subsequently ruled inadmissible under sub-s (2). In principle the prosecution should be able to adduce enough of the tape containing neutral questions and answers to show that Hans speaks English poorly, with a strong German accent.

When a confession appears in a set of prosecution statements you must be able to do three things:

(a) recognise it when you see it;

(b) assess its impact on the case as a whole; and

(c) work out what arguments are available to you to get it excluded.

RECOGNISING THE CONFESSION

There is a partial definition of a confession in s 82(1) of PACE. 'Confession' includes any statement wholly or partly adverse to the person who made it, whether made to a person in authority or not and whether made in words or otherwise. Note that a statement only *partly* adverse to its maker comes within this definition. Thus, 'I admit I was at the robbery with Fred, but I only went with him because he threatened to shoot me if I didn't help' is a confession. It must be a question of fact whether a particular statement contains something that is adverse to its maker, and borderline cases could arise. What would be the effect, for example, of an admission that the defendant was in the area where a crime was committed, even though he denied having anything to do with its commission? Almost certainly the size of the area would be crucial. A defendant who admitted being in the same house as the deceased at the time of the murder would have made a statement that was partly adverse, but what of a defendant who admitted being only in the same city?

It is important to remember that a 'mixed' statement, containing partly favourable and partly adverse matters, is evidence of the truth of *all* its contents.[6] This means that in the unlikely event of the defendant's failure to testify, there will still be evidence of the favourable matters for the jury to consider, because those matters will have been referred to by the police witnesses. It is the duty of the prosecution to present the case fairly; to exclude answers that were favourable to the defendant while admitting those that were unfavourable would be misleading.[7]

If a defendant does not give evidence, his advocate may wish to argue that a statement made by his client contains inculpatory as well as exculpatory matters so as to have the whole statement admitted as evidence of the truth of its contents. The prosecution may then argue that the statement is purely exculpatory, because such a statement, though admissible as evidence of the accused's reaction to incriminating facts, is not admissible as evidence of the truth of its contents.[8] This is likely to be a hard distinction for a jury to appreciate, but the practical significance is that if the statement of a defendant who gives no evidence is mixed, and the defendant is of good character, the judge must direct the jury that his good character is relevant both to disposition and to credibility.[9] Further, such a statement is likely to satisfy any evidential burden that the defendant may have: for example, in relation to self-defence.

A situation of this kind arose in *Western v DPP*,[10] where the defendant was charged with using threatening behaviour, contrary to s 4 of the Public Order Act 1986. Police had found the defendant fighting with another man in an alley. When interviewed, he admitted that he had hit the other man, but said that he had done so in self-defence. At trial, the defendant gave no evidence, but it was argued that what he had said when interviewed raised the issue of self-defence. The magistrates took the view that it had not, on the basis that it was a purely exculpatory statement. The defendant was convicted. On appeal, it was argued that the magistrates had been wrong, because the defendant had admitted his presence in the alley and his participation in fighting. That was sufficient to make the statement mixed. The prosecution argued that a statement is mixed only if the prosecution relies on inculpatory parts of it. In this case, it was argued, the prosecution was not relying on admissions about presence in the alley or participation in fighting: there was ample evidence of those matters from police witnesses. But the Divisional Court observed that there had been no finding by the magistrates that the prosecution did not rely on the defendant's admissions. 'Indeed,' said Butterfield J, 'it is highly likely that the prosecution did rely on those admissions. Not only had the defendant

---

6   *R v Sharp* (1988) 86 Cr App R 274 (HL); *Sourcebook*, p 190; followed *R v Aziz* [1996] AC 41 (HL).

7   *R v Pearce* (1979) 69 Cr App R 365; *Sourcebook*, p 357.

8   *R v Storey and Anwar* (1968) 52 Cr App R 334.

9   See Chapter 11.

10 [1997] 1 Cr App R 474.

admitted presence at the scene and fighting, but had also admitted a series of earlier exchanges with the other man that could have given rise to an inference that he was angry, ready and willing to fight, and was far from acting in self-defence.'

On that narrow ground, the Divisional Court was prepared to allow the appeal, but the Court added that it had grave doubts about the correctness of the prosecution's argument. Whether a statement is mixed or not should not depend on whether other evidence is available to the prosecution, but on an examination of the statement itself. This view seems, tacitly at least, to have been adopted in *R v Garrod*,[11] in which the Court of Appeal said that where a statement contains an admission of fact that is *capable* of adding *some* degree of weight to the prosecution case, the statement must be regarded as mixed.[12]

But suppose a statement appears to be *purely* exculpatory. Then, later, it can be shown to be a lie and thus incriminating. Will this make it a confession? In two cases, the Court of Appeal has said that this will not make a confession out of an apparently wholly exculpatory statement. In *R v Sat-Bhambra*,[13] the court had to consider the admissibility of a number of tape recorded interviews between customs officers and the defendant. Defence counsel admitted that the answers given by his client were exculpatory, but he argued that they had a damaging effect because they showed the defendant to be evasive and prevaricating, and because many of the statements which he made proved eventually to be false. The court took the view, *obiter*, that purely exculpatory statements were not within the scope of s 82(1). Section 76 was aimed at excluding confessions obtained by words or deeds likely to render them unreliable, that is, admissions or partial admissions contrary to the interests of the defendant and welcome to the interrogator. The section 'can hardly have been aimed at statements containing nothing which the interrogator wished the defendant to say and nothing apparently adverse to the defendant's interests'. As Lord Lane observed, to hold otherwise would mean that the statement 'I had nothing to do with it,' might in due course become a 'confession', which, he thought, would be surprising.[14]

This interpretation was adopted by the Court of Appeal in *R v Park*.[15] The defendant had been stopped by police while driving a car with defective rear lights. During a roadside conversation the police came to suspect that he was carrying stolen goods, and a conversation then took place in which the defendant made only exculpatory statements, some of which were later shown to be false. The court held that these statements did not amount to

---

11   [1997] Crim LR 445.
12   My emphasis. See Birch, D, 'The sharp end of the wedge: use of mixed statements by the defence' [1997] Crim LR 416.
13   (1989) 88 Cr App R 55; *Sourcebook*, p 187.
14   (1989) 88 Cr App R 55, p 61.
15   (1994) 99 Cr App R 270; *Sourcebook*, p 188.

confessions, because s 82(1) was not aimed at statements that the maker intended to be exculpatory, that were exculpatory on their face, but that could later be shown to be false or inconsistent with the maker's evidence on oath.[16]

Section 82(1) establishes that a confession can be made 'in words or otherwise' and whether or not the person to whom it is made is 'a person in authority'. The definition thus assumes that a statement can be made by non-verbal means. While this clearly includes a gesture intended to acknowledge guilt, such as a nod of the head when an accusation is put, it might also include an action that was not so intended, but from which a confession is capable of being *inferred*. If there can be an implied assertion by conduct for the purpose of the hearsay rule, as was suggested in *Wright v Doe d Tatham*,[17] a potentially incriminating act of the defendant, such as running away or attempting to bribe witnesses, might amount to a confession.

In *R v Hazy and Collins*, the defendants' flight when detected in the act of lopping a tree was held to be capable of showing that they were acting without authorisation.[18] In *Moriarty v London, Chatham and Dover Railway Co*,[19] a plaintiff's attempts to persuade several persons to give false evidence in support of his claim was held to be evidence of an admission by conduct that the case he was putting forward was untrue. More recently, in *Parkes v R*,[20] a girl had been stabbed to death and the defendant was charged with murdering her. The mother of the girl testified that when she found that her daughter had been injured, she accused the defendant to his face. He made no reply, whereupon she threatened to detain him until the police could arrive. He then attempted to stab her. The Privy Council held that the defendant's reaction to the accusation was evidence from which the jury could infer that he acknowledged the truth of the accusation.[21]

It was emphasised in *Parkes v R* that the defendant's reaction had not been one of *mere* silence, and thus the Privy Council appeared to leave undecided the effect of silence alone in the face of an accusation. But if silence could be interpreted as an adoption of an allegation made against a suspect, it could in principle amount to a confession, since by s 82(1) a confession may be made 'in words or otherwise'. Whether silence is capable of amounting to an

---

16 The decisions in *R v Sat-Bhambra* and *R v Park* appear to support the view taken in *Western v DPP* that the nature of a statement depends on its contents, rather than on the use made of them.

17 (1837) 7 A&E 313. See also *R v Kearley* [1992] 2 AC 228.

18 (1826) 2 C&P 458. But the decision was of a trial judge on assize and the defendant was unrepresented.

19 (1870) LR 5 QB 314.

20 [1976] 1 WLR 1251.

21 See also *Preece and Others v Parry* [1983] Crim LR 170, where the Divisional Court held that the defendants' violent and abusive behaviour to the police when arrested for committing criminal damage and assault in a public house earlier that evening was capable of constituting an admission to those offences.

adoption of an accusation will be a question of fact in each case. But old civil cases dealing with admissions show that this is possible, and 'confessions' are just admissions (partial or complete) made by the defendant in a criminal case.[22]

Two cases often contrasted are *Bessela v Stern*[23] and *Wiedemann v Walpole*.[24] The first of these was an action for breach of promise of marriage. The plaintiff testified that the defendant had seduced her, had made her pregnant, and had repeatedly promised to marry her. Her sister gave evidence that she had overheard a conversation between the plaintiff and the defendant after the child had been born. During this encounter, the plaintiff had said to the defendant, 'You always promised to marry me and you don't keep your word'. The defendant's response was to say that he would give her some money to go away. Statute required that in a breach of promise case there had to be material evidence in support of the promise, apart from that of the plaintiff, and the question arose whether the evidence of the defendant's response satisfied this requirement.

The Court of Appeal held that it did. Cockburn CJ pointed out that the defendant had made no answer to the allegation. True, he had offered her money to go away, and that might have been done even if there had been no promise to marry. But on the other hand, the jury could infer from his silence that he admitted the promise. And Bramwell LJ said: 'If a statement is such that a denial of it is not to be expected, then silence is no admission of its truth; but if two persons have a conversation, in which one of them makes a statement to the disadvantage of the other, and the latter does not deny it, there is evidence of an admission that the statement is correct.'[25]

In *Wiedemann v Walpole*, the Court of Appeal was concerned with another breach of promise case. Here the plaintiff claimed that she and the defendant had had sexual intercourse at a hotel in Constantinople and that he had promised to marry her. The plaintiff produced at trial copies of three letters that she and others on her behalf had later sent to the defendant alleging his promise of marriage. The defendant had not answered any of these letters and the question arose of whether his silence was capable of being construed as an admission of the allegation.

Lord Esher MR said that the context was not the same as a commercial one, where silence following an allegation in correspondence that a promise had been made might amount to an admission. Such cases as those were 'wholly unlike the case of a letter charging a man with some offence or meanness'. According to the ordinary practice of mankind, an admission of guilt could not be inferred from failure to answer.

---

22 Stone, J and Wells, W, *Evidence*, 1991, pp 345–46.
23 (1877) 2 CPD 265.
24 (1891) 2 QB 534.
25 (1877) 2 CPD 265, p 272.

If it were so, life would be unbearable. A man might day by day write such letters, which, if they were not answered, would be brought forward as evidence of the truth of the charges made in them. The ordinary and wise practice is not to answer them – to take no notice of them.[26]

But Lord Esher emphasised the importance of the circumstances; the effect might be different if the allegation were contained in one letter which went unanswered as part of a continuing correspondence between a man and a woman.

A comparison of *Bessela v Stern* and *Wiedemann v Walpole* suggests that silence in the face of an *oral* accusation will be more readily interpreted as acknowledgment of its truth than silence in the face of a written accusation. The reason for this is probably that the greater immediacy of an accusation made face to face is thought to make failure to respond more suspicious than failure to reply to a letter. A recent case has shown that an oral assertion need not even be made in circumstances where one person accuses another for silence to be interpreted as acknowledgment of guilt. In *R v Batt*,[27] the failure by one defendant to dissociate himself from something said to him by another defendant in a conversation was interpreted as acknowledging an allegation of a criminal offence to be true. Ashley and Kerry Batt were charged with robbery. There was evidence that one of the robbers had been holding a gun concealed by some material. While they were on remand in custody the two men shared a cell at the police station. A policeman reported a lot of shouting. He said he heard Kerry say, 'They'll fuck themselves if they show that gun in court. It's not the one used'. Kerry added, 'I've got a friend ID'ing [identifying] me. He is very frightened. He won't pick me out. He knows better than that'.

At trial the judge, when summing up, merely observed that there was nothing recorded of anything said by Ashley in that conversation. It was argued on appeal for Ashley that the judge should have directed the jury that anything Kerry might have said was not evidence against Ashley. But the prosecution argued that the evidence was admissible against Ashley as well as Kerry because Ashley had been present when the words were shouted, had heard what was said, and had failed to dissociate himself from it. The Court of Appeal upheld the prosecution's argument.

IMPACT OF A CONFESSION ON THE CASE AS A WHOLE

The impact is obvious where a defendant has said something that incriminates him in relation to the offence charged. But suppose a defendant says

---

26 [1891] 2 QB 534, p 538.
27 [1995] Crim LR 240.

something that incriminates not only himself but also his co-defendant. Where such a statement was made in the presence of the co-defendant, it may be possible to argue that the latter, by his own words or actions or by his silence, adopted what was said so as to make the statement his own. But if what was said was not in the presence of the co-accused, this is not possible. Then, because of the hearsay rule, what was said outside court will be evidence against the speaker only and not against the co-defendant.[28] This does not mean that the statement will inevitably be excluded at trial, either wholly or in part. Sometimes in the past the judge has agreed to 'edit' a record of a statement or interview so as to omit references to co-defendants. But it is clear that this practice will not be adopted where the defendant who made the remarks does not agree to editing.

The leading authority is now the decision of the Privy Council in *Lobban v The Queen*.[29] Three robbers had entered a house with guns and had killed three victims during the robbery. Lobban and another man named Russell were charged with their murder. About six weeks after the killings, Russell made a statement to the police in which he admitted being the driver of the car in which the robbers had made their journey. But he said that he had not known what the men intended to do. He had seen the guns only when his passengers came out of the house to which they had told him to drive. He added that they had forced him to drive them away. In the final paragraph of his statement, he explained that some time later he had seen a photograph of Lobban in a newspaper and had then recognised him as one of the men involved. The prosecution tendered this statement as part of the evidence against Russell. Counsel for Lobban asked the trial judge to exclude the final paragraph implicating his client. Counsel for Russell objected and the judge refused to exclude it. His refusal was the basis of subsequent appeals after Lobban's conviction.

The Privy Council held that the final part of the statement was relevant to Russell's defence because it might have helped to explain the gap of six weeks between the murders and Russell's report to the police. His reference to Lobban was an integral part of that explanation and was put forward as a sign of frankness. It was therefore relevant. Given its relevance, the judge had no discretion to exclude it. The discretionary power to exclude relevant evidence applies only to evidence on which the *prosecution* proposes to rely. It exists to ensure a fair trial to the defendant or, in a joint trial, to each defendant. But it does not extend to the exculpatory part of a mixed statement on which one of the *defendants* proposes to rely. Any suggestions to the contrary in earlier cases were wrong.

---

28 *R v Gunewardene* [1951] 2 KB 600. Of course, the same is also true of a statement which is wholly exculpatory in relation to its maker and in which all the blame is put on a co-defendant.

29 [1995] 2 Cr App R 573.

So far I have been concerned with what one defendant says *outside court* concerning another. What one defendant says *in court* about another is treated differently. Evidence given by one defendant in his own defence at trial is evidence against co-defendants whom it implicates just as much as the evidence from prosecution witnesses.[30] Suppose a defendant (D1) makes a statement outside court to a policeman (P) about another defendant (D2). D1's statement cannot be evidence against D, when repeated by P in court, because of the hearsay rule. But if D1 makes the same allegation against D2 from the witness box at trial, the evidence of D1 will not be hearsay. D1 may, of course, be cross-examined on it by counsel for D2 and it is for this reason that a distinction is drawn between a statement by one defendant about another made *outside court* and a similar statement made by that defendant from the witness box *in court*.

EXCLUDING THE CONFESSION

A confession can be open to attack under s 76(2)(a) or (b). Section 76(2)(a) provides for exclusion where the confession was, or may have been, obtained by oppression. Under s 76(2)(b), a confession will be excluded where it was, or may have been, obtained 'in consequence of anything said or done which was likely, in the circumstances existing at the time, to render unreliable any confession which might be made by [the defendant] in consequence thereof'.

Section 76(2)(a)

It is sometimes assumed that *any* police impropriety amounts to oppression. This is not the case: attention should be paid to the partial definition of oppression in s 76(8)[31] and to two cases where the meaning of oppression was discussed by the Court of Appeal.

In *R v Fulling*,[32] Lord Lane CJ said that the word should be given its ordinary dictionary meaning. He cited a definition from the *Oxford English Dictionary*: 'Exercise of authority or power in a burdensome, harsh or wrongful manner; unjust or cruel treatment of subjects, inferiors, etc; the imposition of unreasonable or unjust burdens.' He also cited an illustrative quotation from the dictionary entry: 'There is not a word in our language which expresses more detestable wickedness than oppression.' Lord Lane thereby emphasised the seriousness of the conduct envisaged and added that

---

30 *R v Rudd* (1948) 32 Cr App R 138; *Sourcebook*, p 78.

31 By s 76(8) oppression 'includes torture, inhuman or degrading treatment, and the use or threat of violence (whether or not amounting to torture)'.

32 [1987] QB 426; *Sourcebook*, p 196.

the court found it hard to think of circumstances in which there would be oppression without some impropriety on the part of the interrogator.[33]

But the case of *R v Paris and Others*[34] shows that even in the absence of physical violence an interview can be oppressive. The Lord Chief Justice said that, on hearing one of the interview tapes, each member of the court had been horrified. The defendant Miller, the admissibility of whose confessions was in issue, had been 'bullied and hectored'. The officers were not questioning him so much as shouting at him what they wanted him to say. Short of physical violence, it was hard to conceive of a more hostile and intimidating approach by officers to a suspect. The court said that the tapes made it clear that for extended periods Miller was crying and sobbing, yet he was not given any respite.

The court had no doubt that there had been oppression. A confession obtained in such circumstances would have been unreliable even with a suspect of normal mental capacity. In fact, Miller was on the borderline of mental handicap with an IQ of 75, a mental age of 11 and a reading age of eight. There had been a solicitor present, but he had scarcely intervened at all. The Lord Chief Justice pointed out that Law Society guidelines for solicitors advising a suspect in the police station had apparently been ignored and added, 'We can only assume that, in the present case, the officers took the view that unless and until the solicitor intervened, they could not be criticised for going too far. If that is so, they were wholly wrong'.[35] Although the court did not expressly say so, it seems clear from these words that police officers conducting an interrogation have a duty of fairness to suspects which they break at their peril. The presence of a legal adviser does not diminish this duty one jot, let alone extinguish it. The appeal was allowed and the court ordered that copies of the relevant tape be sent to the DPP.

Section 76(2)(b)

The test that has to be applied under this provision is not a test of *actual* reliability. Instead, the question the court has to ask is a *hypothetical* one: might what was said or done have been likely, in the circumstances, to make *any* confession by that defendant unreliable?

The hypothetical nature of this question can be seen in *R v Cox*.[36] The defendant, who was mentally handicapped, was interviewed by police in the

---

33 So it is clear that not everything in Lord Lane's dictionary definition will be 'oppression' for these purposes. The exercise of power might be wrongful (because, eg, of an honest mistake) but not oppressive.

34 (1993) 97 Cr App R 99; *Sourcebook*, p 199.

35 (1993) 97 Cr App R 99, p 110.

36 [1991] Crim LR 276.

absence of an 'appropriate adult', in breach of Code of Practice C. During the interview, he admitted being a party to two burglaries. The defence applied to exclude his confession under s 76(2)(b), but when the defendant gave evidence on the *voir dire* as part of this application, he admitted his involvement in one of the burglaries. This led the judge to conclude that the confession was reliable and should therefore be admitted. The Court of Appeal held that the judge had applied the wrong test. The essential question was not whether the confession was true, but whether the breach of the Code was likely in the circumstances to produce an unreliable confession. In *R v Bow Street Magistrates' Court ex p Proulx*,[37] the Divisional Court held that 'any confession' referred to *any such a confession as the defendant had made*. Thus, the subject matter of the confession cannot be disregarded when applying the test Were it otherwise, it would always be possible to think of some confession by the defendant that would be likely to be unreliable as a consequence of what was said or done. For example, a trivial breach of Code C might make a confession to a trivial offence unreliable because the defendant might have thought that a conviction for such an offence did not matter. However, the same would not be true of a confession to a much graver offence.

For sub-s (2)(b) to apply, it must be shown, as with sub-s (2)(a), that the matters complained of *did in fact cause the confession to be made*. It is particularly important to remember this when considering sub-s (2)(b) because a confession that may very well be unreliable is not covered by that sub-section unless it was made as a result of something 'said or done' by a person other than the suspect. In *R v Goldenberg*,[38] it was argued that a defendant's confessions ought to have been excluded because he was a heroin addict who had been in custody for some weeks, so that it might have been expected that he would say anything to get bail and feed his addiction. No submission had been made at trial to exclude under s 78, but there had been a submission under s 76(2)(b). It was argued that 'anything said or done' could include things said or done by the suspect. Here the suspect had requested an interview. In the court's view, however, the language of the statute did not extend so far. The words were limited to something external to the person making the confession.[39]

But once you can show that an external factor may have caused the confession, the purely personal circumstances of the defendant *can* be taken into account to determine whether that external factor was likely to render unreliable any confession that the accused might make in consequence. This is so because the accused's personal circumstances are *at that stage* part of what

---

37 [2001] 1 All ER 57.

38 (1989) 88 Cr App R 285; *Sourcebook*, p 204.

39 In similar circumstances s 78 should be used: see *R v Anderson* [1993] Crim LR 447 (chronic alcoholism). But see *R v Walker* [1998] Crim LR 211, where the Court of Appeal appears to have taken the view that the mere interviewing of the suspect is capable of being something 'said or done'.

s 76(2)(b) refers to as 'the circumstances existing at the time', in the light of which reliability has to be tested.[40]

For example, in *R v McGovern*,[41] the appellant relied on four grounds for saying that a confession had been made in consequence of things said or done which were likely in the circumstances existing at the time to make any confession unreliable:

(a) The appellant had unlawfully been denied access to a solicitor.

(b) There had been a breach of Code C in relation to notes of the interview.

(c) The appellant was peculiarly vulnerable because of her low IQ and mental age.

(d) The physical condition of the appellant at the time of her interview. She was six months pregnant and had been vomiting in her cell before interview.

The Court of Appeal remarked that although items (c) and (d) were not within the scope of 'anything said or done', they did form the background upon which the submission was made that the confession was unreliable.

This was another of those cases where the police evidence itself lifts the curtain slightly so that we get a glimpse of another world. This was one of the officers giving evidence on the *voir dire*:

> The lady [meaning the defendant] didn't understand all the questions. She didn't even know why she was in the police station. In the last part of the interview she was crying; she was clearly upset; she was crying heavily. Yes, I carried on questioning her. She was not offered a break to compose herself, not even a glass of water. I never offered her a solicitor until she confessed.[42]

In *R v McGovern*, there was a second interview the following day. This was conducted in accordance with the provisions of Code C and in the presence of a solicitor. The defendant made a full confession. Could the prosecution rely on *that* interview, even if they could not rely on the first? The Court of Appeal said they could not. When an accused person has made a series of admissions at a first interview, the very fact that those admissions have been made is likely to have an effect on the second interview. The second interview must therefore be tainted if the first was.

However, what was said on this point has to be read in the light of *R v Neil*,[43] where the Court of Appeal considered earlier decisions and said that

---

40　Because the court will be concerned with the reliability of the confession, which can be affected without improper behaviour by the police, these personal circumstances need not have been known to the police. If they were known and advantage was taken of them there would have been impropriety as well as possible unreliability, and in a serious case there might even have been oppression.

41　(1991) 92 Cr App R 228; *Sourcebook*, p 206.

42　(1991) 92 Cr App R 228, p 233.

43　[1994] Crim LR 441. See also *R v Nelson* [1998] 2 Cr App R 379.

whether a later, unobjectionable, interview should be excluded is a matter of fact and degree. The answer will depend, first, on whether the matters that led to the exclusion of the earlier interview were of a 'fundamental and continuing nature'. The meaning of this expression is unclear. An example might be where an officer who had used oppression in the first interview also conducted the second. If the matters that led to the exclusion of the earlier interview were not of a fundamental and continuing nature, admissions in the second interview would presumably be admitted. If they were of such a nature, a second question has to be asked: did the arrangements for the later interview give the accused sufficient opportunity to exercise an informed and independent choice about whether to adopt or retract what he had said earlier, or to say nothing?

An argument frequently found in connection with both s 76 and s 78 is that the challenged item of evidence was obtained by breach of the defendant's right to legal advice. There is no doubt that a breach of this right, or of some provision under one of the Codes, counts as something 'said or done' for the purposes of s 76. The right in question is set out in s 58 of PACE.

The fundamental provision, contained in s 58(1), is that a person arrested and held in custody in a police station or other premises shall be entitled, if he so requests, to consult a solicitor privately at any time. By sub-s (4), if a person makes such a request, he must be permitted to consult a solicitor as soon as is practicable unless delay is permitted. In any case he must be permitted to consult a solicitor within 36 hours from 'the relevant time', which is likely to be the time of arrival at the police station.[44]

Delay is usually permitted only in the case of a person who is in police detention for a 'serious arrestable offence'[45] and if an officer of at least the rank of superintendent authorises it. By sub-s (8), an officer may authorise delay only where he has reasonable grounds for believing that to permit consultation with a solicitor will lead to interference with or harm to evidence connected with a serious arrestable offence, or interference with or physical injury to other persons; or will lead to the alerting of other persons suspected of having committed such an offence but not yet arrested; or will hinder the recovery of any property obtained as the result of such an offence.

The importance of the right to consult a solicitor was emphasised in *R v Samuel*,[46] where it was described in the judgment of the Court of Appeal as 'one of the most important and fundamental rights of a citizen'. Breach is therefore very likely to lead to the exclusion of a confession, either under s 76 or s 78. An exceptional case is *R v Alladice*.[47] The defendant was convicted of

---

44 See PACE, ss 58(5) and 41(2).
45 See PACE, s 116 and Sched 5, Part I.
46 [1988] QB 615; *Sourcebook*, p 217.
47 (1988) 87 Cr App R 380; *Sourcebook*, p 220. See also *R v Gerald* [1999] Crim LR 315.

robbery. The prosecution relied on admissions which, according to the defence, should have been excluded because he had been wrongfully denied a solicitor. The Court of Appeal agreed that there had been a breach of s 58, but said that the question then arising was whether the confession been obtained *as a result of that breach*[48] and, if so, whether that was likely in all the circumstances to render the confession unreliable. The defendant had given evidence on the *voir dire*. He had said that he was well able to cope with interviews, that he had been given the appropriate caution before each of them, that he had understood the caution and had been aware of his rights. His reason for wanting a solicitor had been to have some sort of check on the conduct of the police during the interview. The trial judge concluded that the only difference the presence of a solicitor would have made would have been to provide additional advice as to the appellant's right to say nothing. This right the defendant knew and understood and, at times during the interview, had exercised. The Court of Appeal commented that 'it may seldom happen that a defendant is so forthcoming about his attitude towards the presence of a legal adviser'.[49]

Not surprisingly, the court concluded on these facts that there was no case for exclusion, either under s 76 because of the absence of causation, or under s 78 on the fairness principle. But this kind of situation is rare. It certainly does not follow that a suspect with previous convictions can safely be denied a solicitor because he is supposed to know his rights.[50]

SECTION 78(1)

Section 78(1) provides:

> In any proceedings the court may refuse to allow evidence on which the prosecution proposes to rely to be given if it appears to the court that, having regard to all the circumstances, including the circumstances in which the evidence was obtained, the admission of the evidence would have such an adverse effect on the fairness of the proceedings that the court ought not to admit it.

---

48   See the wording of s 76(2)(b). There was no suggestion of oppression.

49   (1988) 87 Cr App R 380, p 386.

50   The right to legal advice must also be considered in the light of the European Convention on Human Rights, but the impact of the Convention has so far been almost entirely on special provisions contained in anti-terrorist legislation. See *Magee v United Kingdom* [2000] Crim LR 681 and *Averill v United Kingdom* [2000] Crim LR 682. It also led to the passing of s 34(2A) of the Criminal Justice and Public Order Act 1994: see below, p 242.

Interpretation

There are several points to be made about the interpretation of this provision:

(a) 'In any proceedings': 'proceedings' means criminal proceedings, whether in the Crown Court or in magistrates' courts.[51]

(b) 'The court may refuse to allow evidence ... to be given': the idea of discretion appears at first sight to be expressed in two ways. Section 78(1) provides that, in the circumstances subsequently set out, 'the court *may* refuse to allow evidence on which the prosecution proposes to rely to be given ...'. Those circumstances are where 'the admission of the evidence would have such an adverse effect on the fairness of the proceedings *that the court ought not to admit it*'. It seems curious that, if the court decides that these circumstances exist, there should remain any room for the exercise of further discretion. On this view, in the opening words of the sub-section, 'may' means 'shall'. This approach has now been adopted by the Court of Appeal.[52]

(c) 'Evidence on which the prosecution proposes to rely': the evidence must not have been admitted already. In *R v Sat-Bhambra*,[53] it was only after evidence of a confession had been given, and further evidence had been heard, that application was made for the confession to be excluded. The Court of Appeal held that at that stage it was too late for either s 76 or s 78 to apply; the wording of both sections shows that the court's power exists only where the evidence in question has not yet been given. Section 76 contemplates a situation where 'the prosecution *proposes to give in evidence* a confession by an accused person', and s 78 contemplates a situation where evidence on which the prosecution '*proposes to rely*' has yet to be given.[54]

(d) 'Such an adverse effect on the fairness of the proceedings that the court ought not to admit it':

- It is not enough that the admission of the evidence will have *some* adverse effect; the adverse effect must be so great that the court ought not to admit the evidence. So you can have an adverse effect on the fairness of the proceedings that is not substantial enough to lead to exclusion.[55]

- The 'fairness of the proceedings' refers only to that part of the criminal proceedings taking place in court.[56]

---

51 See s 82(1) and *R v King's Lynn JJ ex p Holland* (1993) 96 Cr App R 74.

52 *R v Middlebrook* (1994) unreported; *R v Chalkley and Jeffries* [1998] 2 All ER 155, p 178.

53 (1989) 88 Cr App R 55; *Sourcebook*, p 187.

54 In *R v Sat-Bhambra*, the problem was solved by relying on s 82(3), which preserves the common law power to exclude prosecution evidence. See below, p 239.

55 *R v Walsh* (1990) 91 Cr App R 161.

56 *R v Mason* (1988) 86 Cr App R 349, p 354; *DPP v Marshall* [1988] 3 All ER 683, p 688.

- It is fairness of the *proceedings* that the judge has to consider. Fairness to the defendant is part of this, but the section is not directed solely towards fairness to the defendant. Fairness of the proceedings requires the judge to take into account fairness to the prosecution as well as to the defence. In *R v O'Loughlin*,[57] Kenneth Jones J said in relation to s 78(1): 'I therefore have to balance matters having regard, on the one hand, to the interests of the defendant; on the other hand, to the interests of the public as represented by the prosecution.'[58] This conveys something of the right idea, but is misleading in that it ranges public interest solely on the side of the prosecution. It is obvious today, even if in 1987 it was not, that the public has a significant interest in the avoidance of wrongful convictions.

Exercise of the discretion

The Court of Appeal has given trial judges a very free hand in their operation of s 78(1) and subjects their decisions to a minimum of review. In *R v Samuel*,[59] the Court of Appeal said that it was undesirable to attempt any general guidance as to the way in which a judge's discretion under s 78 should be exercised because circumstances varied infinitely. And in *R v Jelen and Katz*,[60] the Court of Appeal made the same point, saying that this was not an apt field for hard case law and well founded distinctions between cases.

It is now clear that a judge's exercise of discretion under this provision can be faulted only on the basis of '*Wednesbury* unreasonableness'.[61] This is a concept drawn from administrative law and is based on the decision in *Associated Provincial Picture Houses v Wednesbury Corporation*.[62] This case decided that where an authority had a discretion, the courts, in the absence of error in law or fact, could interfere with its exercise only if the decision made in exercise of the discretion was so unreasonable that no reasonable authority could ever have made it. Under this principle, 'the court does not decide what the reasonable authority *would* do, but only what no reasonable authority *could* do. In other words, a court should not strike down a decision ... on substantive grounds just because it does not agree with it'. In practice, however, in the field of administrative law 'it seems clear that even when a court purports to quash a decision because it is "*Wednesbury* unreasonable", it

---

57 (1987) 85 Cr App R 157.

58 *Ibid*, p 163.

59 [1988] QB 615; *Sourcebook*, p 217.

60 (1989) 90 Cr App R 456, pp 464–65; approved in *R v Roberts* [1997] 1 Cr App R 217, p 231.

61 *R v Christou* [1992] 1 QB 979, p 989; *R v Rankin* (1995) *The Times*, 5 September; *R v McCarthy* [1996] Crim LR 818; *R v McEvoy* [1997] Crim LR 887.

62 [1948] 1 KB 223.

may be applying a standard of unreasonableness less stringent than that specified'.[63] Michael Zander has noted that 'as a matter of impression' the Court of Appeal seems readier to take a different view from that adopted by the trial judge than in some other areas of law where the *Wednesbury* principle is relevant.[64] In practice, therefore, it may be slightly easier to overturn a trial judge's decision than the words of the judges in the Court of Appeal suggest.

Different considerations apply where the judge fails to exercise his discretion at all: for example, where he takes the view that there has been no breach of the Code when in fact there has. The Court of Appeal can then exercise the discretion in his place.[65]

Perhaps a good way of explaining the concept of unfairness embodied in s 78(1) is to compare it with a similar provision in a different area of law. In the administration of a company under the Insolvency Act 1986 a judge may have to decide in an application under s 27(1) of that Act whether the company's affairs are being managed 'in a manner which is unfairly prejudicial' to the interests of some part of its creditors. In *Re Charnley Davies Ltd (No 2)*, Millett J said that the concept of unfairly prejudicial management was a matter of perspective. The appropriate metaphor was 'not a supermarket trolley but a hologram'.[66] This metaphor fits the concept of unfairness under s 78 as well.

What Millett J meant was that there are at least two radically different ways of determining whether a particular legal state of affairs exists. With some you have a shopping list of items, and when you have collected them all you have a particular state of affairs. Has there been theft? You apply the checklist contained in s 1 of the Theft Act 1968. Has there been an appropriation of property belonging to another? Was it dishonest? Was there an intention to deprive permanently? To establish negligence in a civil action you push your trolley round the supermarket in a similar way, taking a duty of care from one shelf, breach from another, causation from a third and loss and damage from a fourth.

But a court that is looking to see if there has been unfairly prejudicial management in an application under the Insolvency Act, or a sufficiently adverse effect on the fairness of the proceedings under s 78(1) of PACE, approaches the problem in a quite different way. Now there is no shopping list to be checked or supermarket trolley to be filled. Instead, there are all the circumstances, which, like a hologram, have to be viewed from one point and then another. It is, as Millett J said, all a matter of perspective. From the standpoint of one set of creditors, there will appear to have been unfairly

63 Cane, P, *An Introduction to Administrative Law*, 2nd edn, 1992, pp 208–09.

64 Zander, M, *The Police and Criminal Evidence Act 1984*, 3rd edn, 1995, p 245.

65 *R v Samuel* [1988] QB 615; *Sourcebook*, p 217.

66 [1990] BCLC 760, p 783. I am indebted to Mark Phillips QC for this reference.

prejudicial management, but if you take the standpoint of other creditors there will not. From the standpoint of a defendant in a criminal trial, the admission of some evidence may well appear to have such an adverse effect on the fairness of the proceedings that it ought to be excluded. From the standpoint of others with an interest in the proceedings, things may appear very differently.

Having said that, there are some general points that can still be made about the exercise of the discretion under s 78(1):

(a) According to the Court of Appeal in *R v Anderson*,[67] it is not entirely clear where the burden of proof lies on all the issues raised by the sub-section. But at least it seems clear from the decision of the Divisional Court in *Vel v Owen*[68] that the prosecution does not have a burden to disprove unfairness in the way that it has a burden to disprove matters relied on by the defence under s 76. However, in *R v Stagg*,[69] very experienced prosecuting counsel accepted that it was for the prosecution to demonstrate either that there was no unfairness, or that its degree did not warrant the exclusion of the evidence.

(b) Although the sub-section would not be one's *first* choice for the exclusion of a confession (because of the burden placed on the prosecution by s 76), it has frequently been relied on by the courts in connection with this sort of evidence. It may be particularly helpful where you want to exclude a confession for unreliability but cannot point to anything said or done by someone other than the defendant so as to trigger s 76.

A good example is *R v Brine*.[70] In that case, the defendant, who suffered from stress, was accused of indecent assault on a child. He was interviewed with his solicitor present for five hours and made no admissions. After the solicitor had left, he did make some admissions and was interviewed further. The total interview time was eight hours. There had been breaches of Code C because of insufficient breaks in questioning and the provision of insufficient meals, but none of these breaches was attributed to deliberate misconduct by the police and, in any case, there was no causal link between these breaches and the defendant's confessions.

The defence called a psychologist on the *voir dire* who said that the defendant, when making his admissions, had been suffering from a mild form of paranoid psychosis. The effect of this condition was that the defendant would have felt very threatened and would have been likely to tell lies and make untrue admissions. In his opinion the confession was unreliable. But the police had not known of the defendant's condition, and

---

67 [1993] Crim LR 447.

68 [1987] Crim LR 496.

69 (1994) unreported, 14 September. See further *R (Saifi) v Governor of Brixton Prison and Another* [2001] 1 WLR 1134.

70 [1992] Crim LR 122.

the trial judge took the view that because there was no improper conduct which had caused the defendant to make his admissions, there was no room for exclusion under s 76, or, apparently, under s 78.

The Court of Appeal, however, said that s 78 was certainly available in circumstances where, although the police had behaved properly, the defendant's psychological condition made his confession unreliable. For this reason, to admit evidence of the confession would have had such an adverse effect on the fairness of the proceedings that the court ought not to have admitted it. Thus, no external element is *essential* to trigger the operation of the sub-section; in this respect it differs importantly from s 76.

(c) A breach of one of the Codes may *help* to get evidence excluded under s 78(1). The importance of the Codes was emphasised by the Court of Appeal in *R v Elson*:[71] they are there to protect the individual against the might of the State. The individual, the court added, is at a great disadvantage when arrested by the police, and this is so whether or not the police behave with the utmost propriety.

But Code breach will not lead to *automatic* exclusion.[72] This was made clear in *R v Keenan*[73] where there had been breaches of provisions of Code C in relation to recording and authenticating interviews. Hodgson J said in the Court of Appeal that, in cases where there had been 'significant and substantial' breaches of the 'verballing' provisions of the Code, evidence would frequently be excluded. But not every breach, or combination of breaches, of the Code would justify exclusion. The courts should not undertake the task of punishing the police for failure to observe the Codes.

An argument for exclusion based on Code breach may have to consider whether the provision relied on did in fact apply. The position of the person who has not been arrested, but who is 'assisting the police with their inquiries', is problematic.

Note 1A of Code C states:

> Although certain sections of this Code (eg, s 9 – treatment of detained persons) apply specifically to persons in custody at police stations, those there voluntarily to assist with an investigation should be treated with no less consideration (eg, offered refreshments at appropriate times) and enjoy an absolute right to obtain legal advice or communicate with anyone outside the police station.

---

71 (1994) *The Times*, 30 June.

72 It would be absurd, eg, to argue that evidence should be excluded because the suspect's period of rest lasted seven hours and 55 minutes instead of eight hours. (See Code C, para 12.2.)

73 [1989] 3 All ER 598. See also *R v Kelly* (1998) *The Times*, 23 February, in relation to breaches of Code D.

Two questions arise here:

- Does 'should' govern 'enjoy an absolute right', so that it expresses a mere wish? Or does 'should' govern only 'be treated with no less consideration', so that the note appears to be declaratory of an existing right to obtain legal advice or communicate with someone outside the police station?

- In either case, what is the status of a note for guidance in the Code?

The answer to the second question appears clearly at para 1.3, which says that the notes are *not* provisions of the Code, but are 'guidance to police officers and others about its application and interpretation'. However, there are parts of the Code that must apply to persons not yet arrested as well as to those who have been: para 10 (dealing with the caution) is an obvious example.

In *R v Christou*,[74] there are *dicta* supporting an argument that a person not yet arrested has the protection of the Code. Lord Taylor said:

> In our view, although the Code extends beyond the treatment of those in detention, what is clear is that it was intended to protect suspects who are vulnerable to abuse or pressure from police officers or who may believe themselves to be so. Frequently, the suspect will be a detainee. But the Code will also apply where a suspect, not in detention, is being questioned about an offence by a police officer acting as a police officer for the purpose of obtaining evidence. In that situation, the officer and the suspect are not on equal terms. The officer is perceived to be in a position of authority; the suspect may be intimidated or undermined.[75]

Evidence obtained by a trick

In addition to these general points about the operation of s 78(1), one particular topic requires consideration: the application of the sub-section where evidence has been obtained by a trick.[76] For example, in *R v Bailey*,[77] two suspects, who had exercised their rights to silence in police interviews, were placed together in a bugged police cell after the police had pretended to be unwilling to leave them together. Their subsequent incriminating conversation was recorded and later held admissible in evidence. The judge's decision was upheld by the Court of Appeal, which observed, however, that

74 [1992] 1 QB 979; *Sourcebook*, p 223.

75 [1992] 1 QB 979, p 991.

76 See Sharpe, S, 'Covert police operations and the discretionary exclusion of evidence' [1994] Crim LR 793; Robertson, G, 'Entrapment evidence: manna from Heaven or fruit of the poisoned tree?' [1994] Crim LR 805; Birch, D, 'Excluding evidence from entrapment' (1994) 47 CLP Pt 2, p 73; Noorlander, P, 'Covert policing and the Convention: entrapment' (1998) 148 NLJ 511.

77 [1993] 3 All ER 513.

such methods were to be used only in grave cases, and where there was no suggestion of oppression or unreliability. But in *R v Mason*,[78] the police trick was too much for the Court of Appeal. In that case, a police officer had lied to a suspect and to his solicitor about the existence of incriminating evidence. It was held that the suspect's subsequent confession should have been excluded.

The use of intrusive surveillance devices, such as telephone tapping or bugging, has sometimes given rise to submissions based on s 78(1). Here again the European Convention may be relevant. Article 8 provides as follows:

1   Everyone has the right to respect for his private and family life, his home and his correspondence.

2   There shall be no interference by a public authority with the exercise of this right except such as is in accordance with the law and is necessary in a democratic society in the interests of national security, public safety or the economic well-being of the country, for the prevention of disorder or crime, for the protection of health or morals, or for the protection of the rights or freedoms of others.

In *Khan v United Kingdom*,[79] the European Court had to consider the case of an applicant in the following circumstances. The applicant had been sentenced to imprisonment for drug dealing on the basis of evidence improperly obtained by a listening device attached by police to a private house without the knowledge of the owners or occupiers. The applicant's appeal against conviction was ultimately dismissed by the House of Lords.[80] Lord Nolan said that there were two separate issues involved in the appeal. First, was the evidence admissible at all? Secondly, if it was, should it have been excluded, either under the judge's common law discretion or under s 78(1)?[81] On the first issue, the House of Lords held that there was no right to privacy in English law. Even if there had been, the common law rule was that evidence obtained improperly, or even unlawfully, could still be admitted. On the second issue, it was held that the fact that evidence had been obtained in breach of Art 8 of the Convention was *relevant* to the exercise of the judge's discretion under s 78(1), but did not *determine* the way in which that discretion should be exercised. On the facts, the trial judge had been entitled to conclude that s 78(1) did not require exclusion. In due course, it was argued for the applicant before the European Court that there had been a breach of his right to a fair trial under Art 6(1) of the Convention in that there had been a breach of his rights under Art 8.

The European Court held that his rights under Art 8 had been violated because United Kingdom domestic law did not at the relevant time regulate

---

78   [1988] 1 WLR 139.

79   [2000] Crim LR 684.

80   *R v Khan (Sultan)* [1997] AC 558.

81   *Ibid*, p 573. For the common law discretion, see the reference to *R v Sang* [1980] AC 402 below.

the use of covert listening devices. The interference with the applicant's rights had thus not been 'in accordance with the law', as required by Art 8(2), but a majority of the Court held that a violation of Art 6(1) had not been established. The Court relied on earlier decisions[82] to the effect that it would not decide as a matter of principle that unlawfully obtained evidence should never be admissible. Although, in this case, the recording was in effect the only evidence against the applicant, there was no risk of its being unreliable. The need for supporting evidence was therefore weaker. The central question was whether the proceedings as a whole were fair. The applicant had had ample opportunity to challenge both the authenticity and the use of the recording. He had not challenged its authenticity and the evidence could have been excluded under s 78(1).

Part III of the Police Act 1997, which came into force on 22 February 1999, now regulates the use of intrusive surveillance devices and thus attempts to provide the proper legal basis that had earlier been lacking. It applies to police and to Customs and Excise officers, and is accompanied by a Code of Practice. Any act of intrusive surveillance in breach of the statute or the Code is likely to be in breach of Art 8, but whether it would lead to exclusion of evidence must, in view of the European Court's broad approach to Art 6(1), remain uncertain.[83]

Other problems have arisen in connection with evidence obtained by what may loosely be called 'entrapment'. The leading common law authority on this subject before the Police and Criminal Evidence Act 1984 was the decision of the House of Lords in *R v Sang*.[84] The defendant had been charged with conspiring to utter counterfeit American bank notes. He pleaded not guilty and, in the absence of the jury, alleged through his counsel that he had been induced to commit the offence by an informer, who had been acting on police instructions. In the absence of that inducement, he would not have committed any offence of the kind with which he was charged. His counsel acknowledged that the trial judge was bound by recent decisions of the Court of Appeal to the effect that entrapment was not a defence to a criminal charge. But he went on to submit that if the judge was satisfied at a 'trial within a trial' that the facts relied on by the defendant were true, he would have a discretion to exclude prosecution evidence that had been obtained in such a way. The trial judge ruled that even if the facts were as alleged, he had no such discretion. The House of Lords reaffirmed the rule that entrapment was not a defence under English law. On the judicial discretion to exclude prosecution evidence, Lord Diplock stated the law in this way:

---

82 Such as *Schenk v Switzerland* (1988) 13 EHRR 242 and *Teixeira de Castro v Portugal* [1998] 4 BHRC 533.

83 For a critical account of this legislation see Colvin, M, 'Part III Police Act 1997' (1999) 149 NLJ 311.

84 [1980] AC 402.

(1) A trial judge in a criminal trial has always a discretion to refuse to admit [prosecution] evidence if in his opinion its prejudicial effect outweighs its probative value.

(2) Save with regard to admissions and confessions and generally with regard to evidence obtained from the accused after the commission of the offence, he has no discretion to refuse to admit relevant admissible evidence on the ground that it was obtained by improper or unfair means. The court is not concerned with how it was obtained. It is no ground for the exercise of discretion to exclude that the evidence was obtained as the result of the activities of an *agent provocateur*.[85]

Although a more liberal approach to the use of discretion can be seen in the speech of Lord Scarman, *R v Sang* was generally regarded as authority for the propositions stated by Lord Diplock.[86]

What was the impact of s 78(1) on this position? In *R v Smurthwaite*,[87] the Court of Appeal clearly took the view that s 78(1) had extended the judicial discretion to exclude prosecution evidence, and that there might be cases where evidence obtained by an agent provocateur should be excluded. The court listed some of the factors to be regarded when considering the admissibility of evidence obtained during an undercover operation. They are as follows:

- Was the officer acting as an *agent provocateur* in the sense that he was enticing the defendant to commit an offence he would not otherwise have committed?[88]

- What was the nature of the entrapment?

- Does the evidence consist of admissions to a completed offence, or does it consist of the actual commission of an offence?

- How active or passive was the officer's role in obtaining the evidence?

- Is there an unassailable record of what occurred, or is it strongly corroborated?

- Did the officer abuse his undercover role to ask questions which ought properly to have been asked as a police officer, and in accordance with the Codes?

In *R v Smurthwaite*, the defendant was alleged to have solicited another person to murder his wife. That other person was, in fact, an undercover police officer, who pretended to be a contract killer, and who surreptitiously recorded two incriminating conversations with the defendant. During the

---

85 [1980] AC 402, p 437.

86 But see Polyviou, PG, 'Illegally obtained evidence and *R v Sang*', in Tapper, CFH (ed), *Crime, Proof and Punishment: Essays in Memory of Sir Rupert Cross*, 1981, pp 226–47.

87 (1994) 98 Cr App R 437, p 440; *Sourcebook*, p 223.

88 Another way of putting this is to ask whether the suspect was tricked, or voluntarily applied himself to the trick: *R v Christou* [1992] QB 979.

second meeting, the defendant made a part payment of £10,000 for the proposed murder. The trial judge ruled the recorded conversations admissible. The Court of Appeal upheld his decision, saying that the officer had not been a true *agent provocateur*; the defendant had been making the running throughout.[89] But in *R v Stagg*,[90] Ognall J excluded undercover evidence obtained 'by a substantial attempt to incriminate a suspect by positive and deceptive conduct of the grossest kind', which he also described as 'a skillful and sustained enterprise to manipulate the accused'. The case had involved a woman police officer, who for a period of seven months pretended to befriend the suspect, but who in fact was operating under the instructions of a psychologist. Their object had been to try to obtain from the suspect a pattern of sexual fantasies that would match the 'psychological profile' of the person who had committed a particular murder. A significant factor in the decision was the judge's finding that 'the increasingly extreme character of the fantasies was the product of deliberate shaping by the policewoman and encouragement by her'.

Entrapment must now be studied in the light of the European Convention on Human Rights. In *Teixeira de Castro v Portugal*,[91] the European Court of Human Rights had to consider the application of a person who had convicted of drug dealing in the following circumstances. The applicant had no previous criminal record and had been previously unknown to the police. A third party introduced him to two undercover police officers, who told him that they wanted to buy a quantity of heroin. The applicant bought the drugs for them. He was convicted on the evidence of the undercover officers.

The Court held that in these circumstances, there had been a violation of the applicant's right to a fair trial under Art 6(1). The public interest could not justify the use of evidence obtained as a result of police incitement. There had been no evidence that the applicant was predisposed to crime. The officers had incited the commission of an offence that would not have been committed without their intervention. The Court distinguished the facts of this case from the situation where an undercover officer tries to buy drugs from someone known to be already engaged in selling.

The emphasis placed by the European Court on the need for the victim of the trap to be predisposed to commit the type of offence in question suggests that the earlier decision of the Court of Appeal in *Williams and O'Hare v DPP*[92] may have to be reconsidered. In that case, police had left an insecure and unattended van in a busy shopping area where crimes involving vehicles were frequent. The van contained what appeared to be a valuable load of cigarettes, which was visible through a partly opened shutter at the back. The

---

89   See also *R v Christou* [1992] QB 979.
90   (1994) unreported, 14 September.
91   [1998] Crim LR 751.
92   (1994) 98 Cr App R 208.

defendants saw the van, became interested, and ultimately removed some cartons from it. The Divisional Court held that the police had not been acting as *agents provocateurs* because they had not been participating in, inciting, procuring or counselling the commission of the offence. But would this sort of random 'virtue testing' be acceptable after *Teixeira*? The police had not *incited* the offence but, equally, they had no knowledge of any predisposition on the part of the persons who gave way to temptation.

However, the significance of the decision in *Teixeira* was diminished in *R v Shannon*.[93] In that case, the Court of Appeal refused to accept *Teixeira* as authority for the wide proposition that police incitement of a person not predisposed to crime would make unfair from the start any trial of that person for the crime incited. Instead, the court said that while the circumstances constituting a particular entrapment can be taken into account, the 'principal' focus of the judge's attention must be on *procedural* fairness. So if the circumstances of the entrapment affect the reliability of the prosecution evidence, or the extent to which the defendant has an opportunity to deal with it, there might be exclusion under s 78(1), but unless the circumstances have *some* impact on procedural fairness, there is no room for exclusion.[94] In *Shannon*, the Court of Appeal tried to close a door that *Smurthwaite* had left open. We shall not know if it succeeded until we know the outcome of the struggle between two views of the scope of s 78(1) as a whole.[95]

THE RATIONALE OF S 78(1)

A submission about the application of a statutory provision is always helped if it can be shown that the rationale of the provision is relevant to the facts in question. Unfortunately, the rationale of s 78(1) and cases involving its application show that judicial attitudes to the discretion have been intuitive: there has been little if any attempt to apply analysis to the operation of the sub-section. At this stage I want to suggest an approach that may be helpful in argument.

At the root of s 78(1) is the idea that the admission of certain evidence is capable of adversely affecting the fairness of the proceedings. It is clear from the sub-section that the court is required to assume that the fairness of the proceedings is not an all-or-nothing affair, but something that may be affected by degrees. The court is directed to attend to 'all the circumstances', but

---

93   [2001] 1 Cr App R 168.

94   It might be argued that the reference to procedural fairness as the 'principal' focus of the judge's attention does leave room for other considerations. But there is no hint of what these might be. It is unclear what force, if any, the court intended to give to the word.

95   See below.

specifically to 'the circumstances in which the evidence was obtained', when considering the exercise of the discretion. Some guidance about ideas of fairness that can be used in interpreting the sub-section can be obtained from these directions.

It is beyond controversy that one of the objects of our criminal trials is to secure rectitude of decision – the right answer – and a criminal trial will therefore cease to be fair to the extent that the likelihood of attaining this end diminishes. So one way in which the fairness of the proceedings can be adversely affected is by inviting the jury to convict on the basis of unreliable evidence. Many cases show the significance of reliability when considering the s 78(1) discretion.

In *R v O'Connor*,[96] for example, the Court of Appeal held that the trial judge ought to have excluded, under s 78(1), evidence of a former co-accused's conviction for conspiring with the defendant. The reason was that the effect of admitting this evidence had been to enable the prosecution to put before the jury a statement, made by the former co-accused in the absence of the defendant, without having the maker of the statement available for cross-examination. Similarly, in *R v O'Loughlin*,[97] it was held that had the depositions of certain absent witnesses been admissible, they should have been excluded under s 78(1) because, although they were probative of guilt, the jury would have had little or no guidance in deciding what weight should be attached to them.

Evidence that might ordinarily be reliable may be made unreliable by the way in which it has been obtained, and s 78(1) has been used to exclude it in these circumstances. In *R v Keenan*,[98] for example, it was said that the provisions of Code C, ensuring that interviews were fully recorded and the suspect given an opportunity to check the record, should be strictly followed, and that the courts should not be slow to exclude evidence following substantial breaches by the interrogator. The importance of the reliability of evidence in exercising the power under s 78(1) can be seen from many cases. It was highly significant, as we have seen, in *R v Khan*.

Where evidence has been obtained by entrapment, admissibility has in part depended on reliability. The factors referred to in *R v Smurthwaite*[99] included whether there was an unassailable record of what had occurred, whether it was strongly supported by other evidence, and whether the evidence consisted of admissions to a completed offence.

It may be difficult to present an argument based on fairness where evidence has been improperly obtained but is nevertheless reliable. Some

96 (1987) 85 Cr App R 298.
97 (1987) 85 Cr App R 157.
98 [1989] 3 All ER 598.
99 (1994) 98 Cr App R 437; *Sourcebook*, p 223.

cases appear to suggest that provided reliability has not been impaired by the impropriety, any unfairness will not be substantial enough to lead to exclusion. *R v Khan*[100] is an example. Other cases besides *R v Khan* suggest that the courts regard drug dealing as an offence that threatens the fabric of society,[101] and in such cases, it is not surprising to find crime control values winning in any struggle with process values. A similar approach was taken in *R v Cooke*.[102] In this case, rape and kidnapping were alleged, and the question arose whether s 78(1) should be used to exclude evidence of a sample of hair, because it might have been improperly taken from the defendant. The Court of Appeal agreed with the trial judge's decision to admit the evidence, regardless of any possible assault on the defendant. The court pointed out that the vast majority of cases under s 78(1) concerned confessions obtained in breach of Code C. In such cases, the impropriety involved in obtaining the confession affected its reliability as an incriminating item of evidence. But in this case, the evidence was of a different nature. The reliability of the DNA tests, which strongly supported the prosecution case, was unaffected by the impropriety of the way in which the sample had been obtained.

In both these cases, a serious crime was alleged and, once it was clear that any impropriety had not affected reliability, the evidence was admitted. But the importance of reliability for admissibility has been shown in far less serious cases. In *R v Stewart*,[103] the defendant was convicted of abstracting electricity and stealing gas. Electricity company officials, accompanied by police, entered the defendant's house in circumstances that were arguably unlawful. There they found a mechanical apparatus used to bypass the meters. The Court of Appeal held that it was unnecessary to decide about the lawfulness of the entry. Even assuming there had been breaches of Code B, the admission of the evidence had not had any effect on the fairness of the proceedings because the apparatus had been there for all to see, whether the entry had been unlawful or not. It was quite a different case from one involving evidence of admissions where there had been a breach of Code C. The basis of the distinction was clearly that in this case, unlike the case of an admission obtained through a breach of Code C, there was no doubt about the reliability of the evidence.

So is reliability the *sole* consideration under s 78? A significant number of decisions show that it is not, and that the operation of s 78(1) can best be understood if 'fairness of the proceedings' takes into account justifiability as well. Rectitude of decision is necessary, but it is also necessary to be able to

---

100 [1996] 2 Cr App R 440.
101 See also, eg, *R v Latif* [1996] 2 Cr App R 92.
102 [1995] 1 Cr App R 318.
103 [1995] Crim LR 500.

justify the decision to the defendant and to the public at large. This cannot be done if the verdict rests on reliable evidence that has been obtained by iniquitous means. 'Apparently reliable evidence may need to be excluded if it carries significant risks of impairing the moral authority of the verdict.'[104]

An obstacle, though not an insuperable one, in the way of this approach is the unfortunate decision of the Court of Appeal in *R v Chalkley and Jeffries*.[105] The defendants had been charged with conspiracy to rob. At trial, the prosecution wished to rely on covertly obtained tape recordings of conversations between them. To obtain these recordings, the police had arrested Chalkley and his partner in connection with another matter, and in their absence had entered their house and planted a listening device. The Court of Appeal later found that this other matter was not a 'trumped up' allegation, although neither Chalkley nor his partner were ever charged in respect of it. At the trial of Chalkley and Jeffries for conspiracy to rob, the judge was asked to exclude the taped conversations under s 78(1). He looked for guidance to cases relating to the dismissal of prosecutions for abuse of process, and concluded that he should conduct a balancing exercise with the circumstances. Did the balance come down in favour of the effective prosecution of crime? Or did it favour instead the public interest in discouraging abuse of police power? Having conducted this exercise, he decided to admit the evidence. The defendants, solely as a result of this ruling, changed their pleas to guilty. They then appealed. The primary question that the Court of Appeal had to consider was whether it had power to quash a conviction based on a plea of guilty in these circumstances. The court held that it had not.

That was enough to decide the appeal. Nevertheless, the court went on to consider the arguments that had been put forward in relation to s 78(1). It concluded that there was no basis for the submission that admitting the tapes would have had such an adverse effect on the fairness of the proceedings that they ought to have been excluded. Accordingly, the appeals were dismissed on that ground also. However, the court also disapproved of the way in which the trial judge had reached the same conclusion, and made further observations about the scope and effect of s 78(1). In particular, the court said that the reference to 'the circumstances in which the evidence was obtained' was not intended to widen the common law rule stated by Lord Diplock in *R v Sang*.[106] Save in the case of admissions and confessions and generally as to evidence obtained after the commission of the offence, there was no discretion to exclude evidence unless its quality was or might have been affected by the way in which it was obtained. The trial judge had therefore been wrong to

---

104 Dennis, IH, 'Reconstructing the law of criminal evidence' (1989) *Current Legal Problems* 21, pp 35–44. See also Duff, RA, *Trials and Punishments*, 1986, pp 99–143.

105 [1998] 2 All ER 155.

106 [1980] AC 402.

apply the balancing process that was appropriate to abuse of process cases when considering the operation of s 78(1).

Shortly after s 78(1) had become law there were suggestions that it had not altered the common law as stated in *R v Sang*.[107] But this narrow construction was rejected in other decisions,[108] and several decisions of the Divisional Court and Court of Appeal have shown that s 78(1) can be used in circumstances lying outside the scope defined in *R v Sang*. For example, in *Matto v Wolverhampton Crown Court*,[109] the Divisional Court held that evidence of breath specimens should have been excluded under s 78(1) because they had been obtained in bad faith and as the result of oppression.[110]

In *R v Smurthwaite*,[111] which was not referred to in *R v Chalkley and Jeffries*, among factors relevant to the reliability of evidence obtained by entrapment were factors that were relevant to *the degree of impropriety* involved in collecting the evidence. Had the police enticed a defendant to commit a crime that he would not otherwise have committed? Had the police *abused their role* by asking questions that ought properly to have been asked only at a police station and in accordance with the Codes?[112]

Further, although the Court of Appeal has said on several occasions that it is not the function of the court to discipline the police, it is clear that the presence of bad faith on their part will make exclusion more likely. Thus, in *R v Walsh*,[113] it was said that bad faith might make 'substantial or significant' a breach that might not otherwise be so. And in *R v Alladice*,[114] the Court of Appeal said that a distinction was to be drawn when considering the effect of refusing access to a solicitor between cases where the police had acted in good faith and cases where they had acted in bad faith. But bad faith is irrelevant if the court is concerned solely with reliability.

Thus *R v Chalkley and Jeffries* is at odds, on this point, with many other decisions of the Court of Appeal and Divisional Court. More recently, the

---

107 See, eg, *R v Mason* (1988) 86 Cr App R 349, 354.

108 See, eg, *R v Fulling* (1987) 85 Cr App R 136, 141; *R v O'Leary* (1988) 87 Cr App R 387, p 391.

109 [1987] RTR 337.

110 See also *Sharpe v DPP* [1993] RTR 392. In *DPP v McGladrigan* [1991] RTR 297, the Divisional Court said that s 78(1) could be used even in the absence of deliberate misconduct. And in *R v Khan and Others* [1997] Crim LR 508, the Court of Appeal accepted that s 78(1) was capable of being used to exclude evidence obtained by an illegal search, though on the facts it upheld the trial judge's decision to admit the evidence. Even in *R v Shannon* [2001] 1 Cr App R 168 the Court of Appeal referred to s 78(1) as having 'superseded' *Sang*: see *per* Auld LJ at p 183.

111 [1994] 1 All ER 898.

112 In *R v Lin* [1995] Crim LR 817, the Court of Appeal said that there would be a strong reason for exclusion if a judge found that the use of undercover officers had been purely in order to get round the requirements of the Code.

113 (1990) 91 Cr App R 161. See also *R v Sanghera* [2001] Crim LR 480.

114 (1988) 87 Cr App R 380.

House of Lords in *R v Khan*[115] accepted that a breach of the defendant's right to privacy under Art 8 of the European Convention on Human Rights was at least a *relevant* consideration under s 78(1); yet how could it be, if the sole concern of the court is with the reliability of evidence, however improperly obtained? A final consideration is that in saying that s 78(1) merely restated the common law, the court failed to account for s 82(3) of the Act.[116] Dennis[117] has suggested that the observations of the Court of Appeal in *R v Chalkley and Jeffries* on s 78(1) were *per incuriam*, and there seems little doubt that he is right. It is submitted that on a correct view of the law, judges are entitled to take process values into consideration under s 78(1), and that reliability, though important, is not the only factor to be taken into consideration.[118]

THE COMMON LAW DISCRETION TO EXCLUDE

Section 82(3) of the Police and Criminal Evidence Act 1984 provides as follows:

> Nothing in this Part of this Act shall prejudice any power of a court to exclude evidence (whether by preventing questions being put or otherwise) at its discretion.

The effect of this provision is to retain the common law discretion to exclude evidence on the ground that its probative value is outweighed by its likely prejudicial effect.[119] This discretion can still be seen at work in relation to the prosecution's right to cross-examine a defendant under s 1(3)(ii) of the Criminal Evidence Act 1898.[120] Although potentially available in other circumstances, this is the only area where it is much used.

USE OF CONFESSIONS BY A CO-DEFENDANT

Where a defendant's confession has been excluded under s 76 or s 78(1), it is no longer available to the prosecution. But in *R v Myers*,[121] the House of Lords held that such a confession may still be available to a co-defendant.

Myers and her co-defendant were charged with murder. At trial, they ran 'cut-throat' defences. Myers had made confessions on two occasions to the

---

115 [1997] AC 558.
116 See below.
117 Dennis, IH, *The Law of Evidence* (1999) p 77.
118 See also Choo, A and Nash, S, 'What's the matter with section 78?' [1999] Crim LR 929.
119 See, eg, *R v O'Leary* (1988) 87 Cr App R 387, p 391.
120 See below, Chapter 11.
121 [1997] 3 WLR 552.

police, but because of Code breach, the prosecution decided that they could not use them. Myers gave evidence and the trial judge permitted her to be cross-examined about these confessions by counsel for her co-defendant. She was convicted and appealed, arguing that evidence of her confessions was inadmissible for *all* purposes – not just those of the prosecution.

Her appeals were unsuccessful. The House of Lords held that a defendant in a joint trial has the right to question witnesses about a *voluntary* statement made by a co-defendant outside court, even though that statement incriminated the co-defendant and even though it was not relied on by the prosecution. The only requirement was that the statement should be relevant to the defence of the party who wanted to ask questions about it. A defendant had an unquestionable right to adduce relevant evidence in his defence, and the trial judge had no discretion to rule such evidence inadmissible so as to protect a co-defendant.[122] But it is important to note that there was no suggestion in *R v Myers* that the confessions had been obtained in the sort of circumstances referred to in s 76(2) of PACE, and the House of Lords was careful to refer to the admissibility of 'voluntary' statements of a co-defendant. The House acknowledged that there might be a distinction between confessions inadmissible on grounds of oppression or unreliability, and confessions held inadmissible on other grounds.[123]

FAILURE TO ANSWER QUESTIONS OR MENTION FACTS

The initial part of this chapter included a discussion of circumstances in which a suspect's silence might amount to a confession. Under the Criminal Justice and Public Order Act 1994, there may be circumstances in which a suspect's silence, though not amounting to a confession, may be used by magistrates or juries as the basis for making inferences at trial. I have already dealt, in Chapter 3, with the effect of s 35 on a defendant's failure to testify at trial, but three other sections need consideration here.

By s 34, a court or jury may draw such inferences as appear proper from evidence that the defendant failed, on being questioned under caution or on being charged with the offence, to mention any fact relied on in his defence if it was a fact which, in the circumstances existing at the time, he could reasonably have been expected to mention. Inferences may be drawn when determining either whether there is a case to answer or the question of guilt.

---

122 The Law Commission has recommended that the judge should have a discretion: see Law Com No 245 (1997), para 8.95. For further discussion of *R v Myers*, see the commentary in [1997] Crim LR 888, pp 889–91.

123 [1997] 3 WLR 552, pp 564, 572. In *R v Corelli* [2001] 6 Archbold News 2, the Court of Appeal held that the observations in *Myers* about the worthlessness of an involuntary confession related only to the question whether it was possible to adduce evidence of such a confession by a co-accused *from someone other than that co-accused*. An involuntary confession can still be put to the co-accused himself in cross-examination as to credit.

Section 36 deals with situations where a suspect is arrested and cautioned and fails to answer questions about apparently incriminating circumstantial evidence. If the constable who arrests him, or another constable investigating the case, reasonably believes that the presence of an 'object, substance or mark' may be attributable to participation in the offence specified, he may tell the suspect of his belief and ask him to account for its presence. If the suspect fails to do so, the court or jury may draw such inferences as appear proper in determining either whether there is a case to answer or the question of guilt. By s 36(1), the provision is applicable only where the object, substance or mark is on his person, or in or on his clothing or footwear, or otherwise in his possession, or in any place in which he is at the time of arrest.

Example

A country house has been burgled. Entry was gained by breaking a window; a safe has been blown open and antique silver taken. Charlie is arrested for the burglary. The arresting officer finds him carrying a bag containing antique silver. In his pocket is a stick of gelignite and there are recent cuts to his fingers. Charlie's failure to account for any or all of these may allow proper inferences to be drawn.

Section 37 deals similarly with failure by an accused to account for his presence at a particular place at or about the time of the alleged commission of the offence for which he has been arrested.

Example

As above; Charlie is found hiding in the grounds of the house shortly after the burglary took place, and fails to account for his presence.

The operation of s 78(1) of PACE

In relation to ss 34–37 inclusive, the accused's failure will form an item of evidence on which the prosecution proposes to rely. There will accordingly be a discretion to exclude it under s 78 of PACE. It follows that the court may have to consider whether the circumstances are such that to admit the evidence of silence would have such an adverse effect on the fairness of the proceedings that it ought to be excluded. What might such circumstances be? One suggestion is that since silence is going to be used for purposes *similar* to a confession, the principles developed by the courts in relation to confessions should apply here as well.[124]

Suppose that, at trial, the accused relies on certain facts for his defence. He says he mentioned them to the police in an interview that was not taped. The officer's notebook records that questions under caution were put to which the accused made no reply. The accused did not sign this record, nor was it

---

124 Dennis, I, 'The Criminal Justice and Public Order Act 1994: the evidence provisions' [1995] Crim LR 4, pp 14–15.

shown to him. There has been a breach of para 11.10 of Code C, which provides that, unless it is impracticable, the person interviewed shall be given the opportunity to read the interview record and to sign it as correct or to indicate the respects in which he considers it inaccurate. The breach is significant and substantial, because it affects the reliability of the evidence against the accused. There is a strong case for exclusion under s 78.

An important amendment to s 34, prompted by concerns that the section might be incompatible with the implied right to silence contained in Art 6 of the European Convention on Human Rights, is sub-s (2A). This provides that where the accused is not at an authorised place of detention at the time of his silence, no inference can be drawn under s 34 unless he has been allowed an opportunity to consult a solicitor before being questioned.

The conditions for allowing an inference to be drawn

Sections 34, 36 and 37 set out conditions that have to be satisfied before an inference can be made. The conditions in s 34 were discussed by the Court of Appeal in *R v Argent*.[125] Most were referred to without comment, but the court did expand on the requirement that the unmentioned fact must be one which, in the circumstances existing at the time, the defendant could reasonably have been expected to mention when questioned. When considering reasonableness, the court must take into account all relevant circumstances at the time of questioning: for example, the time of day and personal characteristics of the defendant such as age, experience, mental capacity, state of health, sobriety, tiredness, and his personality generally. Consideration has to be taken, not of some hypothetical reasonable defendant of ordinary fortitude, but of the actual defendant, with such qualities, knowledge, apprehensions and advice as he is shown to have had at the time.

Whether the defendant knew the grounds of suspicion against him when questioned must also be important. A person cannot be expected to mention a fact when he has no means of telling whether it is relevant or not. Despite this, the Court of Appeal has held that the police have no duty to provide a suspect's legal advisers with a full disclosure of their case prior to an interview.[126]

In *R v Mountford*[127] and *R v Gill*,[128] the Court of Appeal developed a restriction on the use of s 34. According to these decisions, where the truth of an unmentioned fact is the central issue in the trial, so that its resolution will determine the verdict, a s 34 direction should not be given. The reason is that

125 [1997] 2 Cr App R 27.
126 *R v Imran and Hussein* [1997] Crim LR 754.
127 [1999] Crim LR 575.
128 [2001] 1 Cr App R 160.

in these circumstances the s 34 issue cannot be resolved as an independent one, and therefore cannot amount to additional support for the prosecution case. For example, in *R v Gill*, the defendant was charged, together with a man called Taylor, with possession of heroin with intent to supply. The police had visited Gill's flat, where he and Taylor were present. As the police entered, Taylor threw a bag of heroin out of a window. It was the prosecution case that both men were in possession of all the heroin with the intention of supplying it to others. When interviewed, Gill said that the heroin was for his own use. He said that he was using four or five bags each week and that he had bought four bags earlier that day. He declined to say who the supplier was, and later he refused to answer any further questions. In evidence, Gill said that it was Taylor who had supplied him. He added that during the interview he had been prepared to answer only questions about his own use of drugs. He had refused to answer any more questions because he did not want to implicate anyone else, including Taylor. The trial judge gave a direction under s 34 in respect of his silence, but the Court of Appeal held this to have been wrong. In deciding whether Gill could reasonably have been expected to mention during interview that Taylor was his supplier, the jury could only be sure that he was lying, and so reject his explanation for silence, if they concluded, independently of s 34, that Gill was a dealer.

When does a defendant rely on a fact?

For s 34 to apply, the defendant must have failed to mention some fact that he relies on in his defence, but it may not always be easy to determine whether this basic condition has been satisfied. In *R v Moshaid*,[129] the defendant gave a 'no comment' interview, and at trial he gave no evidence and called no witnesses. The Court of Appeal held that the trial judge should not have allowed the jury to consider the possibility of drawing an inference under s 34. The section did not apply because there were no facts relied on by the defendant. So if the defence does no more than put the prosecution to proof of its case, s 34 will not apply. However, because there are no *witnesses* for the defence it will not always follow that there are no *facts relied on* by the defence. In most trials, evidence of such facts will, of course, come from the defendant and perhaps from other defence witnesses. But they can also come from prosecution witnesses, either during cross-examination or even during examination-in-chief.[130] If a defendant who gives no evidence relies in his defence on facts established in this way, s 34 could apply as well as s 35.

In *R v Nickolson*[131] the Court of Appeal emphasised the distinction between facts and theories. Section 34 applies to facts alone. In that case, a

---

129 [1998] Crim LR 420.
130 *R v Bowers and Others* [1998] Crim LR 817.
131 [1999] Crim LR 61.

child claimed that the defendant had sexually abused her in the premises where they both lived. The police took a nightdress that belonged to her which, when analysed, was shown to have been stained by semen. The defendant was interviewed before this was discovered. He denied any indecency with the child, but told the police that he habitually masturbated in his bedroom and in the bathroom. He was asked during cross-examination if he could think of any way in which semen stains might have appeared on the nightdress. He suggested that the child could have gone to the bathroom after he had masturbated there and have come into contact with semen on the lavatory seat. The trial judge gave a s 34 direction on the basis that this explanation had not been put forward at the interview. The Court of Appeal held that this was wrong. The defendant had not asserted *as a fact* that the stains had been caused in this way. What he said had been more in the nature of a theory, or a speculation.[132]

It is for the jury to decide whether the defendant has relied on a particular fact and, if so, whether he failed to mention it. But there may be some trials where it is proper for the judge to decide, as a matter of law, whether there is any evidence on which a jury could conclude that these conditions have been satisfied. If a judge rules that there is no such evidence, he ought to direct the jury that they should not draw any inferences from the defendant's silence.[133]

The effect of legal advice on silence

In *R v Argent*, the Court of Appeal said that legal advice was something the court might have to consider when deciding whether a suspect could reasonably have been expected to mention a particular fact. The significance of legal advice was more fully discussed by the Court of Appeal in *R v Condron*,[134] a case where the defendants had refused to answer questions on the advice of their solicitor. The court gave the following guidance to cover similar cases.

If the defendant says that he failed to answer questions on legal advice, that bare assertion is unlikely to be regarded as a sufficient reason for failure to mention matters relevant to the defence. In practice, therefore, the defendant will have to go further and provide, either through his own testimony or that of the legal adviser, the reasons for the advice.[135] The

---

132 But theories are based on facts, and there may be circumstances where a theory put forward at trial is so dependent on specific facts that both facts and theory might reasonably be expected to be mentioned. See the Commentary on *R v Nickolson* and *R v B(MT)* [2000] Crim LR 181.

133 *R v McGarry* [1998] 3 All ER 805.

134 [1997] 1 Cr App R 185.

135 A defendant who gave evidence of what his solicitor said to him would not, of course, infringe the rule against hearsay. He would not be relying on the truth of what the solicitor said to him. He would be relying on the effect of the solicitor's words on his own decision whether or not to answer questions. See *R v Davis* [1998] Crim LR 659; *R v Daniel* [1998] 2 Cr App R 373.

prosecution will then be able to cross-examine the relevant witness with a view to discovering whether there were any merely tactical reasons for the advice.[136]

Directions to the jury under s 34

The leading case on this subject is *R v Gill*.[137] The Court of Appeal, influenced by the decision of the European Court of Human Rights in *Condron v UK*,[138] set out the duties of a judge giving a s 34 direction as follows:

- He must identify the fact on which the defendant relies.
- He must direct the jury that: (a) it is for them to decide whether in the circumstances it was something that the defendant could reasonably have been expected to mention; and (b) if they think it was, that they are not *obliged* to draw any inferences but that they have a *discretion* to do so.

The Court went on to cite *R v Cowan*[139] and to summarise the essential elements of a direction under s 35 set out in that decision.[140] It seems clear from this that the safeguards provided by *R v Cowan* are to be applied also to directions under s 34. Accordingly, in giving a direction under that section, a judge must also tell the jury that a suspected person is not bound to answer police questions, and that an inference from silence cannot on its own prove guilt. Further, the jury must be satisfied that the prosecution has shown that there is a case to answer before drawing any adverse inference from silence. Finally, they should be directed that they can draw an adverse inference only if they are satisfied that the defendant was silent because he had no answers, or none that would stand up to cross-examination.

Preservation of some existing common law

Section 34 has no effect on any common law principles that already allow inferences to be drawn from silence under accusation or questioning. It remains the law that a failure to deny an accusation or answer questions about an offence *may* amount to an acknowledgment of the truth of the

---

136 The advice given by a solicitor to a client could not normally be the subject of questioning in court because of the client's 'legal professional privilege': see below, Chapter 13. But this privilege would have been 'waived' by a defendant who chose to give evidence about the advice he had received.

137 [2001] 1 Cr App R 160. See also *R v Milford* [2001] Crim LR 330.

138 [2000] Crim LR 679.

139 [1996] QB 373.

140 See Chapter 5.

accusations.[141] If situations like those in *Parkes v R* or *R v Batt*[142] were to recur, the result in each case would be the same.

It was noted above, in Chapter 3, that in a case where an inference can be drawn under s 35 of the Criminal Justice and Public Order Act 1994 from a defendant's failure to give evidence, the jury must be directed that an inference from silence cannot on its own prove guilt. That is the effect of s 38(3), which also provides that a person shall not have a case to answer solely on the basis of such an inference. The sub-section also applies to inferences that may be drawn under ss 34, 36 and 37. However, since an inference drawn under s 34 is relevant only to the credibility of a fact relied on in defence, it is difficult to see how such an inference could be the *only* reason for a conclusion that there is a case to answer, or a conviction.

THE *VOIR DIRE*

Where the admissibility of a confession or other item of prosecution evidence is disputed, the judge will often hear evidence in the absence of the jury before deciding the question. This procedure is known as a *'voir dire'* after the type of oath administered to witnesses who give evidence during it.[143] Where the admissibility of a confession is disputed, the defendant will usually give evidence about the circumstances which led him to make it. If he also gives evidence later in front of the jury, the prosecution may want to cross-examine him about discrepancies between what he said on the *voir dire* and what he said to the jury. It was decided by the Privy Council in *Wong Kam-Ming v R*[144] that this was permissible only where the judge had decided on the *voir dire* that the confession was *admissible*. It was also decided in *Wong Kam-Ming v R* that:

(a) since the *voir dire* was concerned with the *admissibility* of a confession and not with its *truth*, a defendant giving evidence on the *voir dire* should not be cross-examined about whether his confession was true or not; and

(b) in order to maintain the distinction between the issue of admissibility, which has to be decided on the *voir dire*, and the issue of guilt, which has to be decided in the main part of the trial, the prosecution may not call evidence before the jury of anything said by the defendant on the *voir dire*.

R v Wong Kam-Ming was decided before PACE, and it is possible that it no longer represents the law, because the effect of ss 76(1) and 82(1) of that Act is

---

141 See above, pp 214–16.

142 [1976] 1 WLR 1251; [1995] Crim LR 240.

143 See above, Chapter 1, p 25. It is improper for the judge to tell the jury about his ruling during a *voir dire* on the admissibility of a confession: *Mitchell v The Queen* [1998] 2 Cr App R 35 (PC).

144 [1980] AC 247.

to make admissible any statements by the defendant on the *voir dire* that are wholly or partly adverse to him. The fact that there has been no decision on this point after more than 10 years suggests either that the problem does not arise in practice or that, if it does, judges are willing to preserve the distinction between the issue on the *voir dire* and the issues in the rest of the trial by using their exclusionary discretion under s 78(1).

CHAPTER 10

SIMILAR FACT EVIDENCE[1]

NATURE AND DEVELOPMENT OF THE LAW

'Similar fact evidence' is an expression that refers to evidence which one party wishes to adduce as part of its case against another party, and which shows that other party to be guilty of some other misconduct than that primarily alleged, or shows him to have some discreditable propensity or interest.[2] In the context of a criminal trial, which is where the problem almost invariably arises, such evidence will usually be offered by the prosecution as part of an argument to support the conclusion that the defendant committed the particular offence with which he is charged. The expression 'similar fact evidence' was adopted because the question of admissibility typically arose where an offence had been committed in an idiosyncratic way, and where previous behaviour by the defendant showed a propensity to indulge in similar behaviour. But the problem is not confined to such situations and can also arise, for example, where articles of an incriminating nature are found in the defendant's possession, or where the defendant admits interests, such as paedophilia, which may be relevant to the charge alleged against him.

Problems associated with similar fact evidence can also arise where a defendant is charged on an indictment containing several counts. The normal rule in such a situation is that each count has to be separately considered; the evidence on one count is inadmissible in relation to another. But where similar fact features can be found among the counts, evidence on one count may be admissible in relation to others.

---

1   See, generally: *Evidence in Criminal Proceedings: Previous Misconduct of a Defendant*, Law Com No 141 (1996), pp 162–93; Eggleston, Sir R, *Evidence, Proof and Probability*, 2nd edn, 1983, Chapter 7; Stone (1932) 46 Harv LR 954; Hoffmann (1975) 91 LQR 193; Williams (1979) 5 Dalhousie LJ 281; Carter (1985) 48 MLR 29; Allan (1985) 48 MLR 253; Zuckerman (1987) 103 LQR 187; Tapper (1992) 108 LQR 26; Nair [1993] Crim LR 432; Nair (1996) 112 LQR 262; Pattenden (1996) 112 LQR 446; Munday [1999] 58 CLJ 45.

2   An interest will not, of course, be in itself criminal. Even in a criminal trial, the discreditable propensity need not be to commit criminal acts, nor need the other misconduct relied on amount to a criminal offence. For example, in *R v Lewis* (1983) 76 Cr App R 33 the prosecution were allowed to call evidence that the defendant possessed literature from a paedophile society. Similarly, in *R v Barrington* [1981] 1 WLR 419, evidence was given that the defendant possessed indecent photographs. In neither case did the prosecution attempt to rely on the fact that possession of the material in itself constituted a criminal offence. In *R v Butler* (1987) 84 Cr App R 12, evidence was given of consensual sexual acts between the defendant and his former girlfriend similar to those alleged to have been forced on a rape victim.

When details of a defendant's previous convictions are admitted as similar fact evidence, the judge must give a careful direction about their significance during the summing-up. In particular, he should:

- state that, depending on how the jury feels, the convictions *might*, not *must*, be relevant;

- direct the jury as to what issue the similar fact evidence is said to be relevant;

- direct the jury that the fact that a defendant has previous convictions does not mean that he is guilty of the current charge, and that they should approach the evidence with caution.[3]

For some time, it was thought that similar fact evidence could not be adduced where it was evidence of circumstances that had led to a criminal charge in respect of which the defendant was later acquitted. This view was rejected by the House of Lords in *R v Z*.[4] However, while such evidence is in principle admissible, the facts of each case will need to be examined with special care. A wide variety of circumstances is possible. At one end of the spectrum,[5] there may be a man who has had to face a series of similar allegations of rape made by different women. Suppose that on each occasion his defence was consent, or a belief that the woman consented. Such defences might well succeed at first but later become implausible through repetition. If he is charged again with rape and raises the same defence as before, it is likely that the earlier occasions could be used in rebuttal. But suppose the earlier acquittals had come about in a variety of ways. For example, at one trial there might have been a successful submission of no case to answer; at another, a defence of consent succeeded; at yet another, a defence of mistaken identity. The probative worth, at his fourth trial, of the circumstances leading to those acquittals is by no means clear. Another relevant consideration is likely to be the number of previous acquittals; one alone, in the absence of other similar fact evidence, would almost certainly be insufficient. Yet another consideration could be the distance in time between the earlier alleged offences and the current one.[6]

Similar fact problems rarely arise in civil proceedings. There are probably two reasons for this. The first is a belief that judges sitting alone are not prone to the prejudices that may affect members of a jury and, because of their experience of trying cases, are far more likely than juries to be able to assess the weight that should be attached to evidence of a potentially prejudicial nature. The test for excluding similar fact evidence depends on an assessment

---

3   *R v Soffe* (2000) *The Times*, 5 April.
4   [2000] 3 All ER 385.
5   See the speech of Lord Hobhouse at p 407.
6   For commentaries on *R v Z*, see Munday, R, 'Admitting acquittals as similar fact evidence of guilt' [2000] 59 CLJ 468; Tapper, C, 'Clouded acquittal' [2001] 117 LQR 1.

that its probative worth is outweighed by its likely prejudicial effect on the triers of fact hearing it. The less impressionable the latter, the more similar fact evidence can be safely admitted. The second reason why similar fact evidence so rarely creates problems in civil cases is that a judge who tries a case alone delivers a reasoned judgment; so even if he has been influenced by evidence that he ought to have ruled inadmissible, he can cover his tracks by producing a decision that appears not to have relied on it. Where this happens a dissatisfied litigant might have his suspicions, but he is unlikely to have grounds for an appeal.

Not surprisingly, therefore, it has been said that civil courts will admit similar fact evidence wherever it is relevant in determining the matter in issue, provided it would not be oppressive or unfair to the other side.[7] The stricter approach of the criminal courts will, however, be found on the rare occasions when a civil action is tried by a jury.[8]

The problem presented by similar fact evidence is that the evidence may be both relevant and of some weight. But there may be a danger that a jury hearing it will convict improperly, either because they will give it more weight than they should, or because they will decide not to apply the proper standard of proof when considering the case against such a person as the similar fact evidence shows the defendant to be.[9]

During the 19th century, this problem was discussed, if at all, in terms of relevance.[10] Partly for that reason, and partly because there was no effective system of criminal appeals in England until the Court of Criminal Appeal was established in 1907, the problem was dealt with on a case by case basis, usually at first instance only. After 1907, similar fact evidence, like other branches of criminal evidence law, developed as a system of rules based on precedent. What had previously been governed by considerations of relevance came to be governed by an exclusionary rule of law limited by an elaborate range of exceptions.

After the decision of the House of Lords in *DPP v Boardman*[11] in 1975, this rule-based structure began to be dismantled, and increasing emphasis was placed on the balancing of principles in the context of the case being tried. One principle was that a jury should not be deprived of evidence that had significant probative value. Another was that defendants should be protected from the danger of being convicted for the wrong reason as a result of allowing the jury to hear evidence that they might not be able to handle. Gradually it has become clear that in every case it is necessary to try to assess

---

7   *Mood Music Publishing Co Ltd v De Wolfe Publishing Ltd* [1976] 1 Ch 119.

8   *Thorpe v Chief Constable of Greater Manchester Police* [1989] 1 WLR 665.

9   The first type of prejudice has been called 'reasoning prejudice' and the second 'moral prejudice': Law Com No 141 (1996), pp 124–26.

10   Stone, J, 'The rule of exclusion of similar fact evidence: England' (1932) 46 Harv LR 954.

11   [1975] AC 421; *Sourcebook*, p 234.

the probative value of the disputed item of evidence, and to weigh this value against any danger that the jury will misuse the evidence. It is this misuse of evidence by the jury that is referred to when courts speak of the 'prejudicial effect' of an item of similar fact evidence. In a colloquial sense, all sound prosecution evidence is 'prejudicial' to the defendant because it makes a conviction more likely. But the prejudice with which the courts are concerned is the *improper* prejudice that might arise because of misuse of the evidence in question.

This balancing exercise can be illustrated by the approach taken by courts to cases concerning the admissibility of evidence of what are literally similar facts. When Charlie is charged with burglary of a tobacconist's shop the jury is not allowed to know about his 27 previous convictions for burglary of other tobacconists' shops. The reason for this is that the jurors might say, 'Well, it's obvious. He's always doing this. He must be the one who broke in'. They might even say, 'This man needs putting away regardless of this case; he's a public nuisance who has probably done even more crimes for which he hasn't been caught. The easiest way to put him away is to find him guilty on this charge. Don't let's waste time talking about the evidence'. The fact that Charlie has burgled tobacconists' shops on at least 27 previous occasions is not *irrelevant*. A person with that history is more likely than someone without it to have committed the particular burglary with which the court is concerned. That does not go very far towards proving that Charlie, as opposed to some other burglar, committed the crime in question. But it is thought that juries would be unlikely to appreciate this, so the information is kept from them.

Now suppose rather more. When Charlie committed his earlier burglaries, he wrote on every occasion on one of the shop walls five lines from Homer's *Odyssey* in the original Greek and in sequence. A piece of writing which fits this pattern was found on the wall of the premises to which the present charge relates. At once the probative value of Charlie's previous history increases greatly because it puts Charlie in a very much narrower range of potential burglars – almost certainly in a class of one. It is, of course, possible that someone framed him. But similar fact evidence, like any other evidence, does not have to be *conclusive* to be admitted. No evidence given in court can be conclusive. For example, the testimony of someone claiming to be an eye witness is not conclusive, because the witness may be mistaken or committing perjury. Nor is the defendant's own confession conclusive; it might have been untrue and made only as a result of inducements or threats.

In both stories about Charlie I was relying for the relevance of the previous convictions on an assumption that people tend to follow patterns of behaviour. The first pattern was one followed by quite a large number of persons and so did not point at all clearly to Charlie as having been the burglar on the occasion in question. The second pattern, however, was so peculiar to Charlie that it would defy belief to suggest that there might have been someone else operating in the same way.

I have gone into what must appear a rather obvious comparison because I wanted to show how to set about assessing the probative worth of an item of evidence. Such an assessment depends, of course, not on law but on a mixture of logic and general experience. What was said in Chapter 1 about relevance is of vital importance here. To argue effectively, you need to clarify the basic assumptions about the way things are in the world which would have to be true if a particular piece of information is to be relevant at all. If you need to attack the admissibility of a piece of similar fact evidence, the best approach may often be to attack the generalisation upon which your opponent must rely to establish its relevance. Remember that if evidence is not relevant, it must be excluded. In such a case, the judge will never reach the stage where probative value has to be balanced against possible prejudicial effect.

Because an argument about similar fact evidence should be founded on an assessment of its probative worth and likely prejudicial effect in the context of the particular case being tried, references to decisions in other cases will be of little use, and there can be no question now of using them as 'precedents'.[12] Nevertheless, even quite old reports may be useful *as examples of reasoning with facts*, and because of this should not be wholly ignored. It is important, however, when reading earlier cases, to have in mind the legal context in which they were decided. For this reason some knowledge is necessary of the development of similar fact evidence from the end of the 19th century.

Makin v AG for New South Wales[13]

This leading case, decided in 1894, concerned a husband and wife tried for the murder of a child whose body had been found buried on premises occupied by the defendants. The trial judge allowed evidence to be given that other bodies of children had been found at premises that had also been occupied by the defendants. In addition, he allowed evidence to be given by women who had entrusted their children to the defendants' care and had never seen those children again. Had the trial judge been right to admit these various items of evidence?

The Privy Council held that he had. In delivering its decision, Lord Herschell LC used words that have been relied on, though in different ways, on innumerable occasions since then:

It is undoubtedly not competent for the prosecution to adduce evidence tending to shew that the accused has been guilty of criminal acts other than those covered by the indictment, for the purpose of leading to the conclusion that the accused is a person likely from his criminal conduct or character to have committed the offence for which he is being tried. On the other hand, the

---

12 *R v Butler* (1987) 84 Cr App R 12, p 16.
13 [1894] AC 57; *Sourcebook*, p 228.

mere fact that the evidence adduced tends to shew the commission of other crimes does not render it inadmissible if it be relevant to an issue before the jury, and it may be so relevant if it bears upon the question whether the acts alleged to constitute the crime charged in the indictment were designed or accidental, or to rebut a defence which would otherwise be open to the accused.[14]

Lord Herschell's statement has been interpreted in three ways.[15] According to one interpretation there was a general rule, stated in the first proposition, requiring the exclusion of similar fact evidence. But to this rule of exclusion there were exceptions referred to in the second proposition. These exceptions were not exhaustive and the courts gradually developed others: for example, to prove identity, to prove knowledge or intent, to rebut a defence of mistake or involuntary conduct, to establish a consistent system of conduct, and to rebut a defence of innocent association. The effect was to encourage a simplistic view of admissibility. Problems were resolved by asking whether the facts fitted one of several established categories. This approach was later rejected by the House of Lords in *DPP v Boardman*.

A second interpretation of Lord Herschell's words treated as crucial the distinction between evidence that was relevant merely because it established the defendant's propensity to commit acts similar to those charged, and evidence that was relevant for some other reason. If the evidence was relevant *only* through an argument based on propensity, it was excluded by Lord Herschell's first proposition. If the evidence possessed relevance other than through propensity, it was admissible under the second proposition. If evidence was relevant for some reason other than propensity – for example, because it rebutted a defence of mistake or established identity – it was not made inadmissible because it *also* had relevance through propensity. But a judge had a discretion to exclude such evidence if he thought its prejudicial effect outweighed the probative worth that the evidence had otherwise than through propensity. For a time this was a popular approach and is reflected, for example, in the speech of Lord Hailsham in *DPP v Boardman*, where he referred to reasoning from propensity to guilt as an 'inadmissible chain of reasoning'.[16]

The difficulty with an approach based on a distinction between relevance through propensity and relevance by some other route is that there clearly have been cases where similar fact evidence derived its only relevance from an argument based on propensity. In *R v Straffen*,[17] for example, the sole probative force of the similar fact evidence was to show that the accused was

---

14 [1894] AC 57, p 65.

15 Williams, CR, 'The problem of similar fact evidence' (1979) 5 Dalhousie LJ 281, pp 283–90; *Sourcebook*, p 229.

16 [1975] AC 421, p 453.

17 [1952] QB 911.

likely to have committed the crime charged because he had a highly unusual propensity to strangle little girls without any attempt to conceal their bodies, and without any apparent motive. Further, Lord Hailsham's distinction tends to conceal the fact that the *way* in which a defence is rebutted will often be *by showing propensity*. For example, if Marmaduke is charged with the attempted murder of a clergyman by driving at him on a pedestrian crossing, his defence of accident may be rebutted by showing that he has driven at four other clergymen on pedestrian crossings in the previous 24 hours. The rebuttal works by showing Marmaduke's *propensity* to drive at clergymen on pedestrian crossings.

The third approach – the one that has gained ground since *DPP v Boardman* until now it has clearly overtaken the other two – treats the balance between probative worth and the risk of improper prejudice to the accused as the key to determining questions of admissibility. This involves treating Lord Herschell's formula as containing two *competing* (not conflicting) principles. The first proposition refers to the principle that evidence showing the accused to be of bad character and disposition is inadmissible to prove his guilt of the crime charged. The second proposition refers to the principle that relevant evidence ought to be admitted. *DPP v Boardman* has not led to the total abandonment of traditional categories of the kind listed under the first approach to Lord Herschell's formula, because those categories tend to include situations where similar fact evidence is likely to have a high degree of probative value. Pre-*Boardman* cases are still worth looking at as examples of relevance and reasoning with facts, but they no longer have the status they formerly had when they encapsulated exceptions to a general exclusionary rule.

DPP v Boardman

Boardman was tried on three counts. Offences were alleged to have been committed against boys at an English language school of which he was headmaster. Count 1 charged the defendant with buggery of a boy referred to as S on a day in October or November 1972. Count 2 charged him with inciting a boy referred to as H to commit buggery with him on a day in January 1973. A conviction on a third count in relation to another boy was subsequently quashed by the Court of Appeal.

The trial judge ruled that the evidence on count 2 was similar fact evidence in relation to count 1, and vice versa. Accordingly, he directed the jury that in deciding whether the prosecution had proved that the defendant had buggered S, they were entitled to take into account the evidence about inciting H to commit buggery; and in deciding whether the defendant had incited H to commit buggery, they were entitled to take into account the evidence about the buggery of S. The Court of Appeal upheld his decision. The case went to the House of Lords.

The prosecution did not argue that homosexuality was ever sufficient *of itself* to justify the admission of similar fact evidence. In other words, it was not saying that where X is charged with buggery, the prosecution are entitled to support their case by showing simply that X has in the past committed homosexual acts or that in sexual orientation he is homosexual rather than heterosexual. However, they argued that the judge's ruling could be supported on the basis that the evidence of S and H showed several striking similarities in the accused's behaviour. The features relied on were the defendant's waking the boys in the middle of the night, taking them to his sitting room, and requesting that the boys should penetrate him rather than vice versa.

The House of Lords upheld this contention and the following points were made in the speeches:

(a) There is no closed list of cases where similar fact evidence will be admissible.[18]

(b) Ordinary principles apply where homosexual conduct is alleged. The idea, current earlier in the 20th century, that there was a special rule allowing the admission of similar facts in such cases was rejected as obsolete.[19]

(c) The key to admissibility is whether the similar fact evidence has a really material bearing on the issues to be decided. It may have, if between the two sets of facts (facts relating to the count and the similar facts, which may or may not be the subject of another count), there is a close or striking similarity, or an underlying unity.[20]

(d) In each case, it is necessary to consider the weight of the similar fact evidence and the prejudice that it may cause to the accused if it is admitted.[21]

(e) Lord Hailsham emphasised that the similarities should be more than commonplace ones. 'For instance, whilst it would certainly not be enough to identify the culprit in a series of burglaries that he climbed in through a ground floor window, the fact that he left the same humourous limerick on the walls of the sitting room, or an esoteric symbol written in lipstick on the mirror, might well be enough.'[22]

(f) Admissibility is a question of law, not discretion, but the question is one of degree on the facts.[23]

Several of the Law Lords used the expression 'striking similarity' in relation to the test for admissibility.[24] For a time it seemed as if *an example of probative*

---

18 [1975] AC 439, pp 452, 456.
19 *Ibid*, pp 441, 443, 461.
20 *Ibid*, pp 438, 452.
21 *Ibid*, p 438.
22 *Ibid*, p 454.
23 *Ibid*, pp 442, 444.
24 *Ibid*, pp 439, 444, 462.

worth, taken from the facts of a particular case, was going to be elevated into *a rule of admissibility*, with a corollary that in the absence of this feature, potential similar fact evidence would be inadmissible. However, cases since *DPP v Boardman* have re-emphasised the principle that the admissibility of similar fact evidence depends simply on relevance, and on assessing the weight of such evidence and the risk of improper prejudice to the defendant if it is admitted.

For example, in *R v Scarrot*,[25] Scarman LJ said that the admissibility of similar fact evidence depended on its 'positive probative value'. The expression 'strikingly similar' was, he said, no more than a label, and like all labels it could mislead. Whether such 'positive probative value' existed depended on the facts of each case, but plainly some circumstances would be too distant in time or place to have such value. Equally plainly, it was not possible to isolate the bare bones of a criminal offence from its surrounding circumstances and say that it was only within those confines that admissibility was to be determined. Some surrounding circumstances had to be considered in order to understand either the offence charged or the nature of the similar fact evidence. In each case it was a matter of judgment where the line was drawn.

The significance of relevance and probative weight was emphasised again in *R v Lunt*.[26] Neill LJ said that, in order to decide whether proposed similar fact evidence was positively probative in regard to the crime charged, it was first necessary to identify the issue to which the evidence was directed. It might be put forward, for example, to support an identification, to prove intention, or to rebut a possible defence of accident or innocent association. Whether the evidence was or was not positively probative would be governed by the issue to which it was related, not some quality which the evidence was thought to possess in itself.

Neill LJ was one of several judges who assumed that even under the *DPP v Boardman* principles a judge might make a decision in favour of admissibility but still leave room for the exercise of an overriding discretion to exclude evidence whose prejudicial effect was likely to outweigh its probative value.[27] It is clear that such a discretion does exist at common law,[28] but it is impossible that there should be any room for its exercise now in a similar fact case, because the consideration governing the exercise of the *discretion* will already have been taken into account in reaching the *judgment* on the question of admissibility. If the judgment to admit or exclude evidence depends on a balancing of prejudicial effect against probative value, prejudicial effect is

---

25 [1978] 1 QB 1016, pp 1022–23, 1025; *Sourcebook*, p 241.
26 (1986) 85 Cr App R 241, p 245; *Sourcebook*, p 243.
27 See *R v Lunt* (1986) 85 Cr App R 241; see also *R v Burns* [1996] Crim LR 322.
28 See, eg, *R v Sang* [1980] AC 402.

taken into account before the judgment is made; there can be no reason to take it into account again afterwards.

DPP v P[29]

In 1991, the key concept of relevance was re-emphasised by the House of Lords. In this case the defendant was charged with four offences of rape and four offences of incest in respect of each of his two daughters, referred to as B and S. At the start of his trial, an application was made that the counts in the indictment relating to daughter B should be tried separately from those concerning daughter S. This was refused on the basis that the evidence of B was admissible as similar fact evidence in relation to the count concerning S, and vice versa. After the defendant had been convicted, the trial judge's ruling was the basis of a successful appeal to the Court of Appeal.

In giving the judgment of the court, Lord Lane CJ said that the similar fact doctrine seemed to require some feature of similarity beyond what had been described as the paederast's or incestuous father's 'stock in trade'.[30] The court had been unable to find similarities in the two daughters' accounts in respect of any unusual features. It followed that the evidence of one daughter was inadmissible in relation to the counts affecting the other.

Leave was granted to the DPP to appeal to the House of Lords, and two questions were certified for consideration:

(a) Where a father is charged with sexually abusing a young daughter of the family, is evidence that he similarly abused other young members of the family admissible, assuming there to be no collusion and in the absence of any other 'striking similarities'?

(b) Where a defendant is charged with sexual offences against more than one child or young person, is it necessary, in the absence of striking similarities, for the charges to be tried separately?

Lord Mackay LC, in a speech with which the other Law Lords agreed, said it was not appropriate to single out striking similarity as an essential element in every case before allowing the evidence of one complainant to support the testimony of another. In every case it was probative force that had to be weighed, and there was no single way of doing this. Previous cases that had required more than the paederast's or incestuous father's stock in trade had been wrongly decided.

---

29 [1991] 2 AC 447; *Sourcebook*, p 245.

30 This refers to the idea expressed by Lord Hailsham in *DPP v Boardman* that common similarities in the mode of committing burglary would not be sufficient for admissibility. See also *R v Brown* (1963) 47 Cr App R 204; *Sourcebook*, p 259.

Similar fact evidence after *DPP v P*

After *DPP v P*, it was thought for a short period by some judges that Lord Mackay had left striking similarity as an essential test in trials where identification was in dispute. But in *R v W (John)*[31] the Court of Appeal held that this was a misinterpretation, and that there is no special rule in identification cases requiring striking similarity. In delivering the judgment of the Court, Hooper J emphasised the basic test: does the similar fact evidence have such weight that it would be fair to use it, notwithstanding its prejudicial effect? Similar fact evidence that is relevant to identification may acquire its weight from features that are strikingly similar, but that is not the only way in which it may do so. He also emphasised another basic principle: evidence that is merely of disposition or bad character will lack sufficient weight to be admitted as similar fact evidence. A similar point was made in *R v Musquera*,[32] where the Court of Appeal said that while the decision in *DPP v P* had eliminated the necessity to identify a striking similarity, it was still necessary to be able to point to some common feature or features constituting a significant connection between the similar fact evidence and the evidence in the current trial, and going beyond mere propensity or coincidence.

Any presentation of similar fact cases runs the risk of appearing to classify the subject matter. This may be helpful as a short term device to aid memory. But even for so limited a purpose, classification may confuse, because classes will often overlap and it may be tempting to fall into the error of assuming that, to be admitted, evidence must fit into at least one of them.

How should a similar fact problem be approached in practice? You should begin with an argument about relevance in which you will refer to basic principles: if the disputed evidence has greater danger of prejudice than probative value it should not be admitted. At this stage your argument will be confined to the facts of the particular case and may by itself be enough. If the judge seems reluctant to accept your argument, you may be able to push him in the right direction by drawing his attention to a decided case if it appears to be very much in point. But decided cases are no more than illustrations of the basic principles. They should never be treated as 'precedents' which have to be 'followed'. Above all, never try to play a game of 'snap' based on the comparison of features in a particular problem with those in earlier cases.

Earlier cases should be read for their reasoning rather than for their results. They should be read critically because you do not have to look very far before coming across approaches which have become misleading in light

---

31   [1998] 2 Cr App R 289.
32   [1999] Crim LR 857.

of later developments.[33] The Court of Appeal has acknowledged that *DPP v P* has enlarged considerably the scope of similar fact evidence.[34]

With these reservations, I turn to some of the various uses to which similar fact evidence can be put.

PROOF AND SIMILAR FACT EVIDENCE

To prove motive

In a case decided in 1911, *R v Ball*,[35] a brother and sister were charged with incest. Evidence was given that they lived together, sharing a bedroom and a bed. Evidence of earlier sexual relations between them at a time when such relations did not constitute an offence was held admissible to prove 'that they had a guilty passion towards each other', and that the proper inference from their occupying the same bed was that they were guilty as charged. As Lord Loreburn LC said, 'Their passion for each other was as much evidence as was their presence together in bed of the fact that when they were there they had guilty relations with each other'.[36]

More usually the relevant motive will be the defendant's antipathy towards the victim of the crime charged. During the course of argument in *R v Ball* Lord Atkinson remarked that it would be absurd if, in a trial for murder, the prosecution were not allowed to prove previous words or acts of the accused to show that he had feelings of enmity towards the deceased. The reason, he said, was that it was more probable that men were killed by those who had some motive for killing them than by those who had not.[37] Evidence of similar facts to prove motive was admitted in *R v Williams*,[38] where the defendant was charged, under s 16 of the Offences Against the Person Act 1861, with making a threat to kill. The section required the prosecution to prove that the threat was made with the intention that the person threatened would fear that the threat would be carried out. Evidence of previous threatening and violent conduct by the defendant towards the victim was held to have been rightly admitted, because the history of their relationship helped to prove this intention.

---

33 A good example is Lord Hailsham's reference to the 'inadmissible chain of reasoning' in *DPP v Boardman*.

34 *R v Kidd* [1995] Crim LR 406. See also Lord Griffiths in *R v H* [1995] 2 Cr App R 437, p 453 and *R v Groves* [1998] Crim LR 200.

35 [1911] AC 47; *Sourcebook*, p 249.

36 [1911] AC 47, p 71.

37 *Ibid*, p 68.

38 (1987) 84 Cr App R 298.

Evidence was admitted for a similar purpose in *R v Fulcher*.[39] The defendant was charged with the murder of his infant son, who had died from a fractured skull. Evidence was given for the prosecution that the child's medical condition made him more fractious than if he had been healthy, and that when the child cried the defendant used to get aggravated, upset and annoyed. The Court of Appeal held that this evidence had been properly admitted. The prosecution was entitled to adduce evidence to show how on other occasions the defendant had reacted to the crying baby. In giving the judgment of the court, Kennedy LJ said that the relevance of this evidence was that it was possible for the jury to infer from it that on the critical occasion the defendant was so irritated by the child that he resorted to gross violence. The evidence in question was evidence of motive which went to both *actus reus* and *mens rea*.[40]

In *R v Williams* and *R v Fulcher*, evidence of disposition was admitted as similar fact evidence because it showed a highly particularised disposition directed towards a single person. The line between a general and a particular disposition was neatly drawn in the Canadian case of *R v Drysdale*.[41] The defendant in this case was living with a woman and several children of the family. He was charged with the murder of one of them, a girl called Angela. The prosecution was allowed to call evidence to show that the defendant had assaulted Angela on previous occasions, that he had assaulted other children of the family, and that on one occasion he had also attacked a dog which they kept as a pet. The defendant was convicted, but his appeal was successful. The Manitoba Court of Appeal held that the evidence of earlier assaults on Angela was admissible to show a specific antipathy towards her, but evidence of the other matters amounted to no more than evidence of a general disposition to violence, and had been improperly admitted.[42]

But the basis for admitting evidence to prove motive is still not wholly clear. In *R v Williams*, the Court of Appeal adopted a distinction between evidence of similar facts, which the court said usually related to offences against persons other than the alleged victim of the offence charged, and evidence of motive that consisted of other acts or declarations of the accused indicating a desire to commit, or motive for committing, the particular offence

---

39 [1995] 2 Cr App R 251.

40 Kennedy LJ went on to say that it was not intended as evidence of similar facts, but he may to have been using this expression in the narrow sense to refer to evidence of actions following a strikingly similar pattern of behaviour. It was not suggested that the defendant had assaulted the child on any earlier occasions when he had become irritated.

41 (1969) 66 WWR 664.

42 The cases referred to suggest that evidence of antipathy should be admissible only if directed towards a single person. But suppose a defendant is charged with assaulting a member of the staff of a particular public house. His defence is accident. Couldn't this be rebutted by showing that he had previously quarrelled with the manager and told him that he would 'get even' with his staff?

charged. Evidence of the latter type is sometimes admitted now as 'background evidence', which is said to be governed by its own rules, and unconnected with similar fact evidence. It is possible to see *R v Williams* and *R v Fulcher* as resting either on a similar fact or background evidence basis, and other decisions sometimes blur the distinction.[43]

To prove identification

The best identification evidence will be that of reliable witnesses who saw the defendant committing the crime with which he is charged. But the evidence even of honest eye witnesses can be far from reliable. Witnesses may be uncertain, and, even where they appear certain, juries are encouraged to look for other evidence in support. Sometimes support can come from evidence of earlier misconduct by the defendant, or from the discovery of incriminating articles in the defendant's possession.

Where the prosecution rely on other misconduct to help identify the defendant, the jury may be invited to adopt one of two different approaches to the evidence. Rosemary Pattenden has called these the 'sequential' and the 'pooling' approaches.[44] The other misconduct will usually be another crime. Where this is the case, it may be the subject of a previous conviction recorded against the defendant, or of another count in the indictment on which the defendant is currently being tried.

In the sequential approach, the judge first decides whether the crime for which the defendant is being tried and the other misconduct are 'strikingly similar'.[45] If he thinks they are, the jury must consider whether the current offence and the other misconduct were committed by the same person. If their answer is yes, they must next ask whether the defendant committed the other misconduct. If the answer to that is yes, the last stage, in light of their answer to the second question, is the conclusion that the defendant is guilty of the offence charged.

The pooling approach has been applied only in cases where the other misconduct is the subject of other counts in the same indictment. The first question for the jury is whether the same person committed all the offences charged in the indictment. If their answer to that is yes, they may then add together evidence relevant to the issue of identity from each count in order to establish the identity of the culprit. It does not matter that, in relation to any one count, the identification evidence would be insufficient to establish the

---

43 Background evidence is further discussed below.

44 Pattenden, R, 'Similar fact evidence and proof of identity' (1996) 112 LQR 446.

45 Where similar fact evidence of conduct is relied on, the courts must consider any significant dissimilarities when assessing its probative worth. But the mere fact that there are some dissimilarities will not lead inevitably to exclusion: *R v Johnson* [1995] 2 Cr App R 41; *R v West* [1996] 2 Cr App R 374.

identity of the culprit. Lastly, it follows from the first stage that if the accumulated evidence points to the defendant as the culprit, he is guilty on all counts.

These different approaches may be illustrated by reference to two recent decisions of the Court of Appeal. The first of these, *R v McGranaghan*,[46] shows the sequential approach. The defendant was tried on an indictment that contained counts covering offences of burglary, indecent assault, rape and robbery committed on three separate occasions: in May 1978, in October 1978 and in December 1979. Witnesses had made weak identifications of the defendant in respect of each occasion. The Court of Appeal agreed with the trial judge that there were features of striking similarity shared by all three that made evidence in relation to one offence admissible in relation to the others. However, the purpose for which such evidence was admissible was to support the weak identifications of the defendant by the witnesses. In giving the judgment of the court, Glidewell LJ said that no use of similar fact evidence for this purpose could be justified unless the jury was first satisfied that at least one of those offences had been committed by the defendant.

The pooling approach can be seen in *R v Barnes*.[47] In October 1993, there were several assaults on women in the Tufnell Park area of London. The defendant was charged on an indictment containing counts which related to three of those attacks. It was the prosecution's case that the circumstances of the attacks were strikingly similar, and three other incidents were also relied on as similar fact evidence. The prosecution submitted that there was overwhelming evidence that all the attacks were the the work of the same man. They relied on the proximity in time and space of the attacks, the description given by each victim of her assailant and the identical way in which the approach was made in each case. Identification parades had been held and the complainants in respect of the three counts had identified the defendant. The defence accepted that there was sufficient striking similarity for similar fact evidence to be admissible. But an appeal against conviction was based on an alleged misdirection by the judge in relation to identification. It was argued, following *R v McGranaghan*, that the jury should have been told to consider first a single count, and, in doing so, to have regard only to the identification evidence of the complainant in respect of that count. Only if the jury were sure on that count could they use it to help identification on others.

The Court of Appeal distinguished *R v McGranaghan* on the basis that, in that case, the court was considering the propriety of using similar fact evidence to support a doubtful identification. Here the question was a different one, namely, whether identifications by several victims could be used cumulatively, once the jury were satisfied that other evidence showed all

---

46 [1995] 1 Cr App R 559.
47 [1995] 2 Cr App R 491.

the offences to have been committed by one man. The defence proposition would have led to an unreal exercise by the jury in trying to compartmentalise the evidence before them.

On both the sequential and the pooling approaches the first and last questions are the same: on each approach the first thing for the jury to consider is whether the same man was responsible for all the misconduct; the last question is whether the defendant is guilty on each count in the indictment. The difference between the two approaches lies in the way the intermediate stages are handled. On the sequential approach, illustrated by *R v McGranaghan*, once the jury decides that one man has committed all the offences their attention shifts immediately to the question of who committed the offence charged in any *one* count. A decision having been made in relation to the one count, that answers the question in respect of all the others. But on the pooling approach, illustrated by *R v Barnes*, the jury will be told that if they decide that all the offences were committed by the same person, they must try to establish the identity of that person. And to do this they can look at the overall picture created by the evidence on *all* counts. Pooling the available evidence will produce the same result as the sequential approach when the responsibility of the defendant for similar conduct has already been conclusively decided by an earlier conviction. But where this is not so, the pooling and sequential approaches may produce different results on the same set of facts.

The approach to be applied is a matter for the trial judge to decide. There is a danger that weak identification by witnesses may acquire spurious support from coincidences. The choice of approach is therefore likely to be governed by the strength of the identifying evidence and the risk of coincidence involved in the similar fact evidence. In *R v McGranaghan* the witnesses' identifications were weak and the incidents took place over a period of 18 months in south west London and Surrey. In those circumstances, the sequential approach was required to protect the defendant. In *R v Barnes*, by contrast, the witnesses' identifications were strong, and the offences took place during a period of only one month in one area of London. In those circumstances the pooling approach was appropriate, for the reasons given by Lord Taylor CJ.[48]

Striking similarity will often provide the necessary probative weight for similar fact evidence that is used to support an identification. But the House of Lords did not establish in *DPP v P* that similar fact evidence must *always* show striking similarity, in the sense of a 'signature', where it is adduced for that purpose. In *R v Lee*,[49] the Court of Appeal emphasised that the test of

---

48   For the difficulties that arise where sequential and cumulative approaches are applied to crimes committed by a gang, see *R v Lee* [1996] Crim LR 825 and *R v Brown and Others* [1997] Crim LR 502.

49   [1996] Crim LR 825. *R v W (John)* [1998] 2 Cr App R 289.

admissibility for similar fact evidence in identification cases was, as in other types of case, the balancing of probative weight against prejudice to the defendant in the particular circumstances of the case. The court said that similar fact evidence could be used to identify the defendant as the wrongdoer by means of a 'signature' *or by some other special feature*. Sometimes another special feature has been the discovery of incriminating articles in the possession of the defendant.

One of the earliest examples is *Thompson v R.*[50] The defendant was charged with committing an act of gross indecency in a public lavatory with two boys. The case for the prosecution was that the acts in question had been committed on 16 March and the person who committed them had made an appointment to see the boys again at the same place on 19 March. On the second occasion, members of the police kept watch with the boys. In due course the defendant arrived. After he had been identified by the boys and arrested, he claimed to be the victim of mistaken identification. Evidence was given at trial that, when arrested, the defendant had been in possession of powder puffs, and that when his rooms were searched indecent photographs of boys had been found. The House of Lords held that this evidence, showing the accused to be homosexual, was admissible to support the boys' identification. If the boys' identifications had not been accurate, it was an unbelievable coincidence that the man they had mistakenly identified had also been a homosexual. Yet powder puffs and indecent photographs were relevant to homosexual *propensity* rather than to homosexual *activity*.[51]

Where discovery of incriminating articles is relied on to support the prosecution case, there is clearly a danger that, unless some limitation is put on the type of articles admissible, the defendant will be convicted merely because the articles suggest that he is likely to commit offences of the type in question. It used to be said that the articles found must have had some connection with the crime charged. In *R v Taylor*,[52] the defendant was charged with shopbreaking. A police officer gave evidence that, at about midnight, he had seen the defendant and another man outside a shop, had heard the door being forced open, and had seen the defendant and another man run out. On arrest, the defendant told the officer that the affair was a drunken escapade and that he and the other man had charged one another against the door and broken it. There were no marks of any kind on the door and nothing had been stolen, but at trial evidence was given that when the defendant's house was later searched, a jemmy had been found. It was argued on appeal that no connection had been shown between the jemmy and what the defendant was alleged to have done. For this and other reasons his appeal was allowed.

---

50 [1918] AC 221.

51 Compare, eg, the evidential value of discovering a tin of lubricant instead of powder puffs in the defendant's possession.

52 (1923) 17 Cr App R 109; *Sourcebook*, p 250.

Similarly, in the Australian case of *Thompson v The Queen*,[53] the defendants were charged with burglary from two safes, which had been blown open by explosives. The prosecution was allowed to call evidence to show that the accused had in their possession a collection of instruments for opening safes by blowing, by drilling, or by picking the locks. The court held that evidence of possession of articles that *might* have been used in the commission of the offence was admissible. But the extent of the evidence admitted was too wide and the appeal was allowed.

Even in the absence of an apparent connection between the incriminating articles and the offence, evidence of their discovery may be given if it has some bearing on a defence put forward by the defendant. In *R v Da Silva*,[54] for example, the defendant was charged with armed robbery. Two masked men had entered the bedroom of a hotel owner at about 1.00 am and had made off with about £8,500 in cash. The prosecution alleged that the defendant was one of those involved. They relied, amongst other things, on a search of the defendant's room, which had revealed one of the hotel's brochures, £1,200 in cash and a dagger, which the hotel owner said resembled the one he had been threatened with. The police also found a meat cleaver, a knife and a truncheon hidden under the floorboards. Were these items also admissible? There was no evidence that they had been used in the robbery. But the defendant had already provided an explanation for his possession of the dagger: according to him, he had it as part of his equipment for martial arts training. The trial judge held that evidence of the discoveries under the floorboards could be given, because that evidence tended to show that the defendant's explanation for his possession of the dagger was untrue. The Court of Appeal upheld his decision.

To rebut a defence

R v Da Silva is an example of a case where similar fact evidence was admitted because of the nature of the defence. Defences in cases of drug importation have, on several occasions, let in evidence about incriminating materials discovered in addition to the drugs which were the subject of the charge. For example, in *R v Sokialiois*,[55] the defendant was charged with importing cocaine. A packet had been posted from Holland to an address in Dover. It was intercepted, and a co-defendant who attempted to retrieve it from the post office was arrested. The defendant was arrested a little later. In his possession was a piece of paper containing the Dover address where the packet was to be delivered, and a diary with a note of the same address and

---

53 (1968) 117 CLR 313.
54 [1990] 1 WLR 31.
55 [1993] Crim LR 872.

the words 'Uncle Charlie' (slang for cocaine). When interviewed, the defendant denied any knowledge of the address and said, 'I am not a drug dealer. I don't deal in drugs. I don't even take drugs'. His holdall was later recovered from a hotel and found to contain a further quantity of cocaine of similar purity. His defence was that the paper containing the address and the drugs in the holdall had been planted on him by one of the co-accused.

The judge admitted the evidence of finding the holdall on the ground that it was relevant to the defendant's replies given in the interview. On appeal it was argued that the discovery of the additional stock of cocaine went only to propensity, and in effect amounted merely to evidence of bad character. The Court of Appeal rejected this, saying it was clear that the evidence rebutted what had been said in the interview, and that what had been said in the interview had been designed to bolster the defence that he had been framed.

A more difficult case is *R v Peters*.[56] The defendant was charged with importing amphetamine by concealing it in his car. In police interviews he denied any knowledge of the presence of the drugs, and said that he had no connection with drugs in any form. A search of his home revealed small quantities of cannabis and some drug-related equipment. Was this evidence admissible? The Court of Appeal held that it was. It was relevant to show that his denial of any connection with drugs was untrue. But the court added that it would have been admissible even if in interview he had merely denied knowledge of how the drugs had come to be concealed in the car. In effect, the defendant was saying that he was the innocent victim of someone who had used his car to smuggle drugs. According to the court, the defendant's own connection with drugs was relevant and admissible to rebut this defence. It was not necessary for the drugs found at his home to be the same as those imported. But the court noted that it was 'clear, of course,' that evidence of previous convictions for drug offences could not have been given for this purpose.[57]

Similar fact evidence is often admitted to rebut a defence that the defendant had no criminal intent. An old but vivid example is *R v Mortimer*.[58] The defendant was charged with the murder of a woman cyclist. The case for the prosecution was that on the morning of 8 August 1935, he had deliberately driven his motor car at a woman riding a bicycle and had knocked her down,

---

56 [1995] 2 Cr App R 77.

57 The reasoning is obscure. What generalisations about the way things are in the world were tacitly assumed when the court said that the chances of the defendant's being an innocent victim of a drug smuggler must depend greatly on whether he had any contact, even if only as a customer, with persons who handled unlawful drugs? (*R v Peters* [1995] 2 Cr App R 77, pp 81–82.) The truth appears to be that evidence of disposition will be readily admitted to rebut a defence of innocent association or lack of knowledge in trials involving dealing in drugs. See also *R v Yalman* [1998] 2 Cr App R 269; *R v Groves* [1998] Crim LR 200. For a commentary on *Yalman*, see Redmayne (1999) 3 E&P 128.

58 (1936) 25 Cr App R 150; *Sourcebook*, p 250.

with fatal results. His defence was accident. In the light of this, the prosecution were allowed to prove that on two occasions during the previous evening he had knocked down two other women cyclists in a similar way, and had stopped his car to assault them. Evidence was also admitted to show that on the afternoon of 8 August, he had knocked down another woman cyclist and stolen her handbag, and that later he had driven directly at three different parties of police officers who had tried to stop his car. The Court of Criminal Appeal held that all this evidence had been properly admitted, because it was of crucial importance to show that what had been done to the murder victim was deliberate.

More recently, in *R v Kidd*,[59] the defendant was seen lying face down in a field which was protected under legislation designed to preserve ancient monuments and archeological sites. He had with him a metal-detector, and was charged with going equipped for theft. His defence was that he had been drinking, had decided to walk to a friend's house, and had taken the metal-detector with a view to selling it. Once in the field he had stopped for a cigarette and fallen asleep. The trial judge admitted evidence of previous convictions of theft from archaeological sites involving use of a metal-detector. The defendant's appeal was dismissed. The Court of Appeal said that on these facts the previous convictions were highly relevant to rebut the defence that the defendant had been innocently sleeping.

R v Lewis[60] shows the difficulties that can arise where an indictment contains several counts and there are different defences in respect of them. The defendant was tried in connection with four different incidents involving himself and the children of a woman he was living with. In relation to one of the incidents, the defence was a complete denial that the action in question had taken place. The defences in relation to the other three were either accidental touching of a child, or touching for the proper purpose of drying the child after a bath.

The prosecution was allowed to call evidence to show that the defendant possessed magazines, letters and posters from a paedophile society; that in interviews with police he had referred to himself as a paedophile; and that he had asked the children's mother if she could live with a paedophile. The evidence tended to show, therefore, not that he was guilty of other criminal acts, but that his disposition was such that he was likely to have committed the offences for which he was being tried, and in relation to which he had provided a defence of accident or innocent purpose. The Court of Appeal held that the judge had rightly admitted the evidence. It was not rendered inadmissible in relation to all the counts merely because it was inadmissible in

---

59 [1995] Crim LR 406.

60 (1983) 76 Cr App R 33; *Sourcebook*, p 260. See also Carter, PB, 'Forbidden reasoning permissible: similar fact evidence a decade after Boardman' (1985) 48 MLR 29, pp 35–41; *Sourcebook*, pp 263–65.

relation to one count where there had been a straight denial of the *actus reus*, or because in relation to the others there was some degree of denial of the basic facts. In relation to three of the counts, the jury clearly had to consider the possibility of accident and innocent explanation, and the evidence was relevant to these issues.

It is clear, however, that where the issue is whether the alleged offence ever took place at all, evidence of disposition will be inadmissible to support an argument that it did. So where allegations of buggery and gross indecency were made by schoolboys against their headmaster and his defence was that their stories were fabricated, the Court of Appeal held that evidence should not have been admitted of articles found in his possession tending to show that he had homosexual inclinations.[61]

THE POSSIBILITY OF CONCOCTION

Where two or more persons give evidence of similar conduct on the part of a defendant, there may be a danger either that they have conspired together to tell a false story, or that their stories are not truly independent because, though honestly told, they depend in fact on some common source such as rumour or the unconscious influence of one witness on another. The approach of the courts to this problem has varied in the past, but the position is now governed by the decision of the House of Lords in *R v H*.[62] The general rule is now that where an application is made to admit similar fact evidence, the judge should decide the question on the assumption that the facts alleged are true, and ignore any allegation of collusion between witnesses. Save in exceptional circumstances, the question of collusion is a matter for the jury, not the judge, to consider. Where it is raised as an issue by the defence, the judge should tell the jury that they must be satisfied that the similar fact evidence is free from collusion before it can be relied on to support the prosecution case.

SECTION 27(3) OF THE THEFT ACT 1968

Where a person is being proceeded against for handling stolen goods (but not for any offence other than handling stolen goods), then at any stage of the proceedings, if evidence has been given of his having or arranging to have in his possession the goods the subject of the charge, or of his undertaking or

---

61 *R v Wright* (1990) 90 Cr App R 325. See also *R v B(RA)* [1997] 2 Cr App R 88. For criticism of the survival of categories as a means of analysing similar fact evidence, see the commentary on this decision, reported as *R v Burrage* [1997] Crim LR 440.

62 [1995] 2 AC 596. See Law Com No 141 (1996), pp 184–89.

assisting in, or arranging to undertake or assist in, their retention, removal, disposal or realisation, the following evidence shall be admissible for the purpose of proving that he knew or believed the goods to be stolen goods:

(a) evidence that he has had in his possession, or has undertaken or assisted in the retention, removal, disposal or realisation of, stolen goods from any theft taking place not earlier than 12 months before the offence charged;[63] and

(b) (provided that seven days' notice in writing has been given to him of the intention to prove the conviction) evidence that he has within the five years preceding the date of the offence charged been convicted of theft or handling stolen goods.

The effect of the words in brackets in the opening paragraph is that the sub-section cannot be used where a charge of handling is joined with another charge, such as theft.

The sub-section can be used solely for the purpose of proving guilty knowledge on a handling charge. What happens when the defendant is charged with several counts of handling, and in relation to some he denies guilty knowledge, but in relation to others he denies possession? In such a case the trial judge should consider excluding altogether the evidence allowed by the sub-section so as to avoid any possible misuse of it by the jury. If he does allow such evidence to be admitted, the jury must be clearly warned of the limited use that can be made of it.[64]

The sub-section has been restrictively construed. Sub-section (3)(a) does not permit evidence to be given of the transaction which led to stolen property coming into the possession of the defendant on the earlier occasion.[65] Sub-section (3)(b) is to be read subject to s 73(2) of the Police and Criminal Evidence Act 1984 (PACE). This provides that a certificate of conviction of an offence on indictment must give the substance and effect of the indictment and conviction. It follows that the details of the previous conviction appearing on the certificate are admissible under sub-s (3)(b).[66]

Unlike the common law test for the admissibility of similar fact evidence, the sub-section makes no provision for balancing the probative worth of potential evidence against its prejudicial effect. But this consideration can still be taken into account by the judge, because evidence permitted by the sub-section can be excluded either at common law or under s 78 of PACE.[67]

---

63 Note that the sub-section permits evidence to be given of a possession later than the offence charged: *R v Davies* [1972] Crim LR 431. Under the sub-section the mere fact of possession is enough; there is no need for the possessor to have been prosecuted.

64 *R v Wilkins* (1975) 60 Cr App R 300.

65 *R v Bradley* (1979) 70 Cr App R 200.

66 *R v Hacker* [1994] 1 WLR 1659.

67 *Ibid.*

PROPOSALS FOR REFORM

The Law Commission has recently considered reform of the law relating to the evidence that can be given in criminal proceedings of a defendant's previous misconduct.[68] The bulk of the Consultation Paper dealing with this subject is concerned with proposals for the reform of s 1(3) of the Criminal Evidence Act 1898, but some minor amendments to similar fact evidence were proposed for discussion.

The Commission favoured a fundamental proposition that, with certain exceptions, evidence should be inadmissible if it would be prejudicial. Evidence would be regarded as prejudicial if there were a risk that the fact finders might treat it as more probative of guilt than it really was ('reasoning prejudice'), or there was a risk that the evidence might lead the fact finders to convict the defendant without being satisfied that he was guilty as charged ('moral prejudice').[69]

The Commission provisionally proposed that prejudicial evidence should be admissible as part of the prosecution's case if it was relevant to a specific issue, *and* its probative value outweighed its likely prejudicial effect and any other factors militating against its admission. In other words, the Commission broadly endorsed the law as stated in *DPP v P*. But that test was said to be unsatisfactory to the extent that it failed to give sufficient guidance to courts on how to carry out the prescribed balancing exercise. The Commission therefore suggested that legislation should expressly set out the conditions that must be satisfied before such evidence could be admitted, and the factors that the court should consider in deciding whether those conditions were satisfied.[70] The proposal that there should be conditions to be satisfied before similar fact evidence is admitted suggests that there might be a return to the pre-*Boardman* rule-based approach to this problem. Whether this would make for any greater certainty or consistency is doubtful.

SIMILAR FACT EVIDENCE AND CO-DEFENDANTS

A defendant may want to rely on similar fact evidence against a co-defendant in an attempt to show that it was the co-defendant, and not himself, who committed the offence. I have already argued that the test for admitting similar fact evidence itself involves a balancing of probative worth and prejudicial effect on a defendant. If that argument is right, that will be the test applied in all cases, and it will make no difference that the application to

---

68   Law Com No 141 (1996).
69   *Ibid*, paras 7.7–7.15 and 9.92.
70   *Ibid*, paras 10.73–10.82.

admit the evidence is made by a co-defendant rather than the prosecution. But it has also been shown that judges have from time to time expressed the view that there is a judicial discretion to exclude similar fact evidence that may be operated once it has been shown that the evidence is, as a matter of law, admissible.[71] If a judge takes that view, the position of a defendant who makes an application to admit similar fact evidence will be stronger than that of a prosecutor, because a judge has no discretion to exclude admissible evidence called by one defendant, even where it has the effect of prejudicing another.[72]

BACKGROUND EVIDENCE

According to *R v Pettman*,[73] a decision of the Court of Appeal in 1985, evidence showing the defendant's commission of an offence with which he is not charged can be admitted if it is necessary to place it before the jury as part of a continual background, or history, that is relevant to the offence charged, so that the account placed before the jury would be incomplete or incomprehensible without it. So, for example, in *R v M(T) and Others*,[74] in which *R v Pettman* was applied, evidence that M had from a young age been taught by a member of his family to abuse his sisters sexually was held admissible to explain, among other things, why one of M's sisters had made no attempt to obtain help when M had abused her on later occasions that were the subject of the indictment. A similar decision was reached in *R v Sawoniuk*,[75] where the defendant was charged with murders alleged to have been committed by him in 1942 in Belorussia during the German occupation. Two witnesses were able to give evidence that the defendant had been a local police officer involved in a 'search and kill' operation against the Jewish population. The Court of Appeal held, following *R v Pettman*, that this evidence was probative and admissible to support evidence of identification. In both cases, the Court of Appeal drew a clear distinction between similar fact evidence and background evidence when analysing the grounds for admissibility.

A potential difficulty created by lapse of time was highlighted in *R v Butler (Diana)*,[76] where the defendant was charged with the murder of the man with whom she was living. Her defence was provocation. The prosecution was

---

71 See, eg, *R v Lunt* (1986) 85 Cr App R 241; *R v Burns* [1996] Crim LR 322.
72 *R v Lobban* [1995] 2 Cr App R 573. For *dicta* supporting this approach to a defendant's application, see *R v Neale* (1977) 65 Cr App R 304, p 306.
73 (1985) unreported, 2 May.
74 [2000] 1 All ER 148.
75 [2000] 2 Cr App R 220.
76 [1999] Crim LR 835.

allowed to adduce evidence of previous acts of violence committed by her against him three years earlier. The Court of Appeal held on the facts that events at such a distance in time could not come within the concept of background history that was relevant to the offence charged, although the Court recognised that evidence of the relationship between a defendant and a deceased person, and of their conduct towards each other, was in principle admissible in a murder trial.

Although not specifically referred to, the *Pettman* principle seems to have been relied on in *R v Underwood*.[77] The defendant was charged with offences of violence against a woman with whom he was living. The prosecution was allowed, as part of the background history, to adduce evidence of another act of violence not covered by the indictment, evidence that the defendant had prevailed on the complainant to have an abortion, and evidence of the defendant's knowledge of the effect of his violence after the complainant had a stroke. The Court of Appeal upheld the admissibility of all three items of evidence as part of the essential background to the relationship between the parties, and also as rebutting the defence of accident raised by the defendant in relation to one of the counts.

Cases such as *R v Underwood* and *R v Fulcher*[78] suggest that there may be a danger of letting in as background evidence matters that would be inadmissible as similar fact evidence.[79] In theory, the danger ought not to exist; indeed, in theory, there should be no need for a separate category of background evidence. If, as *DPP v P* shows, all that is required for the admissibility of similar fact evidence is a balance of probative worth over prejudicial effect, the test for admissibility is effectively the same because background evidence can always be excluded, in the exercise of the judge's common law discretion, on the basis that its prejudicial effect outweighs its probative worth.[80] Possibly the distinction has been allowed to develop because judges, whether consciously or not, still tend to think of similar fact evidence in terms of categories rather in terms of the broad principle that *DPP v P* settled.

This possibly accounts for the decision of the Court of Appeal in *R v Sidhu*.[81] The defendant was charged with conspiracy to possess explosives contrary to s 4(1) of the Explosive Substances Act 1883. He had been seen with co-defendants at a house where explosives were found, and there was other evidence against him. In his police interview, he denied any knowledge that the explosives were in the house. He said that he was a law-abiding citizen.

---

77 [1999] Crim LR 227.

78 [1995] 2 Cr App R 251, referred to above, p 261.

79 See the commentary on the report of *R v Underwood*.

80 See *R v Sang* [1980] AC 402. The common law discretion to exclude was retained by s 82(3) of the Police and Criminal Evidence Act 1984.

81 (1994) 98 Cr App R 59.

He denied being involved in any terrorist organisation, and said that he did not believe in violence because it was against his religious beliefs. The trial judge allowed the prosecution to adduce in evidence a video film. This showed the defendant in a group of armed people, who were practising with weapons and singing in support of a revolutionary organisation. The Court of Appeal upheld the judge's ruling on the basis, *inter alia*, that the video was background evidence that was relevant to the defendant's part in the conspiracy. The events shown in the video were not, on the facts, too remote in time, and without it the information before the jury would have been incomplete. But the court said that the evidence was not admissible to disprove the defendant's assertion that he was a law-abiding citizen, who was opposed to violence on religious grounds. Those assertions amounted to little more than an emphatic denial of guilt, and to admit the video in rebuttal would be going too far. Quite why this should have been so is unclear. The approach is more lenient than that adopted in drugs cases such as *R v Sokialiois*[82] and *R v Peters*.[83] If this conclusion was based on a judgment that the prejudicial effect of the evidence exceeded its probative worth, this should have defeated the application to admit it as background evidence also. One is left with the impression that the court did regard background evidence as more readily admissible, not least because of the argument that without it, the jury would have been left with an incomplete picture. The potential for this development was probably embedded in *R v Pettman*, which provided two very different tests for admissibility. One was that without such evidence the account placed before the jury would be *incomprehensible*. But the other was merely that the account would be *incomplete*. If the latter test is applied, and if insufficient consideration is given to the exercise of the common law exclusionary discretion, there is a danger that background evidence will become a ticket of admission for a far wider range of evidence than has been previously allowed.

---

82   [1993] Crim LR 872.
83   [1995] 2 Cr App R 77.

CHAPTER 11

CHARACTER EVIDENCE[1]

Evidence about character may be relevant in either a civil or criminal trial in two ways. First, it may be relevant to an issue. For example, in a criminal trial for theft it would be relevant to show that the defendant had a reputation for honesty and had never been convicted before of any criminal offence. The purpose of proving this would be to try to establish that the defendant was not a person likely to commit theft, and that the allegation was therefore likely to be untrue. Evidence of good character could similarly be called for a plaintiff in a civil action for defamation where justification had been pleaded as a defence.[2]

Secondly, evidence of character may be relevant to credibility. The theory – a relic from earlier centuries – remains that a conviction for *any* offence is, in principle, relevant to credibility because of what it is supposed to reveal about the moral character of the person testifying. Subject to some exceptions, *any* witness testifying in *any* case may be cross-examined about his bad character. So, for example, in a civil case, either side may attempt to discredit the other side's witnesses, whether or not they are parties to the action, by proving their bad character. Typically, this will be done by showing that the witness in question has a criminal record, but other evidence may also be admissible. The same is true of criminal cases, save that the right to adduce such evidence in respect of a witness who is also a defendant is restricted. This means that, in principle, you are entitled to shake the credit of any prosecution witnesses by showing that they have previous convictions, and the prosecution have a free hand to do the same with any defence witnesses who are not themselves defendants.

On this last point mistakes are often made. Suppose you are defending Charlie on a burglary charge and his defence is an alibi: he says that he spent the night in question with his girlfriend, Dolly, in a motel near Birmingham. In support of the alibi you call both Charlie and Dolly. Unfortunately, Dolly

---

1   *Evidence in Criminal Proceedings: Previous Misconduct of a Defendant,* Law Com No 141 (1996); Munday [1985] 44 CLJ 62; Munday [1986] Crim LR 511; Mirfield [1991] 50 CLJ 490; Elliott [1991] Crim LR 5; Munday [1994] 53 CLJ 303; Munday [1997] Crim LR 247; Murphy (1998) 2 E&P 71.

2   There is old authority for the proposition that, in civil proceedings, evidence of a party's good character is inadmissible because it is irrelevant: see, eg, *AG v Radloff* (1854) 10 Exch 84, p 97. However, in civil cases where the act complained of was a crime as well as a tort, such evidence might well be relevant. In any event, exclusionary rules of evidence have now a very limited part to play in civil actions. Although the admissibility of good and bad character evidence is strictly governed in criminal cases, in practice a far more flexible approach is likely to be adopted in civil cases tried by a judge alone.

has previous convictions for prostitution, handling stolen goods and dealing in cocaine. In principle, she can be cross-examined about all these offences in an attempt to show that she is not the sort of woman whose word the jury can trust. As will appear later, she is not protected by the Criminal Evidence Act 1898 because she is not a defendant. Because of the theoretical connection between criminal convictions and moral standing, the prosecution are not confined to questioning her about offences involving dishonesty; the offences involving prostitution and drug dealing, as well as the offence of handling, are relevant to her credibility.[3]

There are two restrictions that apply to witnesses generally in respect of cross-examination about previous convictions. The first is a judge-made restriction and the second a statutory one. The judge-made restriction is set out in *Hobbs v Tinling*.[4] In brief, a question as to credit will be proper if the information that the question is designed to elicit would seriously affect the court's opinion as to the credibility of the witness on the matter to which he is testifying. Such a question will be improper if designed to elicit information about matters so remote in time, or of such a character, that the truth of the imputation would not affect, or would affect only in a slight degree, the opinion of the court about the witness's credibility on the matter to which he is testifying.

As Sir James Stephen put it:

> The fact that a woman had an illegitimate child at eighteen is hardly a reason for not believing her at forty, when she swears that she locked up her house safely when she went to bed at night, and found the kitchen window broken open and her husband's boots gone when she got up in the morning.[5]

The statutory restriction is in the Rehabilitation of Offenders Act 1974. Section 1(1) of that Act allows a person's convictions to be 'spent' after a certain period of time has gone by. Where a person's convictions are spent, there is a general prohibition under s 4(1) against referring to them in judicial proceedings. This general prohibition is limited by s 7(2), which in effect gives free scope for reference to spent convictions in criminal proceedings. But an attempt to maintain the spirit of the Act was made in a Practice Direction[6] to the effect that no one should refer in open court to a spent conviction without

---

3   See, eg, *Clifford v Clifford* [1961] 1 WLR 1274, p 1276, where Cairns J said, 'It has never, I think, been doubted that a conviction for any offence could be put to a witness by way of cross-examination as to credit, even though the offence was not one of dishonesty'.

4   [1929] 2 KB 1; *Sourcebook*, p 318.

5   Stephen, Sir JF, *A History of the Criminal Law of England*, 1883, Vol I, p 435.

6   [1975] 2 All ER 1072; *Sourcebook*, p 319.

the authority of the judge, who should not give authority unless the interests of justice require it.[7]

The general prohibition under s 4(1) is also subject to s 7(3) of the Act. This provides:

> If at any stage in any proceedings before a judicial authority in Great Britain ... the authority is satisfied, in the light of any considerations which appear to it to be relevant ... that justice cannot be done in the case except by admitting or requiring evidence relating to a person's spent convictions ... that authority may admit ... the evidence in question ...

One effect of this sub-section is that in a civil trial spent convictions may be admitted, subject to the judge's discretion, when credit is in issue and the convictions are relevant to credit. For example, in *Thomas v Commissioner of Police of the Metropolis*,[8] the plaintiff claimed damages against the defendant for assault, false imprisonment and malicious prosecution. The case was heard by a judge and jury and the judge allowed the plaintiff to be cross-examined about his spent convictions under s 7(3). A majority of the Court of Appeal upheld his decision on the basis that it was a case in which the credibility of the plaintiff on the one hand, and of two police officers on the other, was crucial.

EVIDENCE OF GOOD CHARACTER IN CRIMINAL PROCEEDINGS

The defence will wish, where possible, to give evidence of their client's good character in order to establish the improbability of his having committed the alleged offence. But it is not always appreciated that there are limitations on the sort of evidence that can be adduced for this purpose.

The nature of the evidence

The rule is that only evidence of general reputation is admissible as evidence of good character; evidence of the opinions of specific persons, or evidence of

---

7 In *R v Lawrence* [1995] Crim LR 815, the Court of Appeal said that this gave a wide discretion, but that the judge should not give the same latitude to cross-examining counsel where convictions are spent as where they are not. This was a case concerning cross-examination of a defendant by the prosecution. If the defence wanted to cross-examine a prosecution witness about spent convictions, a judge would probably be reluctant to refuse leave from concern that the defendant's case should be fully put. Similar considerations would apply if counsel for one defendant wished to cross-examine another defendant about the latter's spent convictions. In this situation the position of the cross-examiner would be even stronger, because a judge has no discretion to disallow cross-examination under s 1(3)(iii): *Murdoch v Taylor* [1965] AC 574. This cannot have been changed by a Practice Direction. See *R v Corelli* [2001] Archbold News 2, CA.

8 [1997] 2 WLR 593.

specific acts performed by the accused, is inadmissible. This rule was laid down in *R v Rowton*.[9] In that case, evidence had been called of the defendant's good character and the prosecution had been allowed to call evidence to rebut this by proving that the accused was in fact of bad character. The witness who was called for this purpose was asked what was the accused's general character for decency and morality. The answer was as follows: 'I know nothing of the neighbourhood's opinion, because I was only a boy at school when I knew him; but my opinion, and the opinion of my brothers who were pupils of his, is that his character is that of a man capable of the grossest indecency and the most flagrant immorality.'

A majority of the Court for Crown Cases Reserved held that this testimony should not have been admitted. These points emerge from the majority judgments:

(a) Character evidence is confined to evidence of general reputation; the accused may not give evidence of particular facts for the purpose of showing that he was not the sort of person to commit the offence charged.

(b) It is quite true that character evidence is most cogent when accompanied by evidence showing that the witness has had opportunities of acquiring information beyond what the man's neighbours in general would have acquired. In practice, the admission of such evidence is often carried beyond the letter of the law in the accused's favour.

(c) Evidence of bad character called to rebut evidence of good character is subject to the same restrictions.

In this case, the witness had disclaimed all knowledge of the defendant's general reputation. His answer was therefore inadmissible.

The rule in *R v Rowton* has been much criticised. It was based on a practice, current at the time, which was justified in at least two ways. First, it was said that evidence of particular facts lacked weight, because even the worst criminal could perform acts of generosity. Secondly, it was argued that to allow such evidence to be given would raise issues of which the prosecution had no notice, and on which they could not enter into argument. A third justification may have been that to allow such evidence could unduly prolong trials.

R v Rowton indicated that some flexibility was, in practice, shown in admitting evidence of good character. But the practice is not reliable, as appears from *R v Redgrave*.[10] The defendant was charged with an offence involving homosexual activity in a public lavatory. As part of his defence he wished to adduce evidence, including love letters, Valentine cards and photographs, to show that he had been very actively involved in relationships

---

9   (1865) Le&Ca 520; *Sourcebook*, p 267.
10   (1981) 74 Cr App R 10.

with women. The trial judge held this evidence inadmissible. The defendant was convicted and appealed. Lawton LJ emphasised, relying on *R v Rowton*, that it was not open to a defendant to call evidence of particular facts to show that he had a disposition that made his commission of the offence unlikely.

Counsel for the appellant had brought to the court's attention the fact that defendants accused of homosexual offences were often allowed in practice to say that they were happily married and having a normal sexual relationship with their wives. Lawton LJ recognised this practice, but said that it was 'an indulgence on the part of the court'. Defendants did not have the *right* to give such evidence.

The significance of good character

Where evidence of good character is given, its significance must be explained to the jury. Such evidence was originally relevant to guilt or innocence alone. It could not have been relevant to the defendant's credibility as a witness, because the defendant was not competent to give evidence in his own defence. The right to testify was not granted to defendants generally until the Criminal Evidence Act 1898. But once the defendant was allowed to give evidence, it was clear that good character could have a double function: not only did it make it less likely that the defendant had done what the prosecution alleged, but it meant that he was a more credible witness than someone who was not of good character.

For a long time there were no binding rules about what a judge should say to a jury in summing up on these matters. But wide judicial discretion led to anomalies, and in 1993 the Court of Appeal laid down rules in *R v Vye*.[11] In this case the court recognised two 'limbs' in any direction about good character: the first limb dealt with the relevance of good character to credibility, and the second with the relevance of good character to the question whether the defendant was likely to have behaved as alleged by the Crown. The court then proceeded to consider three problems in connection with directions to a jury about a defendant's good character.

The first problem was whether a first limb direction on credibility needed to be given in a case where the defendant did not give evidence, but at an earlier stage in the investigation had made exculpatory statements to the police or others.

Evidence of what any defendant has said to the police will generally be admissible in one of three ways. A wholly inculpatory statement will be admissible as a confession. A mixed statement, containing both inculpatory and exculpatory parts, will be admissible as evidence of the truth of all those

---

11   (1993) 97 Cr App R 134; *Sourcebook*, p 273.

things that were said.[12] A wholly exculpatory statement will be admissible, not as evidence of the truth of the matters contained in it, but as evidence of the accused's reaction to incriminating facts.[13]

In *R v Vye* the Court of Appeal said that when a defendant has not given evidence at trial, but relies in support of his defence on exculpatory statements made to the police or others, the judge should direct the jury to have regard to the defendant's good character when considering the credibility of those statements. As appears from *R v Storey and Anwar*, a wholly exculpatory statement is not admissible as evidence of the truth of its contents, but only as evidence of the accused's reaction to incriminating facts. It is not clear whether a first limb direction should be given about the defendant's good character in such a case. Even where the value of what the defendant said is only, as Widgery LJ said in *R v Storey and Anwar*, 'evidence of the reaction of the accused which forms part of the general picture to be considered by the jury at the trial',[14] the good character of the defendant is capable of being relevant to the credibility of the reaction and should probably be given.

The second problem the court considered was whether the second limb of the direction – on the relevance of good character to the question of guilt or innocence – was mandatory or discretionary. The court concluded that this direction *must* be given where the defendant is of good character. No distinction should be made between cases where the defendant has given evidence and those where he has not. The judge should indicate that good character is relevant to propensity, but the actual words used should be a matter for the judge in each case.

The third problem the court considered was the position where some defendants were of good character and others were not. The court's decision was that a defendant of good character is entitled to a full direction, even if jointly tried with someone of bad character. In dealing with the co-defendant with bad character, the judge has two choices. In some cases it will be best to grasp the nettle and tell the jury that they have heard nothing about the co-defendant's character and must not speculate or take the absence of information as evidence against him. In other cases it might be better to make no reference to the subject.

If a *Vye* direction should be given, but is omitted, the crucial question for the Court of Appeal will be whether the omission rendered the verdict unsafe.[15]

---

12   *R v Sharp* (1988) 86 Cr App R 274; *Sourcebook*, p 358; *R v Aziz* [1996] AC 41.

13   *R v Storey & Anwar* (1968) 52 Cr App R 334; *Sourcebook*, p 357.

14   (1968) 52 Cr App R 334, p 338.

15   *R v Kamar* (1999) *The Times*, 14 May.

In *R v Cain*,[16] it was held that in cases where, for any reason, the previous convictions of a defendant become known to the jury – for example, because defence counsel thought it necessary to reveal them or because the prosecution were allowed to cross-examine about them – the judge should warn the jury in summing up of the limited use that can be made of them. In particular, the court highlighted the danger that a jury may think convictions that are relevant only to credibility are relevant also to guilt.

Doubtful cases of good character

In *R v Aziz*,[17] the House of Lords said that, generally, a person with no previous convictions was to be treated as being of good character. Sometimes, however, a defendant will admit, as part of his defence, to *some* wrongdoing, though not that alleged by the prosecution. For example, in *R v Aziz*, one of the defendants admitted making a false mortgage application in connection with a matter that was not the subject of the indictment. The House of Lords ruled that in such cases, the *Vye* directions should still be given, accompanied by some appropriate qualification to present a fair and balanced picture to the jury. Exceptionally, it was said, a judge may dispense with the *Vye* directions where it would be an insult to common sense to give them. This might be the case, for example, where a defendant with no convictions was shown to have committed a serious crime similar to the offence charged, but not the subject of the indictment.

When a defendant has already pleaded guilty to one or more counts on the indictment, but is contesting others, the earlier pleas will generally mean that he is no longer of good character. What direction, if any, about character should be given will be a matter for the judge's discretion.[18]

In giving a *Vye* direction, a trial judge is entitled to take into account the fact that the defendant has been formally cautioned by the police, instead of being charged, in connection with another matter. For a formal caution to be given, the suspect must admit his guilt of the offence in question. Accordingly, it would be proper to direct the jury as to the relevance of the defendant's lack of previous convictions in relation to his credibility, but refuse to give the second limb of the direction in relation to propensity.[19]

---

16 [1994] 2 All ER 398.
17 [1996] AC 41.
18 *R v Challenger* [1994] Crim LR 202; cf *R v Teasdale* [1993] 4 All ER 290.
19 *R v Martin* [2000] 2 Cr App R 42.

Spent convictions and good character

Can a defendant with spent convictions hold himself out to the jury as a person of good character? The answer appears to be yes, with the leave of the judge, provided the jury is not lied to or misled.[20] So, a jury cannot be told that a defendant has no convictions when he has.[21] But it is considered legitimate to say that the defendant is 'a man of good character with no relevant convictions'.[22] Even if a conviction is not spent, it may be similarly overlooked if it is minor and of no special significance in the context of the current charge.[23] If an earlier conviction is ignored, or, though mentioned, is treated as irrelevant, the judge should give the *Vye* directions about good character.[24]

EVIDENCE OF BAD CHARACTER IN CRIMINAL PROCEEDINGS

Where the defendant is of bad character, the prosecution may be able to introduce this as similar fact evidence. In these cases the evidence will be adduced as part of the prosecution case, and the question of admissibility will not be affected by the decision of the defendant to testify or remain silent. But suppose similar fact evidence is not admissible. Evidence of the defendant's bad character may still be adduced if he puts his own character in issue by the way in which the defence is run. Two situations must be distinguished. Where the accused himself testifies, the Criminal Evidence Act 1898 applies. But where he does *not*, even though other defence witnesses may have testified, the position is governed by common law.

The position at common law

Where a defendant does not give evidence, but puts his character in issue, either by calling evidence of his own good character or by cross-examining witnesses for the prosecution to that effect, evidence in rebuttal can be called by the prosecution to show that the defendant is in fact of bad character. But if the defendant merely attacks the witnesses for the prosecution in cross-examination in an attempt to show that *they* are of bad character, and so not to be believed, he has not put his own character in issue, and evidence of his bad character cannot then be called.[25]

---

20 *R v Nye* (1982) 75 Cr App R 247; *R v Bailey* [1989] Crim LR 723.
21 *R v O'Shea* (1993) *The Times*, 8 June.
22 May, R, *Criminal Evidence*, 4th edn, 1999, p 130.
23 *R v Timson* [1993] Crim LR 58; *R v H* [1994] Crim LR 205.
24 *R v H* [1994] Crim LR 205.
25 *R v Butterwasser* [1948] KB 4; *Sourcebook*, p 280.

The background to s 1 of the 1898 Act

The section made the defendant a competent witness for the defence in all criminal cases. But to have put the defendant in the same position as any other witness would have created problems. We have already noted the general rule that a witness may be cross-examined about his bad character, and in particular about any previous convictions, with a view to shaking his credibility. A defendant with previous convictions would have been deterred from testifying if this rule had been applied to him. There is another rule for the protection of witnesses, which allows them to claim a 'privilege against self-incrimination' and refuse to answer any questions tending to show that they have committed a criminal offence. If a defendant in the witness box had been allowed to take advantage of this privilege, the prosecution's task of cross-examination would have been made impossible.

Special provisions were therefore necessary for defendants called as witnesses. These are contained in s 1(2) and 1(3).[26] Section 1(3) restricts the prosecution's right to cross-examine about a witness's previous convictions. Section 1(2) removes the privilege against self-incrimination from a defendant who gives evidence by providing that he may be asked any question in cross-examination 'notwithstanding that it would tend to criminate him as to the offence charged'.

The relation between sub-ss (2) and (3)

As the background to s 1 shows, sub-ss (2) and (3) were designed to cover two different situations. Sub-section (3) permits cross-examination on the current charges. Sub-section (2) is a general prohibition, with exceptions, on cross-examination about other offences, previous convictions, or bad character. But questions about previous convictions or bad character may be matters from which guilt of the current charges can be inferred. If 'tend to criminate' in sub-s (3) meant 'tend to convince or persuade the jury that the defendant is guilty', a conflict between the sub-sections could arise, because a line of questioning might be permitted under sub-s (2) but forbidden under sub-s (3).

This problem arose in *Jones v DPP*.[27] The defendant was charged with the murder of a Girl Guide. During the investigation, he gave a false alibi to the police. At his trial he gave evidence, and explained the false alibi by admitting that he had previously been in trouble with the police and did not want to be

---

26 The designation of these provisions was changed by Sched 4, para 1(7) of the Youth Justice and Criminal Evidence Act 1999. Section 1(2) of the 1898 Act was formerly s 1(e) and s 1(3) was s 1(f). This wholly unnecessary change has created a problem for anyone writing about this topic. Accuracy demands that when giving an account of what judges ruled in pre-1999 Act decisions the old designation should be used, because that was the way judges stated the law. Simplicity of presentation demands a uniform reference throughout. I have preferred simplicity, even though it involves anachronism.

27 [1962] AC 635; *Sourcebook*, p 288.

in trouble with them again. He then put forward another alibi, saying that he had been in London with a prostitute at the time when the murder had been committed. This new account included details of his wife's angry reaction to his late return home and her continuing complaints to him in conversations on the two following days.

Some three months before his trial on the charge of murder, the defendant had been convicted of raping another girl. In relation to this offence, he had given an account of his movements on the evening when it had been committed, and of his wife's reactions, that had been almost identical to his account of the evening when the murder victim had last been seen alive. At trial, the prosecution was allowed to cross-examine him about the almost identical conversations with his wife on the earlier occasion. The purpose of this cross-examination was to discredit his alibi by showing the improbability of identical conversations having taken place on two different occasions. But this line of questioning *also* showed that the accused had been suspected of a serious offence on the earlier occasion. Should the trial judge have allowed the cross-examination?

A majority of the House of Lords held that the cross-examination was not admissible under sub-s (2) because it was not *directly* relevant to the offence charged.[28] A majority also held that sub-s (3) always prevails over sub-s (2) and that if cross-examination tends to show that the accused has committed other offences, it can be permitted only in the circumstances set out in provisos (i), (ii) and (iii).

What saved the case for the prosecution was the further majority decision that cross-examination prohibited under s 1(3) is cross-examination that tends to show *for the first time* the commission of another offence. The defendant's reference to previous trouble with the police had been imprecise, but a majority of the House thought it would have been reasonable for the jury to have understood from it that he had had a previous conviction at some time. For this reason the fact that the questions in cross-examination indicated that the defendant had been involved in some unspecified prior charge did not reveal anything new to the jury. The questions were therefore not caught by s 1(3).

The opening words of sub-s (3)

These words prohibit questions tending to show, amongst other things, that the defendant has been 'charged with any offence other than that wherewith he is then charged'. In this context 'charged' means 'accused before a court', and not merely 'suspected or accused without prosecution'.[29]

---

28 The minority thought it was directly relevant because it disproved the alibi.

29 *Stirland v DPP* [1944] AC 315; *Sourcebook*, p 285. As Viscount Simon said, 'The most virtuous may be suspected, and an unproved accusation proves nothing against the accused'.

The word 'charged' is capable of letting in questions about a previous *acquittal*. But it may be difficult to satisfy the general test of relevance where a previous charge resulted in acquittal. In *Maxwell v DPP*,[30] the defendant was convicted of manslaughter and of using on the deceased an instrument to procure a miscarriage. He gave evidence denying the offences and said that he had lived a good, clean, moral life. He thereby put his character in issue. The prosecution was allowed to cross-examine him about a previous occasion when he had been charged with a similar offence but acquitted. The House of Lords held that this had been improper. According to Viscount Sankey, 'The mere fact that a man has been charged with an offence is no proof that he committed the offence'. An acquittal was irrelevant to both guilt and credibility. However, he added that there might be occasions when it would be relevant to ask about a previous acquittal: for example, to obtain evidence about testimony given by a defendant at an earlier trial which tended to throw doubt on his testimony in a current trial.

In sub-s (3), 'character' refers to both reputation *and* disposition.[31] The effect of this is that a defendant may bring himself within s 1(3)(ii) if he gives evidence of specific creditable acts performed by himself, or of discreditable ones performed by prosecution witnesses. It would seem to follow that the prosecution could cross-examine a defendant who had lost the protection of the statute about discreditable acts which were not the subject of any criminal prosecution or conviction. Thus, in *R v Marsh*,[32] a defendant, charged with inflicting grievous bodily harm in the course of a rugby match, wished to adduce evidence that he had no previous criminal convictions. The trial judge ruled that this would entitle the prosecution to cross-examine him about his bad disciplinary record for violent play in previous rugby matches, and the Court of Appeal upheld this ruling.

Character is said to be 'indivisible'. This means that if a defendant puts his character in issue in any respect, the prosecution is entitled to refer to the *whole* of his character; he cannot say that he has a good character in some respects without exposing himself to inquiry about the rest of his character. In *R v Winfield*,[33] for example, the defendant was charged with committing an indecent assault on a woman. He called a witness and asked her questions designed to establish his good character with regard to sexual morality. However, he had previous convictions for dishonesty. The judge held that he

---

30 [1935] AC 309; *Sourcebook*, p 282.

31 *R v Dunkley* [1927] 1 KB 323, p 329; *Stirland v DPP* [1944] AC 315, p 325; *R v Carter* [1997] Crim LR 505.

32 [1994] Crim LR 52. See also *R v Carter* [1997] Crim LR 505; *R v Wright* (2000) *The Times*, 31 May. But since these would be questions on collateral matters, the defendant's answer would be final, ie, no evidence could be called to rebut his denials: see *AG v Hitchcock* (1847) 1 Exch 91. The exception to this rule provided by Criminal Procedure Act 1865, s 6, applies only to the denial of convictions. See above, Chapter 4.

33 [1939] 4 All ER 164.

could be cross-examined about them under s 1(3)(ii). The Court of Criminal Appeal upheld this decision. As Humphreys J said: '[T]here is no such thing known to our procedure as putting half your character in issue and leaving out the other half.' A defendant who has a bad character for dishonesty is not entitled to say that he has never acted indecently towards women and claim that he has not put the rest of his character in issue.[34]

Section 1(3)(i)

This proviso to the sub-section applies where the proof that the defendant has committed or been convicted of another offence is admissible evidence to show that he is guilty of the offence with which he is then charged. It follows that cross-examination under s 1(3)(i) is relevant to the defendant's guilt and not to his credibility alone.

Cross-examination under this proviso is limited by its own wording to cases where the prosecution wish to prove that the accused has *committed* or *been convicted of* an earlier offence. It follows that, under this proviso, cross-examination about occasions when the defendant was merely charged and acquitted is not permitted.

In *R v Cokar*,[35] for example, the defendant was charged with entering a dwelling house by night with intent to steal. The evidence for the prosecution was that at about midnight he had climbed through an open window into a room where the complainant had been sleeping. The complainant woke up shortly afterwards and found the defendant asleep in an armchair. The defence was that the defendant had entered the room to sleep because he had been feeling unwell, and had not intended to steal anything. The prosecution wanted to cast doubt on this story by showing that the defendant knew it was no offence to be found on private premises for an innocent purpose. To this end they applied to cross-examine him about a previous occasion when he had been found on private premises, had been charged with entering with intent to steal, and acquitted when he gave a similar explanation.

The Court of Criminal Appeal held that the questions should not have been put. Lord Parker CJ pointed out that the exception under s 1(3)(i) contained no reference to proof that the defendant had been *charged*. Accordingly, the prohibition against any of the matters referred to in the opening of s 1(3) could be lifted only in order to prove that the defendant had *committed* or been *convicted of* other offences.

---

34 [1939] 4 All ER 164, p 165. The principle was approved by the House of Lords in *Stirland v DPP* [1944] AC 315.

35 [1960] 2 QB 207; *Sourcebook*, p 287.

In practice, s 1(3)(i) is little used. Since *Jones v DPP*,[36] a defendant against whom similar fact evidence has already been admitted can be cross-examined about it without relying on this exception. Sometimes, however, reference for the first time to previous misconduct has been necessary in cross-examination because the defendant has given evidence that takes the prosecution by surprise.

This was the case in *R v Anderson*.[37] The defendant was charged with conspiracy to cause explosions. She had been arrested with others at a flat where much incriminating evidence had been found. Forged documents, such as passports and driving licences, were found in her possession. She gave evidence, and explained the presence of the evidence incriminating her by saying that she was not part of a conspiracy to cause explosions, but of a conspiracy to help people who had escaped from prison in Ireland to get to Scotland and afterwards to the continent.

In due course counsel for the Crown asked for leave to cross-examine her about the fact that she was wanted by the police in Northern Ireland. The relevance of this was that it was highly unlikely that someone wanted by the police there would be used as an escort for escaped prisoners. The trial judge gave leave. The defendant was convicted and appealed.

The Court of Appeal accepted that this evidence would have tended to show that she was guilty of another offence. But the court thought the questioning correct for various reasons. One of those reasons was that if the prosecution had known in advance what the defence was going to be, they could have rebutted it (on the principle in *Makin v AG for New South Wales*[38]) by adducing evidence that she was wanted by police in Northern Ireland. Plainly, the defendant could then have been cross-examined about the similar fact evidence called by the prosecution. Here, the prosecution did not know of the defence in advance. They could have called evidence to rebut it, and then the defendant could have been recalled to deal with that rebutting evidence. The judge had merely taken a permissible short cut.

It seems likely that this approach would now solve the problem caused by the restricted wording of s 1(3)(i). If the facts of *R v Cokar* were to be repeated today, and the prosecution knew in advance what the defence was to be, they would almost certainly be allowed to call evidence of the previous incident as part of their own case in order to rebut the defence.[39] In those circumstances,

---

36 [1962] AC 635.

37 [1988] 2 All ER 549; *Sourcebook*, p 296.

38 [1894] AC 57; *Sourcebook*, p 228.

39 In *R v Kidd* [1995] Crim LR 406 the Court of Appeal acknowledged that since *DPP v P* [1991] 2 AC 447 (*Sourcebook*, p 245) the scope of similar fact evidence had been extended. Thus an argument on these lines would be even more readily accepted today. The provisions for advance disclosure of the defence case contained in Part I of the Criminal Procedure and Investigations Act 1996 now make it much less likely that the prosecution will be taken by surprise.

the questions asked in cross-examination of the defendant about the earlier incident would not tend to show *for the first time* that he had been charged with another offence,[40] and, although the charge had resulted in an acquittal, it would be arguable that the acquittal was relevant to the prosecution's purposes and so admissible.[41]

Section 1(3)(ii) in practice

Assume that you are acting for Charlie who has several recent convictions for burglary. He is being prosecuted for another burglary and part of the prosecution evidence comes from Charlie's ex-girlfriend, Bessie. She says that shortly after the burglary took place Charlie admitted his part in it to her. Charlie denies making any admission, and says that Bessie has made her statement to the police out of spite because she found out that he had been sleeping with someone else.

You will have to put this allegation to her in cross-examination and doubtless it will be denied. Nothing will follow from this line of cross-examination if Charlie gives no evidence himself. He is not 'a person charged *and called as a witness*' within s 1(3) of the 1898 Act, and the position is governed by common law, not the statute. At common law he has not put *his* character in issue by suggesting that a prosecution witness is committing perjury. The prosecution are therefore powerless to call evidence of Charlie's previous convictions.

If Charlie does give evidence, the position is different. He will deny the account given by Bessie and will describe her jealousy at discovering that he had another partner. At the end of his evidence-in-chief, counsel for the prosecution will say, 'Your Honour, at this stage there is a matter of law that arises'. This is coded language for, 'I want to ask leave to cross-examine the defendant about his previous convictions'. It is coded because, of course, the jury must not know yet that the defendant has previous convictions, and the defence will probably have some submissions to make to dissuade the judge from allowing the prosecution to take this course. (The judge is likely to know of a defendant's previous convictions. In *R v Ewing*,[42] O'Connor LJ said that it was desirable, in the interests of a fair trial, that a judge should have this information so that he might 'fire a warning shot' if it seemed that cross-examination of the prosecution witnesses was going to let in the defendant's character.) The judge will send the jury out.[43]

---

40 *Jones v DPP* [1962] AC 635; *Sourcebook*, p 288.

41 *Maxwell v DPP* [1935] AC 309; *Sourcebook*, p 282.

42 [1983] 2 All ER 645, p 649.

43 This is what should happen. Defence advocates will need to be firm if they encounter the sort of judge who glances at them while the jury is still present, saying abruptly 'You can't possibly object, can you?'.

Now counsel for the prosecution must establish that a s 1(3)(ii) situation has arisen. In Charlie's case he will argue that the nature or conduct of the defence is such as to involve an imputation on the character of a witness for the prosecution. It seems that this condition is satisfied. Charlie's own evidence and the cross-examination of Bessie have clearly involved an imputation on Bessie's character.

Even if it is established that a s 1(3)(ii) situation has arisen, all is not entirely lost for the defence. The reason for this is that the judge has a discretion to disallow cross-examination under this provision. At this stage, therefore, you will make submissions in an attempt to persuade the judge to exercise his discretion in your favour. No doubt you will say what you can about the almost impossible task the jury will have in doing justice when they learn that not only does your client have previous convictions, but that they are convictions for burglary – the very offence with which he is currently charged. The judge then makes a decision, the jury returns, and the cross-examination begins, either with or without reference to Charlie's previous convictions.

It is useful to have this picture in mind when you are dealing with a problem containing a s 1(3)(ii) point because it should remind you of the arguments that must be presented:

(a) Is this a s 1(3)(ii) situation at all?

(b) If it is, what arguments are available to each side about the way in which the discretion should be exercised?

This second step is often forgotten. In particular, you need to ask whether the previous convictions are spent. Spent convictions are not automatically excluded, but they will make the exercise of discretion in the defendant's favour more likely.[44]

The first limb of s 1(3)(ii)

There are two ways in which a s 1(3)(ii) situation can arise. The first is by the defendant's attempting to establish his own good character. He may do this by cross-examining prosecution witnesses with this objective, by giving evidence himself of his good character, or by calling character witnesses.

It is sometimes difficult to tell whether a defendant who denies the charge and gives evidence has in doing so given evidence of his own good character. The essential test appears to be the nature of the connection between the assertion, express or implied, of good character and the allegations of the prosecution. The defendant will have to counter the prosecution's version of events. In doing so he may give evidence that has the effect of showing his

---

44   *R v Lawrence* [1995] Crim LR 815 (CA); *R v Barratt* [2000] Crim LR 847.

character in a good light. This should not come within the exception. If, however, what the defendant says goes beyond his need to meet the prosecution case about the facts in issue, so as to raise the issue of his good character independently, then he may be caught. Another way of putting it is: does he give direct evidence of good character, from which it may be inferred that he did not do what was alleged? If so, he will have brought himself within the first limb of s 1(3)(ii). Or does he give evidence that he did not do what was alleged, from which it may be inferred that he is of good character? In that case he will not have brought himself within the first limb.

The distinction can be illustrated by a story of two defendants charged on different occasions with theft from a supermarket. X says, 'I put the gin in my own holdall because I didn't want it to break the eggs in the supermarket's wire basket. I had forgotten it was there by the time I reached the checkout because I was worrying about my wife who was due to have an operation that day'. X has not brought himself within the first limb of s 1(3)(ii). The prosecution rely on the facts that the gin did not go into the wire basket and was not produced at the checkout. The defendant produces a neutral explanation so far as s 1(3)(ii) is concerned for putting the gin in his own holdall. He meets his failure to produce it at the checkout by saying that he forgot it was there and he supports this by describing what was dominating his mind at the time. The fact that it happened to be something that shows him in a good light is subsidiary to his defence.

Compare this case with that of Y, who finds himself in a very similar situation. His reasons for putting the gin in his own holdall and for failing to produce it at the checkout are the same as those given by X. But he also adds, 'I would never do a thing like that. It's against the Ten Commandments'. Y has given *an additional* reason, based on his character, for the jury to acquit him: he respects the Ten Commandments and is the sort of person who would never break any of them. A person like that is unlikely to have committed theft. He *has* given evidence of his own good character and will be caught by the proviso in s 1(3)(ii).

These distinctions can be supported by reference to *Malindi v The Queen*.[45] The defendant was charged with conspiracy to commit arson. The prosecution relied on evidence from co-conspirators, who had been present at a meeting with the defendant when a political campaign of arson was allegedly discussed and approved by him. The defendant gave evidence. He admitted that he had met the co-conspirators. He said they had proposed an arson campaign to him, but he had declined to participate. He had pointed out the illegality of what they suggested and had recommended a political procession instead. This had angered the others, who had accused him of being a moderate and a police informer, and had walked out. The trial judge ruled

---

45 [1967] AC 439; *Sourcebook*, p 300.

that he had thereby given evidence of his own good character, which allowed him to be cross-examined under s 1(3)(ii). By his evidence, he had put himself forward as a person who was, and was regarded by others, as being a moderate and a man of peace.

The Privy Council rejected this view. All the defendant had done was to give a narrative of what he said took place at the meeting. He had given his version of events and conversations but had done no more. He had not made any independent assertion of good character, and so had not brought himself within s 1(3)(ii).

The scope of the second limb of s 1(3)(ii)

The defendant could originally be cross-examined on the matters referred to in the opening words of s 1(3) where 'the nature or conduct of the defence' was 'such as to involve imputations on the character of the prosecutor[46] or the witnesses for the prosecution'. The scope of the original provision has been extended by s 31 of the Criminal Justice and Public Order Act 1994 to include imputations on the deceased victim of the alleged crime. This will cover, for example, the situation where a defendant in a murder case claims that he was defending himself from an attack by the deceased.[47] In R v Miller,[48] the Court of Appeal held that a 'witness' for the purposes of s 1(3)(ii) is simply a person with material evidence to give. It makes no difference whether that evidence is given orally or in some other way. Thus, a witness whose evidence is admitted as documentary hearsay evidence under s 23 or 24 of the Criminal Justice Act 1988 is covered, as is a witness who is subject to a conditional witness order only, and whose statement is therefore read under s 9 of the Criminal Justice Act 1967.

An imputation can be made even when its truth is not disputed. In R v Wainwright,[49] the defendant, who was serving a term of imprisonment, was charged with the murder of a fellow prisoner. The prosecution made formal admissions concerning the deceased's prison record, which indicated that he had been involved in violence while in prison. The defendant said that he had been acting in self-defence by adopting a 'pre-emptive strike' against the

---

46 The reference to imputations on the character of 'the prosecutor' is a reference to the character of the testifying complainant in a criminal case and is a relic from the time when the prosecution was not always represented by a lawyer.

47 But imputations under s 1(3)(ii) are not confined to imputations of criminal offences: see, eg, R v Bishop [1975] QB 274. Would a defendant accused of murder bring himself within the expanded version if his defence was that the deceased had committed suicide? If not, would it make any difference if the reason for the suicide was alleged to have been impending bankruptcy, or the ending of a homosexual or adulterous relationship?

48 [1997] 2 Cr App R 178.

49 [1998] Crim LR 665.

deceased, who he believed intended to kill him. He gave evidence that another prisoner had told him that he had seen the deceased sharpening a knife, and that he had heard from another source that the deceased was going to stab him. The trial judge allowed cross-examination under s 1(3)(ii). On appeal, it was argued that no imputations had been made because the deceased's bad character was common ground, but the Court of Appeal held that this did not affect the application of the sub-section. There is one exception to this. A judge is most unlikely to regard cross-examination on the previous convictions of an accomplice who has turned Queen's evidence as justification for permitting cross-examination under s 1(3)(ii).[50]

A major difficulty for the defence can be presented by the fact that the second limb of s 1(3)(ii) applies even where the imputation is an essential part of the defence. The leading case is *Selvey v DPP*.[51] The defendant was charged with buggery of another man. He denied the offence. But there was medical evidence to show that the complainant had recently been buggered. The defendant met this evidence by giving the following account. He said that he had known the complainant; that the complainant had offered himself to the defendant for £1, and, apparently by way of encouragement, had told the defendant that he had already earned £1 that afternoon with another man. The defendant said that he had rejected the complainant's suggestions.

It was argued for the defendant that an accused person might, without losing the protection of the Criminal Evidence Act, ask a prosecution witness all questions that the nature of his defence necessitated. The House of Lords rejected this argument, holding that s 1(3) permitted cross-examination even where the imputations had been necessary to establish the defence.[52]

Nevertheless, Viscount Dilhorne confirmed that in rape cases the accused could allege consent without exposing himself to cross-examination, either because such cases stood on their own, or because lack of consent was an element which the prosecution had to prove.

He also confirmed that if what was said amounted in reality to no more than a denial of the charge in emphatic language, it should not be regarded as coming within the section. He was referring to a problem considered in

---

50 *R v Taylor and Goodman* [1999] 2 Cr App R 163. Strictly speaking, this is not a legal exception but an indication of how judges should exercise their discretion to exclude cross-examination under this provision (for the discretion, see below). As the Court of Appeal observed, it is standard practice where reliance is placed on such a witness for the prosecution to offer to disclose the witness's convictions at the start of the trial unless the defence asks that this should not be done.

51 [1970] AC 304; *Sourcebook*, p 302.

52 This interpretation is strengthened by a comparison of the two limbs of s 1(3)(ii). Under the first limb – evidence given 'with a view to establish his own good character' – the accused is not caught merely by adducing evidence that happens incidentally to show his character in a good light: see *Malindi v The Queen* [1967] AC 439; *Sourcebook*, p 300. But evidence 'such as to involve imputations' under the second limb suggests that a defendant will be caught wherever such imputations are in fact made, regardless of the defendant's intention in making them.

several old cases, the best known of which were *R v Rouse*[53] and *R v Rappolt*.[54] In *R v Rouse*, the defendant, giving evidence, said of the chief prosecution witness's evidence, 'It is a lie, and he is a liar'. This was held not to be an imputation, because it was simply 'a plea of not guilty put in forcible language such as would not be unnatural in a person in the defendant's rank in life'. In *R v Rappolt*, the allegation made by the defendant while giving evidence was that a prosecution witness was such a horrible liar that not even his brother would speak to him. The Court of Criminal Appeal agreed with the trial judge that this *was* an imputation.

Students interpret these cases in various ways. Some think they are in conflict, so that you can never tell whether or not an allegation that a witness is lying will be caught. Others think that *R v Rouse* is authority for the proposition that it is never an imputation to allege merely that someone is lying. Both interpretations are wrong and result from attaching too much importance to the particular words used, and not enough to their context and the intention of the speaker. What happened in *R v Rouse* was that, on the facts of that case, the Court of Criminal Appeal recognised that the defendant did not intend to cast an imputation on the prosecution witness, because he did not intend to assert that the witness was a person who had *knowingly* said something untrue. But in *R v Rappolt* the court had to interpret different words uttered in a different context; not surprisingly, it reached a different conclusion. The reference to the brother's behaviour was clearly intended to support an allegation of habitual untruthfulness on the part of the witness. That *was* an imputation.

It remains difficult to predict whether a defendant will bring himself within s 1(3)(ii) by references to 'lying' or the use of similar language. In *R v Desmond*,[55] a prosecution witness gave an account of events that differed significantly from that in his witness statement and, in doing so, implicated the defendant further in the robbery that was alleged. In cross-examination, defence counsel suggested to him that he was lying under oath. The trial judge allowed cross-examination under s 1(3)(ii), but the Court of Appeal held that the matters put did not go beyond an emphatic denial of the charge.[56]

Unfortunately, in *R v Britzman*,[57] the Court of Appeal appeared to forget the importance of interpreting words in context. In a discussion of how a judge should exercise his discretion to exclude cross-examination under

---

53 [1904] 1 KB 184.

54 (1911) 6 Cr App R 156.

55 [1999] Crim LR 313.

56 See also *R v Wignall* [1993] Crim LR 62: allegations by defence counsel that a prosecution witness was concocting her evidence, telling an untruth, and making up her evidence as she went along so as to bolster her case all amounted to no more than an emphatic denial.

57 [1983] 1 All ER 369; *Sourcebook*, p 308.

s 1(3)(ii), Lawton LJ referred to cases where there was nothing more than a denial, however emphatic or offensively made, of an act or even a short series of acts amounting to one incident, or of what was said to have been a short interview, as a case where discretion should be exercised in favour of the defendant.[58] But to be able to exercise discretion, a s 1(3)(ii) situation must already have arisen and there will be cases where, on facts like those in *R v Rouse*, it has not.

A good point made in *R v Britzman* was that if what is alleged amounts *in effect* to an allegation of lying in its strict sense – saying something to be the case that you know to be false – then even if the allegation is put politely, and the word 'lie' avoided, the defendant will still be caught under s 1(3)(ii). That was the point in *R v Britzman* of drawing a distinction between denials of single incidents and short interviews, as opposed to denials of the whole of a long conversation or of a long, detailed observation. Denials of the second type *must* in essence be allegations of deliberate fabrication, but a denial of the first type can be made consistently with the witness's being honest but mistaken. As Lawton LJ said in that case, 'Cross-examination should only be allowed if the judge is sure that there is no possibility of mistake, misunderstanding or confusion and that the jury will inevitably have to decide whether the prosecution witnesses have fabricated evidence'. Unfortunately, this was said only in the context of the exercise of discretion. But these matters are relevant at the earlier stage, when it is being considered whether a s 1(3)(ii) situation has arisen at all.

What amounts to an imputation will therefore be governed by interpreting what the accused says in its context, and by trying to take into account current opinion. The latter may be difficult, because what is an imputation in one part of society or at one period of time might not be so in another part of society, or at a different time. For this reason caution is needed when reading earlier cases. In *R v Bishop*,[59] for example, the defendant, who was charged with burglary, accounted for the presence of his fingerprints in the bathroom of the complainant's premises by saying that he had had a homosexual relationship with the complainant. This was held then to involve an imputation. Would it today? If it *might* not, would our answer depend on the character of the witness? We might say one thing if he were a married High Court judge, another if he were an actor who was openly gay, and something else if he were an unmarried vicar who said of his own sexuality that it was 'a grey area'. But this would lead to an undesirable investigation of witnesses' characters. Sometimes it may be possible to avoid the problem because the clash of testimony will mean that one of the witnesses must be lying, but this will not always be the case.

---

58 This error has been perpetuated by the Law Commission: see Law Com No 141 (1996), paras 12.26 and 12.29.

59 [1975] QB 274.

The extent of questioning under s 1(3)(ii)

It is clear that cross-examination under s 1(3)(ii) is relevant only to credibility, not to guilt, and that the jury must be told this in the summing up.[60] It is obviously relevant to credibility that the defendant pleaded not guilty at the earlier trial, and gave evidence on oath that must have been disbelieved; these have always been legitimate subjects for cross-examination under s 1(3)(ii). But may questions also be asked about details of the mode of commission of earlier offences or of defences raised in relation to them?

The question was most recently considered in *R v McLeod*.[61] The defendant was charged with robbery of a Securicor van. He pleaded not guilty and gave evidence, his defence being one of alibi and an allegation that the police had created a false case against him. That clearly brought him within s 1(3)(ii), and so his own counsel, as a tactical measure, raised the matter of his previous convictions for several offences, including robbery, as part of his examination-in-chief. In cross-examination, counsel for the Crown was allowed to ask further questions about the defendant's previous convictions. Those questions were designed to bring out a number of details: for example, that his defence to an earlier charge of robbery had been an alibi and that he had been involved in two earlier offences involving motor cars with false registration plates – a feature of the current allegations against him.

The Court of Appeal, in dismissing the appeal, affirmed the following principles:

(a) The 'primary' purpose of cross-examination under s 1(3)(ii) is to show that the accused is not worthy of belief, not to show that he has a disposition to commit the type of offence with which he is charged. But the mere fact that the offences are of a similar type to that charged will not make questions improper.

(b) Unless the earlier offences are relied on as similar fact evidence, prosecuting counsel should not try to bring out similarities between the underlying facts of previous offences and the instant offence.

(c) Two specific lines of questioning may be relevant to credibility:

- questions about similar defences which have been rejected by juries on previous occasions: for example, false alibis, or the defence that an incriminating substance has been planted;

- questions about whether the accused pleaded guilty on the earlier occasions, or whether he pleaded not guilty and gave evidence on oath.

---

60 *R v McLeod* [1994] 3 All ER 254; *Sourcebook*, p 314. This case concerned the second limb, but it is very likely that the same principle applies to the first.

61 [1994] 3 All ER 254; *Sourcebook*, p 314.

(d) Underlying facts showing particularly bad character over and above the bare facts of the earlier case are not necessarily to be excluded. But the judge should be careful to balance the gravity of the attack on the prosecution against the degree of prejudice that will result from disclosure of the facts in question.

(e) Objections to a particular line of cross-examination should be taken as soon as it is apparent to defence counsel that counsel for the prosecution is in danger of going too far. There is little point in objecting when the questions have been asked and answered, since it will not usually be a ground for discharging the jury.

(f) In every case where there has been cross-examination under s 1(3)(ii) the judge must, in summing up, warn the jury that the questioning goes only to credit and instruct them that they should not consider that it shows a propensity to commit the offence they are considering.

Judicial discretion to exclude s 1(3)(ii) cross-examination

Current guidelines, based on earlier cases, appear in *R v Owen*[62] and can be summarised as follows:

(a) When it is clear that a s 1(3)(ii) situation has arisen, the judge must weigh the prejudicial effect of the proposed questions against the damage done by the attack on the prosecution witness and must generally exercise his discretion so as to secure a trial that is fair to both prosecution and defence.

(b) The general principle is that the jury should know about the character of the man who is saying things to the discredit of the character of the prosecution witness.

(c) The fact that the accused's previous convictions are not for offences of dishonesty, or may be for offences bearing a close resemblance to the offence charged, are matters for the judge to take into account when exercising his discretion. But they do not oblige the judge to disallow the proposed cross-examination.

(d) The Court of Appeal will not interfere with the exercise of the judge's discretion, unless he has erred in principle or there was no material on which he could properly have reached his decision. The court will not quash a conviction merely because its members would have exercised the discretion differently.

These guidelines assume a situation where the defendant has come within the second limb of s 1(3)(ii). Situations where a defendant is caught by the first limb are relatively rare and there has not been a similar opportunity to

---

62 (1985) 83 Cr App R 100; *Sourcebook*, p 311.

develop guidelines for the exercise of discretion in such cases.[63] But considerations (c) and (d) would clearly be taken into account under the first limb also, as would the need to preserve a fair trial.

In *R v Taylor and Goodman*,[64] the Court of Appeal, giving further guidance, made two points:

- Where a defendant has a particularly bad or damaging record, the judge is likely to admit it only if the imputations made against the prosecution witness or witnesses are correspondingly grave.

- However, the mere fact that a record is very bad does not mean that it should never be revealed. Otherwise, a professional criminal 'would eventually build himself a sanctuary from which he could with impunity advance allegations of the utmost seriousness against each and any prosecution witnesses ...'.

However, these guidelines must now be read in the light of the decision of the Court of Appeal in *R v Davison-Jenkins*.[65] In that case, the defendant was charged with theft involving shoplifting. She put her character in issue, and the judge allowed her to be cross-examined under s 1(3)(ii) about five previous convictions involving dishonesty, two of which were also for shoplifting. The Court of Appeal said that, despite a satisfactory direction about the use of cross-examination under s 1(3)(ii), it had been effectively impossible for the jury to disregard propensity once they had heard about the previous convictions for shoplifting. No direction could negate the overwhelming prejudice caused, and it had been wrong to allow the defendant's convictions for those offences to go before the jury. The credibility of the defendant could have been effectively questioned by referring to the three previous convictions for other forms of dishonesty. It is too early to say whether this decision marks the beginning of a more interventionist and realistic approach by the Court of Appeal to the problems raised by s 1(3)(ii) where previous convictions are for offences bearing a close resemblance to that currently charged. It is also unclear whether the decision was based on the fact that the previous convictions were not referred to merely as convictions for theft, but for theft involving shoplifting. Nor is it clear what the position would have been had all the previous convictions been for theft, and not for any other forms of dishonesty.

---

63 One reason for this may be that defence advocates tend to rely on the prosecution for information about their clients' previous convictions.

64 [1999] 2 Cr App R 163, p 172, *per* Judge LJ.

65 [1997] Crim LR 816.

Section 1(3)(iii)

Under this provision a defendant who gives evidence may be questioned about the matters referred to in the opening words of s 1(3) where he has given evidence against any other person charged in the same proceedings.[66] There is no discretion to disallow a co-defendant's application to cross-examine under s 1(3)(iii), so argument in court will generally be confined to the question of whether the appropriate situation has arisen.

The leading case on this topic is *Murdoch v Taylor*.[67] Murdoch and his co-accused, Lynch, were tried together on an indictment which alleged that they had received three cameras, knowing that they had been stolen. Both pleaded not guilty. The case for the prosecution was that both Lynch and Murdoch had been involved in an attempt to sell the cameras at a watchmaker's shop. Murdoch gave evidence in his own defence. In examination-in-chief he stated that he had seen a box in Lynch's possession, but had discovered that it contained cameras only when Lynch had called him into the watchmaker's shop after first entering and spending some time there himself. Under cross-examination by counsel for Lynch, he asserted that he had had nothing to do with the stolen cameras and that they had been entirely Lynch's responsibility. Counsel for Lynch claimed to be entitled to cross-examine Murdoch under s 1(3)(iii). The trial judge permitted this and both men were subsequently convicted.

Murdoch's appeal reached the House of Lords, where the following principles were established:

(a) The Act does not require any investigation of the motives or wishes which may have prompted the evidence in question. As Lord Morris said, it is the nature of the evidence that has to be considered; its character does not change depending on whether it is the product of pained reluctance or malevolent eagerness.

(b) There is no discretion to disallow cross-examination under s 1(3)(iii) by counsel for a co-defendant. But counsel who wishes to rely on this provision should obtain a ruling from the judge that a s 1(3)(iii) situation has arisen before proceeding. Where counsel for the prosecution, rather than counsel for a co-defendant, wishes to use s 1(3)(iii), the judge *does* have a discretion to disallow cross-examination.

(c) No distinction is to be made between evidence given in chief and evidence given in cross-examination for the purpose of deciding if a s 1(3)(iii) situation has arisen.

(d) The relevance of such cross-examination is to credit only.

---

66 This appears to permit D3 to cross-examine D1 who has given evidence against D2. See Law Com No 141 (1996), para 13.12.

67 [1965] AC 574; *Sourcebook*, p 320.

The Law Lords also discussed what amounted to 'evidence against' a co-defendant. They concluded that evidence which does no more than contradict something that a co-defendant has said, without further advancing the prosecution's case to any significant degree, will not come within s 1(3)(iii). But any evidence which, taken in the context of the whole case, *supports the prosecution's case or undermines the defence of the co-defendant*, will be caught.

On the facts of the case, the evidence given by Murdoch was evidence against Lynch. It put Lynch in sole possession and control of property which, according to the rest of the evidence, had been stolen the day before, and which Lynch had tried to sell for a fraction of its true value.

What amounts to giving 'evidence against' a co-defendant has been discussed in a number of later cases.

In the first place, it is clear that, for the evidence of one defendant to support the prosecution case so as to bring s 1(3)(iii) into operation, it must do so in relation to a matter that is contested between the prosecution and the other defendant. So, for example, if the prosecution says that X was in Gray's Inn Place at 10.00 pm on 3 January, *and X agrees that she was*, defendant Y does not bring s 1(3)(iii) into operation by testifying that X was in that place, on that date, and at that time.[68]

Secondly, it is clear that, where the evidence of one defendant, if believed, inevitably entails the guilt of another, the proviso will apply. For example, in *R v Varley*,[69] the defendant Varley and a man named Dibble were jointly charged with robbery. At trial, Dibble's defence was that he had taken part in the robbery with Varley, but had done so only under duress because of threats made against his life by Varley. Varley gave evidence that he had not been present at the commission of the crime at all. The trial judge held that Varley had brought himself within s 1(3)(iii). Both were convicted. Varley appealed, arguing that he had not given evidence against Dibble.

Clearly, Dibble had given evidence against Varley. But was the converse true? The court laid down these further guidelines:

(a) Inconvenience to, or inconsistency with, a co-defendant's defence is not itself sufficient; in particular, mere denial of participation in a joint venture is not in itself sufficient to rank as evidence against a co-defendant.

(b) For the proviso to apply, the denial must lead to the conclusion that if the witness did not participate, then it must have been the other defendant who did.

On the facts of this case, Varley *had* given evidence against Dibble. Varley was saying that he had not gone with Dibble, and had not forced Dibble to go. The

---

68 *R v Crawford* [1998] 1 Cr App R 338.
69 [1982] 2 All ER 519; *Sourcebook*, p 326.

effect of this evidence was not only that Dibble was telling lies, but that Dibble was left as a participant on his own, and not acting under duress.

What is the position where the evidence of one defendant will, if believed, discredit another's defence in the eyes of the jury, but will not inevitably entail that other's guilt? The application of s 1(3)(iii) in such circumstances is not easy to predict. At least two cases suggest that this will *not* be enough for the proviso to apply.

In *R v Bruce*[70] the defendant, another man named McGuinness and some others were charged with robbery. The case for the prosecution was that they had frightened a passenger in a train into giving them money. McGuinness's evidence supported the prosecution case that there had been an agreement to rob. According to him, they had all gone to Hampstead that night to look for a Pakistani to rob. On failing to find anyone who appeared to fit that description, they had boarded a train and found a victim there. McGuinness said that he had played no part in the robbery. Bruce said in his evidence that there had never been a plan to rob anyone. The trial judge ruled that he had thereby given evidence against McGuinness, and so had brought himself within s 1(3)(iii).

The Court of Appeal disagreed. The evidence of Bruce that there had been no conspiracy to rob certainly contradicted part of McGuinness's evidence and damaged his credibility. But it did not contradict McGuinness's evidence that he had taken no part in the robbery. Moreover, Bruce's evidence undermined the case for the prosecution, because what he said made it not *more* but *less* likely that there had been a robbery for which McGuinness could be convicted. In one way Bruce had given evidence against McGuinness, but in another he had not. The court concluded that, on balance, what Bruce said exculpated McGuinness from the robbery and did not incriminate him. Usually evidence that undermines the defence of a co-defendant supports the prosecution's case against him. But here the evidence did more to undermine the prosecution's case than to undermine the co-defendant's defence.

A similar conclusion was reached in *R v Kirkpatrick*.[71] In that case, two defendants, K and B, were charged with indecently assaulting a woman. A third man, L, who was charged with them, pleaded guilty. It was alleged that the complainant had been indecently assaulted in a bedroom by K, B, L, and another man, who was not tried. B was the first defendant to give evidence. He said that L, after kissing and cuddling the complainant, had gone into a bedroom with her. B's story was that he himself had fallen asleep, but had been woken up by screams. He denied participating in the indecent assault. K's story was that B and another man were indecently assaulting the complainant, when K intervened to put a stop to what was happening. The

70 [1975] 1 WLR 1252; *Sourcebook*, p 324.
71 [1998] Crim LR 63.

trial judge held that B had not given evidence against K for the purposes of s 1(3)(iii). The Court of Appeal upheld his ruling. B's evidence had not implicated K. B's defence was inconsistent with that of K, but this did not amount to undermining K's defence. Even if the jury accepted what B said, that did not prevent them from acquitting K.

R v Crawford[72] suggests, however, that s 1(3)(iii) *may* apply where the evidence of one defendant does merely jeopardise the credibility of another. In that case there was evidence to suggest that a robbery with which the two defendants were charged had been committed by a third person, who had not been prosecuted. When one defendant gave evidence denying participation in the robbery it did not, therefore, follow inevitably that the other defendant must have done what was alleged. The Court of Appeal said that the guidelines in *R v Varley*, though helpful, were not to be construed as if they were statutory provisions. It was enough, for s 1(3)(iii) to apply, that the evidence of one defendant should jeopardise the credibility of the other, and so make the prosecution case against the other more likely to be true.

Just as the details of previous offences may be relevant to credibility under s 1(3)(ii), so they may be under s 1(3)(iii). An example of a case where this was so is *R v Reid*.[73] A minicab driver was robbed by four men. Two men – Reid and the co-defendant – were arrested. Reid's defence was that he was the last passenger to get into the car and only then discovered that a robbery had taken place. When cross-examined on behalf of the co-defendant, he said that it was the co-defendant who had been holding a knife to the driver's throat. Counsel for the co-defendant argued successfully that Reid had brought himself within s 1(3)(iii). But he wanted to cross-examine Reid about the details of one of his previous convictions. That conviction had also been for robbery of a taxi driver and the defence then put forward had been similar to Reid's defence in the present case. At that earlier trial Reid had given evidence to the effect that he had been in the car, but had left it before the robbery occurred. The judge allowed Reid to be cross-examined about this. The Court of Appeal upheld this decision. The details of the earlier case were relevant in two ways:

(a) Reid had tried to run the same sort of defence on the earlier occasion;

(b) the earlier defence had also involved Reid in attempting to incriminate others falsely.

It was legitimate for the co-defendant to undermine what Reid had said about him by referring to his earlier attempt to implicate co-defendants.

---

72   [1998] 1 Cr App R 338.
73   [1989] Crim LR 719.

Cross-examination of a co-defendant at common law

Cross-examination of a co-defendant is not governed solely by s 1(3)(iii) of the 1898 Act. An advocate for one defendant may need to bring out matters to the discredit of another defendant in support of his own case, both during examination-in-chief and during cross-examination. This is permissible, provided the judge is satisfied that the matters covered are relevant. Once satisfied of this, the judge has no discretion to exclude the evidence. For example, in *R v Miller*,[74] a decision at first instance, three defendants (Miller, Mercado and Harris) were charged with conspiracy to evade customs duties on the importation of nylon stockings. Mercado's defence was that he had not been concerned in the illegal importations. He said that Harris, one of his employees, had posed as Mercado and used Mercado's office for the illegal transactions. In order to establish that it was Harris, and not Mercado, who had been involved, counsel for Mercado wanted to prove that Harris had been in prison during a period when the illegal importations had been suspended. Devlin J held that, in the light of Mercado's defence, the evidence was relevant and admissible. He said that a judge had no discretion to exclude *defence* evidence that prejudiced another defendant on the basis that its prejudicial effect outweighed its probative worth.

This ruling was adopted as an accurate statement of law by the Court of Appeal in *R v Bracewell*.[75] In that case, two men, Lockwood and Bracewell, were charged with the murder of a man in a house where they had committed a burglary. Neither denied the burglary, but each blamed the other for the murder. Lockwood was allowed to give evidence to the effect that he was an experienced burglar of a strictly non-violent type, with a cool head in emergencies, whereas Bracewell was inexperienced, nervous, excitable, and possibly under the influence of drink (and so, by implication, the man more likely to have panicked and committed the murder). The Court of Appeal held that this evidence entitled Bracewell to cross-examine Lockwood about occasions when Lockwood had been violent to his mistress, and to call evidence in rebuttal of any denial.

PROPOSALS FOR REFORM

The Law Commission has recognised, in its Consultation Paper No 141 (1996), that the law about character evidence rests on some dubious assumptions. Especially problematic are the ideas that character is indivisible and that a distinction can properly be made between evidence that is relevant to

---

74 [1952] 2 All ER 667; *Sourcebook*, p 334.
75 (1978) 68 Cr App R 44; *Sourcebook*, p 336. See also *Lowery v R* [1974] AC 85.

credibility and evidence that is relevant to guilt. In the light of these and other concerns, the Commission has made provisional recommendations for reform of the law on this subject, with special reference to s 1(3) of the 1898 Act. What follows is only an outline of the Commission's criticisms and proposals and students should read the Consultation Paper itself for greater detail.

Indivisibility of character

The idea that character is indivisible assumes that a person who behaves immorally in one way will behave immorally in other ways as well. A classic example of this attitude can be found in *R v Jenkins*[76] where it emerged that a prosecution witness had committed adultery with the defendant. The Court of Criminal Appeal said that cross-examination about this had been designed to show her to be 'a worthless and abandoned woman whose evidence ought not to be relied upon by the jury'. But judicial opinion has not always been unanimous on the indivisibility of character. The effect of adultery on a witness's credibility was the subject of this comment by Cockburn CJ in his summing-up in *R v Castro*:

> There are crimes and offences which savour so much of falsehood and fraud that they do go legitimately to the credit of witnesses. There are offences of a different character, and grievous offences if you will, but which do not touch that particular part of a man's moral organisation, if I may use the phrase, which involves truth, and there is an essential distinction between this species of fault and those things which go to the very root of honesty, integrity, and truth, and so do, unfortunately, disentitle witnesses to belief. A man may have committed a breach of morality, who yet would scorn to tell a lie, as base and dishonourable, and who would shrink with horror from committing wilful and deliberate perjury.[77]

Psychological research does not support the indivisibility of character.[78] The Commission has therefore suggested that English law should follow developments that have already taken place in Australia. The effect of these is that where evidence of a defendant's good character has been limited in a particular respect, evidence of bad character may be given in rebuttal only where it tends to disprove the good character of the defendant *in that respect*.[79]

The effect of this recommendation would be that if the situation in *R v Winfield*[80] were to recur, the defendant would be allowed to adduce evidence of his good character with regard to sexual morality without being exposed to

---

76 (1945) 31 Cr App R 1, p 11.

77 *Charge of the Lord Chief Justice of England in the Case of The Queen against Thomas Castro ... printed from the shorthand writer's notes,* 1874, Vol II, p 4764.

78 Law Com No 141 (1996), paras 6.23–6.34.

79 *Ibid*, para 11.8.

80 [1939] 4 All ER 164.

cross-examination about his previous convictions for dishonesty. Of course, not every question could be so easily resolved. Suppose a defendant is charged with offences of dishonesty. He has no previous convictions for dishonesty but he has one for rape. On that earlier occasion he pleaded not guilty and gave evidence in his own defence. It must follow from his conviction that on that occasion he was disbelieved on his oath. Would this make the conviction for rape available to rebut evidence of his lack of convictions for dishonesty?

The varied nature of previous convictions

Courts have from time to time suggested that cross-examination under s 1(3)(ii) of the 1898 Act should not take place about previous convictions for offences other than dishonesty, especially where the prejudicial effect on the jury might be great. In *R v Watts*,[81] for example, the defendant was charged with indecent assault on a young woman. He claimed that the police evidence was fabricated. The judge then allowed the prosecution to cross-examine him about his convictions for indecent assaults on his young nieces some years before. The Court of Appeal allowed his appeal, on the basis that what was revealed almost certainly did not affect his credibility, as the previous offences did not involve dishonesty. But there is no doubt that in this case the court was generous to the defendant. The decision was at odds with *Selvey v DPP*[82] and in *R v Owen*,[83] the Court of Appeal stated that a judge is not obliged to exclude cross-examination under s 1(3)(ii) about previous convictions for offences not involving dishonesty.

The provisional view of the Law Commission was that the probative value of previous convictions when assessing credibility would vary substantially according to the nature of the conviction and the plea entered.[84] The misconduct most relevant to credibility would be convictions for perjury. Convictions for dishonesty might be relevant in some circumstances, but behaviour not involving dishonesty was unlikely to be relevant to credibility. However, the Commission did not think it appropriate to prescribe by legislation the kinds of conviction that should be probative or otherwise.[85]

---

81 (1983) 77 Cr App R 126.

82 [1970] AC 304; *Sourcebook*, p 302. In a trial for buggery, the judge, whose decision was upheld by the House of Lords, told counsel for the prosecution that his cross-examination under s 1(3)(ii) should be confined to questions about previous convictions for homosexual conduct. See *Selvey v DPP* [1970] AC 304, p 330.

83 (1985) 83 Cr App R 100; *Sourcebook*, p 300.

84 Law Com No 141 (1996), para 6.50.

85 *Ibid*, para 6.63.

The provisional view of the Commission was that a previous plea might be relevant to credibility where it could be inferred that on an earlier occasion the defendant had lied to a court.[86]

Relevance to guilt and relevance to credibility

The clear view of the Commission was that it was hopeless to try to maintain this distinction. Directions based on it were likely to be ignored by both juries and magistrates[87] and the distinction itself was sometimes impossible to make. For example, the Commission suggested that where the prosecution is allowed to cross-examine under the first limb of s 1(3)(ii), it is in effect adducing evidence to show not only that the defendant lacks credibility as a witness, but also to show that he is likely to have committed the offence.[88] In addition, imputations against a prosecution witness might be relevant not just to credibility but to the witness's own propensities, and so relevant to the defendant's guilt. Thus, where self-defence is raised in an assault case and the alleged victim has numerous convictions for serious assaults, this would obviously be relevant to more than the mere credibility of the witness.[89]

Section 1(3)(ii)

The Commission noted that the existing law presented a number of difficulties. Among them were the following:

(a) The existence of a judicial discretion undermines this provision and makes its application difficult to predict in a particular case.[90]

(b) It is not easy for defence advocates to predict in a particular case what they may ask in cross-examination without bringing this provision into play.[91] One reason for this is that the existing law leaves unclear exactly what kind of allegation counts as an imputation.[92]

(c) The jury may be unable to follow the judge's direction about the relevance of information obtained as a result of cross-examination under this provision.[93]

---

86 Law Com No 141 (1996), para 6.70.
87 *Ibid*, para 6.84.
88 *Ibid*, para 6.77.
89 *Ibid*, para 6.78.
90 *Ibid*, paras 12.26–12.27.
91 *Ibid*, para 12.28.
92 *Ibid*, paras 12.31–12.33.
93 *Ibid*, para 6.84.

In relation to the first limb of s 1(3)(ii), the Commission thought that the existing law was unsatisfactory, not least because of lack of clarity. It recommended, amongst other things, loss of protection where there was an express or implied assertion of good character, including non-verbal assertions, giving as an example the wearing of 'a Securicor-style uniform' in court.[94]

In relation to the second limb, the Commission provisionally recommended that imputations should result in loss of the defendant's shield *only if they do not relate to the conduct of the witness in the incident or investigation in question*.[95]

Section 1(3)(iii)

Among defects in existing law the Commission noted the following:

(a) Unfairness may result because there is no judicial discretion to exclude cross-examination by a co-defendant. In particular, there is no scope for the court to protect a defendant where the probative value of his criminal record is small, but its likely prejudicial effect is great.[96]

(b) It is impossible to keep the evaluation of a defendant's guilt separate from the evaluation of his truthfulness.[97]

(c) The application of s 1(3)(iii) may result in the court's being misled. Suppose defendant X gives evidence which does not amount to 'evidence against' defendant Y. X's record will not emerge. Y then gives evidence which does amount to 'evidence against' X. Y's record will be admitted. But X's record will remain hidden, even though it may be much worse than Y's.[98]

The provisional recommendations of the Commission include one to the effect that evidence given by one defendant of a co-defendant's conduct in the incident or investigation in question should not result in loss of protection. Where that protection *is* lost, the court should have a discretion to exclude cross-examination on the first defendant's previous convictions.[99]

The Commission has also proposed the abolition of the rule whereby evidence admitted under s 1(3)(iii) is directly relevant only to credibility.[100]

---

94 Law Com No 141 (1996), paras 11.15–11.31. Cf *R v Robinson (Michael)* [2001] Crim LR 478.
95 *Ibid*, paras 12.71–12.79.
96 *Ibid*, paras 13.5–13.9.
97 *Ibid*, para 13.10.
98 *Ibid*, para 13.11.
99 *Ibid*, paras 13.41–13.46.
100 *Ibid*, paras 13.51–13.53.

CHAPTER 12

OPINION EVIDENCE[1]

The main topics of importance are:

(a) the circumstances in which opinion evidence is generally admissible;

(b) analysing the basis on which an opinion has been given; and

(c) the extent to which the evidence of psychiatrists or psychologists is admissible in criminal trials.

WHEN IS OPINION EVIDENCE ADMISSIBLE?

The fundamental rule is that witnesses testify about facts and not about the opinions they have formed from facts. The reason for this is that it is the job of the 'tribunal of fact' (a judge or, very occasionally, a jury in a civil case, and magistrates or a jury in a criminal case) to hear the evidence, find facts, and make inferences from them. It is thought that the tribunal may be misled and hindered in its work if opinion evidence is too freely received. The pervasiveness of the rule can sometimes be forgotten in cross-examination. A witness should not generally be asked to give his opinion about what another witness has said. For example, in *R v Windass*[2] an appeal against conviction was allowed where a defendant had been asked during cross-examination to interpret entries that his girlfriend had made in her diary without any contribution from him.

A distinction between fact and opinion lies at the heart of the rule and its rationale. Arguably, the distinction cannot be sustained. Believing that something in the case involves making a judgment – an assent to a proposition. Sense awareness involves us in being receptive to objects and events in our surroundings. But belief that something is, or was, the case involves more than just receptivity. It involves acts of mind, in which the material provided by sense awareness is interpreted.[3] If an opinion is an inference from facts, there may be difficulty in finding a fact that is untainted by any element of opinion. Suppose I say that I saw my neighbour Mary in the

---

1 Law Reform Committee, 17th Report, Cm 4489, 1970; Royal Commission on Criminal Justice, Cm 2263, 1993, pp 144–59; Law Commission, *Evidence in Criminal Proceedings: Hearsay and Related Topics*, Cm 3670, 1997, Part IX; *Learned Hand* (1901) 15 Harv LR 40; Kenny [1983] 99 LQR 197; Pattenden [1986] Crim LR 92; Mackay and Colman [1991] Crim LR 800; Mirfield [1992] 109 LQR 528; Jack (1994) 144 NLJ 1099; Spencer (1992) 45 CLP, Part 2, 213.

2 (1989) 89 Cr App R 258. See also *R v Gray and Evans* [1998] Crim LR 570.

3 Cf Landesman, C, *An Introduction to Epistemology*, 1997, pp 6–7.

supermarket. There lurks behind this apparent statement of fact an opinion based on my knowledge of Mary and comparisons I have made between her characteristics and those of the person whom I saw in the supermarket. Sometimes an expression of opinion may be a shorthand way of stating perceived facts. If, at the scene of a motor accident, a bystander who observed what happened says, 'That pedestrian never gave the driver a chance to stop', he probably intends to convey his perception that the pedestrian walked into the road quickly and without paying any attention to the traffic. The fundamental rule is not pressed too far; in the example given, the witness would probably be allowed to state the opinion, but would be required afterwards to state, so far as he could, the facts on which his opinion was based.[4]

Fortunately, the problem of classification is not one that bothers the courts much in practice. What they are mainly concerned with is the exception to the rule against opinion evidence which allows an expert to give evidence of his opinion in certain circumstances. This exception allows an expert to give the court the benefit of his expertise, including his opinion, where the matters on which he testifies are likely to be outside the experience of judge or jury. In each case it is for the judge to decide:

(a) whether the issue is one on which the court could be assisted by expert evidence; and,

(b) whether the expert tendered has the expertise to provide such evidence.[5]

In an age in which professional experts of all kinds proliferate, it is almost inconceivable that an expert witness should be called who is an amateur. But the possibility remains, and perhaps if the area of expertise is sufficiently recondite it might be necessary to rely on one. In *R v Silverlock*,[6] the Court for Crown Cases Reserved had to consider whether a witness giving his opinion about samples of handwriting needed to be a professional expert, or at least a person whose ordinary business led him to have special experience in questions of handwriting, or whether the evidence of any person who had merely studied handwriting for some years would suffice. The court held that while a witness giving such evidence should be skilled in the subject, there were no restrictions on the *manner* in which that skill had to be acquired. The evidence of a person without professional qualifications could be admitted, provided the judge was satisfied that the witness was sufficiently skilled.

---

4   Cf *R v Davies* [1962] 3 All ER 97, where the Courts Martial Appeal Court held that, on a charge of drunken driving, a witness who is not medically qualified can give his general impression as to whether a driver has taken drink but must describe the facts on which he relies. The common law rule allowing such 'shorthand' expressions of opinion remains applicable in criminal cases, but received statutory recognition so far as civil proceedings were concerned in s 3(2) of the Civil Evidence Act 1972.

5   *R v Stockwell* (1993) 97 Cr App R 260, p 264, *per* Lord Taylor CJ.

6   [1894] 2 QB 766.

A witness who has acquired his expertise in the course of his daily work may certainly give expert evidence, even though he lacks paper qualifications. In *R v Murphy*,[7] for example, a police constable who was a traffic accident expert was allowed to give evidence of his opinion as to the nature of a collision, the course of one of the vehicles involved and other matters said to be deducible from marks in the road and damage to the vehicles. The Court of Appeal upheld the judge's ruling. Provided the judge was satisfied that these matters were within his expertise, his evidence was admissible.

A witness who is otherwise not specially qualified may be an 'expert ad hoc' where he has special knowledge acquired by study of materials that are relevant in a particular case, such as video recordings or photographs. In *R v Clare and Peach*,[8] a police officer had made a special study of video recordings showing people arriving at a football match and later scenes of disorder in a town centre. He was permitted to give evidence identifying the defendants as persons shown on the film committing offences. The appellants argued that his evidence was inadmissible, because he was in no better position than the members of the jury to make identifications from the video recordings. The Court of Appeal rejected this argument. It held that, as a result of his study, the officer had special knowledge which the jury did not possess. To give the jury similar time and facilities to conduct the same research would have been utterly impracticable. It was therefore legitimate for the officer to assist them in his evidence by pointing to what he believed to be happening in scenes shown on the film.

Although it is clear that the object of expert evidence is to provide the court with information that is outside the experience of judge or jury, there is little authority on how to determine whether particular information falls within this class. But in practice the question rarely arises. In most cases it is clear whether the question is one that requires expert evidence or not. A case where a problem did arise (though it was not the central problem) was *R v Stagg*.[9] In that case Ognall J expressed a strong doubt whether evidence obtained from the technique known as 'psychological profiling' was expert evidence of a kind recognised by the courts. Where the question is admittedly one for an expert, and the court is satisfied that the witness is qualified as an expert, the employment of an unorthodox technique is more likely to affect weight than admissibility. Thus in *R v Robb*[10] a phonetician was allowed to express an opinion on voice identification, although he relied on a technique that had only minority support within his profession.

---

7   [1980] 1 QB 434.

8   [1995] 2 Cr App R 333. In a decision at first instance it was held that, as a matter of public policy, where there exists a relationship between the proposed expert and the party calling him which a reasonable observer might think was capable of affecting the expert's opinion, that expert's evidence should not be admitted, however unbiased his conclusions might probably be. See *Liverpool Roman Catholic Archdiocesan Trust v Goldberg* (2001) 151 NLJ 1093.

9   (1994) unreported, 14 September. See also *R v Gilfoyle* [2001] 2 Cr App R 57.

10 (1991) 93 Cr App R 161.

THE BASIS OF THE OPINION

An expert gives his opinion on the basis of facts in a particular case, but those facts must themselves be proved by admissible evidence. However, if the rule against hearsay were strictly applied, an expert would often be prevented from giving an opinion because his reasoning and conclusions will be governed by matters that he has learned in the course of his training and experience, either from what he has read or from others who share his specialisation. The courts have therefore relaxed the hearsay rule to take this into account. So, for example, an expert in property valuations is not confined to giving evidence based on comparables of which he has first hand knowledge. Of course, a surveyor who is asked to express a view on the open market value of a particular property will have regard to any relevant personal experience. But he will also have regard to the sales experience of his office, whether that is within his own first hand knowledge or not, and to all sources from which information can be obtained about market trends and conditions.[11]

Experts may support their opinions by referring to articles, letters to journals and other materials, whether published or not, when giving their testimony.[12] An example of this practice can be seen in *R v Abadom*.[13] The appellant had been convicted of robbery, and his appeal raised a question about the materials that could be used by expert witnesses when giving evidence. The main evidence against him was that a pair of his shoes had fragments of glass embedded in them; it was the prosecution's case that the glass came from a window broken during the robbery. One of the prosecution expert witnesses relied, in support of this contention, on statistics collated by the Home Office Central Research Establishment in relation to the refractive index of broken glass.[14] The point taken on appeal was that the evidence of this expert was inadmissible hearsay because the expert had no personal knowledge of the analyses whose results were collated in these statistics. The Court of Appeal rejected this contention on the ground that experts must be entitled to draw on material produced by others in their field of expertise. Indeed, it is part of their duty to consider any material that might be available and not to draw conclusions based solely on their own experience, which will inevitably be limited. The court emphasised that the primary facts on which

---

11 *Abbey National Mortgages plc v Key Surveyors Nationwide Ltd* [1996] 3 All ER 184, p 189, *per* Sir Thomas Bingham MR. This Court of Appeal decision shows a greater readiness to accept hearsay than the decision of Megarry J in *English Exporters (London) Ltd v Eldonwall Ltd* [1973] Ch 415.

12 *H v Schering Chemicals Ltd* [1983] 1 WLR 143; *Sourcebook*, p 390.

13 [1983] 1 All ER 364; *Sourcebook*, p 391.

14 The refractive index is a measure of the extent to which light is bent when it passes into a particular piece of glass.

an expert's opinion is based must be proved by admissible evidence. So here, for example, it was necessary to show by admissible evidence that glass from the broken window and glass from the appellant's shoes had the same refractive index. But once the primary facts have been proved, experts are entitled to draw on the work of others, whether published or unpublished, as part of their own experience in that field. Where they have done so, however, this should be mentioned in their evidence so that it can be taken into account when considering the probative worth of their opinion as a whole.

Sometimes the primary facts of a case are not established by the expert himself, but by other members of a team, which the expert leads. In such a case, the evidence of the other relevant team members must be available (in the absence of formal admissions),[15] so that the primary facts can all be proved by admissible evidence.[16] The distinction between primary facts and other facts relied on by an expert to interpret primary facts (which may be called 'expert's facts') is that only primary facts are peculiar to the investigation being carried out. For example, in *R v Abadom*, primary facts included the location of the glass fragments and the refractive index of those fragments, and in *R v Jackson*, they included the location of blood stains and their blood groupings. Expert's facts come from other factual situations. Often they are facts about experiments used to test and substantiate a particular hypothesis. So in *R v Abadom*, the Home Office statistics, based on tests carried out in different situations, were expert's facts, and could be relied on without formal proof by the expert when interpreting primary facts of that case, namely, the location and refractive index of the glass fragments. But in *R v Jackson*, the facts about the blood stains were primary, because it was the blood that was being investigated for the purpose of the trial. So those facts had to be formally proved, in the absence of admissions.

By s 30(1) of the Criminal Justice Act 1988, an 'expert report' (that is, a written report by a person dealing wholly or mainly with matters on which he is, or, if living, would be, qualified to give expert evidence)[17] shall be admissible as evidence in criminal proceedings, whether or not the person making it attends to give oral evidence. If it is proposed that the person making the report shall not give oral evidence, the report shall be admissible only with leave of the court. It seems most unlikely that a court would allow an expert report to be adduced without calling the maker if the opposing party had a genuine desire to cross-examine on it. The effect of this provision is that if an expert gives evidence, his report is admissible as evidence of the facts and opinions that it contains. The jury can therefore be given copies, and the expert does not have to read it aloud, or cover all the matters contained in

---

15 See below, Chapter 14.
16 *R v Jackson* [1996] 2 Cr App R 420.
17 Criminal Justice Act 1988, s 30(5).

it during examination-in-chief. There are provisions, affecting the defence as well as the prosecution, for advance disclosure of expert evidence.[18]

In its report on hearsay and related topics, the Law Commission considered the problem arising from the fact that very often an expert's opinion will be based on the investigation of primary facts by members of his team. In order to save time and money, the Commission recommended that the present disclosure requirements should be extended. The advance notice would include a list of any persons who had supplied information on which the expert relied, and a brief description of the information that each person had supplied. Any other party to the proceedings could apply for a direction that a person named in this way should give oral evidence. But a direction could be made only if the applicant satisfied the court that there was a real issue that could be pursued better with the assistant than with the expert. In the absence of any application in relation to a named assistant, a new hearsay exception would operate. This would allow the expert to base his evidence on any information supplied by that assistant on matters of which that assistant had (or might reasonably be supposed to have had) personal knowledge. Any information relied on in this way would be admissible as evidence of its truth. If a direction were made that the assistant should give evidence in person, the exception would not apply.[19]

EVIDENCE FROM PSYCHIATRISTS AND PSYCHOLOGISTS

According to Lord Campbell, '[H]ardly any weight is to be given to the evidence of what are called scientific witnesses; they come with a bias on their minds to support the cause in which they are embarked ...'.[20] Judicial attitudes have not greatly changed where the witnesses are experts in psychiatry or psychology. To some extent judges recognise that a psychiatrist or psychologist may be able to provide useful testimony about matters that are outside the experience of judge or jurors.[21] At the same time, they tend to

---

18 Crown Court (Advance Notice of Expert Evidence) Rules, SI 1987/716, as amended by the Crown Court (Advance Notice of Expert Evidence) (Amendment) Rules, SI 1997/700; Magistrates' Court (Advance Notice of Expert Evidence) Rules, SI 1997/705. If the notice is not given, the leave of the court is needed to adduce the evidence.

19 Law Com No 245 (1997), paras 9.23–9.29.

20 *The Tracy Peerage* (1839) 10 Cl&F 154, p 191.

21 For an example of psychiatric evidence that was of assistance to the court, see *DPP v A and BC Chewing Gum Ltd* [1968] QB 159; *Sourcebook*, p 395, where the Divisional Court held that magistrates hearing an information under the Obscene Publications Act 1964 should have heard the expert evidence of psychiatrists who had been available at trial to give their opinion about the tendency of certain articles to deprave and corrupt children. Lord Parker CJ observed that while the effect of a publication on an adult might well be capable of being assessed without expert evidence, where the effect on children was in issue the justices needed all the help they could get.

think there is a danger that mental experts will usurp the role of the jury or other triers of fact unless a clear line is drawn between abnormal and normal mental states. The latter are taken to include lust, anger, and other undesirable emotions which, judges believe, are perfectly capable of being understood by ordinary people without expert assistance. The attempt to make such a distinction has led to some unhappy compromises, the most unhappy being the distinction drawn between expert evidence relevant to the reliability of a confession, and expert evidence relevant to *mens rea*.

In *R v Raghip and Others*,[22] the Court of Appeal acknowledged that it was the regular practice of judges to admit psychiatric or psychological evidence when considering submissions about the admissibility of confessions. The reason for this is that the mental condition of the defendant at the time of interview is one of the circumstances to be considered by the trial judge on a submission under s 76(2)(b) of the Police and Criminal Evidence Act 1984.[23] But the court also said that a distinction must be made between the admission of such evidence for that purpose and its admission where it is relevant to the defendant's *mens rea*. Following this distinction, the Court of Appeal in *R v Coles*[24] held that expert evidence is inadmissible to enable a jury to reach a decision about the existence of *mens rea, unless related to the mental health or psychiatric state of the defendant*. The defendant was charged with arson. After he had given evidence himself, his counsel applied for leave to call the expert evidence of a psychologist. The trial judge held the evidence inadmissible because it was not evidence of any mental abnormality, merely that the defendant was of low average mental capacity. The Court of Appeal upheld his decision, observing that, 'Adolescents of varying stages of maturity and brightness are all within the common experience of jurors'.

The 'common experience of jurors' had been established in *R v Turner*[25] as a key concept in determining the admissibility of psychiatric or psychological evidence on the issue of *mens rea*. The defendant was charged with the murder of his girlfriend, and the defence was provocation. It was said that the defendant had been deeply in love with the girl and had believed her to be pregnant by him. One day he was sitting in a motor car with her when she told him, with a grin, that while he had been in prison she had been sleeping with two other men, that she could make money in that way, and that the child she was carrying was not his. The defendant claimed that he had been

---

22 (1991) *The Times*, 9 December.

23 But note *R v O'Brien* (2000) *The Times*, 16 February, where the Court of Appeal put limits on expert evidence concerning the type of personality associated with those who make false confessions. (1) The abnormal disorder must not only be of the type which might render a confession unreliable, but there must also be a very significant deviation from the norm. (2) There should be a history of admissions pre-dating the making of the confession which is not based solely on a history given by the subject, and which points to or explains the abnormality.

24 [1995] 1 Cr App R 157; *Sourcebook*, p 405.

25 [1975] QB 834; *Sourcebook*, p 401.

very upset by what she told him. His hand had come across a hammer by the side of the seat and he had hit her with it. He said, 'It was never in my mind to do her any harm. I did not realise what I had in my hand. I knew it was heavy ... When I realised it was a hammer I stopped'.

The psychiatrist would have said that the defendant's relationship with his girlfriend was such as to make him likely to be overwhelmed by anger as a result of what she had said to him. In his opinion, the defendant's personality was such that he could have killed her in an explosive release of blind rage. He added, however, that the defendant showed no signs of mental illness. While he would obviously benefit from psychotherapeutic counselling, there was no need for psychiatric treatment.

In the Court of Appeal, Lawton LJ referred to the well established rule[26] that an expert's opinion is admissible to furnish the court with scientific information which is likely to be outside the experience and knowledge of a judge or jury. But he said that the opinion of an expert is unnecessary if a judge or jury can form their own conclusions on the facts without help. In particular, they do not need the help of experts 'on matters of human nature and behaviour within the limits of normality'. In relation to the evidence in this case, Lawton LJ said:

> We all know that both men and women who are deeply in love can, and sometimes do, have outbursts of blind rage when discovering unexpected wantonness on the part of their loved ones ... Jurors do not need psychiatrists to tell them how ordinary folk who are not suffering from any mental illness are likely to react to the stresses and strains of life.[27]

It followed that the psychiatrist's evidence was not admissible to establish that the defendant was likely to have been provoked.

In the course of argument *Lowery v The Queen*[28] was cited as part of the appellant's submission. This case, which the court in *R v Turner* said was 'decided on its special facts', involved two defendants, Lowery and King, who were convicted of the sadistic and otherwise motiveless murder of a girl aged 15. At trial they ran 'cut-throat' defences, each saying that the other was solely responsible for the crime. King called in his defence a psychologist whose testimony supported King's evidence against Lowery. In the event, both defendants were convicted. Lowery appealed, arguing that the psychologist's evidence should not have been admitted. The Privy Council upheld the trial judge's decision to admit the evidence and dismissed Lowery's appeal.

The evidence on behalf of King had been given by a Professor Cox, a psychologist. He had had interviews in turn with both Lowery and King, and in each case he had applied certain tests. These were partly intelligence tests,

---

26 See the decision of Lord Mansfield in *Folkes v Chadd* (1782) 3 Doug KB 157.

27 [1975] QB 834, p 841.

28 [1974] AC 85; *Sourcebook*, p 397.

but in the main were tests as to the general personality of the person interviewed. Among other things, he had found a callousness and a sadistic tendency in Lowery that were not present in King.

The main reason why the Privy Council held this evidence admissible for King seems to have been that the situation was analogous to one where there was a relevant physical disparity between two co-defendants. Evidence would have been admissible to show that one defendant had greater physical capacity to commit the crime than the other. The Privy Council held in effect that no logical distinction could be drawn between physical capacities and mental ones. Professor Cox had provided scientific evidence as to the respective personalities of the two accused. That kind of information was not within the knowledge of judges or jurors and it was therefore appropriate to admit expert evidence on the subject. The opinion of the Privy Council shows that it was *influenced* by the fact that Lowery had put his own character in issue both by attacking King, and by claiming that he was less likely by reason of his character and circumstances to have committed the crime than his co-defendant. But however relevant and necessary that evidence might have been to King's defence, this consideration could not have been conclusive of *admissibility*.[29] For the evidence to be admissible, the Privy Council had to accept the argument that expert evidence about relevant characteristics of a defendant's personality could be received by analogy with expert evidence about relevant physical characteristics. In both cases the evidence was necessary, and so admissible, to assist the jury in matters beyond their own experience.

Another argument in *R v Turner* was that the psychiatrist's evidence was relevant and admissible to help the jury in relation to the credibility of the defendant's evidence. The Court of Appeal rejected this on the basis that the defendant was not mentally disordered. This test was followed in *R v Mackenney and Pinfold*,[30] in which the Court of Appeal said that if a witness is suffering from some defect or abnormality of mind it may well be permissible to call *psychiatric* evidence to show that the witness is incapable of giving reliable evidence.[31] The mental illness need not be such as to make the witness totally incapable of giving accurate evidence, but it must substantially affect the witness's capacity to do so. This is very different from calling psychiatric evidence with a view to warning a jury that a witness who is capable of giving reliable evidence may be choosing not to do so. If a witness is mentally capable of giving reliable evidence, it is for the jury to decide whether that

29 In *R v Theodosi* [1993] RTR 179, the Court of Appeal emphasised that a trial judge had no discretion to admit inadmissible opinion evidence merely because the defendants were running cut-throat defences.

30 (1981) 76 Cr App R 271.

31 The evidence of a psychologist is inappropriate because it is psychiatry, not psychology, that is the branch of medical science dealing with diseases and disorders of the mind: *ibid*, p 275.

evidence is reliable, and they do not need the assistance of a psychiatrist.[32] Similarly, in *R v Browning*[33] it was held that evidence from a psychologist about the deterioration of memory was inadmissible because the subject matter of the proposed testimony was within the jury's experience.

Whether an expert could give his opinion on what has been called 'the ultimate issue' – that is to say, the very question to be decided by the court – was a vexed question for a long time. So far as civil proceedings are concerned, the question is now answered by s 3 of the Civil Evidence Act 1972, which provides that where a person is called as a witness in civil proceedings, his opinion on any relevant matter, including an issue in the proceedings, shall be admissible if he is qualified to give expert evidence on it. In criminal cases, evidence of an expert on a particular matter is sometimes excluded on the ground that it would be providing an opinion on the ultimate issue.[34] However, the rule is frequently ignored. The rationale behind the supposed prohibition is that the expert should not usurp the functions of the jury. But the rule is of little use, because counsel can bring a witness so close to giving his opinion on the ultimate issue that the inference as to his view is obvious. In *R v Stockwell*,[35] the Court of Appeal said that an expert is called to give his opinion and should be allowed to do so. What is important is that the judge should make it clear to the jury that they are not bound by an expert's opinion.

---

32 (1981) 76 Cr App R 271, p 276.
33 [1995] Crim LR 227.
34 See, eg, *R v Theodosi* [1993] RTR 179.
35 (1993) 97 Cr App R 260.

CHAPTER 13

PRIVILEGE AND PUBLIC INTEREST IMMUNITY[1]

This chapter deals with reasons for excluding evidence that are unlike any previously encountered. Other exclusionary rules or principles have as the reason for their existence the need to secure a fair trial. Relevant evidence can be excluded because it is likely to mislead the jury[2] or because it would have an adverse effect on the fairness of the proceedings.[3] The justification for the rules relating to privilege and public interest immunity has nothing to do with the fairness of the trial but with some other benefit that is thought to be more important. The rules about privilege and public interest immunity acknowledge that the public have interests that must occasionally be allowed to prevail over their interest in securing fair trials at which all relevant and otherwise admissible evidence can be heard. Although these topics have this understanding in common, they operate differently. A *privilege* is a *right which the law gives to a person* allowing him to refuse to testify about a particular matter or to withhold a document. Effect is given to *public interest immunity* by means of a *power which the courts have* to exclude evidence on the ground that disclosure of information would be damaging to the general good.

PRIVILEGE

There are three main privileges: privilege against self-incrimination, legal professional privilege, and the privilege arising from statements made 'without prejudice'.

---

1   Law Reform Committee, Sixteenth Report, Cmnd 3472, 1967, London: HMSO; CLRC, 11th Report, paras 169–73 and 272–76; Helmholz, RH *et al*, *The Privilege against Self-Incrimination*, 1997; Zuckerman, AAS, 'Privilege and public interest', in Tapper, CFH (ed), *Crime, Proof and Punishment*, 1981, pp 248–95; Tapper (1974) 37 MLR 92; Tapper (1978) 41 MLR 192; Heydon (1971) 87 LQR 214; Allan (1985) 101 LQR 200; Allan (1987) CLJ 43; Andrews (1988) 104 LQR 410; Andrews (1989) CLJ 43; Brown [1994] PL 579; Scott [1996] PL 427; Tapper (1996) 1 E&P 5; Forsyth (1997) CLJ 51; Passmore (1999) 3 E&P 71; Pattenden (2000) 4 E&P 213.

2   See, eg, the law relating to hearsay, similar fact evidence or the exclusion of confessions under s 76(2)(b) of the Police and Criminal Evidence Act 1984 (PACE).

3   See, eg, s 78(1) of PACE or the common law discretion to exclude evidence whose prejudicial effect outweighs its probative value.

Privilege against self-incrimination

Section 14(1) of the Civil Evidence Act 1968, which is declaratory of the common law,[4] describes the privilege as the right of a person in any legal proceedings, other than criminal proceedings, to refuse to answer any question, or produce any document or thing, if to do so would tend to expose that person to proceedings for an offence or for the recovery of a penalty. Section 14 extends the privilege in civil proceedings to protect a person's spouse. At common law the privilege was restricted to the person claiming it.[5]

The consequences of exercising the privilege may be considerable. As Templeman LJ said:

> Where a defendant in a civil action relies on the doctrine against self-incrimination and insists on remaining silent and on concealing documents and other evidence relevant to the action, he is relying on his own wrongdoing or on his own apparent or possible wrongdoing to hamper the [claimant] in the proof of his just claims in the suit.[6]

Statutes have abolished the privilege in certain cases. Sometimes that has been done by providing that a person may be questioned, but that only a limited use may be made of his answers. For example, by s 31 of the Theft Act 1968, the privilege may not be claimed in proceedings for the recovery or administration of any property on the ground that to answer questions would expose the person questioned to proceedings under the Theft Act. But the section goes on to provide that no statement or admission made by anyone answering questions in such proceedings shall be admissible in evidence against that person in proceedings for an offence under the Act.[7] At one time it was thought that the scope of the privilege could be cut down by the courts in a similar way, but it is now accepted that where statute has not limited the use to which such evidence can be put, the civil courts have no power to impose a limit of their own devising.[8] The Youth Justice and Criminal

---

4   *Rio Tinto Zinc Corpn v Westinghouse Electric Corpn* [1978] AC 547, p 636.

5   The origins of the privilege were traditionally said to be the reaction of common lawyers against the prerogative courts of Star Chamber and High Commission during the time of the Civil Wars and Commonwealth in the mid 17th century. More recently it has been argued that the privilege developed at a later stage as the result of the rise of adversary procedure at the end of the 18th century: see Langbein, JH, 'The privilege and common law criminal procedure: the sixteenth to the eighteenth centuries', in Helmholz, RH *et al*, *The Privilege against Self-Incrimination*, 1997, Chapter 4. Another view is that the privilege came into English law via European and canon law: see Macnair, MRT, 'The early development of the privilege against self-incrimination' (1990) 10 OJLS 66.

6   *Rank Film Distributors v Video Information Centre* [1980] 2 All ER 273, 291.

7   The section also covers questioning in proceedings for the administration of any property, for the execution of any trust or for an account of any property or dealings with property. Provisions of a similar kind can be found under s 9 of the Criminal Damage Act 1971, s 98 of the Children Act 1989 (in relation to proceedings relating to the care, supervision and protection of children), s 72 of the Supreme Court Act 1981 (proceedings for the infringement of intellectual property rights), and in various statutes relating to the investigation of fraud.

8   *Bishopsgate Investment v Maxwell* [1992] 2 All ER 856, pp 866–67.

Evidence Act 1999 amends various statutory provisions so as to restrict the use that may be made in criminal proceedings of answers and statements given under compulsion by virtue of those provisions.[9]

As well as cases where the privilege has been expressly removed by statute, there are cases where statutes have impliedly removed it. For example, in *Re London United Investments plc*,[10] the Court of Appeal held that the privilege was not available to persons who were being examined by inspectors appointed by the Department of Trade and Industry under s 432 of the Companies Act 1985, and in *Bank of England v Riley*,[11] the Court of Appeal held that it was not available to persons being examined under the Banking Act 1987. In the *Bishopsgate*[12] case, the Court of Appeal held that the privilege was not available where inquiries were being conducted by persons such as liquidators under s 235 of the Insolvency Act 1986, or by the court under s 236.

The privilege has to be claimed on oath by the person who wishes to rely on it. Thus, where the privilege was claimed by a solicitor on his client's behalf, it was held that the claim had not been properly made. But a person who claims the privilege does not have to show in detail why disclosure might incriminate him, because such a requirement might expose him to the peril against which the privilege is designed to protect him.[13]

Legal professional privilege

The scope of legal professional privilege at common law is reflected in s 10 of the Police and Criminal Evidence Act 1984.[14] There are three categories:

(a) Communications between a professional legal adviser and his client, or any person representing his client, made in connection with the giving of legal advice to the client. Here the communication is a two-way system and can be thought of in the form of a straight line, with the client or his agent at one end and the legal adviser at the other. The legal advice can be of any kind and does not have to be connected with litigation or the prospect of it. The protection is available even where the lawyer is an 'in-house' lawyer advising his employers.[15] In *Balabel v Air India*,[16] Taylor LJ

---

9 Youth Justice and Criminal Evidence Act 1999, s 59 and Sched 3.

10 [1992] 2 All ER 842.

11 [1992] 1 All ER 769.

12 See above, fn 8.

13 *Downie v Coe* (1997) *The Times*, 28 November.

14 *R v Central Criminal Court ex p Francis and Francis* [1988] 3 WLR 989. The section defines 'items subject to legal privilege' in the context of powers of entry, search and seizure.

15 *Alfred Crompton Amusement Machines Ltd v Customs and Excise Commrs* [1972] 2 QB 102, p 129. The decision of the Court of Appeal on this point was not challenged in the subsequent appeal to the House of Lords.

16 [1988] Ch 317.

said that, although the test for a privileged communication was whether it had been made confidentially for the purpose of obtaining legal advice, this purpose was not to be narrowly construed and should be taken to include practical advice about what should be done in the relevant legal context. In line with this approach, Colman J, in *NRG v Bacon and Woodrow*,[17] observed that a solicitor's duty frequently includes advising on the commercial wisdom of entering into a transaction in relation to which legal advice has been sought.

(b) Communications between lawyer, client *and third parties* for the purpose of pending or contemplated litigation. It is enough if the litigation is contemplated only by the party asking for advice; the other prospective party to the litigation can be totally ignorant of the fact that litigation might arise.[18] The lines of communication can be seen as forming a triangle so as to involve three parties instead of two. Here the communications with the third parties – often other professionals such as surveyors, doctors or accountants – will be protected only if the *dominant purpose* is for use in litigation, pending or contemplated.

The 'dominant purpose' test was settled by the House of Lords in *Waugh v British Railways Board*.[19] The appellant's husband was employed by the British Railways Board. A train that he was driving collided with another and he died as a result. His widow brought an action under the Fatal Accidents Acts. This appeal arose from an interlocutory application by the plaintiff for disclosure by the Board of a report, called 'the joint inquiry report', made by officers of the Board two days after the accident. The Board had resisted, claiming legal professional privilege for it. The document had been prepared for a dual purpose: for railway operation and safety purposes and for the purpose of obtaining legal advice in anticipation of litigation. Both purposes were of equal weight. The House of Lords held that this was not enough to support a claim for privilege. For privilege to be available, the purpose of preparing for litigation had to be the sole or dominant purpose of the document under consideration. Since the purposes in this case were of equal weight, there was no dominant purpose and the report was ordered to be disclosed.

(c) Items enclosed with or referred to in communications of types (a) or (b), *provided the items came into existence in connection with the giving of legal advice* and are in the possession of a person who is entitled to possession of them. The point here is that the privilege exists to protect communications between client, legal adviser and, sometimes, third parties. It does not exist to protect evidence from production. To take an obvious example, suppose Charlie murders Bertie after planning the crime carefully on paper. He

---

17 [1995] 1 All ER 976.

18 *Plummers Ltd v Debenhams plc* [1986] BCLC 447 (Ch D).

19 [1980] AC 521; *Sourcebook*, p 420.

cannot prevent the police from obtaining this document by handing it to his solicitor. Even if an object or document is placed in a solicitor's hands for the legitimate purpose of obtaining advice in connection with the defence case, privilege will not protect it. In *R v King*[20] the defendant had been charged with conspiracy to defraud. He sent some documents to his solicitors so that they could obtain the opinion of a handwriting expert on them. The defence later decided not to call the expert, but the prosecution served him with a subpoena compelling him to produce in court the documents that he had received from the defence solicitors.[21] The Court of Appeal upheld the trial judge's decision that legal professional privilege did not protect them. *They had not been brought into existence for the purpose of the solicitor and client relationship.*

Copies of original documents are, of course, frequently brought into existence in the course of this relationship. Whether *their* disclosure can be compelled depends on whether the *originals* would have been privileged or not. If the originals would not, the copies will not attract privilege just because they are part of a set of instructions to enable the client to obtain legal advice.[22]

Legal professional privilege will not protect a communication to facilitate crime or fraud. The principle is easy to state but not always easy to apply. 'Fraud' is very widely defined to include, in addition to the tort of deceit, 'all forms of fraud and dishonesty such as fraudulent breach of contract, fraudulent conspiracy, trickery and sham contrivances'.[23] It may be difficult in a particular case to determine whether a client was obtaining advice to *facilitate* a fraud in this wide sense or to *avoid* one. A solicitor, of course, can quite properly be asked for advice about the effect of a proposed transaction by a client who wishes to avoid prosecution or civil litigation. But in a doubtful case it will be easier to argue that the communication was not to facilitate a crime or fraud where the lawyer is asked to explain the effect of what has already been done, rather than to advise about the structuring of a transaction that has yet to be carried out.[24]

This exception to the scope of legal professional privilege has more recently been expressed by saying that for the privilege to apply there must be

---

20 [1983] 1 WLR 411.

21 There was, of course, no attempt to get him to disclose the instructions he had received from the defence solicitors or his own advice to them.

22 *Dubai Bank v Galadari* [1989] 3 All ER 769.

23 *Crescent Farm (Sidcup) Sports Ltd v Sterling Offices Ltd* [1972] Ch 553, p 565, *per* Goff J. Cf s 10(2) of PACE, which provides that items held with the intention of furthering a criminal purpose are not subject to legal professional privilege. Perhaps surprisingly, this has been interpreted to include items that were the subject of a third party's intention to further a criminal purpose: *Central Criminal Court v Francis and Francis* [1989] AC 346.

24 *Barclays Bank v Eustice* [1995] 1 WLR 1238, pp 1249–50, *per* Schiemann LJ; *Sourcebook*, p 417.

'absence of iniquity'.[25] The breadth of this concept is illustrated by *Barclays Bank v Eustice*.[26] In that case 'iniquity' was held to include obtaining advice about how to structure a series of transactions at an undervalue that would have had the effect of prejudicing the interests of creditors.[27] The Court of Appeal held that it made no difference that neither the solicitor nor even the client realised that this would be the effect of what was proposed.[28] It has been held at first instance that criminal or fraudulent conduct undertaken by private investigators in the conduct of litigation can also cause the privilege to be lost. In *Dubai Aluminium Co Ltd v Al Alawi*,[29] Dubai sued the defendant in respect of his conduct while he was its sales manager and obtained a worldwide Mareva, or 'freezing', injunction against him. The defendant applied to have the injunction discharged on the ground that, while investigating his finances and assets, Dubai's agents had contravened the Data Protection Act 1984 and Swiss laws on banking secrecy. In pursuit of his claim to discharge the injunction, he applied for an order requiring Dubai to disclose the documents relating to their investigation. He accepted that these were *prima facie* subject to legal professional privilege, but he argued that the privilege did not attach to them because they were part of, or relevant to, iniquitous acts by Dubai. Rix J found on the facts that there was a strong *prima facie* case of criminal or fraudulent conduct in the obtaining of information about the defendant's accounts. He held that such conduct constituted 'crime, fraud or iniquity' so as to remove the protection of legal professional privilege, saying that if investigative agents employed by solicitors for the purpose of litigation were permitted to indulge in criminal or fraudulent conduct without any consequence for the conduct of the litigation, the courts would be going far towards sanctioning such conduct. The defendant had also complained that his dustbins had been searched, and documents taken from them and copied before being put back, but Rix J held that such civil wrongs did not amount to 'crime, fraud or iniquity'.

Expert reports prepared for the purpose of current litigation will normally be covered by legal professional privilege. But reports from experts such as doctors and psychiatrists brought into existence by parties to cases involving the welfare of children are an exception. The overriding duty to regard the welfare of a child as paramount in such cases will not allow the parties to suppress 'unfavourable' reports. However, only reports of third parties are

---

25 *Ventouris v Mountain* [1991] 1 WLR 607, p 611, *per* Bingham LJ; *Barclays Bank v Eustice* [1995] 1 WLR 1238, p 1252, *per* Schiemann LJ.

26 [1995] 1 WLR 1238.

27 See Insolvency Act 1986, s 423.

28 If it were otherwise, the communications between a client and an incompetent solicitor might be protected, while those between a client and a competent one would not.

29 [1999] 1 All ER 703.

affected by this rule. Privilege continues to apply to communications between legal advisers and their clients in actions of this kind.[30]

Duration of the privilege

The general rule is, 'once privileged, always privileged'.[31] So documents prepared for one action will continue to be privileged in subsequent litigation, even though the subject matter or the parties may be different. A good example of this is *The Aegis Blaze*.[32] The defendants were the owners of the vessel *Aegis Blaze*. In December 1980, a cargo was damaged while being carried in that vessel. In March 1981, proceedings in respect of that loss were in contemplation and the defendants' solicitors instructed surveyors to inspect the vessel (which lay at Sibenik in Yugoslavia) for the purpose of obtaining evidence. The surveyors reported to the solicitors in the same month. It was common ground that their report ('the Sibenik report') was privileged from production, at least in the litigation then contemplated.

In July 1981, another cargo was damaged while being carried in the vessel on another voyage. Two lots of different cargo owners sued to recover in respect of this loss. They knew of the Sibenik report and wanted it to be disclosed to them. It was agreed that it was relevant to their case, but the defendants claimed that because it was privileged in relation to the first proceedings it was privileged in relation to the second also.

The Court of Appeal upheld the defendants' argument. Parker LJ said that if a party claiming privilege in a second action is the party entitled to privilege in an earlier action, but there is no connection of subject matter whatever, it is most improbable that a question of privilege will arise, because in such circumstances the document will not be relevant, and so not disclosable. But if there is a sufficient connection for the document to be relevant, then the party entitled to the privilege will be able to assert it in the second action. If this were not the case, the court would again and again have to become involved on discovery in balancing the interests of the public in protecting access to legal advice against the interests of the public in having all relevant information available at the trial of actions.

Another example of the maxim 'once privileged, always privileged' is the rule whereby documents concerning property rights that are privileged in the hands of one owner are privileged in the hands of that person's successors in title.[33]

---

30 *Oxfordshire County Council v M* [1994] Fam 295.
31 *Calcraft v Guest* [1898] 1 QB 759, p 761, *per* Lindley MR; *Sourcebook*, p 411.
32 [1986] 1 Lloyd's Rep 203.
33 *Minet v Morgan* (1873) 8 Ch App 361.

It used to be thought that where the holder of a privilege could derive no further benefit from its exercise, the privilege could be defeated by the interest of another person who needed to have access to the information, particularly where this was needed to defeat a criminal charge.[34] However, since the decision of the House of Lords in *R v Derby Magistrates ex p B*,[35] it is clear that this is not the case. The problem in this case stemmed from the murder, in April 1978, of a girl of 16. Shortly afterwards, the applicant, B, was arrested. At first he denied involvement, but subsequently admitted sole responsibility. He was charged with murder. Preparations for trial were well advanced when, in October 1978, he was seen by a psychiatrist. Following that interview, he changed his story and made a statement to the effect that his stepfather had killed the girl. He admitted being present at the time and to taking some part, but he said that he had been under duress. At his trial in November, he relied on this account and was acquitted.

In July 1992, the stepfather was arrested and charged with the murder. Committal proceedings were begun, and the applicant was called on behalf of the prosecution to give evidence. In the course of cross-examination on behalf of his stepfather, he was asked about instructions that he had given the solicitors acting for him in 1978. The question arose whether he could still maintain the legal professional privilege attaching to those communications. The magistrate, following earlier cases, decided that he had to balance the two public interests[36] and decided in favour of disclosure. But the House of Lords said that earlier decisions had been wrong. The principle remains that a man must be able to consult his lawyer in confidence, since otherwise he might hold back half the truth. The client must be sure that what he tells his lawyer will never be revealed without consent. Legal professional privilege is much more than an ordinary rule of evidence; it is a fundamental condition on which the administration of justice rests.

Bypassing the privilege via secondary evidence

Legal professional privilege prevents facts *from having to be disclosed*. It does not prevent the facts *from being proved* if any other means of doing so can be found. For example, in *Calcraft v Guest*,[37] the appellant had obtained copies of certain privileged documents and so was in a position to prove the contents of the originals by means of secondary evidence. Was he entitled to do so? The Court of Appeal held that he was, and approved an earlier *dictum* of Parke B

34　*R v Barton* [1973] 1 WLR 115; *R v Ataou* [1988] QB 798.

35　[1995] 3 WLR 681; *Sourcebook*, p 424.

36　In protecting access to legal advice and in having all relevant and admissible evidence available at trial.

37　[1898] 1 QB 759.

to the effect that even if the original had been stolen, a correct copy of it could be admitted.

It may be possible to block this escape route if the party who stands to lose the benefit of the privilege can obtain an injunction to restrain the use of the copies. This is what happened in *Ashburton v Pape*,[38] in which Cozens-Hardy MR explained the decision as follows:

(a) *Calcraft v Guest* establishes only that if a litigant wants to prove a particular document whose original he cannot produce because of privilege, he may produce a copy as secondary evidence even though the copy has been obtained by improper, even criminal, means. The reason why he can do so is that in the main action, in which the copy is to be used, the court is not concerned with the circumstances in which the evidence was obtained.

(b) The situation is different where proceedings are brought that have those circumstances as their central concern, such as proceedings for an injunction to restrain the use of the copy document. In other words, the question is one of *relevance*.

In *Ashburton v Pape*, Swinfen Eady LJ said that the basis of the remedy is the principle, on which the Court of Chancery acted for many years, that allows a court to restrain the publication of confidential information improperly or surreptitiously obtained, or of information imparted in confidence that ought not to be divulged. The fact that an original or copy document is *admissible* according to evidence law is no answer to the demand of the lawful owner for delivery up of the document, and no answer to the application of the lawful owner of confidential information to restrain it from being published or copied.[39] However, in *Goddard v Nationwide Building Society*,[40] Nourse LJ took the view that the basis of relief was not the confidential nature of the communications but the legal professional privilege attaching to them. The importance of this distinction may lie in the fact that on the more recent view there appears to be less scope for a judge to exercise his discretion when deciding whether to grant the injunction. It had been suggested that a judge should conduct a balancing exercise, taking into account, for example, the way in which the information had been obtained and its importance to the issues being tried.[41] But in *Derby and Co Ltd v Weldon (No 8)*,[42] the Court of Appeal held that such an exercise was inappropriate where the court was being asked for an injunction in support of legal professional privilege.

---

38 [1913] 2 Ch D 469; *Sourcebook*, p 412.

39 See the judgment of Swinfen Eady LJ in *Calcraft v Guest*. Separate proceedings are not necessary and an application can be made at any time up to the point when the copies are used by the party who has obtained them: *Webster v James Chapman and Co* [1989] 3 All ER 939.

40 [1986] 3 All ER 264.

41 *Webster v James Chapman and Co* [1989] 3 All ER 939 (Scott J).

42 [1990] 3 All ER 762.

Where a privileged document, or a copy, has been obtained by trickery or by some other improper means, a party wishing to prevent its use must apply for an injunction. But sometimes, privileged documents are accidentally included among documents that a party has a duty to disclose to his opponent under r 31 of the CPR. Where this happens, the party who has seen the document may use its contents only with the court's permission.[43] It is likely that in deciding whether to grant permission the court will be guided by cases decided before the Civil Procedure Rules came into force. The principle formerly applied was that where it was obvious that the document had been disclosed by mistake the privilege continued to apply. But if the person examining the document might reasonably have concluded that the privilege was being waived, it would be lost.[44]

In *Butler v Board of Trade*,[45] it was held that public policy would prevent an injunction of this kind from being granted where its effect would be to restrain the prosecution from adducing admissible evidence in criminal proceedings. In a case where the prosecution obtained a privileged communication by accident rather than impropriety, the Court of Appeal held that it could be used during the cross-examination of the defendant.[46]

Journalists' sources

There are no other types of communication protected by privilege, but there is a special provision for the protection of journalists' sources in s 10 of the Contempt of Court Act 1981. This provides:

> No court may require a person to disclose, nor is any person guilty of contempt of court for refusing to disclose, the source of information contained in a publication for which he is responsible, unless it be established to the satisfaction of the court that disclosure is necessary in the interests of justice or national security or for the prevention of disorder or crime.

The burden is on the party who wishes to obtain disclosure to prove that one or more of the conditions is satisfied.[47] In order to show that an order for disclosure is necessary, a claimant must show that all other reasonable means have been employed to identify the source, but without success.[48]

---

43 CPR, r 31.20.

44 Compare *IBM Corpn v Phoenix International (Computers) Ltd* [1995] 1 All ER 413 and *Pizzey v Ford Motor Co Ltd* (1993) *The Times*, 8 March.

45 [1971] Ch 680.

46 *R v Tompkins* (1977) 67 Cr App R 181. See also *R v Cottrill* [1997] Crim LR 56.

47 *Secretary of State for Defence v Guardian Newspapers Ltd* [1985] AC 339.

48 *Ashworth Hospital Authority v MGN Ltd* [2001] 1 All ER 991, p 1011, *per* Lord Phillips MR.

The meaning of 'necessary' has been considered in several cases. In *Re An Inquiry Under the Company Securities (Insider Dealing) Act 1985*,[49] Lord Griffiths said:

> I doubt if it is possible to go further than to say that 'necessary' has a meaning that lies somewhere between 'indispensable' on the one hand, and 'useful' or 'expedient' on the other, and to leave it to the judge to decide towards which end of the scale of meaning he will place it on the facts of any particular case. The nearest paraphrase I can suggest is 'really needed'.[50]

In *Camelot Group plc v Centaur Communications Ltd*,[51] there was a continuing threat that further information would be improperly disclosed by an employee, and the unease and suspicion that the leaks had caused was inhibiting good working relationships. Schiemann LJ said that in such cases, the following legal principles applied:

- There is an important public interest in the press being able to protect the anonymity of its sources.

- But the law does not enable the press to protect that anonymity in all circumstances.

- When assessing whether a disclosure order should be made, a relevant but not conclusive factor is that an employer may wish to identify the employee so as to exclude him from future employment.

- Whether sufficiently strong reasons are shown in a particular case will depend on the facts.

- Great weight will be given to judgments in cases, especially if they are recent, where the facts were similar.[52]

Since these decisions, however, the Court of Appeal has emphasised the significance of the European Convention on Human Rights, and it remains to be seen if disclosure would be ordered if similar situations were to recur. Section 10 must be read in the light of Art 10 of the Convention. This provides:

1   Everyone has the right to freedom of expression. This right shall include freedom to hold opinions and to receive and impart information and ideas without interference by public authority and regardless of frontiers ...

2   The exercise of these freedoms, since it carries with it duties and responsibilities, may be subject to such formalities, conditions, restrictions or penalties as are prescribed by law and are necessary in a democratic society, in the interests of national security, territorial integrity or public

---

49   [1988] AC 660.

50   *Ibid*, p 704.

51   [1998] 1 All ER 251.

52   *Ibid*, pp 257–60. See also *Michael O'Mara Books Ltd v Express Newspapers plc* (1998) *The Times*, 6 March, where a court at first instance ordered disclosure because suspicions about the leak of information had affected the reputation of two innocent companies, and where there remained the threat of further leaks.

safety, for the prevention of disorder of crime, for the protection of health or morals, for the protection of the reputation or rights of others, for preventing the disclosure of information received in confidence, or for maintaining the authority and impartiality of the judiciary.

In *Ashworth Hospital Authority v MGN Ltd*,[53] the Court of Appeal held that the interpretation of s 10 of the Contempt of Court Act 1981 should, so far as possible, equate the specific purposes for which an order for disclosure of sources is permitted under the Act with the legitimate aims in Art 10 of the Convention, and should apply the same test of necessity as that applied by the European Court of Human Rights when interpreting that Article. The Court also held that, by analogy with Art 10, 'the interests of justice' is not confined to the administration of justice in courts of law, but covers all interests that are justiciable. Thus where, as in the *Ashworth Hospital Authority* case, there have been leaks of information from confidential hospital records, the health authority can argue that its claim for identification of the source is in the interests of the protection of health, the protection of the rights of others and the prevention of the disclosure of information received in confidence.

But the Court of Appeal pointed out that the approach of the European Court to the question whether an order for disclosure should be made involves something more than deciding whether, on the facts, it is necessary for the achievement of a legitimate aim. It must also be considered whether the achievement of the legitimate aim is, on the facts, so important that it overrides the considerable public interest in protecting journalists' sources. Protecting journalists' sources protects free communication of information to and through the press; orders for source disclosure have a 'chilling effect' on the exercise of that freedom. Lord Phillips MR, in a judgment with which the other members of the court agreed, acknowledged that the decisions of the European Court showed that freedom of the press had in the past carried greater weight in Strasbourg than in the United Kingdom.[54] Thus, earlier decisions under s 10 may have lost some of their authority, and perhaps the courts will be less ready to make disclosure orders in future.

Without prejudice statements[55]

This head of privilege is founded partly on the public policy of encouraging litigants to settle their differences rather than pursuing them to the bitter end. It is founded also on the express or implied agreement of the parties that communications in the course of their negotiations should not be admissible

---

53 [2001] 1 All ER 991.

54 *Ibid*, pp 1010–12.

55 Statements that are 'without prejudice' to their maker if the terms proposed are not accepted. See *Walker v Wilsher* (1889) 23 QBD 335, p 337.

in evidence if the negotiations break down.[56] The rule applies to exclude from evidence all negotiations genuinely aimed at settlement, whether oral or in writing. The application of the rule does not depend on the use of the expression 'without prejudice', though it is no doubt safer to use it. If the circumstances make it clear that the parties were trying to settle a claim, evidence of the negotiations will not generally be admissible to establish an admission. Conversely, the use of the 'without prejudice' label will be of no effect where there is no attempt at settlement.[57]

Evidence of the negotiations will be admissible if it is necessary to show the terms of a settlement that was ultimately reached: for example, where one of the parties wants to sue on that agreement.[58] But it does not follow that the privilege no longer applies just because a settlement has been reached. For example, where several parties are engaged in building construction works, there is a risk that at some stage there will be litigation between two or more of them. Suppose the main contractor makes certain admissions in an attempt to settle a dispute with one of the subcontractors. If those admissions could be used against him by other subcontractors with whom he was also in dispute, this would discourage settlements with *any* of the subcontractors. The House of Lords decided, therefore, in *Rush and Tompkins Ltd v GLC*,[59] that generally the without prejudice rule makes evidence of negotiations inadmissible *in any subsequent litigation connected with the same subject matter*.

PUBLIC INTEREST IMMUNITY

Public interest immunity ('PII'), formerly called 'Crown privilege', is a rule of law that requires the withholding of documents on the ground that it would be harmful to the public interest to disclose them. A convenient starting point for examining this rule is the decision of the House of Lords in *Duncan v Cammell Laird*.[60] That action was brought by the dependants of men who had died when a submarine sank during trials. It was alleged that the defendants, who built the submarine, had been negligent. Among the documents that the plaintiffs wanted to obtain on discovery were contracts between the defendants and the Admiralty, and salvage reports. The Admiralty resisted disclosure on the ground of national security. The House of Lords held that

---

56 *Unilever plc v The Proctor and Gamble Co* [2001] 1 All ER 783, pp 789–90, 796, *per* Robert Walker LJ.
57 *Paddock v Forrester* (1842) 3 Man&G 903; *Oliver v Nautilus SS Co* [1903] 2 KB 639; *Re Daintrey ex p Holt* [1893] 2 QB 116.
58 *Tomlin v Standard Telephones and Cables Ltd* [1969] 1 WLR 1368. For other exceptions, see *Unilever plc v The Proctor and Gamble Co* [2001] 1 All ER 783, pp 792–93.
59 [1989] AC 1280; *Sourcebook*, p 423. Cf *Gnitrow Ltd v Cape plc* [2000] 3 All ER 763.
60 [1942] AC 264; *Sourcebook* p 427.

the court was bound to accept the minister's certificate that disclosure of these documents would be harmful to the public interest. The effect of this decision was that a court could never question a claim of Crown privilege, if made in the proper form, regardless of the nature of the documents that the government wished to keep secret. The House of Lords said that claims to Crown privilege could be put on two alternative grounds:

(a) Disclosure of the *contents* of the particular documents would harm the public interest, for example, by endangering national security or prejudicing diplomatic relations.

(b) The documents belonged to a *class* of documents that had to be withheld in the interests of 'the proper functioning of the public service'.

In 1956, the Lord Chancellor, Viscount Kilmuir, made a statement in the House of Lords indicating that the class of documents routinely withheld to protect 'the proper functioning of the public service' would be narrowed by excluding those categories of documents that appeared to be particularly relevant to litigation, and for which the highest degree of confidentiality was not required in the public interest. These included road accident reports, ordinary contractual documents, and medical records and reports. He added, 'We also propose that if medical documents, or indeed other documents, are relevant to the defence in criminal proceedings, Crown privilege should not be claimed.' In this statement, Kilmuir explained that the reason for claiming Crown privilege on a class, as opposed to a contents basis, was that it was needed to secure 'freedom and candour of communications with and within the public service', so that government decisions could be taken on the best advice and with the fullest information. People advising the government must be able to know that they were doing so in confidence, and that any document containing their advice would not subsequently be disclosed.[61]

The beginning of the modern approach to PII can be seen in the decision of the House of Lords in *Conway v Rimmer*.[62] The plaintiff, who had been a probationary police officer, brought an action against his former superintendent for malicious prosecution. (He had been prosecuted for theft from a fellow probationer and acquitted.) His legal advisers wanted to obtain on discovery a number of confidential reports which had been made on the plaintiff during his probationary period. These were likely to be relevant to the issue of malice, and both sides wanted them to be produced. The Home Secretary objected. The House of Lords took the opportunity to reverse its earlier ruling in *Duncan v Cammell Laird*, and held that in such cases it was for the court to decide where the balance of public interest lay: in protecting a government claim for secrecy, or in upholding a litigant's right to have all relevant materials available for the proper adjudication of his claim. But the

---

61 *HL Deb*, col 741–48, 6 June 1956.
62 [1968] AC 910; *Sourcebook*, p 429.

idea that public interest immunity might be based on a class rather than a contents claim was still accepted, and it was said that the reason for supporting a class claim was that disclosure 'would create or fan ill-informed or captious public or political criticism', or would be 'inimical to the proper functioning of the public service'.[63]

PII can operate in cases not involving the government. In *R v Lewes JJ ex p Secretary of State for the Home Department*,[64] it was said that the old expression 'Crown privilege' was wrong and misleading. While a minister was always an appropriate, and often the most appropriate, person to assert the public interest, it is open to any person to raise the question, and there may be cases where the trial judge should do so if no one else has. So, for example, in *D v NSPCC*,[65] the House of Lords protected the anonymity of an informer who had reported suspicions of child cruelty to the NSPCC.

An important distinction between public interest immunity and the sort of privilege that might be claimed by a private litigant, such as legal professional privilege or the privilege against self-incrimination, used to be that a privilege might be waived, but a claim to public interest immunity could not. As Lord Scarman said in *Air Canada v Secretary of State for Trade*,[66] 'The Crown, when it puts forward a public interest immunity objection, is not claiming a privilege but discharging a duty'. Similarly, in *Makanjuola v Commissioner of Metropolitan Police*,[67] Bingham LJ said that, 'public interest immunity is not a trump card vouchsafed to certain privileged players to play when and as they wish'.[68] It cannot 'in any ordinary sense' be waived, because although rights can be waived, duties cannot. It follows that where a litigant holds documents in a class *prima facie* immune, he should (save in a very exceptional case) assert that they are immune, and decline to disclose them, since the ultimate decision about where the balance of public interest lies is not for him, but for the court. This approach, coupled with a class claim rather than a contents claim, led to undesirably wide public interest immunity claims being made by ministers in a number of trials. The practice was criticised in the Scott report,[69] and the central government has now effectively abandoned class claims.[70]

---

63 [1968] AC 910, pp 952, 993–94.

64 [1973] AC 388, p 400.

65 [1978] AC 171; *Sourcebook*, p 437.

66 [1983] 2 AC 394, p 446; *Sourcebook*, p 444.

67 [1992] 3 All ER 617.

68 *Ibid*, p 623.

69 Report of the Inquiry into the Export of Defence Equipment and Dual-Use Goods to Iraq and Related Prosecutions, 15 February 1996 (HC 115).

70 Attorney General's statement to the House of Commons, *HC Deb*, Vol 287, cols 949–57, and Lord Chancellor's statement to the House of Lords, *HL Deb*, Vol 576, cols 1507–17, 18 December 1996.

Further, in *R v Chief Constable of West Midlands Police ex p Wiley*,[71] the House of Lords held that a class claim cannot be made in respect of documents compiled as part of the investigation of a complaint against the police, and it seems likely that class claims generally will be much reduced in future. In *Ex p Wiley*, Lord Woolf acknowledged that Bingham LJ's *dicta* in *Makanjuola* had provided 'a very clear statement as to the nature of public interest immunity', but suggested that the *dicta* had been applied subsequently in a manner beyond what Bingham LJ had intended.[72] As was shown above, Bingham LJ was not referring to something new when he used the 'trump card' analogy: In *Air Canada,* Lord Scarman had spoken similarly of a duty rather than a right. But after *ex p Wiley,* it is clear that if a minister believes that the overriding public interest requires government documents to be *disclosed,* he is not obliged to request immunity for them. It appears that ministers must now consider, before making a claim for PII, whether the public interest is better served by disclosure than by concealment. It looks very much as if they are expected to exercise a discretion in deciding whether or not to claim PII.

In recent decades, the leading cases on PII in the House of Lords have been concerned with civil claims, and it seems that the judges in those cases did not regard themselves as expressing principles that were equally applicable in criminal trials.[73] In *R v Governor of Brixton Prison ex p Osman,*[74] Mann LJ said that he thought they should apply, although he acknowledged that great weight should be attached in such cases to the need to do justice to the defendant. Sir Richard Scott has argued, however, that this view is contradicted by *dicta* in both old and modern criminal cases.[75]

Suppose a defendant in a criminal case requests information from the prosecution, such as the name of an informer, relating to the methods by which offences are investigated. The prosecution claims PII. This is a good example of a situation where no real balancing of interests is done by a criminal court. While the relevance of such information in a particular case is not uncritically accepted, the line taken is that, if such information is in fact relevant to the conduct of the defence, it must be disclosed. The basic rule is that in public prosecutions witnesses may not be asked, and will not be allowed to disclose, the names of informers or the nature of the information given. Thus in *Marks v Beyfus,*[76] an action for malicious prosecution, the Director of Public Prosecutions was called as a witness by the plaintiff but

---

71 [1995] 1 AC 274.

72 *Ibid,* p 296.

73 Scott, Sir R, 'The acceptable and unacceptable use of public interest immunity' [1996] PL 427, pp 430–32.

74 [1991] 1 WLR 281 (DC).

75 *Ibid,* Scott, pp 432–35.

76 (1890) 25 QBD 494; *Sourcebook,* p 425.

refused on grounds of public policy to give the names of his informers or to produce the statement on which he had acted in directing the earlier unsuccessful prosecution of the plaintiff. His objection was upheld by the trial judge and by the Court of Appeal. The reason for the rule is that informers need to be protected, both for their own safety and to ensure that the supply of information about criminal activities does not dry up.

However, in *Marks v Beyfus*, Lord Esher qualified this basic rule by stating that it could be departed from if the disclosure of the name of the informant was necessary to show the defendant's innocence. In such a case one public policy would be in conflict with another, and the policy that an innocent man should not be condemned when his innocence could be proved had to prevail. But it is for the defendant to show that there is a good reason for disclosure.[77]

An example of a case where disclosure was considered appropriate is *R v Agar*.[78] In that case, a prosecution for possession of drugs, the Court of Appeal said that the trial judge should have ordered the informer's name to be disclosed. The accused's defence was that the informer and the police had acted together to frame him. The information was necessary for a proper presentation of the defence case because disclosure of the informer's identity might have given weight to the defendant's testimony. But disclosure will not be ordered in the usual case, where knowledge of the informer will not affect the defence. An example is *R v Slowcombe*.[79] Following a tip off, the defendant had been arrested in possession of a shotgun outside a sub post office. He claimed to have been recruited by V and to have been told by him that there was an accomplice working in the post office who would hand over the money, but that the gun was necessary for the sake of appearances. The defendant argued that he was not guilty of conspiracy to rob, but only of conspiracy to steal. The judge refused a defence application to ask a police officer whether the informer had been V. The Court of Appeal upheld this decision. If V had not been the informer, the defendant's story could still have been true. If V *had* been the informer, that would not establish that only a theft had been planned. V could have conspired with the defendant to commit the robbery but then have turned informer. Disclosing the name of the informer could therefore contribute little or nothing to the issue the jury had to consider, which was whether the defendant's explanation might reasonably have been true.[80]

The rule in *Marks v Beyfus*[81] also protects the identity of persons who have allowed their premises to be used for police observation, as well as the

---

77 *R v Hennessey* (1978) 68 Cr App R 419. See also *R v Keane* [1994] 1 WLR 746; *R v Menga and Marshalleck* [1998] Crim LR 58.

78 [1990] 2 All ER 442.

79 [1991] Crim LR 198.

80 In *R v Turner* [1995] 1 WLR 264 Lord Taylor CJ said that judges should scrutinise applications for disclosure of informers with very great care and should ensure that the information requested was essential to the running of the defence.

81 (1890) 25 QBD 494; *Sourcebook*, p 425.

identity of the premises from which observation was kept. But even if the defendant argues that identification of the premises is necessary to establish his innocence (because, for example, it has a bearing on the accuracy of witness observations) the judge may still refuse to allow the question to be put. In *R v Johnson*,[82] where the defendant was charged with supplying drugs, the only evidence against him was supplied by police officers who had kept observation from private premises. The defence applied to cross-examine about the exact location in order to test whether the officers could have seen what they said they did. The trial judge ruled that the exact location should not be revealed, and the Court of Appeal upheld his decision. But the prosecution must first provide a proper evidential basis to support their claim for protection of identity. In *R v Johnson*, Watkins LJ stated the following as minimum requirements:

(a) The police officer in charge of the observations must testify that he visited all the observation places to be used and ascertained the attitude of their occupiers, both as to the use to be made of them and to possible subsequent disclosure.

(b) A police officer of at least the rank of chief inspector must testify that immediately prior to the trial he visited the places used for observation and ascertained whether the occupiers were the same as when the observation took place and, whether they were or not, the attitude of those occupiers to possible disclosure of their use as observation points.

The object of keeping the identity of premises secret is to protect the owner or occupier. Where this consideration does not apply, cross-examination may be permitted on the details of surveillance. Thus in *R v Brown*,[83] where officers gave evidence that they had kept observation from an unmarked police vehicle, it was held that the defence were entitled to information relating to the surveillance and to the colour, make and model of the vehicle.

---

82   [1989] 1 All ER 121.
83   (1987) 87 Cr App R 52.

CHAPTER 14

FACTS NOT REQUIRING PROOF

The general rule is that if a party wants to rely on a particular fact in support of his case, that fact must be formally proved by providing evidence of it at trial. To this rule, there are two important exceptions: formal admissions and judicial notice.

FORMAL ADMISSIONS

If one party admits the existence of a fact on which the other proposes to rely, he will do so because his legal advisers see that the fact is not in contention, and that it would be pointless and time wasting to insist that it be proved by evidence. *Formal* admissions, however, must be distinguished from *informal* admissions. The latter are frequently referred to simply as 'admissions' (or, in criminal cases, as 'confessions') and the facts to which they refer require proof like any other item of evidence. The reason for this is the difference between formal and informal admissions. A formal admission is made deliberately, for the purpose of the proceedings, and is binding on the party who makes it (unless he is allowed to withdraw it). An informal admission is not deliberately made for the purpose of the proceedings. Even if proved, it is not binding on the maker, who is entitled to explain it away if he can. There is quite likely, also, to be a dispute about whether an informal admission was made at all, or about its terms, or about the sense in which it should be understood. Formal admissions, which are recorded, are far less likely to give rise to these problems. Of course, the fact that someone has said something contrary to his interest will generally increase the probability that what he said was true. For example, in an action for negligence based on a road traffic accident the claimant might adduce evidence that immediately after the accident the defendant said to him, 'I'm terribly sorry; that was entirely my fault. I was distracted by my children in the back of the car'. That clearly constitutes an admission of liability, but unless (as is extremely unlikely) it is *formally* admitted by the defendant, the claimant will have to prove by evidence that it was the defendant who was solely responsible for the collision. The fact that an admission was made can, of course, be used to prove this. Similarly, in a criminal case, a defendant who was charged with murder might say during an interview with the police, 'All right; I admit I used the dead man's credit card'. That would almost certainly be a confession within the meaning of s 82(1) of the Police and Criminal Evidence Act 1984. But unless the defence formally admitted that the defendant *did* use the dead man's card, that fact would need to be proved by evidence at trial. How, then, are formal admissions made?

FORMAL ADMISSIONS IN CIVIL TRIALS

By r 14.1 of the CPR, a party may admit the whole or any part of another party's case. He may do this by giving notice in writing, for example, in a statement of case or by letter. Admissions can also be made in other ways:

- by default, where a defendant fails to deal in his defence with an allegation made by a claimant;[1]
- in response to a notice to admit facts;[2]
- in response to a written request or court order to give additional information.[3]

FORMAL ADMISSIONS IN CRIMINAL TRIALS

At common law, the rule was that there could be no formal admissions, at least by a defendant, in criminal proceedings. The basis of this was that it was contrary to public interest to waive the rules of evidence by consent in criminal cases. As Sir John Coleridge said in *AG for New South Wales v Bertrand*:

> The object of a trial is the administration of justice in a course as free from doubt or chance of miscarriage as merely human administration of it can be – not the interests of either party. This remark very much lessens the importance of a prisoner's consent, even when he is advised by counsel, and substantially, not of course literally, affirms the wisdom of the common understanding in the profession, that a prisoner can consent to nothing.[4]

A change in this respect was proposed by the Criminal Law Revision Committee in its Ninth Report on Evidence.[5] The Committee thought that if one party was willing to treat something as proved, it was unnecessary for the other party to have the burden of proving it. The existing law could lead to considerable waste of time and money, as, for example, in a conspiracy trial mentioned by the Committee, in which it had been necessary to bring a witness from Los Angeles to England in order to prove a receipt that the defendant did not dispute. (This was before the time when proof could be

---

1   CPR, r 16.5(5).
2   CPR, r 32.18.
3   CPR, rr 18.1 and 26.5(3).
4   (1867) LR 1 PC 520, p 534.
5   Cmnd 3145, 1966.

made by an agreed written statement, a reform that the Ninth Report also recommended.) Effect was given to the Committee's proposals in s 10 of the Criminal Justice Act 1967, which provided as follows:

(1) Subject to the provisions of this section, any fact of which oral evidence may be given in any criminal proceedings may be admitted for the purpose of those proceedings by or on behalf of the prosecutor or defendant, and the admission by any party of any such fact under this section shall as against that party be conclusive evidence in those proceedings of the fact admitted.

(2) An admission under this section:

(a) may be made before or at the proceedings;

(b) if made otherwise than in court, shall be in writing;

(c) if made in writing by an individual, shall purport to be signed by the person making it and, if so made by a body corporate, shall purport to be signed by a director or manager, or the secretary or clerk, or some other similar officer of the body corporate;

(d) if made on behalf of a defendant who is an individual, shall be made by his counsel or solicitor;

(e) if made at any stage before the trial by a defendant who is an individual, must be approved by his counsel or solicitor (whether at the time it was made or subsequently) before or at the proceedings in question.

(3) An admission under this section for the purpose of proceedings relating to any matter shall be treated as an admission for the purpose of any subsequent criminal proceedings relating to that matter (including any appeal or re-trial).

(4) An admission under this section may with the leave of the court be withdrawn in the proceedings for the purpose of which it is made or any subsequent criminal proceedings relating to the same matter.

Where there is a plea of not guilty at a plea and directions hearing, both prosecution and defence are expected to inform the court of facts which are to be admitted and which can be reduced into writing under s 10(2)(b).[6]

JUDICIAL NOTICE

Broadly speaking, 'judicial notice' refers to the acceptance by a judicial tribunal of the truth of a fact without formal proof, on the ground that it is within the knowledge of the tribunal itself.[7] Beyond this, statements of a general nature are hard to make. Judges and writers have commonly referred

---

6 *Practice Direction (Crown Court: Plea and Directions Hearings)* [1995] 1 WLR 1318, para 10(f).

7 Nokes, GD, *An Introduction to the Law of Evidence*, 4th edn, 1967, p 54.

to 'the doctrine of judicial notice', but this is not an apt expression because it suggests a unity and coherence that the topic does not possess. It is not even possible to say whether, in all circumstances, a judge has a duty rather than a discretion to take judicial notice of a particular fact. As will be shown, there are some statutory provisions that require judicial notice to be taken; in those cases a duty will obviously exist, but beyond that the position is unclear. For example, in *R v Aspinall*, Brett JA said that 'judges are entitled *and bound* to take judicial notice of that which is the common knowledge of the great majority of mankind and of the great majority of men of business'.[8] But according to Cross and Tapper,[9] a judge has a discretion whether or not to take judicial notice of any fact, and there is support for this contention in Commonwealth authority. For example, in *R v Zundel*,[10] a decision of the Ontario Court of Appeal, the defendant was charged with an offence, contrary to s 177 of the Criminal Code, of spreading false news by publishing a pamphlet denying that the Holocaust occurred. His defence was, in part, his belief in the truth of what he had published. Among a number of issues raised on appeal was a submission by the prosecution that the trial judge had erred in failing, at the prosecution's request, to take judicial notice of the fact that the Holocaust did occur. The court upheld his refusal to do so, and stated, relying on works by Thayer and Phipson,[11] that judges have a wide discretion as to matters of which they will take judicial notice, and *may* notice matters which they cannot be *required* to notice. The court pointed out that the generally accepted modern view was that where a court takes judicial notice, that is final, in the sense that the court declares that it will find that a fact exists or will direct the jury to do so. The effect of such a direction in this case would have been to tell the jury that they must conclude the fact of the Holocaust to be so notorious as to be indisputable by reasonable men and women. From that they might have inferred that the defendant knew that what he had published was false, and so the operation of judicial notice would have been gravely prejudicial to the defence. Accordingly, the trial judge had exercised his discretion properly.

The idea of taking judicial notice of facts has been familiar to English lawyers for over 650 years.[12] Various rationales for the practice have been suggested, and a writer's favoured rationale tends to affect his view of the scope and effect of judicial notice. It has been suggested, for example, that the

---

8 (1876) 2 QBD 48, pp 61–62. Emphasis supplied. See also the judgment of Clauson LJ in *McQuaker v Goddard* [1940] 1 KB 687.

9 Tapper, C (ed), *Cross and Tapper on Evidence*, 9th edn, 1999, p 67.

10 (1987) 35 DLR (4th) 338. In *Mullen v Hackney LBC* [1997] 1 WLR 1103 the Court of Appeal assumed without argument that a discretion existed.

11 Thayer, JB, *A Preliminary Treatise on the Law of Evidence at the Common Law*, 1898, p 309; *Phipson on Evidence*, 13th edn, 1982, p 26.

12 Nokes, GD, 'The limits of judicial notice' (1958) 74 LQR 59, p 61, citing *Botton v Wilton* (1302) YB 30 & 31 Edw I (RS), pp 256, 258.

purpose of judicial notice is to save the time and expense involved in adducing formal evidence of matters that are simply *likely to be true*.[13] Another, rather different, view is that the practice reduces the risk of diversion and confusion that would result from disputing what is really *indisputable*. This view was best expressed by EM Morgan:

> In the practical operation of our adversary system, where so much does in fact depend upon the financial resources of the respective parties and the comparative diligence, skill and other qualities of contending counsel, it is especially important that a party be prevented from perverting the true function of the court by presenting a moot issue or securing a wrong result by disputing what is demonstrably indisputable among reasonable persons.[14]

Yet another justification is that judicial notice can make for consistency between cases, in particular by operating as a form of judicial control over the jury. For example, courts take judicial notice of the fact that flick knives and butterfly knives are offensive weapons in themselves for the purposes of s 1 of the Prevention of Crime Act 1953, and juries are to be directed accordingly.[15]

Judicial notice may be applied to facts which a judge can be called upon to accept *either* from his general knowledge of them, *or* from inquiries to be made by him for his own information from sources to which it is proper for him to refer.[16] In addition, statutes have sometimes provided that judicial notice be taken of certain matters. I shall therefore consider this topic under the following heads:

(a) Facts judicially noticed without inquiry.

(b) Facts judicially noticed after inquiry.

(c) Some examples of statutory provisions for judicial notice.

(d) Problems associated with judicial notice.

FACTS JUDICIALLY NOTICED WITHOUT INQUIRY

These are facts that are regarded as matters of common knowledge. Thus in *R v Luffe*,[17] the question arose as to a child's legitimacy. The evidence was that the husband did not have access to the wife until a fortnight before the birth, and the court took judicial notice of the fact that he could not have been the father. Lord Ellenborough CJ remarked:

---

13 Thayer, *op cit*, fn 11, p 309.

14 Morgan, EM, *Some Problems of Proof under the Anglo-American System of Litigation*, 1956, p 42.

15 *R v Simpson* [1983] 3 All ER 789; *DPP v Hynde* [1998] 1 All ER 649. For the definition of a butterfly knife, see the schedule to the Criminal Justice Act 1988 (Offensive Weapons) Order (SI 1988/2019).

16 *Commonwealth Shipping Representative v P and O Branch Service* [1923] AC 191, p 212.

17 (1807) 8 East 193.

Here … in nature the fact may certainly be known that the husband, who had no access until within a fortnight of his wife's delivery, could not be the actual father of the child. Where the thing cannot certainly be known, we must call in aid such probable evidence as can be resorted to, and the intervention of a jury must, in all cases in which it is practicable, be had to decide thereupon; but where the question arises as it does here, and where it may certainly be known from the invariable course of nature, as in this case it may, that no birth could be occasioned and produced within those limits of time, we may venture to lay down the rule plainly and broadly, without any danger arising from the precedent …[18]

Similarly, courts have taken judicial notice of the fact that the nature of an opera singer's work differs from that of an ordinary hired labourer;[19] that cats are kept for domestic purposes;[20] that boys have mischievous natures;[21] that there are large numbers of motor cars and motor buses in the streets of London, and that a boy employed to ride a bicycle through London traffic runs the risk of injury by collision with other vehicles;[22] that people who go to hotels do not like having their nights disturbed,[23] and that the reception of television has become a very common feature of domestic life, and is enjoyed almost entirely for recreational purposes.[24]

More recently, judicial notice has been taken of the fact that stripes are often used on football shirts to identify teams;[25] that Elvis Presley was resident in the USA and performed mainly there;[26] and that more men than women leave surviving spouses.[27]

What is common knowledge differs, of course, according to time and place. Thus the common knowledge of Aesop's fables that was assumed in 1848 would not be assumed today.[28] A fact may be common knowledge only among a class of the community, such as those interested in a particular sport or other form of entertainment, and where that is likely to be the case it is best not to assume that judicial notice will be taken.

---

18 (1807) 8 East 193, pp 201–02.
19 *Lumley v Gye* (1853) 2 E&B 216, pp 266–67.
20 *Nye v Niblett* [1918] 1 KB 23.
21 *Clayton v Hardwicke Colliery Co Ltd* (1915) 85 LJKB 292.
22 *Dennis v AJ White and Co* [1916] 2 KB 6; [1917] AC 479, p 491.
23 *Andreae v Selfridge and Co Ltd* [1938] Ch 1.
24 *Bridlington Relay Ltd v Yorkshire Electricity Board* [1965] Ch 436, p 446.
25 *Cook & Hunt's Design Application* [1979] RPC 197.
26 *RCA Corpn v Pollard* [1982] 2 All ER 468.
27 *Turner v The Labour Party* [1987] IRLR 101.
28 *Hoare v Silverlock* (1848) 12 QB 624.

FACTS JUDICIALLY NOTICED AFTER INQUIRY

Whenever the meaning of words arises, however technical or obscure, then, unless there is some dispute about it, it is common practice for the court to inform itself by any means that is reliable and ready to hand. Counsel usually give any necessary explanation, or reference may be made to a dictionary.[29] For the purposes of more complicated inquiries, reference may be made to such sources as reports of earlier cases, certificates from responsible officials, letters from Secretaries of State or statements made in court by counsel on their behalf, works of reference and the oral statements of witnesses. The cases show that such inquiries have generally been made in at least three types of case: where information is required about current political or diplomatic matters; about historical facts; and about customs, including professional practices.

Current political and diplomatic matters

If a court needs information about matters of this kind, it may formally ask a government minister to provide it. The answer will be regarded as conclusive in relation to the matters with which it deals. A leading case that illustrates this approach is *Duff Development Co Ltd v Government of Kelantan*.[30] In 1912, the Government of Kelantan, which was situated in the Malay Peninsula, granted the appellant company certain mining and other rights by an agreement containing an arbitration clause. Disputes later arose. These were referred to an arbitrator, who made an award in favour of the company. The company subsequently obtained a court order giving it leave to enforce the award. The Government applied to set aside the order on the ground that Kelantan was a Sovereign independent State, and so entitled to immunity from legal process. Before setting aside the order, the master asked the Secretary of State for the Colonies for information as to the status of Kelantan. He received in reply an official letter stating that Kelantan was an independent State and its Sultan the sovereign ruler. It was ultimately held by the House of Lords that this letter was conclusive of the question of sovereignty. Viscount Cave stated:

> It has for some time been the practice of our courts, when such a question is raised, to take judicial notice of the sovereignty of a State, and for that purpose (in any case of uncertainty) to seek information from a Secretary of State; and when information is so obtained the court does not permit it to be questioned by the parties.[31]

---

29 *Baldwin and Francis Ltd v Patents Appeal Tribunal* [1959] AC 663, p 691.

30 [1924] AC 797.

31 *Ibid*, pp 805–06.

Judicial notice has similarly been used in determining the extent of the monarch's territorial sovereignty;[32] whether a person was entitled to diplomatic immunity;[33] and whether a state of war existed between this country and a foreign State.[34]

Historical facts

It was held by the Judicial Committee of the Privy Council in *Read v Bishop of Lincoln*[35] that when it is important to ascertain ancient facts of a public nature, the law permits historical works to be referred to. In the opinion delivered by Lord Halsbury LC, reference was made to earlier occasions when such works had been referred to, and in order to resolve questions concerning Church ritual raised by the *Read* case, Lord Halsbury himself referred in his opinion to the first prayer book of King Edward VI, Wither's *Hymns and Songs of the Church*, which had been licensed by James I and Charles I, and to the writings of Plutarch and St Paul.[36]

The view was formerly taken that while judicial notice might be taken of ancient facts of a public nature, it would not extend to facts of a contemporary, or nearly contemporary kind. Thus in *Commonwealth Shipping Representative v P and O Branch Service*[37] Viscount Cave LC said that he knew of no authority for the proposition that the date of a particular event in a modern war might be stated without proof and an inference based on it. A more liberal approach was, however, suggested by Lord Dunedin, who stated that although he would not feel justified in resting any conclusion on such things as the particular dates when certain operations of war were begun or were in progress, when those dates had not been proved but had to be supplied from his own knowledge, nevertheless:

> ... it is settled by authority that a judge may be aware that there is a state of war; and by that I do not understand a vague consciousness such as may have been felt by an ancient Roman when he noticed that the Temple of Janus was open, but an intelligent apprehension of the state of war as it is and the theatre of the operations thereof.[38]

More recent authority suggests that judicial knowledge may be taken of contemporary, or near contemporary, events. In *Monarch Steamship Co Ltd v*

---

32 *The Fagernes* [1927] P 311.
33 *Engelke v Musman* [1928] AC 433.
34 *R v Bottrill ex p Kuechenmeister* [1947] 1 KB 41.
35 [1892] AC 644.
36 *Ibid*, pp 656, 658, 660.
37 [1923] AC 191, p 197. See also Lord Atkinson at p 206.
38 *Ibid*, p 205.

Karlshamns Oljefabriker (A/B),[39] the question arose whether British shipowners who were parties to a charterparty made in April 1939 should have foreseen that war might break out, with the resulting loss or diversion of the vessel. In the House of Lords, Lord du Parcq said that it was not necessary that the outbreak of war should have been contemplated as something certain and unavoidable; it was enough if the parties might reasonably be assumed to have contemplated a war and the likelihood that it would lead to such an embargo as in fact occurred. He continued, 'Your Lordships are entitled ... to take judicial notice of the facts of history, whether past or contemporaneous with ourselves'. Several of the Law Lords did so. Lord du Parcq himself referred to the Prime Minister's announcement on 31 March 1939 of the guarantee given to Poland, and Lord Wright said:

> There was indeed in 1939 the general fear that there might be war. Munich, the Sudetenland, the invasion by Germany of Czechoslovakia, the difficulty about the Polish Corridor, were matters of common knowledge.[40]

Customs

Judicial notice may be taken of general customs that have been proved in earlier cases, despite the rule[41] that a court cannot treat a fact as proved on the basis of evidence heard in a previous case. For example, in *George v Davies,*[42] the plaintiff, a domestic servant, had entered the defendant's service on 3 November 1910 at yearly wages, payable monthly, without an express agreement as to notice. On 17 November, she gave notice to leave at the expiration of the first month of her service. She left on 3 December. The defendant refused to pay her wages for the month during which she had been in service on the ground that she had left without giving one month's notice. The plaintiff brought an action in the county court to recover the wages, alleging a custom that either party to the contract of hire of a domestic servant was entitled, in the absence of an express agreement, to determine the service at the end of the first month by notice given at or before the expiration of the first fortnight. She called no evidence in support of the custom, but the county court judge said that he had taken judicial notice of the custom in previous cases and would do so again in this one. Accordingly, he gave judgment for the plaintiff. On appeal, the Divisional Court[43] held that he had been entitled to do so. Bray J declared, 'A time must come when a county court judge, having had the question of the existence of this custom before him in other

---

39 [1949] AC 196. See also *Cornelius v Banque Franco-Serbe* [1941] 2 All ER 728; *R v Birkenhead Borough JJ ex p Smith* [1954] 1 WLR 471.

40 [1949] AC 196, pp 234, 222. See also pp 214, 215.

41 See, eg *Roper v Taylor's Central Garages (Exeter) Ltd* [1951] 2 TLR 284.

42 [1911] 2 KB 445.

43 The Divisional Court at that time heard appeals from county courts.

cases, is entitled to say that he will take judicial notice of it, and will not require it to be proved by evidence in each case'.[44] Of course, what is judicially noticed is the existence of the custom; this does not preclude evidence that there was a departure from the custom on a particular occasion. Among other customs judicially noticed have been the practice of the Ordnance Survey Office in compiling Ordnance Survey maps[45] and, it seems, good accountancy practices.[46]

STATUTORY PROVISIONS

Several Acts of Parliament direct the courts to take judicial notice of various matters. For example, the Interpretation Act 1978 provides (re-enacting earlier provisions) that every Act passed after 1850 shall be a public Act and judicially noticed as such unless the contrary is expressly provided.[47] By s 3(2) of the European Communities Act 1972, judicial notice is to be taken of various treaties,[48] of the Official Journal of the Communities, and of any decision of, or expression of opinion by, the European Court on questions concerning the meaning or effect of any of the treaties or Community instruments. There is no express provision for taking judicial notice of statutory instruments, but some have been so frequently relied on that judicial notice will be taken of them.[49] Judicial notice will not, however, be taken of foreign law; expert evidence is required on this subject.[50]

PROBLEMS ASSOCIATED WITH JUDICIAL NOTICE

The ground covered so far may appear misleadingly simple. In fact the topic of judicial notice gives rise to a number of problems, which may be grouped together in four categories. These include the relationship of judicial notice and evidence, the effect of judicial notice, the scope of judicial notice, and the

---

44 [1911] 2 KB 445, pp 447–48.
45 *Davey v Harrow Corporation* [1958] 1 QB 60, p 69.
46 *Heather v P-E Consulting Group Ltd* [1973] 1 Ch 189, pp 218, 224.
47 Interpretation Act 1978, ss 3, 22(1) and Sched 2, para 2.
48 European Communities Act 1972, s 1(2) and Part 1 of Sched 1.
49 See, eg, *R v Jones* [1969] 3 All ER 1559 (SI approving the breathalyser Alcotest R 80 device).
50 *R v Ofori* (1994) 99 Cr App R 223; *R v Okolle* (2000) *The Times*, 16 June.

use of personal knowledge by judges, jurors, and others exercising a judicial function.[51]

The relationship of judicial notice and evidence

It has been suggested in the past that judicial notice is a form of proof. Sir JF Stephen changed his mind on the matter. He originally included judicial notice in a chapter of his *Digest of the Law of Evidence* headed, 'Facts which need not be proved – judicial notice'.[52] In the 3rd edition, he changed the heading to 'Facts proved otherwise than by evidence' and this was followed in later editions.[53] The current view, however, is that judicial notice is not properly regarded as a form of *proof*; rather, it is a *substitute* for proof.[54]

Where judicial notice is taken without inquiry, it is clear that no process of proof is involved, because no material containing information is produced by either party. But is judicial notice *after* inquiry based on a process of proof? It has been shown already that the court may accept information as part of its inquiry from such diverse sources as written statements from a minister of the Crown, statements made in court by counsel on behalf of a minister, a court's earlier decision about the existence of a custom, and historical or other works of reference. The opinions of judges on whether judicial notice is a form of proof have not been consistent. In *Duff Development Co Ltd v Government of Kelantan*, Lord Finlay said of cases where a minister of the Crown provides information about the sovereignty of a foreign State, 'Such information is not in the nature of evidence; it is a statement by the sovereign of this country through one of his ministers upon a matter which is peculiarly within his cognisance'. Yet in the same case, Lord Sumner said that the minister's statement was the 'best evidence', and that where such a statement was provided, 'other evidence' was neither admissible nor needed.[55] However, in *Commonwealth Shipping Representative v P and O Branch Service*, Lord Sumner described the taking of judicial notice as involving that 'at the stage when evidence of material facts can be properly received, certain facts may be *deemed* to be established, although not proved by sworn testimony, or by the

---

51   As well as Nokes, *op cit*, fn 12; Morgan, *Some Problems of Proof*; and Thayer, *Treatise*, see also Davis, KC, 'Judicial notice' (1955) 55 Col LR 945; Manchester, C, 'Judicial notice and personal knowledge' (1979) 42 MLR 22; McConville, M, 'The doctrine of judicial notice and its relation to evidence' (1979) 1 Liverpool LR 62; Carter, PB, 'Judicial notice: related and unrelated matters', in Campbell, E and Waller, L (eds), *Well and Truly Tried: Essays on Evidence in Honour of Sir Richard Eggleston*, 1982, pp 88–99.

52   Stephen, JF, *Digest of the Law of Evidence*, 1st and 2nd edns, Chapter VII.

53   See, commenting on the change, Thayer, JB, 'Judicial notice and the law of evidence' (1890) 3 Harv LR 285, p 288, fn 1.

54   See, eg, Carter, PB, *Cases and Statutes on Evidence*, 2nd edn, 1990, p 123; *Cross and Tapper on Evidence*, p 67.

55   [1924] AC 797, pp 813, 824.

production, out of proper custody, of documents which speak for themselves'.[56]

The position was scarcely clarified by the Court of Appeal in *McQuaker v Goddard*.[57] In that case, the plaintiff had been bitten by a camel at Chessington Zoo. As the law then stood, it was necessary to determine, for purposes of liability, whether camels were wild or tame animals. The trial judge concluded that they belonged to the latter class. He reached this conclusion after he had consulted books about camels and had heard witnesses from each party on the nature and habits of camels. The Court of Appeal upheld his decision. The evidential status of the information presented to him was discussed in the judgment of Clauson LJ. He said of the evidence given by the witnesses about camels:

> That evidence is not, it must be understood, in the ordinary sense evidence bearing upon an issue of fact. In my view the exact position is this. The judge takes judicial notice of the ordinary course of nature, and in this particular case of the ordinary course of nature in regard to the position of camels among other animals. The reason why the evidence was given was for the assistance of the judge in forming his view as to what the ordinary course of nature in this regard in fact is, a matter *of which he is supposed to have complete knowledge* ... When that evidence was given and weighed up with the statements in the books of reference which were referred to, the facts became perfectly plain; and the learned judge was able without any difficulty whatever to give a correct statement of the natural phenomena material to the matter in question, of which he was bound to take judicial notice.[58]

Only Clauson LJ relied explicitly on judicial notice as the basis for his judgment. The key to understanding what he said is to realise that he was adopting an old legal fiction that judges have complete knowledge of the ordinary course of nature, and that witnesses and reference books are no more than devices for refreshing the judge's memory.[59] MacKinnon LJ said nothing on the subject, concluding only: 'The learned judge has held, upon overwhelming evidence, that the camel is within the class of tame animals, and not within the class of wild animals.'[60] However, Scott LJ seems to have adopted what Clauson LJ said on the subject, saying in the course of his judgment:

> [I]t is also well to remember that it is the function of the judge and not of the jury to decide whether an animal belongs to the class of domestic animals or to

---

56 [1923] AC 191, p 212. Emphasis supplied.

57 [1940] 1 KB 687.

58 *Ibid*, pp 700, 701. Emphasis supplied. See also *Behrens v Bertram Mills Circus Ltd* [1957] 2 QB 1.

59 Cf Schiff, S, 'The use of out-of-court information in fact determination at trial' (1963) 41 Can Bar Rev 335, p 348.

60 [1940] 1 KB 687, p 699.

the class of wild animals. I need say no more for the moment on this head – I think Clauson LJ will probably add a few words on that aspect of the case.[61]

But it seems as if Scott LJ did accept that taking judicial notice involved a process of proof. When all three judgments had been delivered, counsel for the appellant asked for leave to appeal to the House of Lords. Scott LJ responded:

> I do not think we ought to give that leave. *On the facts proved, of which the learned judge and this court are entitled to take judicial notice,* there is nowhere in the world a camel which is wild and not domesticated and used in the service of man, and the law is clear that in England, as elsewhere, the camel is a domesticated animal. It is not open to you to contend that the camel is a wild animal anywhere.[62]

What is clear from *McQuaker v Goddard* is that where judicial notice is taken after inquiry, that inquiry is not limited by the ordinary rules of evidence. No member of the Court of Appeal, for example, suggested that the trial judge had improperly referred to books of reference on the subject of camels. But where inquiry is made, and particularly where witnesses are heard, it is artificial to regard judicial notice as being wholly divorced from proof.

The effect of taking judicial notice

When judicial notice is taken, is the matter noticed conclusive and indisputable, or is the effect merely to establish a fact that may be rebutted by other evidence? Certainly in some cases judicial notice will be conclusive, as the cases in relation to political and constitutional affairs have shown.[63] The problem arises where judicial notice is taken of facts that are supposed to be part of common knowledge. The answer appears to be that, despite some occasional statements to the contrary,[64] judicial notice is final. It follows that a judge who has taken judicial notice of a fact must instruct a jury, if the case is being tried with one, that they must accept as a fact the matter noticed, and he should not admit evidence to show anything to the contrary.[65] Misunderstanding on this point can arise if the fact of which judicial notice is taken is not defined with sufficient clarity. For example, if a court takes judicial notice that a particular custom exists, that settles that *at the time of the court's decision* the custom did exist. But that will be no bar to proving in a

---

61 [1940] 1 KB 687, p 696.
62 *Ibid*, p 701. Emphasis supplied.
63 See above, pp 341-42.
64 See, eg, Thayer, *Treatise*, pp 308–09.
65 McConville, *op cit*, fn 51, p 72; Nokes, *op cit*, fn 12, pp 70–75.

later case that the custom was not in fact followed,[66] or, where sufficient time has passed, that the custom has changed or has ceased to exist.

The scope of judicial notice

Two main views have been taken of the scope of judicial notice. On one view, which may be called the broad view, judges are taking judicial notice of facts all the time, without any overt reference to the matter. The reason for this is that when conducting a process of judicial reasoning, as of any other reasoning, not a step can be taken without assuming something that has not been proved.[67] This is particularly true, as we have seen above, in Chapter 1, when assessing the relevance or weight of a given item of evidence. The process has been vividly described by Davis:

> When a judge or an officer starts to write findings of fact and conclusions of law, every paragraph necessarily contains facts that have not been proved with evidence. When the judge or officer looks at the testimony of the first witness, he uses extra-record information about the meaning of words in the English language, and this is so whether or not he consults the dictionary, and whether or not the meaning of a word is at issue between the parties. His knowledge of the meaning of the word 'the' comes from beyond the record. He assumes that a man is not 30 ft tall, that trains run on rails, that automobiles are not flying machines, that France is outside the United States, and that coal is a fuel. He assumes the existence of human beings, of organised government, of a legal system, of courts, of businesses, of corporations. Every simple case involves the assumption of hundreds of facts that have not been proved.[68]

If this view is right, then, as Cross and Tapper have stated, 'the tacit applications of the doctrine of judicial notice are more numerous and more important than the express ones'.[69]

There are those, however, who have preferred to maintain a more restrictive view. Sir Richard Eggleston, for example, has acknowledged that a judge or jury must make use of general knowledge to interpret the evidence. But, he continued, 'This is not a question of judicial notice, but of the tribunal relying on its own experience as to the ordinary course of human affairs'.[70] In

---

66 It is in this sense that Lord Goddard CJ's observation in *Davey v Harrow Corporation* [1958] 1 QB 60, p 69, is best understood. He said that the courts could in future take notice of a practice of the Ordnance Survey Office as 'at least *prima facie* evidence' of what a line on an Ordnance Survey map represents. (See Carter, *op cit*, fn 51, p 94.)

67 Thayer, *Treatise*, pp 270, 279.

68 Davis, *op cit*, fn 51, p 975.

69 *Cross and Tapper on Evidence*, p 77. Another effect is that it makes the word 'doctrine' even less appropriate if it refers to such a variety of circumstances.

70 Eggleston, Sir R, *Evidence, Proof and Probability*, 2nd edn, 1983, pp 143–44. See also Carter, *op cit*, fn 51, p 94.

Burns v Lipman,[71] the High Court of Australia observed that while a juror or judge might take into account in a road traffic negligence case what usually occurs on a highway, that knowledge is not properly to be regarded as judicial notice.

But it is difficult to see how this distinction can be maintained, because there seems to be no difference between notorious facts (of which judicial notice will be taken) and general knowledge (which can be used only to help the judge interpret the evidence). As Lord Sumner said in *Commonwealth Shipping Representative v P and O Branch Service,* 'Judicial notice refers to facts, which a judge can be called upon to receive and to act upon, *either from his general knowledge of them,* or from inquiries to be made by himself for his own information from sources to which it is proper for him to refer'.[72] Nor is the distinction always made in practice, as can be seen from the speeches in *Monarch Steamship Co Ltd v Karlshamns Oljefabriker (A/B).*[73]

The division of opinion about the scope of judicial notice is probably a result of different rationales that have been suggested for the practice. If, like Morgan, you regard judicial notice as a device for filtering out evidence about matters that are really unarguable, you will tend to favour restricting its scope to notorious or readily ascertainable facts, making its application mandatory instead of discretionary, and the effect of its application conclusive. If, like Thayer, you prefer to see judicial notice as a labour saving device in litigation, its scope can be wider and its application discretionary. Its effect might even be defeasible in the light of further evidence.[74]

Use of personal knowledge

While it seems clear that a tribunal may make use of its *general* knowledge by virtue of judicial notice, or as part of its interpretation of the evidence if a narrow view of judicial notice is taken, it is also said that neither judges nor jurors can make use of their purely *personal* knowledge in reaching a decision.[75] A line of cases suggests that a county court judge may take into account his own knowledge of labour conditions in the area where he sits. But these cases were all decided under the Workmen's Compensation Acts, under which the judge's function was that of an arbitrator. Even in those cases, a judge was expected to apply the common knowledge of everyone in the

---

71 (1974) 132 CLR 157.
72 [1923] AC 191, p 212. Emphasis supplied.
73 [1949] AC 196.
74 Thayer, *Treatise,* p 309.
75 Formerly, jurors were entitled and expected to use personal knowledge: see *Bushell's Case* (1670) Vaugh 135. But by the early 19th century, the position had changed: *R v Sutton* (1816) 4 M&S 532; *R v Rosser* (1836) 7 C&P 648.

district, and was not supposed to rely on his personal knowledge of highly specialised matters.[76]

The Divisional Court has on several occasions held that magistrates have properly applied their own knowledge of local conditions. In *Ingram v Percival*,[77] the defendant was convicted of an offence under s 11 of the Salmon and Freshwater Fisheries Act 1923, which made it an offence to place a 'fixed engine' of any description for taking salmon or migratory trout in any inland or tidal waters. The justices found that the defendant had used a net for taking salmon and migratory trout in waters near the North Pier at Sunderland, and that the net was a fixed engine within the meaning of the statute. They also found that the net was fixed in the sea about 100 yds from the shore, and that the location was in tidal waters. The sole question in the Divisional Court was whether the justices had been entitled to find that at the position where the net was found there was 'a perceptible, a real, ebb and flow of the tide, notwithstanding that it was fixed ... below low water mark'. The justices in the case stated said:

> We considered that tidal waters consist of waters affected by a lateral or horizontal flow of water as distinct from a vertical rise and fall and it is within our knowledge that such a flow extends beyond low water mark and is experienced at more than 100 yds from the shore. We therefore hold that in this case the net was in tidal waters.

Lord Parker CJ held that the justices were fully entitled to make use of that knowledge which they said they had. 'It has always been recognised,' he said, 'that justices may and should – after all, they are local justices – take into consideration matters which they know of their own knowledge, and particularly matters in regard to the locality, whether it be on land, as it seems to me, or in water'.[78]

This decision has been criticised on the ground that the tidal nature of the waters was apparently not notorious in the locality, and that in this case the justices were not using background knowledge to interpret evidence about the matter because there was no evidence on the question whether the waters were tidal or not. They were therefore using their own private knowledge in the place of evidence in order to find a fact in issue.[79] A better example of justices taking their knowledge of local conditions into account can be found in *Paul v DPP*.[80] The defendant was alleged to have been 'kerb crawling' in his

---

76 *Roberts and Ruthven Ltd v Hall* (1912) 5 BWCC 331; *Peart v Bolckow, Vaughan and Co Ltd* [1925] 1 KB 399; *Keane v Mount Vernon Colliery Co Ltd* [1933] AC 309; *Reynolds v Llanelly Associated Tinplate Co Ltd* [1948] 1 All ER 140. Cf *Mullen v Hackney LBC* [1997] 1 WLR 1103, where these matters were apparently not drawn to the attention of the Court of Appeal. See further Allen, C, 'Judicial notice extended' (1998) 2 E&P 37.

77 [1969] 1 QB 548.

78 *Ibid*, p 555.

79 Carter, *op cit*, fn 51, pp 98–99.

80 (1990) 90 Cr App R 173.

car and to have stopped a woman who was a known prostitute. It was said that after a short conversation she got into his car. Although he was observed by police officers, who followed the car and arrested him, there were no other vehicles or pedestrians in the area at the time. He was charged under s 1(1) of the Sexual Offences Act 1985 with soliciting a woman in a street for the purposes of prostitution in such manner or circumstances as to be likely to cause a nuisance to other persons in the neighbourhood. In reaching their decision that the defendant's actions were likely to cause a nuisance of this kind, the justices took into account their own knowledge that the area had a heavily residential population, and that it was a frequent haunt of prostitutes, who attracted a constant procession of cars at night. The Divisional Court held that the justices had been right to take their local knowledge into account. In this case, of course, it was clear that the justices had the common knowledge of anybody living in that locality; it is at best unclear that the justices in *Ingram v Percival* were in that position.

Other cases suggest that it may be difficult, if not impossible, for magistrates to disregard their own private knowledge, but that their use of it will be legitimate if confined to their interpretation of evidence in the case. In *R v Field and Others ex p White*,[81] a grocer had been prosecuted under s 6 of the Sale of Food and Drugs Act 1875 for selling a packet of cocoa which, when analysed, had been found to contain 80% starch and sugar. Under the statute, an offence was not committed where any ingredient not injurious to health had been added if it was required for the production or preparation of the food or drug as an article of commerce. The justices had all served in the navy, and this had apparently made them experts in the constitution of cocoa. They concluded that it was a matter of common knowledge that cocoa, as an article of commerce, must necessarily contain a large proportion of other ingredients. They therefore dismissed the complaint. Their decision was upheld. In delivering judgment, Wills J said that the justices had:

> ... decided the case as they did upon their own knowledge; and in the nature of things, no one in determining a case of this kind can discard his own particular knowledge of a subject of this kind. I might as well be asked to decide a question as to the sufficiency of an Alpine rope without bringing my personal knowledge into play.[82]

The use by justices of their personal knowledge was considered by the Divisional Court in *Wetherall v Harrison*.[83] The defendant was charged with failing to provide a specimen of blood without reasonable excuse, contrary to s 9(3) of the Road Traffic Act 1972. He had reacted abnormally and struggled when a doctor had tried to take the specimen. The doctor gave evidence to the

---

81 (1895) 64 LJMC 158.
82 *Ibid*, p 160. The judge was a distinguished mountaineer.
83 [1976] 1 QB 773.

effect that the defendant's reaction had not been genuine, and that he had been pretending to have a fit. The defendant in evidence stated that he had been apprehensive in the past when required to have an injection, and that on this occasion he had felt hot and faint and had had difficulty in breathing. He called no expert medical evidence. Among the justices was a doctor who gave his fellow justices his professional opinion as to the genuineness of the defendant's reaction. The justices also had a layman's experience of wartime inoculations and the fear that they could create in certain individuals. They concluded that the defendant had suffered a hysterical reaction from his fear of the needle, and that he therefore had a reasonable excuse for failing to provide the sample. The prosecutor appealed. In dismissing the appeal, Lord Widgery CJ said:

> I do not think the position of a justice of the peace is the same, in this regard, as the position of a trained judge. If you have a judge sitting alone, trying a civil case, it is perfectly feasible and sensible that he should be instructed and trained to exclude certain factors from his consideration of the problem. Justices are not so trained. They are much more like jurymen in this respect. I think it would be wrong to start with the proposition that justices' use of their own local or personal knowledge is governed by exactly the same rule as is laid down in the case of trained judges. I do not believe that a serious restriction on a justice's use of his own knowledge or the knowledge of his colleagues can really be enforced. Laymen (by which I mean non-lawyers) sitting as justices considering a case which has just been heard before them lack the ability to put out of their minds certain features of the case. In particular, if the justice is a specialist ... it is not possible for him to approach the decision in the case as though he had not got that training, and indeed I think it would be a very bad thing if he had to. In a sense, the bench of justices are like a jury, they are a cross-section of people, and one of the advantages which they have is that they bring a lot of varied experience into the court room and use it.[84]

Lord Widgery CJ emphasised, however, that although such special knowledge could be used to *interpret* the evidence given in court, it must not be used to *contradict* it. The same point was made by O'Connor J, who said that a justice with specialised knowledge 'must not start substituting what he might have said in evidence, as opposed to using his knowledge to assess the evidence which is available'.[85] Whether such a distinction can be maintained in practice may well be doubted. Perhaps for this reason it was stated by the Divisional Court in *Bowman v DPP*[86] that justices must be extremely circumspect in using their own local knowledge. They should inform the parties if they are likely to use such knowledge, so as to give an opportunity for comment on the knowledge that they claim to have. Another result of what was said in *Wetherall v Harrison* appears to be that a *judge* who has expert

---

84 [1976] 1 QB 773, pp 777–78.
85 *Ibid*, pp 778, 779.
86 [1990] Crim LR 600.

knowledge is expected to put that knowledge entirely to one side, so that someone in the position of Wills J would have to forget, for the purposes of the trial, his knowledge of Alpine ropes.[87]

The position of members of industrial tribunals was dealt with by the Employment Appeal Tribunal in *Dugdale v Kraft Foods Ltd*,[88] where Phillips J said that members of such tribunals are appointed because of their special knowledge and experience. They are entitled to draw on it in assisting the tribunal as a whole to reach a decision. But he added that while the main use of such knowledge will be to explain and understand the evidence that they hear, members are also entitled to use their knowledge to fill gaps in the evidence about matters which will be obvious to them, but might be obscure to a layman. If evidence is given that appears to be contrary to their knowledge, they ought to draw the witness's attention to the fact so as to give the witness an opportunity to deal with it. Provided, however, that such an opportunity has been given, it seems that they may prefer their own knowledge to that of the witness.[89]

---

87 See *R v Field and Others ex p White* (1895) 64 LJMC 158, p 160.
88 [1977] 1 All ER 454.
89 *Ibid*, p 459.

CHAPTER 15

JUDICIAL FINDINGS AS EVIDENCE

The rule at common law is that a judicial finding in one case is inadmissible, in another case between different parties, to prove the facts on which the first decision was based. The reason for this is that it would be unjust for someone to have his rights affected by litigation to which he was not a party and in which, therefore, he could not be heard. This appears from the unanimous opinion of all the judges in *The Duchess of Kingston's* case,[1] that:

> ... as a general principle ... a transaction between two parties in judicial proceedings ought not to be binding upon a third; for it would be unjust to bind any person who could not be admitted to make a defence, or to examine witnesses, or to appeal from a judgment he might think erroneous; and therefore the depositions of witnesses in another cause in proof of a fact, the verdict of the jury finding the fact, and the judgment of the court upon the facts found, although evidence against the parties and all claiming under them, are not, in general, to be used to the prejudice of strangers.

As a general principle, this is obviously sound. Unfortunately, the principle was applied in such a way that criminal convictions had to be ignored in cases where common sense would have acknowledged them to be both relevant and weighty. Reform in civil cases was achieved by statute in 1968, and in criminal cases in 1984.

CONVICTIONS AS EVIDENCE IN CIVIL CASES

The commission of an offence often gives rise to civil as well as criminal liability. For example, assaults are torts as well as crimes, and acts or omissions constituting the offences of careless or dangerous driving can give rise to actions for damages in negligence, or to claims under the Fatal Accidents Acts. Criminal proceedings are usually completed more quickly than civil proceedings. Where this has happened, what is the status at the subsequent civil trial of an earlier criminal conviction relating to the same facts? The answer given by the common law was that it had no status at all, despite the fact that there might be a defendant common to both proceedings, and this was confirmed in the leading case of *Hollington v F Hewthorn and Co Ltd*.[2] The case arose from a collision between two motor cars in which the plaintiff's son sustained fatal injuries. The plaintiff brought an action under

---

1   (1776) 20 St Tr 355, col 538.
2   [1943] KB 587.

the Fatal Accidents Acts against the defendants on behalf of his son's estate. However, because of his son's death, he had no evidence of the defendant's negligence available except the conviction for careless driving of the second defendant, for whose tort the first defendants were alleged to be vicariously liable. It was argued on his behalf (by AT Denning KC, as he then was) that the conviction was admissible as at least *prima facie* evidence of negligence, but this argument was rejected by the Court of Appeal. In giving judgment, Lord Goddard CJ stated:

> [T]he conviction is only proof that another court considered that the defendant was guilty of careless driving. Even were it proved that it was the accident that led to the prosecution, the conviction proves no more than what has just been stated. The court which has to try the claim for damages knows nothing of the evidence that was before the criminal court. It cannot know what arguments were addressed to it, or what influenced the court in arriving at its decision … It frequently happens that a bystander has a complete and full view of an accident. It is beyond question that, while he may inform the court of everything he saw, he may not express any opinion on whether either or both of the parties were negligent … [O]n the trial of the issue in the civil court, the opinion of the criminal court is equally irrelevant.[3]

He also referred to the impossibility of determining what weight should be given to a conviction without in effect re-trying the criminal case. The father's claim therefore failed. Doubts were expressed about the justice of this result, and these were reflected in the 15th Report of the Law Reform Committee on the subject of what had come to be known as 'the rule in *Hollington v Hewthorn*'.[4] In their Report, the Committee stated:

> Rationalise it how one will, the decision in the case offends one's sense of justice. The defendant driver had been found guilty of careless driving by a court of competent jurisdiction. The onus of proof of culpability in criminal cases is higher than in civil; the degree of carelessness required to sustain a conviction for careless driving is, if anything, greater than that required to sustain a civil cause of action in negligence. Yet the fact that the defendant driver had been convicted of careless driving at the time and place of the accident was held not to amount even to *prima facie* evidence of his negligent driving at that time and place. It is not easy to escape the implication in the rule in *Hollington v Hewthorn* that, in the estimation of lawyers, a conviction by a criminal court is as likely to be wrong as right. It is not, of course, spelt out in those terms in the judgment of the Court of Appeal, although, in so far as their decision was based mainly upon the ground that the opinion of the criminal court as to the defendant driver's guilt was as irrelevant as that of a bystander who witnessed the accident, the gap between the implicit and the explicit was a narrow one.[5]

---

3   [1943] KB 587, pp 594–95.
4   1967, Cmnd 3391.
5   *Ibid*, para 3.

The Committee's criticisms were followed by the enactment of ss 11–13 of the Civil Evidence Act 1968.[6] Section 11 provided, amongst other things, as follows:

(1) In any civil proceedings the fact that a person has been convicted of an offence by or before any court in the United Kingdom or by a court-martial there or elsewhere shall (subject to subsection (3) below) be admissible in evidence for the purpose of proving, where to do so is relevant to any issue in those proceedings, that he committed that offence, whether he was so convicted upon a plea of guilty or otherwise and whether or not he is a party to the civil proceedings; but no conviction other than a subsisting one shall be admissible in evidence by virtue of this section.

(2) In any civil proceedings in which by virtue of this section a person is proved to have been convicted of an offence by or before any court in the United Kingdom or by a court-martial there or elsewhere–

  (a) he shall be taken to have committed that offence unless the contrary is proved; and

  (b) without prejudice to the reception of any other admissible evidence for the purpose of identifying the facts on which the conviction was based, the contents of any document which is admissible as evidence of the conviction, and the contents of the information, complaint, indictment or charge sheet on which the person in question was convicted, shall be admissible in evidence for that purpose.

(3) Nothing in this section shall prejudice the operation of section 13 of this Act or any other enactment whereby a conviction or a finding of fact in any criminal proceedings is for the purposes of any other proceedings made conclusive evidence of any fact.

Similar provisions relating to findings of adultery and paternity as evidence in civil proceedings are contained in s 12.

The Law Reform Committee took the view that in actions other than those for defamation, the relevance of the conviction is to prove that the convicted person's conduct was such as to give rise to a civil liability, either on the part of the convicted person himself or on the part of another person, such as an employer or insurer. Because this liability is additional to the penal consequences of the conviction and may fall on someone other than the convicted person, the Committee concluded that the person on whom civil liability would fall should not be completely precluded from showing that the convicted person's conduct on the occasion in question was not such as the criminal court had found it to be. But the Committee thought that in actions for defamation the only issue, other than that of damages, was whether a person who had been tried for a criminal offence was guilty of that offence. The real purpose of the action was to obtain a re-trial of the criminal proceedings upon different evidence by a court which lacked jurisdiction to

---

6 These are contained in Part II of the 1968 Act, which remains unaffected by the Civil Evidence Act 1995.

try criminal cases, and which applied a procedure and standard of proof regarded by the law as inappropriate in criminal proceedings. As it happened, a few years before the report there had been a much publicised case where the plaintiff had been convicted of robbery and had had the conviction upheld by the Court of Criminal Appeal. Several years later, he brought an action for libel against a defendant who had published a statement that the plaintiff was guilty of the robbery of which he had been convicted. As the law then stood, the defendant had the burden of proving that the plaintiff had in fact been guilty. He failed to discharge it and the plaintiff's claim succeeded.[7]

Accordingly, s 13(1) of the 1968 Act provided:

> In an action for libel or slander in which the question whether a person did or did not commit a criminal offence is relevant to an issue arising in the action, proof that, at the time when that issue falls to be determined, that person stands convicted of that offence shall be conclusive evidence that he committed that offence; and his conviction thereof shall be admissible in evidence accordingly.

Nothing more will be said about s 13(1), but several points need to be made in relation to s 11.

The scope of the section

Section 11(1) refers to proof of 'the fact that a person has been convicted of an offence by or before any court in the United Kingdom ...'. It follows that the rule in *Hollington v Hewthorn* continues to apply to convictions by foreign courts, and they therefore remain irrelevant, and so inadmissible.[8] Nor does the section extend to adjudications of guilt in police disciplinary proceedings.[9] Sub-section (1) provides that 'no conviction other than a subsisting one shall be admissible in evidence'. If a person has been convicted, but there is an appeal pending, the court will not rely on the section. Instead, the civil hearing will be adjourned until the criminal appeal has been determined.[10]

Pleading the section

If the claimant intends to rely on a criminal conviction as evidence under s 11, he must include in his pleading a statement of that intention, with particulars of the conviction and its date, the court that made the conviction, and the issue in the action to which the conviction is relevant. An appropriate paragraph in

---

7   *Hinds v Sparks* (1964) *The Times*, 28, 30 July.
8   This was confirmed by the Court of Appeal in *Union Carbide Corpn v Naturin Ltd* [1987] FSR 538.
9   *Thorpe v Chief Constable of the Greater Manchester Police* [1989] 1 WLR 665.
10 *In Re Raphael, decd* [1973] 1 WLR 998.

a particulars of claim would follow particulars of the negligence alleged, and would read something like this:

> Further, the defendant was convicted on 1 April 1997 by the magistrates' court sitting at Barchester of the offence of driving his motor car on the road without due care and attention contrary to s 3 of the Road Traffic Act 1988. The said conviction is relevant to the issue of negligence and the plaintiff intends to rely on it as evidence in this action.

The effect of the section

Broadly, there are two views about the effect of the section. One is that a conviction merely operates to raise a *presumption* that the facts on which it was based are true.[11] On this view, the conviction itself has no weight as an item of evidence. The other view is that the conviction is in itself an item of evidence to be weighed in the scales against the defendant. Both views found expression in the decision of the Court of Appeal in *Stupple v Royal Insurance Co Ltd*.[12] In that case Buckley LJ said that no weight was to be given to the mere fact of conviction. He was chiefly influenced by the difficulty of assessing weight in such a situation. After saying that weight could not depend on such considerations as the status of the court that convicted, or whether the verdict was unanimous or by a majority, he concluded: 'It remains, I think, as true today as before the Act that mere proof of conviction proves nothing relevant to the plaintiff's claim.'[13] In other words, a conviction is only a trigger that activates the presumption under sub-s (2), so as to place a burden of proof on the defendant to show that he did not commit the offence relied on.

Lord Denning MR took a different view. He said:

> I think that the conviction does not merely shift the burden of proof. It is a weighty piece of evidence of itself. For instance, if a man is convicted of careless driving on the evidence of a witness, but that witness dies before the civil action is heard ... then the conviction itself tells in the scale in the civil action. It speaks as clearly as the witness himself would have done, had he lived. It does not merely reverse the burden of proof. If that was all it did, the defendant might well give his own evidence negativing want of care, and say: 'I have discharged the burden. I have given my evidence and it has not been contradicted.' In answer to the defendant's evidence, the plaintiff can say to him: 'But your evidence is contradicted. It is contradicted by the very fact of your conviction.'[14]

---

11 On presumptions generally, see above, Chapter 5, pp 122–31.
12 [1971] 1 QB 50.
13 *Ibid*, p 76.
14 *Ibid*, p 72. Do not be misled by Lord Denning's references to shifting or reversing the burden of proof. There is more than one issue in the case. The effect of s 11(2) is to place the burden of proof in relation to one of those issues (the commission of the offence) on the defendant, once the plaintiff has proved the fact of conviction. See above, Chapter 5.

Lord Denning's example is a persuasive argument in favour of his interpretation of the section. The editors of *Phipson* have produced further arguments in support, based on the wording of s 11.[15] They point to the fact that sub-s (1) expressly provides: '... the fact that a person has been convicted of an offence ... shall ... be admissible in evidence for the purpose of proving ... that he committed that offence.' The presumption of the correctness of the conviction is not referred to until sub-s (2). They argue that s 11(1) could exist perfectly well in the absence of s 11(2). In that case, its meaning would clearly be the one favoured by Lord Denning. Given that that is so, it is hard to see why the addition of sub-s (2) should change that meaning. Further, 'the fact' of a conviction is, by sub-s (1), admissible *'in evidence'*; the interpretation of Buckley LJ would deprive it of any evidential effect as a fact. They argue that their view is supported by Lord Diplock's approach in *Hunter v Chief Constable of the West Midlands Police*, where he said, 'The burden of proof of "the contrary" that lies upon a defendant under s 11 is the ordinary burden in a civil action: proof on a balance of probabilities; although in the face of a conviction after a full hearing this is likely to be an uphill task'. If the conviction was not an item of evidence, but merely a trigger, a distinction could not have been made between convictions based on a guilty plea and convictions 'after a full hearing'.[16]

In *Stupple v Royal Insurance Co Ltd*,[17] Lord Denning accepted that a distinction could be made. He thought that the weight to be given to a conviction would depend on the circumstances, and that a plea of guilty might have less weight than a conviction after a full trial because sometimes defendants pleaded guilty in error, or to save time and expense where the offence was minor, or to avoid some embarrassing fact coming out. The Law Reform Committee took the same view. They stated in their 15th Report that a conviction after a contested trial, a conviction on a plea of guilty, and an acquittal did not have the same probative value in relation to the question in issue in a civil action.[18] Later, when dealing with the defendant's burden of proof, they drew a distinction between convictions after a contested trial and convictions on a plea of guilty. In the former case, they said, the burden was unlikely to be discharged by the testimony of the convicted person alone; in the latter case they suggested that it could, if he produced a convincing explanation for his plea. Support for Lord Denning's views can also be found in the decision of the Court of Appeal in *Taylor v Taylor*, where Davies LJ said that it was 'obvious that, when a man has been convicted by 12 of his fellow countrymen and countrywomen at a criminal trial, the verdict of the jury is a

---

15 *Phipson on Evidence*, 14th edn, 1990, p 918.

16 [1982] AC 529, p 544.

17 [1971] 1 QB 50.

18 Law Reform Committee, 15th Report, *The Rule in Hollington v Hawthorn*, 1967, Cmnd 3391, para 10.

matter which is entitled to very great weight when the convicted person is seeking, in the words of the statute, to prove the contrary'.[19]

No doubt it may be difficult to assess the weight of a particular conviction, for example, where it was by a majority verdict, or where for some reason the defendant was unrepresented. But it does seem possible to say that some convictions will carry less weight than others, and the arguments in favour of Lord Denning's position are strong.[20]

CONVICTIONS AS EVIDENCE IN CRIMINAL CASES

Some offences presuppose the commission of an earlier offence by someone else. For example, handling presupposes that the property handled has already been stolen. Sometimes the easiest way to prove that goods have been stolen is to prove that someone else has been convicted of their theft. But if the person charged with handling was tried separately from the thief, the handler would not have been a party in the trial for theft, would therefore not have been heard in it, and so would have been powerless to affect its outcome. It was this sort of powerlessness that the common law took into account in the general principle that a judicial finding in one case was inadmissible in another case, between different parties, to prove the facts on which the first decision was based. The application of that principle in the kind of situation just described led courts to treat the earlier conviction as no more than non-expert evidence of opinion,[21] and so inadmissible to establish the fact that the goods were stolen.[22] Similarly, where a defendant was charged with permitting betting on licensed premises, evidence that a bookmaker had been convicted of using the premises on the occasion in question was inadmissible to prove that betting had been taking place there;[23] and where a defendant was charged with living on the earnings of prostitution, evidence that a particular woman had been convicted of practising as a prostitute was inadmissible to prove that she was a prostitute.[24] In cases where two persons were indicted for a criminal offence and one pleaded guilty but the other did not, the judge had to direct the jury that they must pay no attention to the fact that one of the defendants had pleaded guilty. A man's confession was evidence only against himself and not against anyone else.[25]

---

19 [1970] 1 WLR 1148, p 1152.
20 See, further, the note by Zuckerman (1971) 87 LQR 21. For brief arguments in favour of Buckley LJ's view, see *Cross and Tapper*, p 98; Carter, PB, *Cases and Statutes on Evidence*, 2nd edn, 1990, p 433.
21 *R v Shepherd and Shepherd* (1980) 71 Cr App R 120.
22 *R v Turner* (1832) 1 Mood CC 347.
23 *Taylor v Wilson* (1911) 76 JP 69.
24 *R v Hassan* [1970] 1 QB 423.
25 *R v Moore* (1956) 40 Cr App R 50, pp 53–54.

In 1972, the Criminal Law Revision Committee criticised the state of the law in this respect, saying that it was quite wrong that the prosecution should be required to prove again the guilt of the earlier defendant. It appears, however, that the Committee thought that the amended law would apply in only limited circumstances, for they added that their proposed amendment would 'be helpful to the prosecution in various cases where the guilt of the accused depends on another person's having committed an offence', such as handling stolen goods, harbouring offenders and offences under ss 4 and 5 of the Criminal Law Act 1967 of assisting offenders and concealing offences.[26] In fact, when the law in this respect was changed by the Police and Criminal Evidence Act 1984, the scope of the legislation was far wider. Section 74 provided as follows:

(1) In any proceedings the fact that a person other than the accused has been convicted of an offence by or before any court in the United Kingdom or by a Service court outside the United Kingdom shall be admissible in evidence for the purpose of proving, where to do so is relevant to any issue in those proceedings, that that person committed that offence, whether or not any other evidence of his having committed that offence is given.

(2) In any proceedings in which by virtue of this section a person other than the accused is proved to have been convicted of an offence by or before any court in the United Kingdom or by a Service court outside the United Kingdom, he shall be taken to have committed that offence unless the contrary is proved.

(3) In any proceedings where evidence is admissible of the fact that the accused has committed an offence, in so far as that evidence is relevant to any matter in issue in the proceedings for a reason other than a tendency to show in the accused a disposition to commit the kind of offence with which he is charged, if the accused is proved to have been convicted of the offence–

(a) by or before any court in the United Kingdom; or

(b) by a Service court outside the United Kingdom,

he shall be taken to have committed that offence unless the contrary is proved.

(4) Nothing in this section shall prejudice–

(a) the admissibility in evidence of any conviction which would be admissible apart from this section; or

(b) the operation of any enactment whereby a conviction or a finding of fact in any proceedings is for the purposes of any other proceedings made conclusive evidence of any fact.

Section 75(1) applies where evidence that a person has been convicted of an offence is admissible by virtue of s 74. This sub-section provides that, among

---

26 CLRC, 11th Report, paras 217–20.

any other admissible evidence for the purpose of identifying the facts on which the conviction was based, reliance may be placed on the contents of any document which is admissible as evidence of the conviction, and the contents of the information, complaint, indictment or charge sheet on which the person in question was convicted.

Before I turn to a more detailed consideration of the scope of s 74 and its interaction with s 78, which provides a general exclusionary discretion in relation to evidence on which the prosecution proposes to rely, some general points need to be made about these provisions:

(a) The reference to 'proceedings' in s 74 is a reference to criminal proceedings, and the reference to a 'Service court' is a reference to a court-martial or standing civilian court.[27]

(b) It should be noted that under s 74(2) and (3), the burden of proving that a person did not commit the offence for which he has been convicted rests on a defendant who asserts that fact. Proof will be to the civil standard of a balance of probabilities, because that is the standard always applicable where a defendant in a criminal trial bears a burden of proof in relation to any issue.[28]

(c) Section 74(3) would apply, for example, where the prosecution needs to prove that the defendant committed some other offence for which he has been convicted, because that provides an element of the later offence with which he is charged. For example, suppose that after a defendant's conviction for assault, his victim dies. If the defendant were then charged with murder or manslaughter, the fact of the assault could be established merely by proof of the conviction. The sub-section could also apply if a defendant who was being cross-examined under s 1(3)(ii) or (iii) of the Criminal Evidence Act 1898 denied the fact of conviction or any admissible details of the offences.

(d) The way to prove convictions is governed by s 73(1) and (2) of the Act. Whether the conviction was at a summary trial or on indictment, proof may be made (a) by producing a certificate of conviction duly signed by the clerk of the appropriate court; and (b) by proving that the person named in the certificate is the person whose conviction is to be proved. A document purporting to be a duly signed certificate shall be taken to be such unless the contrary is proved.

---

27 Police and Criminal Evidence Act 1984, s 82(1).
28 *R v Carr-Briant* [1943] KB 607.

The scope of s 74(1)

Clearly, proof of the commission of an earlier offence will be 'relevant to any issue' in the current proceedings if it establishes an element of the offence now charged. So, for example, in *R v Pigram*,[29] where two men were charged with handling stolen goods, the plea of guilty made by one of the defendants was held admissible at the trial of the other for the purpose of proving that the goods were stolen. None of the cases decided under the old law that were referred to at the beginning of this section would now be decided in the same way. But the Court of Appeal has held that a wide interpretation should be applied to 'issue', so as to allow it to cover not just essential ingredients of an offence, but evidentiary matters also. In *R v Castle*,[30] for example, C and others, including F, were charged with robbery. F pleaded guilty. The victim had picked out C and F at identification parades, saying 'Yes' when identifying C and 'Possibly' when identifying F. The trial judge admitted evidence of F's guilty plea under s 74(1) and was upheld by the Court of Appeal, on the basis that the plea of guilty by F was relevant to the reliability of the identification of C, which was the 'issue' for the purposes of the subsection. F had, as it were, confirmed an identification made by the victim that had been no more than tentative. If that was correct, then the probability was that the more certain identification of C was correct also.

While the Court of Appeal has said that it does not approve of allowing evidence to go before a jury that is irrelevant, inadmissible, prejudicial or unfair simply on the basis that is convenient for the jury to have 'the whole picture',[31] it has also been said that 'anything which enables a jury better to understand the relevant factual background against which the issue arises is properly to be described as relevant to that issue within the terms of s 74'. So in a case where defendants were charged with conspiracy to pervert the course of justice by obtaining the false evidence of witnesses at an earlier trial, it was held proper to have proved that the earlier trial had resulted in a conviction, and that at a later trial others had already been convicted of conspiracy to pervert the course of justice in relation to the earlier trial.[32] Where there was strong circumstantial evidence linking two defendants to a third in the commission of a burglary, the guilty plea of the third defendant was admissible to show that the other defendants were also involved in its commission.[33] Even the previous convictions of persons other than the co-accused may be relevant to an issue. In *R v Warner and Jones*,[34] the defendants

---

29 [1995] Crim LR 808.
30 [1989] Crim LR 567.
31 *R v Boyson* [1991] Crim LR 274.
32 *R v Buckingham and Others* (1993) 99 Cr App R 303; see particularly the *dicta* of McCowan LJ at p 307.
33 *R v Grey* (1988) 88 Cr App R 375.
34 (1992) 96 Cr App R 324.

were charged with conspiracy to supply heroin. The prosecution case was based in part on police observations at the address of one of the defendants. These revealed that a great many people had visited the house. Eight of the visitors observed by the police had previous convictions for the possession or supply of heroin. The trial judge allowed evidence of these convictions to be adduced under s 74 and was upheld by the Court of Appeal. The previous convictions of the visitors were relevant to the characters of the people that the defendants were letting into the house, and this had a bearing on the nature of the transactions going on there.

It would be possible for a defendant to use s 74(1). Suppose A is charged alone with a particular offence. His defence is that the offence was committed not by him, but by B, who has previous convictions for committing the same type of offence in a similar way. It seems that there would be nothing to stop A from proving this by relying on s 74(1), which does not have the limitation to be found in s 74(3) excluding evidence that is relevant only because it has a tendency to show disposition. If the defendant were not A, but B, the prosecution could not rely on s 74(3) to prove the previous convictions and would have to prove the similar facts by other evidence. But if A and B were charged together, A should be in no worse position because of that and ought to be able to rely on s 74(1). Moreover, the judge would have no discretion to exclude the evidence under s 78, because that section applies only to evidence upon which the *prosecution* proposes to rely, nor are there any other sources of discretion that would enable a judge to exclude relevant evidence which a defendant wished to call.[35]

Interaction with s 78(1)

It has already been shown how s 78 provides a judicial discretion to exclude evidence upon which the prosecution proposes to rely if the admission of that evidence would have such an adverse effect on the fairness of the proceedings that the court ought not to admit it. This section, as well as providing some remedy where evidence has been unfairly obtained, has also been used to mitigate the potential for unfairness contained in s 74(1). It is now settled that once a judge is satisfied that the evidence tendered under s 74(1) has some probative force, careful consideration should be given to s 78(1) to see whether the discretion to exclude should be exercised.[36] It was emphasised above, in Chapter 9, that the wording of s 78(1) does not refer to a balance of prejudicial over probative value to determine exclusion. However, it has to be said that in connection with s 74(1) this is the test that has been assumed to apply by

---

35   See the commentary on *R v Hendrick* [1992] Crim LR 427.

36   *R v Boyson* [1991] Crim LR 274; *R v Skinner and Others* [1995] Crim LR 805; *R v Lee* [1996] Crim LR 825; *R v Mahmoud and Manzur* [1997] 1 Cr App R 414.

virtue of the section.[37] There is a suggestion in *R v Lee*, at least in relation to conspiracy charges, that the greater the probative value of the conviction, the more prejudice will be caused to the defendant by admitting it in evidence, because to adduce evidence in this way denies an opportunity for cross-examination which the defendant would have had if evidence of the commission of an offence had been called in the ordinary way. If evidence is admitted under s 74(1), the jury must always be told to what issues it is relevant, and to what issues it is *not* relevant.[38]

In several cases, the court has suggested that the discretion to exclude ought to be exercised where the earlier conviction was obtained as the result of a guilty plea, rather than a contested trial. Thus in *R v Kempster* Staughton LJ said:

> It may well be true that the other person is unlikely to have pleaded guilty unless he was in fact guilty; but the defence will be deprived of any opportunity to cross-examine him, in particular as to the complicity of the defendant. No doubt such cross-examination may in itself be unlikely in some cases, or else turn out to be a disaster ... But one cannot always assume that.[39]

Further, the use of s 74(1) may give rise to a problem that has not yet been openly considered by the courts. What is the position where the plea may have been the result of plea bargaining? Suppose A, B and C are charged with a joint offence. B and C plead not guilty, but A, as part of a plea bargain involving other outstanding allegations against him, pleads guilty. The weight of the guilty plea as evidence of the commission of the offence is almost bound to be reduced; yet the court trying the case will be in no position to discover whether this has happened or not. Nor, in most cases, will the defendants who plead not guilty. It may be particularly tempting for a prosecutor to use s 74(1), because the Court of Appeal has said that in principle the prosecution should be very careful before deciding to call as a witness an accomplice in the crime in respect of which the defendant is standing trial. Before doing so, there should be a clear indication from the accomplice of willingness to give evidence for the prosecution.[40]

However, the Court of Appeal has not been consistent in its application of s 78(1) where there has been an earlier guilty plea. Thus in *R v Grey*[41] the argument based on lack of opportunity to cross-examine was disregarded. Turner J said that the man whose conviction had been proved under s 74(1)

---

37   See, eg, *R v Boyson* [1991] Crim LR 274; *R v Lee* [1996] Crim LR 825; *R v Mahmoud and Manzur* [1997] 1 Cr App R 414.

38   *R v Kempster* [1989] 1 WLR 1125; *R v Boyson* [1991] Crim LR 274; *R v Skinner and Others* [1995] Crim LR 805; *R v Mahmoud and Manzur* [1997] 1 Cr App R 414.

39   [1989] 1 WLR 1125, p 1134. See also *R v Humphreys and Tully* [1993] Crim LR 288; *R v Lee* [1996] Crim LR 825; *R v Mahmoud and Manzur* [1997] 1 Cr App R 414.

40   *R v Moran* (1985) 81 Cr App R 51, p 52; *R v Sinclair* (1989) *The Times*, 18 April.

41   (1988) 88 Cr App R 375.

could have been called to give evidence for the Crown. 'Had he done so, no sensible objection could have been raised to evidence by [him] that he had been convicted of that offence or, for that matter, that he had pleaded guilty to it.' But the admissibility of a witness's evidence was not the point; what Turner J ought to have been considering was the potential for unfairness to a defendant where there was no witness whom he could cross-examine, especially where the commission of the offence had been established merely by a guilty plea. A similarly blithe approach appears to have been taken in *R v Turner*.[42] In that case, T and another man, L, were in separate cars driving at night down a hill towards a bend in the road. The road was slightly greasy. Both were driving at a slightly excessive speed. L overtook T, cut in sharply on the corner, losing control of his car and colliding with an oncoming vehicle. As a result, L's passenger died. The prosecution alleged that L and T were racing, though not by any previous arrangement. L pleaded guilty to causing death by reckless driving. T was tried on the same charge. His defence was that he was not racing, not reckless, and not contributing to any recklessness by L. The trial judge allowed L's guilty plea to be admitted under s 74(1) to prove that L had been driving recklessly. The Court of Appeal said that provided the judge made it clear, as he had, that L's plea did not amount to an admission that he was racing, but only that he was reckless, there was nothing unfair in admitting the evidence. It was true, the court acknowledged, that since L was not called as a witness it was impossible to cross-examine him as to the basis of his plea. But such a result, they said, was inevitable in cases of this sort.

From time to time, the Court of Appeal does appear to have recognised the potential for unfairness that s 74(1) can create. In *R v Hillier and Farrar*,[43] Watkins LJ said, 'It is the widely held view, which we share, that Parliament cannot have appreciated how wild an animal it was prepared to let loose upon the field of evidence when it enacted s 74'. It has been said that the sub-section should be 'sparingly' used,[44] and in *Warner v Jones*,[45] it was suggested that it might have been wiser not to use it since it added little to an already strong case against the defendants.[46] More importantly, in *R v Kempster*,[47] Staughton LJ, in delivering the judgment of the Court of Appeal, drew attention to an observation of that court in the earlier unreported case of *R v Curry*[48] to the effect that where the evidence that the prosecution wish to

---

42 [1991] Crim LR 57.

43 (1992) 97 Cr App R 349.

44 *R v Robertson* (1987) 85 Cr App R 304; *R v Chapman* [1991] Crim LR 44; *R v Boyson* [1991] Crim LR 274; *R v Humphreys & Tully* [1993] Crim LR 288; *R v Skinner and Others* [1995] Crim LR 805; *R v Mahmoud and Manzur* [1997] 1 Cr App R 414.

45 (1988) 88 Cr App R 375.

46 See also *R v Humphreys and Tully* [1993] Crim LR 288.

47 [1989] 1 WLR 1125.

48 28 April 1988.

adduce under s 74(1) expressly or by necessary inference imports the complicity of the person on trial in the offence with which he is charged, the sub-section should not be used.

It cannot be said that in all cases the Court of Appeal has followed the maxim referred to by Staughton LJ, but the cases on conspiracy show that in that area at least it has very largely done so. In *R v O'Connor*,[49] a case in which conspiracy between only two persons was alleged, the Court of Appeal held that the trial judge should have used s 78(1) to exclude evidence of the co-accused's conviction, because the effect of admitting this evidence had been to allow the prosecution to put before the jury a statement made by the co-accused in the absence of the defendant, without the co-accused being before the court to be cross-examined about the admission that he had made. By contrast, in *R v Robertson*,[50] the conspiracy was alleged to have been between the defendant, two other named men, and other unknown persons. The Court of Appeal held that evidence of the convictions of the other named men had been rightly admitted. In this case, also, it was true that the prosecution had been enabled to put to the jury statements made by the co-accused in the absence of the defendant, without the opportunity for cross-examination. The different conclusions are explicable if one looks at what the evidence in each case was likely to prove. In *R v O'Connor*, where the conspiracy was alleged to have been between the defendant and the co-accused, and no other person, the conviction of the co-accused on his own admission did not just prove the existence of a conspiracy: it proved also that the defendant was a conspirator. This was the very matter that the prosecution had to establish, and it is not surprising that the Court of Appeal appears to have taken the view that the absence of safeguards usually surrounding testimony made the evidence unsafe for consideration by the jury, even after judicial guidance.[51] In *R v Robertson*, however, the co-accused's pleas and convictions did not on their face involve the defendant. Even if the co-accused had given evidence at the defendant's trial in accordance with their pleas, defence counsel would almost certainly not have cross-examined them.[52] The co-accused's pleas were put forward for the limited purpose of establishing the fact that a conspiracy had existed; the defendant's involvement in it had been proved by other means.

R v O'Connor and *R v Robertson* can be seen as standing at opposite ends of a scale of cases concerning the use of s 74(1) in cases of conspiracy. At a point somewhere between them lies *R v Lunnon*.[53] In this case the prosecution set out to prove that on a particular date the defendant had conspired with S Lake, J Lake and Perrey to steal from shops in Watford. Two propositions

49   (1987) 85 Cr App R 298.
50   (1987) 85 Cr App R 304.
51   For a similar case that did not involve conspiracy, see *R v Mattison* [1990] Crim LR 117.
52   (1987) 85 Cr App R 304, p 312.
53   (1989) 88 Cr App R 71.

appear to have been involved: (a) there had been such a conspiracy between the Lakes and Perrey; (b) Lunnon also had been a party to it. The prosecution wanted to prove the first proposition by using s 74(1), but the situation differed in an important respect from that in *R v Robertson*. In the latter case, the defendant had not been mentioned in the counts to which the co-accused had pleaded guilty. Here, however, the position was that S Lake had pleaded guilty to a count, the particulars of which alleged that on the date in question he had conspired with J Lake, Perrey and Lunnon to steal from shops in Watford. If the prosecution could prove the conspiracy by establishing this conviction, with the details of the conspiracy that the indictment would have revealed, would there not be the same danger of insufficiently tested evidence directly implicating the defendant that had existed in *R v O'Connor*?

The trial judge thought not, and the Court of Appeal agreed with him. The court pointed to the fact that the conviction had been adduced only for the purpose of proving the existence of a conspiracy; other evidence had been relied on to show that the defendant had been a party to it. Substantial reliance was placed on the warnings given by the trial judge to the jury about the way in which this evidence could be used. In particular, he had been careful to tell them the limited purpose for which the evidence had been adduced. He had emphasised that the jury could find any of the defendants, or all of them, not guilty of being a part of it. It seems that unless there are only two persons involved in the conspiracy, then, provided a sufficient warning is given to the jury that the evidence can be used solely to show that there was a conspiracy, and not that the defendant was part of it, evidence under s 74(1) is likely to be admitted, in the absence of any other reason to exclude it.

If such evidence is admitted, it is important that the judge should give an accurate direction to the jury on its significance. In particular, he must be careful to direct the jury that evidence of a former co-defendant's conviction is not evidence that the defendant is guilty,[54] and although the conviction is evidence that the offence in question took place, it is not conclusive evidence; it can be rebutted. The issue is one for the jury to decide, and a judge should not by his comments appear to withdraw that issue from them.[55]

EVIDENCE OF PREVIOUS ACQUITTALS

Evidence of previous acquittals will only rarely be admitted in either civil or criminal proceedings. The reason is that the different standards of proof in civil and criminal cases will usually have the effect of making a defendant's

---

54 See *R v Stewart* [1999] Crim LR 746.
55 See *R v Dixon (Sarah Louise)* [2001] Crim LR 126.

previous acquittal on a criminal charge irrelevant in subsequent civil proceedings arising from the same facts. It remains the case that even where what amounts to a serious crime is alleged, the standard in civil proceedings is proof on a balance of probabilities.[56] The defendant's earlier acquittal because the prosecution failed to prove its case *beyond reasonable doubt* will have no effect one way or the other in later civil proceedings. So, for example, where insurers were sued on an insurance policy and claimed that they were not liable because the company insured had been responsible through its principle shareholder and director for itself causing the destruction by fire of the property insured, the trial judge held evidence of the director's earlier acquittal on a charge of arson arising from the same facts irrelevant, and so inadmissible.[57]

As in civil proceedings, so in criminal; the position is that a previous acquittal remains subject to the rule in *Hollington v Hewthorn*: it is irrelevant and inadmissible. A good example of the application of this rule can be found in the decision of the Privy Council in *Hui Chi-Ming v The Queen*.[58] A man named Ah Po, who was carrying a length of water pipe, went to 'look for someone to hit', accompanied by the defendant and four other youths. Ah Po found a victim and hit him with the pipe, thereby causing injuries that proved fatal. In due course, Ah Po was charged with murder. The jury found him not guilty of murder, but guilty of manslaughter. The prosecution had done some plea bargaining with most of the other defendants, but Hui Chi-Ming would not plead guilty to manslaughter. He was therefore tried for the murder of Ah Po's victim, the prosecution arguing that Ah Po had in fact murdered the man and that Hui Chi-Ming had been participating in a joint enterprise. The defence wanted to adduce evidence of Ah Po's acquittal on the charge of murder, but the prosecution objected to its admissibility and was upheld by the trial judge. The Privy Council concluded that the trial judge had been right. Citing *R v Turner*[59] and *Hollington v Hewthorn*,[60] Lord Lowry said that the verdict of a different jury at the earlier trial was irrelevant since it was no more than evidence of their opinion.

A previous acquittal *will* be admissible if it is possible to argue that it is relevant to any of the issues that the court has to decide, and sometimes a court will be satisfied that it is relevant to an issue of credibility. Take the illustration of Parker LJ in *R v Cooke*:[61]

> Suppose a police officer says that he has obtained admissions from seven defendants to a group of offences in a series of interviews conducted over a

---

56 See above, Chapter 5.
57 *TD Radcliffe and Co v National Farmers' Union Mutual Insurance* [1993] CLY 708.
58 [1992] 1 AC 34.
59 (1832) 1 Mood CC 347.
60 [1943] KB 587.
61 (1987) 84 Cr App R 286, p 293.

short period. Suppose all of them say that the interviews never took place. Suppose that six of the seven are all tried separately and that all six are acquitted. Suppose the seventh is then tried. It offends against common sense to say that on the trial of the seventh it is not relevant [to] credibility for the jury to know that the officer's evidence has not been accepted by six separate juries.

That, of course, is an extreme example. As Parker LJ said in the same case, whether evidence of acquittals will be admissible because of relevance to credibility is a matter of degree. One case where such evidence was admitted was *R v Hay*.[62] Hay had signed a statement admitting charges of arson and burglary. Separate trials of the two charges took place. At the first trial, on a count of arson, Hay said that his statement had been fabricated by the police. In due course the jury acquitted him. The judge at the later trial for burglary, at which the prosecution again relied on Hay's statement, refused to allow evidence of Hay's earlier acquittal to be given. The Court of Appeal disagreed with this decision. They held that because the confession to arson had been shown to be untrue by the verdict of the first jury, the whole of the statement was suspect. The acquittal on the arson charge had therefore been relevant in assessing the weight to be given to the confession of burglary. O'Connor LJ said:

> The jury ought to have been told of the acquittal and directed that it was conclusive evidence that the appellant was not guilty of arson, and that his confession to that offence was untrue.[63] The jury should have been directed that in deciding the contest between the appellant and the police officers as to the part of the statement referring to the burglary, they should keep in mind the first part must be regarded as untrue.[64]

In another case an acquittal became relevant because of the way in which the prosecution conducted its case. In *R v Doosti*,[65] the defendant was charged with conspiracy to supply heroin. At a trial six months earlier he had been charged with a drug offence and with obstructing the police; these offences were alleged to have taken place at the same premises as those involved in the conspiracy count. At both trials the same police officer gave evidence about the seizure of drugs. At the first trial the defendant had been acquitted on the drugs charge, but convicted of obstruction. At the later trial his counsel wanted to cross-examine the police officer about the earlier acquittal, but the trial judge refused leave. When the defendant came to give evidence, he was cross-examined under what is now s 1(3)(ii) of the Criminal Evidence Act 1898 about his previous convictions, including the conviction for obstruction. He

---

62 (1983) 77 Cr App R 70.

63 Note carefully that the parties at the second trial were the same as at the first. The Crown was bound by the earlier decision in relation to Hay, and that was why the acquittal was conclusive in the second case. See further below, Chapter 16.

64 (1983) 77 Cr App R 70, p 75.

65 (1985) 82 Cr App R 181.

was not allowed to give evidence on re-examination of his acquittal on the drugs charge at the earlier trial.

The Court of Appeal said that the earlier acquittal did not necessarily mean that the police officer had been lying or was unreliable; it was consistent with the jury's not being sure that the prosecution case had been made out. Thus the trial judge had been right to stop cross-examination about the previous acquittal because it had not been directed to any relevant issue. But since the prosecution had chosen to cross-examine about the previous conviction for obstruction, the defence ought to have been allowed to adduce evidence of the defendant's acquittal on the drugs charge. The court emphasised that the conviction and acquittal had resulted from the same trial, that the trial had concerned a similar charge in similar circumstances, and that it had involved the same police officer as the chief prosecution witness in the current case. Ewbank J said:

> The prosecution are not obliged to bring out a defendant's conviction. If they choose to do so they, in our judgment, incur the risk that in such circumstances as obtained in this case a defendant will be permitted to refer to an acquittal on another charge which may throw doubt on the reliability of the prosecution witness.[66]

Where an acquittal is too ambiguous, however, it will not be admitted. This was the case in *R v Henri*.[67] The defendant was charged with buggery, attempted rape and indecent assaults on two girls aged eight and nine, the daughters of the woman with whom he cohabited. At the first trial he was acquitted on some counts and the jury failed to agree on others. He was retried on six counts of buggery and indecent assault in respect of which the first jury had failed to agree. Both girls gave evidence at the re-trial. Defence counsel asked leave to adduce evidence of the earlier acquittals as being relevant to the reliability of one of the girls. The trial judge refused, and the Court of Appeal upheld his decision on the basis that there could have been several reasons, apart from the witness's unreliability, why the first jury had acquitted on some counts. The trial judge had rightly held that to allow the evidence to be given would have encouraged the jury to speculate about why the first jury had reached the decision they had, rather than concentrating on the evidence in the trial before them. As the commentary in the *Criminal Law Review* states, the case is 'a neat illustration of the principle that the relevance of evidence in law is determined not simply by the dictates of logic, but is affected by other factors such as fairness, and the need to avoid the proliferation of side issues which may serve to confuse the jury'.[68]

---

66 (1985) 82 Cr App R 181, p 185.

67 [1990] Crim LR 51.

68 See also above, Chapter 1, and the discussion of cross-examination on previous acquittals, above, Chapter 4, pp 70–73.

CHAPTER 16

ESTOPPEL

An 'estoppel' exists when, *in consequence of some previous act or statement to which he is either a party or a privy*,[1] a person is precluded from afterwards showing the existence of a different state of affairs than that indicated by the previous act or statement.[2] The rule is based on considerations of justice and public policy. It would be *unjust* to allow someone to do or say something, yet afterwards try to obtain an advantage by denying the validity of what he did earlier, or the truth of what he said earlier. It would be *contrary to public policy* to allow identical claims to be repeatedly litigated. But estoppel cannot be used to authorise illegality.[3] For example, if powers that are *ultra vires* are assumed by a person or body, estoppel cannot be used to authorise what has been done.[4] Similarly, the courts have refused to allow an estoppel to prevent the application of the Moneylenders Acts.[5] It is a matter of interpretation in each case whether a statute has made a transaction absolutely illegal or void, or merely voidable; in the latter case, it may be possible to plead estoppel successfully.[6]

It has been a matter of some controversy whether estoppel forms part of adjective or substantive law. Some judges have insisted that it is merely a rule of evidence, and so belongs exclusively to adjective law.[7] Others have pointed out that while a party cannot found a cause of action on an estoppel, he may, as a result of being able to rely on an estoppel, succeed in a cause of action where otherwise he would have failed; for this reason, it is said, estoppel is more correctly viewed as a substantive rule of law.[8] The truth of the matter is that in some contexts estoppel will appear to operate more as a rule of

---

1   A 'privy' is someone who has a type of legal connection to another person; for example, for some purposes an agent is the privy of his principal, and vice versa. See further, below, pp 375–76.

2   The definition of estoppel by Diplock LJ in *Thoday v Thoday* [1963] P 181, p 197, is too wide to differentiate this rule of exclusion from others.

3   *Re A Bankruptcy Notice* [1924] 2 Ch 76, p 97, *per* Lord Atkin.

4   See, eg, *Ministry of Agriculture and Fisheries v Matthews* [1950] 1 KB 148.

5   *Hoare v Adam Smith (London) Ltd* [1938] 4 All ER 283.

6   *Western Fish Products Ltd v Penwith District Council* [1981] 2 All ER 204, p 221, *per* Megaw LJ. A party relying on estoppel must plead it; failure to do so may amount to a waiver of the estoppel: *Vooght v Winch* (1819) 2 B&Ald 662.

7   See, eg, *Low v Bouverie* [1891] 3 Ch 82, p 105, *per* Bowen LJ; *Maritime Electric Company Ltd v General Dairies Ltd* [1937] AC 610, p 620, *per* Lord Maugham.

8   See, eg, *Canada and Dominion Sugar Co Ltd v Canadian National (West Indies) Steamships Ltd* [1947] AC 46, p 56, *per* Lord Wright; *Amalgamated Investment and Property Co Ltd v Texas Commerce International Bank Ltd* [1982] 1 QB 84, pp 131–32, *per* Brandon LJ.

substantive law; in others it will appear predominantly to be a rule of evidence, and so part of adjective law. This chapter is concerned only with those features that belong to adjective law. In particular, no reference is made to 'equitable estoppel', which is more appropriately seen as part of substantive law.

In accordance with my aim of covering estoppel only to the extent that it operates as a rule of evidence, I have divided this chapter into three parts. The first, and largest, part deals with estoppels that arise from previous judicial proceedings. This is followed by shorter sections on estoppel by deed and estoppel by representation.

ESTOPPEL BY PREVIOUS JUDICIAL PROCEEDINGS

A judgment is conclusive against everyone in relation to the *legal state of affairs* that it produces. This is of special importance where the judgment affects the status of a person or thing (a 'judgment *in rem*'), for example, a judgment to the effect that a person is divorced, or that a ship seized in wartime is not a neutral vessel. A judgment also has the effect of preventing the parties to an action, or their privies,[9] from *denying the facts on which it is based*. This form of estoppel may operate either as 'cause of action estoppel' or as 'issue estoppel', and is based on two policy considerations. The first is that litigation should be final; the second, that nobody should be harassed twice in respect of the same cause of action.[10]

Cause of action estoppel

This prevents a party to an action from asserting or denying, as against the other party, the existence of a particular cause of action, the existence of which has already been determined in a final judgment on the merits in previous litigation between the same parties. If judgment was given for the plaintiff in the earlier action, the cause of action no longer exists (and so cannot be sued on again) because the judgment has taken its place. If judgment was given for the defendant in the earlier action, the effect is that the earlier court has found the cause of action not to exist. As a result, the unsuccessful plaintiff can no longer assert that it does. Suppose, for example, that Alice sues Bertie for repayment of a loan of £10,000, which she alleges was made to Bertie on 1

---

9 See below, pp 375–76.

10 See, eg, *Carl Zeiss Stiftung v Rayner and Keeler Ltd (No 2)* [1967] AC 853, p 946, *per* Lord Upjohn; *C (A Minor) v Hackney London Borough Council* [1996] 1 WLR 789, p 792, *per* Simon Brown LJ. Some judges and writers refer to these policies in their Latin forms: *'Interest republicae ut sit finis litium'* and *'Nemo debet bis vexari pro una [et eadem] causa'*.

April 2001. Bertie, by his defence, denies the fact of the loan and says that the money was a gift. In due course, the county court judge hears the action, decides that the transaction was a gift rather than a loan, and gives judgment for Bertie. Alice cannot later sue Bertie again to recover the same sum on the basis that it was a loan. If she tries to do so, Bertie will apply successfully to have her action struck out as an abuse of the process of the court, on the ground that she is estopped by the judgment in the first action from making the allegation that she loaned him the money.[11]

Originally, this form of estoppel was known as 'estoppel by record' (the record being that of the court delivering the judgment), but it is now immaterial whether the judicial decision has been pronounced by a tribunal that is required to keep a written record of its decisions or not.[12] A final judgment 'on the merits' means a judgment on the cause of action that cannot be varied, re-opened or set aside by the court delivering it, or by any other court of co-ordinate jurisdiction, although it may be subject to appeal to a court of higher jurisdiction.[13] There will be no judgment on the merits when an action is dismissed for want of prosecution.[14] Default judgments and judgments by consent, however, are treated as judgments 'on the merits'.[15] A judgment obtained by fraud or collusion will not give rise to an estoppel.[16]

Cause of action estoppel applies also to 'privies' of (or to persons who are 'in privity with') the parties to the original action.[17] The term 'privity' refers to a type of relation between two or more parties that is recognised by the law, and is said to be either of blood (for example, between ancestor and heir), of title (for example, between vendor and purchaser), or of interest.[18] The difficulty with this description is the potentially wide concept of 'interest'. It is clear that privity for this purpose is not established merely by having some interest, in the sense of mere curiosity or concern, in the outcome of the original litigation. The sense of 'interest' is narrower than that, and is governed by the fundamental principle that nobody should be harassed twice in respect of the same cause of action. This principle requires some degree of identity between the successful defendant in the first action and the party who is being sued in the later action. For example, in an action relating to trust property, there will normally be sufficient privity between the trustees and the

---

11 See CPR, r 3.4(2) and PD, para 1.5.

12 *Carl Zeiss Stiftung v Rayner and Keeler Ltd (No 2)* [1967] AC 853, p 933, *per* Lord Guest.

13 *The Sennar (No 2)* [1985] 1 WLR 490, p 494, *per* Lord Diplock.

14 *In Re Orrell Colliery and Fire-Brick Company* (1879) Ch D 681.

15 *In Re South American and Mexican Company ex p Bank of England* [1895] 1 Ch 37; *Kinch v Walcott* [1929] AC 482; *Kok Hoong v Leong Cheong Kweng Mines Ltd* [1964] AC 993, pp 1010–12, *per* Lord Radcliffe.

16 *The Duchess of Kingston's* case (1776) 20 St Tr 355, pp 478–81.

17 *C (A Minor) v Hackney London Borough Council* [1996] 1 WLR 789, p 792, *per* Simon Brown LJ.

18 *Ibid*; *Carl Zeiss Stifftung v Rayner and Keeler Ltd (No 2)*, p 910, *per* Lord Reid.

beneficiaries to make a decision that is binding on the trustees binding on the beneficiaries, and vice versa. In deciding whether or not privity exists, it is important to remember that privity with a party to earlier proceedings will apply whether that party won or lost. This consideration requires a narrow construction of 'interest', because:

> Any contention which leads to the conclusion that a person is liable to be condemned unheard is plainly open to the gravest of suspicions. A defendant ought to be able to put his own defence in his own way, and to call his own evidence. He ought not to be concluded by the failure of the defence and evidence adduced by another defendant in other proceedings unless his standing in those other proceedings justifies the conclusion that a decision against the defendant in them ought fairly and truly to be said to be in substance a decision against him. Even if one leaves on one side collusive proceedings and friendly defendants, it would be wrong to enable a plaintiff to select the frailest of a number of possible defendants, and then to use the victory against him not merely *in terrorem* of other and more stalwart possible defendants, but as a decisive weapon against them.[19]

Issue estoppel

There are many causes of action that can be established only by proving that two or more different conditions are fulfilled. Such causes of action involve as many separate issues between the parties as there are conditions to be fulfilled by the plaintiff in order to establish his cause of action. If, in litigation on one cause of action, any of the separate issues as to whether a particular condition has been fulfilled is determined by a court of competent jurisdiction, neither party can, in subsequent litigation between one another on *any* cause of action that depends on the fulfilment of the identical condition, assert that the condition was fulfilled if the court in the first action determined that it was not. Nor can either party subsequently deny that such a condition was fulfilled if the court in the first action determined that it was.[20] In order to see whether issue estoppel applies, the facts established and reasons given by the judge, his judgment, the pleadings, the evidence, and even the history of the matter may be taken into account.[21] For issue estoppel to apply, three conditions must be satisfied:

(a) the same issue must have been decided in the earlier case;

(b) the judicial decision in the earlier case must have been final; and

---

19 *Gleeson v J Wippell and Co Ltd* [1977] 1 WLR 510, p 516, *per* Megarry VC.

20 *Thoday v Thoday* [1963] P 181, p 198, *per* Diplock LJ.

21 *Carl Zeiss Stiftung v Rayner and Keeler Ltd (No 2)* [1967] AC 853, p 946, *per* Lord Upjohn.

(c) the parties to the decision, or their privies, must be the same persons as the parties to the proceedings in which the estoppel is raised, or their privies.[22]

The difference between cause of action estoppel and issue estoppel is that in cause of action estoppel, the cause of action has merged in the judgment and no longer has any independent existence. In issue estoppel, for the purpose of some *other* claim or cause of action, a state of fact or law is alleged or denied, the existence of which is a matter necessarily decided by the prior judgment, and it cannot afterwards be raised between the same parties or their privies. It has been suggested that one test for the operation of issue estoppel is that a party will be estopped from bringing an action which, if it succeeds, will result in a judgment conflicting with an earlier judgment.[23]

Issue estoppel, like cause of action estoppel, is a feature of adversary procedure.[24] Where proceedings have an inquisitorial element, therefore, issue estoppel will not be strictly applied. So, for example, issue estoppel could rarely, if ever, apply to proceedings for divorce, or to children's cases.[25] Another example occurred in *The European Gateway*.[26] In this case, Steyn J held that a court set up to conduct a formal investigation into a collision at sea under the Merchant Shipping Act 1894 was a court of competent jurisdiction in exercising its powers to order a master's certificate to be suspended or cancelled. But he held that in other matters its role was purely investigatory, with the result that it was not a court of competent jurisdiction in relation to the shipowners' civil liability. Matters litigated before the court of formal investigation could accordingly be litigated again in High Court Admiralty proceedings, and were not barred by issue estoppel.

Issue estoppel has been extended to cover not only the case where a particular point has been raised and specifically determined in the earlier proceedings, but also the case where a party later attempts to raise a point that might have been, but was not, raised in the earlier proceedings. This extension is based on *dicta* in *Henderson v Henderson*, where Wigram VC said:

> I believe I state the rule of the court correctly when I say that, where a given matter becomes the subject of litigation in, and of adjudication by, a court of competent jurisdiction, the court requires the parties to that litigation to bring forward their whole case, and will not (except under special circumstances) permit the same parties to open the same subject of litigation in respect of matter which might have been brought forward as part of the subject in contest, but which was not brought forward, only because they have, from

---

22 *Carl Zeiss Stiftung v Rayner and Keeler Ltd (No 2)* [1967] AC 853, p 935, *per* Lord Guest.

23 *Port of Melbourne Authority v Anshun Proprietary Limited* (1981) 147 CLR 589, pp 597, 603, *per* Gibbs CJ, Mason and Aickin JJ.

24 See above, p 38.

25 See, eg, *Thoday v Thoday* [1964] P 181; *B v Derbyshire County Council* [1992] 1 FLR 538; *In Re B* [1997] 3 WLR 1.

26 [1987] QB 206.

negligence, inadvertence, or even accident, omitted part of their case. The plea of *res judicata* applies, except in special cases, not only to points upon which the court was actually required by the parties to form an opinion and pronounce a judgment, but to every point which properly belonged to the subject of litigation, and which the parties, exercising reasonable diligence, might have brought forward at the time.[27]

Although the court in *Henderson* was considering cause of action estoppel, it is clear that Wigram VC's observations apply to issue estoppel also.[28] They were spoken of as 'settled law' by Lord Shaw when delivering the opinion of the Privy Council in *Hoystead v Commissioner of Taxation.*[29]

The rule in *Henderson* thus falls into two parts. The first relates to those points actually decided by the court. Secondly, the rule extends to those points which might have been brought forward at the time, but were not. This is founded on the principle of public policy in preventing multiplicity of actions.[30] Thus in *Greenhalgh v Mallard,*[31] it was held that if, in one action for damages for conspiracy, acts done in combination are alleged, a plaintiff cannot bring a second action on the same facts, even though in the first action the claim was formulated on the basis of an unjustified ultimate purpose only, without reliance on the means by which it was to be achieved, and in the second action the means were alleged to be unlawful, but no challenge was made to the legitimacy of the ultimate purpose.

A further example of the operation of the rule can be seen in the decision of the High Court of Australia in *Port of Melbourne Authority v Anshun Proprietary Ltd.*[32] Under an agreement for the hire of a crane, Anshun agreed to indemnify the Port Authority against any claims that might be made against the Authority arising from the use of the crane. A workman suffered injury arising from Anshun's use of the crane, and he sued Anshun and the Authority for damages. The defendants served contribution notices on each other, but the Authority's notice was confined to a claim for contribution. Damages were awarded against both defendants, and between them it was ordered that the Authority pay 90% and Anshun 10%. The Authority then brought a separate action against Anshun, claiming an indemnity under the agreement in respect of all amounts that it had paid to the workman as damages and costs. The judge ordered that the action be stayed on the ground that the claim under the agreement should have been raised in the original action, with the result that the Authority was estopped from raising it in the

---

27 (1843) 3 Hare 100, pp 114–15.
28 *Arnold v National Westminster Bank plc* [1991] 2 AC 93, p 107, *per* Lord Keith of Kinkel.
29 [1926] AC 155, p 170.
30 *Talbot v Berkshire County Council* [1994] QB 290, p 296, *per* Stuart-Smith LJ.
31 [1947] 2 All ER 255.
32 (1981) 147 CLR 589.

current litigation. The majority of the High Court[33] held that this reasoning was correct. The Authority had been unreasonable in failing to raise the indemnity agreement in the first action, as that agreement was a defence to Anshun's claim for contribution, and was so closely connected with the subject matter of that action that it was to be expected that the Authority would raise it as a defence and as a basis of recovery from Anshun. A decision that the Authority was not entitled to an indemnity against Anshun had not been a necessary step to the judgment in the first action that Anshun was entitled to contribution, and the judgment did not, therefore, effect an issue estoppel in the strict sense, but it did in the extended sense based on the rule in *Henderson*. The High Court noted that the application of the rule to issue estoppel was to be treated with caution, and said that there should be no estoppel unless it appeared that the matter relied upon as a defence in the second action was so relevant to the subject matter of the first that it would have been unreasonable not to rely on it.[34]

The English Court of Appeal has held that the rule in *Henderson* should apply in actions for personal injury. A classic problem was presented in *Talbot v Berkshire County Council*.[35] A was a passenger in a motor car driven by B, which was involved in a collision caused partly by the fault of B and partly by the fault of C, the local authority, which was responsible for the maintenance of the highway. A and B were both injured in the collision. A sued B for damages for personal injury. B issued third party proceedings against C, claiming a contribution in respect of A's claim, but making no claim against C in respect of B's own injuries. Judgment was given in A's favour against both B and C, who were each held partly to blame. B subsequently brought a fresh action against C in respect of his own personal injuries. The Court of Appeal held that he was estopped from doing so. The court said that the rule in *Henderson* was valuable, because it avoided unnecessary expense to the parties and the waste of court time that could be available to other litigants. A further argument in its favour was that it had the advantage, particularly important in personal injury claims, of preventing stale claims from being brought long after the event; it enabled a defendant to know the extent of his potential liability in respect of any one event, which was important for insurance companies, who had to make provision for claims; it might also affect their conduct of negotiations, their defence and any question of appeal. The court said that the *Henderson* rule should not be restricted to those cases where points could have been taken, but were not, in relation to one particular cause of action and defence. B's own personal injury claim should have been brought at the time of the original action. A safeguard to prevent injustice existed in that the court would not apply the rule in its full rigour if there were

---

33   Gibbs CJ, Mason and Aickin JJ.
34   (1981) 147 CLR 589, p 602.
35   [1994] QB 290.

special circumstances why it should not do so. But no such circumstances existed in this case:

> The mere fact that a party is precluded by the rule from advancing a claim will inevitably involve some injustice to him, if it is or may be a good claim; but that cannot of itself amount to a special circumstance, since otherwise the rule would never have any application. The court has to consider why the claim was not brought in the earlier proceedings. The plaintiff may not have known of the claim at that time ... or there may have been some agreement between the parties that the claim should be held in abeyance to abide the outcome of the first proceedings; or some representation may have been made to the plaintiff on which he has relied, so that he did not bring the claim earlier. These would be examples of special circumstances, though of course they are not intended to be an exhaustive list.[36]

The court acknowledged that the negligence or inadvertence of which Wigram VC had spoken would often be that of legal advisers rather than of the party himself, but added that 'the action or inaction of the agent is that of the principal'.[37]

In reaching this decision, the Court of Appeal dealt with one aspect of a problem that had arisen from the requirement that for issue estoppel to operate, there must be an identity of issues as well as parties. The question whether there is identity of issues depends on whether the issues are analysed broadly or minutely. In road accident cases, the issue may be seen as, 'Who caused the collision?'. Alternatively, it may be argued that because negligence requires a breach of duty owed to a particular individual[38] there are different issues for each particular duty of care, so that identity of issues will be rare. Several cases at first instance show different approaches to the problem.[39] So far as personal injury cases are concerned, it appears that the Court of Appeal favours the use of the rule in *Henderson* to bypass undesirable effects of minute analysis. But in other types of litigation this approach may not be possible. For example, in *New Brunswick Railway Co v British and French Trust Corporation Ltd*,[40] the House of Lords held that a judgment delivered on the construction of one bond would not operate as an estoppel to prevent one of the parties to that action raising a defence as to the construction of another bond in a different action, even though the two bonds were in identical terms. The House was of the opinion that if in an action the question of the

---

36 [1994] QB 290, p 299.

37 *Ibid*. See also *Wain v F Sherwood and Sons Transport Ltd* (1998) *The Times*, 16 July. But the rule in *Henderson v Henderson* has been held not to extend to prevent a defendant from bringing a subsequent action when he could have claimed an indemnity or contribution in earlier proceedings in which he was sued with a co-defendant. See *Sweetman v Shepherd and Others* (2000) *The Times*, 29 March (CA).

38 *Bourhill v Young* [1943] AC 92.

39 See, eg, *Randolph v Tuck* [1962] 1 QB 175; *Wood v Luscombe* [1966] 1 QB 169; *Wall v Radford* [1991] 2 All ER 741.

40 [1939] AC 1.

construction of a particular document had been decided, each party to that action was estopped from subsequently litigating the same question of construction of that particular document. But the parties would not be estopped from subsequently litigating the question of construction of another document, even though the second one was in substantially identical words. 'For the documents are two distinct documents, and the questions of their construction are two distinct questions.'[41]

The parties to the earlier decision must not only have been the *same persons* as the parties to the later action in which the estoppel is raised. They must also be suing or being sued in the later action in the *same capacities* as in the first. In *Marginson v Blackburn Borough Council*,[42] the plaintiff was a passenger in a motor car owned and driven by his wife. The car was involved in a collision with a bus driven by an employee of the defendants. As a result of the collision, the plaintiff suffered personal injuries, his wife was killed, and two nearby houses were damaged. The owners of the houses sued both Marginson and the council, alleging that the damage to their houses had been caused by the negligence of both drivers, Marginson being vicariously liable (as the law then stood) for the negligence of his wife, and the council for that of its employee. There were third party proceedings between Marginson and the council. The county court judge held Marginson and the council equally liable. Subsequently, Marginson brought a High Court action against the council. He claimed in two capacities. First, he claimed damages in his own right for the injuries that he had suffered. He also claimed as the administrator of his wife's estate for the benefit of her estate, and on his own and his daughter's behalf as dependants of his deceased wife. The Court of Appeal held that Marginson was estopped from pursuing his personal claim by virtue of the county court judgment (the law then being that contributory negligence was a complete defence to a claim in negligence), but the court held that he was not estopped from pursuing the claims that he was making in a representative capacity, as administrator of his wife's estate.

Identity of parties was a crucial factor in *C (A Minor) v Hackney London Borough Council*,[43] in which the Court of Appeal distinguished *Talbot v Berkshire County Council*.[44] The plaintiff, a minor, lived in a council house where her mother was the tenant. The house was damp and in a state of disrepair. An action by the plaintiff's mother against the council, based on these facts, was disposed of by way of a consent order specifying the works necessary to put the house into repair and providing for payment of damages. Afterwards, the plaintiff brought proceedings against the council by her stepfather as next friend, claiming damages for negligence and breach of

---

41 [1939] AC 1, p 43, *per* Lord Romer.
42 [1939] 2 KB 426.
43 [1996] 1 WLR 789.
44 [1994] QB 290.

statutory duty under the Defective Premises Act 1972. She alleged ill health from the disrepair. It was argued for the council that she was estopped from bringing the action by virtue of the consent order made in the earlier action brought by her mother. The court rejected this argument. It could not be right, it said, that her dependence on her mother created such a nexus between them that they should be regarded effectively as the same party. If that were so, it would be right equally in the context of a road accident case where a mother and infant child were both injured by the defendant's negligence. If the mother sued and obtained judgment on her own behalf, it could not be the case that her child would be thereby barred from making a subsequent claim. The court said that the critical difference between this case and the *Talbot* case was that in the latter the parties were the same; in this case they were not.

Does the fact that the first judgment was obtained by default make any difference to the application of the rule in the *Henderson* case? There are various *dicta* to suggest that it does. In *New Brunswick Railway Co v British and French Trust Corporation Ltd*, Lord Maugham LC said:

> In my opinion we are at least justified in holding that an estoppel based on a default judgment must be very carefully limited. The true principle in such a case would seem to be that the defendant is estopped from setting up in a subsequent action a defence which was necessarily, and with complete precision, decided by the previous judgment ...[45]

In the same case, Lord Wright said that all necessary effect was given to a default judgment by treating it as conclusive of what it directly decided; a further effect by way of estoppel would be an illegitimate extension of the doctrine.[46]

A similarly cautious approach was suggested by Lord Radcliffe when delivering the opinion of the Privy Council in *Kok Hoong v Leong Cheong Kweng Mines Ltd*.[47] After stating that there was no doubt that a default judgment could give rise to an estoppel, he said that the question was not whether there could be such an estoppel, but rather what the judgment should be treated as deciding. 'There is obvious and, indeed, grave danger in permitting such a judgment to preclude the parties from ever reopening before the court on another occasion, perhaps of very different significance, whatever issues can be discerned as having been involved in the judgment so obtained by default.' From one point of view, a default judgment was like a judgment by consent, but from another, it 'speaks for nothing but the fact that a defendant, for unascertained reasons, negligence, ignorance or indifference, has suffered judgment to go against him in the particular suit in question'. In his opinion, when judgment had been obtained by default, it would be wrong to apply the full rigour of any principle as widely formulated as that in

45 [1939] AC 1, p 21.
46 *Ibid*, p 38.
47 [1964] AC 993, pp 1010–12.

Henderson; a much more restricted operation should be given to any estoppel arising from a default judgment. In *Arnold v National Westminster Bank plc* Lord Keith of Kinkel suggested that, where the earlier proceedings had resulted in a default judgment, this might amount to special circumstances that would prevent the rule in *Henderson* from applying.[48]

It is plain from *Henderson* that the discovery of new material will not by itself suffice to avoid issue estoppel. The point was further explained by Lord Cairns LC in *Phosphate Sewage Co Ltd v Molleson*, where he said that a party who had been unsuccessful in litigation could not be allowed to reopen that litigation merely by saying that, since the former case, there had emerged another fact going in exactly the same direction as the facts stated before, leading up to the same relief asked for before, but additional to facts already relied on. The only way litigation could be reopened was if the new fact entirely changed the aspect of the case, and it could not by reasonable diligence have been discovered before.[49] In *Arnold v National Westminster Bank plc*, Lord Keith of Kinkel suggested that it should be easier to overcome an issue estoppel than a cause of action estoppel where a party relies on further relevant material which he could not by reasonable diligence have adduced in the earlier proceedings. The underlying principles on which estoppel is based – public policy and justice – have, he said, greater force in cause of action estoppel, where the subject matter of the two proceedings is identical, than they do in issue estoppel, where the subject matter is different.[50]

There are signs that the rule in *Henderson v Henderson* may now be applied more flexibly. In *Johnson v Gore Wood & Co*,[51] the House of Lords held that the raising of a matter in later proceedings will not necessarily be an abuse of process just because it could have been raised in earlier proceedings. Whether there is an abuse of process will not depend on a dogmatic approach, but on a broad, merits-based judgment. It is preferable to ask whether in all the circumstances, a party's conduct was an abuse of process than to ask whether it was an abuse and then, if it was, whether it was excused or justified by special circumstances. It remains to be seen whether this approach will in practice produce different results.

Analogous provisions in criminal proceedings

We have seen that, in civil cases, cause of action estoppel will prevent a defendant from being sued twice in respect of the same cause of action. A

---

48 [1991] 2 AC 93, p 107.
49 (1879) 4 App Cas 801, p 814. Lord Cairns's test was applied by the Court of Appeal in *Ashmore v British Coal Corporation* [1990] 2 QB 338, and in *Smith v Linskills* [1996] 1 WLR 763, and by the House of Lords in *Hunter v Chief Constable of the West Midlands Police* [1982] AC 529.
50 [1991] 2 AC 93, p 108.
51 (2000) *The Times*, 22 December.

similar principle operates in criminal law, in which the pleas of *autrefois acquit* and *autrefois convict* are available to prevent a defendant's being put in what is sometimes called 'double jeopardy'. The leading authority on the scope of these pleas at common law is the speech of Lord Morris of Borth-y-Gest in *Connelly v DPP*.[52] In this speech, Lord Morris laid down a number of propositions, of which the following are the most important:

(a) A man cannot be tried for a crime in respect of which he has previously been acquitted or convicted.

(b) A man cannot be tried for a crime in respect of which he could on some previous indictment have been convicted.

(c) The same rule applies if the crime in respect of which he is being charged is in effect the same, or substantially the same, as a crime in respect of which he has been acquitted, or could have been convicted, or has been convicted.

(d) One test as to whether the rule applies is whether the evidence that is necessary to support the second indictment, or whether the facts that constitute the second offence, would have been sufficient to procure a conviction on the first indictment, either in relation to the offence charged, or in relation to an offence of which, on that indictment, the accused could have been found guilty.

A substantial inroad on the common law has been made in ss 54–57 of the Criminal Procedure and Investigations Act 1996. These sections introduce the concept of 'tainted acquittals' and apply to acquittals in respect of offences alleged to have been committed on or after 15 April 1997.[53]

The provisions apply where (a) a person has been acquitted of an offence, and (b) a person has been convicted of an 'administration of justice offence' involving interference with or intimidation of a juror or a witness, or potential witness, in any proceedings that led to the acquittal.[54] Where it appears to the court before which the person was convicted that there is a real possibility that, but for the interference or intimidation, the acquitted person would not have been acquitted, the court shall certify that it so appears, unless it would be contrary to the interests of justice to take proceedings against the acquitted person for the offence of which he was acquitted, whether because of lapse of time, or for any other reason.[55] Where a court has certified under these provisions, an application may be made to the High Court for an order quashing the acquittal. Where such an order is made, proceedings may be

---

52 [1964] AC 1254.

53 Criminal Procedure and Investigations Act 1996 (Appointed Day No 4) Order (SI 1997/1019).

54 Criminal Procedure and Investigations Act 1996, s 54(1). The definition of an 'administration of justice offence' is contained in s 54(6).

55 Criminal Procedure and Investigations Act 1996, s 54(2) and (5).

taken against the acquitted person for the offence in respect of which he was acquitted.

The High Court shall not make an order quashing an acquittal unless four conditions are satisfied:

(a) It appears to the High Court likely that, but for the interference or intimidation, the acquitted person would not have been acquitted.

(b) It does not appear to the court that, because of lapse of time or for any other reason, it would be contrary to the interests of justice to take proceedings against the acquitted person for the offence of which he was acquitted.

(c) It appears to the court that the acquitted person has been given a reasonable opportunity to make *written* representations to the court.

(d) It appears to the court that the conviction for the administration of justice offence will stand. In determining whether this condition is satisfied, the court shall take into account all the information before it, but shall ignore the possibility of new factors coming to light.[56]

The pleas of *autrefois acquit* and *autrefois convict* provide in a criminal context something analogous to cause of action estoppel in civil proceedings. Is there anything analogous to issue estoppel?[57] Some authorities suggest that the prosecution may be estopped from adducing evidence that either contradicts, or is at least inconsistent with, a defendant's innocence of an earlier offence for which he has been tried and acquitted. The principal authority was formerly the decision of the Privy Council in *Sambasivam v Public Prosecutor*.[58] In that case, the Privy Council held that the effect of an acquittal was not just that the person acquitted could not be tried again for the same offence. In addition, the verdict was binding and conclusive in all subsequent proceedings between the parties to the adjudication. The defendant had originally been charged on two counts, one in relation to possession of a firearm and the other in relation to possession of ammunition. He had signed a statement admitting both offences, but repudiated this at trial. He was acquitted of the charge relating to ammunition, but the court disagreed on the other charge, and a re-trial was ordered. At the re-trial, the whole confession was once again put in evidence. The parts dealing with possession of ammunition were, of course, inconsistent with the defendant's previous acquittal, but the court was not told of the acquittal, and it convicted the defendant on the firearms charge. The Privy Council held that the conviction should be set aside. Lord MacDermott said:

> Here, the appellant having been acquitted at the first trial on the charge of having ammunition in his possession, the prosecution was bound to accept the

---

56 Criminal Procedure and Investigations Act 1996, s 55.

57 See Mirfield, P, 'Shedding a tear for issue estoppel' [1980] Crim LR 336; Hirst, M, 'Contradicting previous acquittals' [1991] Crim LR 510.

58 [1950] AC 458.

correctness of the verdict, and was precluded from taking any step to challenge it at the second trial. And the appellant was no less entitled to rely on his acquittal in so far as it might be relevant in his defence.[59]

The *Sambasivam* rule was unlike issue estoppel because it was one-sided. An accused person is not prevented from denying that he committed an offence for which he has been convicted; he has only to overcome a presumption of guilt under s 74 of the Police and Criminal Evidence Act 1984. By contrast, a true estoppel is mutual: it binds both parties.

But the rule was capable of leading to difficulties, as Hirst pointed out:

> Imagine that D has been charged with a murder, and acquitted in controversial circumstances; imagine then that some months later a similar offence is committed, and that it is clear for various reasons that whoever committed the first offence also committed the second. Moreover, D seems to be the only person who could have been involved in both incidents. The *Sambasivam* rule would preclude use of that crucial similar fact evidence.[60]

Hirst's hypothetical problem arose in *R v Z*.[61] The defendant was charged with rape. His defence was that the complainant had consented to intercourse, alternatively, that he believed that she had consented. In order to rebut these defences, the prosecution wished to call four women who had made previous complaints of rape against the defendant. Each complaint had given rise to a separate trial. In one, the defendant had been convicted, but in the other three, he had been acquitted. At a preparatory hearing, the judge ruled that the one conviction was insufficient to be admitted as similar fact evidence, and the prosecution did not challenge that. The judge also ruled that the four sets of circumstances, taken together, shared enough common features to be admissible as similar fact evidence, but that evidence of the circumstances surrounding allegations that had led to acquittals was inadmissible because of the rule in *Sambasivam*. On an interlocutory appeal by the prosecution, the Court of Appeal reluctantly upheld this ruling, but that court's decision was subsequently reversed by the House of Lords, which held that the principle of double jeopardy does not render relevant evidence inadmissible merely because that evidence tends to show that a defendant was in fact guilty of an offence of which he was earlier acquitted. Such evidence is admissible because the defendant is not being put on trial again for the offence of which he has been acquitted, nor does he stand in jeopardy of being punished for it on some other ground.

---

59 [1950] AC 458, p 479.

60 Hirst, *op cit*, fn 57, p 517.

61 [2000] 3 All ER 385. See Roberts, P, 'Acquitted misconduct evidence and double jeopardy principles, from *Sambasivam* to *Z*' [2000] Crim LR 952; Mirfield, P, '*Res judicata* rejected' [2001] 117 LQR 194.

ESTOPPEL BY DEED

Where an action is brought on a deed, the parties to the deed and those claiming through them, such as successors in title, are estopped from denying the truth of the facts stated in the deed. An early example of the application of this rule is *Bowman v Taylor*.[62] The plaintiff claimed as patentee the rent under a licence to use certain looms for weaving, called 'power looms', which had been granted to the defendants. The licence had been granted by a deed, which recited that the plaintiff had invented power looms, for which he had obtained a patent. The defendants by their plea denied, amongst other things, that the plaintiff was the inventor, or that the power loom was a new invention. The plaintiff alleged that those pleas were bad, because the defendants were estopped by the recitals in the deed to which they were parties. The Court of King's Bench held that where a person has entered into a deed, by which, in express terms, he has admitted certain facts to exist, he is estopped from afterwards disputing those facts. The recitals were so bound up in the deed that they were essentially part of the deed itself. Accordingly, the defendants were estopped from denying either that the power loom was a new invention, or that the plaintiff was its inventor.

However, in *Greer v Kettle*,[63] Lord Maugham said that while he did not doubt the correctness of the result in *Bowman v Taylor*, he did doubt whether the recital considered in that case could properly be taken to be a statement on behalf of the licensee, who could have had little knowledge of the matters contained in it. The decision was better explained on the ground that the deed was entered into on the footing that the recital, whether true or not, must be taken during the continuance of the licence as true. Thus, the licensee of a patent right was bound on the same principle and in the same way as a tenant who has taken a lease of lands from another, and who is estopped during the lease from denying his landlord's title.[64]

Recitals will not always bind both parties to a deed. The law was explained by Patteson J in *Stroughill v Buck* as follows:

> When a recital is intended to be a statement which all the parties to the deed have mutually agreed to admit as true, it is an estoppel upon all. But, when it is intended to be the statement of one party only, the estoppel is confined to that party, and the intention is to be gathered from construing the instrument.[65]

This statement of the law was approved by the House of Lords in *Greer v Kettle*.

---

62 (1834) 4 LJKB 58.
63 [1938] AC 156.
64 *Ibid*, pp 169–70.
65 (1850) 14 QB 781, p 787.

For recitals to be binding, they must relate to specific facts, and be certain, clear and unambiguous.[66] Estoppel by deed will not operate so as to prevent a party from relying on fraud, duress, illegality, or any other fact entitling him to rescission or rectification of the deed.[67] An example of such a case is *Wilson v Wilson*.[68] The defendant, Lascelles Wilson, wanted to buy a house with the help of a building society loan. His personal earnings did not meet the society's requirements, so he invited his brother, Donald Wilson, to become a co-purchaser. The transfer, by which the vendor transferred his interest in the property to the two brothers, stated that the transferees should stand possessed of the property as joint tenants upon trust for sale, with a power to postpone sale. The title was registered in the brothers' joint names subject to a registered charge to the building society, both brothers being joined as mortgagors. The plaintiff later served a notice purporting to sever the joint tenancy and began an action claiming that, pursuant to the transfer, he was entitled to an undivided share in half the property.

Buckley J held that the common intention of the brothers at the time of purchase was that the beneficial ownership should be vested solely in the defendant, and that the plaintiff had joined in the transaction merely in order to help his brother to obtain a mortgage. The two brothers had not appreciated the effect of the declaration of beneficial interest, or had even appreciated that it was in the deed at all. Accordingly, he concluded that there should be rectification of the transfer, and the parties were not estopped by the declaration of beneficial interest that it contained.

ESTOPPEL BY CONDUCT

An estoppel may arise where it would be unconscionable for a person to deny a representation of fact that is implicit in his conduct. Such an estoppel may arise from agreement, from an express or implied representation, or from negligence. For there to be estoppel by conduct, the representation must relate to an existing fact and be unambiguous.

Agreement

An old example is *Cooke v Loxley*.[69] This was an action for use and occupation of land let to the defendant by the plaintiff's predecessor in title. The defendant had paid rent not only to the plaintiff's predecessor in title, but also

---

66   *Greer v Kettle* [1938] AC 156, p 170, *per* Lord Maugham.

67   *Ibid*, p 171.

68   [1969] 1 WLR 1470.

69   (1792) 5 TR 4.

to the plaintiff. At trial, the defendant wanted to call evidence that the plaintiff had no title to the land. The evidence was rejected, and the trial judge's decision was upheld by the Court of King's Bench. Lord Kenyon CJ said that in an action for use and occupation, a tenant who occupies land by agreement with another, ought not, as a matter of convenience and public policy, to be permitted to call upon that other person to show the title under which he let the land.

For similar reasons bailees, licensees and agents cannot deny the title of their bailors, licensors or principals after having effectively acknowledged them in the transactions carried out on their behalf.[70]

Express or implied representation

In *Pickard v Sears*,[71] the rule was laid down that where a person by words or conduct wilfully causes another to believe in a certain state of things, and thereby induces him to act or to alter his own previous position, the representor will be estopped from alleging that a different state of affairs existed at the time when the representation was made. By 'wilfully', it is meant either that the representor alleges something to be true that he knows to be false, or that he means his representation to be acted upon, and it is acted upon accordingly. 'If, whatever a man's meaning may be, he so conducts himself that a reasonable man would take the representation to be true, and believe that it was meant he should act upon it, and did act upon it as true, the party making the representation would be equally precluded from contesting its truth.'[72]

In *Greenwood v Martins Bank Ltd*,[73] for example, the plaintiff's wife had forged her husband's signature on cheques drawn on the defendant bank. The husband discovered that his wife had been forging his signature, but at first said nothing about it to the bank. Eventually, he threatened to do so, and the wife killed herself. The husband then sued the bank for the amounts that it had paid out of his account on the authority of the forged cheques, but it was held by the House of Lords that he was estopped from relying on the fact of the forgery. It was acknowledged that mere silence could not amount to a representation. When, however, there was a duty of disclosure, deliberate silence might become significant and amount to a representation. A bank's customer had a duty to disclose the fact of forgery to his bank, if he discovered it. The plaintiff's silence in this case therefore amounted to a representation that the forged cheques were in order. Assuming that detriment to the bank followed, all the elements essential to estoppel were present.

---

70 See, eg, *Gosling v Birnie* (1831) 7 Bing 399; *Crossley v Dixon* (1863) 10 HL Cas 293.
71 (1837) 6 A&E 469.
72 *Freeman v Cooke* (1848) 18 LJ Ex 114, pp 119–20, *per* Parke B.
73 [1933] AC 51.

Negligence

To establish estoppel by negligence, it has to be proved that a duty of care was owed to the person who has suffered loss,[74] and that there has been a breach of that duty. In *Coventry, Sheppard and Co v Great Eastern Railway*,[75] both conditions were satisfied. A railway company had negligently issued two delivery orders in respect of one consignment of wheat. This had enabled a swindler to obtain two advances of money, as if there had been two separate consignments. It was held that the railway company's negligence estopped it from denying that there had been two consignments.[76]

---

74 For a case where this could not be established, see *Moorgate Mercantile Co Ltd v Twitchings* [1977] AC 890.

75 (1883) 11 QBD 776.

76 Cf *Mercantile Bank of India Ltd v Central Bank of India Ltd* [1938] AC 287, where a plea of estoppel failed because there had been no breach of a duty of care.

CHAPTER 17

DOCUMENTARY AND REAL EVIDENCE

DOCUMENTARY EVIDENCE

A party who wishes to rely on a statement contained in a document as evidence supporting his case needs to consider, in addition to any other relevant evidence law, at least one further matter: proof of the contents of the document. In some cases, proof of due execution may have to be considered also.[1] So far as criminal cases are concerned, the basic provision that deals with proof of the contents of a document is s 27 of the Criminal Justice Act 1988. This provides that where a statement contained in a document is admissible as evidence in criminal proceedings, it may be proved either by the production of that document, or, whether or not the document is still in existence, by the production of a copy. A copy may be authenticated in such manner as the court may approve. It is immaterial how many removes there are between a copy and the original.[2] A 'statement' is any representation of fact, however made; a 'document' is anything in which information of any description is recorded; and a 'copy', in relation to a document, is anything onto which information recorded in the document has been copied, by whatever means and whether directly or indirectly.[3] Since the Civil Evidence Act 1995 has provisions in the same terms,[4] proof of the contents of a document is now essentially the same in both civil and criminal proceedings. Where a copy is produced, the courts appear to have a wide discretion as to the manner in which it may be authenticated, but the best method is likely to be proof by the evidence of a person with custody and control of the copy that it is a true copy of the original.[5] Given the broad terms of the present law, it is likely that the special provisions of the Bankers' Books Evidence Act 1879, regulating proof of the contents of such books by a system of examined copies, will fall into disuse, and the rather complex provisions of that Act are therefore not considered further.

---

1   This chapter deals only with proof of the contents of private documents; there are special rules for the proof of various public documents, details of which may be found in standard practitioners' works.

2   By the Criminal Procedure and Investigations Act 1996, Sched 2, para 31, s 27 has no application to proceedings before a magistrates' court inquiring into an offence as examining justices. The appropriate provision in those circumstances is s 71 of the Police and Criminal Evidence Act 1984, as amended by the 1996 Act.

3   Criminal Justice Act 1988, Sched 2, para 5, as amended by the Civil Evidence Act 1995, Sched 1, para 12.

4   Civil Evidence Act 1995, ss 8 and 13.

5   The strict approach adopted in *R v Collins* (1960) 44 Cr App R 170 is unlikely now to be followed.

It will be noted that where an original document is not available, s 27 of the Criminal Justice Act 1988 and s 8 of the Civil Evidence Act 1995 do not go so far as to allow proof of the contents of the original by oral evidence. At this point there remains a divergence between civil and criminal evidence law. In civil proceedings, although s 8 of the 1995 Act does not sanction the admission of oral evidence, oral hearsay evidence of the contents of a document that would itself be admissible if it were available can be given under the general provision for the admission of hearsay evidence contained in s 1. In criminal proceedings, however, the admissibility of oral evidence of the contents of a document is governed by common law. For this purpose it is necessary to look at the exceptions to the common law rule that only primary evidence of the contents of a document (that is, the original document itself) is admissible. There are four exceptions:

(a) *Destruction or loss of original.* Destruction by fire was one of the earliest acceptable excuses for failure to produce an original,[6] and the principle was afterwards extended to cover other circumstances in which the original had been lost or destroyed.[7] Before the exception can be applied where a document is missing, proof must be given that an adequate search has been made.[8] In such a case, the court must be reasonably satisfied that due diligence has been used: '... it is not necessary to negative every possibility – it is enough to negative every reasonable probability – of anything being kept back.'[9]

(b) *Other impossibility or inconvenience.* Production of a document may be excused, and secondary evidence given of its contents, when it is impossible for reasons other than destruction or loss to produce it, or even when it would be highly inconvenient to do so. Thus secondary evidence can be admitted of writing on a wall and of an inscription on a tombstone.[10] Similarly, secondary evidence has been admitted of inscriptions on flags and banners;[11] and of the contents of a placard on a wall;[12] of a document in the custody of a foreign court;[13] and of a notice that was required by statute to be fixed permanently to a wall.[14] In *R v*

---

6   *Leyfield's Case* (1611) 10 Co Rep 88a, pp 92b, 93a.

7   *Read v Brookman* (1789) 3 TR 151; *Pooley v Millard* (1831) 1 Cr&J 411; *Blackie v Pidding* (1848) 6 CB 196.

8   *Brewster v Sewell* (1820) 3 B&Ald 296.

9   *M'Gahey v Alston* (1836) 2 M&W 206, p 214.

10 *Mortimer v M'Callan* (1840) 6 M&W 58, pp 63, 68, 72. But a tombstone has been produced in evidence on at least one occasion: see *Boosey v Davidson* (1849) 13 QB 257, p 265.

11 *R v Hunt* (1820) 3 B&Ald 566. But see the criticism of this decision in Nokes, GD, 'Real evidence' (1949) 65 LQR 57, pp 65–66.

12 *R v Fursey* (1833) 6 C&P 81, p 84; *Bruce v Nicolopulo* (1855) 11 Exch 129.

13 *Alivon v Furnival* (1834) 1 Cr M&R 277.

14 *Owner v Bee Hive Spinning Co Ltd* [1914] 1 KB 105.

Nazeer,[15] information contained in a computer at the record department of the Department of Social Security was used by the prosecution to produce a schedule of cashed orders from pension and allowance books that had been reported as lost or stolen. The Court of Appeal held that the information contained in the schedule, and the oral testimony of DSS employees about the checks that they had made comparing the paid orders with the information contained in the computer, was admissible as secondary evidence of that information. The computer was a 'document' for the purposes of s 24 of the Criminal Justice Act 1988. It was wholly impracticable for it to be produced in court, and the prosecution could rely on the common law exceptions allowing secondary evidence of documents to be admitted; admissibility of such evidence was not exclusively governed by s 27 of the 1988 Act.

(c) *Non-production by opponent after service of notice to produce.* This exception is unlikely to be of importance in criminal cases.

(d) *Lawful non-production by a stranger.* Secondary evidence will be admissible where a stranger to the litigation lawfully declines to produce a document in his possession or control. (A witness with no such justification can, in theory, be compelled to produce a document at trial by a witness summons.) Thus, secondary evidence has been given of the contents of a document where the original was unavailable because of privilege;[16] because the document was in the possession of a stranger outside the jurisdiction;[17] and because the document was in the possession of a person entitled to diplomatic immunity.[18]

Even where secondary evidence is admissible at common law, care must be taken to ensure that the evidence does not infringe the rule against hearsay. For example, oral evidence might be given of the contents of a document by a witness who examined the original and could remember its contents, perhaps with the help of a memory-refreshing contemporaneous note. But suppose the witness's knowledge of the contents of the document was obtained solely from hearing some other person read it aloud. In that case the rule against hearsay would operate to exclude the evidence.

The party who adduces a document in evidence must usually, in the absence of an admission by his opponent, prove that it was duly executed. This obligation may simply require evidence that the document was signed by the person whose signature it purports to bear. Sometimes, it may be necessary to prove the handwriting of the whole of a disputed document. Proof of execution may also require proof of attestation.

---

15 [1998] Crim LR 750.
16 *Mills v Oddy* (1834) 6 C&P 728.
17 *Kilgour v Owen* (1889) 88 LT Jo 7.
18 *R v Nowaz* [1976] 1 WLR 830.

Proof of a signature or of handwriting may be made in one or more of the following ways:

(a) By evidence of the writer, or of someone else who saw the maker of the document write it or put his signature on it.

(b) By evidence of opinion, given by an ordinary witness. Such evidence is admissible even where the evidence of the writer is available. Thus on a charge of forgery, it is not necessary to call the person whose signature is alleged to have been forged.[19] Such an opinion will be based on the witness's recollection of having seen a particular person's writing or signature before, as was described by Coleridge J in *Doe d Mudd v Suckermore*:

> Either the witness has seen the party write on some former occasion, or he has corresponded with him, and transactions have taken place between them upon the faith that letters purporting to have been written or signed by him have been so written or signed. On either supposition, the witness is supposed to have received into his mind an impression, not so much of the manner in which the writer has formed the letters in the particular instances, as of the general character of his handwriting; and he is called on to speak as to the writing in question by a reference to the standard so formed in his mind ... The test of genuineness ought to be the resemblance, not to the formation of the letters in some other specimen ... but to the general character of writing, which is impressed on it as the involuntary and unconscious result of constitution, habit, or other permanent cause, and is therefore itself permanent.[20]

(c) By an actual comparison, often aided by expert opinion evidence. Section 8 of the Criminal Procedure Act 1865 applies to both civil and criminal proceedings and provides that:

> Comparison of a disputed writing with any writing proved to the satisfaction of the judge to be genuine shall be permitted to be made by witnesses; and such writings, and the evidence of witnesses respecting the same, may be submitted to the court and jury as evidence of the genuineness or otherwise of the writing in dispute.

In civil proceedings, the judge has to be satisfied on the balance of probabilities as to the genuineness of the writing that is to be used as a standard for comparison. In criminal proceedings, he must be satisfied beyond reasonable doubt.[21] The statute does not expressly require the evidence of witnesses. Once a document has been proved to the judge's satisfaction to be a genuine sample of handwriting from the person who is alleged to have written the disputed document, it may apparently simply be compared with the disputed document. But it has been held that, in criminal

---

19 *R v Hurley* (1843) 2 Mood & Ry 473.
20 (1837) 3 A&E 703, p 705.
21 *R v Ewing* [1983] 2 All ER 645.

cases, expert evidence should also be available. Thus in *R v Harden*,[22] the defendant was charged with obtaining money by false pretences. The prosecution alleged that he had sent fictitious agreements to a finance company, and the jury was invited by the trial judge to compare peculiarities in the handwriting of various documents. The defendant was convicted, but his appeal was allowed; the Court of Criminal Appeal held that the jury should have had the assistance of expert evidence.[23]

'Attestation' refers to the signature of a document by a person who is not a party to it, but who is a witness to the signature of one of the parties. By s 3 of the Evidence Act 1938, any document required by law to be attested, with the exception of a will or other testamentary document, 'may, instead of being approved by an attesting witness, be proved in the manner in which it might be proved if no attesting witness were alive'. The effect of this provision is that non-testamentary documents required by law to be attested may now be proved by showing that the signature is in fact that of the attesting witness. Where the court is asked to pronounce for a will in solemn form, the general practice is for at least one of the attesting witnesses to be called to give evidence of execution. But a will can be pronounced for where both attesting witnesses are proved to be dead, or even if the evidence shows merely that they cannot be traced, if the court is satisfied in all the circumstances that the will was duly executed.[24]

There is said to be a presumption that a document was made on the date that it bears.[25] In any proceedings, proof of execution may be dispensed with in the case of 'ancient documents', which, by s 4 of the Evidence Act 1938, are documents more than 20 years old. For this rule to apply, the document must appear to be regular on the face of it, and must be produced from proper custody. 'Proper custody' is any custody that is consistent with the genuineness and legitimate origin of the document. Thus, in *Bishop of Meath v Marquess of Winchester*,[26] documents that had belonged to a deceased bishop by virtue of his office, which had been found among his private papers in the possession of his family, were held to have been produced from proper custody, even though they should have been in the custody of his successor as bishop. As Tindal CJ said: 'It is not necessary that they should be found in the best and most proper place of deposit.'[27]

---

22 [1963] 1 QB 8.

23 See also *R v Tilley* [1961] 1 WLR 1309.

24 *Re Lemon's Estate* (1961) 105 SJ 1107.

25 *In the Goods of Adamson* (1875) LR 3 P&D 253, 256. This is no more than a presumption of fact – an inference that may be drawn. See *Anderson v Weston* (1840) 6 Bing NC 296, where Bosanquet J referred to the date as *'prima facie'* evidence of the date of execution, pp 300–01.

26 (1836) 3 Bing NC 183.

27 *Ibid*, p 200.

Statements in documents produced by computers

There are now no special conditions to be satisfied before admitting in evidence documents produced by a computer. The provisions contained in Part I of the Civil Evidence Act 1968 were repealed by s 15(2) and Sched 2 of the Civil Evidence Act 1995. The provisions contained in s 69 of the Police and Criminal Evidence Act 1984 were repealed by s 60 of the Youth Justice and Criminal Evidence Act 1999.

REAL EVIDENCE

'Real evidence' is an ill-defined concept. There is general agreement that it includes physical objects produced for the inspection of the court. If a document is adduced in evidence, the question whether it is 'real' or 'documentary' evidence depends on the purpose for which it is adduced. If the purpose is to establish its contents, it is classed as an item of documentary evidence; if the purpose is to establish its condition or appearance (for example, to show that it has been damaged, or to show its size or shape), it is classed as an item of real evidence. The distinction was formerly of some importance because of the rule that the original of an item of documentary evidence had to be produced (or the foundation laid for the admission of secondary evidence), whereas it was not essential to produce items of real evidence in court. At the risk of reducing the weight of the evidence, oral evidence could be given about the state of a physical object. As was shown earlier, statutes have now removed almost completely the requirement to produce original documentary evidence, and one result is that the question whether a piece of evidence is to be classified as 'real' or 'documentary' has lost much of its former importance.

Beyond physical objects produced for the inspection of the court there was room for argument about what else might count as 'real evidence'. The arguments about classification are of limited importance now; indeed, their major significance is probably to provide a useful checklist of occasions when direct perception by a trier of fact can be part of the evidence in the case.

Demeanour of the witness

The traditional view of demeanour is that it may be relevant to credibility. One of the standard arguments against the admissibility of hearsay evidence has been that the court is unable to see the demeanour of the person making the original statement.[28] The weight attached to demeanour can also be

---

28 *Teper v R* [1952] 2 AC 480, p 486. But see Stone, M, 'Instant lie detection? Demeanour and credibility in criminal trials' [1991] Crim LR 821; Law Com No 245 (1997), paras 3.9–3.12.

perceived in the reluctance of appellate courts to interfere with the conclusions of trial judges who have seen and heard the witnesses.[29]

Physical appearance of a person or animal in court

In *Line v Taylor*,[30] a dog was brought into court to display its good temper. More recently, a parrot's display of affection in court towards a particular person was used as evidence that the parrot belonged to that person.[31] In another case, in which the plaintiff was suing for damages and for the return of cats which she claimed belonged to her, the judge agreed that the cats should be present in open court when the case was heard so that their reactions to the plaintiff and her children could be observed.[32]

It appears that before defendants in criminal trials were allowed to give evidence, the jury might take into account their reactions in the dock at various stages of the trial. In *AG for New South Wales v Bertrand*,[33] the Privy Council had to consider a case where there had been a re-trial after a jury had disagreed. At the second hearing, the trial judge had attempted to shorten the proceedings by reading back to the prosecution witnesses the notes of their evidence at the first trial and asking them if what he had read was true. After that, he had permitted fresh oral examination-in-chief and cross-examination. The Privy Council, allowing the appeal, disapproved of this course and emphasised the value of 'open oral examination of the witness in the presence of prisoner, judge, and jury'. According to Sir John Coleridge:

> The most careful note must often fail to convey the evidence fully in some of its most important elements ... It cannot give the look or manner of the witness: his hesitation, his doubts, his variations of language, his confidence or precipitance, his calmness or consideration; *it cannot give the manner of the Prisoner, when that has been important, upon the statement of anything of particular moment.*[34]

The resemblance of a child, produced to the court, to a person alleged to be its father has in some cases been held to be evidence, albeit slight, of parentage.[35]

---

29 *SS Hontestroom v SS Sagaporack* [1927] AC 37, pp 47, 48; *Hvalfangerselskapet Polaris A/S v Unilever Ltd* (1933) 46 Ll L Rep 29; *Yuill v Yuill* [1945] P 15; *In the Estate of Bercovitz, decd* [1962] 1 All ER 552, p 558.

30 (1862) 3 F&F 731.

31 (1995) *The Times*, 16 February, p 5.

32 (1995) *The Times*, 26 April, p 3.

33 (1867) LR 1 PC 520.

34 *Ibid*, p 535. Emphasis supplied.

35 *Slingsby v AG* (1916) 33 TLR 120, p 122; *Russell v Russell and Mayer* (1923) 129 LT 151, p 153; *C v C and C* [1972] 1 WLR 1335.

Views[36]

Things and places outside court may be inspected during the course of a trial. For example, members of a jury in one case viewed reconstructions of events, enacted outside court in a Range Rover motor car, to assist them in determining whether police had seen an act of oral intercourse in a similar car on an earlier occasion.[37] In a trial for murder, a jury inspected a house, where the bodies of nine victims had been unearthed, to determine whether the wife of a man living there might have failed to notice her husband's activities on the premises.[38] During the course of hearing *Tito v Waddell*,[39] the trial judge visited Ocean Island in the Pacific Ocean, which was the subject of the litigation.

The legal status of a view was settled by the Court of Appeal in *Buckingham v Daily News Ltd*.[40] The case concerned an employee of the defendants who had been injured when cleaning one of his employer's machines. During the course of an action for negligence against the employers, the judge inspected the machine and watched a demonstration by the plaintiff of how he cleaned it. The Court of Appeal held that the inspection was part of the evidence in the case: it was as if the machine had been brought into court and the plaintiff had there demonstrated what took place. In the course of his judgment, Birkett LJ referred to occasions when, as a judge of first instance, he had visited factories, workshops, shops and cinemas in order to see the nature of the place where an accident had occurred.[41] The parties, their legal representatives and the judge (or judge and jury) should all be present at the view.[42]

Automatic recordings

Where the recording device operates as no more than a calculator, the print-out or other reading is an item of real evidence. An obvious example is the print-out produced by a breathalyser.[43] In *R v Spiby*,[44] the Court of Appeal had to consider whether the rule against hearsay applied to the print-out from a device which monitored telephone calls and recorded the numbers to which

---

36 See Ormerod, D, 'A prejudicial view' [2000] Crim LR 452.
37 (1994) *The Times*, 13 January, p 3.
38 (1995) *The Times*, 20 October, p 5.
39 See *Tito v Waddell* [1975] 3 All ER 997.
40 [1956] 2 QB 534.
41 *Ibid*, p 542.
42 *Salusbury v Woodland* [1970] 1 QB 324, p 343; *R v Hunter* [1985] 1 WLR 613; *R v Ely JJ ex p Burgess* [1992] Crim LR 888.
43 *Castle v Cross* [1984] 1 WLR 1372.
44 (1990) 91 Cr App R 186.

calls were made and their duration. The court held that the print-out was an item of real evidence, and not caught by the hearsay rule, because the recording was entirely automatic and did not depend on anything that had passed through a human mind.

The contents of tape recordings may be admitted as evidence of what was said on a particular occasion. In *R v Maqsud Ali*, where a conversation between defendants had been surreptitiously obtained, Marshall J said:

> For many years now photographs have been admissible in evidence on proof that they are relevant to the issues involved in the case and that the prints are taken from negatives that are untouched. The prints as seen represent situations that have been reproduced by means of mechanical and chemical devices. Evidence of things seen through telescopes or binoculars which otherwise could not have been picked up by the naked eye have been admitted, and now there are devices for picking up, transmitting, and recording, conversations. We can see no difference in principle between a tape recording and a photograph.[45]

The voices recorded must, of course, be identified by admissible evidence, and if there is a challenge to the authenticity of the recording, the court must be satisfied on this matter before admitting it. However, it seems that it is enough merely to establish a *prima facie* case for authenticity.[46] The recording is a document within the meaning of s 27 of the Criminal Justice Act 1988, and a transcript of the recording will be admissible as a copy under the same section.

In *R v Rampling*,[47] the Court of Appeal gave guidance on the use in court of tape recordings of police interviews:

(a) The tape can be produced and proved by the interviewing officer or any other officer present when it was taken.

(b) The officer should have listened to the tape before the trial so that he can, if necessary, deal with any objections to authenticity or accuracy.

(c) The transcript of the recording can be produced by the officer. He should have checked this against the recording for accuracy before the trial.

(d) The defendant is entitled to have any part of the tape played to the jury.

(e) If any part of the tape is played, it is for the judge to decide whether the jury should have a transcript to enable them to follow more clearly.

Subject to any necessary editing to remove inadmissible evidence, a jury in retirement may, on request, be allowed to hear a tape recording of a police interview with the defendant, where the tape has been made an exhibit, even though the tape has not been played earlier during the trial.[48] Any playing of

---

45 [1966] 1 QB 688, p 701. See also *R v Senat and Sin* (1968) 52 Cr App R 282.

46 *R v Robson and Harris* (1972) 56 Cr App R 450.

47 [1987] Crim LR 823.

48 *R v Riaz and Burke* (1991) 94 Cr App R 339.

the tape after the jury has retired should be in open court, with judge, counsel and the defendant present.[49] A jury may also want, after retirement, to see once again a video tape of an interview with a child admitted under s 27(1) of the Youth Justice and Criminal Evidence Act 1999. It is a matter for the judge's discretion whether this should happen. He must have in mind the need to avoid unfairness from replaying only the complainant's evidence-in-chief. Usually, if the jury simply wish to be reminded of what the witness said, it will be sufficient for the judge to remind them of this from his own note. A jury should only rarely be permitted to retire with a transcript of a child complainant's video interview. Where that does happen, the judge should give warnings to the jury which would prevent their giving disproportionate weight to the transcript.[50] But if the question of how the words were spoken is important to the jury, the judge may allow the video, or the relevant part of it, to be replayed. If there is a replay, the following rules apply:

(a) It must be in court, with judge, counsel and defendant present.

(b) The judge should warn the jury that because they are hearing the evidence-in-chief of the complainant a second time, well after all the other evidence, they should guard against the risk of giving it disproportionate weight simply for that reason, and should bear well in mind the other evidence in the case.

(c) To assist in maintaining a fair balance, when the video has been replayed the judge should remind the jury from his own notes of the cross-examination and re-examination of the complainant, whether the jury ask him to do so or not.[51]

A film or photograph may be admitted to prove the commission of an offence and the identity of the offender. For example, in *R v Dodson*,[52] photographs taken at half second intervals by a security camera at a building society office were held admissible to show an offence being committed. It is necessary, of course, in such a case to adduce oral evidence to authenticate the video recording or still photographs. In *The Statue of Liberty*,[53] Sir Jocelyn Simon P admitted a cinematograph film of radar echoes, recorded mechanically by a shore radar station. Films or photographs are treated as if they are extensions of human perception.[54] In *Taylor v Chief Constable of Cheshire*,[55] police officers saw a video recording made by a security camera of someone picking up an item in a shop and putting it in his jacket. The police identified the man as

---

49   *R v Hagan* [1997] 1 Cr App R 464, p 470.
50   *R v Morris* [1998] Crim LR 416.
51   *R v Rawlings and Broadbent* [1995] 2 Cr App R 222, pp 227–28; cf *R v Horley* [1999] Crim LR 488.
52   [1984] 1 WLR 971.
53   [1968] 1 WLR 739.
54   See the judgment of Marshall J in *R v Maqsud Ali* [1966] 1 QB 688, referred to above.
55   [1986] 1 WLR 1479.

Taylor. The film was later accidentally erased, but the Court of Appeal held that the officers' evidence of what they had seen on the tape had been properly admitted: they were in effect in the position of bystanders who had witnessed the event.

BIBLIOGRAPHY

Allan, TRS, 'Similar fact evidence and disposition' (1985) 48 MLR 253.

Allan, TRS, 'Abuse of power and public interest immunity' (1985) 101 LQR 200.

Allan, TRS, 'Privilege and confidentiality' [1987] CLJ 43.

Allen, C, 'Discretion and security: excluding evidence under section 78(1)' [1990] CLJ 80.

Allen, C, *Sourcebook on Evidence*, 1996, London: Cavendish Publishing.

Allen, C, *The Law of Evidence in Victorian England*, 1997, Cambridge: CUP.

Allen, C, 'Judicial notice extended' (1998) 2 E&P 37.

Allen, CK, *Law in the Making*, 7th edn, 1964, Oxford: Clarendon Press.

Anderson, T and Twining, W, *Analysis of Evidence*, 1991, London: Weidenfeld and Nicolson.

Andrews, JA, 'Public interest and criminal proceedings' (1988) 104 LQR 410.

Andrews, NH, 'Privileged documents' [1989] CLJ 43.

Andrews, JA and Hirst, M, *Criminal Evidence*, 3rd edn, 1997, London: Sweet & Maxwell.

Richardson, P et al (eds), *Archbold: Criminal Pleading, Evidence and Practice*, 2001, London: Sweet & Maxwell.

Ashworth, A, *The Criminal Process: An Evaluative Study*, 2nd edn, 1998, Oxford: OUP.

Ashworth, AJ and Pattenden, R, 'Reliability, hearsay evidence and the English criminal trial' (1986) 102 LQR 292.

Austin, JL, *How to Do Things with Words*, 2nd edn, 1975, Oxford: Clarendon Press.

Austin, JL, *Philosophical Papers*, 3rd edn, 1979, Oxford: OUP.

Baker, JH, *An Introduction to English Legal History*, 3rd edn, 1990, London: Butterworths.

Baker, JH, 'Criminal courts and procedure at common law 1550–1800, in Cockburn, JS (ed), *Crime in England 1550–1800*, 1977, London: Methuen.

Baldwin, J and McConville, M, *Jury Trials*, 1979, Oxford: Clarendon Press.

Beattie, J, 'Scales of justice: defence counsel and the English criminal trial in the eighteenth and nineteenth centuries' (1991) 9 Law and History Review 221.

Bentham, J, 'Anarchical Fallacies', Article II, in Waldron, J (ed), *Nonsense Upon Stilts: Bentham, Burke and Marx on the Rights of Man*, 1987, London: Methuen.

Bentham, J, 'Rationale of Judicial Evidence', in Bowring, J (ed), *The Works of Jeremy Bentham, 1838–43*, Vol 6, Edinburgh: William Tait.

Best, WM, *A Treatise on the Principles of Evidence*, 4th edn, 1866, London: H Sweet.

Birch, D, 'Hunting the snark' [1988] Crim LR 221.

Birch, D, 'The Criminal Justice Act 1988: (2) documentary evidence' [1989] Crim LR 15.

Birch, D, 'Children's evidence' [1992] Crim LR 262.

Birch, D, 'Excluding evidence from entrapment' (1994) 47 CLP, Part 2, 73.

Birch, D, 'The sharp end of the wedge: use of mixed statements by the defence' [1997] Crim LR 416

Birch, D, 'Suffering in silence: a cost-benefit analysis of section 34 of the Criminal Justice and Public Order Act 1994' [1999] Crim LR 769.

Birch, D, 'A better deal for vulnerable witnesses' [2000] Crim LR 223.

Birch, D, and Leng, R, *Blackstone's Guide to the Youth Justice and Criminal Evidence Act 1999*, 2000, London: Blackstone Press.

Blackstone, Sir W, *The Commentaries on the Laws of England*, Kerr, RM (ed), 1876, London: John Murray.

Boon, A, *Advocacy*, 1993, London: Cavendish Publishing.

Brown, The Rt Hon Lord Justice S, 'Public interest immunity' [1994] PL 579.

Cairns, DJA, *Advocacy and the Making of the Adversarial Criminal Trial 1800–1865*, 1998, Oxford: Clarendon Press.

Campbell, J (1st Baron Campbell), *The Lives of the Chief Justices of England*, 1849-57, London: John Murray.

Campbell, K, 'Offence and defence' in Dennis, I (ed), *Criminal Law and Justice*, 1987, London: Sweet & Maxwell.

Cane, P, *An Introduction to Administrative Law*, 2nd edn, 1992, Oxford: Clarendon Press.

Carr, EH, *What Is History?*, 2nd edn, 1987, Harmondsworth: Penguin Books.

Carter, PB, 'Judicial notice: related and unrelated matters', in Campbell, E and Waller, L (eds), *Well and Truly Tried: Essays on Evidence in Honour of Sir Richard Eggleston*, 1982, Sydney: LBC.

Carter, PB, 'Forbidden reasoning permissible: similar fact evidence a decade after Boardman' (1985) 48 MLR 29.

Carter, PB, 'Hearsay, relevance and admissibility' (1987) 103 LQR 106.

Carter, PB, *Cases and Statutes on Evidence*, 2nd edn, 1990, London: Sweet & Maxwell.

Carter, PB, 'Hearsay: whether and whither' (1993) 109 LQR 573.

Carter, PB, 'Evidence obtained by use of a covert listening device' (1997) 113 LQR 468.

Charge of the Lord Chief Justice of England in the Case of *The Queen against Thomas Castro ... printed from the shorthand writer's notes*, 1874, London: Vacher and Sons.

Choo AL-T, 'Confessions and corroboration: a comparative perspective' [1991] Crim LR 867.

Choo, AL-T, 'The notion of relevance and defence evidence' [1993] Crim LR 114.

Choo, AL-T, *Hearsay and Confrontation in Criminal Trials*, 1996, Oxford: Clarendon Press.

Choo, AL-T, and Nash, S, 'What's the matter with section 78?' [1999] Crim LR 929.

Clark, DH, 'The last word on the last word' (1969) 32 MLR 142.

Colvin, M, 'Part III of the Police Act 1997' (1999) 149 NLJ 311.

Cottu, C, *On the Administration of Criminal Justice in England; and the Spirit of the English Government*, translated from the French, 1822, London: for Richard Stevens.

Creighton, P, 'Spouse competence and compellability' [1990] Crim LR 34.

Criminal Law Revision Committee, 11th Report, *Evidence (General)*, 1972, Cmnd 4991, London: HMSO.

Cullen, T, *Crippen: The Mild Murderer*, 1988, Harmondsworth: Penguin Books.

Damaska, MR, *The Faces of Justice and State Authority: A Comparative Approach to the Legal Process*, 1986, New Haven and London: Yale UP.

Daniel, WTS, *The History and Origin of the Law Reports*, undated, London: Wildy & Sons.

Darbyshire, P, 'Previous misconduct and magistrates courts' [1997] Crim LR 105.

Darbyshire, P, 'An essay on the importance and neglect of the magistracy' [1997] Crim LR 627.

Davis, KC, 'Judicial notice' (1955) 55 Col LR 945.

Dennis, I, 'Reconstructing the law of criminal evidence' (1989) CLP 21.

Dennis, I, 'Miscarriages of justice and the law of confessions' (1993) PL 291.

Dennis, I, 'Instrumental protection, human right or functional necessity?' [1995] CLJ 342.

Dennis, I, 'The Criminal Justice and Public Order Act : the evidence provisions' [1995] Crim LR 4.

Dennis, IH, *The Law of Evidence*, 1999, London: Sweet & Maxwell.

Devlin, P, *Easing the Passing: the Trial of Dr John Bodkin Adams*, 1986, London: Faber & Faber.

Duff, RA, *Trials and Punishments*, 1986, Cambridge: CUP.

Duman, D, 'Pathway to professionalism: the English Bar in the eighteenth and nineteenth centuries' (1980) Journal of Social History 615.

Dummett, M, *Frege: Philosophy of Language*, 2nd edn, 1981, London: Duckworth.

Dworkin, R, 'Is law a system of rules?', in Dworkin, R (ed), *The Philosophy of Law: Oxford Readings in Philosophy*, 1977, Oxford: OUP.

Dworkin, R, *Taking Rights Seriously*, 1977, London: Duckworth.

Dworkin, R, 'Principle, policy, procedure', in *A Matter of Principle*, 1986, Oxford: Clarendon Press.

Easton, S, 'Legal advice, common sense and the right to silence' (1998) 2 E&P 109

Edwards, P (ed), *The Encyclopedia of Philosophy*, 1967, London: Collier-Macmillan Limited.

Eggleston, Sir R, *Evidence, Proof and Probability*, 2nd edn, 1983, London: Weidenfeld and Nicolson.

Elliott, DW, 'Cut-throat tactics: the freedom of an accused to prejudice a co-accused' [1991] Crim LR 5.

Evans, J, 'Change in the doctrine of precedent in the nineteenth century', in Goldstein, L (ed), *Precedent in Law*, 1987, Oxford: OUP.

Fielding, H, *The History of Tom Jones*, Signet Classics Series, 1963, London: The New English Library.

Forsyth, C, 'Public interest immunity: recent and future developments' (1997) CLJ 51.

Friedman, RD, 'Thoughts from across the water on hearsay and confrontation' [1998] Crim LR 697.

Geddes, A, 'The exclusion of evidence relating to a complainant's sexual behaviour in sexual offence trials' (1999) 149 NLJ 1084.

Gilbert, Sir J, *The Law of Evidence*, Capel Lofft (ed), 1791, London: A Strahan and W Woodfall.

Gooderson, RN, '*Res gesta* in criminal cases' [1956] CLJ 199; [1957] CLJ 55.

Guest, S, 'The scope of the hearsay rule' (1985) 101 LQR 385.

Guest, S, 'Hearsay revisited' (1988) 41 CLP 33.

Hale, Sir M, *The History of the Pleas of the Crown*, G Wilson (ed), 1778, London: for T Payne *et al*.

Hand, L, 'Historical and practical considerations regarding expert testimony' (1901) 15 Harv L Rev 40.

Hart, HLA, *Essays on Bentham*, 1982, Oxford: Clarendon Press.

Healy, P, 'Proof and policy: no golden threads' [1987] Crim LR 355.

Helmholz, RH *et al*, *The Privilege against Self-Incrimination: Its Origins and Development*, 1997, London and Chicago: The University of Chicago Press.

Heydon, JD, 'Statutory restrictions on the privilege against self-incrimination' (1971) 87 LQR 214.

Hirst, M, 'Contradicting previous acquittals' [1991] Crim LR 510.

Hirst, M, 'Conduct, relevance and the hearsay rule' (1993) 13 LS 54.

Hoffmann, LH, 'Similar facts after *Boardman*' (1975) 91 LQR 193.

Holdsworth, Sir WS, *A History of English Law*, 1903–72, London: Methuen and Sweet & Maxwell.

Hoyano, L, 'Variations on a theme by Pigot: special measures directions for child witnesses' [2000] Crim LR 250.

Hunter, M, 'Judicial discretion: section 78 in practice' [1994] Crim LR 558.

Imwinkelreid, EJ, 'The worst evidence principle: the best hypothesis as to the logical structure of evidence law' (1992) U Miami L Rev 1069.

Jack, A, 'Lord Woolf and expert evidence' (1994) 144 NLJ 1099.

Jackson, JD, 'Hearsay: the sacred cow that won't be slaughtered?' (1998) 2 E&P 166.

James, GF, 'Relevancy, probability and the law' (1941) 29 Cal L Rev 689.

Jennings, A *et al*, 'Silence and safety: the impact of human rights law' [2000] Crim LR 879.

Kant, I, 'Foundations of the Metaphysics of Morals', trans Beck, LW, *The Library of Liberal Arts*, 2nd edn, 1990, London: Collier-Macmillan.

Kean, AWG, 'The history of criminal liability of children' (1937) 53 LQR 364.

Keane, A, *The Modern Law of Evidence*, 5th edn, 2000, London: Butterworths.

Kenny, A, 'The expert in court' (1983) 99 LQR 197.

Kibble, N, 'The sexual history provisions ...' [2000] Crim LR 274.

Landesman, C, *An Introduction to Epistemology*, 1997, Oxford: Blackwells.

Landsman, S, 'The rise of the contentious spirit: adversary procedure in eighteenth-century England' (1990) 75 Cornell L Rev 497.

Landsman, S, 'From Gilbert to Bentham: the reconceptualization of evidence theory' (1990) 36 Wayne L Rev 1149.

Langbein, JH, 'The criminal trial before the lawyers' (1978) 45 U Chi L Rev 236.

Langbein, JH, 'Shaping the eighteenth-century criminal trial: a view from the Ryder sources' (1983) 50 U Chi L Rev 1.

Langbein, JH, 'Historical foundations of the law of evidence: a view from the Ryder sources' (1996) 96 Columbia Law Rev 1168.

Law Commission No 29, *Offences of Damage to Property*, 1970, London: HMSO.

Law Commission No 202, *Corroboration of Evidence in Criminal Trials*, 1991, London: HMSO.

Law Commission No 216, *The Hearsay Rule in Civil Proceedings*, 1993, London: HMSO.

Law Commission No 245, *Evidence in Criminal Proceedings: Hearsay and Related Topics*, 1997, London: The Stationery Office.

Law Commission Consultation Paper 138, *Evidence in Criminal Proceedings: Hearsay and Related Topics*, 1996, London: HMSO.

Law Commission Consultation Paper 141, *Evidence in Criminal Proceedings: Previous Misconduct of a Defendant*, 1996, London: HMSO.

Law Commission Consultation Paper 145, *Legislating the Criminal Code: Corruption*, 1997, London: HMSO.

Law Reform Committee, 15th Report, *The Rule in Hollington v Hewthorn*, 1967, Cmnd 3391, London: HMSO.

Law Reform Committee, 16th Report, *Privilege in Civil Proceedings*, 1967, Cmnd 3472, London: HMSO.

Law Reform Committee, 17th Report, *Evidence of Opinion and Expert Evidence*, 1970, Cmnd 4489, London: HMSO.

Lieberman, D, *The Province of Legislation Determined: Legal Theory in Eighteenth-Century Britain*, 1989, Cambridge: CUP.

Lobban, M, *The Common Law and English Jurisprudence 1760–1850*, 1991, Oxford: Clarendon Press.

Lowndes, J, *A Few Brief Remarks on Lord Denman's Bill for Improving the Law of Evidence*, 1843, London: Saunders and Benning.

Macaulay, TB (Lord Macaulay), *The History of England from the Accession of James II*, 1849–55, repr 1880, London: Longmans, Green.

McConville, M, 'The doctrine of judicial notice and its relation to evidence' (1979) 1 Liverpool LR 62.

McEwan, J, *Evidence and the Adversarial Process: the Modern Law*, 1992, Oxford: Blackwells.

McEwan, J, 'In defence of vulnerable witnesses: the Youth Justice and Criminal Evidence Act 1999' (2000) 4 E&P 1.

Mackay, RD and Colman, AM, 'Excluding expert evidence' [1991] Crim LR 800.

Macnair, MRT, 'The early development of the privilege against self-incrimination' (1990) 10 OJLS 66.

Manchester, C, 'Judicial notice and personal knowledge' (1979) 42 MLR 22.

May, R, *Criminal Evidence*, 4th edn, 1999, London: Sweet & Maxwell.

Megarry, Sir R, *A Second Miscellany-at-Law: A Further Diversion for Lawyers and Others*, 1973, London: Stevens.

Milsom, SFC, *Historical Foundations of the Common Law*, 2nd edn, 1981, London: Butterworths.

Mirfield, P, 'Shedding a tear for issue estoppel' [1980] Crim LR 336.

Mirfield, P, 'The argument from consistency for overruling Selvey' (1991) CLJ 490.

Mirfield, P, 'Expert evidence and unreliable confessions' [1992] 108 LQR 528.

Mirfield, P, '"Corroboration" after the 1994 Act' [1995] Crim LR 448.

Mirfield, P, *Silence, Confessions and Improperly Obtained Evidence*, 1997, Oxford: Clarendon Press.

Mirfield, P, '*Res judicata* rejected' [2001] 117 LQR 194.

Morgan, EM, *Some Problems of Proof under the Anglo-American System of Litigation*, 1956, New York: Columbia University Press.

Munday, R, 'Similar fact evidence: identity cases and striking similarity' [1999] 58 CLJ 45.

Munday, R, 'Admitting acquittals as similar fact evidence of guilt' [2000] 59 CLJ 468.

Munday, RJC, 'Reflections on the Criminal Evidence Act 1898' (1985) CLJ 62.

Munday, RJC, 'Stepping beyond the bounds of credibility' [1986] Crim LR 511.

Munday, RJC, 'The paradox of cross-examination to credit' [1994] CLJ 303.

Munday, RJC, 'What constitutes a good character?' [1997] Crim LR 247.

Murphy, P, 'Hearsay: the road to reform' (1997) 1 E&P 107.

Murphy, P, *Murphy on Evidence*, 7th edn, 2000, London: Blackstone Press.

Murphy, P, 'Character evidence: the search for logic and policy continues' (1998) 2 E&P 71.

Nance, DA, 'The best evidence principle' (1988) 73 Iowa L Rev 227.

Nair, RL, 'Similar fact evidence: prejudice and irrelevance revisited' [1993] Crim LR 432.

Nair, RL, 'Weighing similar fact and avoiding prejudice' (1996) 112 LQR 262.

Nokes, GD, *An Introduction to the Law of Evidence*, 4th edn, 1967, London: Sweet & Maxwell.

Nokes, GD, 'Real evidence' (1949) 65 LQR 57.

Nokes, GD, 'Professional privilege' (1950) 66 LQR 88.

Nokes, GD, 'The limits of judicial notice' (1958) 74 LQR 59.

Nokes, GD, '*Res gestae* as hearsay' [1954] 70 LQR 370.

Noorlander, P, 'Covert policing and the Convention: entrapment' (1998) 148 NLJ 511.

Ormerod, D, 'Redundant *res gestae*?' [1998] Crim LR 301.

Ormerod, D, 'A prejudicial view' [2000] Crim LR 452.

Ormerod, DC, 'The hearsay exceptions' [1996] Crim LR 16.

Osborne, C, 'Hearsay and the European Court of Human Rights' [1993] Crim LR 255.

Packer, HL, 'Two models of the criminal process' (1964) 113 U of Pa L Rev 1.

Park, RC, 'McCormick on Evidence and the concept of hearsay' (1981) 65 Minn LR 423.

Parkinson, GRH (ed), *An Encyclopaedia of Philosophy*, 1988, London: Routledge.

Passmore, C, 'The future of legal professional privilege' (1999) 3 E&P 71.

Pattenden, R, 'Conflicting approaches to psychiatric evidence in criminal trials' [1986] Crim LR 92.

Pattenden, R, 'Should confessions be corroborated?' (1991) 107 LQR 317.

Pattenden, R, 'Similar fact evidence and proof of identity' (1996) 112 LQR 446.

Pattenden, R, 'Litigation privilege and expert opinion evidence' (2000) 4 E&P 213.

Peysner, J, 'Hearsay is dead! Long live hearsay!' (1998) 2 E&P 232.

Phillipps, SM, *A Treatise on the Law of Evidence*, 7th edn, 1829, London: William Benning.

Polyviou, PG, 'Illegally obtained evidence and *R v Sang*', in Tapper, CFH (ed), *Crime, Proof and Punishment: Essays in Memory of Sir Rupert Cross*, 1981, London: Butterworths.

Post, JB, 'The admissibility of defence counsel in English criminal procedure' (1984) 5 J Leg Hist 23.

Postema, GJ, *Bentham and the Common Law Tradition*, 1986, Oxford: Clarendon Press.

Redmayne, M, 'Drugs, money and relevance' (1999) 3 E&P 128.

Rein, A, 'The scope of hearsay' (1994) 110 LQR 431.

Report to the Secretary of State for the Home Department of the Departmental Committee on Evidence of Identification in Criminal Cases, 1976, London: HMSO.

Roberts, P, 'Taking the burden of proof seriously' [1995] Crim LR 783.

Roberts, P, 'Acquitted misconduct evidence and double jeopardy principles, from *Sambasivam* to *Z*' [2000] Crim LR 952.

Robertson, G, 'Entrapment evidence' [1994] Crim LR 793.

Royal Commission on Criminal Justice, Report, 1993, Cm 2263, London: HMSO.

Royal Commission on Criminal Procedure, Report, 1981, Cmnd 8092, London: HMSO.

Schiff, S, 'The use of out-of-court information in fact determination at trial' (1963) 41 Can Bar Rev 335.

Scott, the Rt Hon Sir R, *Report of the Inquiry into the Export of Defence Equipment and Dual-Use Goods to Iraq and Related Prosecutions*, 1996, HC 115, London: HMSO.

Scott, the Rt Hon Sir R, 'The acceptable and unacceptable use of public interest immunity' [1996] PL 427.

Seabrooke, S, 'The vanishing trick - blurring the line between credit and issue' [1999] Crim LR 387.

Shapin, S, *A Social History of Truth: Civility and Science in Seventeenth-Century England*, 1994, Chicago and London: The University of Chicago Press.

Sharpe, S, 'Covert police operations and the discretionary exclusion of evidence' [1994] Crim LR 793.

Sharpe, S, 'Judicial discretion and investigative impropriety' (1997) 1 E&P 149.

Simpson, AWB, 'The rise and fall of the legal treatise' (1981) 45 U Chi L Rev 632.

Smith, JC, 'The presumption of innocence' (1987) 38 NILQ 223.

Smith JC, 'Sections 23 and 24 of the Criminal Justice Act 1988' [1994] Crim LR 426.

Smith, JC, 'Proving conspiracy' [1996] Crim LR 386.

Smith, JC, 'More on proving conspiracy' [1997] Crim LR 333.

Spencer, JR, 'Court experts and expert witnesses' (1992) 45 CLP, Part 2, 213.

Spencer, JR, 'Orality and the evidence of absent witnesses' [1994] Crim LR 628.

Spencer, JR, 'Hearsay reform: a bridge not far enough?' [1996] Crim LR 29.

Starkie, T, *A Practical Treatise on the Law of Evidence*, 3rd edn, 1842, London: V and R Stevens and GS Norton.

Stein, A, 'After Hunt: the burden of proof, risk of non-persuasion and judicial pragmatism' (1991) 54 MLR 570.

Stephen, Sir JF, *A History of the Criminal Law of England*, 1883, repr 1973, New York: Burt Franklin.

Stephen, Sir JF, *A Digest of the Law of Evidence*, 2nd edn, 1876, London: Macmillan.

Stone, J, '*Res gesta reagitata*' [1939] 55 LQR 66.

Stone, D, 'The presumption of death: a redundant concept?' (1981) 44 MLR 516.

Stone, J, 'The rule of exclusion of similar fact evidence' (1932) 46 Harv LR 954.

Stone, J and Wells, WAN, *Evidence: Its History and Policies*, 1991, Sydney: Butterworths.

Stone, M, *Cross-Examination in Criminal Trials*, 1988, London: Butterworths.

Stone, M, 'Instant lie detection? Demeanour and credibility in criminal trials' [1991] Crim LR 821.

Sugarman, D, 'Legal theory, the common law mind and the making of the textbook tradition', in Twining, W (ed), *Legal Theory and Common Law*, 1986, Oxford: Blackwell.

Tapper, C, 'Privilege and policy' (1974) 37 MLR 92.

Tapper, C, 'The open society and its enemy' (1978) 41 MLR 192.

Tapper, C, 'The probative force of similar fact evidence' (1992) 108 LQR 26.

Tapper, C, 'Prosecution and privilege' (1996) 1 E&P 5.

Tapper, C, *Cross and Tapper on Evidence*, 9th edn, 1999, London: Butterworths.

Tapper, C, 'Clouded acquittal' [2001] 117 LQR 1.

Taylor, JP, *Treatise on the Law of Evidence*, 6th edn, 1872, London: William Maxwell.

Temkin, J, 'Sexual history evidence' [1993] Crim LR 3.

Thayer, JB, *A Preliminary Treatise on Evidence at the Common Law*, 1898, Boston: Little, Brown.

Trautman, HL, 'Logical or legal relevancy – a conflict in theory' (1952) 5 V and L Rev 385.

Tribe, LH, 'Triangulating hearsay' (1974) 87 Harv LR 957.

Twining, W, *Theories of Evidence: Bentham and Wigmore*, 1985, London: Weidenfeld and Nicolson.

Twining, W, *Rethinking Evidence: Exploratory Essays*, 1994, Evanston, Illinois: Northwestern University Press.

Waldron, J (ed), *Theories of Rights: Oxford Readings in Philosophy*, 1984, Oxford: OUP.

Weinberg, M, 'Implied assertions and the scope of the hearsay rule' (1973) 9 Melb U L Rev 268.

Weyrauch, WO, 'Law as mask – legal ritual and relevance' (1978) 66 Cal L Rev 699.

Wigmore, JH, *Treatise on Evidence in Trials at Common Law*, 3rd edn rev, 1940, Boston: Little, Brown.

Wigmore, JH, *The Principles of Judicial Proof*, 2nd edn, 1931, Boston: Little, Brown.

Williams, CR, The problem of similar fact evidence' (1979) 5 Dalhousie LJ 281.

Williams, CR, 'Offences and defences' (1982) 2 LS 233.

Williams, CR, 'Issues at the penumbra of hearsay' (1987) 11 Adel LR 113.

Williams, G, *Criminal Law: The General Part*, 2nd edn, 1961, London: Stevens.

Williams,G, 'The evidential burden: some common misapprehensions' (1977) 127 NLJ 156.

Williams, G, 'Evidential burdens on the defence' (1977) 127 NLJ 182.

Williams, G, 'The logic of "exceptions"' (1988) CLJ 261.

Winder, WHD, 'The courts of requests' (1936) 52 LQR 369.

Wittgenstein, L, *Philosophical Investigations*, trans Anscombe, GEM, 3rd edn, 1967, Oxford: Blackwells.

Woffinden, B, *Miscarriages of Justice*, 1989, London: Coronet.

Zander, M, *The Police and Criminal Evidence Act 1994*, 3rd edn, 1995, London: Sweet & Maxwell.

Zuckerman, AAS, 'Previous convictions as evidence of guilt' (1971) 87 LQR 21.

Zuckerman, AAS, 'Privilege and public interest', in Tapper, CFH (ed), *Crime, Proof and Punishment: Essays in Memory of Sir Rupert Cross*, 1981, London: Butterworths.

Zuckerman, AAS, 'Similar fact evidence – the unobservable rule' (1987) 103 LQR 187.

Zuckerman, AAS, *The Principles of Criminal Evidence*, 1989, Oxford: Clarendon Press.

INDEX